Baseball: A Comprehensive Bibliography
Supplement 2 (1992 through 1997)

Baseball

A Comprehensive Bibliography

◆

Supplement 2
(1992 through 1997)

◆

Compiled by
Myron J. Smith, Jr.

with a foreword by
JOHN KUENSTER

McFarland & Company, Inc., Publishers
Jefferson, North Carolina, and London

British Library Cataloguing-in-Publication data are available

Library of Congress Cataloguing-in-Publication Data

    Baseball : a comprehensive bibliography.   Supplement 2,
1992 through 1997 / compiled by Myron J. Smith, Jr. ; with
a foreword by John Kuenster.
       p.   cm.
    Includes indexes.
    ISBN 0-7864-0531-7 (library binding : 50 # alkaline paper) ∞
    1. Baseball—United States—Bibliography.   2. Baseball—
Canada—Bibliography.   I. Title.
Z7514.B3S64   1998
[GV863.A1]
016.796357'0973—dc21   98-14523
                                            CIP

Manufactured in the United States of America

McFarland & Company, Inc., Publishers
  Box 611, Jefferson, North Carolina 28640

For Dennie

Contents

List of Journals Consulted

AB Bookman Weekly
Academy of Management
Journal
Accent on Living
Across the Board
Adirondac
Aethlon: The Journal of
Sport Literature
Airman
Alaska
Albany Law Review
American Banker
American Demographics
The American Economist
American History
American History Illus-
trated
American Jewish History
American Journal of Oph-
thalmology
American Journal of
Physics
American Journal of Soci-
ology
American Journal of
Sports Medicine
American Journal of Trial
Advocacy
The American Legion
American Legion Maga-
zine
American Poetry Review
The American Scholar
American School and Uni-
versity
The American Spectator
American Statistician

American Studies
American Teacher
American Visions
Americas
Amusement Business
Annals of Biomedical En-
gineering
Annals of Emergency
Medicine
Antiques and Collecting
Hobbies
APG Quarterly
Applied Economics/Applied
Economics Letters
Architectural Record
The Arithmetic Teacher
Arizona Highways
Arkansas Historical Quar-
terly
Arkansas Law Notes
Army
Athletic Business
Atlanta
Atlanta History
Atlantic Economic Journal
Aussie Sport Action
Australian Journal of Jew-
ish Studies
Australian Leisure
Australian Magazine
Baltimore Business Journal
Baseball Australia
Baseball Digest
Baseball History
Baseball Research Journal
Beckett Baseball Card
Monthly

Beckett Focus on Future
Stars
Beckett Future Stars &
Sports Collectibles
Beckett Vintage Sports
Bench & Bar of Minnesota
Better Homes and Gardens
Biological Cybernetics
Black Enterprise
Black Issues in Higher
Education
Boston
Boston Bar Journal
Boy's Life
Broadcasting
Broadcasting & Cable
Bulletin (Australia)
Bulletin of the Psycho-
nomic Society
Business First-Columbus
Business History Review
Business Journal–Milwau-
kee
The Business Journal–
Serving Phoenix & the
Valley of the Sun
Business Week
Buzz
CA Magazine
Cable Vision
California
California Engineer
California History
California Lawyer
The Californians: The
Magazine of California
History

The Canadian Historical Review
Canadian Journal of Psychiatry
Canadian Journal of the History of Sport
Career World
Carologue: A Bulletin of South Carolina History
Catholic University Law Review
CATO Journal
Challenge
Chance
Chicago
Child Life
Christian Century
The Chronicle of Higher Education
Chronicles of Oklahoma
Cineaction
Clearing House
Cleveland
Clinical Journal of Sport Medicine
Cobblestone
Colby Quarterly
The College Mathematics Journal
Colorado Business Magazine
Colorado Heritage
Columbia Journalism Review
Communication
Compressed Air Magazine
Computer Life
Concrete International
Confluencia
Connecticut Law Practice
Constitution
Contemporary Thought on Performance Enhancement
Cornell Journal of Law and Public Policy
Country Home
Crain's Chicago Business
Crain's Cleveland Business
Critique-Studies in Contemporary Fiction
Cultural Critique
Current Health
Cycle World
D Magazine
Delaware History
Denver Corporate Connection

Denver Magazine
Detroit
Dialectical Anthropology
Discovery
Dispute Resolution Journal
Dissent
Diversity
Dugout (Canada)
Eastern Economic Journal
Ebony
Ecological Psychology
Economic Development Quarterly
Economic Inquiry
Economic Journal
Editor & Publisher
Elysian Fields Quarterly
Emerge
Emmy
English Today
Entertainment and Sports Lawyer
Entrepreneur
Environment & Behavior
E.P.S. Education Physique et Sport (France)
Esquire
Essence
Europe
Events USA
The Exceptional Parent
Family Circle
Family Life
Family Safety and Health
Far Eastern Economic Review
Feminisms
Film and History
Film Comment
Financial World
First Aider
Florida Law Review
Florida Sports Fan
Florida State University Law Review
For the Record
Forbes
Fordham Intellectual Property, Media, and Entertainment Law Journal
Fordham International Law Journal
Fordham Urban Law Journal
Fortune
Free China Review
Friends of Financial History

Gateway Heritage
The Geographical Bulletin
The George Washington Journal of International Law and Economics
The Gettysburg Review
Golf
Good Housekeeping
Good Old Days
Gourmet
Governing
GQ: Gentlemen's Quarterly
Greeley Style Magazine
Harper's
Hastings Communications and Entertainment Law Journal
Hawaii Business
Heating, Piping, and Air Conditioning
The Hemingway Review
High Plains Literary Review
Hispanic
History of Education Quarterly
Hitotsubashi Rouse (Japan)
Home Office Computing
Honolulu
Hoosierisms Quarterly
Hot Wire
Houston Metro
Hudson Review
Human Relations
Humanity & Society
IBA World Baseball
Illinois Issues
Illustrated Librarian
Inc
Indiana Law Review
Industrial and Labor Relations Review
Industrial Relations: A Journal of Economy and Society (Great Britain)
Inland Architect
Inside Sports
Inside Sports (Australia)
Institutional Investor
International Journal of Instructional Media
International Journal of Sport Psychology
International Journal of the History of Sports (Great Britain)

International Review of the Sociology of Sport (Germany)
Interview
Jack & Jill
Japan and the World Economy
Japan Echo
Japanese Journal of Psychology
JEN, Journal of Emergency Nursing
Jet
Journal of Advertising Research
Journal of Aging and Physical Activity
Journal of American Culture
Journal of American History
Journal of Applied Biomechanics
Journal of Applied Psychology
Journal of Applied Social Psychology
Journal of Applied Sport Psychology
Journal of Athletic Training
Journal of Black Studies
Journal of Business
Journal of Business Strategy
Journal of Comparative Psychology
Journal of Consumer Research
The Journal of Dispute Resolution
Journal of Economic Education
Journal of Economic Literature
Journal of Experimental Psychology: Human Perception & Performance
Journal of Finance
Journal of Gambling Studies
Journal of Hospitality & Leisure Marketing
Journal of Human Movement Studies
Journal of Labor Economics

Journal of Labor Research
The Journal of Legal Studies Education
Journal of Market Research Society
The Journal of Narrative Technique
Journal of Negro History
Journal of Orthopaedic & Sports Physical Therapy
Journal of Policy Analysis
Journal of Popular Culture
Journal of Psychology
Journal of Recreational Mathematics
Journal of Social Behavior & Personality
Journal of Sport and Exercise Psychology
Journal of Sport and Social Issues
Journal of Sport Behavior
Journal of Sport History
Journal of Sport Management
Journal of Sports Philately
Journal of Strength and Conditioning Research
Journal of the American Academy of Religion
Journal of the American Chamber of Commerce
Journal of the American Dental Association
Journal of the American Statistical Association
Journal of the History of Medicine and Allied Sciences
Journal of the Japanese and International Economic Association
Journal of the Mississippi Academy of Sciences
The Journal of the Philosophy of Sport
Journal of the West
The Journal of Undergraduate Research in Physics
Journal of Urban History
Journalism and Mass Communications Quarterly
Kansas History
KidSports
Labor Law Journal
Labor's Heritage

Ladies Home Journal
Landscape Architecture
Landscape Management
Latin American Perspectives
Law and Order
Law Practice Management
Leadership Quarterly
Learn 94
Legal Reference Services Quarterly
Life
Living Bird
Look Japan
Los Angeles
Los Angeles Business Journal
Louisiana History
Louisiana Law Review
Loyola Entertainment Law Journal
Loyola of Los Angeles Law Review
The Lutheran
M
Maclean's
Mainstream
Maledicta
Managerial and Decision Economics
Marquette Sports Law Journal
Maryland Historical Magazine
Maryland Magazine
Mathematical and Computer Modelling
Mathematical Teaching in the Middle School
The Mathematics Teacher
Meat Business Magazine
Mechanical Engineering
Media History Digest
Media Week
Medicine, Exercise, Nutrition, and Health
Men's Fitness
Men's Health
Men's Journal
Mercury
Metropolis
Michigan History
Milwaukee
Minneapolis
The Minneapolis Review of Baseball
Minnesota Medicine

Minnesota Monthly
Mississippi
Missouri HIstorical Re-
  view
Modern Maturity
Modern Fiction Studies
Money
Montana: The Magazine of
  Western History
Morbidity and Mortality
  Weekly Report
Mother Earth News
Motor Boating & Sailing
Muscle and Nerves
Names
Narrative
The Nation
National Geographic Trav-
  eler
National Geographic World
The National Law Journal
National Pastime
The National Review
Nation's Business
Nevada
Nevada Magazine
New Jersey Monthly
The New Leader
New Mexico Business
  Journal
New Mexico Magazine
The New Republic
New York
New York Law School
  Journal of International
  and Comparative Law
New York Times Magazine
The New Yorker
Newsweek
Nine: A Journal of Base-
  ball History and Social
  Policy Perspective
North American Review
North Carolina Central
  Law Journal
Northern Kentucky Law
  Review
The Northern Logger and
  Timber Processor
Northwestern University
  Law Review
Nova Law Review
OAH Magazine of History
Ohio
OMEGA: The Journal of
  Death and Dying
Online

Operations Research Let-
  ters
Outside
Ovation
Pacific Northwest Quar-
  terly
Parents
Parnassus: Poetry in Re-
  view
Pediatric Exercise Science
Pediatrics
Pennsylvania Journal of
  Health, Physical Educa-
  tion, Recreation, and
  Dance
Pennsylvania Heritage
Penny Power
Penthouse
People Weekly
Pepperdine Law Review
Perceptual & Motor Skills
Performance and Instruc-
  tion
Personality and Social
  Psychology Bulletin
Perspective
Petersen's Photographic
  Magazine
Pharmacy Times
Philadelphia
Physician and Sports
  Medicine
Physics Today
Pittsburgh
Pittsburgh History
Play and Culture
Playboy
PM, Public Management
Poets and Writers
Policy Review
Popular Culture in
  Libraries
Popular Mechanics
Popular Music and Society
Popular Science
Population Studies
Premiere
Proceedings of the Ameri-
  can Antiquarian Society
The Professional Photog-
  rapher
The Progressive
Prospects
PSA Journal
Psychological Reports
Psychology and Aging
Psychology Today

Public Culture
Public Finance Review
Publisher's Weekly
Publishing Research Quar-
  terly
Puget Sound Business
  Journal
Pulp and Paper
Purple Sages Review
Qualitative Sociology
Quarterly Journal of Busi-
  ness and Economics
Quarterly Review of Eco-
  nomics and Finance
Queen's Quarterly
Reader's Digest
Reading Teacher
Real Estate Issues
Reason
Redbook
Referee
Research in Urban Policy
Research Quarterly for
  Exercise and Sport
Restaurants and Institu-
  tions
The Review of Academic
  Life
The Review of Economics
  and Statistics
Review of Industrial Orga-
  nization
Review of Litigation
Runner's World
San Francisco Business
Santa Clara Law Review
The Saturday Evening Post
Saturday Night
Scholastic Coach
Scholastic Coach & Ath-
  letic Director
Scholastic Scope
Science
Scott Stamp Monthly
Serials Librarian
Seton Hall Journal of
  Sport Law
Sewanee Review
Small Press
Smart Money
Smithsonian
Social Education
Social Science Quarterly
Sociologie et Societes
Sociological Focus
Sociology of Sport Journal
South Florida

Southern Communication
Journal
Southern Economic Jour-
nal
Southern Living
Sport
Sport Marketing Quarterly
The Sport Psychologist
SportEurope (Italy)
Sporting Goods Business
Sporting Traditions (Aus-
tralia)
Sports Canada Magazine
(Canada)
Sports Illustrated
Sports Illustrated Australia
Sports Illustrated Canada
Sports Illustrated for Kids
The Sports Lawyers Jour-
nal
Sports Link (Australia)
Sports Weekly (Australia)
SportsTURF
Spotlight
St. Louis
St. Louis Business Journal
Stanford Law Review
State and Local Govern-
ment Review
Stetson Law Review
Strength and Conditioning
Studies in American Indian
Literature
Studies in Latin American
Popular Culture
Studies in Popular Culture
Studies in Symbolic Inter-
action
Success
Supervisory Management
Syntax and Semantics
Syracuse Law Review

Tampa Bay Business Jour-
nal
Tampa Bay History
Tax Notes
TCI
Television Quarterly
Tennessee Journal of
Health, Physical Educa-
tion, Recreation, and
Dance
Texas Coach
Texas Monthly
Texas Tech Law Review
Threads Magazine
Time
Time (Canada)
Timeline
Topps Magazine
Toronto Life
Traces of Indiana and
Midwestern History
Tradition: A Journal of
Orthodox Jewish
Thought
Trailer Life
Trains
Travel in Taiwan
Tulsa Journal of Compara-
tive and International
Law
TV Guide
UCLA Entertainment Law
Review
UMKC Law Review
University of Colorado
Law Review
University of Kansas Law
Review
Urban Affairs Review
USA Weekend
U.S. News & World Report
Vanderbilt Law Review

Vanity Fair
Vermont Law Review
The Virginia Quarterly
Review
Vital Speeches of the Day
Vudei Revuew
Washington Business Jour-
nal
Washington University
Quarterly Review
The Washingtonian
Weatherwise
Welding Journal
Western Humanities Re-
view
Western Journal of Com-
munications
Western States Jewish His-
tory
Westways
Where the Trails Cross
Whittier Law Review
Whole Earth Review
Win
Wisconsin Law Review
Wisconsin Magazine of
History
Wisconsin Trails
Women Lawyer's Journal
Women's Sports and Fit-
ness
The Woodworker's Journal
The World & I
World Baseball Magazine
(Switzerland)
World Press Review
Worth
Yale Journal of Law and
the Humanities
Yale Law Journal
Yale Review
Yankee

Foreword

Baseball: A Comprehensive Bibliography, with its supplements, represents a basic and invaluable resource for the staff of *Baseball Digest*. We recommend it highly to baseball fans, researchers, and writers alike.

John Kuenster, Editor
Baseball Digest
November 23, 1997

Introduction

Objectives/Selection Criteria

With an inclusion deadline of January 1985, the main volume of *Baseball: A Comprehensive Bibliography* was published in 1986. Despite addenda, that 21,251-citation compilation was, like all published literature guides, almost instantly outdated. Many thousands of items were penned on baseball in the seven years after that first edition appeared. Consequently, a first supplement was published in 1993 covering the period 1985 to May 1992. The time is right for a second supplement.

Covering the period from June 1992 through December 1997, the citations in this supplement allow us to point out primarily English-language (with some Spanish, French, and Japanese language) coverage of baseball materials appearing in a variety of sources, including some periodicals not founded or in their infancy before our first supplement.

Additionally, this supplement backtracks to include a number of titles omitted for one reason or another in the first two volumes, with special attention paid to newer interest areas such as baseball cards, Rotisserie leagues, the diamond overseas, and the rise of the Internet. This work contains over 5,100 new references.

As a reference tool, this book aims to perform for its users the same kind of service as the titles it supplements, namely, the quick identification of materials of interest and the provision of assistance in establishing further research agendas. In general, the items cited are, once again, those the user might reasonably expect to find in large university, public, or government libraries and those specialized repositories noted for their acquisition of sports resources.

If not immediately available in local libraries, many of the references cited (especially non-reference books and photocopies of periodical articles) can be obtained in the United States (and a few other nations) through interlibrary loan, details of which service can be provided by the libraries approached. Runs of certain journals, such as *Baseball Digest*, are available in microform from such firms as University Microfilms. Bookstores and mail-order distributors remain an excellent source for specific titles. Increasingly, full-text articles are also available directly or via subscription services over the Internet.

The criteria for selection in this supplement are broad and essentially the same as those employed in the giant 1986 volume and its 1993 offspring. The following types of published materials are represented: books and monographs, periodical articles exceeding a page in length, and documents, such as World Series programs.

A considerable amount of spade work has also been done in the garden of printed, if not strictly "published," materials and a selection is here served, most notably of doctoral dissertations and masters' theses. References are also provided to World Wide Web sites and to a number of periodical articles available via the net.

Although much is included, the categories of exclusion have been retained from the older volumes: newspaper articles (unless reprinted in anthologies or free standing as special supplements), poetry and fiction. All of these are worthy of special bibliographies outside the scope of this work and, indeed as we note in Section A:1 Bibliographies and Indexes below, my colleagues are working diligently on several, especially fiction.

Despite vigorous research, it is probable that a number of published sources, paper and electronic, are missing. In the event that users have or find material fitting the inclusion criteria which was nevertheless left out, it would be helpful to have it forwarded to the compiler for use in our next supplement. Many users responded generously in this manner following the appearance of our earlier works and we thank them.

Arrangement

With minor modifications, the arrangement in this supplement is the same as that of the 1986 master volume and the 1993 supplement. The main sections presented in the Contents table, with their subsections, form something of a classified index of this work, providing the key to its layout. Annotations are provided for references when the titles are not clear. The lengthy introductions provided for sections and subsections in the main volume are, in the interests of space and price, cut down or entirely omitted here. Together with a list of journals consulted, the two indexes complete this work.

Acknowledgments

Fewer people and organizations were involved with this supplement than before; however, those who did help were even more generous this time than last. In no particular order, these individuals and libraries include the following: Myles Friedman, editor, *Spring Training*; *The Sporting News*, St. Louis, Mo.; Bob Kuenster, Century Publications; Bob Carroll, N. Huntingdon, Pa.; David Q. Voigt, Albright College; Mike Shannon,

Spitball Magazine; John R. Schmidt, Park Ridge, Ill.; Cynthia Harris, reference editor, Greenwood Publications; Joe Horrigan, vice president, Pro Football Hall of Fame; SABR Bibliography Committee member Ted Hathaway, Minneapolis; Wayne County Public Library, Wooster, Ohio; Cleveland (Ohio) Public Library, Cleveland, Ohio; Greeneville–Greene County (Tenn.) Public Library; University of Tennessee Library, Knoxville; the Library of Congress; and the New York Public Library.

In April 1997, all of the 28 major league teams (and the two expansion organizations) were again approached for assistance, together with the National Baseball Hall of Fame and Museum, the league offices, and the office of the Commissioner of Baseball. In response, the following teams supplied copies of their 1997 media guides (those * starred also sent yearbooks, which are indexed below):

Kansas City Royals*, Baltimore Orioles*, Texas Rangers*, Cleveland Indians, Florida Marlins, New York Yankees, Oakland A's, San Francisco Giants, Pittsburgh Pirates, Anaheim Angels, New York Mets, Milwaukee Brewers, and Detroit Tigers. As was the case in 1986 and 1993, no team was more helpful than the Los Angeles Dodgers, whose executive vice president, Fred Claire, has been a long-time supporter of these bibliographic endeavors.

The Montreal Expos and St. Louis Expos offered to sell us copies of their printed material, while the other teams, the league offices, the Office of the Commissioner, and the National Baseball Hall of Fame and Museum failed to respond at all. It is perhaps a commentary on the present state of public relations in Major League Baseball that we have received considerably less support for this bibliographic effort in 1997 than in 1992 and less than when it was originally undertaken a decade and a half ago. Indeed, certain libraries and writers associated with professional football offered more help than many directly involved with baseball. Perhaps when a full second edition is undertaken in about 2002, assistance will be more generous—one can hope.

Special appreciation is reserved for my colleagues at Tusculum College, without whose backing and aid this project would remain undone. Robert E. Knott, president, and Jim Reid, vice president, provided the freedom and encouragement to proceed. Oriole fan and history professor Fred Kaufmann cheered the project on while Tate Library colleagues Charles Tunstall, Carolyn Parker, Regina Settle, and Susan Gibson provided a sounding board and interlibrary loan support.

Hearty thanks is also due to *Baseball Digest* editor John Kuenster, whose endorsement constitutes our foreword. These comments set a tone for which we are grateful.

Myron J. Smith, Jr.
Chuckey, Tennessee
Spring 1998

A. Reference Works

Aside from general studies of the game and its history which are cited in the next chapter, the sources noted here are concerned with items which may be considered to have ready-reference value. Section 1 provides data on those bibliographies, indexes, and services which may be employed to update this guide in future years while Section 2 includes information on books and articles which contain definitions of the game's various aspects and quotes about it. Section 3 covers a variety of topics, including annuals and guides, discussions of scoring and scheduling, guides to records and stats (statistics), and works filled with detail for baseball trivia fans. Finally, Section 4 addresses the growing literature surrounding the hobbies of baseball collectibles, e.g., baseball cards, autographs, buttons, stamps, and so forth.

1. Bibliographies and Indexes

The sources in this part offer significant assistance to those who would attempt to keep abreast of both current and historical writings on baseball and is designed specifically to update the citations provided on pages 9–13 of *Baseball: A Comprehensive Bibliography*. The bibliographies contained in certain of the general works and histories cited in Chapter B:1 are particularly helpful as are those in some of the individual biographies covered in Chapter F. These should be examined in addition to the titles noted here.

Additionally, both the serious and casual researcher can utilize the many computerized databases (on-line and CD-ROM) found commercially and in librar-

ies to search for topics on the various aspects of baseball. Those seeking more information, particularly in such specialized areas as sports law and sports medicine, should search the on-line indexes to various databases available commercially via the Internet. Indeed, many of the databases noted as being in paper or CD-ROM format in our original work or its first supplement are now available through the World Wide Web. Examples include products of the H.W. Wilson Company and the Information Access Company. Because database proprietors and search services add, delete, and modify the databases they offer, users should check with their vendors to learn which are available on the service they use. We note a few in this work.

1. Akin, W. E. "Where Baseball Can Still Be Fun: The Flowering of Minor League Baseball Research." *Nine: A Journal of Baseball History and Social Policy Perspective*, V (Fall 1996), 130–138.

2. Barra, Allen. "The Cutting Edge of Baseball Research." *Inside Sports*, XIV (September 1992), 14–15. SABR, the Society for American Baseball Research.

3. Bjarkman, Peter C. "Grizzled Veterans and Bullpen Gems: Baseball's Books on the Art of Pitching." *Elysian Fields Quarterly*, XIV (Spring 1995), 82–88.

4. ____. "Today's Boom Industry in 'Women and Baseball' Histories." *Elysian Fields Quarterly*, XIII (Fall 1994), 94–98.

5. Brewster, Todd. "Baseball's Motherlode." *M*, IX (April 1992), 51+. The National Baseball Library, a unit of the National Baseball Hall of Fame and Museum.

6. Carroll, Bob. *The Sports Video Resource Guide: A Fan's Sourcebook for All the Best in Sports Videos*. New York: Simon & Schuster, 1992. 254p.

7. Clermont, Susan. "*A Bibliography of Baseball Music Titles.*" 1997. <**http://www2.ari.net/home/idenwald/ballb/intro.htm**>. References to 400 works compiled from Library of Congress records.

8. Eley, Stephen. *Padwick's Bibliography of Cricket*. 2 vols. London, Eng.: The Library Association, 1991.

9. Hodgins, Laurence. "Baseball on Video." *Baseball Australia*, VIII (June–August 1995), 14–15.

10. Hoffman, Sharon. "The 'Ins' and 'Outs' of Baseball and Books." *Illustrated Librarian*, LXXII (April 1990), 334+.

11. Information Access Company. *Searchbank*. Infotrac now offers its valuable subscriptions via the WWW under this title. The most useful for purposes of baseball research are: General Reference Center (Magazine Index), Health Reference Center, Business Index ASAP, Legaltrac, Books-in-Print, PAIS International, and ISI Current Contents.

12. Jones, Donald G., with Elaine L. Daley. *Sports Ethics in America: A Bibliography, 1970–1990*. Westport, Conn.: Greenwood Press, 1992.

13. Kahn, Lawrence M. "Discrimination in Professional Sports: A Survey of the Literature." *Industrial and Labor Relations Review*, XLIV (April 1991), 395–418.

14. Lenskyj, Helen J., comp. *Women, Sport and Physical Activity: Selected Research Themes*. Gloucester, Ont.: Sport Information Resource Centre, 1994. 46p.

15. Lewis, Robert M. "American Sport History: A Bibliographic Guide." *American Studies International*, XXIX (April 1991), 35–59.

16. McEvoy, Dave. "Baseball Fights Back." *Publisher's Weekly*, CCXLI (February 14, 1994), 28–30. Contest with popularity of basketball literature.

17. Millman, B. "North American Information Sources." In: M. Shoebridge, ed. *Information Sources in Sports and Leisure*. London, Eng.: Bowker-Sauer, 1992. pp. 279–306.

18. Miranda, M. A. "An Evaluation of Journals in Physical Education, Athletics, and Sports." *Serials Librarian*, XXI, no. 1 (1991), 89–99.

19. National Baseball Hall of Fame and Museum. Library. *Women in Baseball: A Selective Bibliography*. Cooperstown, N.Y., 1997. 11pp. Also available from the Hall of Fame Website <**http://www.enews.com/bas_hall_fame/library/bibs/womenbib.html**>.

20. Phelps, Frank. *The Index to The Sporting News Baseball Registers, 1940–1995*. Cleveland, Oh.: SABR, 1996. 78p.

21. Riess, Steven A. "The Historiography of American Sport." *OAH Magazine of History*, VII (Summer 1992), 10–14.

22. Smith, Myron J., Jr. *Baseball: A Comprehensive Bibliography—Supplement I (1985–May 1992)*. Jefferson, N.C.: McFarland & Co., Inc., 1993.

422p. Adds another 7,771 citations to the 21,251 in the 1985 original work.

23. Society of American Baseball Research. Bibliography Committee. *Baseball on the Net* <**http://www.skypoint.com/~ashbury/_hhdir/hhhotlinks2.html**> is a compilation of 1,200 baseball resources on the Internet accessible via a search engine. Although last updated on June 12, 1996 and currently dormant, the site is still active (as of July 1997) and valuable.

24. *RBI: Research in Baseball Index—A Database for Baseball Research* <**http://student-www.uchicago.edu/users/tmc5/dataserv.htm**> is an ongoing volunteer project designed to catalog all books, pamphlets, magazine and feature newspaper articles, recordings, musical scores, dissertations, films and television about baseball. Under the able direction of Ted Hathaway in Minneapolis, this source adds several thousand titles per year. The fee-based database is not interactive; requests for citations on various topics may, however, be sent to RBI at 5645 Fremont Ave., S., Minneapolis, MN 55419 or e-mailed to hathae@msus1.msus.edu.

25. Sport Information Resource Centre. *The Baseball File: A Comprehensive Bibliography of America's National Pastime.* Gloucester, Ont., 1992. 176p. Includes 5,000 citations for the period 1981–1991.

26. _____. *Sport Database.* An outgrowth of the *Sport Discus* CD-ROM project, this database is updated monthly and is available for fees through a variety of on-line venders: Knight-Rider Information's *Data Star/Dialog* <*http://www.dialog.com*>; The Library Corporation's *NlightN* <*http://www.nlightn.com*>; Ovid Technologies' *Ovid Online* <*http://www.ovid.com*>; CompuServe's *IQUEST* or *Knowledge Index* <*http://www.compuserve.com*>; and, in the Republic of China, through *STICNET.*

27. _____. *Sport Quest.* An outgrowth of the previous citation, this fee-based indexing service is entirely based on the WWW from the publisher's URL <**http://www.SPORTQuest.com**>.

28. Walker, Donald and B. Lee Cooper. *Baseball and American Culture: A Thematic Bibliography of Over 4,500 Works.* Jefferson, N.C.: McFarland & Co., Inc., 1995. 257p.

2. Dictionaries, Glossaries, and Quotations

The sources in this part are designed to assist users in understanding the terminology of the game (sometimes called "baseballese") or to facilitate the identification of famous and infamous quotes, remarks, insults, and wisecracks uttered about it by the great and unknown since the mid–19th Century. Glossaries are also presented in some of the titles presented in Chapter B, parts 1 and 2, as well as in Chapter F.

29. Blount, Roy. "Sports Proverbs Are Profound and Existentially Useful; Sports Proverbs Are Banal and Make Little Sense." *Esquire,* CXX (October 1993), 94–95.

30. "Fungo Lingo: A Baseball Guide." *People Weekly,* XXXI (May 1, 1989), 93+.

31. Freeman, Criswell, comp. *The Wisdom of Old-Time Baseball: Common Sense and Uncommon Genius from 101 Baseball Greats.* Nashville, Tn.: Walnut Grove Press, 1996. 163p. Quotes.

32. Herskowitz, Mickey. "Here are Bits of Baseball Wisdom That Belong to the Ages." *Baseball Digest,* LII (December 1993), 86–89.

33. Hoffman, Sanford and Michael J. Pellowski. *Baseball's Funniest People.* New York: Sterling, 1997. Quotes.

34. Liebman, Glenn. "Baseball 'Greybeards' Often Targets of Choice Quips." *Baseball Digest,* LII (June 1993), 62–64.

35. _____. *Baseball Shorts: 1,000 of the Game's Funniest One-Liners.* Chicago, Ill.: Contemporary Books, 1994. 230p.

36. _____. "Here's Some Wit and Wisdom

from Hall of Fame Members." *Baseball Digest,* LI (December 1992), 72–74.

37. ____. "Here's What Hall of Famers Say About Each Other." *Baseball Digest,* LI (June 1992), 62–65.

38. Liu, Delian and Bryan Farka. "Three Strikes and You're Out: A Look at Baseball and Football Jargon in American English." *English Today,* XII (January 1996), 36+.

39. McBride, Joseph. *High and Inside: An A to Z Guide to the Language of Baseball.* Chicago: Contemporary Books, 1997.

40. Nelson, Donald. *Baseball's Even Greater Insults.* New York: Simon & Schuster, 1994. 230p.

41. Oldfather, Chad H. "The Hidden Ball: A Substantive Critique of Baseball Metaphors in Judicial Opinions." *Connecticut Law Practice,* XXVII (Fall 1994), 17+.

42. Olney, Buster. "Creative Players Put Their Own Spin on Baseball Lingo." *Baseball Digest,* LIII (August 1994), 46–49.

43. Plaut, David, ed. *Speaking of Baseball.* Philadelphia, Pa.: Running Press, 1993. 413p.

44. Safire, William. "The Spinner Spun." *The New York Times Magazine,* (December 22, 1996), 18+.

45. "Sports Slang: The Language of Baseball, Basketball, Football, and Surfing." *Scholastic Scope,* XXXIX (April 19, 1991), 11+.

46. Stewart, Wayne. "Colorful Quotes Have Always Been Part of Game's History." *Baseball Digest,* LI (June 1992), 52–55.

47. ____. "Humorous Side Remarks Enliven Big League Baseball Scene." *Baseball Digest,* LII (June 1993), 60–61.

48. Sullivan, Mike. "Baseball Chitchat Often Borders on the Outrageous." *Baseball Digest,* LVI (November 1997), 66–71.

49. Wells, Malcolm. *Baseball Talk: What Do They Really Mean by That, Anyway?* Minocqua, Minn.: Willow Creek Press, 1997.

3. Annuals and Guides, Scoring and Scheduling, Records, Stats and Trivia

This part is a composite designed to cover several related topics, both general and specific, which nevertheless, for ease of handling, is subdivided into three subsections: annuals and guides; scoring and scheduling, records and stats; and trivia. Citations revealed by SABR colleagues as missed in Baseball: A Comprehensive Bibliography are included. Information relative to some of these topics is also contained in certain general works in other sections, e.g., Chapter B: 1; Chapter C; and Chapter F.

a. Annuals and Guides

Users should note that certain annuals are found elsewhere in this supplement as appropriate to the topics covered, e.g., annual guides to the value of fantasy league teams and players are covered in Chapter B:2:1 ("Rotisserie Leagues and Fantasy Baseball, Including Adult Baseball Camps") below.

50. *Australian Sports Directory.* Canberra: Australian Sports Commission, 1992—. Annual.

51. Aylesworth, Thomas G., ed. *Kids World Almanac of Baseball.* New York: World Almanac, 1996—. Annual.

52. Bauer, David, ed. *Sports Illustrated Presents Baseball.* New York: SI, 1996—. v. 1—.

53. Delavan, John, ed. *Gold Collectors Series Baseball Magazine.* Northbrook, Ill.: H & S Media, 1997—. v. 1—. This new (192-page) annual also has a World Wide Web site **<http://www.gcsmag.com>**.

54. DeMarco, Tony. "Parallel Paths to 3,000 [Hits]." *Beckett Baseball Card Monthly,* IX, no. 90 (September 1992), 8–12.

55. Dewan, John and Dom Zminda. *Stats Baseball Scorecard.* New York: Stats Publishing, 1990—. v.1—.

56. Gervino, Tony, ed. *Hardball.* New York: Harris Pub. Co., 1996—. v. 1—.

57. *The Official Baseball Atlas: A Sports Travel Book.* Chicago, Ill.: Rand McNally, 1993—. Annual.

58. Quinn, Robert J. "Having Fun With Baseball Statistics." *Mathematical Teaching in the Middle School,* I (May 1996), 780+.

59. Rosner, Bernard, *et al.* "Modeling Pitching Performance and the Distribution of Runs Per Inning in Major League Baseball." *The American Statistician,* L (November 1996), 352+.

60. Starr, Mark. "Kiss Those Babies Goodbye." *Newsweek,* CXXIII (June 13, 1994), 58–60. Records under assault.

61. Wheatley, Tom. "A Series of [World Series] Records." *Beckett Baseball Card Monthly,* IX, no. 9 (October 1992), 16–24.

62. White, Paul, ed. *The USA Today Baseball Weekly Almanac.* New York: Hyperion, 1994–. Annual.

b. Scoring and Scheduling, Records and Stats

Certain other references to the four topics covered here are also found elsewhere in subject-specific parts. Examples include Chapter B:2:c ("Championships") and Chapter F:1 ("Rookies") below.

63. Aboufadel, E. "A Mathematician Catches a Baseball." *American Mathematical Monthly,* CIII (December 1996), 870–878.

64. Albert, Jim. "Exploring Baseball Hitting Data: What About Those Breakdown Statistics?" *Journal of the American Statistical Association,* LXXXIX (September 1994), 1066–1075.

65. Albright, S. Christian. "A Statistical Analysis of Hitting Streaks in Baseball." *Journal of the American Statistical Association,* LXXXVIII (December 1993), 1175+.

66. "Baseball by the Numbers." *Sport,* LXXXV (May 1994), 66+.

67. Bortstein, Larry. "How Many Hallowed Records Are Really Unassailable?" *Baseball Digest,* LIV (September 1995), 40–44.

68. Boswell, Thomas. "Total Average: A Real Swingin' Time." *Inside Sports,* XVIII (January 1996), 52–61.

69. ____. "Total Average: Giants Among Men." *Inside Sports,* XVI (March 1994), 33+.

70. ____. "Total Average: Puttin' a Big Hurt on History." *Inside Sports,* XVII (February 1995), 46–56. Ranks Frank Thomas first among 100 hitters.

71. Brody, Susan. "Go Figure." *Sports Illustrated for Kids,* IX (June 1997), 74–75.

72. Brown, A. "The Probability of Breaking Sports Records." *Journal of Recreational Mathematics,* XXVI, no. 1 (1994), 42–47.

73. Browne, M. "Re-reading Bill James." *Elysian Fields Quarterly,* XI (Winter 1992), 78–82.

74. Childress, C. "Working with the Scorekeeper." *Referee,* XVIII (April–May 1993), 42–43, 46–47, 42–45.

75. Costa, Gabriel B. "The Numbers Game: Baseball's Greatest Hitter— Williams or Ruth?" *Elysian Fields Quarterly,* XII (Fall 1993), 89–91. Draw.

76. ____. "The Numbers Game: Was Cobb's Batting More Dominant Than Ruth's Slugging?" *Elysian Fields Quarterly,* XIII (Summer 1994), 60–61. In a word, No!

77. Daniels, Curt. "Clone the Baseball Team." *Win,* XIV (June 1993), 56+. Streaks and records.

78. Day, George. "Baseball by the Numbers: The Science of Sabermetrics." *Dugout,* II (April and August 1994), 22–24, 21–24.

79. Debs, Victor, Jr. *Still Standing After All These Years: Twelve of Baseball's Longest Standing Records.* Jefferson, N.C.: McFarland & Co., Inc., 1997. 254p.

80. Dickson, Paul. *The Joy of Keeping Score: How Scoring Has Influenced and Enhanced the History of Baseball.* New York: Walker, 1996. 117p.

81. Dittmar, Joseph J. *Baseball Records Registry: The Best and Worst Single-Day Performances and the Stories Behind Them.* Jefferson, N.C.: McFarland & Co., Inc., 1997. 544p.

82. Doyle, Al. "Low Batting Averages Don't Always Curtail RBI Totals." *Baseball Digest,* LVI (May 1997), 54–57.

83. Ehret, S. "Baseball: (When to) Score That Run." *Referee,* XX (December 1995), 62–64.

84. Flanagan, Jeffrey. "Time-Tested Major League Records May Stand Forever." *Baseball Digest,* LII (August 1993), 62–63.

85. Goldberg, Suzanne. "Making a Hit with Percentages." *Learn 94,* XXII (February 1994), 58–59.

86. Heaton, E. E. and A. W. "Total Production Average: The Best Overall Batting Performance Measure—So Far." *Baseball Research Journal,* XXIV (1995), 127–130.

87. Holway, John B. "Games Won at Bat, Key State in Rating a Hitter's Value." *Baseball Digest,* LIII (June 1994), 20–26.

88. James, Bill. "Answering Questions About Baseball Using Statistics." *Chance,* VI, no. 2 (1993), 17+.

89. Knowles, Glenn, Keith Sherony, and Mike Haupert. "The Diamond for Major League Baseball: A Test of the Uncertainty of Outcome Hypothesis." *The American Economist,* XXXVI (Fall 1992), 72+.

90. Kuenster, John. "Complete-Game Averages by Starting Pitchers Continue to Plummet." *Baseball Digest,* LV (February 1996), 17–19.

91. Lanoue, H. R. and J. J. Revetta, Jr. "An Analytical Hierarchy Approach to Major League Baseball Performance Ratings." *Mathematical and Computer Modelling,* XVII, nos. 4–5 (1993), 195+.

92. Lewis, Allen. "These Six Records Appear Beyond Challenge in the Majors." *Baseball Digest,* LI (December 1992), 78–80.

93. McClellan, S. "Standardized Range Factor: A New Method of Measuring Defense." *Baseball Research Journal,* XXIV (1995), 113–116.

94. Moran, N. "Streaks: Statistics vs. Serendipity." *Baseball Research Journal,* XXIV (1995), 79–80.

95. Muscat, Carrie. "Sometimes the Numbers *Do* Lie." *Inside Sports,* XVII (August 1995), 10–12. Statistical and endorsement competition between *The Baseball Encyclopedia* and *Total Baseball,* by John Thorn and Pete Palmer.

96. Nighttingale. Dave. "Score It an Error: A Veteran Sportswriter Blasts the Standards in Major League Official Scoring." *Inside Sports,* XVI (July 1994), 52–55.

97. "Numbers Game." *Sports Illustrated for Kids,* VIII (April 1996), 42–43.

98. Olson, Stan. "Total Baseball Player Ratings Place Ruth, Lajoie at Top." *Baseball Digest,* LV (March 1996), 56–58.

99. Paulson, Richard A. "A Comment on the Misperception of Streaks." *Journal of Gambling Studies,* X (Summer 1994), 199–205.

100. Rosenberg, Mitchell. "Learn About Statistics: Math League Baseball." *Arithmetic Teacher,* XLI (April 1994), 459–461.

101. Rosner, B., F. Mosteller, and C. Youtz. "Modeling Pitcher Performance and the Distribution of Runs Per Inning in Major League Baseball." *American Statistician,* L (November 1996), 352–360.

102. Rozema, Edward. "Round-off, Batting Averages, and Ill-Conditioning." *The College Mathematics Journal,* XXV (September 1994), 314–317.

103. Rubin, Bob. "Crunch Time in the Numbers Game: By Turning the Sports World's Raw Data Into Detailed Analyses, STATS, Inc., Keeps Everyone From Rotisserie Players to Major League Managers on the Figurative Cutting Edge." *Inside Sports,* XVII (June 1995), 22–25.

104. Rundquist, Willie. *Baseball by the Numbers: How Statistics Are Collected, What They Mean, and How They Reveal the Game.* Jefferson, N.C.: McFarland & Co., Inc., 1995. 190p.
105. Russell, Robert A. and Janny M. Y. Leung. "Devising a Cost-Effective Schedule for a Baseball League." *Operations Research Letters,* XLII (July 1994), 614–625.
106. Seeman, Corey. "Drowning by Numbers: The State of Baseball History." *Pittsburgh History,* LXXVI (Summer 1993), 76–78.
107. Stone, Larry. "RBI and Runs Scored, Clues to a Hitter's True Value." *Baseball Digest,* LV (July 1996), 54–57.
108. Swetman, D. L. "RBI Average: A New Statistic for Baseball." *Baseball Research Journal,* XXIV (1995), 123–126.
109. Szetela, Walter. "Baseball." *The Arithmetic Teacher,* XLI (March 1994), 382–390.
110. Thomley, S. "On the Hot Seat: Official Scorers and No-Hitters." *National Pastime,* XV (1995), 127–128.
111. Vass, George. "Playing Streaks: What Do They Really Mean in the Majors?" *Baseball Digest,* LIV (July 1995), 22–26.
112. Yellon, A. "Team All-Time Records: Clubs May Move, But Records Should Follow." *National Pastime,* XIV (1994), 31–33.
113. Zentall, Thomas R. "'Bouncing Back' from a Loss: A Statistical Artifact." *Bulletin of the Psychonomic Society,* XXIX (September 1991), 384–386.

c. Trivia

Other citations to trivia will be found in certain subject-specific parts below, e.g., Chapter B:2:d ("The World Series").

114. Alley, Robert S. *Baseball Trivia: So You Think You Know Baseball.* Indianapolis, Ind.: Masters Press, 1994. 149p.
115. "The Amazing World Series Quiz." *Sports Illustrated for Kids,* VIII (October 1996), 54–59.
116. Ariel Books Staff. *Fantastic Baseball Quiz Book.* Kansas City, Mo.: Andrews & McMeel, 1997. 374p.
117. Banks, Kerry. *The Glory Years: Old Time Baseball Trivia.* New York: Sterling Publishing, 1997.
118. Debs, Victor, Jr. *Baseball Tidbits.* Indianapolis, Ind.: Masters Press, 1997.
119. Floatow, Scott and Ken Samuelson. *The Baseball Encyclopedia Quiz Book.* New York: Macmillan, 1997.
120. Forker, Dom. *1,001 Baseball Questions Your Friends Can't Answer.* New York: Signet, 1997. 235p.
121. ____. *Test Your Baseball IQ.* New York: Sterling, 1993. 128p.
122. Herzog, Brad. *7th Inning Stretch: Time Out for Baseball Trivia.* New York: Bantam, 1994. 76p.
123. Hoppel, Joe and the Editors of *The Sporting News. Baseball: A Doubleheader Collection of Facts, Feats & Firsts.* New York: Galahad Books, 1994. 260p.
124. Malkovich, A. J. *The Ultimate Sports Trivia Encyclopedia.* Aurora, Colo.: Field Productions, 1991. 287p.
125. Martinez, David H. *The Book of Baseball Literacy: What Every Baseball Fan Needs to Know.* New York: Plume, 1996. 382p.
126. Nash, Bruce M. and Allan Zullo. *Nash & Zullo's Believe It or Not: Baseball Edition.* New York: Dell, 1992. 165p.
127. Nemec, David. *Great Baseball Feats, Facts, and Firsts.* New York: Signet Books, 1995. 409p.
128. ____. ____. New York: Signet Books, 1997. 426p.
129. Phillips, Louis. *Ask Me Anything About Baseball.* New York: Avon Books, 1995. 118p.
130. Rosjhowski, Mark. *Spalding Baseball Crosswords.* 2nd ed. Indianapolis, Ind.: Masters Press, 1994. 179p.
131. Skloot, Floyd. "Trivia Tea: Baseball

as Balm." *The Gettysburg Review,* V (Summer 1992), 377+.

132. Vickery, A. Lou. *Answers to Baseball's Most Asked Questions.* Indianapolis, Ind.: Masters Press, 1995. 138p.

133. Weber, Bruce. *Baseball Trivia and Fun Book.* New York: Scholastic, 1993. 63p.

4. Baseball Cards, Autographs, and Collectibles

In the eleven years since the publication of *Baseball: A Comprehensive Bibliography,* the literature on hobby aspects of baseball, including especially baseball cards (now often seen as a business or investment), has grown significantly. The citations in this part are, for ease of handling, divided into three parts, the size of which reflect publication growth: autographs; baseball cards; and collectibles and computer program reviews. It should be noted that a few citations relative to this topic are found elsewhere, e.g., references to the baseball cards of certain players are found in Chapter G ("Individual Biography") below.

a. Autographs

134. Chen, Theo. "Sign Language." *Beckett Baseball Card Monthly,* XI, no. 112 (July 1994), 120–121.

135. Duncan, David J. "A Mickey Mantle Koan: The Obstinate Grip of an Autographed Baseball." *Harper's,* CCLXXXV (September 1992), 65–72.

136. Moe, Rita. "[Autograph] Hounds of the Metrodome." *The Minneapolis Review of Baseball,* X (Fall 1991), 18–21.

137. Nash, Bruce M., Allan Zullo, and Michael Bernard. *The Insider's Guide to Baseball Autographs.* Kansas City, Mo.: Andrews and McMeel, 1994. 173p.

138. Regli, Phil. "Autographs: *Sports Illustrated* Covers." *Beckett Vintage Sports,* I, no. 7 (June 1997), *passim.*

<http://www.beckett.com/products/vtpd.html>.

139. Rudolph, Benjamin. "Exploding Ink: The Undeniable Allure of Autographs Has Blown Up Into the Hobby's Hottest Trend." *Beckett Baseball Card Monthly,* VII, no. 147 (June 1997), *passim.* <http://www.beckett.com/products/bbpd.html>.

140. Ryan, Steve. "Leaving Their Marks." *Beckett Baseball Card Monthly,* XI, no. 107 (February 1994), 18–23.

141. Seigerman, David. "Say 'Please.'" *Beckett Focus on Future Stars,* III, no. 27 (July 1993), 20–21. Collecting autographs at minor league parks.

b. Baseball Cards

142. Allison, Will. "Trailblazing Cardboard." *Beckett Focus on Future Stars,* III, no. 26 (June 1993), 20–22.

143. "The Baseball Card Market." *Pulp and Paper,* LXIII (August 1989), 102+.

144. *Beckett Almanac of Baseball Cards and Collectibles, No. 2.* Dallas, Tx.: Beckett Publications, 1997. 400p.

145. Bloom, John. *"Cardboard Images of the Past: Baseball Card Collecting and the Politics of Sports."* Unpublished Ph.D. Dissertation, University of Minnesota, 1991.

146. ____. *A House of Cards: Baseball Card Collecting and Popular Culture.* American Culture, v. 12. Minneapolis: University of Minnesota Press, 1997. 142p. Based on the previous entry.

147. Brill, Bob. "Parallel Challenge." *Beckett Baseball Card Monthly,* XI, no. 116 (November 1994), 106–113. Keeping interest up re: card trading during baseball strike.

148. ____. and Steve Ryan. "'94 Card Preview." *Beckett Baseball Card Monthly,* XI, no. 108 (March 1994), 14–23.

149. Broome, Tol. "The Boom in Bowman." *Beckett Baseball Card Monthly,* XI, no. 106 (January 1994), 20–23.

150. ____. *From Ruth to Ryan: Unbeatable Card Buys.* Iola, Wisc.: Krause Publications, 1993. 160p.

151. ____. "Heavy Metal [in Baseball Cards]." *Beckett Baseball Card Monthly,* XII, no. 119 (February 1995), 120–123.

152. ____. "Mini [Topps 1975 Rookie Card] Sensation." *Beckett Baseball Cards Monthly,* XII, no. 118 (January 1995), 114–119.

153. Brown, Chip. "Honus Wagner Strikes Out." *Forbes,* CLI (January 4, 1993), 266–267+.

154. Burrell, Chris. "Dreams for Sale: The Commerce of Card Collecting." *The Minneapolis Review of Baseball,* X (Fall 1991), 13–15.

155. Chen, Theo. "Learning by the Cards: The Sports Card Hobby Has a Lot to Offer Those Interested in Reading, Writing, and Arithmetic." *Beckett Baseball Card Monthly,* X, no. 101 (August 1993), 16–19.

156. ____. "Pure Premium." *Beckett Baseball Card Monthly,* X, no. 94 (January 1993), 14–17. 1990 Leaf set.

157. ____. "Trendy Ten [Collecting Trends]." *Beckett Baseball Card Monthly,* XI, no. 116 (November 1994), 16–23.

158. Childress, Casey and Linda McKenzie. *A Kid's Guide to Collecting Baseball Cards.* Rev. ed. Tucson, Ariz.: Harbinger AZ, 1994. 80p.

159. Consumer Guide. *Baseball Card Price Guide.* Lincolnwood, Ill.: Publications International, 1996–. Annual. Both the 1996 and 1997 editions have 640 pages.

160. Cooper, Joseph H. "Cards for Kids." *Beckett Baseball Card Monthly,* IX, no. 93 (December 1992), 14–17; X, no. 105 (December 1993), 108–111; XI, no. 114 (December 1994), 118–125.

161. ____. "Inside the [Uniform] Numbers." *Beckett Baseball Card Monthly,* III, no. 97 (April 1993), 22–23.

162. Craft, David. *Baseball Cards.* New York: Mallard Press, 1992. 117p.

163. Crouch, Gary. "Collecting in the '90s." *Beckett Baseball Card Monthly,* XI, no. 109 (April 1994), 120–121.

164. Derris, Robert. "An American Hobby: Baseball Card Collecting." *Antiques and Collecting Hobbies,* XCV (July 1990), 23+.

165. Dodgen, Lynda and Adrian Rapp. "An Analysis of Personality Differences Between Baseball Card Collectors and Investors Based on the Myers-Briggs Personality Inventory." *Journal of Social Behavior & Personality,* VII, no. 2 (1992), 355–361.

166. Farris, P. J. "On Baseball Cards and Literacy Acquisition." *Reading Teacher,* XLVIII (April 1995), 626–627.

167. Fitts, Robert K. "Baseball Cards and Race Relations." *Journal of American Culture,* XVII (Fall 1994), 75+.

168. Garrity, John. "House of Cards: Driven by Greed, the Sports-Trading-Card Industry All But Collapsed. Can It Rebuild Itself?" *Sports Illustrated,* LXXXV (July 29, 1996), 104–106, 108, 110.

169. Gill, Andrew M. and Victor Brazer. "Baseball Stars and Baseball Cards: A New Look at Monopsony in Major League Baseball." *Social Science Quarterly,* LXXV (March 1994), 195+.

170. Gordon, James D., 3rd. "Cardozo's Baseball Cards." *Stanford Law Review,* XLIV (April 1992), 899+.

171. Green, Keith. "Carbonated Cardboard." *Beckett Baseball Card Monthly,* XII, no. 123 (June 1995), 100–103. Baseball cards from Pepsi and Coca Cola.

172. Green, Paul M. *The Complete Price Guide to Baseball Cards Worth Collecting.* Chicago, Ill.: Contemporary Books, 1994. 310p.

173. "He Shoots Baseball Cards: Tips From Spring Training." *Petersen's Photographic Magazine,* XVIII (May 1989), 32+.

174. Hines, Catharine. "Minor League Cards, Major League Excitement." *Beckett Future Stars,* VII, no. 73 (May 1997), *passim.* **<http://www.beckett.com/products/fspd.html>.**

175. Hoffman, Frank W. "The Baseball Card Collecting Phenomenon: An Historical Overview." *Popular Culture in Libraries,* I, no. 3 (1993), 59–64.

176. ____. and William G. Bailey. "Baseball Card Collecting." In: their *Sports and Recreation Fads*. Binghampton, N.Y.: Haworth, 1991. pp. 39–42.

177. "Hot Hobby!" *National Geographic World*, no. 190 (June 1991), 23+.

178. Kaufman, James and Nathan Stone. "Spinning the [Old] Toppers." *Beckett Baseball Card Monthly*, III, no. 97 (April 1993), 16–19.

179. Klein, Rich. "Expanding Potential." *Beckett Baseball Card Monthly*, X, no. 98 (May 1993), 108–109. Cards from the N.L. expansion teams in Colorado and Florida.

180. Klemm, Alisia. "Trading Up." *Sporting Goods Business*, XXIX (June 1996), 58–59.

181. Kull, Andrew. "Unilateral Mistake: The Baseball Card Case." *Washington University Law Quarterly*, LXX (Spring 1992), 57+.

182. Larson, Mark K. *Minor League Baseball Card Price List*. Iola, Wis.: Krause Publications, 1993. 480p.

183. Liebenson, Donald. "The Guys Who Make Topps Click." *Topps Magazine*, (Summer 1991), 58–59.

184. ____. "Lost and 'Find.'" *Topps Magazine*, (Spring 1992), 18, 21.

185. ____. "Take a Second Look." *Topps Magazine*, (Fall 1992), 18–21.

186. Lipset, Lew. "The Old Judge." *Beckett Vintage Sports*, I, no. 7 (June 1997), *passim*. **<http://www.beckett.com/products/vtpd.html>**. The Topps T206 series.

187. Liss, Kenneth M. "Journey Into the Unknown." *Topps Magazine*, (Spring 1992), 24–25.

188. ____. "The 'Mod' and Colorful Sizzling '70s: 1975 Topps Set Was the Decade's Best." *Topps Magazine*, (Summer 1991), 52–53.

189. Montague, John. "It's in the Cards." *Topps Magazine*, (Fall 1992), 64–65.

190. Moriah, Dave. "Royalty." *Beckett Baseball Card Monthly*, X, no. 95 (February 1993), 10–16. Donruss Diamond King art cards.

191. O'Shei, Tim. "The Making of a Card." *Beckett Baseball Card Monthly*, XI, no. 108 (March 1994), 106–110.

192. ____. "Truly Limited." *Beckett Baseball Card Monthly*, X, no. 102 (September 1993), 108–113.

193. Owens, Thomas S. *The Book of 1993 Baseball Cards*. Lincolnwood, Ill.: Publications International, 1993. 320p.

194. ____. *The Book of 1994 Baseball Cards*. Lincolnwood, Ill.: Publications International, 1994. 320p.

195. Payne, Mike. "No. 1 Picks." *Beckett Baseball Cards Monthly*, no. 148 (July 1997), *passim*. **<http://www.beckett.com/products/bbpd.html>**.

196. ____. "One Hundred Great Cards." *Beckett Baseball Cards Monthly*, III, no. 100 (July 1993), 10–20.

197. ____. "Q & A: Dr. James Beckett." *Beckett Baseball Cards Monthly*, X, no. 100 (July 1993), 22–23.

198. Pearlman, Donn. "The Innovative '80s." *Topps Magazine*, (Winter 1992), 66–67.

199. ____. "Yesterday's Novelties, Today's Bargains." *Topps Magazine*, (Summer 1991), 66–67.

200. Portantiere, Nick. "Peripheral Vision." *Beckett Baseball Card Monthly*, VII, no. 147 (June 1997), *passim*. **<http://www.beckett.com/products/bbpd.html>**. People in the background of cards.

201. Pueschel, Brad. "Have Mighty Baseball Cards Struck Out?" *Beckett Baseball Cards Monthly*, XII, no. 118 (January 1995), 20–23. Because of the 1994-95 strike.

202. Rapp, Adrian and Lynda Dodgen. "The Who, What, and Whys of Baseball Card Collecting." *Popular Culture in Libraries*, I, no. 3 (1993), 65+.

203. Regoli, Bob. "Racism in Baseball Card Collecting: Fact or Fiction?" *Human Relations*, XLIV (March 1991), 255–264.

204. Rosen, Alan "Mr. Mint," with T. S. O'Connell. *True Mint: Mr. Mint's Price & Investment Guide to True Mint Baseball Cards*. Iola, Wisc.: Krause Publications, 1994. 304p.

205. Roush, Chris. "All-Star Appeal." *Beckett Baseball Card Monthly,* IX, no. 88 (July 1992), 8–9. All-Star cards.

206. Ruth, Amy. "Victorian Scraps." *Antiques and Collecting Magazine,* XCIX (February 1995), 38+. Early baseball cards.

207. Ryan, Steve. "Insertmania." *Beckett Baseball Card Monthly,* X, no. 99 (June 1993), 112–113.

208. Savage, Kevin. "Hobby on the Move." *Beckett Baseball Card Monthly,* X, no. 94 (January 1993), 10–13.

209. Sliepka, Dave and Theo Chen. "Cards That Never Were [Issued]." *Beckett Baseball Card Monthly,* XII, no. 119 (February 1995), 18–23.

210. Slocum, Frank. *Baseball Cards of the Sixties: The Complete Topps Cards, 1960–1969.* New York: Simon and Schuster, 1994. Unpaged.

211. Smith, Greg. "Baseball Cards." *Petersen's Photographic Magazine,* XX (April 1992), 28+.

212. *Sports Collectors Digest & Sports Cards Magazine,* Editors of. *Getting Started in Card Collecting.* Iola, Wisc.: Krause Publications, 1993. 208p.

213. Stewart, Mark. *The Ultimate Insider's Guide to Baseball Cards.* New York: Crown, 1993. Unpaged.

214. Towey, Michael P. *Baseball Rookie Run Down: A Unique Rookie Card–First Card Index, 1991–1992.* Lincoln, Neb.: Pop Fly Publications, 1994. 53p.

215. "The Ups and Downs of Collecting Baseball Cards." *Penny Power,* IX (June 1989), 10+.

216. Vest, J. "Lawyers Hold All the Cards." *U.S. News & World Report,* CXXI (December 2, 1996), 57+. Charges against Topps Co. for promoting gambling among children.

217. Weikle, David. "Base Ball Umpires: In the Cards." *Referee,* XX (May 1995), 36–40.

218. Whalen, Dwight. "Collecting the World's Most Bizarre Trading Cards." *Fate,* XLVIII (March 1995), 42–46.

219. White, Michael K. "Playing Cards." *Greeley Style Magazine,* VIII (August 1991), 15+.

220. Williams, Pete. *Card Sharks: How Upper Deck Turned a Child's Hobby Into a High-Stakes, Billion-Dollar Business.* New York: Macmillan, 1995. 278p.

c. Collectibles and Computer Program Reviews/Internet Sites

1. Collectibles

221. Aldridge, Gwen. *Baseball Archaeology: Artifacts From the Great American Pastime.* Photos by Bret Wills. San Francisco, Ca.: Chronicle Books, 1993. 111p.

222. Baker, Mark Allen and Mark K. Larson. *Team Baseballs: A Comprehensive Guide to the Identification, Authentication, and Value of Autographed Baseballs.* Iola, Wis.: Krause Publications, 1992. 544p.

223. *The Baseball and Sports Publications Price Guide.* Tampa, Fla.: Century of Sports Pub. Co., 1996–. Annual.

224. Bevans, Don. *Baseball Team Collectibles.* Radnor, Pa.: Wallace-Homestead Book Co., 1994. 241p.

225. Broome, Tol. "Call Them Collectibles." *Beckett Baseball Card Monthly,* XII, no. 124 (July 1995), 116–123. Phone cards.

226. ____. "A Real Gamer." *Beckett Baseball Card Monthly,* XII, no. 123 (June 1993), 10–15. Game-used memorabilia.

227. Chadwick, Bruce. "Color-Blind Collectibles." *Topps Magazine,* (Fall 1992), 42–43.

228. ____. "Doing Pennants." *Topps Magazine,* (Winter 1992), 22–23.

229. ____. "Games People Played." *Topps Magazine,* (Spring 1992), 22–23.

230. ____. "Get with the Program." *Topps Magazine,* (Summer 1992), 20–21.

231. ____. "That's the Ticket." *Topps Magazine,* (Fall 1991), 20–21.

232. "Collectors and Their Collections:

Baseball Memorabilia." *Maryland Magazine,* XXVIII (April 1996), 38+.

233. Cooper, Mark, with Douglas Congdon-Martin and special contributions by Vincent F. Hink and William E. Howard. *Baseball Games: Home Versions of the National Pastime, 1860s–1960s—Price Guide.* Atglen, Pa.: Schiffer Pub., 1995. 158p.

234. Cox, A. J. "Baseball's Passionage Collectors: A Psychosocial Perspective of the Quest for Memorabilia." *Nine: A Journal of Baseball History and Social Policy Perspective,* III (Spring 1995), 248–260.

235. Crispell, Diane. "Collecting Memories." *American Demographics,* X (November 1988), 38+.

236. Evans, M. K. "The Memorabilia Bust." *GQ: Gentlemen's Quarterly,* LXV (April 1995), 92+.

237. Gabriel, Paul E. "An Examination of Customer Racial Discrimination in the Market for Baseball Memorabilia." *Journal of Business,* LXVIII (April 1995), 215+.

238. Graham, Tim. "Show Me the Memorabilia." *Beckett's Baseball Cards Monthly,* VII, no. 148 (July 1997), *passim.* **<http://www.becketts.com/products/bbpd.html>.**

239. Halper, Barry, with Bill Madden. "Baseball Collecting." In: John Thorn and Pete Palmer, eds. *Total Baseball.* 3rd ed. New York: HarperPerenial, 1993. pp. 596–600.

240. Herndon, Myrtis Elizabeth. *"The Sporting Spirit: Perceptions in Philatelic Art Iconography and Sports Philately, 1896–1974."* Unpublished Ph.D. dissertation, the Ohio State University, 1991.

241. Huffman, Francis. "Where Does It Come From?" *Entrepreneur,* XVII (June 1989), 90+. Collecting memorabilia.

242. Kent, David A. "As American as Baseball." *Scott Stamp Monthly,* XI (September 1993), 14+. Collecting baseball stamps.

243. Larson, Mark K. *The Complete Guide to Baseball Memorabilia.* 2nd ed., expanded and rev. Iola, Wis.: Krause Publications, 1994. 464p.

244. ____. ____. Expanded, rev., 3rd ed. Iola, Wis.: Krause Publications, 1996. 480p.

245. McQuarrie, Jack. "Got It? Flaunt It." *Beckett Baseball Card Monthly,* X, no. 94 (January 1993), 104–107. Displaying collectibles.

246. Menchine, Ron. *A Picture Postcard History of Baseball.* Vetal, N.Y.: Almar Press, 1992. 135p.

247. ____. "Yearbooks." *Beckett Vintage Sports,* I, nos. 5–7 (April–June, 1997), *passim.* **<http://www.beckett.com/products/vtpd.html>.**

248. Miller, Stuart. "Supply, Demand, and the Souvenir." *Inside Sports,* XVI (September 1994), 10–11.

249. Nathans, Aaron. "Hungry for Collectibles." *Beckett Baseball Card Monthly,* XI, no. 113 (August 1994), 20–23. Nontraditional items.

250. Raycraft, Don and Craig. *Value Guide to Baseball Collectibles.* Paducah, Ky.: Collector Books, 1992. 215p.

251. Reed, Fred. "Stand-Up Comics." *Beckett Vintage Sports,* I, no. 7 (June 1997), *passim.* **<http://www.beckett .com/products/vtpd.html>.** Sports comic book collecting.

252. Sgroi, Peter. "How It Became Legal to Keep Baseball Souvenirs." *Baseball Digest,* LIV (August 1995), 34–37.

253. Thompson, Jim. "'Gram Crackers." *Beckett Baseball Card Monthly,* VII, no. 148 (July 1997), *passim.* **<http://www.beckett.com/products/bbpd. html>.** Collecting programs.

254. ____. "Mediums, Well Done." *Beckett Baseball Card Monthly,* VII, no. 147 (June 1997), *passim.* **<http://www.beckett.com/products/bbpd. html>.** Collecting media guides.

2. Computer Program Reviews/ Internet Sites

Internet Sites

There are, according to John Skilton's massive list, almost 3,000 sites on the

World Wide Web devoted to baseball. If some of those were broken down by sub-pages, there would be even more. We offer only a few at this point, and recommend that initial users employ the Skilton guide, as well as the SABR sites as their entry-ports into the colorful world of baseball on the net. Seamus Kearney's original essay *Baseball on the Net: A Primer for Computer Access to Baseball Information* **<http://www.skypoint.com /~ashbury/_bbotn/linkonnet.html>** in its revised December 1994 edition is still a helpful guide.

255. *Baseball Parent* **<http://members. aol.com/baseparent/index.html>** offers articles from past issues, youth baseball links, and subscription information.

256. *Beckett Products.* In addition to his print magazines, Dr. James Beckett has offered, until recently, his current issues at his website:
Beckett Baseball Card Monthly **<http:/ /www.beckett.com/products/bbpd. html>**.
Beckett Future Stars & Sports Collectibles **<http://www.beckett.com/ products/fspd.html>**.
Beckett Vintage Sports **<http://www. beckett.com/products/vtpd.html>**.

257. *Bigleague.com*, not to be confused with the next entry, provides links to a number of sports sites on the Internet, including baseball, football, hockey, golf, UK News and Sports, and basketball, courtesy of Monte Cristo, based in Falls Church, Va. **<http://www.bigleague.com>**.

258. *Bigleaguers.com* **<http://www.big leaguers.com>** allows, via a search engine, access to the personal sites of all players who are represented by the Major League Players Association. Many of the sites are maintained by players themselves.

259. *CBS Sportline* **<http://cbs.sports line.com>** is one of the most popular locations for sports information, featuring a sports wire and profiles, chat,

contests, etc. Similar in intent to the Foxsport site noted below.

260. *CNNSI* **<http://CNNSI.com>** is a joint, interactive service provided by Cable News Network and *Sports Illustrated*. One feature of note is provision of statistics on 15,000 players.

261. *ESPN Sportzone* **<http://www. espnsportzone.com>** ruled the roost of sports sites until the appearance of CBS Sportline, above.

262. *Fastball.com* **<http://www.fast ball.com>** is a premiere site for current information on baseball game results, stats, standings, dugout chatter, and team coverage. Regular updates of scores from games in progress can be had together with the latest columns from the pressbox. Net surfers can check this source as their grandfathers used to check the headlines of the sports page in the newspaper.

263. *Foxsports* **<http://www.foxsport .com>** offers late news, scores, profiles, and, with the Fox network hosting a baseball game of the week on tv, an expanded look at baseball. Compare with CBS Sportline above.

264. *Home Plate: Baseball in the 1930s* **<http://rampages.onramp.net/~word work/index.html>** is Larry S. Bonura's shrine to recording WWW information on baseball in the glory years.

265. *TheInsidePitch* **<http://pegasus. rutgers.edu/~tarose>** is "a major league baseball zin," with stats and commentary.

266. *John Skilton's Baseball Links* **<http: //www.baseball-links.com>** is the single most comprehensive collection of W3 baseball links available (2,839 in July 1997), indexed into 21 different categories. This is THE STARTING PLACE for anyone employing the web for current baseball research.

267. *National Baseball Hall of Fame and Museum* at Cooperstown, N.Y., maintains a website which lists its enshrinees, offers special bibliographies, and reports on other nuggets of baseball

heritage <http://www.enews.com/bas_hall_fame/overview.html>.

268. *NandoNet's Press Box* <http://www2.nando.net:80/newsroom/sports/PressBox.html> presents daily columns.

269. *Nerd World: Baseball* <http://207.159.105.133/cgi-bin/vdata.cgi?BASEBALL/145> when printed out offers 14 pages of links and rivals the number of individual sites noted by John Skilton.

270. *RotoBall* <http://rotoball.com>. Rotisserie baseball.

271. *RotoNews Fantasy Baseball Report* <http://futures.net/roto.

272. *The Society for American Baseball Research (SABR)* has and does offer a number of exciting sites and services which describe not only its own activities and products, but offers some actual assistance.

SABR Homepage <http://www.sabr.org> is a guide to mission and products.

SABR Bibliography Committee. This active division maintains its own home page <http://student-www.uchicago.edu/users/tmc5/bibcomm.htm#tsn> from which sample copies of its *Current Baseball Publications, Newsletter,* and *Bibliography of Reviews* of recent baseball publications can be viewed. It also announces its *Research in Baseball Index* which we cover above under Bibliographies.

273. *Search Sport* <http://www.oldsport.com/search/main.htm> is a directory of sports arranged alphabetically; by clicking your choice, e.g., baseball, a list of links appears. Fast.

274. *Sport Information Resource Centre* <http://www.sirc.ca> maintains its own site where it describes its products and offers news on conferences.

275. *The Sporting News* <http:thesportingnews.com> maintains its baseball coverage excellence and its "Archives" sub-page is filled with topics of historical interest. We have noted

several in the appropriate topical locations in the main portions of the bibliography below.

276. *Sports Illustrated for Kids* <http://www.pathfinder.com@@zidULwYAK@fn3efa/SIFK>.

277. *The Unofficial Sports Links Page* <http://www.cybergate.net/%Ekcarter/links/links.html> not only offers links to 15 sites, but to a number of general sites, plus other sports.

278. *USA Today Baseball Weekly* <http://www.usatoday.com/bbw/front.htm> is the same quality weekly journal online as it is in print.

Computer Program/ Internet Print Materials

279. Delavan, John, ed. *Web Guide Sports: More Than 2,000 Sports Sites in 70 Categories Featured.* Northbrook, Ill.: H & S Media, 1997—. v. 1—. Biannual.

280. Godfrey, John. "Batter Up!: Baseball Rotisserie League Assistance on the Internet." *Home Office Computing,* XV (April 1997), 46–47.

281. Herther, N. K. "Play Ball: Microsoft's First Experiment with Consumer Online Services." *Online,* XVIII (September–October 1994), 18–26.

282. Hiltner, Judith R. and James R. Walker. "Super Frustration Sunday: The Day *Prodigy's* Fantasy Baseball Died—An Analysis of the Dynamics of Electronic Communication." *Journal of Popular Culture,* XXX (Winter 1996), 103–118.

283. Humber, B. "Virtual Baseball: The Grand Old Game Meets the Information Super Highway." *Dugout,* II (December 1994), 11–14.

284. Jaroslovsky, Rich. "Major League Baseball Sportsguide: Review." *Computer Life,* I (October 1994), 126–127.

285. Johnston, B. L. "Sports on the Internet." *Tennessee Journal of Health, Physical Education, Recreation, and Dance,* XXXIV (Spring 1996), 36+.

286. Maloni, Kelly, Ben Greenman, and Kristin Miller. "Baseball." In: their *Netsports: Your Guide to Sports Mania on the Information Highway.* New York: Michael Wolff & Co., 1995. pp. 34–57. Updates are on the Web **<http://www.ypn.com>.**

287. "Play Ball." *Sports Illustrated for Kids,* IX (June 1997), 36+. Computer baseball programs.

288. Rothenberg, Robert. "Strangers in a Strange Land." *Esquire,* CXXV (June 1996), 58–61. ESPN SportZone website.

289. Seglin, J. L. "Scoring on the Net: Sometimes Shopping [for Baseball Cards] On-line Can Be a Hit Out of the Park." *Inc,* XVIII (November 19, 1996), 107–108.

290. Tedesco, Richard. "Baseball Teams Wait for the Sign: TV May Provide the Model for Local, National Webcast Rights." *Broadcasting & Cable,* CXXVII (May 26, 1997), 35–36.

291. Temple, Bob. "Pro Baseball." In: his *Sports on the Net.* Indianapolis, Ind.: Que Corp., 1995. pp. 77–106.

292. Trivette, Don. "Microsoft's Complete Baseball Guide: A Review." *Computer Life,* II (August 1995), 122–123.

293. Wiener, L. "The Grand Old Game on the Internet." *U.S. News & World Report,* CXXI (July 1, 1996), 63+.

B. General Works,
History, and Special Studies

The references in this chapter cover a variety of topics which are categorized here for purposes of organization. Section 1 provides coverage of baseball history in general with parts on general studies of the game and its background; early history to 1901; modern history from 1901 through 1997; studies of blacks, women, and other minorities in baseball, including the Negro Leagues and the All-American Girls Professional Baseball League; and examinations of baseball lore and literature, art and music, film, superstitions, nicknames, and mascots. Section 2 gives sources for such diverse baseball events as spring training and opening day; All-Star games from 1933 through 1997, and World Series contests through 1997. In addition, this section lists works examining the economic side of the game; broadcasting and baseball journalism; and baseball fans. Two new parts are mixed in relating to strikes and to salaries, arbitration, and collective bargaining.

1. General Works and Histories

The sources in this part are designed to draw together in one place as many of the recent general works and histories of the game as possible. Here the user can find information on the history of the game since the beginning as well as data on blacks and minorities. Users should note that most of the other sections of this guide inevitably contain historical information.

a. General Works and Histories

The sources here are those general works providing multi-level examinations of the game and its history which cover more than one era or time frame.

23

294. Adomites, Paul and Saul Wisnia, eds. *Best of Baseball.* Lincolnwood, Ill.: Publications International, 1997. 384p. First published in a 216-page 1996 edition.

295. ____, et al., eds. *Treasury of Baseball: A Celebration of America's Pastime.* Lincolnwood, Ill.: Publications International, 1994. 300p.

296. Almonte, Paul. *Get Inside Baseball.* New York: Silver Moon Press, 1994. 74p.

297. Altherr, T. L. "Pitching the Game from the Past: Teaching a Baseball History Course." *Nine: A Journal of Baseball History and Social Policy Perspective,* II (Spring 1994), 197–208.

298. Alvarez, Mark, ed. *The Perfect Game.* Dallas, Tx.: Taylor Publishing Co., 1993. 262p.

299. Anderson, Dave. *Pennant Races: Baseball at Its Best.* Garden City, N.Y.: Doubleday, 1994. 421p.

300. *Baseball Legends of All Time.* Lincolnwood, Ill.: Publications International, 1994. 238p.

301. Benson, John and Tony Blengino. *Baseball's Top 100: The Best Individual Seasons of All Time.* Wilton, Conn.: Diamond Library, 1995. 317p.

302. Brown, Bill. "Waging Baseball, Playing War: Games of American Imperialism." *Cultural Critique,* no. 17 (Winter 1990), 51+.

303. Bucek, Jeanine, ed. *The Baseball Encylopedia.* 10th ed. New York: Macmillan, 1996. 3,026p. A supplement, *The Baseball Encyclopedia Update,* was issued in early 1997. covering the season.

304. Buege, Bob. "Who'll Stop the Game?: Ballgames Have Been Halted by a Variety of Circumstances, Including Irate Fans." *Beckett Baseball Card Monthly,* IX, no. 91 (October 1992), 100–104.

305. Burke, Larry. *The Baseball Chronicles: A Decade-by-Decade History of the All-American Pastime.* New York: Smithmark Publishers, 1995. 176p.

306. Burns, Ken. "Baseball: The American Epic." *Proceedings of the American Antiquarian Society,* CIV, no. 2 (1994), 243–260.

307. Cahan, Richard and Mark Jacob. "Baseball's Family Album." *Chicago,* XLIV (April 1995), 75+. Brief history of baseball in Chicago, previewing the next entry.

308. ____. *The Game That Was: The George Brace Baseball Photo Collection.* Chicago, Ill.: Contemporary Books, 1996. 256p.

309. Caraher, Brian G. "The Poetics of Baseball: An American Domestication of the Mathematically Sublime." *American Studies,* XXXII (Spring 1991), 85–100.

310. Christopher, Matt. *Great Moments in Baseball History.* Boston, Mass.: Little, Brown, 1995. 112p.

311. Cosgrove, Ben. *Covering the Bases: The Most Unforgettable Moments in Baseball in the Words of the Writers and Broadcasters Who Were There.* San Francisco, Ca.: Chronicle Books, 1997. 208p.

312. Doogan, Mike. "Sideways Baseball." *Alaska,* LX (August 1994), 14+.

313. Dugan, Ellen, ed. *The Sporting Life, 1878–1991.* Atlanta, Ga.: High Museum of Art, 1992. 128p.

314. Engel, Robert. "Swatting Flies: Baseball in the Adirondacks." *Adirondac,* LVIII (July 1995), 14+.

315. Fletcher, Rickie D. *"'Play Ball!': A Sociological Analysis of America's Game."* Unpublished Ph.D. Dissertation, Texas A & M University, 1993. 240p.

316. Frommer, Harvey. *Big Apple Baseball: An Illustrated History from the Boroughs to the Ballparks.* Dallas, Tx.: Taylor, 1995. 212p.

317. Gammons, Peter. "Diamond Notes." *Sport,* LXXXVII (September 1996), 100+.

318. Gibson, Campbell. "Competitive Imbalance: A Study of the Major Leagues from 1876 to 1993." *Baseball Research Journal,* XXIV (1995), 153–156.

319. Gilbert, Thomas. *Deadball: Major League Baseball Before Babe Ruth.* New York: Watts, 1996. 124p.

320. Gold, Eddie. "Memorable Pitching Duels Enliven Big League History." *Baseball Digest,* LIV (April 1995), 42–50.

321. Goldstein, Warren. "Inside Baseball." *The Gettysburg Review,* V (Summer 1992), 410+.

322. Gutman, Dan. *Baseball's Greatest Games.* New York: Viking Press, 1994. 212p.

323. Helyar, John. *Lords of the Realm: The Real History of Baseball.* New York: Villard Books, 1994. 576p.

324. Holway, John B. *Baseball Bizarre: Mystifying But True Tales from Baseball's Hidden History.* Madison, Wisc.: Brown & Benchmark, 1992.

325. Howerton, D. "Basketball—Our New National Pastime." *Sport,* LXXXV (March 1994), 34–38+. According to the 1997 *USA Today* poll, Football ranks first, with basketball second and baseball third.

326. Italia, Bob. *100 Unforgettable Moments in Pro Baseball.* Minneapolis, Minn.: Abdo & Daughters, 1996. 48p.

327. Kelley, Leo. "Oklahoma Baseball." *Chronicles of Oklahoma,* LXX (Spring 1992), 46–65.

328. "Let's Move It!: Once a Real Plus, Baseball's Lack of a Time Constraint Has Evolved Into One B-o-r-i-n-g Delay After Another." In: Joe Hoppel, ed. *The Sporting News 1993 Baseball Yearbook.* St. Louis, Mo.: TSN, 1993. pp. 18–21.

329. Light, Jonathan Fraser. *The Cultural Encyclopedia of Baseball.* Jefferson, N.C.: McFarland & Co., Inc., 1997. 904p.

330. Lipsyte, Robert. "The Dying Game." *Esquire,* CXIX (April 1993), 100–105.

331. Marshall, Joe Douglas, ed. *Home Field: Nine Writers at Bat.* Seattle, Wash.: Sasquatch Books, 1997. 214p. A history of baseball in the Northwest.

332. Mead, William B. and Paul Dickson. *Baseball: The Presidents' Game.* Washington, D.C.: Farragut Publishing Co., 1993. 224p.

333. Neft, David S. and Richard M. Cohen. *The Sports Encyclopedia: Baseball, 1997.* New York: St. Martin's Press, 1997. 715p.

334. Nemec, David and Saul Wisnia. *Baseball: More Than 150 Years.* Lincolnwood, Ill.: Publications International, 1996. 576p.

335. Owens, Thomas S. *Remember When: A Nostalgic Look at America's National Pastime, Featuring Photographs from Corbis-Bettmann.* New York: MetroBooks, 1996. 176p.

336. Patell, Cyrus. "Baseball and the Cultured Logic of American Individualism." *Prospects,* XVIII (1993), 401+.

337. Phillips, John, ed. *CPC Baseball Almanac.* Cabin John, Md.: Capital Publishing Co., 1993. 64p.

338. Pietrusza, David. *Lights On: The Wild Century-Long Saga of Night Baseball.* American Sports History Series, no. 7. Lanham, Md.: Scarecrow Press, 1997. 257p.

339. Rader, Benjamin G. "Baseball." In: David Levinson and Karen Christensen, eds. *Encyclopedia of World Sport from Ancient Times to the Present.* 3 vols. Santa Barbara, Ca.: ABC/CLIO Press, 1996. I, 77–99.

340. Robertson, John G. *Baseball's Greatest Controversies: Rhubarbs, Hoaxes, Blown Calls, Ruthian Myths, Managers' Miscues, and Front-Office Flops.* Jefferson, N.C.: McFarland & Co., Inc., 1995. 198p.

341. Santa Maria, Michael and James Costello. *In the Shadows of the Diamond: Hard Times in the National Pastime.* Dubuque, Iowa: Elysian Fields Press, 1992. 267p.

342. Seaver, Tom, with Marty Appel. *Great Moments in Baseball.* Sessacus, N.J.: Carroll Publishing Group, 1995. 339p.

343. Shannon, Mike. *Tales from the*

Dugout: The Greatest True Baseball Stories Ever Told. Chicago, Ill.: Contemporary Books, 1997.

344. Skeeter, Brent R. "The Climatically Optimal Major League Baseball Season in North America." *The Geographical Bulletin,* XXX (November 1988), 97+.

345. Skolnik, Richard. *Baseball and the Pursuit of Innocence: A Fresh Look at the Old Ball Game.* College Station: Texas A & M University Press, 1994. 257p.

346. Solomon, Burt. *The Baseball Timeline: The Day-to-Day History of Baseball, from Valley Forge to the Present Day.* New York: Avon Books, 1997. 1,082p.

347. Sullivan, Dean A., ed. *Early Innings: A Documentary History of Baseball, 1825–1908.* Lincoln: University of Nebraska Press, 1995. 312p.

348. Thomas, Georges. "Un Peu d'Histoire." *E.P.S. Education Physique et Sport (France),* XLIV (Janv./Fevr. 1994), 34–35. "A Little History."

349. Thorn, John, Pete Palmer, and Michael Gershman. *Total Baseball: The Offical Encyclopedia of Major League Baseball.* 5th ed. New York: Viking Press, 1997.

350. Tiano, Charles. *More Balls Than Strikes: 120 Years of Baseball in New York's Hudson Valley.* Saugeteris, N.Y.: Hope Farm Press, 1995. 136p.

351. Verdi, Bob. "Build 'Em Up and Tear 'Em Down." *Inside Sports,* XV (February 1993), 62–65. Sports teams and heroes in Chicago.

352. Wallace, Joseph E., ed. *The Baseball Anthology: 125 Years of Stories, Poems, Articles, Photographs, Drawings, Interviews, Cartoons, and Other Memorabilia.* New York: Abrams, 1994. 296p. This official MLB publication covers material published in 1868–1993.

353. Ward, Geoffrey C. *Baseball: An Illustrated History.* New York: Alfred A. Knopf, 1994. 486p. Companion

volume to Ken Burn's monumental PBS television series.

354. Wimmer, Dick, ed. *The Sandlot Game: An Anthology of Baseball Writings.* Indianapolis, Ind.: Masters Press, 1997.

355. Young, Chip. "The National Pastime: Past Its Time?" *TV Guide,* XLI (July 10, 1993), 18–21.

356. Zoss, Joel and John Bowman. *Diamonds in the Rough: The Untold Story of Baseball.* Chicago, Ill.: Contemporary Books, 1996. 433p.

b. Early Baseball to 1901

The entries in this part are directly concerned with baseball's antecedents and growth in the years to 1901, when the American League was formed. They concern not only controversies, but early stats, play in assorted cities and states, and the development of the sport in relationship to society as a whole.

357. Anderson, Will. *Was Baseball Really Invented in Maine?* Portland, Me.: W. Anderson, Pub., 1992. 180p.

358. Anderson, William M. "Manistee's Field of Dreams." *Michigan History,* LXXVIII (May 1994), 49–51. Reenactments of pre-1901 baseball by the Manistee Salt City Base Ball Club.

359. Baker, William J. "Disputed Diamonds: The Y.M.C.A. Debate Over Baseball in the Late 19th Century." *Journal of Sport History,* XIX (Winter 1992), 257+.

360. Baldassarre, Joseph A. "Baseball's Ancestry." In: John Phillips, ed. *CPC Baseball Almanac.* Cabin John, Md.: Capital Publishing Co., 1993. pp. 7–11.

361. "Baseball's Early Days." *Country Home,* XIV (June 1992), 124–127.

362. Bass, Cynthia. "The Double Game." *Elysian Fields Quarterly,* XII (Summer 1993), 28–35. How, in 1890, the simultaneous games of the New York Giants (N.L.) at the Polo Grounds and those of the Players' Association team at their park were separated by a single

fence; fans from Coogan's Bluff could see both at the same time.

363. ____. "The World Tour of Eighty Eight." *Elysian Fields Quarterly*, XII (Spring 1993), 49–58.

364. Boston, Talmage. "Lincoln and Baseball: The Truth." *Elysian Fields Quarterly*, XII (Summer 1993), 64–67.

365. Bready, James H. "Play Ball!: The Legacy of 19th Century Baltimore Baseball." *Maryland Historical Magazine*, LXXXVII (Summer 1992), 127–146.

366. Brock, D. "Mark Twain and the Great Base Ball Match: Big Doin's in Hartford." *National Pastime*, XIV (1994), 55–58.

367. Cardello, Joseph. "Game 6: The Greatest Game of Them All." *Elysian Fields Quarterly*, XI (Spring 1992), 44–55. October 6, 1889 World Series contest between the New York Giants (N.L.) and Brooklyn Bridegrooms (A.A.).

368. Cash, Jon D. "Origins—The Spirit of St. Louis in the History of Professional Baseball: May 4–8, 1875." *Gateway Heritage*, XV (Spring 1995), 4–17. Based on the next entry.

369. ____. *"The Spirit of St. Louis in the History of Major League Baseball, 1875–1891."* Unpublished Ph.D. Dissertation, University of Oregon, 1995. 403p.

370. Cline, Scott. "'To Foster Honorable Pastimes': Baseball as a Civic Endeavor in 1880s Seattle." *Pacific Northwest Quarterly*, LXXXVII (Fall 1996), 171–179.

371. "Early Pullman Baseball Team." *Where the Trails Cross*, XIX (Spring 1989), 94+.

372. Foster, Mark S. "Playing by the Rules: The Evolution of Baseball in the 19th Century." *Colorado Heritage*, (Spring 1995), 44–51.

373. Franks, J. S. "Whose Baseball?: Baseball in 19th Century Multicultural California." *Nine: A Journal of Baseball History and Social Policy Perspective*, IV (Spring 1996), 248–262.

374. "Frontier Baseball." *Nevada*, L (March 1990), 27+. 1860s.

375. Gilbert, Thomas. *Elysian Fields: The Birth of Baseball.* New York: Watts, 1996. 120p.

376. Greenberg, K. S. "Honor and Slavery: Lies, Duels, Noses, Masks, Dressing as a Woman, Gifts, Strangers, Humanitarianism, Death, Slave Rebellions, the Proslavery Argument, Baseball, Hunting and Gambling in the Old South." *American Historical Review*, CII (June 1997), 894–895+.

377. Griffith, William R. "The Early History of Amateur Base Ball in the State of Maryland." *Maryland Historical Magazine*, LXXXVII (Summer 1992), 201–208.

378. Hoffman, Frank W. and William G. Bailey. "The Rise of Baseball." In: their *Sports and Recreation Fads.* Binghamton, N.Y.: Haworth, 1991. pp. 35–37.

379. Jayroe, Walt. "The Boys of Summer: Pro Baseball Experiment Strikes Out in the Southwest." *New Mexico Magazine*, LXXII (May 1994), 22+.

380. Kissel, T. "Bound for the Klondike: The Canadaigua Rustlers of 1897–1898." *National Pastime*, XV (1995), 131–132.

381. ____. "The Pumpkin and Cabbage Tournament of 1866: High Scoring and Discord in Upstate New York." *Baseball Research Journal*, XXIV (1995), 30–33.

382. Massengill, Patrick. "Vintage Baseball in Colorado." *Colorado Heritage*, (Spring 1995), 52+.

383. McCulloch, Ron. *How Baseball Began.* Los Angeles, Ca.: Warwick Publications, 1995. 140p.

384. Melville, Tom. "Cricket, Anyone?" *Pennsylvania Heritage*, XVII (Summer 1991), 32–37.

385. Moore, Glenn. "The Great Baseball Tour of 1888–1889: A Tale of Image-Making, Intrigue, and Labour Relations in the Gilded Age." *International Journal of the History of Sport*, XI (December 1994), 431+.

386. Moore, Jim. "Mark Twain and the Em Quads: A Square Deal." *The Californians: The Magazine of California History,* IX (May 1991), 48+. Twain joined the San Francisco Em Quads in 1864 at the behest of right fielder Lew Ward.

387. Nemec, David. *The Great Encyclopedia of 19th Century Major League Baseball.* New York: D. I. Fine Books, 1997. 852p.

388. Olson, James S. "Review Essay— The Creation of American Team Sports: Baseball and Crickett, 1838–72." *Journal of Urban History,* XIX (November 1992), 127–130.

389. Pearson, Daniel Merle. *Baseball in 1889: Players vs. Owners.* Bowling Green, Oh.: Popular Press, Bowling Green State University, 1993. 234p.

390. Pope, Steven W. "Amateurism and American Sports Culture: The Invention of an Athletic Tradition in the United States, 1870–1900." *International Journal of the History of Sport,* XIII (December 1996), 290–309.

391. Schaefer, John. "Baseball History Prior to 1900." *Texas Coach,* XXXV (April 1991), 34+.

392. Smith, Duane A. "Mighty Casey Matches the Mountains: The Origins of Baseball in Colorado." *Colorado Heritage,* (Spring 1995), 4–43.

393. Stempel, Carl W. *"Towards a Historical Sociology of Sport in the United States, 1825–1875."* Unpublished Ph.D. dissertation, University of Oregon, 1992.

394. Story, Ronald. "The Country of the Young: The Meaning of Baseball In Early American Culture." In: D. K. Wiggins, ed. *Sport in America: From Wicked Amusement to National Obsession.* Champaign, Ill.: Human Kinetics Pub., 1995. pp. 121–132.

395. Townes, Clayton C. and William A. Hoffman, eds. *Official Guide of the Cleveland Amateur Base Ball Association.* Cleveland, Oh.: A. G. Spalding & Bros., 1914. 119p.

396. Vermilyea, Natalie. "Krank's De-

light: California Baseball, 1858–1888." *The Californians: The Magazine of California History,* VIII (March 1991), 31+.

397. Warnock, James. "Entrepreneurs and Progressives: Baseball in the Northwest, 1900–1901." *Pacific Northwest Quarterly,* LXXXII (July 1991), 92–100.

398. Wright, J. J. "Brother Against Brother: Events and Final Days of Professional Baseball's 1879 Season." *Nine: A Journal of Baseball History and Social Policy Perspective,* III (Spring 1995), 204–217.

399. Zweig, Jason. "Wild Pitch: How American Investors Financed the Early Growth of Baseball." *Friends of Financial History,* LIX (Summer 1997), 18+.

c. The Modern Era

In the introduction to this part in *Baseball: A Comprehensive Bibliography*, we noted in general the compact between the National League and American League which launched pro baseball in this country onto its modern path. In an effort to better present the numerous citations here relative, this part is subdivided into two sections: general works and selected seasonal references, the latter entered by date.

1. General Works

400. Ahrens, Art. "Long-Ago Game in Wrigley Field Remains Vivid for Fan." *Baseball Digest,* LIV (August 1995), 64–70.

401. Bedingfield, Gary. "Taking Baseball to War." *Army,* XLVI (September 1996), 42+. As played in Northern Ireland in 1942.

402. Blake, Mike. *Baseball Chronicles, September 17, 1911 to October 24, 1992: An Oral History of Baseball Through the Decades.* Cincinnati, Oh.: Betterway Books, 1994. 324p.

403. Blount, Roy, Jr., *et al.* "The Great-

est Game I Ever Saw." *Sports Illustrated,* LXXIX (July 19, 1993), 38–45.

404. Briley, Ron. "More Legacy of Conquest: Long-Term Ramifications of the Major League Baseball Shift to the West." *Journal of the West,* XXXVI (April 1997), 68–78.

405. Brown, W. E., Jr. "Sunday Baseball Comes to Boston." *National Pastime,* XIV (1994), 83–85.

406. Cataneo, David. *Hornsby Hit One Over My Head: A Fan's Oral History of Baseball.* New York: Harcourt, Brace & Co., 1997.

407. Cebulash, Mel. *Bases Loaded: Great Baseball of the 20th Century.* Syracuse, N.Y.: New Readers Press, 1993. 64p.

408. Cole, Robert C. "The End of the Sticks: The Last Days of Baseball Barnstorming." *Elysian Fields Quarterly,* XIII (Winter 1994), 17–25. Post-World Series tours.

409. Cunningham, Bob. "Big League General Managers See Brighter Future for the Game." *Baseball Digest,* LV (December 1996), 78–82.

410. Darby, William and David. *Major League Baseball, 1979–1992: A Year-by-Year History Using Fan Oriented Statistics.* Jefferson, N.C.: McFarland & Co., Inc., 1993. 646p.

411. Downey, Mike. "Foul Ball." In: Gerald Kavanagh, ed. *Street and Smith's Baseball '97.* New York: Street and Smith, 1997. pp. 52–57. Baseball in the strike years of 1994–1995.

412. Feinstein, John. "What the Game Can Be: The Heroism of Cal Ripken and Mickey Mantle Shows Us Why, for All Its Flaws, We Still Love Baseball." *Inside Sports,* XVII (December 1995), 68–71.

413. "Forty Pictures to Remember, 1954–1994." *Sports Illustrated,* LXXXI (November 14, 1994), 53–63+.

414. Fraley, Gerry. "Pennant Pressure: When the Heat Is On." *Inside Sports,* XVIII (October 1996), 58–62.

415. Frommer, Harvey. *New York City Baseball, the Last Golden Age, 1947–1957.* San Diego, Calif.: Harcourt, Brace, Jovanovich, 1992. 219p.

416. Gerlach, Larry R. "Not Quite Ready for Prime Time: Baseball History, 1983–1993." *Journal of Sport History,* XXI (Summer 1994), 103–137.

417. Gilbert, Thomas W. *Baseball at War: World War II and the Fall of the Color Line.* New York: Franklin Watts, 1997. 144p. 1940–1947.

418. _____. *The Good Old Days: Baseball in the 1930s.* New York: Franklin Watts, 1996. 124p.

419. _____. *The Soaring Twenties: Babe Ruth & the Home Run Decade.* New York: Franklin Watts, 1996. 130p.

420. Gowdy, Curt and John Powers. *Seasons to Remember: The Way It Was in American Sports, 1945–1960.* New York: HarperCollins, 1993.

421. Graber, Ralph S. "Two Men [Jimmy O'Connell and Cozy Dolan] Out: The Bribery Scandal of 1924." *Elysian Fields Quarterly,* XII (Spring 1993), 59–63.

422. Gutman, Dan. *Baseball Babylon: From the Black Sox to Pete Rose, the Real Stories Behind the Scandals That Rocked the Game.* New York: Viking Penguin, 1992. 336p.

423. _____. *Baseball's Biggest Bloopers: The Games That Got Away.* New York: Viking Penguin, 1993. 200p.

424. Hirshberg, Dan. "Five Base Path Collisions Rank Among the Most Memorable." *Baseball Digest,* LIII (June 1994), 30–34.

425. Hoffman, T. "Games of Our Lives: Baseball and Hockey." *Queen's Quarterly,* CII (September 1995), 662–672.

426. Ingham, A. "The Industrialization of the United States and the 'Bourgeoisification' of American Sport." In: E. G. Dunning, *et al.,* eds. *The Sports Process: A Comparative and Developmental Approach.* Champaign, Ill.: Human Kinetics Pub., 1993. pp. 169–206.

427. Kolbert, J. B. "Major League Baseball During World War II: The Changing Game." *National Pastime,* XIV (1994), 102–105.

428. Kuenster, John. "Major League Baseball Will Survive Its Many Problems." *Baseball Digest,* LIV (November 1995), 19–21.

429. Livingston, Bill. "Was Big League Play Really Better in the Old Days?" *Baseball Digest,* LVI (February 1997), 78–81.

430. Macht, Norman L. "Baseball of Another Era Left Some Golden Memories." *Baseball Digest,* LIV (August 1995), 61–62.

431. McGuire, Mark. "Baseball Played a Special Role During World War II." *Baseball Digest,* LIII (June 1994), 66–73.

432. McLeary, Kathleen. "Basketball vs. Baseball." *USA Weekend,* (June 4, 1993), 4–6.

433. Moffi, Larry. *This Side of Cooperstown: An Oral History of Major League Baseball in the 1950s.* Iowa City: University of Iowa Press, 1996. 262p.

434. Oakley, J. Ronald. *Baseball's Last Golden Age, 1946–1960: The National Pastime in a Time of Glory and Change.* Jefferson, N.C.: McFarland & Co., Inc., 1994. 384p. Includes information on the rise of air travel and competition from professional football.

435. Okkonen, Marc. *Baseball Memories, 1900–1909.* New York: Sterling Publishing Co., 1992. 234p.

436. ____. *Baseball Memories, 1950–1959: An Illustrated Scrapbook of Baseball's Fabulous 50s—All the Players, Managers, Cities & Ballparks.* New York: Stering Publishing Co., 1993. 210p.

437. Olson, James S. "Review Essay: Sports as Cultural Currency in Modern America." *Journal of Urban History,* XIX (November 1992), 127–130.

438. Peary, Danny, ed. *We Played the Game: 65 Players Remember Baseball's Greatest Era, 1947–1964.* New York: Hyperion, 1994. 643p.

439. Pelissero, John P., Beth M. Henschen, and Edward I. Sidlow. "The New Politics of Sports Policy Innovation in Chicago." *Research in Urban Policy,* no. 4 (1992), 57–78.

440. Regalado, Samuel O. "'Play Ball!': Baseball and Seattle's Japanese-American Courier League, 1928–1941." *Pacific Northwest Quarterly,* LXXXVII (Winter 1995-1996), 29–37.

441. Rushin, Steve. "1954–1994: How We Got Here." *Sports Illustrated,* LXXXI (April 16, 1994), 35–52.

442. ____. "What Might Have Been." *Sports Illustrated,* LXXIX (July 19, 1993), 96–105.

443. Rutkoff, Peter H. "Two-Base Hit: Baseball and New York, 1945–1960." *Prospects,* XX (1995), 285+.

444. Sands, Jack and Peter Gammons. *Coming Apart at the Seams: How Baseball Owners, Players, and Television Executives Led Our National Pastime to the Brink of Disaster.* New York: Macmillan, 1993. 266p.

445. Schroeder, S. E. "When Technology and Culture Collide: The Advent of Night Baseball." *Nine: A Journal of Baseball History and Social Policy Perspective,* III (Fall 1994), 85–106.

446. Skipper, John C. *Inside Pitch: A Closer Look at Classic Baseball Moments.* Jefferson, N.C.: McFarland & Co., Inc., 1996. 192p.

447. Smith, Robert. *Baseball in the Afternoon: Tales from a Bygone Era.* New York: Simon & Schuster, 1993. 272p.

448. ____. "Can You Spare a Dime?" In: Charles Einstein, ed. *The New Baseball Reader: An All-Star Lineup from the Fireside Book of Baseball.* New York: Penguin, 1992. pp. 395–406. 1930s' game.

449. Stewart, Wayne. "Closing Days of the Season Feature Oddities and Drama." *Baseball Digest,* LIV (October 1995), 44–49.

450. Sullivan, Neil J. *The Diamond Revolution: The Prospects for Baseball After the Collapse of Its Ruling Class.* New York: St. Martin's Press, 1992. 232p.

451. Van Blair, Rick. "What Some Old-Timers Think of the Major Leagues Today." *Baseball Digest,* LIV (November 1995), 50–55.
452. Vanderburg, Bob. *Minnie & Mick: The Go-Go White Sox Challenge the Fabled Yankee Dynasty, 1951–1964.* South Bend, Ind.: Diamond Communications, 1996. 272p.
453. Vass, George. "Baseball's Shrunken Seasons: What Might Have Been...." *Baseball Digest,* LIV (January 1995), 32–39. The seasons of 1901, 1904, 1918, 1919, 1972, 1981, and 1994.
454. ____. "Pennant Races Don't Really Begin Until the Month of July." *Baseball Digest,* LV (July 1996), 24–31.
455. ____. "These Were the Ten Oddest Plays in Baseball History." *Baseball Digest,* LIV (February 1995), 44–53.
456. Ward, Geoffrey C. and Ken Burns. "The Capital of Baseball." *U.S. News & World Report,* CXVII (August 29, 1994), 90+. New York City MLB teams in the 1940s and 1950s.
457. Wear, Ben. "In a League of Its Own: Despite Its Glory Days, Alaska Baseball Faces an Uncertain Future." *Alaska,* LIX (May–June 1993), 41+.
458. Wenner, Lawrence A. "Passed Balls: The Unraveling Seams and Themes of Baseball." *Journal of Sport and Social Issues,* XX (May 1996), 115–117.
459. White, G. Edward. *Creating the National Pastime: Baseball Transforms Itself, 1903–1953.* Princeton, N.J.: Princeton University Press, 1996. 368p.

2. Selected Seasonal References

1911
460. Malley, T. "Ring Lardner and the 'Br'er Rabbit Ball': The Power Surge of 1911." *National Pastime,* XV (1995), 19–20.

1912
461. Bass, Cythia. "One-Nothing." *Elysian Fields Quarterly,* XIII (Summer 1994), 35–43. Smokey Joe Wood's Boston (A.L.) defeats Walter Johnson's Washington (A.L.) in the September 6 "Game of the Century."

1916
462. Lewis, Allen. "This Was the Majors' Strangest of All Seasons." *Baseball Digest,* LIII (March 1994), 93–95.

1935
463. Krevisky, S. "The A.L.'s 1935 Batting Races: Down to the Final Day." *National Pastime,* XV (1995), 114–117.

1939
464. Katz, Lawrence S. *Baseball in 1939: The Watershed Season of the National Pastime.* Jefferson, N.C.: McFarland & Co., Inc., 1995. 202p.

1944
465. Borst, Bill. *The Best of Seasons: The 1944 St. Louis Cardinals and St. Louis Browns.* Jefferson, N.C.: McFarland & Co., Inc., 1995. 321p.

1946
466. Klein, Alan H. "The Baseball Wars: The Mexican Baseball League and Nationalism in 1946." *Studies in Latin American Popular Culture,* XIII (1994), 33+.
467. Leslie, J. Paul. "'Say It Ain't So': The 1946 Houma Indians and the Baseball Scandals." *Louisiana History,* XXXV (Spring 1994), 163–181.
468. Turner, Frederick W. *When the Boys Came Back: Baseball and 1946.* New York: Holt, 1996. 290p.

1951
469. Lowe, S. R. "The Kid on the Sandlot: Public Policy, Congress, and Organized Baseball, 1951." *Nine: A Journal of Baseball History and Social Policy Perspective,* III (Spring 1995), 218–234.

470. Rosenfeld, Harvey. *The Great Chase: The [Brooklyn] Dodgers-[New York] Giants Pennant Race of 1951.* Jefferson, N.C.: McFarland & C., Inc., 1992.

1961

471. Hoffman, Frank W. and William G. Bailey. "The M & M Boys Race with Ruth." In: their *Sports and Recreation Fads.* Binghampton, N.Y.: Haworth, 1991. pp. 205–209. Mantle and Maris pursue the home run record.

1962

472. Ladson, William. "Dodgers vs. Giants: 1962." *Sport,* LXXXIII (October 1992), 22–23.

1968

473. Gleisser, Benjamin. "1968: The Summer of Slumbering Lumber." *Beckett Baseball Card Monthly,* XI, no. 117 (December 1994), 100–105.

474. Rushin, Steve. "The Season of High Heat." *Sports Illustrated,* LXXIX (July 19, 1993), 30–37.

1969

475. Briley, R. "Baseball and America in 1969: A Traditional Institution Responds to Changing Times." *Nine: A Journal of Baseball History and Social Policy Perspectives,* IV (Spring 1996), 263–281.

1978

476. Bradley, Mark. "New York vs. Boston, 1978: Bucky Dent Propels Yankees to Eastern Division Title." *Sport,* LXXXIV (October 1993), 70+.

1979

477. Ryan, Jeff. "Philadelphia vs. Chicago, 1979: Phillies Outslug Cubs, 23–22, in 10 Innings." *Sport,* LXXXV (July 1994), 26–27.

1991

478. "1991 Baseball Chronology." In: Myles Friedman, ed. *Spring Training:* *Grapefruit and Cactus League Yearbook.* Chapel Hill, N.C.: Vanguard Publications, 1992. p. 82+.

1992

479. "Baseball 1992." Sports Illustrated, LXXVI (April 6, 1992), 32–110.

480. Brown, Bill. "The Meaning of Baseball in 1992." *Public Culture,* IV (Fall 1991), 43+.

481. Davids, Bob. "Some Odds and Ends Left Over from the '92 Season." *Baseball Digest,* LI (March 1993), 32–36.

482. DeLand, Dave. "Coming on Strong." *Beckett Baseball Card Monthly,* IX, no. 93 (December 1992), 21–23.

483. Hersch, Hank. "Bang-Bang Play." *Sports Illustrated,* LXXVI (June 29, 1992), 38–41.

484. Horgan, Sean. "A Polite Bashing." *Sports Illustrated,* LXXVII (November 16, 1992), 38–39. American pro-players make their annual tour of Japan.

485. Klapisch, Bob. and Ringolsby, Tracy. "Baseball Ratings and Inside Stuff." Inside Sports, XIV (February 1992), 52–59.

486. Levin, Bob. "Season of Dreams." *Maclean's,* CV (September 28, 1992), 48–49.

487. "1992 Baseball Preview." *Inside Sports,* XIV (March 1992), 26–45.

488. Stewart, Wayne. "Here's One Writer's Diary of the 1992 Major League Season." *Baseball Digest,* LII (January 1993), 32–37.

489. Vass, George. "How the Division Races Shape Up for '92 Season." Baseball Digest, LI (April 1992), 20–59.

490. Wheatley, Tom. "Stranger Than Fiction." *Beckett Baseball Card Monthly,* IX, no. 93 (December 1992), 18–20.

491. Wulf, Steve. "I Got It...I Got It...Oops: With an Unsightly Rash of Bobbies and Boots, Baseball Is Suffering Through a Plague of Errors." *Sports Illustrated,* LXXVI (May 18, 1992), 46–48, 50, 53.

1993

492. Aschburner, Steve. "Indians, Mariners, and Rangers: Still Chasing a Division Title." *Baseball Digest,* LII (September 1993), 68–72.

493. Baker, John. "1993: Baseball's Year of Hard Knocks." *TV Guide,* XLI (October 16, 1993), 43+.

494. "Baseball '93." *Sports Illustrated,* LXXVIII (April 5, 1993), 34–50+.

495. Crasnick, Jerry. "Long Gone." *Beckett Baseball Card Monthly,* XI, no. 106 (January 1994), 10–19.

496. Davids, Bob. "Some Odds and Ends Left Over from the '93 Season." *Baseball Digest,* LIII (April 1994), 60–63.

497. Deacon, James. "A Time to Play." *Maclean's,* CVI (April 5, 1993), 48–50.

498. Dubroff, Rick. *How Was the Game?: A Fan's Journey Around Baseball.* Baltimore, Md.: Diamond Pub. Co., 1994. 169p.

499. Feinstein, John. "Baseball Wrap-up: Beginnings and Endings." *Inside Sports,* XVI (January 1994), 58–61.

500. Hirdt, Peter. "A Newcomer's Guide." *Sports Illustrated,* LXXVIII (April 12, 1993), 40–41. The expansion season.

501. Kurkijan, Tim. "And What a Year It Was." *Sports Illustrated,* LXXIX (October 4, 1993), 60–62+.

502. ____. "The Big Bang." *Sports Illustrated,* LXXIX (September 13, 1993), 32–34, 39–40. Hitting during this season.

503. "1993 Annual Baseball Roundup." *Ebony,* XLVIII (June 1993), 110–112+.

504. "The 1993 *Sport* Magazine Baseball Preview." *Sport,* LXXXIV (April 1993), 20–24+.

505. Rushin, Steve. "Last Shot." *Sports Illustrated,* LXXIX (October 4, 1993), 42–44.

506. Shapiro, Walter. "The Last Great Season." *Time,* CXXXVII (April 12, 1993), 60–65. Published simultaneously in *Time (Canada),* CXLI (April 12, 1993), 54–59.

507. Stewart, Wayne. "Here's a Month-by-Month Recap of '93 Major League Season." *Baseball Digest,* LIII (February 1994), 57–76.

508. ____. "Here's a Recap of a Few Zany Moments from Last Season." *Baseball Digest,* LIII (April 1994), 71–73.

509. Vass, George. "Keep an Eye on These Young, Up-and-Coming Clubs in '93." *Baseball Digest,* LII (January 1993), 38–42.

510. Wheatley, Tom. "Best/Worst '93: Predictably Unpredictable." *Beckett Baseball Card Monthly,* X, no. 105 (December 1993), 20–21.

511. Wulf, Steve. "The A.L. Feast." *Sports Illustrated,* LXXIX (August 9, 1993), 12–19.

1994

512. Angell, Roger. "Mind Game." *The New Yorker,* LXXI (April 10, 1995), 5–6. July 5 game between New York (A.L.) and Oakland (A.L.).

513. Cafardo, Nick. "'94 Season Preview: New Frontier [of Divisional Play]." *Beckett Baseball Card Monthly,* XI, no. 109 (April 1994), 20–24.

514. Crothers, Tim. "Bronx Zoo Revisited." *Sports Illustrated,* LXXXVII (July 14, 1997), 56–57.

515. Davids, Bob. "Some Odds and Ends Left Over from the '94 Season." *Baseball Digest,* LIV (April 1995), 82–83.

516. Dolgan, Bob. "Players' Strike Thwarted Longball Hitters in '94." *Baseball Digest,* LIV (May 1995), 64–68.

517. Garrity, John. "Crunch Time." *Sports Illustrated,* LXXXI (August 1, 1994), 20–22+. Cleveland vs. Chicago in the A.L. Central Division.

518. Himes, Larry and Bob Costas. "Pro & Con: Will Baseball's Divisional Realignment Make for Better Regular-Season Play?" *Inside Sports,* XVI (March 1994), 14–15.

519. Hitzges, Norm and Dave Lawson. *Essential Baseball 1994: A Revolu-*

tionary New Method of Evaluating Major League Teams, Players, and Managers. New York: Plume, 1994. 369p.

520. Hoffer, Richard. "Too Good to Be True." Sports Illustrated, LXXXI (August 22, 1994), 14–21. Imaginary end of the season.

521. Kuenster, John. "New Faces in New Places Give Some Teams Fresh Outlook on Pennant Races." Baseball Digest, LIII (June 1994), 17–19.

522. Kurkijan, Tim. "Surprise, Surprise, Surprise." Sports Illustrated, LXXX (April 18, 1994), 36–38+. The season's opening week.

523. "Mean Season." Maclean's, CVII (September 26, 1994), 30–35.

524. "'94—A Year to Remember? A Year to Forget?: An Emphatic Yes to Both." Sport, LXXXVI (January 1995), 52–56.

525. Palmer, Jim. "The Inside Pitch." Inside Sports, XVI (May 1994), 48–51.

526. ____. "Making the Final Stride." Inside Sports, XVI (April 1994), 28–51.

527. Perlstein, Steve. Rebel Baseball: The Summer the Game Was Returned to the Fans. Onion Press, 1994. 256p.

528. Rose, Pete. "Rose's Crystal Ball: The All-Time Hit King Picks the Division Winners." Sport, LXXXV (May 1994), 15–16.

529. Stewart, Wayne. "Here's a Month-by-Month Recap of the '94 Major League Season." Baseball Digest, LIV (February 1995), 58–64.

530. Vass, George. "How Major League Pennant Races Shape Up for '94 Season." Baseball Digest, LIII (April 1994), 20–55.

531. ____. "Major League Baseball Embarks on a New Era in '94." Baseball Digest, LIII (January 1994), 40–45.

532. Wheatley, Tom. "'94 Best & Worst: Double Dip." Beckett Baseball Card Monthly, XI, no. 117 (December 1994), 20–23.

1995

533. Angell, Roger. "Called Strike." The New Yorker, LXXI (May 22, 1995), 46–53. End of the strike allows the season to begin.

534. Boswell, Thomas. "Baseball's Season of Pennance." TV Guide, XLIII (July 8, 1995), 8–11.

535. Davids, Bob. "Some Facts and Figures Left Over from the '95 Season." Baseball Digest, LV (April 1996), 77–80.

536. Deane, Bill. "Here Are a Few Statistical Odds and Ends from '95 Season." Baseball Digest, LV (March 1995), 74–78.

537. Fraley, Gerry and Tracy Ringolsby. "Getting into the Swing." Inside Sports, XVII (June 1995), 36–40.

538. Modono, Bill. "April Showers." Pittsburgh, XXVI (April 1995), 40+. Strike prospects of the season.

539. "101 Reasons Baseball Is Dead." GQ: Gentlemen's Quarterly, LXV (April 1995), 196–197.

540. Stewart, Wayne. "Month-by-Month Review of the '95 Major League Season." Baseball Digest, LV (February 1996), 54–63.

541. Vass, George. "'95 Season Puts a Dozen Major Leaguers 'On the Spot.'" Baseball Digest, LIV (August 1995), 20–24.

542. Verducci, Tom. "Anybody Home?: There Were Lots of Empty Seats and Angry Fans as the Baseball Season Began." Sports Illustrated, LXXII (May 8, 1995), 18–23.

543. ____. "The Best: In Digging Itself Out of a Hole with Fans, Baseball Might Well Celebrate the Little Things That Make the Game Great—and the Players Are Masters of Those Fundamentals." Sports Illustrated, LXXXII (May 1, 1995), 64–70, 72.

544. ____. "The Wild Card Crunch." Sports Illustrated, LXXXIII (August 21, 1995), 50–52.

545. Weinberg, Rick. "A New Ball Game." Sport, LXXXVI (April 1995), 26–28+.

1996

546. Barra, Allen. "Baseball's Glory Days Are...Now." *The New York Times Magazine,* (October 6, 1996), 60–61.

547. Callahan, Gerry. "Ole! No Way!" *Sports Illustrated,* LXXXV (August 26, 1996), 18–22. Three game series in Monterrey, Mexico, between the Mets and Padres.

548. Fraley, Gerry. "A Comforting Chaos: The Hot Topics in Baseball for 1996 Deal With — Thank Goodness — On-the-Field Craziness." *Inside Sports,* XVIII (May 1996), 38–47.

549. Kurkjian, Tim. "The Best and the Worst [Midseason]." *Sports Illustrated,* LXXXV (July 15, 1996), 88+.

550. ____. "Nothing But Offense: A Storm of Offense in Both Leagues." *Sports Illustrated,* LXXXIV (April 15, 1996), 66–67.

551. Martin, J. "Can Baseball Make It in Mexico?" *Fortune,* CXXXIV (September 30, 1996), 32+. The Monterrey exhibition.

552. Ringolsby, Tracy and Gerry Fraley. "1996 Baseball Preview." *Inside Sports,* XVIII (April 1996), 28–49.

553. Starr, Mark. "Diamond Jubilee." *Newsweek,* CXXVIII (September 16, 1996), 78–79. 1996 season.

554. Stewart, Wayne. "Month-by-Month Diary: A Look Back at the '96 Season." *Baseball Digest,* LVI (February 1997), 43–55.

555. Vass, George. "Here's How A.L., N.L. Division Races Shape Up for the '96 Season." *Baseball Digest,* LV (April 1996), 18–33.

556. Verducci, Tom. "The Race Is On." *Sports Illustrated,* LXXXIV (June 17, 1996), 62–64, 67. A.L. Central Division.

557. "What a Week: Seven Days in September Were Filled with Feats on the Field and Pennant Fever from Coast to Coast, Just Like the Old Days." *Sports Illustrated,* LXXXV (September 30, 1996), 30–34, 37–40.

1997

558. *Beckett Preview: Baseball '97.* Dallas, Tx.: Beckett Publications, 1997. 128p.

559. Boswell, Thomas. "Baseball '97: It's Rally Time." *Inside Sports,* XIX (April 1997), 30–31.

560. Callahan, Gerry. "Nice to Meet You." *Sports Illustrated,* LXXXVI (June 23, 1997), 62–65. Interleague play.

561. Fraley, Gerry and Tracy Ringolsby. "1997 Baseball Preview." *Inside Sports,* XIX (April 1997), 32–71.

562. La Russa, Tony and Joe Torre. "They're Leagues Apart." *Sports Illustrated,* LXXXVI (March 31, 1997), 95–96. Interleague play.

563. McKelvey, Steve and David Menzies. "Fair or Foul?" *Inside Sports,* XIX (May 1997), 68–74.

564. Schwarz, Alan. "Baseball Hot Topics for 1997." *Inside Sports,* XIX (May 1997), 58–67.

565. Vass, George. "Here Are the Nine Biggest Surprises of the '97 Season." *Baseball Digest,* LVI (November 1997), 26–33.

566. ____. "Here's How the Pennant Chases Shape Up in A.L. and N.L. for '97 Season." *Baseball Digest,* LVI (April 1997), 20–36.

567. ____. "Will Power Surge in the Majors Continue During '97 Season?" *Baseball Digest,* LVI (January 1997), 60–67.

568. Verducci, Tom. "Spring Classic." *Sports Illustrated,* LXXXVI (June 23, 1997), 66–70. June interleague series between the Baltimore Orioles and the Atlanta Braves.

d. Blacks, Women, and
Other Minorities in Baseball,
Including the Negro Leagues

Citations in this part concern the challenges of racism and inequality found by blacks, women, and other minorities throughout pro baseball's history and the manner by which they have been addressed; additionally, they mark the strides made recently by all minorities entering the sport and the newfound pride in those who were not earlier able to participate. Three parts are here provided: General Works; Negro League teams; and the All-American Girls Professional Baseball League. References to women's college teams are located in Section D:1, High School and College Baseball, below.

1. General Works

569. Abrams, Calvin R. and May. "Interviews with Jewish Major Leaguers of the Post World War II Baseball Era." *American Jewish History,* LXXXIII (March 1995), 109–122.

570. Ardell, Jean Hastings. "Baseball Is a Man's Game: Or Is It?" *Elysian Fields Quarterly,* XII (Summer 1993), 8–10.

571. Ashe, Arthur. *A Hard Road to Glory—Baseball: The African-American Athlete in Baseball.* New York: Amistad, 1993. 260p. The baseball sections extracted from the 3 volume work, *A Hard Road to Glory.*

572. Ballenberg, Bill and Shelley Smith. "Remembering Their Game: There Used to Be Two Games of Professional Baseball, the Major Leagues and the Negro Leagues. They Were Separate and Most Definitely Not Equal. The Men of the Negro Leagues Performed With Skill and Passion, but for Nickels and Dimes. Yet Their Memories of Those Days Are Rich." *Sports Illustrated,* LXXVII (July 6, 1992), 80–92.

573. "Baseball's Century: 'Color Barrier." *Hispanic,* X (May 1997), 14+. Focuses on Latinos.

574. "Baseball's Subtle Prejudice: Racial Report Card." *Sports Illustrated,* LXXXIII (September 25, 1995), 15–16.

575. Beran, Jamie A. "Diamonds in Iowa: Blacks, Buxton, and Baseball." *Journal of Negro History,* LXXV (Summer-Fall 1990), 81+.

576. Berlage, Gai. "Women Baseball

Stars of the Swinging 1920s and 1930s." *Nine: A Journal of Baseball History and Social Policy Perspective,* V (Fall 1996), 77–93.

577. ____. *Women in Baseball: Forgotten History.* Westport, Conn.: Praeger, 1994. 208p.

578. Berry, Charmaine H. "Indian Men with Baseball Caps." *Studies in American Indian Literature,* VII (Spring 1995), 25+.

579. Billet, Bret L. and Lance J. Formwalt. *America's National Pastime: A Study of Race and Merit in Professional Baseball.* Westport, Conn.: Praeger, 1995. 161p.

580. Bjarkman, Peter C. "Diamonds are a Gal's Worst Friend: Women in Baseball History and Fiction." *Elysian Fields Quarterly,* XII (Summer 1993), 93–105. First appeared in a 1989 issue of the *SABR Review of Books.*

581. ____. "Six-Pointed Diamonds and the Ultimate Shiksa: Baseball and the American-Jewish Immigrant Experience." *Elysian Fields Quarterly,* XI (Fall 1992), 49–79.

582. ____. "The Yiddish Connection: Jewish Ball Players and the National Pastime." *Dugout,* III (August 1995), 15–20.

583. "Black and White: Two Former Players Recall the Negro Baseball Leagues." *Airman,* XXXVIII (August 1994), 42+.

584. Boren, Stephen D. and Thomas. "Early Black Batteries in the Major Leagues: By No Means an Overnight Phenomenon." *Baseball Research Journal,* XXI (1992), 107–109.

585. Brashler, William. *The Story of Negro League Baseball.* New York: Ticknor & Fields, 1994. 166p.

586. Chadwick, Bruce. *When the Game Was Black and White: The Illustrated History of Baseball's Negro Leagues.* New York: Abbeville Press, 1992. 191p.

587. Chamberlin, Mitchell B. and Bruce J. Arneklev. "Macro-Social Determinants of the Racial Composition of Major League Baseball Teams." *Soci-*

ological Focus, XXVI (February 1993), 65+.

588. Clerk, Dick and Larry Lester, eds. *The Negro Leagues Book.* Cleveland, Oh.: SABR, 1994. 382p.

589. Corbett, M. L. "Building the Champions." *Black Enterprise,* XXV (July 1995), 84–87. Retired black athletes as team executives.

590. Craft, David. *The Negro Leagues: 40 Years of Black Professional Baseball in Words and Pictures.* New York: Crescent Books, 1993. 112p.

591. Davis, J. E. "Baseball's Reluctant Challenge: Desegregating Major League Spring Training Sites, 1961–1964." *Journal of Sport History,* XIX (Summer 1992), 144–162.

592. Derby, R. E. "House of David Baseball: The Bearded Beauties." *National Pastime,* XIV (1994), 7–10.

593. Dixon, Phil and Patrick J. Hannigan. *The Negro Baseball Leagues, 1867–1955: A Photographic History.* Mattituck, N.Y.: Amereon House, 1992. 329p.

594. Feldman, E. "Of Pennants and Penitents: Baseball, The World Series, and Yielding to Temptation—A Jewish Morality Tale." *Tradition: A Journal of Orthodox Jewish Thought,* XXX (March 1996), 1–5.

595. Finerty, J. D. "Race Discrimination in Hiring Major League Baseball Managers." *For the Record,* III (June–July 1992), 2–3, 8.

596. Fremon, David K. *The Negro Baseball Leagues.* New York: New Discovery Books, 1994. 96p.

597. Frias, Ramon. "Latin Stars More Abundant Than Ever in the Big Leagues." *Baseball Digest,* LII (July 1993), 20–23.

598. Gardner, Robert and Dennis Shortelle. *The Forgotten Players: The Story of Black Baseball in America.* New York: Walker, 1993. 120p.

599. Giancaterino, Randy. "A Pitch for Black History." *American Visions,* VIII (June 1993), 22+. A Negro Leagues museum at Kansas City.

600. Gilbert, Thomas W. *Baseball and the Color Line.* New York: Franklin Watts, 1995. 176p.

601. Gomez, Pedro. "Squeeze Play." *Hispanic,* X (July 1997), 34+. Cuban players.

602. Gonzalez, G. Leticia. *"Beyond Black and White: A Comprehensive Study of the Stacking of Latinos in Major League Baseball, 1950–1992."* Unpublished Ph.D. Dissertation, University of Iowa, 1994.

603. ____. "The Stacking of Latinos in Major League Baseball: A Forgotten Minority?" *Journal of Sport and Social Issues,* XX (May 1996), 134–160.

604. Gould, Todd. "Life in the Negro Leagues." *Hoosierisms Quarterly,* I (Summer 1996), 4–8.

605. Gregorich, Barbara. "From Bloomer Girls to Silver Bullets: A Short History of Women in Baseball." *Dugout,* II (December 1994), 5–10.

606. ____. *Women at Play: The Story of Women in Baseball.* San Diego, Ca.: Harcourt, Brace, Jovanovich, 1993. 214p.

607. ____. "Women in Baseball: Indiana's Dynamic Heritage." *Traces of Indiana and Midwestern History,* V (Spring 1993), 26+.

608. Guss, Greg. "Skin Game." *Sport,* LXXXIX (May 1997), 52–58, 84.

609. Heaphy, Leslie Anne. *"Shadowed Diamonds: The Growth and Decline of the Negro Leagues."* Unpublished Ph.D. Dissertation, University of Toledo, 1995. 436p.

610. Hochberg, Barry. "Make Room on the Bench." *South Florida,* XLVI (July 1993), 51+. Cuban players.

611. Kalmut, A. R. "The Turnstiles Clicked, the Lights Went Out: A History of Black Baseball Teams That Crossed Borders But Not Barriers." *Dugout,* II (April 1994), 16–21.

612. Kelley, Brent. *Voices from the Negro Leagues: Conversations with 51 Baseball Standouts of the Period 1924–1951.* Jefferson, N.C.: McFarland & Co., Inc., 1997. 304p.

613. Lapchick, R. E. "Professional Sports: The Racial Report Card." In: D. S. Eitzen, ed. *Sport in Contemporary Society: An Anthology.* 4th ed. New York: St. Martin's Press, 1993. pp. 355–371.

614. Lawrence, Merlisa. "The Silent Minorities: Baseball's Black and Hispanic Stars Have to Speak Up If Their Brethren Are to Get Front-Office Jobs." *Sports Illustrated,* LXXVIII (April 5, 1993), 108+.

615. Leavy, Walter and Ahmad Rashad. "50 Years of Blacks in Sports." *Ebony,* L (October 1995), 131–134+; LI (November 1995), 156+.

616. Levine, Peter. *Ellis Island to Ebbets Field: Sport and the American Jewish Experience.* New York: Oxford University Press, 1992. 326p.

617. Malloy, Jerry. "The 25th Infantry Regiment Takes the Field: A Salute to Baseball in the Army's Black Infantry, 1894–1919." *National Pastime,* XV (1995), 59–64.

618. Margolies, Jacob. *The Negro Leagues: The Story of Black Baseball.* New York: Watts, 1993. 128p.

619. McKissack, Patricia C. and Frederick, Jr. *Black Diamond: The Story of the Negro Baseball Leagues.* New York: Scholastic, 1994. 184p.

620. McPhillips, Matthew J. "The Girls of Summer: A Comprehensive Analysis of the Past, Present, and Future of Women in Baseball." *Seton Hall Journal of Sport Law,* VI, no. 1 (1996), 301+.

621. Moffi, Larry and Jonathan Kronstadt. *Crossing the Line: Black Major Leaguers, 1947–1959.* Iowa City: University of Iowa Press, 1996. 254p.

622. Ogden, R. Dale and J. Ronald Newlin. "Race and Sport in Indiana: Before and After Jackie Robinson." *Hoosierisms Quarterly,* I (Summer 1996), 9–14.

623. Otto, F. "Playing Baseball in America: Puerto Rican Memories." *Nine: A Journal of Baseball History and Social Policy Perspective,* IV (Spring 1996), 362–376.

624. Pendleton, Jason. "Jim Crow Strikes Out: Interracial Baseball in Wichita, Kansas, 1920–1935." *Kansas History,* XX (Summer 1997), 86+.

625. Phillips, John C. "The Integration of Central Positions in Baseball: The Black Shortstop." *Sociology of Sport Journal,* VIII (June 1991), 161–167.

626. Pratkanis, A. R. and M. E. Turner. "Nine Principles of Successful Affirmative Action: Mr. Branch Rickey, Mr. Jackie Robinson, and the Integration of Baseball." *Nine: A Journal of Baseball History and Social Policy Research,* III (Fall 1994), 36–65.

627. "Replacement Players, Circa 1883." *Harper's,* CCXC (April 1995), 24–25. Women's exhibition game.

628. Retort, Robert D. *Pictorial Negro Leagues Album.* New Castle, Pa.: RDA Enterprises, 1992. 260p.

629. Ribowsky, Mark. *A Complete History of the Negro Leagues, 1884 to 1955.* Secaucus, N.J.: Carol Pub. Group., 1995. 332p.

630. Richardson-James, Sharon. "Race and Baseball: Getting Beyond 'Business as Usual.'" *Journal of Sport and Social Issues,* XVII (April 1993), 67+.

631. Riley, James A. *The Negro Leagues.* New York: Chelsea House, 1997. 102p.

632. Ritter, Lawrence S. *Leagues Apart: The Men and Times of the Negro Baseball Leagues.* New York: Morrow Junior Books, 1995. Unpaged.

633. Rodriguez, Roberto. "Before Canseco: The Early History of Latinos in Baseball was Full of Hits and Runs Around the Colorline." *Black Issues in Higher Education,* XIII (April 18, 1996), 18+.

634. Rolbein, Seth. "Playing Beisbol." *Boston,* LXXXVII (August 1995), 53–56. Cuban players.

635. Rossi, John P. "Blacks in Major League Baseball: The Experience of the First Generation, 1947–61." *International Journal of the History of Sport,* XIII (December 1996), 397–403.

636. Rozin, Skip. "Two Worlds." *Topps Magazine,* (Fall 1992), 36–39. Black and white leagues.

637. Ruck, Rob. "Baseball in Its Heyday." *Pittsburgh,* XXIV (February 1993), 36+. The city's Negro League teams; excerpted from the next entry.

638. ____. *Sandlot Seasons: Sport in Black Pittsburgh.* Urbana, Ill.: University of Illinois Press, 1993.

639. ____. and Christopher Fletcher. "Playing Ball in the 'Burgh." *Pittsburgh,* XXV (December 1994), 44–52.

640. Sailes, Gary A. "The Myth of Black Sports Supremacy." *Journal of Black Studies,* XXI (June 1991), 480–487.

641. Santa Maria, Michael. "One Strike and You're Out: Baseball Has Always Been a Reliable Mirror of Race Relations in America." *American Vision,* V (April 1990), 16+.

642. Sport Information Resource Centre. *Making an Informed Decision About Girls' Participation on Boys' Teams.* Gloucester, Ont., 1995. 26p.

643. Stanford, J. "African-American Baseballists and the *Denver Post* Tournament." *Colorado Heritage,* (Spring 1995), 20–34.

644. "Surviving Negro Leaguers Celebrate Black Baseball's 75th Anniversary." *Jet,* LXXXIX (November 20, 1995), 46–47.

645. "Taking Charge on the Field: After Years of Being Shut Out, Blacks and Hispanics Are Finally Getting Some of the Game's Top Jobs." *Ebony,* XLVIII (May 1993), 110–112, 114.

646. Tygiel, Jules. "The Negro Leagues." *OAH Magazine of History,* VII (Summer 1992), 24–27.

647. Ward, Geoffrey C. and Ken Burns, With Jim O'Connor. *Shadow Ball: The History of the Negro Leagues.* New York: Knopf, dist. by Random House, 1994. 79p. Abridged in *U.S. News & World Report,* CXVII (August 29, 1994), 83–84.

648. "What's Behind the Shrinking Number of African-American Players?" *Ebony,* XLVII (June 1992), 112–114+.

649. White, Sol. *History of Colored Base Ball, with Other Documents on the Early Black Game, 1886–1936.* Compiled and introduced by Jerry Malloy. Lincoln: University of Nebraska Press, 1995. 187p. A revision and reprinting of the 1907 ed., complete with bibliography.

650. Wiggins, D. K. "'The Year of Awakening': Black Athletes, Racial Unrest, and the Civil Rights Movement of 1968." *International Journal of the History of Sports,* IX (August 1992), 188–208.

2. Negro League Teams, Arranged Alphabetically

BALTIMORE ELITE GIANTS

651. Leffler, Robert R., Jr. "Boom and Bust: The Elite Giants and Black Baseball in Baltimore, 1936–1951." *Maryland Historical Magazine,* LXXXVII (Summer 1992), 171–186.

CLEVELAND BUCKEYES

652. Kleinknecht, M. F. "Building a Champion: Wilbur Hayes and the Cleveland Buckeyes." *National Pastime,* XV (1995), 136–140.

DETROIT STARS

653. Bak, Richard. *Turkey Stearnes and the Detroit Stars: The Negro Leagues in Detroit, 1919–1933.* Detroit, Mich.: Wayne State University Press, 1994. 298p.

HILLDALE FIELD
CLUB OF PHILADELPHIA

654. Lanctot, Neil. *Fair Dealing and Clean Playing: The Hilldale Club and the Development of Black Professional Baseball, 1910–1932.* Jefferson, N.C.: McFarland & Co., Inc., 1994. 304p.

INDIANAPOLIS ABCs

655. Debono, Paul. *The Indianapolis ABCs: History of a Premier Team in the Negro Leagues.* Jefferson, N.C.: McFarland & Co., Inc., 1997. 280p.

KANSAS CITY MONARCHS

657. Campbell, Janet B. "Beyond the Box Score: The Kansas City Monarchs." *History News,* XLVII (March–April 1992), 6–11.

LONG ISLAND CUBAN GIANTS

658. Malloy, Jerry. "The Birth of the Cuban Giants: The Origins of Black Professional Baseball." *Nine: A Journal of Baseball History and Social Policy Perspective,* II (Spring 1994), 233–247.

NEWARK EAGLES

659. Overmyer, James. *Effa Manley and the Newark Eagles.* Metuchen, N.J.: Scarecrow Press, 1993. 297p.

PITTSBURGH CRAWFORDS

660-1. Shannon, Mike. *The Day Satchel Paige and the Pittsburgh Crawfords Came to Herford, N.C.* Jefferson, N.C.: McFarland & Co., Inc., 1992.

ST. LOUIS BLACK BRONCHOS

662. Debono, Peter. "1910: The St. Louis Black Bronchos." *American Visions,* VIII (June–July 1993), 26–27.

YORK MONARCHS

663. Wright, J. J. "The Giants to Monarchs: The 1890 Season of the Colored Monarchs of York, Pennsylvania." *Nine: A Journal of Baseball History and Social Policy Perspective,* II (Spring 1994), 248–259.

3. All-American Girls Professional Baseball League

664. Brownie, Lois. *Girls of Summer in Their Own League.* New York: Harper-Collins, 1992. 212p.

665. Helmer, Diana Star. *Belles of the Ballpark.* Brookfield, Ct.: Millbrook Press, 1993. 96p. Racine Belles, first AAGPBL champions.

666. ____. "Force Out." *Elysian Fields Quarterly,* XII (Summer 1993), 18–21.

667. Johnson, Susan E. *When Women Played Hardball: Professional Lives and Personal Stories from the All-American Girls Professional Baseball League, 1943–1954.* Seattle, Wash.: Seal Press, 1994. 292p.

668. Kiefer, Michael. "Hard Ball: The World's Only Professional Women's Baseball League." *Women's Sports and Fitness,* XIV (April 1992), 56+.

669. Laughlin, Kathleen. "Sports-Minded All Their Lives: Female Professional Baseball Players in the All American Girls Baseball League." *Feminisms,* III (July 1994), 8+.

670. Macy, Sue. *A Whole New Ball Game: The Story of the All-American Girls Professional Baseball League, 1943–1954.* New York: Holt, 1993. 140p.

671. Pratt, M. "The All-American Girls Professional Baseball League." In: G. I. Cohen, ed. *Women in Sport: Issues and Controversies.* Newbury Park, Calif.: Sage Publications, 1993. pp. 49–58.

672. Weiller, Karen H. "The All American Girls Professional Baseball League, 1943–1954: Gender Conflict in Sport?" *Sociology of Sport Journal,* XI (September 1994), 289+.

673. ____. and Catriona T. Higgs. "Living the Dream: A Historical Analysis of Professional Women Baseball Players, 1943–1954." *Canadian Journal of the History of Sport,* XXIII (May 1992), 46–54.

674. Zipter, Yvonne. "The All American Girls Baseball League." *Hot Wire,* IX (January 1993), 24+.

e. Baseball Lore and Literature,
Art and Music, Film, Superstitions,
Nicknames and Mascots

BASEBALL-related aspects of several of the humanities are provided in this large part. Here the reader will find subparts devoted not only to general works which emphasize baseball's place in our culture, but concerning art and photography, film, lore and literature, music, superstitions, nicknames, and even mascots. As noted in our introduction to this part in *Baseball: A Comprehensive Bibliography*, our purpose, especially with regards to adult and juvenile baseball novels, is not to review the many hundreds of fictional works of baseball (although in our first outing, a few of the more interesting or important adult-oriented baseball novels were cited with annotation). Rather, because such a listing had already been provided by Anton Grobani and was (and is) being updated by others, we chose then—as we choose now—to concentrate on citing references which themselves analyze. We again direct our readers to those of our colleagues who, by their citations in our 1986 bibliography and below, do the good work of covering baseball's fictional literature title by title.

1. General Works

675. Ardolino, F. "Dives, Dark Clubhouses, Deceptive Dreamscapes, and Clean, Well-Lighted Places in Sports Literature and Film." *Aethlon, the Journal of Sports Literature,* VIII (Spring 1991), 1–13.
676. Berlage, Gai I. "Women's Professional Baseball Gets a New Look: On Film and In Print." *Journal of Sport History,* XIX (Summer 1992), 110–129.
677. Chidester, D. "The Church of Baseball, the Fetish of Coca-Cola, and the Potlatch of Rock-n-Roll: Theoretical Models for the Study of Religion in American Popular Culture." *Journal of the American Academy of Religion,* LXIV (December 1996), 743–765.
678. Early, G. "Birdland: 2 Observations on the Cultural Significance of Baseball." *American Poetry Review,* XXV (July 1996), 9–12.
679. Heilman, Robert D. "Baseball: Random Connections." *Sewanee Review,* CXXXIV (Fall 1996), 550+.
680. McLuhan, Marshall. "Baseball Is Culture." In: William Humber and John St. James, eds. *All I Thought About Was Baseball: Writings on a Canadian Pastime.* North York, Ont.: University of Toronto Press, 1996. pp. 209–214.
681. Ruscoe, Michael, ed. *Baseball: A Treasury of Art and Literature.* New York: Macmillan, 1993. 376p.
682. Stewart, Wayne. "Embarrassing Moments Are Part of Major League Lore." *Baseball Digest,* LI (December 1992), 75–77.

2. Art, Including Photography

683. *Baseball Days—From the Sandlots to the Show: Photographs by Henry Horenstein, Essays and Stories by Bill Littlefield.* Boston, Mass.: Little, Brown, 1993. 151p.
684. Benger, Brent. "Fall Classics." *Sports Illustrated,* LXXIX (August 23, 1993), 38–45. Reproductions of paintings.
685. Ferguson, Gretje. "Baseball in America." *Petersen's Photographic Magazine,* XXI (June 1992), 44+.
686. Harrison, Robert L. "Painting the Game: A Conversation with Mike Schacht." *Elysian Fields Quarterly,* XIII (Winter 1994), 85–90.
687. Holtzman, Bud. "Diamond Fantasies: Baseball Camps Offer New Market for Studio Professionals." *The Professional Photographer,* CXVIII (June 1991), 50+.
688. Horenstein, Henry. "The Old Ball

Game." *Life,* XVI (June 1993), 44–51.

689. Iooss, Walter and Thomas Boswell. *Diamond Dreams: 30 Years of Baseball Through the Lens of Walter Iooss.* Boston, Mass.: Little, Brown, 1995. 160p.

690. Mandrake, Mark. "This Guy Has Seen 'Em All—Literally." *Inside Sports,* XVII (April 1995), 18–19. Photographer George Brace.

691. Mantoani, T. J. "Making the Ordinary Extraordinary." *Petersen's Photographic Magazine,* XXIV (August 1995), 22–23. Baseball photography.

692. McCabe, Neal and Constance. *Baseball's Golden Age: The Photographs of Charles M. Conlon.* New York: Harry N. Abrams, 1993. 198p.

693. "Miracle Mitts." *Sport,* LXXXVII (October 1996), 84–85.

694. Moore, Steve. *Back to the Bleachers: Baseball Cartoons.* New York: Macmillan, 1995. 95p.

695. "The National Pastime: How to Photograph Amateur Baseball Games." *PSA Journal,* LVIII (April 1992), 14+.

696. O'Connell, T. S. "Legacy of the Picture Man." *Beckett Baseball Card Monthly,* X, no. 95 (February 1993), 90–96. Photographer Charles Conlon.

697. Ralph, John. "All-Star Baseball Art." In: John Blake, *et al. Texas Rangers 1995 Yearbook.* Arlington, Tex.: Public Relations Dept., Texas Rangers, 1995. pp. 35–49.

698. Stoddard, M. G. "The Art of the Athlete." *Saturday Evening Post,* CCLXVIII (July–August 1996), 58–63. SEP covers.

699. Sugar, Bert R. *Great Baseball Players in Historic Photographs.* New York: Dover Books, 1996. 128p.

3. Film

The Ken Burns documentary *Baseball* is referenced under Burns, below in Individual Biography.

700. Baker, Aaron B. *"Contested Identities: Sports in American Film and Television."* Unpublished Ph.D. Dissertation, Indiana University, 1994.

701. Booth, Stephen A. "Hollywood Goes to Bat." *Video Review,* X (September 1989), 44+.

702. Edelman, Rob. *The Great Baseball Films: From Silent Days to the Present.* Secaucus, N.J.: Carol Pub. Group, 1994. 231p.

703. Erickson, Hal. *Baseball in the Movies: A Comprehensive Reference, 1915–1991.* Jefferson, N.C.: McFarland & Co., Inc., 1992. 402p.

704. Good, Howard. *Diamonds in the Dark: America, Baseball, and the Movies.* Lanham, Md.: Scarecrow Press, 1997. 185p.

705. Gretton, Viveca. "You Could Look It Up: Notes Towards a Reading of Baseball, History, and Ideology in the Dominant Cinema." *Cineaction,* no. 21 (Summer 1990), 70+.

706. Griffin, Nancy. "Clean Up Women." *Premiere,* V (July 1992), 76+. "A League of Their Own."

707. "Lights, Cameras, Action: Films Turn the Game into a Reel Art Form." In: Joe Hoppel, ed. *The Sporting News 1995 Baseball Yearbook.* St. Louis, Mo.: TSN, 1995. pp. 42–45.

708. Lyons, Jeffrey. "A Requiem for Innocence Lost: *"When It Was a Game II."* *Inside Sports,* XV (October 1993), 22–23. HBO documentary.

709. Stevens, John D. "A Note on Hollywood and Baseball." *Film and History,* XIX (September 1989), 69+.

710. Torres, Richard. "'The Truest Form of Theater.'" *Inside Sports,* XVIII (October 1996), 18, 20.

711. Tudor, Deborah V. *"Hollywood and the Representation of Team Athletics in Recent Films."* Unpublished Ph.D. Dissertation, Northwestern University, 1992.

712. Vantornhout, K. L. *"Film Analysis of 'A League of Their Own' Myths and Portrayals of Heroines in Sport."* Unpublished M.A. Thesis, San Jose State University, 1996. 250p.

4. Lore and Literature

713. Bachner, Saul. "Sports Literature for the At-Risk Student." *Clearing House,* LXVII (March–April 1994), 200–203.

714. Barra, Allen. "Writing with a Ring in It." *Inside Sports,* XIV (October 1992), 13–14. Tales of Ring Lardner.

715. *Baseball Tales—Major League Writers on the National Pastime: Photographs by Terry Heffernan, Introduction by Lawrence S. Ritter.* New York: Viking Penguin, 1993. 100p. With emphasis on Heffernan's photos, the stories are: "How I Got My Nickname," by W. P. Kinsella; "You Could Look It Up," by James Thurber; "The Rollicking God," by Nunnally Johnson; "Bush League Hero," by Edna Ferber; and "Baseball Hattie," by Damon Runyon.

716. Bjarkman, Peter C. *Baseball and the Game of Ideas: Essays for the Serious Fan.* Delhi, N.Y.: Birch Brook Press, 1993. 21lp.

717. ____. "Bats, Balls, Books, and Boxscores: The Nature and Appeal of Baseball's Literature." *Nine: A Journal of Baseball History and Social Policy Perspective,* V (Fall 1996), 116–129. Keynote address at the Indiana State University Baseball Literature Conference, April 1995.

718. ____. "Major League Hits from Minor League Players: Small Presses and the Baseball Book Industry." *Small Press,* VII (June 1989), 26+.

719. ____. "A True Mythical Nine: Baseball Fiction's All-Time All-Star Team." *Elysian Fields Quarterly,* XIII (Summer 1994), 62–66.

720. ____. "The Writer's Game: Jewish-American Novelists and the National Pastime." *Dugout,* III (August 1995), 39–43.

721. Blaisdell, Lowell D. "Legends as an Expression of Baseball Memory." *Journal of Sport History,* XIX (Winter 1992), 227–256.

722. Blake, Mike. *Baseball's Bad Hops and Lucky Bounces.* Cincinnati, Oh.: Betterway Books, 1995. 243p. Anecdotes.

723. Caracher, Brian G. "The Poetics of Baseball: An American Domestication of the Mathematically Sublime." *American Studies,* XXXII (Spring 1991), 85+.

724. Carino, P. "Fields of Imagination: Ballparks as Complex Pastoral Metaphors in Kinsella's *Shoeless Joe* and the *Iowa Baseball Confederacy.*" *Nine: A Journal of Baseball History and Social Policy Perspective,* II (Spring 1994), 287–299.

725. Carney, Gene. *Romancing the Horsehide: Baseball Poems on Players and the Game.* Jefferson, N.C.: McFarland & Co., Inc., 1993. 120p.

726. Cataneo, David. *Peanuts and Crackerjack: A Treasury of Baseball Legends and Lore.* Nashville, Tn.: Rutledge Hill Press, 1991.

727. Christopher, Matt. *Matt Christopher's All-Star Lineup: Five Volumes in One.* New York: Black Dog and Leventhal, 1997. 703p. An anthology of stories.

728. Citron, Jo Ann. "Running the Basepaths: Baseball and Jane Austin." *The Journal of Narrative Technique,* XVIII (Fall 1988), 269+.

729. De Avila, Liliana. "The Selection of Statistics in a Baseball Outcome Predictive Pitching Form Is Within the Subject Matter of Copyright." *Seton Hall Journal of Sport Law,* II (Spring 1992), 233+.

730. Duvall, J. N. "Baseball as Aesthetic Ideology: Cold War History, Race, and DeLillo's 'Pafko at the Wall.'" *Modern Fiction Studies,* XLI (June 1995), 285–313.

731. Early, G. "Birdland: Two Observations on the Cultural Significance of Baseball." *American Poetry Review,* XXV (July 1996), 9–12.

732. Egan, Terry, Stan Friedman, and Mike Levine, eds. *The Macmillan Book of Baseball Stories.* New York: Macmillan, 1992. 127p.

733. Fehler, Gene. *I Hit the Ball: Base-ball Poems for the Young.* Jefferson, N.C.: McFarland & Co., Inc., 1996. 120p.

734. Folsom, Ed. *Walt Whitman's Native Representations.* New York: Cambridge University Press, 1994. 194p.

735. Frisch, Mark F. "Self-Definition and Redefinition in the New World: Coover's 'The Universal Baseball Association' and Borges." *Confluencia,* IV (Spring 1989), 13+.

736. Gardner, Martin, ed. *The Annotated Casey at the Bat: A Collection of Ballads About the Mighty Casey.* 3rd rev. ed. New York: Dover Publications, 1995. 231p.

737. Gaughran, Richard. "The Hero as Outlaw: Jerome Charyn's *The Seventh Babe.*" *Elysian Fields Quarterly,* XI (Spring 1992), 90–96.

738. ____. "Yellow Ribbons, Homers for America, and Roy Hobbs." *The Minneapolis Review of Baseball,* X (Fall 1991), 33–36.

739. Gleason, William A. *"Playing for Keeps: Recreation and Re-Creation in American Literature, 1840–1940."* Unpublished Ph.D. dissertation, U.C.L.A., 1993.

740. Grey, Zane. *The Redheaded Outfield and Other Baseball Stories.* New York: Gramercy Books, 1995. 178p. Originally written almost a century earlier.

741. Harris, Mark. *Diamond: Baseball Writings of Mark Harris.* New York: David I. Fine, 1994. 289p.

742. Harrison, Robert L. "Center Field Poet: An Interview with Gene Fehler." *Elysian Fields Quarterly,* XIV (Spring 1995), 67–75.

743. ____. *Green Fields and White Lines: Baseball Poems.* Jefferson, N.C.: McFarland & Co., Inc., 1995. 141p.

744. Henry, H. "'Them Dodgers Is My Gallant Knights': Fiction as History in *The Natural.*" *Journal of Sport and Social Issues,* XVI (December 1992), 149–152.

745. Hunt, Moreau C. *"Frozen Moments in the Interior Stadium: Style in Contemporary 'Proseball.'"* Unpublished Ph.D. Dissertation, Middle Tennessee State University, 1993.

746. Hurley, C. Harold. "Baseball in Hemingway's *The Three Day Blow*: The Way It Really Was in 1916." *The Hemingway Review,* XVI (Fall 1996), 43+.

747. ____. *Hemingway's Debt to Baseball in "The Old Man and the Sea":* *A Collection of Critical Readings.* Lewiston, Idaho: E. Mellen Press, 1992. 117p.

748. Isaacs, N. D. "Is the Key to the Batter's Box Under Iron John's Pillow?" *Aethlon: The Journal of Sport Literature,* XII (Spring 1995), 45–49.

749. Jenkins, Clarence W. *"Heading Home—Baseball Fiction and the American Experience: A Study of Baseball Fiction from the Gilded Age to the Jazz Age."* Unpublished Ph.D. dissertation, University of Wisconsin at Milwaukee, 1996.

750. Katovich, Michael A. "Humor in Baseball: Functions and Dysfunctions." *Journal of American Culture,* XVI (Summer 1993), 7–15.

751. Kinsella, W. P. *Box Socials.* New York: Ballantine Books, 1991. 225p. Fictional account of a Canadian's 1945 or '46 journey to try out with the St. Louis Cardinals.

752. ____. *Diamonds Forever: Reflections from the Field, the Dugout, and the Bleachers.* Toronto and New York: HarperCollins, 1997.

753. ____. *The Dixon Cornbelt League and Other Baseball Stories.* New York and Toronto: HarperCollins, 1993. 180p. Canadian emphasis.

754. ____. *Go the Distance: Baseball Stories.* Dallas, Tx.: Southern Methodist University Press, 1995. 179p. First published as *Further Adventures of Slugger McBatt.*

755. Klinkowitz, Jerry. "Philip Roth's Anti-Baseball Novel." *Western Humanities Review,* XLVII (Spring 1993), 30+.

756. Kriegel, Leonard. "From the Catbird Seat: Football, Baseball, and Language." *Sewanee Review,* CI (Spring 1993), 213–225.

757. Lardner, Ring W. *Ring Around the Bases: The Complete Baseball Stories of Ring Lardner.* Edited by Matthew J. Bruccoli. New York: Charles Scribner's Sons, 1992. 609p.

758. ____. *Short Stories/Selections: The Annotated Baseball Stories of Ring W. Lardner, 1914–1919.* Edited by George W. Hilton. Stanford, Ca.: Stanford University Press, 1995. 63 1p.

759. Lauricella, John A. *"In Play: Baseball in American Fiction."* Unpublished Ph.D. dissertation, Cornell University, 1993.

760. Marshall, Tod. "Of Baseball, Clarity, and Emotion." *High Plains Literary Review,* IX (August 1994), 125+.

761. Meissner, Bill. *Hitting into the Wind: Baseball Stories.* New York: Random House, 1994. 205p.

762. Miguelalfonso, R. "Mimesis and Self-Consciousness in Robert Coover's *The Universal Baseball Association." Critique-Studies in Contemporary Fiction,* XXXVII (December 1996), 92–107.

763. Moore, Jim and Natalie Vermilyea. *Ernest Thayer's "Casey at the Bat": Background and Characters of Baseball's Most Famous Poem.* Jefferson, N.C.: McFarland & Co., Inc., 1994. 360p.

764. Morris, T. "'Forget It Means Fuck It': Hispanic Stereotypes in Baseball Fiction." *Aethlon: The Journal of Sport Literature,* XII (Spring 1995), 63–70.

765. Mueller, Lavonne, ed. *Baseball Monologues.* Portsmouth, N.H.: Heinemann, 1996. 155p.

766. Nauen, Elinor, ed. *Diamonds are a Girl's Best Friend: Women Writers on Baseball.* Boston: Faber & Faber, 1994. 295p.

767. Olenik, Michael. "The Literary Heritage of Baseball." *AB Bookman's Weekly,* XCIX (April 21, 1997), 1297+.

768. Orodenker, Richard. *The Writers' Game: Baseball Writing in America.* Twayne's United States Authors Series, no. 663. New York: Twayne Publishers, 1996. 248p.

769. Perilli, Paul. "Sports and the Literary Writer." *Poets and Writers,* XXII (July 1994), 18+.

770. Poff, John. "Casey Revisited: The Culture of Baseball." *Elysian Fields Quarterly,* XIII (Special Issue 1994), 3–5.

771. Roberts, F. M. "Dem Bums Become the Boys of Summer: Remembering Baseball in American Popular Culture and Sports Literature—From Comic Caricatures to Sacred Icons of the National Pastime." *American Jewish History,* LXXXIII (March 1995), 51–63.

772. Salisbury, L. "Baseball Purists Purify." *Nine: A Journal of Baseball History and Social Policy Perspective,* III (Spring 1995), 235–247.

773. Segrave, J. O. "'Playball!': Baseball Lingo in the Language of Sexual Relations." *Aethlon: The Journal of Sport Literature,* XII (Fall 1995), 117–123.

774. Schaap, Dick, ed. *Joy in Mudville: The Big Book of Baseball Humor.* Garden City, N.Y.: Doubleday, 1992. 424p.

775. Simmons, Carl. "An American Fascination: Books and Stories on Baseball." *AB Bookman Weekly,* LXXXIX (March 30, 1992), 1245+.

776. Solomon, Eric. "Memories of Days Past; or, Why Eric Rolfe Greenberg's *The Celebrant* Is the Greatest (Jewish) Baseball Novel." *American Jewish History,* LXXXIII (March 1995), 83+.

777. Staudohar, Paul D., ed. *Baseball's Best Short Stories.* Chicago, Ill.: Chicago Review Press, 1995. 387p.

778. Thomas, Brook. "Stanley Fish and the Uses of Baseball: The Return of 'The Natural.'" *Yale Journal of Law and the Humanities,* II (Winter 1990), 59+.

779. Toropov, Brandon. *The Fifty Biggest Baseball Myths.* Secaucus, N.J.: Carol Publishing Group, 1997.

780. Trujillo, Nick. "Interpreting (The Work and Talk of) Baseball: Perspectives on Ballpark Culture." *Western Journal of Communications,* LVI (Fall 1992), 350+.

781. Tuttle, Dennis. "The Great Work of Homers." *Inside Sports,* XVII (June 1995), 20–21. Mike Shannon's *Spitball* magazine.

782. Warde, Robert. "Mind Games." *Elysian Fields Quarterly,* XI (Winter 1992), 17–22. Value of literature.

783. Westbrook, Deeanne. *Ground Rules: Baseball and Myth.* Urbana: University of Illinois Press, 1996. 348p.

5. Music

784. Cooper, B. Lee, Donald E. Walker, and William L. Schurk. "The Decline of Contemporary Baseball Heroes in American Popular Recordings." *Popular Music and Society,* XV (Summer 1991), 49+.

785. Kraft, R. E. and J. E. Crothers. "The Music of Baseball: A Historical Perspective." *Nine: A Journal of Baseball History and Social Policy Perspective,* V (Spring 1997), 316–336.

786. Wells, John D. and James D. Skipper, Jr. "The Soup of Summer: A Sociological Study of Songs About Baseball and the Play Element in Culture." *Popular Music and Society,* XII (Winter 1988), 25+.

6. Superstitions, Nicknames, and Mascots

787. Banks, D. J. "Trivial Names and Mascots in Sports." *Journal of Sport and Social Issues,* XVII (April 1993), 5–8.

788. "Baseball Nicknames from the Good Old Days." *Good Old Days,* XXX (April 1993), 20+.

789. Brill, Howard W. "The Name of the Departed Team: Who Can Use It?" *Whittier Law Review,* XV (Winter 1994), 1003–1016.

790. Clifton, Merrill. "Perjorative Nicknames of Baseball All-Stars." *Maledicta,* X (1988), 78+.

791. Davis, L. R. "Protest Against the Use of Native American Mascots: A Challenge to Traditional American Identity." *Journal of Sport and Social Issues,* XVII (April 1993), 9–22.

792. Finnigan, Bob. "Is the Cy Young Award Jinx a Fact or Fallacy?" *Baseball Digest,* LIV (July 1997), 48–51.

793. Gmelch, George. "Superstition and Ritual in American Baseball." *Elysian Fields Quarterly,* XI (Spring 1992), 25–36.

794. Graham, Stedman. "What's in a Name? Plenty." *Inside Sports,* XVIII (June 1996), 8, 10.

795. Guilfoile, William J. "Hall of Famers Name Their Toughest Diamond Foes." *Baseball Digest,* LI (August 1992), 28–31.

796. Keetz, F. "Aliteration and Initials." *National Pastime,* XIV (1994), 74–76.

797. Lessiter, Mike. "What's in a Name." *Beckett Baseball Card Monthly,* IX, no. 89 (August 1992), 16–19.

798. Long, Sam. "Weather Names and Baseball Games: Lots and Lots of Weather Names." *Weatherwise,* XLIV (August 1990), 184+.

799. Maestri, Vic. "Names: A Fascinating Part of Baseball Tradition." *Baseball Digest,* LV (January 1996), 61–63.

800. Nuessel, Frank. "Objectionable Sport Team Designations." *Names,* XLII (June 1994), 101–199.

801. Skipper, James K., Jr. "Placenames Used as Nicknames: A Study of Major League Baseball Players." *Names,* XXXVIII (March 1990), 1+.

802. Sloan, C. J. and C. S. Watts. *College Nicknames & Mascots.* Northport, Ala.: Vision Press, 1992. Unpaged.

803. Slowikowski, S. S. "Cultural Performance and Sport Mascots." *Journal of Sport and Social Issues,* XVII (April 1993), 23–33.

804. "Superstitious!" *Sports Illustrated for Kids,* VIII (August 1996), 24–28.

805. Verducci, Tom. "Martinez Mania." *Sports Illustrated,* LXXXIII (July 24, 1995), 26–28+. Names.

806. Wenner, L. A. "The Real Red Face of Sports." *Journal of Sport and Social Issues,* XVI (April 1993), 1–4. Focus on team names like the Braves and Indians.

807. Wilson, Brenda and James K. Skipper, Jr. "Nicknames and Women Professional Baseball Players." *Names,* XXXVIII (December 1990), 305+.

2. Special Studies

The parts here bring together a number of diverse but interconnected subjects. For example, the business of professional baseball may be examined in relation to spring training and the World Series while baseball fans may be seen in the light of business or All Star Game balloting. For this supplement, we have added two new sub-parts: Strikes and Salaries, Salary Arbitration, and Collective Bargaining

a. Spring Training and Opening Day

Like the rite of Opening Day, the tradition of spring training in pro baseball dates back into the last century. By the 1990s, it was possible to play ball all year long as many players took advantage of winter ball in Latin America, a phenomenon which is covered in Chapter D:3:f ("Baseball in Latin America").

808. Ames, K. "One Strike and They're Out." *Newsweek,* CXX (February 27, 1995), 82+. Spring training opens with replacement players.

809. Anderson, Joan. *Batboy: An Inside Look at Spring Training.* New York: Lodestar Books, 1996. Unpaged.

810. Angell, Roger. "Warming Up." *The New Yorker,* LXXIII (April 7, 1997), 39–40.

811. "Baseball Mania: Fans and Players Warm Up Together During Spring Training." *Trailer Life,* L (May 1990), 73+.

812. Bjarkman, Peter C. "A Spring Like No Other." *Dugout,* III (April–May 1995), 2–7. 1995.

813. Brooks, Patricia. "Take Me South to the Ballgame." *Events USA,* I (February–March 1993), 23+.

814. Dagostino, Paul. "The Boys of Spring: Valley Scores Huge Win from Cactus League Economics." *The Business Journal—Serving Phoenix & the Valley of the Sun,* XVII (March 28, 1997), 21–22.

815. DeGeorge, G. "Let's See Some Hustle Out There." *Business Week,* (March 21, 1992), 100+. The economics of spring training.

816. Ehret, S. "The Strangest Spring." *Referee,* XX (June 1995), 28–32.

817. Fioto, Lou. "Talk About Time Off." *Accent on Living,* XL (Summer 1995), 114–115. Opening day baseball.

818. Friedman, Myles. "The Stars of Spring Training." *Spring Training: Grapefruit and Cactus League Yearbook,* V (1992), 50–53; VI (1993), 50–59; VII (1994), 50–51+; VIII (1995), 50–51+.

819. Hall, Stephen S. "Souvenirs from the Land of Meaningless Games." *National Geographic Traveler,* VI (March 1989), 80+.

820. Helyar, John. "Field of Dreams." *Smart Money,* I (April 15, 1992), 177–179. Spring training.

821. Jennings, Jay. "When Baseball Sprang for Hot Springs: Nearly a Century Ago, the Springtime Mecca for Many Major League Players Was a Spa in Arkansas." *Sports Illustrated,* LXXVIII (March 22, 1993), 90–93.

822. Keller, Melissa L. "Pitching for St. Petersburg: Spring Training and Publicity in the Sunshine City, 1914–1918." *Tampa Bay History,* XV (Fall-Winter 1993), 35–53.

823. Krabbenhoft, Herman. "Opening Day Grand Slams Remain Baseball Rarities." *Baseball Digest,* LIII (April 1994), 84–86.

824. Kurkjian, Tim. "Now Hear This."

Sports Illustrated, LXXXIV (March 4, 1996), 40–48. Spring training.

825. LaZebnik, Jack. "Season Opener: 'I Don't Hate It! I Don't Hate It!'" *Elysian Fields Quarterly,* XIII (Summer 1994), 87–89. St. Louis (N.L.), April 1994.

826. Lewis, Michael. "Signs of Spring." *Beckett Baseball Card Monthly,* XI, no. 107 (February 1994), 12–17. Spring training.

827. McGregor, Ed. *The History of Opening Day.* Alexandria, Va.: Time, Inc., 1997. 5p. Special advertising supplement to the March 31, 1997 issue of *Sports Illustrated.*

828. Phillips, John. *Opening Day: The Season Openers of Cleveland's Teams Since 1889.* Cabin John, Md.: Capital Publishing Co., 1993. 100p.

829. Piotrowski, Michael A. "Arizona's Cactus League: A Needle in Florida's Side?" *Tampa Bay Business Journal,* XV (January 16, 1995), 1–3.

830. Rubin, Bob. "An Opening Day Press Box Potpourri." *Inside Sports,* XV (May 1993), 16–19.

831. Rushin, Steve. "The Wrongs of Spring." *Sports Illustrated,* LXXVI (April 6, 1992), 132+.

832. Smith, Katherine Snow. "Spring Fever: A Homerun for Retail." *Tampa Bay Business Journal,* XIV (April 1, 1994), 11–12.

833. Spatz, Lyle. *New York Yankee Openers: An Opening Day History of Base-*

ball's Most Famous Team. Jefferson, N.C.: McFarland & Co., Inc., 1997. 416p.

834. Stewart, Wayne. "Baseball Hopes in Spring Often Dimmed by Harsh Reality." *Baseball Digest,* LIV (April 1995), 26–28.

835. ____. "Here Are Some Opening Day Oddities and Heorics." *Baseball Digest,* LIV (May 1995), 32–35.

836. ____. "Managers' Hopes in Spring are Often Rudely Demolished." *Baseball Digest,* LIII (March 1994), 66–70.

837. Walburn, Lee. "An April Fool's Day." *Atlanta,* XXXIII (April 1994), 10+.

838. Weinberg, Rick. "Spring Training '94." *Sport,* LXXXV (March 1994), 76–81.

839. Will, George F. "Reunion in the Desert." *Newsweek,* CXXI (April 5, 1993), 62–63. Spring training, Cactus League.

840. Wright, J. J. "Cape May and Points South: The Origin and Early Application of Training Principles and Practices for Professional Baseball's Spring Training Institution." *Nine: A Journal of Baseball History and Social Policy Perspective,* V (Fall 1996), 61–76.

841. Wulf, Steve. "Ball One." *Sports Illustrated,* LXXVIII (April 12, 1993), 84–90, 92–94, 99–100. A history of throwing out the first pitch on Opening Day.

b. All-Star Games,
Including Old-Timers Games

MAJOR LEAGUE
ALL STAR GAMES, 1992–1997

Year	League Winner	Score	Game Location
1992	American	13–6	San Diego
1993	American	9–3	Baltimore
1994	National	8–7	Pittsburgh
1995	National	3–2	Texas
1996	National	6–0	Philadelphia
1997	American	3–1	Cleveland

842. Abrams, Roger I. "The All Star Baseball Team Law." *Seton Hall Journal of Sport Law,* I (Summer 1991), 201+.
843. Browne, M. "All Star Digressions." *Elysian Fields Quarterly,* XI (Spring 1992), 79–83.
844. Fletcher, Christopher. "Pittsburgh Scrapbook: All-Star Moments." *Pittsburgh,* XXV (July 1994), 96+.
845. Green, Keith. "Voice of the Fan." *Beckett Baseball Card Monthly,* XII, no. 124 (July 1995), 18–19. Fan voting.
846. Modeno, Bill. "A Mid Summer Night's Bore." *Pittsburgh,* XXV (July 1994), 26–29.
847. Palmer, Jim. "The True All-Star Game." *Inside Sports,* XVI (August 1994), 74–77.
848. Schreiber, Lee R. "All-Star Game to All-Star Week." In: John Blake, *et al. Texas Rangers 1995 Yearbook.* Arlington, Tx.: Public Relations Dept., Texas Rangers, 1995. pp. 62–67.
849. *The Sporting News. Archives. History of the All-Star Game, 1933–1996* **<http://www.thesportingnews.com/features/all-star/archive.html>** is an Internet site with yearly coverages.
850. Wheatley, Tom. "Seeing Stars." *Beckett Baseball Card Monthly,* XI, no. 112 (July 1994), 10–19.

1970
851. Ryan, Jeff. "All-Star Game, 1970." *Sport,* LXXXV (August 1994), 87–88.

1971
852. Ryan, Jeff. "All-Star Game." *Sport,* LXXXIV (August 1993), 102+.

1992
853. Brass, Kevin. "Our Own Field of Dreams." *San Diego Magazine,* XLIV (July 1992), 66+.

1993
854. "Kirby Puckett Wins All-Star MVP Honors as AL Beats NL, 9–3." *Jet,* LXXXIV (August 2, 1993), 46–48+.

1994
855. Leavy, Walter. "McGriff 's Home-run in Ninth Helps National League All-Stars Gain the Edge in 65th Clash." *Jet,* LXXXVI (August 1, 1994), 50–53.

1995
857. "Frank Thomas Shines in 66th All-Star Game." *Jet,* LXXXVIII (July 31, 1995), 46–47.

1996
858. "National League Wins All-Star Game; Retiring Ozzie Smith Applauded." *Jet,* XC (July 29, 1996), 49–50.

1997
859. "American League Wins 3–1 at All-Star Game Dedicated to Larry Doby." *Jet,* XCII (July 28, 1997), 46–48.
860. Crothers, Tim. "Whose All-Stars?" *Sports Illustrated,* LXXXVII (July 7, 1997), 82–83.
861. Kiefer, Kit. "The Party of a Pastime: Baseball's Biggest Celebration—The Pinnacle All-Star Fan Fest—Readies for Its Seventh Edition in Cleveland." *Beckett's Baseball Card Monthly,* no. 148 (July 1997), *passim.* **<http://www.beckett.com/products/bbpd.html>.**

c. Championships

In the 1986 main volume of *Baseball: A Comprehensive Bibliography*, we chose not to separate out from our World Series section the literature concerning baseball's postseason league championship contests. To better present material relative to these annual events, we now exhibit our citations in three parts: general works, the American League Championship Series (ALCS) by year, and the National League Championship Series (NLCS) by year.

1. General Works

862. Angell, Roger. "The Game's the Thing." *The New Yorker,* LXXI

(November 27, 1995), 74–80. Post-season play.

863. Barry, Daniel and J. A. Hartigan. "Choice Models for Predicting Divisional Winners in Major League Baseball." *Journal of the American Statistical Association,* LXXXVIII (September 1993), 766+.

864. Boswell, Thomas. "Seven Ways to Save Baseball." *TV Guide,* XLIII (October 7, 1995), 26–28+. Post-season series.

865. Fagan, Garth. "Going, Going, Gone." *TV Guide,* XLI (October 16, 1993), 26–29. New playoff formula.

866. Feinstein, John. "A Glimmer of Hope." *Inside Sports,* XVIII (January 1996), 48–51. Excellent quality of 1995 postseason play.

867. James, Bill. "1996 Baseball Playoffs Preview." *Inside Sports,* XVIII (November 1996), 60–65.

868. Kelly, Tom and Jim Leyland. "An Insider's October." *Inside Sports,* XVII (November 1995), 52–57. Play-offs.

869. Keown, Tim. "Winning with Aces." *TV Guide,* XLV (September 27, 1997), 38+. Preview of the 1997 playoffs.

870. Lowe, John. "A Question of Crunch Time." *Inside Sports,* XVII (October 1995), 70–73.

871. Robinson, C. W. "Baseball Playoff Eliminations: An Application of Linear Programming." *Operations Research Letters,* X (March 1991), 67+.

872. Rushin, Steve. "Octoberfest." *Sports Illustrated,* LXXXVII (October 13, 1997), 28–35.

873. Smith, Curt. "Where Have All the Children Gone?" *Reader's Digest,* CXLIII (October 1993), 61–63. How league championship and world series games are played so late that children cannot stay up to watch on TV.

874. Sowell, Mike. *One Pitch Away: The Players' Stories of the 1986 League Championships and World Series.* New York: Macmillan, 1995. 312p.

875. Verducci, Tom. "Game Show." *Sports Illustrated,* LXXXV (Octo-

ber 14, 1996), 22–27. Report on the '96 ALCS/NLCS.

876. Weiss, Peter. *Longshots: The Most Unlikely Championship Teams in Baseball History.* Holbrook, Mass.: Bob Adams, 1992. 180p.

877. Woody, Clay. "When a One-Game Playoff Decided the A.L. Pennant." *Baseball Digest,* LII (September 1993), 62–67. Cleveland vs. Boston in 1948.

2. American League Championship Series (ALCS) by Year

ALCS RESULTS, 1992–1997

1992	Toronto 4, Oakland 2
1993	Toronto 4, Chicago 2
1994	Strike Year
1995	Cleveland 4, Seattle 2
1996	New York 4, Baltimore 1
1997	Cleveland 4, Baltimore 2

1976

878. Adelson, Bruce. "Chris Chambliss Recalls Dramatic Home Run That Won 1976 A.L. Playoffs." *Baseball Digest,* LI (October 1992), 46–48.

1978

879. Ballew, Bill. "Bucky Dent's '78 Playoff Homer: A Haunting Memory in Boston." *Baseball Digest,* LII (October 1993), 46–50.

1993

880. Deacon, James. "A Lakeside Series." *Maclean's,* CVI (October 11, 1993), 66+.

881. Verducci, Tom. "Backs to the Wall." *Sports Illustrated,* LXXIX (October 18, 1993), 44–46, 51.

1995

882. Verducci, Tom. "Five Days of Hardball." *Sports Illustrated,* LXXXIII (October 16, 1995), 22–28+. Seattle over New York.

1996

883. Verducci, Tom. "Legend of the Fall." *Sports Illustrated,* LXXXV

(October 21, 1996), 28–33. New York over Baltimore.

1997
884. Verducci, Tom. "Tribal Warfare." *Sports Illustrated,* LXXXVII (October 20, 1997), 46–54.
885. ____. and Johnette Howard. "Octoberfest: American League." *Sports Illustrated,* LXXXVII (October 13, 1997), 48–57.

3. National League Championship Series (NLCS) by Year

NLCS RESULTS, 1992–1997

1992	Atlanta 4, Pittsburgh 3
1993	Philadelphia 4, Atlanta 2
1994	Strike Year
1995	Atlanta 4, Cincinnati 0
1996	Atlanta 4, St. Louis 3
1997	Florida 4, Atlanta 2

1972
886. Flowers, Kevin M. "'72 Playoff Victory Served as a Springboard for the Reds." *Baseball Digest,* LI (July 1992), 54–59.

1992
887. Henneman, Jim. "Braves Playoff Comeback in '92 Ranks with the Classics." *Baseball Digest,* LI (March 1993), 79–81.
888. Kurkijan, Tim. "The Cruelest Game." *Sports Illustrated,* LXXVII (October 26, 1992), 20–23. Loss by Pittsburgh in Game 4.
889. Rushin, Steve. "Unbelievable." *Sports Illustrated,* LXXVII (October 26, 1992), 16–20. Atlanta comeback over Pittsburgh.

1993
890. Kirkpatrick, Curry. "Straight, No Philter." *Newsweek,* CXXII (October 25, 1993), 48–49.
891. Rushin, Steve. "Stretching It Out." *Sports Illustrated,* LXXIX (October 18, 1993), 36–38, 43.

1995
892. Verducci, Tom. "World Class." *Sports Illustrated,* LXXXIII (October 23, 1995), 26–38, 41–42. Braves defeat Cincinnati.

1996
893. Callahan, Gerry. "Credit the Cards." *Sports Illustrated,* LXXXV (October 21, 1996), 34–36. Initial Cardinal onslaught.
894. Keown, Tim. "Can Anyone Beat Atlanta?" *TV Guide,* XLIV (September 28, 1996), 30–31+.

1997
895. Crothers, Tim. "Hardball." *Sports Illustrated,* LXXXVII (October 20, 1997), 54–59.
896. Farber, Michael and Tim Crothers. "Octoberfest: National League." *Sports Illustrated,* LXXXVII (October 13, 1997), 48–57.

d. The World Series

Interest in the October extravaganza called the World Series remains high, doubtless due in part to the cancellation of the long-running classic because of the 1994 strike and several well-fought contests. We continue in this update the pattern in Supplement I by departing from the arrangement in *Baseball: A Comprehensive Bibliography*. The second of our two subparts here is not arranged by decade, but again by year.

WORLD SERIES, 1992–1997

1992	Toronto 4, Atlanta 2
1993	Toronto 4, Philadelphia 2
1994	Strike Year
1995	Atlanta 4, Cleveland 2
1996	New York 4, Atlanta 2
1997	Florida 4, Cleveland 3

1. General Works

897. Brown, Brian. "The Average Length of a World Series: Teams Match Up

Well." *Baseball Research Journal,* XXIV (1995), 144–145.

898. Canter, George. *"Inside Sports" World Series Factbook.* Detroit, Mich.: Visible Ink Press, 1996. 617p.

899. Conangelo, Jerry and Bill Giles. "Pro & Con: Should the World Series Be Played in a Neutral Site?" *Inside Sports,* XVIII (June 1996), 22–23.

900. Croucher, J. S. "How History Repeats Itself in the U.S. Baseball World Series." *International Journal of the History of Sport,* XII (April 1995), 169–172.

901. Fimrite, Ron. *"Sports Illustrated," the World Series: A History of Baseball's Fall Classic.* Birmingham, Ala.: Oxmoor House, 1993. 224p.

902. Gentelle, Andrew. *All-Time Great World Series.* New York: Grosset & Dunlap, 1994. 47p.

903. George, M. "Just Maybe the World Series Imitates Life: Two Decades of North American Culture and the Fall Classic." *Dugout,* I (October 1993), 8–12.

904. Gutman, Dan. *World Series Classics.* New York: Viking Penguin, 1996. 256p.

905. Hoppel, Joe. *The Series: An Illustrated History of Baseball's Postseason Showcase.* St. Louis, Mo.: The Sporting News, 1993. 399p.

906. *KidSports,* Editors of. "World Series Guide." *KidSports,* IV, no. 5 (1992), 20–23.

907. Kuenster, John. "Former Major League Stars Reveal Their Favorite World Series Memories." *Baseball Digest,* LVI (October 1997), 17–23.

908. ____. "World Series Highlights by the Decade, 1907–1997." *Baseball Digest,* LVI (October 1997), 80–86.

909. Nahinsky, Irwin D. "'Bouncing Back' in the World Series." *Bulletin of the Psychonomic Society,* XXIX (March 1991), 131–132.

910. Pascarelli, Peter. "World Series: Was 1991 the Greatest Ever? Or Was 1975?" *Sports Illustrated,* LXXVII (October 5, 1992), 39+.

911. Schwartz, Alan. "Fall Classics: Here are the Greatest October Moments Since Baseball Entered the TV Era Two Decades Ago." *Inside Sports,* XIX (November 1997), 66+.

912. Snyder, John S. *World Series: Great Moments and Dubious Achievements.* San Francisco, Ca.: Chronicle Books, 1995. Unpaged.

913. Vass, George. "Here Are the Seven Greatest World Series Relief Appearances." *Baseball Digest,* LIV (October 1995), 18–25.

914. ____. "These Are the Greatest World Series of Each Decade." *Baseball Digest,* LV (October 1996), 26–36.

915. ____. "World Series Base Running Feats and Blunders." *Baseball Digest,* LVI (October 1997), 26–31.

916. Vene, Juan. *La Historia de Las Series Mundiales de Beisbol, 1968–1993.* Guadalajara, Mexico: Editorial Agata, 1993. 327p.

917. Wulf, Steve. "Is This the Year?" *Sports Illustrated Canada,* I (April 5, 1993), 30–34, 36, 38. For a Blue Jays-Expos series.

918. "You Are the Manager." *Sports Illustrated for Kids,* IX (October 1997), 50–57.

2. The World Series by Year

1919
For studies of fictionalized works on this "Black Sox" series, please see Chapter B:1:e:4 "Lore and Literature," above.

919. Algren, Nelson. "The Silver-Colored Yesterday." In: Charles Einstein, ed. *The New Baseball Reader: An All-Star Lineup from the Fireside Book of Baseball.* New York: Penguin, 1992. pp. 1–7.

920. Nathan, D. A. "Anti-Semitism and the Black Sox Scandal." *Nine: A Journal of Baseball History and Social Policy Perspective,* IV (Fall 1995), 94–100.

921. Smith, James D., 3rd. "Five Old-Timers [Chester Cornelius 'Red' Hoff,

Bob Wright, Eddie Gill, Joseph 'Unser Choe' Hauser, and James Reese] Recall 1919 and the Series." *Elysian Fields Quarterly,* XII (Spring 1993), 64–66.

922. Ward, Geoffrey C. and Ken Burns. "'The Faith of 50 Million.'" *U.S. News & World Report,* CXVIII (August 29, 1994), 71+.

1920

923. Holway, John B. "All-in-One Game: The 1920 World Series." *Timeline,* XII (September–October 1995), 16–23.

924. Tru-Fit Screw Products Corporation. *1920 World Series Scrap Book.* Cleveland, Oh.: P.R. Dept., Tru-Fit Screw Products Corp., 1953. 72p.

1941

925. Borst, Bill. "The Best of Seasons: When Even a World War Couldn't Stop the World Series." *Dugout,* II (October 1994), 3–7.

1954

926. Woody, Clay. "World Series Flashback: A Difference of 200 Feet Highlight '54 Fall Classic." *Baseball Digest,* LI (October 1992), 24–29.

1962

927. Klink, Bill. "World Series Flashback: In '62, Ralph Terry Got a Chance to Redeem Himself." *Baseball Digest,* LI (October 1992), 30–35.

1964

928. Halberstam, David. *October 1964.* New York: Villard Books, 1994. 380p. New York/St. Louis series.

1965

929. Farley, Harrison. "The Surprise Visit." *Minnesota Medicine,* LXXVIII (December 1995), 8+.

1969

930. Ziegel, Vic. "Miracle at Shea." *New York,* XXVI (April 19, 1993), 116–118.

1972

931. Holway, John B. "World Series Flashback: A's Finessed Johnny Bench on Called Third Strike in '72." *Baseball Digest,* LI (October 1992), 36–38.

1975

932. Blount, Roy, Jr. "The Greatest Game I Ever Saw." *Sports Illustrated,* LXXIX (July 19, 1993), 38–39. Oct. 21, between Red Sox and Reds.

933. Fimrite, Ron. "Everything Came Up Reds." *Sports Illustrated,* LXXXI (October 10, 1994), 48–50+.

1977

934. Lupica, Mike. "Reggie's Triple-Header." *New York,* XXVI (April 19, 1993), 158–160.

935. Verducci, Tom. "Reggie Jackson Recalls a Moment of Glory in '77 World Series." *Baseball Digest,* LII (May 1993), 43–45.

1980

936. Caroulis, Jon. "How Phillies Finally End World Series Title Drought." *Baseball Digest,* LIV (September 1995), 58–63.

937. McGraw, Tug and Diane V. Smart. "We Were the Champions." *Philadelphia,* LXXXII (October 1991), 39+. Over Kansas City.

1986

938. Gordon, Stephen. "Boston vs. New York, 1986: [Bill] Buckner's Error Propels Mets Past Red Sox in One of the Most Dramatic Comebacks in World Series History." *Sport,* LXXXV (November 1994), 95+.

1989

939. Wenner, Lawrence A. "'We Are the World, We Are the Quake!': The Redefinition of Fans as Interpretive Community in Sportswriting About the 1989 Bay Area World Series and Earthquake Disaster." *Journal of Sport and Social Issues,* XVII (December 1993), 181–205.

1991

940. Kuenster, John. "Twins and Braves Provided Great Theater in '91 World Series." *Baseball Digest,* LI (February 1992), 15–21.

941. Lopresti, Mike. "A Series That Twinkled." In: George Leonard, ed. *Athlon's 1992 Pro Baseball.* Nashville, TN.: Athlons, 1992. pp. 11–17.

942. Ringolsby, Tracy. "Beyond Money." *Inside Sports,* XIV (February 1992), 60–62.

943. Verducci, Tom. "Last to First World Series a Fitting End to '91 Season." *Baseball Digest,* LI (March 1992), 56–59.

1992

944. Angell, Roger. "Shades of Blue." *The New Yorker,* LXVIII (December 7, 1992), 124–147.

945. Deacon, James. "The Passport Series." *Maclean's,* CV (October 26, 1992), 86–89+.

946. ____., Bob Levin, and Mary Nemeth. "There Is Joy in Hogtown." *Maclean's,* CV (November 2, 1992), 58–60, 62+.

947. Gordon, Alison. "Canada from Eh to Zed." *Sports Illustrated,* LXXVII (October 26, 1992), 40–42, 45. Reprinted in William Humber and John St. James, eds. *All I Thought About Was Baseball: Writings on a Canadian Pastime.* North York, Ont.: University of Toronto Press, 1996. pp. 121–126.

948. Kuenster, John. "Devon White's Catch a Turning Point in '92 World Series." *Baseball Digest,* LII (February 1993), 15–21.

949. Levin, Bob. "Baseball Heaven." *Maclean's,* CV (November 2, 1992), 56–57.

950. Perkins, Dave. "Blue Jays Again?" *Beckett Baseball Card Monthly,* IX, no. 9 (October 1992), 8–11.

1993

951. Angell, Roger. "Oh, What a Lovely War." *The New Yorker,* LXIX (November 22, 1993), 90–99.

952. Buschel, Bruce. "Whoot, There It Was." *Philadelphia,* LXXXV (March 1994), 50+.

953. "Carter Bats Blue Jays to Second Consecutive World Series Championship." *Jet,* LXXV (November 8, 1993), 55–56.

954. Deacon, James. "A Clash of Cultures." *Maclean's,* CVI (October 25, 1993), 42+. Philadelphia and Toronto.

955. Feestern, John. "WOW!: What a Way to End It." *Inside Sports,* XVI (January 1994), 58–61.

956. Holtzman, Jerome. "'World's Worst' Series Game Recalled by Plate Ump [Charlie Williams]." *Baseball Digest,* LIII (April 1994), 68–69. Game four.

957. "Jays, Phillies Battle in Annual Fall Classic." *Jet,* LXXXV (November 1, 1993), 48+.

958. "Jumping for Joy." *Maclean's,* CVI (November 1, 1993), 62–66+.

959. Kuenster, John. "Which Way, Jose?: And a Few Other Whimsical Questions for '93." *Baseball Digest,* LII (April 1993), 15–17.

960. Rochmis, Jon, ed. *A Series to Remember: The Official Book of the 1993 World Series.* San Francisco, Ca.: Woodford Press, 1993. 144p.

961. Rushin, Steve. "Home Sweet Homer." *Sports Illustrated,* LXXIX (November 1, 1993), 18–23+.

962. ____. "Slam-Bang Series." *Sports Illustrated,* LXXIX (October 25, 1993), 16–20+.

963. Vass, George. "How Division Races Shape Up for the 1993 Season." *Baseball Digest,* LII (April 1993), 18–46.

964. Zuckerman, Ethan R. "October, 1993: The Sixth Game of the Recently Concluded World Series, as Viewed from the Bar of the American Club in Accra, Ghana, West Africa, 5,417 Statute Miles from the Toronto Skydome." *Elysian Fields Quarterly,* XIII (Winter 1994), 16–21.

1995

965. Croucher, John S. "'Now History Repeats Itself in the U.S. Baseball

World Series'" *International Journal of the History of Sport,* XII (April 1995), 169–172.

966. Fimrite, Ron. *A Series for the Fans—The Indians and the Braves Meet Again After 47 Years: The Official Book of the 1995 World Series.* San Francisco, Ca.: Woodford Press, 1995. 144p.

967. Hoynes, Paul. "Indians' World Series Hopes Spoiled by Braves' Pitching." *Baseball Digest,* LV (February 1996), 20–27.

968. Kuenster, John. "Pitching, as Usual, Will Determine Outcome of Divisional Races." *Baseball Digest,* LIV (July 1995), 15–17.

969. Verducci, Tom. "Brave Hearts." *Sports Illustrated,* LXXXIII (November 6, 1995), 26–32, 36.

970. ____. "Nailed." *Sports Illustrated,* LXXXIII (October 30, 1995), 34–39.

971. Weinberg, Rick. "World Series Roundup." *Sport,* LXXXVI (November 1995), 26+.

1996

972. Angell, Roger. "One for the Good Guys." *The New Yorker,* LXXII (November 25, 1996), 52–56+.

973. Callahan, Gerry. "No Nonsense." *Sports Illustrated,* LXXXV (October 28, 1996), 36–39.

974. Grayson, Robert. "Is the Bronx Bombers' Win Habit-Forming?" *Baseball Illustrated Annual,* XXXII (1997), 64–69.

975. Kelly, Rob, ed. *A Series for New York: The Official Book of the 1996 World Series.* San Francisco, Ca.: Woodford Press, 1996. 144p.

976. Kuenster, John. "It Seemed Written in the Stars That the Yankees Would Win." *Baseball Digest,* LVI (February 1997), 17–20.

977. "New York Yankees Capture World Series in Come-from-Behind Victory Over Atlanta Braves." *Jet,* XC (November 11, 1996), 52–53.

978. Verducci, Tom. "Stroke of Fate." *Sports Illustrated,* LXXXV (November 6, 1996), 24–32+. Yankees comeback.

979. Weir, Tom. "World Series Commentary: Yankee 1–0 Win in Game 5 Was a Classic in Pitching and Defense." *Baseball Digest,* LVI (February 1997), 21–27.

980. Wulf, Steve. "A True Classic." *Time,* CXLVIII (November 4, 1996), 86–87.

1997

981. Price, S. L. "High Standards." *Sports Illustrated,* LXXXVII (October 27, 1997), 52–55.

982. Verducci, Tom. "The Faux Classic." *Sports Illustrated,* LXXXVII (October 27, 1997), 42–47.

983. ____. "Happy Ending." *Sports Illustrated,* LXXXVII (November 3, 1997), 30–42.

984. Wulf, Steve. "Fish Are Jumpin'." *Time,* CL (October 27, 1997), 129+.

e. The National Baseball
Hall of Fame and Museum

During the years since the publication of *Baseball: A Comprehensive Bibliography* in 1986, a significant body of literature has been developed on the founding of this famous repository while writings on the criteria for inclusion have continued apace from earlier times. Citations to players included in the Hall are found in both Chapter F ("Collective Biography") and Chapter G ("Individual Biography") below.

985. Alexander, Charles C. "Triple Play: Cleveland's Hall of Fame Triumvirate." *Timeline,* IX (April–May 1992), 2–17.

986. Barney, R. K. "Hallowed Halls and Baseball History: The Evolution of the Canadian and American Baseball Halls of Fame." *Nine: A Journal of Baseball History and Social Policy Perspective,* IV (Fall 1995), 11–33.

987. Bradley, Michael. "No Soup for You." In: Tony Gervino, ed. *Hardball.*

New York: Harris Pub. Co., 1997. pp. 70–75.

988. Field, R. "Into the Hallowed Halls: Baseball Honors the Game's Greats." *Dugout,* III (April–May 1995), 8–10.

989. Findlay, David W. and Clifford E. Reid. "Voting Behavior, Discrimination, and the National Baseball Hall of Fame." *Economic Inquiry,* XXXV (July 1997), 562+.

990. Fruehling-Springwood, Charles. *Cooperstown to Dyersville: A Geography of Baseball Nostalgia.* Boulder, Colo.: Westview Press, 1996. 217p.

991. Gafur, R. A. S. *Cooperstown Is My Mecca.* Agincourt, Ont.: Priv. print., 1995. Unpaged.

992. Gelbert, Doug. *Sports Halls of Fame: A Directory of Over 100 Sports Museums in the United States.* Jefferson, N.C.: McFarland & Co., 1992. 176p.

993. Griffith, J. L. "A Pilgrimage to the Baseball Mecca." *Tennessee Journal of Health, Physical Education, Recreation, and Dance,* XXX (Spring 1992), 17–18.

994. Grody, Carl W. "Stall of Fame." In: Gerald Kavanagh, ed. *Street and Smith's Baseball '97.* New York: Street and Smith, 1997. pp. 44–47. Slowness to admit players, particularly Don Sutton and Tony Perez.

995. Holoway, John B. "More Negro Leaguers for the Hall." *National Pastime,* XV (1995), 91–95.

996. Holtzman, Jerome. "Are the Baseball Writers Short-Changing Hall of Fame Candidates?" *Baseball Digest,* LV (April 1996), 62–67.

997. ____. "How Poem Helped Elect Infield Trio to the Hall of Fame." *Baseball Digest,* LI (March 1993), 70–73. Franklin P. Adam's 1908 "Tinkers to Evers to Chance."

998. International Association of Sports Museums and Halls of Fame. *I.A.S. M.H.F. Membership Directory.* Wilmington, Del., 1992. 31p. An annual guide; includes baseball museums in foreign countries.

999. James, Bill. *The Politics of Glory: How Baseball's Hall of Fame Really Works.* New York: Macmillan, 1994. 452p.

1000. Kaufman, J. C. "Applying Multiple Regression Analysis to Baseball Hall of Fame Membership." *Perceptual and Motor Skills,* LXXXI (December 1995), 1328–1330; LXXXII (June 1996), 883–889.

1001. Kelly, Brent P. *The Case For: Those Overlooked by the Baseball Hall of Fame.* Jefferson, N.C.: McFarland & Co., Inc., 1992. 324p.

1002. Kuenster, John. "Mike Schmidt Heads 1995 Slate of Hall of Fame Candidates." *Baseball Digest,* LIII (December 1994), 17–19.

1003. ____. "Scouts and Coaches Should Be Eligible for the Hall of Fame." *Baseball Digest,* LI (December 1992), 17–21.

1004. Lang, Jack. "Call to the Hall." *Beckett Vintage Sports,* I, no. 7 (June 1997), *passim.* <**http://www.beckett.com/products/vtpd.html**>. Memories of special phone calls to baseball's greats.

1005. ____. "Has Veterans Committee Cheapened Hall of Fame Standards?" *Baseball Digest,* LIV (July 1995), 34–35.

1006. ____. "Lasting Memories of Calls to Hall of Fame Electees." *Baseball Digest,* LVI (September 1997), 84–87.

1007. Lundquist, Carl. "Carlton, Rizzuto, Durocher: Diverse Trio to Be Inducted Into the Hall of Fame." *Baseball Digest,* LIII (July 1992), 70–75.

1008. Miller, Stuart. "Closed Gates for the Near-Greats?" *Inside Sports,* XVII (September 1995), 14–18.

1009. Noden, Merell. "Home Run." *Runner's World,* XXIX (May 1994), 68+.

1010. Passy, Charles. "Cooperstown, New York: Baseball, Opera, and American History Meet in a Bucolic Setting." *Ovation,* X (July 1989), 38–41.

1011. Pietrusza, David. "These Were 'Near-Misses' in Hall of Fame Voting." *Baseball Digest,* LII (November 1993), 56–59.

1012. *Players of Cooperstown: Base-ball's Hall of Fame.* Lincolnwood, Ill.: Publications International, 1992. 256p.

1013. Pope, S. W. "Sports Films and Hall of Fame Museums: An Editorial Intro-duction." *Journal of Sport History,* XXIII (Fall 1996), 309–312.

1014. *Pro Sports Halls of Fame.* 8 vols. New York: Grolier, 1996. Includes two volumes for Baseball.

1015. Shapiro, David W. and Steven Sei-dman. "Brainstorming Interactive Exhibits for the Baseball Hall of Fame." *International Journal of Instructional Media,* XXIII, no. 2 (1996), 173+.

1016. Sheed, Wilfrid. "An American Place." *Life,* XVI (August 1993), 78–80.

1017. Silverman, Jeff. "Short Stop, Long Run." *Westways,* LXXXIX (August 1997), 38+.

1018. "Sliding Into Cooperstown: A Look Into the Future of Hall of Fame Admissions." In: Myles Friedman, ed. *Spring Training: Grapefruit and Cac-tus League Yearbook.* Chapel Hill, N.C.: Vanguard Publications, 1996. pp. 64–67.

1019. Springwood, Charles F. *Cooper-stown to Dyersville: A Critical Geog-raphy of Baseball Nostalgia.* Boulder, Col.: Westview Press, 1995. 232p.

1020. Vass, George. "Baseball Hall of Fame Thrives on Controversy." *Base-ball Digest,* LVI (June 1997), 26–27.

1021. ____. "Why Do Hall of Fame Vot-ers Diminish Defensive Skills?" *Base-ball Digest,* LIV (May 1995), 22–26.

f. The Business of
Professional Baseball, Including
Economic and Legal Issues, Trades
and Drafts, and the Reserve Clause

Professional baseball today is a huge entertainment business where thousands of people in other industries join game attendees in investing and reaping large sums of money. As noted in the intro-duction to this part in *Baseball: A Com-prehensive Bibliography,* today's students of the pro segment of "the national pas-time" must concern themselves not only with managerial firings and player trades, but on topics as different as stadium leases and collective bargaining.

The sources in this part address, often in great specificity, a wide range of top-ics related to the business of baseball. Because of their notoriety, the issues of strikes, salaries, salary arbitration, and collective bargaining, drugs and violence, and gambling have been separated out for review below.

1022. Abramson, Dan. "Baseball and the Court." *Constitution,* IV (Fall 1992), 68–75.

1023. Armstrong, Jim. "Late-Round Draft Choices Defy the Odds to Make Majors." *Baseball Digest,* LV (De-cember 1996), 62–67.

1024. Arte, Tuskar, *et al.* "Sports Stocks and Bonds: The High Stakes Game of Team Ownership." *Financial World,* CLXV (May 20, 1996), 53–64.

1025. Baldo, A. "Secrets of the Front Office: What America's Pro Teams Are Worth." In: D. S. Eitzen, ed. *Sport in Contemporary Society: An Anthology.* 4th ed. New York: St. Martin's Press, 1993. pp. 187–195.

1026. Bale, John and Joseph Maguire, eds. *The Global Arena: Sports Talent Migration in an Interdependent World.* New York: Isbs/Frank Cass & Co., 1993.

1027. Bevis, Charles W. "A Home Run by Any Measure: The Baseball Play-ers' Pension Plan." *Baseball Research Journal,* XXI (1992), 64–70.

1028. "The Beginning of the End: The Giants' Signing of Bud Black Was the Defining Moment in Baseball's Calamitous Economic Folly." In: Joe Hoppel, ed. *The Sporting News 1995 Baseball Yearbook.* St. Louis, Mo.: TSN, 1995. pp. 22–27.

1029. Blair, John P. "Benefits from a

Baseball Franchise: An Alternative Methodology." *Economic Development Quarterly,* VI (February 1992), 91+.

1030. Blass, Asher A. "Does the Baseball Labor Market Contradict the Human Capital Model of Investment?" *The Review of Economics and Statistics,* LXXIV (May 1992), 261+.

1031. Blum, Debra E. "Coaches Fear Changes in Major League Draft Will Hurt College Baseball and Its Athletes." *The Chronicle of Higher Education,* XXXVIII (May 6, 1992), A41–A42.

1032. ____. "Major League Draft Is Big Headache for College Baseball." *The Chronicle of Higher Education,* XL (September 8, 1993), A36+.

1033. Boone, Louis E. "Applying the Brand Equity Concept to Major League Baseball." *Sport Marketing Quarterly,* IV (September 1995), 33–42. Team marketing.

1034. Boroughs, D. L. "Playing the Money Game." *U.S. News & World Report,* CXVIII (May 15, 1995), 59–60+.

1035. Brand, Stanley. "Baseball's Antitrust Exemption: Don't Repeal the Field of Dreams." *Elysian Fields Quarterly,* XIII (Summer 1994), 12–14.

1036. Branvold, S. E. "The Use of Promotions in College Baseball." *Sport Marketing Quarterly,* I (October 1992), 19–24.

1037. ____. "The Utilization of Fence Signage in College Baseball." *Sport Marketing Quarterly,* I (December 1992), 29–32.

1038. Braver, Andrew F. "Baseball or Besoburo: The Implications of Antitrust Law on Baseball in America and Japan." *New York Law School Journal of International and Comparative Law,* XVI, no. 3 (1994), 421+.

1039. Brill, Howard W. "Baseball and the Legal Profession." *Arkansas Law Notes,* (1990), 81–83.

1040. Bruggink, Thomas H. "National Pastime to Dismal Science: Using Baseball to Illustrate Economic Principles." *Eastern Economic Journal,* XIX (Summer 1993), 275+. Also published in *Elysian Fields Quarterly,* XII (Spring 1993), 14–28, under the title "The Value of Diamonds: Using Baseball Examples to Teach Economics."

1041. Burk, Robert F. *Never Just a Game: Players, Owners, and American Baseball to 1920.* Chapel Hill, N.C.: University of North Carolina Press, 1994. 284p. Economic emphasis.

1042. Burns, Charles M. "The Scope of Major League Baseball's Antitrust Exemption." *Stetson Law Review,* XXIV (Spring 1995), 495+.

1043. *The Business of Baseball 1996.* Carmel, Calif.: Paul Kagan Associates, 1996. Unpaged.

1044. *The Business of Baseball 1997.* Carmel, Calif.: Paul Kagan Associates, 1997. Unpaged.

1045. Butter, Michael R. "Competitive Balance in Major League Baseball." *American Economist,* XXXIX (Fall 1995), 46–53.

1046. Callahan, Gerry. "A League of Their Own." *Sports Illustrated,* LXXII (April 17, 1995), 36–38. Free agents.

1047. ____. "Signed, Sealed, and Delivered." *Sports Illustrated,* LXXXVI (February 17, 1997), 36–39. Player draft.

1048. Cameron, Christopher D. "The Plays of Summer: Antitrust, Industrial Investment, and the Case Against a Salary Cap for Major League Baseball." *Florida State University Law Review,* XXII (Spring 1995), 827–884.

1049. Carothers, Tim. "The Skinny on Expansion." *Sports Illustrated,* LXXXVII (September 1, 1997), 36–37.

1050. Caroulis, Jon. "Luck Still a Big Factor in Amateur Player Draft." *Baseball Digest,* LIV (February 1995), 20–25.

1051. Catanoso, Justin. "Loading the Bases in North Carolina: The Sports-Hungry Triad Area Has a Real Shot at a Ball Club." *Sports Illustrated,* LXXXVI (April 7, 1997), 98, 102. Expansion.

1052. Chalpin, Marc. "It Ain't Over 'Til Its Over: The Century-Long Conflict Between the Owners and the Players in Major League Baseball." *Albany Law Review,* LX (Fall 1996), 205–238.

1053. Champion, W. T. *Sports Law in a Nutshell.* St. Paul, Minn.: West Pub. Co., 1993. 325p.

1054. Cozzillo, Michael J. "From the Land of Bondage: The Greening of Major League Baseball Players and the Major League Baseball Players Association." *Catholic University Law Review,* XLI (Fall 1991), 117+.

1055. Crasnick, Jerry. "Take Me Out to the Ball Game." In: Tim Polzer, ed. *Beckett's Baseball 1997 Preview.* Houston, Tx.: Beckett Publications, 1997. pp. 16–25. Promotions.

1056. Crawford, S. A. G. M. "Early Advertising (1892–1932) on Recreational Sports: Thematic Possibilities of the D'Arcy Collection at the University of Illinois." *Sporting Traditions (Australia),* IX (November 1992), 17–33.

1057. "Dad Just Got Traded!" *Sports Illustrated for Kids,* VI (August 1994), 42–45.

1058. DeLand, Dave. "All the Right Moves." *Beckett Baseball Card Monthly,* IX (April 1992), 8–13. Trades.

1059. Dodge, John. "Regulating the Baseball Monopoly: One Suggestion for Governing the Game." *Seton Hall Journal of Sport Law,* V, no. 1 (1995), 35+. Also published in *Elysian Fields Quarterly,* XIII (Winter 1994), 8–9.

1060. Dorst, Julie. "Franchise Relocation: Reconsidering Major League Baseball's *Carte Blanche* Control." *Seton Hall Journal of Sport Law,* IV (Summer 1994), 553–594.

1061. Eisenhammer, Fred and Jim Binkley. *Baseball's Most Memorable Trades: Superstars Swapped, All-Stars Copped, and Megadeals That Flopped.*

Jefferson, N.C.: McFarland & Co., Inc., 1997. 233p.

1062. Euchner, Charles C. *Playing the Field: Why Sports Teams Move and Cities Fight to Keep Them.* Baltimore, Md.: Johns Hopkins University Press, 1993.

1063. Fehr, Donald. "Major League Baseball Player Association." *World Baseball Magazine (Switzerland),* I (1994), 14–17.

1064. Field, Robert. "The Business of Baseball: Greedy Owners & Selfish Players." *Dugout,* II (April 1994), 3–6.

1065. Finn, Marie T., ed. *Who Runs Professional Sports: Major League Baseball.* Sacramento, Ca.: Forster-Long, 1992. 307p.

1066. Fizel, John L., Elizabeth Gustafson, and Lawrence Hadley, eds. *Baseball Economics: Current Research.* Westport, Conn.: Praeger, 1996. 228p.

1067. Gaspard, James G., 2nd. "Spectator Liability in Baseball: 'Nobody Told Me I Assumed the Risk!'" *Review of Litigation,* XV (Winter 1996), 229–250.

1068. Gebroe, Linda. "Stepping Up to the Plate." *San Francisco Business,* XXVIII (May 1993), 14+. Baseball's business aspects.

1069. Gergen, Joe. "Expansion." In: Joe Hoppel, ed. *The Sporting News 1992 Baseball Yearbook.* St. Louis, Mo.: The Sporting News, 1992. pp. 16–20.

1070. Gold, Eddie. "These Were the Ten Most Lopsided Trades Ever." *Baseball Digest,* LV (August 1995), 30–37.

1071. Gould, Mark T. "Baseball's Antitrust Exemption: The Pitch Gets Closer and Closer." *Seton Hall Journal of Sport Law,* V, no. 1 (1995), 273–289.

1072. ____. "Fantasy Revisited: Baseball's Antitrust Exemption Gets Hit by a Pitch." *Entertainment and Sports Lawyer,* XI (Fall 1993), 11–14. Piazza v. Major League Baseball.

1073. ____. "Real Fantasy Baseball: Will the Antitrust Exemption Ever End?"

Entertainment and Sports Lawyer, XI (Spring 1993), 3–8. No.

1074. Gramlich, Edward H. "A Natural Experiment in Styles of Capitalism: Professional Sports." *Quarterly Review of Economics and Finance,* XXXIV (Summer 1994), 121–131.

1075. Greenberg, M. J. *Sport Law Practice.* 2 vols. Charlottesville, Va.: The Michie Company, 1992. See especially Chpt. 5: "Baseball Contracts."

1076. Greising, David and Irene Recio. "Baseball's Owners Are Finally Taking a Whack at the Ball: They're Facing Up to the Problems Plaguing the Sport, Especially Financial Inequality Among Teams." *Business Week,* (April 12, 1993), 66–69.

1077. Grosse, W. "The Regulation, Control, and Protection of Athletic Agents." *Northern Kentucky Law Review,* XIX (Fall 1991), 49–80.

1078. Grossman, V. Shukie. "Antitrust and Baseball: A League of Their Own." *Fordham Intellectual Property, Media, and Entertainment Law Journal,* IV (Fall 1993), 563+.

1079. Halbantian, Haig R. and Andrew Schotter. "Matching and Efficiency in the Baseball Free Agent System: An Experimental Examination." *Journal of Labor Economics,* XIII (January 1995), 1–32.

1080. Harris, Nancy S. *"The Class and Status Conversion Process: The Case of Professional Baseball Players."* Unpublished Ph.D. Dissertation, New York University, 1993.

1081. Herman, Bruce. "Trading Places." *Beckett Focus on Future Stars,* II, no. 20 (December 1992), 14–17. Trades of minor leaguers.

1082. Hoffman, Frank W. and William G. Bailey. "Franchise Shifting in Major League Baseball." In: their *Sports and Recreation Fads.* New York: Haworth, 1991. pp. 145–147.

1083. Horowitz, Ira. "The Increasing Competitive Balance in Major League Baseball." *Review of Industrial Organization,* XII, no. 3 (1997), 373+.

1084. ____. "On the Persistence of Business Alliances: The Case of Major League Baseball Trading Patterns." *Review of Industrial Organization,* VIII, no. 4 (1993), 491+.

1085. Huffman, Francis. "Play Ball!" *Entrepreneur,* XX (April 1992), 90+. Business aspects of the game.

1086. Hylan, Timothy R., Maureen J. Lage, and Mitchell Treglia. "The Case Theorem, Free Agency, and Major League Baseball: A Panel Study of Pitcher Mobility from 1961 to 1992." *Southern Economic Journal,* LXII (April 1996), 1029–1042.

1087. ____. "Institutional Change and Invariance of Behaviour in Major League Baseball." *Applied Economics Letters,* VI (May 1997), 311–314.

1088. Hyman, M. "Old Timers Take a Swing at Baseball: Disgruntled Players from the Past Are Suing Over Royalties and Griping About Pensions." *Business Week,* (June 9, 1997), 78–79.

1089. Irani, D. S. *"Three Essays on Sports Economics."* Unpublished Ph.D. Dissertation, University of California at Santa Barbara, 1996. 79p.

1090. Juarez, Michael H. "Baseball's Antitrust Exemption." *Hastings Communications and Entertainment Law Journal,* XVII (Spring 1995), 737–762.

1091. Kahane, Lawrence. "Team Roster Turnover and Attendance in Major League Baseball." *Applied Economics,* XXIX (April 1997), 425–431.

1092. Kalamut, A. R. "What's in a Name?: The Multi-Million Dollar Marketing of Baseball's Second Cities." *Dugout,* III (August 1995), 27–29.

1093. Kessler, Remy. "Baseball Remains Exempt from Antitrust Laws." *Loyola Entertainment Law Journal,* IV (1984), 197–203.

1094. Knowles, Glen, *et al.* "Baseball Attendance and Outcome Uncertainty: A Reply." *The American Economist,* XXXIX (Fall 1995), 87+.

1095. Kochman, Ladd. "Major League

Baseball: What Really Puts Fans in the Stands?" *Sport Marketing Quarterly,* IV (March 1995), 9–11.

1096. _____. and Ravija Badarinathi. "Baseball Attendance and Outcome Uncertainty: A Note." *The American Economist,* XXXIX (Fall 1995), 87–89.

1097. Kohm, Joseph A., Jr. "Baseball's Antitrust Exemption: It's Going ... Going...Gone!" *Nova Law Review,* XX (Spring 1996), 1231–1254.

1098. Krause, K. M. "Regulating the Baseball Cartel: A Reassessment of the National Commission, Judge Landis, and the Antitrust Exemption." *International Journal of the History of Sport,* XIV (April 1997), 55–77.

1099. Krautmann, A. C. "Free Agency and the Allocation of Labor in Major League Baseball." *Managerial and Decision Economics,* XV (September 1994), 459–478.

1100. Kuenster, John. "Orioles and Cardinals Bolstered Pennant Hopes with Player Acquisitions." *Baseball Digest,* LV (April 1996), 15–17. Trades.

1101. _____. "These Player Trades May Change Course of Division Races." *Baseball Digest,* LI (April 1992), 17–19.

1102. _____. "These Player Transactions Promise to Make an Impact on '97 Season." *Baseball Digest,* LVI (April 1997), 15–19.

1103. Kurkjian, Tim. "Ball of Confusion: With an Imposed Salary Cap in Place and Court Battles Looming, Baseball Spins Out of Control." *Sports Illustrated,* LXXXII (January 9, 1995), 58–63.

1104. _____. "Feeding Frenzy: The Big-Revenue Sharks Swooped in and Snatched Up the Bait—Some of the Best Players the Small Revenue Clubs Could No Longer Afford." *Sports Illustrated,* LXXXII (April 17, 1995), 24–26, 29–31.

1105. _____. "Inside the Baseball Draft." *Sports Illustrated,* LXXVIII (June 14, 1993), 68–69.

1106. Lavelle, Lydia. "From the Diamonds to the Courts: MLB v. The Commissioner." *North Carolina Central Law Journal,* XXI, no. 1 (1995), 97–121.

1107. Leonard, Wilbert M., 2nd. "Economic Discrimination in Major League Baseball: Marginal Revenue Products of Majority and Minority Group Members." *Journal of Sport and Social Issues,* XIX (May 1995), 180–190.

1108. Leonhardt, David. "Baseball's Slump Is Far from Over." *Business Week,* (November 4, 1996), 82–83.

1109. Levin, Bob and James Deacon. "Of Mice and Money: Cash Registers Ring in Hockey and Baseball." *Maclean's,* CV (December 21, 1992), 27–28.

1110. Lowe, Stephen R. *"Congress and Professional Sports."* Unpublished Ph.D. Dissertation, Ohio University, 1993.

1111. Mack, Connie and Michael M. Blau. "The Need for Fair Play: Repealing the Federal Baseball Antitrust Exemption." *Florida Law Review,* XLV (April 1993), 201+.

1112. Maier, Harold G. "Baseball and Chicken Salad: A Realistic Look at Choice of Law." *Vanderbilt Law Review,* XLIV (May 1991), 827+.

1113. "Major League Cities: More Than Baseball." *Better Homes and Gardens,* LXX (May 1992), 183+.

1114. "Major Leagues [Major League Baseball Properties] to License Negro Leagues Memorabilia." *Jet,* LXXXV (December 6, 1993), 46–47.

1115. Mann, Steve and David Pietrusza. "The Business of Baseball." In: John Thorn and Pete Palmer, eds. *Total Baseball.* 3rd ed. New York: HarperPerenial, 1993. pp. 554–571.

1116. Marburger, Daniel R. *"Stee-Rike Four!": What's Wrong with the Business of Baseball?* New York: Praeger, 1997.

1117. _____. and John F. Scoggins. "Risk and Final Offer Arbitration Usage

Rates: Evidence from Major League Baseball." *Journal of Labor Research,* XVII (Fall 1996), 735+.

1118. "Marketing Baseball on a Shoestring Budget." *Athletic Business,* XIII (April 1989), 34+.

1119. Martens, Kevin E. "Fair or Foul?: The Survival of Small-Market Teams in Major League Baseball." *Marquette Sports Law Journal,* IV (Spring 1994), 323+.

1120. McCarthy, Eugene J. "Baseball, Deregulation, and Free Enterprise." *Elysian Fields Quarterly,* XII (Spring 1993), 8–10.

1121. McEvoy, Sharlene A. "The Legal Environment of Baseball." *The Journal of Legal Studies Education,* XII (Summer 1994), 197+.

1122. Meissner, Nancy Jean. "Nearly a Century in Reserve: Organized Baseball, Collective Bargaining, and the Antitrust Exemption Enter the '80s." *Pepperdine Law Review,* VIII (January 1981), 313–336.

1123. Miller, Marvin. "Baseball Revenue Sharing: Brother, Can You Spare a Dime?" *Sport,* LXXXV (May 1994), 12+. Between rich teams and poor.

1124. Mirabito, Laura. "Picking Players in the College Draft Could Be Picking Trouble with Antitrust Law." *Santa Clara Law Review,* XXXVI, no. 3 (1996), 823+.

1125. Mixon, Frank. "Baseball Bonanza." *Enterpreneur,* XVII (April 1989), 80+. Baseball-related business ventures.

1126. Mullin, B. J. *Sport Marketing.* Champaign, Ill.: Human Kinetics Pub., 1993. 296p.

1127. Nalbantian, Harry R. and Andrew Schotter. "Matching and Efficiency in the Baseball Free Agent System: An Experimental Examination." *Journal of Labor Economics,* XIII (January 1995), 1–31.

1128. Nemeth, M. "A Battle for the Bucks." *Maclean's,* CVI (October 18, 1993), 60–61. The sale of paraphernalia by Major League Baseball Properties.

1129. Pastier, John. "The Business of Baseball." *Inland Architect,* XXXIII (January 1989), 56+.

1130. Petit, P. "Baseball and the American Legal Mind." *Law Practice Management,* LV (January–February 1997), 23+.

1131. Picher, Thomas C. "Baseball's Antitrust Exemption Repealed: An Analysis of the Effect on Salary Cap and Salary Taxation Provisions." *Vermont Law Review,* XX (Winter 1995), 559–617.

1132. "Play Ball!: Demographics and Baseball." *Population Today,* XXIV (April 1996), 3+.

1133. Prebut, D. "Best Interests or Self Interests: Major League Baseball's Attempt to Replace the Compulsory Licensing Scheme with Retransmission Consent." *Seton Hall Journal of Sport Law,* III, no. 1 (1993), 11–147.

1134. Rimer, Edward. "Discrimination in Major League Baseball: Hiring Standards for Major League Managers, 1975–1994." *Journal of Sport and Social Issues,* XX (May 1996), 118–133.

1135. Ringolsky, Tracy. "Can Baseball Clubs Buy a World Series Championship?" *Baseball Digest,* LVI (August 1997), 38–41.

1136. ____. "What Does $95 Million Buy These Days?" *Inside Sports,* XIV (December 1992), 8–9. Expansion.

1137. Robinson, Mark A. "Injunctive Relief for Trademark Infringement Is Not Available When Likelihood of Confusion Does Not Exist...: 'Major League Baseball Properties, Inc. v. Sed Non Olet Denarius, Ltd.,' 817 F. Supp 1183." *Seton Hall Journal of Sport Law,* IV, no. 1 (1994), 205+.

1138. Robbins, W. S. "Baseball's Antitrust Exemption: A Corked Bat for Owners?" *Louisiana Law Review,* LV (May 1995), 937–972.

1139. Rosenthal, Jeffrey A. "The Football Answer to the Baseball Problem: Can Revenue Sharing Work?" *Seton*

Hall Journal of Sport Law, V, no. 2 (1995), 359+.

1140. Rosentraub, Mark S. *Major League Losers: The Real Cost of Sports and Who's Paying for It.* New York: Basic Books, 1997. 513p.

1141. Rush, Steven. "From Baseball to Business." *Nation's Business,* LXXXIV (October 1996), 48+. Retirement.

1142. Sammons, Jack L. "On Being a Good Christian and a Good Lawyer: God, Man, Law, Lawyering, Sandy Koufax, Roger Maris, Orel Hershiser, Looking at the Catcher, and Corked Bats in the Kingdom (with a Brief Guest Appearance by Ty Cobb." *Texas Tech Law Review,* XXVII (Summer 1996), 1319–1343.

1143. Sands, J. and Peter Gammons. "Can Baseball Survive?" *Journal of Business Strategy,* XIV (July–August 1993), 58–61.

1144. Saporito, Bill. "CEO Owners Eye Baseball's Costs." *Fortune,* CXXVII (April 5, 1993), 10–11.

1145. Schlossberg, Don. "Labor Peace Promotes Flood of New Products." *Baseball Illustrated Annual,* XXXII (1997), 70–75.

1146. Selig, A. "Major League Baseball and Its Antitrust Exemption." *Seton Hall Journal of Sport Law,* IV, no. 1 (1994), 277–286.

1147. Shaler, Mike. "Franchise Stability, Expansion, and Fan Ownership of the Game." *Elysian Fields Quarterly,* XII (Fall 1993), 5–9.

1148. Shea, Charles. "The Hardball Tactics of Baseball and Its Owners." *The Chronicle of Higher Education,* LXXXIX (October 14, 1992), A5+.

1149. Sica, Anthony. "Baseball's Antitrust Exemption: Out of the Pennant Race Since 1972." *Fordham Intellectual Property, Media & Entertainment Law Journal,* VII (Autumn 1996), 295–387.

1150. Siegfried, J. J. "Sports Player Drafts and Reserve Systems." *CATO Journal,* XIV (December 1995), 443–452.

1151. Simon, Ron. *The Game Behind the Game: Negotiating in the Big Leagues.* Stillwater, Minn.: Voyageur Press, 1993.

1152. Sloane, Arthur A. "The Major League Umpires Association: A Study in Pragmatism and Opportunism." *Labor Law Journal,* XLVII (April 1996), 230–238.

1153. Smith, Larry C. "Beyond Peanuts and Cracker Jack: The Implications of Lifting Baseball's Antitrust Exemption." *University of Colorado Law Review,* LXVII (Winter 1996), 113–141.

1154. "So Long, George, But Leave the Key." *Inside Sports,* XVI (March 1994), 18+. Antitrust proceedings.

1155. Soivenski, Michael S. "A Few Thoughts on Expansion: What Can Fans in Florida and Colorado Expect?" *Baseball Research Journal,* XXI (1992), 15–19.

1156. Sommers, Paul M., ed. *Diamonds are Forever: The Business of Baseball.* Washington, D.C.: Brookings Institution, 1992. 208p.

1157. Spander, Deborah L. "The Impact of Piazza on the Baseball Antitrust Exemption." *UCLA Entertainment Law Review,* II (Winter 1995), 113+.

1158. *Sports Advantage: A Comprehensive Guide to Sports Marketing Opportunities.* Wilmette, Ill.: Standard Rate and Data Service, 1992. 622p. Includes those for pro baseball.

1159. "Sport$Money: An Analysis of Recent Free Agent Signings in Major League Baseball." *For the Record,* IV (February–March 1993), 4–6.

1160. St. John, Mary C. "Strike One, and You're Out: Should Ballparks Be Strictly Liable to Baseball Fans Injured by Foul Balls?" *Loyola of Los Angeles Law Review,* XIX (December 1985), 589–620.

1161. Steinbreder, John. "Profits of the Sandlot." *Business Week,* (July 20, 1992), 48, 50.

1162. Stratton, Peter. "Attribution, Baseball, and Consumer Behavior." *Journal* of the Market Research Society, XXXIII (July 1991), 163+.

1163. Sullivan, Barbara K. "Of Pinstripes and Flannel." *Business Week,* (July 20, 1992), 56–57.

1164. Tanick, Marshall H. and Martin D. Munic. "Baseball Law in Minnesota: From Foul Balls to Family Court." *Bench & Bar of Minnesota, XLV* (April 1988), 16–22.

1165. Taylor, Stephanie L. "Baseball as an Anomaly American Major League Baseball Antitrust Exemption: Is the Australian Model a Solution?" *Seton Hall Journal of Sport Law,* V, no. 2 (1995), 359+.

1166. Telser, L. G. "The Ultimate Game and the Law of Demand." *Economic Journal,* CV (November 1995), 1519–1524.

1167. Tiemann, Robert L. and Pete Palmer. "Major League Attendance." In: John Thorn and Pete Palmer, eds. *Total Baseball.* 3rd ed. New York: HarperPerenial, 1993. pp. 143–147.

1168. Topel, Brett. "Wanna Trade?" *Beckett Baseball Card Monthly,* IX (May 1992), 8–10.

1169. Turland, Kathleen L. "Major League Baseball and Antitrust: Bottom of the Ninth, Bases Loaded, Two Out, Full Count and Congress Takes a Swing." *Syracuse Law Review,* XLV (Summer 1995), 1329–1389.

1170. United States. Congress. House. Committee on Education and Labor. Subcommittee on Labor-Management Relations. *The Impact of Collective Bargaining on the Antitrust Exemption: Hearings.* 103rd Cong., 2nd sess. Washington, D.C.: GPO, 1995. 122p.

1171. ____.____.____.____. Committee on the Judiciary. *Baseball Fans and Communities Protection Act of 1994: Report.* 103rd Cong., 2nd sess. Washington, D.C.: GPO, 1994. 45p.

1172. ____.____.____.____. *Professional Sports Franchise Relocation— Antitrust Implications: Hearings.* 104th Cong., 2nd sess. Washington, D.C.: GPO, 1996. 396p.

1173. ____.____.____.____. Subcommittee on Economic and Commercial Law. *Baseball's Antitrust Exemption: Hearings.* 103rd Cong., 1st sess. Washington, D.C.: GPO, 1993. 272p.

1174. ____. ____. Senate. Committee on the Judiciary. *Major League Baseball Reform Act of 1995: Report.* 104th Cong., 2nd sess. Washington, D.C.: GPO, 1995. 31p.

1175. ____.____.____.____. Subcommittee on Antitrust, Monopolies, and Business Rights. *Baseball's Antitrust Immunity: Hearings.* 102nd Cong., 2nd sess. Washington, D.C.: GPO, 1993. 440p.

1176. ____.____.____.____.____. *Professional Baseball Teams and the Antitrust Laws: Hearings.* 103rd Cong., 2nd sess. Washington, D.C.: GPO, 1995. 70p.

1177. Urooman, John "The Baseball Players' Labor Market Reconsidered." *Southern Economic Journal,* LXIII (October 1996), 339–360.

1178. ____. "A United Theory of Capital and Labor Markets in Major League Baseball." *Southern Economic Journal,* LXIII (January 1997), 594+.

1179. Van Dyck, Dave. "Commentary: For Baseball Owners, More Profit Comes Before Tradition." *Baseball Digest,* LII (June 1993), 30–31.

1180. Vass, George. "Is Major League Baseball on the Brink of a Revolution?" *Baseball Digest,* LII (February 1993), 31–39.

1181. ____. "'Pennant Insurance' Deals are 'Old Hat' in the Majors." *Baseball Digest,* LV (August 1996), 22–29. Trades.

1182. Verdi, Bob. "Whose Game Is It, Anyway?: Baseball's Blind Pursuit of the Almighty Dollar Is Driving Away the Fans." *Inside Sports,* XV (July 1993), 64–67.

1183. Verducci, Tom. "Big Deals." *Sports Illustrated,* LXXVIII (June 14, 1993), 61–62+. Baseball player agents.

1184. ____. "Liar's Poker: Anything Goes in Late-Season Waivers." *Sports*

Illustrated, LXXXVII (August 25, 1997), 36–39.

1185. ____. "Trimming the Fat." *Sports Illustrated,* LXXXIII (December 3, 1995), 106+.

1186. Vrooman, John. "A Unified Theory of Capital and Labor Markets in Major League Baseball." *Southern Economic Journal,* LXIII (January 1997), 594–614.

1187. Waddell, Ray. "Half of MLB's Teams Keep Prices at '94 Levels." *Amusement Business,* CVII (May 29, 1995), 39–41.

1188. Wakefield, Kirk L. "The Pervasive Effects of Social Influence on Sporting Event Attendance." *Journal of Sport and Social Issues,* XIX (November 1995), 335–351.

1189. Waller, Spencer W. and Neil B. Cohen. "Run Baseball Just Like Any Other Business?: That's the Last Thing the Owners Should Want." *Elysian Fields Quarterly,* XIII (Summer 1994), 10–11. To do so would cost the game its antitrust advantage.

1190. ____. and Paul Finkelman, eds. *Baseball and the American Legal Mind.* New York: Garland Pub., 1995. 525p.

1191. Willisch, Michael J. "Protecting the 'Owners' of Baseball: A Governance Structure to Maintain the Integrity of the Game and Guard the Principals' Money Investment." *Northwestern University Law Review,* LXXXVIII (Summer 1994), 1619–1650.

1192. Wong, G. M. and L. L. Pike. "Losing Ground: The Pro Leagues Are Taking Their Lumps on Antitrust." *Athletic Business,* XVIII (January 1994), 10–14.

1193. Wulf, Steve. "Can You Win with No $?" In: David Bauer, ed. *SI Presents Baseball 1997.* New York: Sports Illustrated, 1997. pp. 58–67. Fiscal problems of small market teams.

1194. Yablon, Charles M. "On the Contribution of Baseball to American Legal Theory." *Yale Law Review,* CIV (October 1994), 227–242.

1195. Yarborough, Ed and C. T. Morrow. "Baseball and the Law." *Texas Coach,* XLI (February 1997), 24–27.

1196. Yasser, R., *et al. Sports Law: Cases and Materials.* 3rd ed. Cincinnati, Ohio: Anderson Publishing Co., 1997. 830p.

1197. Yaukwitt, Russell M. "Buy Me Some Peanuts and Ownership: Major League Baseball and the Need for Employee Ownership." *Cornell Journal of Law and Public Policy,* V (Spring 1996), 401+.

1198. Zimbalist, Andrew S. *Baseball and Billions: A Probing Look Inside the Big Business of Our National Pastime.* New York: Basic Books, 1992. 270p.

1199. ____. "Baseball Economics and Antitrust Immunity." *Seton Hall Journal of Sport Law,* IV, no. 1 (1994), 287–320.

1200. Zweng, Jason. "Wild Pitch: How American Investors Financed the Growth of Baseball." *Friends of Financial History,* XLIII (Summer 1991), 4+.

g. Strikes

1201. Aiken, P. "Unknown Rights and Baseball Strikes." *Publishing Research Quarterly,* XI (March 1995), 21–26.

1202. Angell, Roger. "Bad Call." *The New Yorker,* LXX (August 15, 1994), 2+. Strike.

1203. Bard, R. L. and L. Kurlantzick. "To the Victor Belongs the Spoiled Game." *Challenge,* XXXVIII (March–April 1995), 63–64.

1204. Bernstein, Aaron. "Owners 1, Players 0." *Business Week,* (April 17, 1995), 32–33. Court injunction ends strike.

1205. Blum, Albert A. "A Panel Shouts 'Play Ball!'" *Labor Law Journal,* XLVII (July 1996), 426–428.

1206. Boyle, Maryellen. "The Sacred Meets the Profane: Baseball on Strike." *Communication,* XIII, no. 4 (1993), 229+.

1207. Bukowski, Douglas. "The State of

the Game: Strikeouts." *Elysian Fields Quarterly,* XIV (Summer 1995), 7–11, 20.

1208. Clinton, Bill. *Proposed Legislation: "Major League Baseball Restoration Act"—Message from the President of the United States Transmitting a Draft of Proposed Legislation....* House doc. 104-30. Washington, D.C.: GPO, 1995. 5p. Concerns the baseball strike; sent to the Committee on Economic and Educational Opportunities of the House of Representatives.

1209. Crasnick, Jerry. "Going…Going…Gone." *Beckett Baseball Card Monthly,* XI, no. 115 (October 1994), 12–18.

1210. ____. "Striking Out." *Beckett Baseball Card Monthly,* XII, no. 118 (January 1995), 10–19.

1211. Dolen, Edward F. *In Sports, Money Talks.* New York: 21st Century Books, 1996. 144p. 1994-95 strike.

1212. Dutch, Sharon. "The Future of Baseball." *American Demographics,* XVIII (April 1996), 22+. Effects of the 1994-95 strike.

1213. Dworkin, James B. and G. S. Jeif. "Social Consequences of Crossing the Picket Line: The 1994-95 Major League Baseball Strike." *Nine: A Journal of Baseball History and Social Policy Perspective,* V (Spring 1997), 242–262.

1214. Fisher, Christopher J. "The 1994-95 Baseball Strike: A Case Study in Myopic Subconscious Macrocosmic Response to Conflict." *Seton Hall Journal of Sport Law,* VI (Winter 1996), 367–395.

1215. Giamporcaro, Peter F. "No Runs, No Hits, Two Errors: How Maryland Erred in Prohibiting Replacement Players from Camden Yards During the 1994-95 Major League Baseball Strike." *Loyola Entertainment Law Journal,* XVII, no. 1 (1996), 123+.

1216. Grover, R., *et al.* "Ste-e-e-rike?" *Business Week,* (August 15, 1994), 26–28.

1217. Gurdah, Natalie M. "Baseball, Hotdogs, Apple Pie, and Strikes: How Baseball Could Have Avoided Its Latest Strike by Studying Sports Law from British Football." *Tulsa Journal of Comparative and International Law,* III (Fall 1995), 121+.

1218. "Hardball." *The New Yorker,* LXX (October 17, 1994), 65–68+. Strike.

1219. Impoco, J. "Down to the Last Out?" *U.S. News & World Report,* CXVIII (February 13, 1995), 66–68.

1220. Jordan, Pat. "Buddy's Boys and Their $100 Million Toys." *New York Times Magazine,* (September 18, 1994), 46–51+. Owners and the strike.

1221. Jordan Lippner, J. "Replacement Players for the Toronto Blue Jays?: Striking the Appropriate Balance Between Replacement Worker Law in Ontario, Canada, and the United States." *Fordham International Law Journal,* XVIII (1995), 2026–2094.

1222. Kuenster, John. "Blame for '94 Strike Falls on Players and Owners Alike." *Baseball Digest,* LIV (January 1995), 17–19.

1223. Kurkijan, Tim. "Ball of Confusion." *Sports Illustrated,* LXXII (January 9, 1995), 58–63.

1224. ____. "Dream On." *Sports Illustrated,* LXXII (February 13, 1995), 30–35.

1225. ____. "Swing Shift." *Sports Illustrated,* LXXII (January 23, 1995), 70–75. Career crises brought on by the strike.

1226. ____. and Tom Verducci. "Time Is Running Out." *Sports Illustrated,* LXXXII (March 20, 1995), 38–40, 45.

1227. Layden, Joe. *The Great American Baseball Strike.* Brookfield, Conn.: Millbrook Press, 1995. 64p.

1228. Mackin, Patrick C. "How Corporate Freeloaders in Stadium Skyboxes Adversely Affect Baseball." *Elysian Fields Quarterly,* XII (Spring 1993), 44–48.

1229. Oorlog, Dale R. "Marginal Revenue and Labor Strife in Major League Baseball." *Journal of Labor Research,* XVI (December 1995), 25–42.

1230. "Opportunities Lost: Can the Opportunities Lost in the '94 Strike Be Regained?" In: Joe Hoppel, ed. *The Sporting News 1995 Baseball Yearbook.* St. Louis, Mo.: TSN, 1995. pp. 37–41.

1231. Ozanian, Michael K. and Brooke Grabarek. "'Foul!'" *Financial World,* CLXIII (September 1, 1994), 18–21. The strike.

1232. Passmore, David L., *et al.* "Ballpark Estimates: Impact of the 1994 Baseball Strike on the Pennsylvania Economy." *Journal of Sport and Social Issues,* XX (May 1996), 161–172.

1233. Patterson, Ted. "Baseball Strikes Out." *The World & I,* X (April 1995), 82+.

1234. Rainie, H. "Where Have You Gone, Joe DiMaggio?" *U.S. News & World Report,* CXVII (August 15, 1994), 8–9. Strike.

1235. Roberts, S. V. "A Bronx Cheer for Baseball." *U.S. News & World Report,* CXVII (August 22, 1994), 24–26+. Strike.

1236. Rushin, Steve. "Casualties of War." *Sports Illustrated,* LXXXI (October 10, 1994), 36–38+. Impact of baseball strike on lower-paid employees, concession operators, etc.

1237. Schalian, John. "Contraria." *GQ: Gentlemen's Quarterly,* LXVI (March 1996), 72+.

1238. Seligman, Dan. "Strange Solidarity." *Fortune,* CXXXI (May 15, 1995), 144+.

1239. Shapiro, Walter. "Bummer of '94." *Time,* CXLIV (August 22, 1994), 68–74.

1240. Starr, Mark. "In This Game, It's Hard to Root for Either Side." *Newsweek,* CCXXIV (August 8, 1994), 58–59. Strike.

1241. ____. "'We Was Robbed!'" *Newsweek,* CCXXIV (August 22, 1994), 46–56.

1242. Sutherland, Billie. "Baseball Is Striking Out at More Than Itself." *San Diego Business Journal,* XV (August 15, 1994), 1–2.

1243. Verducci, Tom. "Brushback: A High, Hard One from a Federal Judge Ended Strike, But the Basic Dispute Remained Unsettled." *Sports Illustrated,* LXXXII (April 10, 1995), 60–62, 67.

1244. ____. "In the Strike Zone." *Sports Illustrated,* LXXXI (August 1, 1994), 26–28.

1245. ____. "Making Small Talk." *Sports Illustrated,* LXXXI (September 12, 1994), 20–24. Strike.

1246. Wanta, Wayne. "The Impact of the Baseball Strike on Newspapers." *Journalism and Mass Communications Quarterly,* LXXIV (Spring 1997), 184+.

1247. Wilentz, Sean. "Labor Reporting and the Baseball Strike." *Dissent,* XLII (Winter 1995), 12+.

1248. Williams, Peter. "Winners and Losers." In: George Leonard, ed. *Athlon's 1997 Baseball.* Nashville, Tn.: Athlon's Pub. Co., 1997. pp. 33–34. From the 1994-95 MLB strike.

1249. Winkler, K. "Baseball, Apple Pie, and Section 10(j): The Americanization of Injunctive Relief Under the NLRA [National Labor Relations Act]." *Labor Law Journal,* XLVI (August 1995), 504–512.

1250. Zimbalist, Andrew S. "Field of Schemes." *The New Republic,* CCXI (August 15, 1994), 11+. strike.

1251. Zipp, John F. "The Economic Impact of the Baseball Strike of 1994." *Urban Affairs Review,* XXXII (November 1996), 157–185.

h. Salaries, Salary Arbitration, and Collective Bargaining

1252. Battista, Leon J., Jr. "Approaching the Economics of Salary Determination in Baseball." *Elysian Fields Quarterly,* XII (Spring 1993), 30–40.

1253. Bevans, Michael. "Let's Make a Deal." *Sports Illustrated,* LXXXII (February 20, 1996), 196+.

1254. "Black Major League Baseball Players Paid Well Despite Strike." *Jet,*

LXXXVII (December 26, 1994), 51–54.

1255. "Blacks May Make Financial Sacrifices If Baseball Season Begins Without Regular Players." *Jet,* LXXXVII (March 20, 1995), 46–47.

1256. Boal, W. M. and M. R. Ransom. "Monopsony in the Labor Market." *Journal of Economic Literature,* XXXV (March 1997), 86–112.

1257. Bretz, Robert D., Jr. and Steven L. Thomas. "Perceived Equity, Motivation, and Final Offer Arbitration in Major League Baseball." *Journal of Applied Psychology,* LXXVII (June 1992), 280–287.

1258. Coleman, B. Jay, *et al.* "Convergence or Divergence in Final-Offer Arbitration in Professional Baseball." *Industrial Relations: A Journal of Economy and Society,* XXXII (Spring 1993), 238–247.

1259. Curie, David. "'On Higher Ground': Baseball and the Rule of Flood v. Kuhn." *Legal Reference Services Quarterly,* VIII (Spring-Summer 1988), 29–62.

1260. Donegan, Frederick N. "Examining the Role of Arbitration in Professional Baseball." *The Sports Lawyers Journal,* I, no. 1 (1994), 183+.

1261. Estenson, I. S. "Salary Determination in Major League Baseball: A Classroom Exercise." *Managerial and Decision Economics,* XV (September 1994), 537+.

1262. Faurot, David J. and Stephen McAllister. "Salary Arbitration and Pre-Arbitration Negotiation in Major League Baseball." *Industrial and Labor Relations Review,* XLV (July 1992), 697+.

1263. Fizel, John L. "Bias in Salary Arbitration: The Case of Major League Baseball." *Applied Economics,* XXVIII (February 1996), 255–265.

1264. _____. "'Play Ball!': Baseball Arbitration at Twenty." *Dispute Resolution Journal,* XLIX (June 1994), 42–48.

1265. Gillard, John P., Jr. "An Analysis of Salary Arbitration in Baseball: Could a Failure to Change the System Be Strike Three for Small Market Franchises?" *The Sports Lawyers Journal,* III, no. 1 (Spring 1996), 125+.

1266. Greenwood, Jon S. "What Major League Baseball Can Learn from Its International Counterparts: Building a Model Collective Bargaining Agreement for Major League Baseball." *George Washington Journal of International Law and Economics,* XXIX (Fall 1995), 259–296.

1267. Gustafson, Elizabeth and Lawrence Hadley. "Arbitration and Salary Caps in Major League Baseball." *Quarterly Journal of Business and Economics,* XXXIV (Summer 1995), 32–47.

1268. Greenwood, Jon S. "What Major League Baseball Can Learn from Its International Counterparts: Building a Model Collective Bargaining Agreement for Major League Baseball." *The George Washington Journal of International Law,* XXIX, no. 2 (1995), 581+.

1269. Hadley, Lawrence, Elizabeth Gustafson, and Mary Jo Thierry. "Who Would Be the Highest Paid Baseball Player?: One Way to Answer the Question, 'How Much Would the Babe Be Worth Today?'" *Baseball Research Journal,* XXI (1992), 86–92.

1270. Hage, David. "The National Pastime: The Rich vs. the Rich." *U.S. News & World Report,* CXVIII (February 20, 1995), 8–9.

1271. Hale, D. "Step Up to the Scale: Wages and Unions in the Sports Industry." *Marquette Sports Law Journal,* V (Fall 1994), 123–139.

1272. Hoaglin, D. C. and P. F. Velleman. "A Critical Look at Some Analyses of Major League Baseball Salaries." *American Statistician,* XLIX (August 1995), 277–285.

1273. Holbrook, M. B. and C. J. Shultz. "An Updating Model of Salary Adjustments in Major League Baseball: How Much Is a Home Run Worth?"

Journal of Sport Management, X (April 1996), 131–148.

1274. Hopkins, T. J. "Arbitration: A Major League Effect on Players' Salaries." *Seton Hall Journal of Sport Law,* II, no. 1 (1992), 301–335.

1275. Howard, Larry W. and James L. Miller. "Fair Pay for Fair Play: Estimating Pay Equity in Professional Baseball with Data Envelopment Analysis." *Academy of Management Journal,* XXXVI (August 1993), 882+.

1276. Hubbard, Steve, David Moore, and Stan Fischler. "Sports Salaries: Rocketing Out of Control?" *Inside Sports,* XVI (April 1994), 58–69.

1277. Jennings, Kenneth M. *Swings & Misses: Moribund Labor Relations in Professional Baseball.* Westport, Conn.: Greenwood Press, 1997.

1278. Johnson, William O. "For Sale." *Sports Illustrated,* LXXVIII (May 17, 1993), 32–34, 39. Advertising.

1279. Kahn, Lawrence M. "Free Agency, Long-Term Contracts, and Compensation in Major League Baseball: Estimates from Panel Data." *The Review of Economics and Statistics,* LXXV (February 1993), 157–164.

1280. Kiersh, Edward and Brad Buchholz. "The Salary Survey." *Inside Sports,* XV (April 1993), 58–71.

1281. Ladewski, Paul. "Hey Big Spenders." *Inside Sports,* XIV (April 1992), 68+. Salaries.

1282. Leonard, Wilbert M., 2nd. "The Influence of Race/Ethnicity in Salary Arbitration." *Journal of Sport Behavior,* XVII (September 1994), 166–177.

1283. MacDonald, D. N. and M. O. Reynolds. "Are Baseball Players Paid Their Marginal Products?" *Managerial and Decision Economics,* XV (September 1994), 443–458.

1284. Marburger, Daniel R. "Bargaining Power and the Structure of Salaries in Major League Baseball." *Managerial and Decision Economics,* XV (September 1994), 433–442.

1285. Marvine, Charles D. "Baseball's Unilaterally Imposed Salary Cap: This Baseball Cap Doesn't Fit." *University of Kansas Law Review,* XLIII (April 1995), 625–660.

1286. Moser, James W. "Evenhandedness in Arbitration: The Case of Major League Baseball." *Eastern Economic Journal,* XV (April 1989), 117+.

1287. Purdy, Dean A., *et al.* "A Reexamination of Salary Discrimination in Major League Baseball by Race/Ethnicity." *Sociology of Sport Journal,* XI (March 1994), 60+.

1288. Seligman, Daniel. "Computers, Baseball, and Guys Named Mike." *Fortune,* CXXVII (May 17, 1993), 139–140. Computerized studies of MLB salaries.

1289. ____. "Strange Solidarity." *Fortune,* CXXXI (May 15, 1995), 144+.

1290. Smith, D. J. and S. J. "Major League Baseball Division Standings, Sports Journalists' Predictions, and Player Salaries." *Managerial and Decision Economics,* XV (September 1994), 421–432.

1291. Sommers, Paul M. "Ticket Prices and Player Salaries in Major League Baseball." *Journal of Recreational Mathematics,* XXVI, no. 4 (1994), 274+.

1292. Swank, Deborah R. "Arbitration and Salary Inflation in Major League Baseball." *Journal of Dispute Resolution,* (1992), 159+.

1293. Verducci, Tom. "The Bad News." *Sports Illustrated,* LXXXIII (July 10, 1995), 32–33. Collective bargaining failure.

1294. Vrooman, John. "The Baseball Players' Labor Market Reconsidered." *Southern Economic Journal,* LXIII (October 1996), 339–360.

1295. Wilson, John. "Efficiency and Power in Professional Baseball Players' Employment Contracts." *Sociology of Sport Journal,* VIII (December 1991), 326+.

i. Drugs and Violence

1296. Achiron, M. "Words to Die For." *People Weekly,* XXXIX (June 7, 1993), 83–84. How Joe Matteucci was murdered at a Little League game in Castro Valley, Calif.

1297. "Brawltimore." *Sports Illustrated,* LXXVIII (June 14, 1993), 22–23. Fight between Orioles and Seattle Mariners.

1298. Dolan, E. F. *Drugs in Sports.* Rev. ed. New York: Watts, 192. 159p.

1299. Hanson, Linda S. and Craig Dernis. "Revisiting Excessive Violence in the Professional Sports Arena: Changes in the Past 20 Years." *Seton Hall Journal of Sport Law,* VI, no. 1 (1996), 127+.

1300. Holtzman, Jerome. "Violence on the Diamond as Old as the Game Itself." *Baseball Digest,* LII (October 1993), 24–26.

1301. Karon, D. R. "Winning Isn't Everything, It's the Only Thing: Violence in Professional Sports." *Indiana Law Review,* XXV (Winter 1991), 147–163.

1302. Macht, Norman L. "Commentary: Ugly Incidents on the Field Have Long Cursed the Majors." *Baseball Digest,* LVI (May 1997), 58–61.

1303. Palmer, C. A. "Drugs vs. Privacy: The New Game in Sports." *Marquette Sports Law Journal,* II (Spring 1992), 175–209.

1304. Rainey, David W. "Assaults on Umpires: A Statewide Survey." *Journal of Sport Behavior,* XVII (March 1994), 148–155.

1305. _____. and Kevin Cherilla. "Conflict with Baseball Umpires: An Observational Study." *Journal of Sport Behavior,* XVI (March 1993), 49–59.

1306. Reifman, Alan S., Richard P. Larrick, and Steven Fain. "Temper and Temperature on the Diamond: The Heat Aggression Relationship in Major League Baseball." *Personality and Social Psychology Bulletin,* XVII (October 1991), 580–586.

1307. Rosenberg, J. M., *et al. Athletic Drug Reference.* Durham, N.C.: Clean Data, Inc., 1992. 265p.

1308. Wallace, Carole J. "The Men in Black and Blue: A Comment on Violence Against Sports Officials and State Legislative Reaction." *Seton Hall Journal of Sport Law,* VI, no. 1 (1996), 341+.

1309. Wulf, Steve. "Basebrawl." *Sports Illustrated,* LXXIX (August 16, 1993), 12–17.

j. Gambling

Gambling is not a new problem for pro baseball; betting has been at the bottom of some of the greatest tragedies in the sport from its beginning right up through the Pete Rose banishment. References to specific gambling episodes like the Black Sox scandal are handled elsewhere; the citations here cover general references, including guides for participants.

1310. Gates, Robert W. "Betting the Big Show: World Series." *Win,* XIV (June 1993), 50–55.

1311. Ginsberg, Daniel E. *The Fix Is In: A History of Baseball Gambling and Game Fixing Scandals.* Jefferson, N.C.: McFarland & Co., Inc., 1995. 317p.

1312. McGraw, D. "The National Bet." *U.S. News & World Report,* CXXII (April 7, 1997), 50–55. Illegal wagering.

1313. Most, Marshall G. and Robert Rudd. "Don't Bet on It: The Representation of Gambling in Baseball America." *The Southern Communication Journal,* LXI (Spring 1996), 233+.

1314. Ostertag, T. J. "From Shoeless Joe to Charley Hustle: Major League Baseball's Continuing Crusade Against Sports Gambling." *Seton Hall Journal of Sport Law,* II, no. 1 (1992), 19–49.

1315. Patrick, John. *John Patrick's Sports Betting: Proven Winning System for Football, Basketball, and Baseball.* Secaucus, N.J.: Carol Pub. Group., 1996. 307p.

1316. Pichette, Jean. "Between Virtual Baseball and the Croupier State: The Depths of the Real." *Sociologie et Societes,* XXVII (Spring 1995), 165–170.

1317. Reilly, Rick. "1-900 Ripoffs." *Sports Illustrated,* LXXV (November 18, 1991), 114–120, 122–124, 126.

1318. Ross, Robert. "Early Baseball Season Baseball Betting Gambits." *Win,* XIII (April 1991), 56+.

1319. Rothchild, John. "Sleaze Play." *Worth,* I (February–March 1992), 61+.

1320. Schureck, George. "Chasing Those Last-Minute, Late-Season Major League Baseball Betting Profits." *Win,* XIV (September 1992), 62+.

1321. Seligman, Dan. "Ask Mr. Statistics." *Fortune,* CXXXIII (May 13 and June 10, 1996), 201–202, 161–162. The first article concerns the market on home-run betting and the second taxes on the income.

1322. Sheridan, Danny. "Baseball Betting Guide." *Sport,* LXXXIV (April 1993), 70–72.

1323. ____. "Sheridan's Best Bets and Busts: Baseball '94." *Sport,* LXXXV (April 1994), 94–96.

1324. ____. "____: Baseball '95." *Sport,* LXXXVI (May 1995), 47–48.

1325. Tuccile, Jerome. "Gambling in Baseball." *Penthouse,* XXIII (November 1991), 18+.

1326. Vass, George. "Should Big Leagues Clamp Down on Team Brawls?" *Baseball Digest,* LII (October 1993), 18–23.

1327. Woodland, Linda H. and Bill M. "Market Efficiency and the Favorite-Longshot Bias: The Baseball Betting Market." *Journal of Finance,* XLIX (March 1994), 269–279.

k. Medical, Fitness, and Nutritional Issues

In Babe Ruth's day, little attention was paid by most pro ball players to matters of fitness and nutrition, while medical issues were only of concern if they pre-

vented play. For the most part, this attitude had completely changed by the 1990s. The literature of medical, fitness, and nutritional issues relative to baseball is immense and much of it is technical. What is cited here consists of general titles (including a few on the subjects of athletic training and sports medicine, both worthy of individual bibliographies) together with a few technical examinations of specific problems, e.g., Little League elbow. The most helpful continuing coverage of these topics is presented in the product of the Sport Information Resource Centre.

1328. Andrews, J. R. and L. A. Timmerman. "Outcome of Elbow Surgery in Professional Baseball Players." *American Journal of Sports Medicine,* XXIII (July 1995), 407–413.

1329. Armstrong, Jim. "Health and Desire Are Big Factors in Setting Career Records." *Baseball Digest,* LVI (May 1997), 48–53.

1330. Broeg, Bob. "Fatal Tragedies to Players Are Part of Game's History." *Baseball Digest,* LII (July 1993), 58–61.

1331. Canavan, P. K. "Shoulder Impingement Syndrome a Pitcher's Nightmare." *First Aider,* LXV (Spring 1995), 6, 8, 17.

1332. Chastain, Bill. "Why the Surge in Majors' Disabled Lists?" *Baseball Digest,* LI (September 1992), 40–42.

1333. Ciccantelli, P. "Avoiding Elbow Pain: Tips for Young Pitchers." *Physician and Sports Medicine,* XXII (March 1994), 65–66.

1334. Connolly, G. N. and Joe Garagiola. "It's Time Major League Baseball Made Tobacco History." *Journal of the American Dental Association,* CXXVI (August 1995), 1121–1124. Commentary on chewing tobacco.

1335. Dolgan, Bob. "Why Are So Many of Today's Pitchers Injury-Prone?" *Baseball Digest,* LII (October 1993), 54–59.

1336. Dorfman, Harvey A. "Reflections on Providing Personal and Performance Enhancement Consulting Services in Professional Baseball." *The Sport Psychologist,* IV (December 1990), 341–346.

1337. Eisenbath, Mike. "What Pitchers Fear Most When They're on the Mound." *Baseball Digest,* LVI (September 1997), 76–79. Being hurt by screaming line drives.

1338. Ellenbecker, Todd S. *The Elbow in Sport: Injury, Treatment, and Rehabilitation.* Champaign, Ill.: Human Kinetics Pub., 1997. 202p. Includes Little League elbow.

1339. Etkin, Jack. "Pressure, an Intrusive Foe of Long Hitting Streaks." *Baseball Digest,* LVI (September 1997), 68–71.

1340. Fleisig, G. S., *et al.* "Kinetics of Baseball Pitching with Implications About Injury Mechanisms." *American Journal of Sports Medicine,* XXIII (March 1995), 233–239.

1341. Gordon, Jeff. "Handle with Care: Hot Dogs-and-Beer Diet Seems to Be Food for Thought in View of Weird Injuries That Take Toll on Big League Ballplayers." In: Gary Levy, ed. *The Sporting News 1992 Baseball Yearbook.* St. Louis, Mo.: TSN, 1992. pp. 38–40.

1342. Greene, John C. "A Program to Help Major League Baseball Players Quit Using Spit Tobacco." *Journal of the American Dental Association,* CXXV (May 1994), 559+.

1343. Hart, Edward J. "Little League Baseball and Head Injuries." *Pediatrics,* LXXXIX (March 1992), 520+.

1344. Hicks, Robert A., *et al.* "Do Right-Handers Live Longer?: An Updated Assessment of Baseball Player Data." *Perceptual & Motor Skills,* LXXVIII (June 1994), 1243–1247.

1345. Holtzman, Jerome. "Baseball and Psychiatry Remain an Odd Sort of Mix." *Baseball Digest,* LII (February 1993), 57–58.

1346. Janda, David, Michael McGwire, and Derek Macksey. "Sliding Injuries in College and Professional Baseball:

A Prospective Study Comparing Standard and Break-Away Bases." *Clinical Journal of Sport Medicine,* III (April 1993), 78+.

1347. Kuenster, John. "Players Can Succeed in the Majors Despite Physical Imperfections." *Baseball Digest,* LV (September 1996), 17–19.

1348. Laby, D. M., *et al.* "The Visual Function of Professional Baseball Players." *American Journal of Ophthalmology,* CXXII (October 1996), 476–485.

1349. Laliberte, Richard. "Baseball Dangers." *Parents,* LXX (April 1995), 32–34.

1350. Long, R. R., *et al.* "Pitcher's Arm: An Electrodiagnostic Enigma." *Muscle and Nerve,* XIX (October 1996), 1276–1281.

1351. Nocera, Joseph. "Bitter Medicine." *Sports Illustrated,* LXXXIII (November 6, 1995), 74–76+. Lawsuits against team doctors.

1352. O'Neil, C. "Chewing Tobacco Strikes Out." *First Aider,* LXV (Spring 1995), 7, 13. Reprinted from the February 21, 1995 issue of *The Washington Post.*

1353. Over, Ray. "Age and Level of Performance in Major League Baseball." *Journal of Aging and Physical Activity,* II (July 1994), 221–232.

1354. Pasternack, Joel S., Kenneth M. Veenema, and Charles M. Callahan. "Baseball Injuries: A Little League Survey." *Pediatrics,* XCVIII (September 1996), 445–448.

1355. Paull, Geoffrey and Denis Gleucross. "Expert Participation and Decision Making in Baseball." *International Journal of Sport Psychology,* XXVIII (January 1997), 35+.

1356. Post, Paul. "When Should a Big League Veteran Call It Quits?" *Baseball Digest,* LVI (September 1997), 62–67.

1357. Ramotar, Juliet. "Breakaway Bases Strike Out Injuries." *The Physician and Sportsmedicine,* XXI (September 1993), 10+.

1358. Ranalli, D. N. "Spit Tobacco: Baseball's Hidden Health Hazard." *Scholastic Coach & Athletic Director,* LXV (April 1996), 8–9.

1359. Ravizza, Kenneth. "SportPsych Consultation Issues in Professional Baseball." *The Sport Psychologist,* IV (December 1990), 330–340.

1360. Robertson, P. B., *et al.* "Smokeless Tobacco Use: How It Affects the Performance of Major League Baseball Players." *Journal of the American Dental Association,* CXXVI (August 1995), 1115–1121.

1361. Roisum, T. C. and J. A. Whiteside. "Baseball and Softball." In: M. B. Mellion, ed. *Sports Medicine Secrets.* Philadelphia, Pa.: Hanley & Belfus, 1994. pp. 272–376.

1362. Schultz, Richard and Donala Musa. "The Relationship Between Age and Major League Baseball Performance: Implications for Development." *Psychology and Aging,* IX (June 1994), 274–286.

1363. Sinusas, K. and J. G. Coroso. "Smokeless Tobacco Use and Athletic Performance in Professional Baseball Players." *Medicine, Exercise, Nutrition, and Health,* IV (January–February 1995), 48–50.

1364. Smith, Ronald E. "An Organizational Empowerment Approach to Consultation in Professional Baseball." *The Sport Psychologist,* IV (December 1990), 347+.

1365. ____. and Donald S. Christensen. "Psychological Skills as Predictors of Performance and Survival in Professional Baseball." *Journal of Sport & Exercise Psychology,* XVII (December 1995), 399–415.

1366. Snyder, Eldon E. and Ronald Ammons. "Baseball's Emotion Work: Getting Psyched to Play." *Qualitative Sociology,* XVI (Summer 1993), 111–132.

1367. Stewart, Wayne. "Bizarre Injuries, Off-Beat Humor Are Part of Baseball." *Baseball Digest,* LIII (July 1994), 34–35.

1368. Strauss, R. H. "Spitting Image: Breaking the Sports-Tobacco Connection." *The Physician and Sportsmedicine,* XIX (November 1991), 46, 48.

1369. Todd, Mike. "Overcoming Fear, the Usual Aftermath of a Beaning." *Baseball Digest,* LVI (July 1997), 34–37.

1370. Tuttle, Bill. "My War with a Smoke-Free Killer." *Reader's Digest,* CXLIX (October 1996), 120–125. Chewing tobacco.

1371. United States. Centers for Disease Control and Prevention. "Sliding-Associated Injuries in College and Professional Baseball, 1990–1991." *Morbidity and Mortality Weekly Report,* XLII (April 2, 1993), 223–226.

1372. Vass, George. "Pre-Season Player Mishaps Often Dash Pennant Hopes." *Baseball Digest,* LVI (July 1997), 24–33.

1373. ____. "Who Says Baseball Is a Game for Softies?" *Baseball Digest,* LI (June 1992), 25–30.

1374. ____. "Why the Surge in Placing Players on the Disabled List?" *Baseball Digest,* LII (July 1993), 48–54.

1375. Walk, S., M. A. Clark, and V. Seefeldt. "Baseball and Softball." In: D. J. Caine, *et al.,* eds. *Epidemiology of Sports Injuries.* Champaign, Ill.: Human Kinetics Pub., 1996. pp. 63–85.

1376. Wells, M. J. and G. W. Bell. "Concerns on Little League Elbow." *Journal of Athletic Training,* XXX (September 1995), 249–253.

l. Media: Newspapers, Radio, Television

1377. Altherr, T. L. "Baseball Is Life?: Images of Baseball in *Life* magazine, 1936–1972." *Nine: A Journal of Baseball History and Social Policy Perspective,* V (Fall 1996), 18–47.

1378. "Bad News: A Media Invasion Has Heightened Tensions in Once

Congenial Clubhouses." *Sports Illustrated,* LXXVIII (May 17, 1993), 44, 49.

1379. "Baseball on Cable: A Game of Extra Innings." *Cable Vision,* XII (May 22, 1989), 72+.

1380. Bellamy, R. and J. R. Walker. "Foul Tip or Strike Three?: The Evolving 'Partnership' of Major League Baseball and Television." *Nine: A Journal of Baseball History and Social Policy Perspective,* III (Spring 1995), 261–275.

1381. Berler, Ron. "Here's What Players Look for When Watching a Game on TV." *Baseball Digest,* LIII (October 1994), 49–50.

1382. "The Best Sportscaster." *TV Guide,* XLI (April 17, 1993), 61–62.

1383. Blount, Roy, Jr. "Cheerleaders in the Outfield and Other Ways to Liven Up Baseball on TV." *TV Guide,* XLII (July 9, 1994), 22–24.

1384. Brown, Rich and Geoffrey Foisie. "Baseball Wants More Buck for Its Bang." *Broadcasting,* CXXII (February 24, 1992), 4, 24–26.

1385. Brunelli, R. "Networks Play Bickerball: ABC and NBC Disagree Over Who'll Get the 1995 World Series." *Media Week,* V (June 5, 1995), 5–6.

1386. Burgi, M. "TV Whiffs on Baseball Strike." *Media Week,* IV (September 5, 1994), 6+.

1387. Catsis, John R. *Sports Broadcasting.* Chicago, Ill.: Nelson-Hall, 1996. 275p.

1388. Cohen, Sharon. "Sportswriters and the Color Bar." *Media History Digest,* XII (Fall 1992), 24+.

1389. Dupree, S. "Bidding for Baseball: The Networks Vow Frugality, but the Ratings May Dictate Otherwise." *Media Week,* V (October 15, 1995), 4–5.

1390. "The Enduring Charm of Radio." In: Joe Hoppel, ed. *The Sporting News 1996 Baseball Yearbook.* St. Louis, Mo.: TSN, 1996. pp. 42–49.

1391. Evensen, Bruce J. "Jazz Age Journalism's Battle Over Professionalism, Circulation, and the Sports Page." *Journal of Sport History,* XX (Winter 1993), 229–246.

1392. Freeman, M. "Cashing In on the Series: What It Means to Sales When the Home Team Makes the Big Show." *Media Week,* VI (October 21, 1996), 5–6.

1393. ____. and M. Gimein. "Can Baseball Come Back?: Local TV, Cable Carriers Expect Ratings Rebound, Advertisers Wary." *Media Week,* VI (March 11, 1996), 9+.

1394. Goodman, Tom. "Radio Rooting." *Elysian Fields Quarterly,* XIII (Winter 1994), 59–66.

1395. Gould, Barry. *Superbook of Television Sports.* York, Maine, 1992–. Annual. A directory of organizations and personnel.

1396. Heuton, C. "Tuning Out the Scabs." *Media Week,* V (March 27, 1995), 6+. Televising baseball games that employ replacement players during the '95 strike.

1397. Howerton, David. "America's Teams." *Sport,* LXXXVII (November 1996), 32–34+. Intense media coverage.

1398. Jessell, Harry A. and Kim McAvoy. "Baseball Scores: $315 Million from Rights." *Broadcasting & Cable,* CXXVII (March 31, 1997), 24–25.

1399. Johnson, William O. "Every Day Is Game Day." *Sports Illustrated,* LXXVII (December 21, 1992), 52–58, 63–64. ESPN's SportsCenter.

1400. ____. "For Sale: The National Pastime." *Sports Illustrated,* LXXVIII (May 17, 1993), 32–34, 39. Television contracts.

1401. Knott, Richard D., Jr. *"The Sports Hero as Portrayed in Popular Journalism, 1886–1920."* Unpublished Ph.D. Dissertation, University of Tennessee, 1994.

1402. Lamb, Chris and Glen Bleske. "Covering the Integration of Baseball: A Look Back." *Editor & Publisher, the*

Fourth Estate CXXX (January 27, 1996), 48+.

1403. "Local TV and Radio Lineup." *Broadcasting & Cable,* CXXVII (March 31, 1997), 28–29. MLB games by team.

1404. Lumpkin, Angela and Linda D. Williams. "An Analysis of *Sports Illustrated* Feature Articles, 1954–1987." *Sociology of Sport Journal,* VIII (March 1991), 16–32.

1405. Madden, Bill. "New Yap City." *Sport,* LXXXVI (February 1995), 57–60. Media pressure on MLB players in New York City.

1406. McClellan, S. "Media Face One Strike, No Ball." *Broadcasting & Cable,* CXXV (February 20, 1995), 6–7.

1407. ____. "MLB Gets Its First Start." *Broadcasting & Cable,* CXXIV (March 14, 1994), 30–33. The short-lived The Baseball Network.

1408. ____. "Two Ways to Go on Baseball: CBS vs. ABC-NBC." *Broadcasting & Cable,* CXXIII (May 17, 1993), 6+.

1409. McConville, J. "Fox, CBS Swinging for Baseball [MLB TV Contract]." *Broadcasting & Cable,* CXXV (October 23, 1995), 4+.

1410. Messner, M. A. "Separating the Men from the Girls: The Gendered Language of Televised Sport." In: D. S. Eitzen, ed. *Sports in Contemporary Society: An Anthology.* 4th ed. New York: St. Martin's Press, 1993. pp. 219–233.

1411. Moore, G. "Ideology on the Sportspage: Newspapers, Baseball, and Ideological Conflict in the Gilded Age." *Journal of Sport History,* XXIII (Fall 1996), 228–255.

1412. Neal-Lundstord, J. "Sport in the Land of Television: The Use of Sports in Network Prime-Time Schedules, 1946–1950." *Journal of Sport History,* XIX (Spring 1992), 56–76.

1413. "Networks, Local TV Score with Interleague Baseball." *Mediaweek,* VII (June 23, 1997), 6–8.

1414. Orodenker, Richard, ed. *20th Cen-tury American Sportswriters.* Detroit, Mich.: Gale Research, 1996.

1415. ____. *The Writers' Game: Baseball Writing in America.* Authors Series, no. 663. New York: Twayne, 1996. 248p.

1416. Regalado, Samuel O. "'Image Is Everything': Latin Baseball Players in the United States Press." *Studies in Latin American Popular Culture,* XIII (1994), 101–128.

1417. Reisler, Jim. *Black Writers/Black Baseball: An Anthology of Articles from Black Sportswriters Who Covered the Negro Leagues.* Jefferson, N.C.: McFarland & Co., Inc., 1994. 169p.

1418. Reynolds, Mike. "Mighty [Rupert] Murdoch Swings the Bat." *Mediaweek,* VII (April 14, 1997), 60–61. FX and Fox Sports.

1419. ____. "Home-Team Advantage: Baseball Makes a Comeback on Regional Networks." *Mediaweek,* VII (April 14, 1997), 64–65.

1420. Rubin, Bob. "Breaking Into the Boys' Club: Robin Roberts and Other Women Are Proving That, in the World of Sports Broadcasting, Knowledge, Experience, and Talent No Longer Are Male Preserves." *Inside Sports,* XVII (November 1995), 16–18.

1421. ____. "Critiquing the [Media] Critics." *Inside Sports,* XIV (January 1992), 10–13.

1422. ____. "From Print to TV Demands a Whole New Alphabet." *Inside Sports,* XIV (February 1992), 12–17. Problems for reporters making the switch.

1423. ____. "...Then the Two-Faced, Ignorant, Misogynous Jerk Homered to Left: What Would Journalists Say If They Could Tell the Whole Truth About Jose Canseco and Other Players Who Make Their Jobs a Living Hell?" *Inside Sports,* XV (October 1993), 8–11.

1424. ____. "To Print or Not to Print: When Is News News?" *Inside Sports,* XV (August 1993), 22–25.

1425. Rushin, Steve. "Time Travel on the Tube." *Sports Illustrated Classic,* LXXVII (Fall 1992), 88–93.

1426. Ryan, Marie L. "Narrative in Real Time: Chronicle, Mimesis, and Plot in the Baseball Broadcast." *Narrative,* I (May 1993), 138+.

1427. Shannon, Mike. *Baseball: The Writers' Game.* South Bend, Ind.: Diamond Communications, 1992. 259p.

1428. Smith, Curt. *The Storytellers, from Mel Allen to Bob Costas: 60 Years of Baseball Tales from the Broadcast Booth.* New York: Macmillan, 1995. 278p.

1429. ____. *Voices of the Game: The Acclaimed Chronicle of Baseball Radio and Television Broadcasting, from 1921 to the Present.* Rev. ed. New York: Simon & Schuster, 1992. 623p.

1430. Verducci, Tom. "Bad News." *Sports Illustrated,* LXXVIII (May 17, 1993), 44+. Press-baseball relations.

1431. Victory, D. "Good Sports, Bad Sports." *Washingtonian,* XXXI (May 1996), 86–91. Newspaper sports pages rated by bartenders!

1432. Weinstock, Neal. "Holding Sports Hostage." *Sport,* LXXXIV (March 1993), 42+. How TV has changed baseball.

m. Baseball Fans

Spectators and fans in the 1990s remain the backbone of baseball regardless of its level. Without them, the pro game would wither and, on all levels, only the players would participate in the sport, probably then without compensation and having joy only in the purity of their performance and the perfection of the game. The citations in this part celebrate baseball spectators as a group, with emphasis on fans at professional games. In addition, we again include references to guidebooks and other data compiled in an effort to help those watching to better understand the intricacies of the game.

1433. Allman, Cathy. "A Mother's Point of View." *Elysian Fields Quarterly,* XII (Summer 1993), 11–12.

1434. Bakalar, Nick. *The Baseball Fan's Companion: How to Watch the Game Like an Expert.* New York: Macmillan, 1996. 210p.

1435. Cataneo, David. *Hornsby Hit One Over My Head: A Fan's Oral History of Baseball.* San Diego, Ca.: Harcourt Brace & Co., 1997. 261p. Designed to let the "average fan" tell the story of baseball as he or she remembers it; most stories included are from fans on the East Coast of the U.S.

1436. Champion, W. T. "'At the Ol' Ball Game' and Beyond: Spectators and the Potential for Liability." *American Journal of Trial Advocacy,* XIV (Spring 1991), 495–526.

1437. DePaulo, Lisa. "Rounding Home: Growing Up with the Ultimate Baseball Fan." *Women's Sports and Fitness,* XVI (April 1994), 98+.

1438. Farber, Michael. "The Old Heave-Ho: Fans' Tossing Things, Be They Confections or Critters, Has Lost Whatever Charm It Once Had." *Sports Illustrated,* LXXXIV (May 27, 1996), 88+.

1439. Fimrite, Ron. *Birth of a Fan.* New York: Macmillan, 1993. 214p.

1440. Fleming, Richard C. D. "Like Father, Like Daughters." *Colorado Business Magazine,* XX (April 1993), 23+.

1441. Goodwin, Doris Kearns. *Wait Till Next Year: A Memoir.* New York: Simon & Schuster, 1997. 261p. A famous historian's recollections of growing up a Brooklyn (N.L.) fan and switching to Boston (A.L.).

1442. Jones, Michelle. "On Being a Fan." *Elysian Fields Quarterly,* XII (Summer 1993), 13–17.

1443. Holt, Douglas B. "How Consumers Consume: A Typology of Consumption Practices." *Journal of Consumer Research,* XXII (June 1995), 1–16. Uses MLB as a prime example.

1444. Holtzman, Jerome. "Player Restraint Wears Out When Fans Get Abusive." *Baseball Digest,* LV (September 1996), 55–59.

1445. Kasky, J. "The Best Buys for Fans Today." *Money,* XXIII (October 1994), 158–167+.

1446. Kochman, Ladd M. "Major League Baseball: What Really Puts Fans in the Stands." *Sports Marketing Quarterly,* IV (March 1995), 9+.

1447. Kuenster, John. "Fans Blow Off Steam Against Actions of Baseball Establishment." *Baseball Digest,* LVI (December 1997), 17–21.

1448. _____. "Letters from Readers Reveal What 'Real' Fans Are Thinking." *Baseball Digest,* LII (September 1993), 17–21.

1449. McKelvey, Steve and David Menzies. "Fair or Foul?: As Baseball Stands at the Crossroads, Two Fans Offer Differing Perspectives on the Future and Direction of the National Pastime." *Inside Sports,* XIX (May 1997), 68–74.

1450. Pietrusza, David. "Grace Coolidge: The First Lady of Baseball." *Elysian Fields Quarterly,* XII (Summer 1993), 36–39.

1451. "Purists: Hate the DH? Love Grass, Day Games?: If So, You May Be a Baseball Purist." In: Joe Hoppel, ed. *The Sporting News 1994 Baseball Yearbook.* St. Louis, Mo.: TSN, 1994. pp. 32–35.

1452. Roos, M. "Factors Influencing Spectators' Interest in Baseball: Theory, Empirical Research, and an Inter-Cultural Comparison with Bullfight Spectators." In: B. Svoboda and A. Rychtecky, eds. *Physical Activity in Life, East and West, South and North: Proceedings of the 9th International Society for Comparative Physical Education and Sport Conference, 1995.* Aachen, Germany: Meyer and Meyer Verlag, 1995. pp. 260–264.

1453. Ryan, Jeff. "The Fans: Ballpark Figures Then and Now." *Sport,* LXXXIV (March 1993), 37+.

1454. Sheed, Wilfred. *My Life as a Fan.* New York: Simon and Schuster, 1993. 221p.

1455. Singer, Thomas. "Baseball as the Center of the World: A Condensed Jungian Guide to the Psychological Experience of Baseball Fever." In: Murray Stein and John Hollwitz, eds. *Psyche and Sports.* Wilmette, Ill.: Chiron Publications, 1994. pp. 49–67.

1456. Starr, Mark. "Baseball's Black Problem." *Newsweek,* CXXII (July 19, 1993), 56–57. Paucity of Afro-American fans at MLB games.

1457. Sullivan, Dean A. "Faces in the Crowd: A Statistical Portrait of Baseball Spectators in Cincinnati, 1886–1888." *Journal of Sport History,* XVII (Winter 1990), 354+.

1458. Trujillo, Nick and Bob Kruzek. "Emotionality in the Stands and on the Field: Expressing Self Through Baseball." *Journal of Sport and Social Issues,* XVIII (November 1994), 307+.

1459. Verducci, Tom. "The Play's the Thing: Fans Who Boycott the Ballpark are Missing Surprising Developments on the Field." *Sports Illustrated,* LXXXIII (July 10, 1995), 16–22.

1460. Waddell, Ray. "MLB Winning Back Fans." *Amusement Business,* CIX (May 26, 1997), 1–2.

1461. Weiller, Karen and Catriona T. Higgs. "Fandom in the '40s." *Journal of Sport Behavior,* XX (June 1997), 211+.

n. Rotisserie Leagues and Fantasy Baseball, Including Adult Baseball Camps

What is often described as fantasy baseball was only in its infancy when *Baseball: A Comprehensive Bibliography* appeared in 1986. Today, rotisserie baseball is a thriving enterprise while several hundred dedicated fans are able each year to attend team-sponsored adult baseball camps. The references here examine the literature of fantasy baseball; their number, like those for baseball cards in

Chapter A:4:b above, will grow significantly in the years ahead.

1462. Albert, Joshua, ed. *Power Ranking System Fantasy Baseball Report, 1997.* Shakopee Valley, Minn.: Shakopee Valley Printing, 1997—. v. 1—. This new (102-page) annual also has its own web page <**http://www. jldpub.com**>.

1463. Ambrosius, Greg., ed. *Fantasy Baseball.* Iola, Wisc.: Krause, 1996—. 6 times per year. Issues average 82 pages.

1464. Bloom, John. "'I Don't Know How Fame Feels': Cultural Tension Within Baseball Fantasies at the Minnesota Twins Open Tryout Camp." *Play and Culture,* III (February 1990), 51–63.

1465. *Fantasy Fact Sheets,* Editors of. *Fantasy Baseball Fact Sheet.* Los Angeles, Calif.: Fantasy Fact Sheets, 1991—. v. 1—. Annual.

1466. Friedman, Myles. "The Roto Index: Player Rankings by Position for Rotisserie Leagues." *Spring Training: Grapefruit and Cactus League Yearbook,* V (1992), 42–47; VI (1993), 42–47; VII (1994), 52–59; VIII (1995), 52–59; IX (1996), 96–103; X (1997), 96–103.

1467. Gervino, Tony, ed. *Hardball.* New York: Harris Publishing, 1996—. v. 1—.

1468. Golenbock, Peter. *How to Win at Rotisserie Baseball.* New York: Carol & Graf, 1994—. Annual.

1469. Johnson, Rebecca. "Hoop du Jour." *Women's Sports and Fitness,* XVIII (September 1996), 44–45+. Adult camps in New York City.

1470. Mann, Steve. *Steve Mann's Fantasy Baseball Guide, 1997: Let Major League Baseball's First Professional Analyst Help You Draft a Team That Puts You in the Money.* New York: HarperCollins, 1997.

1471. McCormick, Eileen M. "Memories Are Built at 'Fantasy' Baseball Camp." *Pharmacy Times,* LXIX (June 1993), 48+. That sponsored by the St. Louis Cardinals.

1472. Millburg, S. "Field of Dreamers." *Southern Living,* XXVIII (March 1993), 22+. Adult baseball camps.

1473. Patton, Alex. *Patton's 1995 Predictions for Rotisserie Baseball.* New York: Wings, 1995. 375p.

1474. Rubin, Bob. "Fantasy Baseball Players Are Living a Dream." *Inside Sports,* XV (July 1993), 14–17.

1475. Sutton, Eddie. "Baseball Camp Fund-Raiser." *Scholastic Coach,* LXIII (May–June 1994), 102–103.

1476. Taylor, Bruce, ed. *Fantasy Baseball Index.* Seattle, Wash.: Fantasy Baseball Index, 1997. 154p. Also available at the following World Wide Web site: <**http://www.fantasyindex.com/ baseball**>.

1477. Watt, R. L. "Fantasy Camp: Baseball Addicts' Ultimate High." *Sport,* LXXXV (April 1994), 18+. Camp run by the Los Angeles Dodgers.

C. Professional
Leagues and Teams

The citations in this chapter concern the professional leagues and teams of organized baseball, including those of a "minor" variety. Here the user will find information relative to the surviving National and American Leagues, as well as such doomed efforts as the Federal League. In addition, the majority of this guide's references to individual big league teams are located here, arranged in alphabetical order under either the National or American Leagues. The minor leagues and teams are covered in three parts, including one each devoted to specific leagues and teams. This section is concluded with categories on stadiums and equipment. Here the reader will find information on old and new ballparks, artificial vs. grass surfaces, lighting, scoreboards, the development of baseballs and gloves, uniform changes, and aluminum and wood bats.

1. General Works (All-Star Teams and Doomed Leagues)

The citations here are of two distinct types; however, because as a body neither was sufficient in number to justify a separate section, they are placed together. First, references to what *Baseball: A Comprehensive Bibliography* labeled "doomed" leagues," those 19th and 20th century professional associations or leagues which either "died," or never actually began. Examples include the Players (Brotherhood) league of 1890 and the Federal League of 1914–1915. Entries

related to all-star teams are limited to teams encompassing all positions. All-Star teams of, say, pitchers are entered in the appropriate section of collective biography in Chapter F below.

1478. Acocella, Nicholas. *The Book of Baseball Lineups.* Secacus, N.J.: Carol Pub. Group, 1996. 192p.

1479. ____. and Donald Dewey. *The Greatest Team of All Time, as Selected by Baseball's Immortals from Ty Cobb to Willie Mays.* Holbrook, Mass.: B. Adams, 1994. 180p.

1480. Borges Fallas, Alberto A. *"Fran-*

chise Rules in the Context of Sports Leagues." Unpublished Ph.D. dissertation, Clemson University, 1992.

1481. Cannella, A. A. and W. G. Rowe. "Leader Capabilities, Succession, and Competitive Context: A Study of Professional Baseball Teams." *Leadership Quarterly,* VI (Spring 1995), 69–88.

1482. Chatterjee, Sangit and Mustafa Yelmaz. "Parity in Baseball: Stability of Evolving Systems?" *Chance,* IV (Summer 1991), 37+.

1483. Deacon, James. "Making Their Pitch: Jays and Expos, a Tale of Two Budgets." *Maclean's,* CX (March 31, 1997), 50–51.

1484. Dewey, Donald and Nicholas Acocella. *The Ball Clubs.* New York: HarperCollins, 1996. 604p. Revision of the next entry.

1485. ____. *Encyclopedia of Major League Baseball Teams.* New York: HarperCollins, 1993. 594p.

1486. Filichia, Peter. *Professional Baseball Franchises: From the Abbeville Athletics to the Zanesville Indians.* New York: Facts on File Publications, 1993. 290p.

1487. Fort, R. and J. Quirk. "Cross-Subsidization, Incentives, and Outcomes in Professional Team Sports Leagues." *Journal of Economic Literature,* XXIII (September 1995), 1265–1299.

1488. Fox, Stephen R. *Big Leagues: Professional Baseball, Football, and Basketball in National Memory.* New York: Morrow, 1994. 522p.

1489. Gaylord, J. O. and D. L. Groves. "Framework Development for Isolating the Important Factors in the Formation and Development of Professional Sports Leagues." *Journal of Hospitality & Leisure Marketing,* I (Fall 1993), 11–39.

1490. Hollingsworth, Harry. *The Best and Worst Baseball Teams of All Times.* New York: S. P. I. Books, 1994. 209p.

1491. Jamail, Milton. "Hispanic All-Star Team." *Hispanic,* (April 1989), 60+; (April 1990), 30+; (April 1991), 31+.

1492. James, Bill. "To Have and Have Not: For Now, Baseball's Wealthy Teams Have the Upper Hand—But History Has Shown That Champions Are Built with Brains, Not Bucks." *Inside Sports,* XVII (July 1995), 32–39.

1493. Jennison, Christopher. *Wait 'Til Next Year: The Yankees, Dodgers, and Giants of 1947–1957.* Mattituck, N.Y.: Amereon, 1994. 168p.

1494. Jones, Donald D. *Former Major League Teams: An Encyclopedia.* Jefferson, N.C.: McFarland & Co., Inc., 1995. 233p.

1495. La Blanc, Michael L. *Hotdogs, Heroes & Hooligans: The Story of Baseball's Major League Teams.* Detroit, Mich.: Visible Ink Press, 1994. 581p. Based on the next entry.

1496. ____. and Mary R. Ruby, eds. *Professional Sports Team Histories.* 4 vols. Detroit, Mich.: Gale Research, 1994.

1497. Markus, Robert. "For Expansion Teams, Agony Comes Before the Ecstasy." *Baseball Digest,* LII (April 1993), 58–64.

1498. McCarthy, John P., Jr. *Baseball's All-Time Dream Team.* Crozet, Va.: Betterway Books, 1994, 240p.

1499. Morgan, Bradley J., ed. *Sports Fan's Connection: An All-Sports-in-One Directory to Professional, Collegiate, and Olympic Teams, Leagues, Conferences, and Other Information.* 2nd ed. Detroit, Mich.: Gale Research, 1993.

1500. Nemec, David. *The Great American Baseball Team Book.* New York: Plume, 1992. 399p.

1501. Shaler, Mike. "The Greatest No-Place Teams; or, When the Regular Season Was Hard—Second-Place Teams That Won 100 Games." *Elysian Fields Quarterly,* XIV (Summer 1995), 38–53.

1502. Wright, Russell O. *The Best Teams, the Worst Teams: A Major League Baseball Statistical Reference, 1903–1994.* Jefferson, N.C.: McFarland & Co., Inc., 1995. 189p.

2. The American Association

1503. Mayer, H. C. "They Didn't Know How to Quit: Five Examples of Determination from the American Association." *Baseball Research Journal,* XXIV (1995), 150–152.

1504. Shipley, R. E. "Not Bad for a Beer League: Dusting Off the American Association for a Second Look." *National Pastime,* XV (1995), 55–58.

1505. Wright, Marshall D. *The American Association.* Jefferson, N.C.: McFarland & Co., Inc., 1997.

3. The National League

This part is broken into two main subsections. The first provides sources dealing with the N.L. in general since 1870 and the second provides, in alphabetical order by organization, material on the league's various teams, including those no longer extant. Information here should be compared with that in the following part on the American League.

a. General Works

The citations below concern the National League of Professional Baseball Clubs in general since the 1870s. In addition to history and administration, readers will also find information concerning specific teams, although the use of individual entries is necessary to determine just which ones. Additional general information on the N.L. will be found throughout the team histories below.

1506. Bjarkman, Peter C. "Introduction: Breaking Traditions in the Senior Circuit." In: his *Encyclopedia of Major League Baseball: National League— Team Histories.* Updated and rev. ed. New York: Carroll & Graf, 1993. pp. 1–19.

1507. ____. "The Myth of the Senior Circuit." *Dugout,* II (April 1994), 10–13.

1508. Harshman, Jack E. "In Search Of: The National League in New Eng-

land." *Elysian Fields Quarterly,* XIII (Fall 1994), 30–40. From the beginning to the departure of the Boston Braves.

1509. Vass, George. "A Long, Tough Road Ahead for Two New Expansion Teams." *Baseball Digest,* LI (August 1992), 32–38.

1510. Whitford, David. *Playing Hardball: The High-Stakes Battle for Baseball's New Franchises.* Garden City, N.Y.: Doubleday, 1993. 271p.

b. The Teams, Arranged Alphabetically

The references below are entered, alphabetically, under each National League city. To save space, the introductory historical material provided for each team in *Baseball: A Comprehensive Bibliography* is not updated here.

ATLANTA (N.L.)

1511. Atlanta Braves Staff. *From Home Plate to Home Cooking.* Atlanta, Ga.: PR Dept., Atlanta Braves, 1993. 110p.

1512. Ballew, Bill. "New Blood." *Beckett Focus on Future Stars,* IV, no. 39 (July 1994), 12–15.

1513. Caruso, Gary. *The Braves Encyclopedia.* Philadelphia, Pa.: Temple University Press, 1995. 624p.

1514. Hope, Bob. *We Could've Finished Last Without You: An Irreverent Look at the Atlanta Braves.* Atlanta, Ga.: Longstreet Press, 1991. 192p.

1515. Hosier, Stan. *The Atlanta Braves Album & Autograph Book.* Alpharetta, Ga.: Bookmark GA, 1992. 72p.

1516. Kindred, Dave. "Button Down Baseball." *Atlanta,* XXXI (April 1992), 27+.

1517. Klapisch, Bob. *Braves: An Illustrated History of America's Team.* Atlanta, Ga.: Turner Pub., 1995.

1518. ____. *World Champion Atlanta Braves, 1871–1995.* Atlanta, Ga.: Turner Pub., 1996.

1519. Kurkjian, Tim. "Living on Easy Streak." *Sports Illustrated,* LXXVII (August 3, 1992), 62–63.

1520. Lupica, Mike. "Meet the 'Atlanta Bills.'" *Esquire,* CXXI (April 1994), 71+.

1521. Mabe, Logan D. "Play Ball." *Atlanta,* XXXI (April 1992), 44–51.

1522. Rosenberg, I. J. *Bravo: The Inside Story of the Atlanta Braves, 1995.* Atlanta, Ga.: Longstreet Press, 1995.

1523. ____. "Still Delivering." *Beckett Baseball Card Monthly,* XI, no. 113 (August 1994), 10–13.

1524. ____. "Third Time's a Charm." *Beckett Baseball Card Monthly,* X, no. 98 (May 1993), 19–20.

1525. Rushin, Steve. "Last Shot." *Sports Illustrated,* LXXIX (October 4, 1994), 42–44. Race with San Francisco.

1526. Sink, Richard M., Skip Caray, and Pete Van Wieren. *Chop to the Top: A Behind-the-Scenes Look at the Team and Town That Turned Upside Down.* Cornelius, N.C.: Tomahawk Press, 1992. 336p.

1527. Thorn, John and Pete Palmer. *Total Braves.* New York: Viking Penguin, 1994. 224p.

1528. Toomey, Jim. "How Atlanta Braves Were Originally Cast in N.L. West Division." *Baseball Digest,* LIII (March 1994), 85–88.

1529. Verducci, Tom. "Better Than Ever." *Sports Illustrated,* LXXXVI (May 5, 1997), 32–34, 37.

1530. ____. "Double Trouble." *Sports Illustrated,* LXXIX (September 6, 1993), 26–29.

1531. ____. "Thank You, L.A., from Everyone in Atlanta." *Sports Illustrated,* LXXIX (October 11, 1979), 16–22. Division race won on final day of the season over S.F.

1532. Zack, Bill. *Tomahawked!: The Inside Story of the Atlanta Braves' Tumultuous Season.* New York: Simon and Schuster, 1993. 224p.

BOSTON (N.L.)

1533. Beverage, D. "A Forgotten Boston Pennant Race." *National Pastime,* XV (1995), 13–18.

1534. Buckley, Steve. "The Way They Were." *Boston,* LXXXV (August 1993), 100–107.

1535. Minichino, Camille. "Memoir: The Boston Braves." *Elysian Fields Quarterly,* XII (Summer 1993), 43–45.

BROOKLYN (N.L.)

1536. Cardello, Joseph. "September 16, 1930: The Return of the Daffiness Boys." *Elysian Fields Quarterly,* XIII (Winter 1994), 51–58.

1537. Chadwick, Bruce. *Dodgers: Memories and Memorabilia from Brooklyn to L.A.* New York: Abbeville Press, 1993. 132p.

1538. "The '47 Dodgers in Havana: Spring Training in 1947 Found Baseball at a Crossroads." In: Myles Friedman, ed. *Spring Training: Grapefruit and Cactus League Yearbook.* Chapel Hill, N.C.: Vanguard Publications, 1996. pp. 20–27.

1539. Neft, David S. *The Dodgers Trivia Book.* New York: St. Martin's Press, 1993.

1540. Powell, Larry. "Cal Abrams Recalls Play That Ruined Flag Hopes of Dodgers in 1950." *Baseball Digest,* LI (September 1992), 72–75.

1541. Prince, Carl E. *Brooklyn Dodgers: The Bums, the Borough, & the Neighborhood, 1947–1957.* New York: Oxford University Press, 1996. 224p.

1542. Roberts, Frederic M. "Dem Bums Become the Boys of Summer: From Comic Caricatures to Sacred Icons of the National Pastime." *American Jewish History,* LXXXIII (March 1995), 51–64.

1543. Rosenfeld, Harvey. *Great Chase: The Dodgers-Giants Pennant Race of 1951.* Jefferson, N.C.: McFarland & Co., Inc., 1992. 304p.

1544. Shailer, Kenneth. "Lords of Brooklyn." In: Tony Gervino, ed. *Hardball.* New York: Harris Pub. Co., 1997. pp. 80–83. 1955 club.

1545. Sparks, Barry. "'53 Dodgers Were

Tops in Run Superiority" *Baseball Digest,* LII (May 1993), 46–48.

1546. Wolpin, Stewart. *Bums No More: The Championship Season of the 1955 Brooklyn Dodgers.* New York: St. Martin's Press, 1995. 130p.

CHICAGO (N.L.)

1547. Berler, Ron. "The Forever Cursed." *Inside Sports,* XIV (October 1992), 70–73.

1548. Borden, Jeff. "Turning the Cubs Into a Cash Cow." *Crain's Chicago Business,* XIV (April 4, 1994), 3–5.

1549. Castle, George. "Fans Still Carry the Torch for Also-Ran '69 Cubs." *Baseball Digest,* LII (June 1993), 71–76.

1550. Chadwick, Bruce. *The Chicago Cubs: Memories & Memorabilia of the Wrigley Wonders.* New York: Abbeville Press, 1994. 132p.

1551. ____. *The Chicago Cubs Trivia Book.* New York: St. Martin's Press, 1994. 128p.

1552. Fulk, David. *The Cubs Companion: An All-Purpose Friend and Fan Book for the Fans Who Need It Most.* South Pasadena, Ca.: Keystone Communications, 1993.

1553. Golenbock, Peter. *Wrigleyville: A Magical History Tour of the Chicago Cubs.* New York: St. Martin's Press, 1996. 560p.

1554. Grossman, Ron. "Fifty Years Ago the Cubs Marched to Their Last N.L. Pennant." *Baseball Digest,* LIV (July 1995), 60–67.

1555. Holtzman, Jerome and George Vass. *The Chicago Cubs Encyclopedia.* Philadelphia, Pa.: Temple University Press, 1997.

1556. Lanford, Jim. *The Cub Fan's Little Book of Wisdom: 101 Truths Learned the Hard Way.* South Bend, Ind.: Diamond Communications, 1993. 101p.

1557. Montville, Leigh. "Fired Up Again." *Sports Illustrated,* LXXXII (June 5, 1995), 64–66. 71.

1558. Phalen, Rick. *Our Chicago Cubs: Inside the History and the Mystery of Baseball's Favorite Franchise.* South Bend, Ind.: Diamond Communications, 1992. 290p.

1559. Verducci, Tom. "Blown Away." *Sports Illustrated,* LXXXVI (April 14, 1997), 38–40+. Losing streak at the beginning of the '97 season.

CINCINNATI (N.L.)

1560. Bjarkman, Peter C. *The Reds.* New York: Gallery Books, 1991. 77p.

1561. Cardello, J. "The Parker Brothers and Other Cincinnati Oddities." *Baseball Research Journal,* XXIV (1995), 21–24.

1562. Chadwick, Bruce. *The Cincinnati Reds: Memories and Memorabilia of the Big Red Machine.* New York: Abbeville Press, 1994. 156p.

1563. Crothers, Tim. "Alas, the Poor Reds." *Sports Illustrated,* LXXXVI (May 5, 1997), 69+.

1564. Gershman, Michael. "The Big Red Machine." *Beckett Baseball Card Monthly,* IX, no. 88 (July 1992), 16–24. Team of the 1970s.

1565. Gietschier, Steven P. "They Beat the Black Sox: The 1919 Cincinnati Reds." *Timeline,* VIII (October– November 1991), 32–45.

1566. Honig, Donald. *The Cincinnati Reds: An Illustrated History.* New York: Prentice-Hall, 1992. 256p.

1567. Lidz, Franz. "Right Off the Bat." *Sports Illustrated,* LXXXII (June 12, 1995), 44–48.

1568. Melville, Tom. "Red Stockings at the Wicket." *Timeline,* XI (March– April 1994), 50–54.

1569. Reed, William F. "A Red Menance Once Again." *Sports Illustrated,* LXXVII (July 27, 1992), 26–29.

1570. Rhodes, Gregory L., John G. Erardi, and Jerry Dowling. *The First Boys of Summer: The 1869–1870 Cincinnati Red Stockings, Baseball's First Professional Team.* Cincinnati, Oh.: Road West Pub. Co., 1994. 144p.

1571. Ryan, Jeff. "The Big Red Machine." *Sport,* LXXXVI (May 1995), 85–86. 1976 team.

1572. Schnert, Chris W. *Cincinnati Reds.* Minneapolis, Minn.: Aldo & Daughters, 1996. 42p.

CLEVELAND (N.L.)

1573. Grabowski, John J. *Sports in Cleveland: An Illustrated History.* Encyclopedia of Cleveland History, v. 2. Bloomington, Ind.: Indiana University Press, 1992. 150p.

1574. Phillips, John. *Buck Ewing and the 1893 Spiders.* Cabin John, Md.: Capital Publishing Co., 1992. 100p.

1575. ____. *Cleveland Baseball: The 1894 Spiders.* Cabin John, Md.: Capital Publishing Co., 1991. 100p.

1576. ____. *The Spiders Who Was Who.* Cabin John, Md.: Capital Publishing Co., 1988. 100p.

COLORADO (N.L.)

1577. Cady, Lew. *They've Got Rockies in Their Heads: The Colorado Rockies' First Season...From the Fans' Point of View.* Denver, Colo.: Mile High Press, 1993. 253p.

1578. Clark, Nancy. "Lewis and Floorwax Pitch for Baseball." *Denver Magazine,* XXI (May 1991), 28+.

1579. Clarke, Norm. "Will Denver's Light Air Affect Big League Pitching?" *Baseball Digest,* LI (August 1992), 39–41.

1580. Corliss, Richard. "High on the Rockies." *Time,* CXLII (July 19, 1993), 55+.

1581. "Crazy Climate." In: Joe Hoppel, ed. *The Sporting News 1993 Baseball Yearbook.* St. Louis, Mo.: TSN, 1993. pp. 34–37.

1582. Gottlieb, Alan. *In the Shadow of the Rockies: An Outsider's Look Inside a New Major League Baseball Team.* Niwot, Colo.: Roberts Rinehart Pub., 1994. 249p.

1583. Hirdt, Steve. "A Newcomer's Guide." *Sports Illustrated,* LXXVIII (April 12, 1993), 40–41.

1584. Olkowski, Tom. "Moving Mountains; or, the Rockies Are Coming." *Elysian Fields Quarterly,* XI (Spring 1992), 64–66.

1585. Reed, K. B. *"The Major League Baseball Expansion Process: An Interpretive and Evaluative Case Study of Colorado's Acquisition of a National League Franchise."* Unpublished Ed.D. dissertation, University of Northern Colorado, 1995. 337p.

1586. Reilly, Rick. "Rocky Mountain Fever." *Sports Illustrated,* LXXVIII (June 14, 1993), 46–50, 52.

1587. Rothman, Howard. *All That Once Was Good: Inside America's National Pastime.* Denver, Colo.: Pendleton-Clay Publishers, 1995. 262p.

1588. Rundles, Jeff. "The Story Is Baseball." *Denver Corporate Connection,* VIII (November 1993), 10+.

1589. Rushin, Steve. "'Hello, My Name Is...'" *Sports Illustrated,* LXXVIII (March 8, 1993), 28–31.

1590. Verducci, Tom. "No Terrible Twos." *Sports Illustrated,* LXXX (May 23, 1994), 32–35.

1591. ____. "Rocky Mountain Home Run Fever." *Sports Illustrated,* LXXXIII (July 31, 1995), 28–30, 33.

FLORIDA (N.L.)

1592. Farber, Michael. "Deep Six." *Sports Illustrated,* LXXXV (December 23, 1996), 58–60+. Signing free agents.

1593. Hirdt, Steve. "A Newcomer's Guide." *Sports Illustrated,* LXXVIII (April 12, 1993), 40–41.

1594. Kalamut, A. R. "Marlins, Manatees & Miracles: Baseball in the Sunshine State." *Dugout,* III (April–May 1995), 17–20.

1595. Kuenster, Bob. "The Florida Marlins Are Armed for a Run at a Pennant." *Baseball Digest,* LVI (June 1997), 22–25.

1596. Kurkijan, Tim. "A New Big Fish."

Sports Illustrated, LXXXV (July 29, 1996), 100–101.

1597. McCarthy, Kevin. *Baseball in Florida.* Sarasota, Fla.: Pineapple Press, 1996. 262p.

1598. Recio, I. "The Marlins: Bases Loaded with Tie-ins." *Business Week,* (April 12, 1993), 68–69.

1599. Swift, E. M. "Paying Off." *Sports Illustrated,* LXXXVII (August 18, 1997), 32–39.

1600. Verducci, Tom. "No Terrible Twos." *Sports Illustrated,* LXXX (May 23, 1994), 32–35.

HOUSTON (N.L.)

1601. Crothers, Tim. "Working Overtime." *Sports Illustrated,* LXXXVI (May 12, 1997), 92+.

1602. Holtzman, Jerome. "'94 Astros Didn't Magically Become Contenders in the N.L." *Baseball Digest,* LIII (October 1994), 32–33.

1603. Kurkjian, Tim. "Houston Has a Problem." *Sports Illustrated,* LXXXV (September 2, 1996), 50, 52.

1604. Rushin, Steve. "If This Is Thursday..." *Sports Illustrated,* LXXVII (August 24, 1992), 42–42, 45–46.

1605. Sehnert, Chris W. *Houston Astros.* Minneapolis, Minn.: Abdo & Daughters, 1997. 42p.

LOS ANGELES (N.L.)

1606. Callahan, Gerry. "Flying Into First." *Sports Illustrated,* LXXXVII (September 8, 1997), 38–41.

1607. Chadwick, Bruce. *The Dodgers: Memories and Memorabilia from Brooklyn to Los Angeles.* New York: Abbeville Press, 1993. 132p.

1608. Crothers, Tim. "Not-So-Artful Dodgers." *Sports Illustrated,* LXXXVI (June 23, 1997), 72+.

1609. Deadly, Tim. "Dodgers Ticket Policy Spurs Suit." *Los Angeles Business Journal,* XVII (March 13, 1995), 1–2.

1610. Fimrite, Ron. "Dodger Blues."

Sports Illustrated, LXXVII (September 28, 1992), 18–21.

1611. Neft, David S. *Dodgers Trivia Book.* New York: St. Martin's Press, 1993. 100p.

1612. Rifkin, Alan. "Hang Time." *Los Angeles,* XL (May 1995), 32+.

1613. Sehnert, Chris W. *Los Angeles Dodgers.* Minneapolis, Minn.: Abdo & Daughters, 1997. 42p.

1614. Spatz, Lyle. "When Two Cy Young Pitchers Played in the Dodger Outfield." *Baseball Digest,* LV (May 1996), 41–43.

1615. Verducci, Tom. "Dodger Blues." *Sports Illustrated,* LXXXV (August 19, 1996), 38–43.

1616. ____. "Fashionably in First." *Sports Illustrated,* LXXX (May 30, 1994), 26–28+.

1617. Whiteside, Kelly. "Baseball Anonymous." *Sports Illustrated,* LXXXII (March 13, 1995), 28–31. Use of strike replacement players at Dodgertown during spring training.

1618. Young, Peter. "Bleeding Dodger Blue." In: Joe Hoppel, ed. *The Sporting News 1993 Baseball Yearbook.* St. Louis, Mo.: TSN, 1993. pp. 22–25. Reprinted in *Buzz,* IV (August 1993), 101+.

LOUISVILLE (N.L.)

1619. Bailey, B. "The Louisville Colonels of 1889." *National Pastime,* XIV (1994), 14–17.

1620. Von Borries, Philip. *Legends of Louisville: Major League Baseball in Louisville, 1876–1899.* West Bloomfield, Mich.: Altwerger and Mandel Pub. Co., 1993. 153p. The Louisville Colonels began as an American Association club.

MILWAUKEE (N.L.)

1621. Gendzel, Glen. "Competitive Boosterism: How Milwaukee Lost the Braves." *Business History Review,* LXIX (Winter 1995), 530–567.

MONTREAL (N.L.)

1622. Blair, Jeff. "Back from the Dead." *Maclean's,* CVI (September 27, 1993), 67+.

1623. Bjarkman, Peter C. "Bizarre Diamond Traditions North of the Border: 25 Years of the Montreal Expos." *Dugout,* II (August and October 1994), 16–20, 11–14.

1624. Deacon, James. "Play Ball!" *Maclean's,* CVII (April 11, 1994), 46–48.

1625. ____. "Small Markets, Big Bargains." *Maclean's,* CVIII (April 17, 1995), 62+.

1626. Doyle, Al. "Montreal Expos Succeed in the N.L. on a Limited Salary Budget." *Baseball Digest,* LV (December 1996), 58–61.

1627. Farber, Michael. "Exposed." *Sports Illustrated,* LXXXVI (June 30, 1997), 42–43.

1628. ____. "Stars Are Out." *Sports Illustrated,* LXXXII (April 17, 1995), 32, 35. Player purge.

1629. Gallagher, David. "Business Profile: Money Mayhem in Montreal." *Sports Canada Magazine,* I (February–March 1994), 28–30.

1630. Kurkijan, Tim. "Break Up the Expos." *Sports Illustrated,* LXXXIV (May 6, 1996), 70+.

NEW YORK GIANTS (N.L.)

1631. Chadwick, Bruce. *The Giants: Memories & Memorabilia from a Century of Baseball.* New York: Abbeville Press, 1993. 132p.

1632. Hardy, James D., Jr. *The New York Giants Baseball Club: The Growth of a Team and a Sport, 1870–1900.* Jefferson, N.C.: McFarland & Co., Inc., 1996. 272p.

1633. Hynd, Noel. *The Giants of the Polo Grounds: The Glorious Times of Baseball's New York Giants.* Dallas, Tx.: Taylor Pub. Co., 1996. 396p. Reprint of the 1988 Doubleday edition.

1634. Rosenfeld, Harvey. *Great Chase: The Dodgers-Giants Pennant Race of 1951.* Jefferson, N.C.: McFarland & Co., Inc., 1992. 304p.

1635. Whittingham, Richard. *Giants, in Their Own Words: New York Giant Greats Talk About the Team, the Game, the Coaches, and the Times of Their Lives.* Chicago, Ill.: Contemporary Books, 1992. 268p.

1636. Williams, Peter and W. P. Kinsella. *When the Giants Were Giants: Bill Terry and the Golden Age of New York Baseball.* Chapel Hill, N.C.: Algonquin Books of Chapel Hill, 1994. 331p.

1637. Zigler, Jack. "The Last Giants Game in the Polo Grounds." *Elysian Fields Quarterly,* XI (Spring 1992), 57–60.

NEW YORK METS (N.L.)

1638. Allen, Maury. "Amazin'." *Beckett Baseball Card Monthly,* XI, no. 115 (October 1994), 106–115. 1969 club.

1639. Ashburn, Richie. "The '62 Mets: The Best of the Worst." *Topps Magazine,* (Winter 1993), 66–68.

1640. Breslin, Jimmy. "The Worst Baseball Team Ever." *Sports Illustrated,* LXXX (May 30, 1994), 66–68+. Reprint from the 1962 issue.

1641. Chadwick, Burce. "Memories of Expansions Past." *Topps Magazine,* (Spring 1992), 16–17.

1642. Hersh, Hank. "Down-and-Out." *Sports Illustrated,* LXXVII (August 17, 1992), 80–83.

1643. Kalinsky, George. *The New York Mets: A Photographic History.* New York: Macmillan, 1995. 240p.

1644. Kaplan, David A. "Amazin' Disgrace." *Newsweek,* CXXII (July 5, 1964), 64+.

1645. Klapisch, Bob and John Harper. *The Worst Team Money Could Buy: The Collapse of the New York Mets.* New York: Random House, 1993.

1646. Kurkijan, Tim. "View from the Basement." *Sports Illustrated,* LXXX (April 4, 1994), 99+.

1647. Lichtenstein, Grace. "Runs, Hits, Eros: The Nets and the News-Sports Divide." *Columbia Journalism Review,* XXXII (May–June 1992), 22–23.

1648. Rushin, Steve. "Bad Beyond Belief." *Sports Illustrated,* LXXVI (May 25, 1992), 82–88, 90–92, 95.

1649. Sehnert, Chris W. *New York Mets.* Minneapolis, Minn.: Abdo & Daughters, 1997. 42p.

1650. Verducci, Tom. "The Amazing Collapse of the New York Mets." *Sports Illustrated,* LXXIX (December 20, 1993), 78–86+.

1651. ____. "Battle Weary." *Sports Illustrated,* LXXVIII (May 17, 1993), 40–42, 44.

PHILADELPHIA (N.L.)

1652. Alesii, Brenda and Dan Loccche. *Philadelphia Sports Quiz: Phillies, Athletics, Eagles, 76ers, Warriors, Flyers.* New York: Citadel Press, 1993.

1653. Beaton, Rod. "Phillies' Roster Made Up of Some Special Characters." *Baseball Digest,* LII (August 1993), 20–23.

1654. Buckley, Steve. "Wild Things." *Sport,* LXXXIV (September 1993), 65–67.

1655. Caroulis, Jon. "'96 Phillies, Only a Feeble Imitation of 'The Wild Bunch.'" *Baseball Digest,* LV (May 1996), 56–59.

1656. Hochman, Stan. *The Sports Book: Everything You Need to Be a Fan in Philadelphia.* New York: Pocket Books, 1996. 116p.

1657. Honig, Donald. *The Philadelphia Phillies: An Illustrated History.* New York: Prentice-Hall, 1992. 256p.

1658. Kurkjian, Tim. "A Flying Start." *Sports Illustrated,* LXXVIII (May 10, 1993), 22–24, 27.

1659. Merz, Andrew K. *Phillies Wit: Words of Wisdom from the Wild, Wacky, Wonderful '93 Phillies.* Swarthmore, Pa.: WIT Press, 1993. 100p.

1660. Orlando, Lou. *The Ultimate Phillies Trivia Quiz.* Villanova, Pa.: Rockford Associates, 1994. 55p.

1661. Roberts, Robin and C. Paul Rogers, 3d. *The Whiz Kids and the 1950 Pennant.* Philadelphia, Pa.: Temple University Press, 1996. 288p.

1662. Rossi, John. "Chico Ruiz and the Collapse of the '64 Phillies." *Elysian Fields Quarterly,* XIV (Spring 1995), 38–42.

1663. Westcott, Rich. *Phillies '93.* Philadelphia, Pa.: Temple University Press, 1994. 208p.

1664. ____. and Frank Bilovsky. *The New Phillies Encyclopedia.* Philadelphia, Pa.: Temple University Press, 1993. 800p.

1665. Wulf, Steve. "Don't Look Back...." *Sports Illustrated,* LXXIX (September 27, 1993), 22–24, 27.

PITTSBURGH (N.L.)

1666. Baker, S. "Angels in the Outfield: How Kevin McClatchy Kept the Pirates in Pittsburgh." *Business Week,* (December 18, 1995), 86–87.

1667. Doyle, Al. "How Low-Budget Pirates Surprised N.L. Opponents." *Baseball Digest,* LVI (December 1997), 66–71.

1668. Driver, David. "When the Pirates Fielded an All-Minority Team." *Baseball Digest,* LIV (September 1995), 80–82.

1669. Flowers, Kevin. "Former Pirates Recall '71 World Series Championship Season." *Baseball Digest,* LVI (October 1997), 72–79.

1670. Fulton, B. "Pittsburgh, 1887: Discord, Dissension, and Disaster." *National Pastime,* XV (1995), 146–148.

1671. Modeno, Bill. "Design for Winning." *Pittsburgh,* XXIV (December 1993), 26–27. Evolution of the Pirates logo.

1672. O'Brien, Jim. *Maz & the Sixty Bucks: When Pittsburgh and Its Pirates Went All the Way.* Pittsburgh, Pa.: J. P. O'Brien, 1993. 512p. 1960 season.

1673. Ruck, Rob. "Bye, Bye Baseball." *Pittsburgh,* XXIV (August 1993), 38–43. The team's economic difficulties.

1674. Rushin, Steve. "Rundown on the Pirates." *Sports Illustrated,* LXXVI (May 4, 1992), 20–23.

1675. Verducci, Tom. "What a Steal." *Sports Illustrated,* LXXXVI (June 16, 1997), 54–56, 58.

ST. LOUIS (N.L.)

1676. Beaton, Rod. "Cardinals' Outfield Blended Power and Speed in '96." *Baseball Digest,* LV (November 1996), 68–71.

1677. Boren, Stephen D. "The 1942 Pennant Race: The St. Louis Steamroller." *National Pastime,* XV (1995), 133–135.

1678. Chadwick, Bruce. *The St. Louis Cardinals: Over 100 Years of Baseball Memories and Memorabilia.* New York: Abbeville Press, 1995. 132p.

1679. Gottheilf, Josh. "Hot Seats: Cardinals Ticket Sales up 6%." *St. Louis Business Journal,* XVII (February 3, 1997), 1–2.

1680. Kramer, S. D. "Another Newspaper [*St. Louis Post Dispatch*] Buys Into a Baseball Team." *Editor & Publisher, the Fourth Estate,* CXXIX (January 6, 1996), 51+.

1681. Kurkijan, Tim. "New House of Cards." *Sports Illustrated,* LXXXIV (January 22, 1996), 54–55.

1682. Mead, Alden. "The Cardinals in the Forties: A Great Team That Could Have Been Even Greater." *Baseball Research Journal,* XXI (1992), 78–79.

1683. Rains, Rob. *The Cardinal Fan's Little Book of Wisdom.* South Bend, Ind.: Diamond Communications, 1994. 101p.

SAN DIEGO (N.L.)

1684. Baker, Kevin. "The Great San Diego Fire Sale." *Harper's,* CCLXXXVIII (April 1994), 72–73.

1685. Bloom, Barry M. "Mission Accomplished: The Padres Have Practiced Globalization Without the Help of Major League Baseball." *Sport,* LXXXVIII (September 1997), 46–49.

1686. King, Peter. "Padres Hit Parade." *Sports Illustrated,* LXXVI (June 15, 1992), 28–33.

1687. Kurkijan, Tim. "The Penny-Pinchin' Padres." *Sports Illustrated,* LXXVIII (March 29, 1993), 28–32.

1688. Verducci, Tom. "A New Fresh Start." *Sports Illustrated,* LXXXIV (February 26, 1996), 68–71.

SAN FRANCISCO (N.L.)

1689. Bamberger, Michael. "A Giant Question." *Sports Illustrated,* LXXXVI (May 12, 1997), 60–62, 67.

1690. Carrozzi, Craig J. *City Scapes and Giants' Capers.* San Francisco, Calif.: Southern Trails, 1991. 168p.

1691. Chadwick, Bruce. *The Giants: Memories & Memorabilia from a Century of Baseball.* New York: Abbeville Press, 1993. 132p.

1692. Dale, Myron L. and John Hunt. "Antitrust Law and Baseball Franchises: Leaving Your Heart (and the Giants) in San Francisco." *Northern Kentucky Law Review,* XX (Winter 1993), 337+.

1693. Hersch, Hank. "Tale of Four Cities: For Giants Fans in Two Bay Areas, It Is the Best of Times, It Is the Worst of Times." *Sports Illustrated,* LXXVII (August 24, 1992), 24–26, 31.

1694. Hession, Joseph. *Giants: The Collector's Edition.* San Francisco, Calif.: Foghorn Press, 1993. 221p.

1695. Kurkijan, Tim. "103, But It Wasn't to Be." *Sports Illustrated,* LXXIX (October 11, 1993), 20–21.

1696. Madden, Bill. "Giant Steps." *Sport,* LXXXV (June 1994), 54–58.

1697. Mitchell, Russell. "Take Me Out to the Valley?" *Business Week,* (October 12, 1992), 76–77. Threatened move.

1698. Peters, Nick and Martha Jane

Stanton. *Miracle at Candlestick!:
The Dramatic Story of the San
Francisco Giants' Amazing Summer
of '93—of a Season That Almost
Wasn't, a Team That Refused to Quit,
and a Turnaround That Captured
the Imagination of an Entire City.*
Atlanta, Ga.: Longstreet Press, 1993.
140p.

1699. Rushin, Steve. "Interest Bearing
Bonds." *Sports Illustrated,* LXXVIII
(April 26, 1993), 18–21.

1700. Tuckman, Michael. "Sliding
Home: The Inside Story of How
the Real Million-Dollar Players
Saved the San Francisco Giants." *California Lawyer,* XIII (April 1993),
34–42.

1701. Verducci, Tom. "Double Trouble."
Sports Illustrated, LXXIX (September 6, 1993), 26–29. Challenge from
Atlanta Braves.

TAMPA BAY (N.L.)

1702. Andelman, Bob. *Stadium for Rent:
Tampa Bay's Quest for Major League
Baseball.* Jefferson, N.C.: McFarland
& Co., Inc., 1993. 351p.

1703. "First USA Issuing Card for
Tampa Bay Devils." *American Banker,*
CLXII (June 2, 1997), 20+. Affinity
credit card in honor of the expansion
Tampa Bay Devil Rays.

1704. Herman, Bruce. "Baseball Breeding Ground." *Topps Magazine,* (Winter 1992), 62–65. Concerns local interest.

4. The American League

Entries provided here are broken into
two main sections. The first provides
sources dealing with the A.L. in general
since its founding in 1901. The second
gives, in alphabetical order by organization, material on the league's various
teams, including some no longer extant.
Information here should be compared
with that in the part above on the National
League.

a. General Works

The citations listed below concern the
American League of Professional Baseball Clubs in general since 1901. In addition to history and administration, readers will also find information concerning
specific teams, although the use of individual titles is necessary to determine just
which ones.

1705. Bjarkman, Peter C. "Introduction:
Historical Perspectives on the Junior
Circuit." In: his *Encyclopedia of
Major League Baseball: American
League—Team Histories.* Updated and
rev. ed. New York: Carroll & Graf,
1993. pp. 1–15.

1706. Singer, Tom. "Blueprint for Success: If the Marlins and Rockies
Want to Win Quick, the Blue Jays
and Royals Can Provide Tips." *Sport,*
LXXXIV (May 1993), 54–55.

1707. Verducci, Tom. "A Disgrace of a
Race." *Sports Illustrated,* LXXX (May
9, 1994), 34–36+. 1994 A.L. West.

1708. ____. "Trading Places." *Sports
Illustrated,* LXXXV (July 8, 1996),
20–25. Team chemistry of New York
and Baltimore in 1996.

1709. Wulf, Steve. "The A.L. Feast."
Sports Illustrated, LXXIX (August 9,
1993), 12–19. Seeing ten A.L. games
in a week.

b. The Teams,
Arranged Alphabetically

The references below are entered,
alphabetically, under each American
League city. To save space, the introductory historical material provided for each
team in *Baseball: A Comprehensive Bibliography* is not updated here.

ANAHEIM (A.L.)

1710. Crothers, Tim. "Earning Their
Wings." *Sports Illustrated,* LXXXVII
(July 28, 1997), 65–66. See also California (A.L.), below.

BALTIMORE (A.L.)

1711. Alesii, Brenda and Daniel Locche. *Washington-Baltimore Sports Quiz: Colts, Redskins, Senators, Orioles, Capitals.* New York: Carol Publishing Group, 1993.

1712. Callahan, Gerry. "In Flight." *Sports Illustrated,* LXXXVI (May 19, 1997), 46–49, 52.

1713. Chadwick, Bruce. *Baltimore Orioles: Memories & Memorabilia of the Lords of Baltimore.* New York: Abbeville Press, 1995. 132p.

1714. Ey, Craig S. "Playoffs Would Spark Economic Home Run." *Baltimore Business Journal,* XIV (September 27, 1996), 1–2.

1715. Kurkjian, Tim. "As Good as Advertised." *Sports Illustrated,* LXXXIV (April 22, 1996), 48–49.

1716. ____. "Birds of Prey." *Sports Illustrated Canada,* I (April 5, 1993), 58–62, 64.

1717. ____. "Slip Slidin' Away." *Sports Illustrated,* LXXVII (September 21, 1992), 30–32.

1718. "1954–1994: 40 Years of Orioles Memories." In: Bob Brown, ed. *The 1996 Official Yearbook of the Baltimore Orioles.* Baltimore, Md.: Public Relations Dept., Baltimore Orioles, 1996. pp. 54–85.

1719. Patterson, Ted. *The Baltimore Orioles: 40 Years of Magic from 33rd St. to Camden Yards.* Dallas, Tx.: Taylor, 1994. 248p.

1720. Pugh, David and Linda Geeson. *The Book of Baltimore Orioles Lists.* Baltimore, Md.: American Literary Press, 1993. 144p.

1721. Rushin, Steve. "Watch the Birdies." *Sports Illustrated,* LXXIX (September 20, 1993), 38–41.

BOSTON (A.L.)

1722. Buckley, Steve. "What's Wrong with the Red Sox?" *Sport,* LXXXIV (March 1993), 46–48+.

1723. Carney, William J. "Fast Start Boosted Hopes for Red Sox Revival." *Baseball Digest,* LIV (September 1995), 20–23. In 1995.

1724. Chadwick, Bruce. *Boston Red Sox: Memories & Memorabilia of New England's Team.* New York: Abbeville Press, 1992 132p.

1725. Dramin, E. "The 1950 Boston Red Sox: When Great Hitting Wasn't Enough." *National Pastime,* XIV (1994), 90–93.

1726. Kurkjian, Tim. "Mo Town." *Sports Illustrated,* LXXIX (August 2, 1993), 14–19.

1727. ____. "They'll Run, But Can't Hide." *Sports Illustrated,* LXXX (April 4, 1994), 120+.

1728. Neft, David S. *Boston Red Sox Trivia Book.* New York: St. Martin's Press, 1993. 100p.

1729. Reynolds, Bill. *Lost Summer: The '67 Red Sox and the Impossible Dream.* New York: Warner Books, 1992. 293p.

1730. Roderick, Stephen. "The October Surprise." *Boston,* LXXXVII (October 1995), 59+. Boston appearances in the World Series.

1731. Scoggins, Charlie. "BoSox Fans at Long Last Will See Some Speed on Basepaths." *Baseball Digest,* LIII (May 1994), 48–50.

1732. Shaughnessy, Dan. *At Fenway: Dispatches from the Red Sox Nation.* New York: Crown, 1996. 241p.

1733. Smith, Curt. *The Red Sox Fan's Little Book of Wisdom.* South Bend, Ind.: Diamond Communications, 1994.

1734. Verducci, Tom. "Bumble Sox." *Sports Illustrated,* LXXXIV (April 29, 1996), 24–29.

1735. ____. "Going All Out." *Sports Illustrated,* LXXXII (June 19, 1995), 56–58, 60.

CALIFORNIA (A.L.)

1736. Bisheff, Steve. "Earning Their Wings in Anaheim." *Inside Sports,* XV (August 1993), 66–69.

1737. Cole, Jack. *California Angels.* Minneapolis, Minn.: Abdo & Daughters Pub., 1997. 35p.

1738. Fimrite, Ron. "Hell-Raisers in Halos." *Sports Illustrated,* LXXIX (July 19, 1993), 46–57. 1961 club.

1739. ____. "Introducing the Bat Boys." *Sports Illustrated,* LXXVIII (March 15, 1993), 30–33. Dependence on young players.

1740. Kurkijan, Tim. "Vanishing Act." *Sports Illustrated,* LXXXIII (October 2, 1995), 22–26.

1741. Ryan, Bob. "Angels' Outfield Ranks with Best in the Big Leagues." *Baseball Digest,* LV (March 1996), 50–53.

CLEVELAND (A.L.)

1742. Alexander, Charles C. "The 'Cry Baby' Cleveland Indians of 1940." *Nine: A Journal of Baseball History and Social Policy Perspective,* V (Fall 1996), 1–17.

1743. *Akron Beacon Journal,* Editors of. *No. 1 in Our Hearts: The Cleveland Indians, 1995 American League Champions.* Akron, Oh., 1995. 61p.

1744. Boynton, B. "One Team, Two Fields." *National Pastime,* XV (1995), 51–54.

1745. Crothers, Tim. "Full House." *Sports Illustrated,* LXXXIII (July 10, 1995), 24–30.

1746. ____. "Tribe's Tribulations." *Sports Illustrated,* LXXXVII (August 25, 1997), 40, 42.

1747. Dudley, Bruce. *Bittersweet Season: The 1954 Cleveland Indians Revisited.* Annapolis, Md.: Dudley, 1995. 97p.

1748. ____. "The Day [in 1954] the Indians Pocketed a Pennant." *National Pastime,* XIV (1994), 72–73.

1749. ____. *Distant Drums: The 1949 Cleveland Indians Revisited.* Bowie, Md.: Dudley, 1989. 107p.

1750. Glassman, Brian A. "The Zygotes of Summer." *Elysian Fields Quarterly,* XII (Summer 1993), 70–72.

1751. Grabowski, John J. *Sports in Cleveland: An Illustrated History.* Encyclopedia of Cleveland History, v. 2. Bloomington, Ind.: Indiana University Press, 1992. 150p.

1752. Grosshandler, Stanley. "'54 Indians: Their Pitching Staff Was One of the Best Ever." *Baseball Digest,* LIII (May 1994), 58–62.

1753. Hodermarsky, Mark. *The Cleveland Sports Legacy, 1900–1945.* Cleveland, Oh.: Cleveland Landmarks Press, 1992. 109p.

1754. Hoynes, Paul. "Future of the Indians Tied to a Trio of Young Stars." *Baseball Digest,* LIII (July 1994), 22–25.

1755. Johnson, P. M. "Awake by the Lake." *Sport,* LXXXVI (November 1995), 86+.

1756. Keating, W. D. "Cleveland: The 'Comeback City.'" In: M. Lauria, ed. *Reconstructing Urban Regime Theory: Regulating Urban Politics in a Global Economy.* Thousand Oaks, Calif.: Sage Publications, 1997. pp. 189–205.

1757. Kelly, Thomas. *The Summer of '54.* N.p.: Vista Books, 1994. 110p.

1758. ____. and Marc Jaffe. *The Summer of '95.* N.p.: Archives Books, 1995. 169p.

1759. Kuenster, John. "Indians Were a Model of Consistency in Winning A.L. Central Division." *Baseball Digest,* LIV (December 1995), 17–19.

1760. Kurkijan, Tim. "Improved Indian: A Hot Indians Summer." *Sports Illustrated,* LXXXV (September 2, 1996), 52+.

1761. ____. "Tightening the Bond." *Sports Illustrated,* LXXVIII (April 5, 1993), 76–77. As a result of the deaths of pitchers Tim Crews and Steve Olin in a boating accident.

1762. McNichol, Tom. "Here's Hoping." *USA Weekend,* (April 3, 1992), 4–6.

1763. Plummer, W. "A Darkened Spring." *People Weekly,* XXXIX (April 5, 1993), 45–46.

1764. Phillips, John. *The Championship*

Indians of '95. Cabin John, Med.: Capital Publishing Co., 1996. 91p.

1765. ____. *Cleveland Baseball Transactions of the 1990s.* Cabin John, Md.: Capital Publishing Co., 1996. 71p.

1766. ____. *Cleveland Baseball: Who Was Who in 1911–19.* Cabin John, Md.: Capital Publishing Co., 1990. 100p.

1767. ____. *Cleveland Baseball: Who Was Who in the Twenties.* Cabin John, Md.: Capital Publishing Co., 1990. 100p.

1768. ____. *The Crybaby Indians of 1940.* Cabin John, Md.: Capital Publishing Co., 1990. 100p.

1769. ____. *The 1945 Indians.* Cabin John, Md.: Capital Publishing Co., 1992. 100p.

1770. ____. *The 1946 Indians.* Cabin John, Md.: Capital Publishing Co., 1993. 100p.

1771. ____. *The 1947 Indians.* Cabin John, Md.: Capital Publishing Co., 1994. 100p.

1772. ____. *Remember When?: 57 Unforgettable Games Played by Cleveland's Major League Teams.* Cabin John, Md.: Capital Publishing Co., 1993. 72p.

1773. ____. *Who Was Who in Cleveland Baseball, 1901–10.* Cabin John, Md.: Capital Publishing Co., 1989. 100p.

1774. Pluto, Terry. *Burying the Curse: How the Indians Became the Best Team in Baseball.* Akron, Oh.: Beacon Journal Press, 1995. 179p.

1775. ____. *The Curse of Rocky Colavito: A Loving Look at a Thirty-Year Slump.* New York: Simon and Schuster, 1994. 300p.

1776. Powers, Lindy. *The Cleveland Indians: A Family Album.* Hartford, Conn.: MDI Publications, 1996. 117p.

1777. "Pushovers Are Pushing Back." In: Joe Hoppel, ed. *The Sporting News 1993 Baseball Yearbook.* St. Louis, Mo.: TSN, 1993. pp. 26–29.

1778. Rogan, Mike. *Cleveland Indians '93.* New York: Bantam Books, 1993. 40p.

1779. Rogers, Mike. *Inside Pitch: Cleveland Indians '93.* New York: Bantam Books, 1993. 40p.

1780. Ryan, Jeff. "Laughing Matters." *Inside Sports,* XVI (March 1994), 61–65.

1781. Sailsbury, Luke. *The Cleveland Indians: The Legend of King Saturday.* Urbana, Ohio.: Smith Pub., 1992. 288p.

1782. Schneider, Russell J. *The Cleveland Indians Encyclopedia.* Philadelphia, Pa.: Temple University Press, 1996. 574p.

1783. ____. *The Glorious Indian Summer of 1995: When a Season of Dreams Became Reality in Cleveland.* Cleveland, Oh.: Russell Schneider Enterprises, 1995. 259p.

1784. Smith, Gary. "The Ripples from Lake Little." *Sports Illustrated,* LXXIX (July 12, 1993), 18–28+. Effects of the deaths of pitchers Steve Olin and Tim Crews on the team's 1993 season.

1785. Thorn, John, *et al.,* eds. *Total Indians.* New York: Penguin Books, 1996. 224p.

1786. Tomsic, Tony. "Indian Summer." *Cleveland,* XXIV (October 1995), 56–63. 1995 season.

1787. Torry, Jack. *Endless Summers: The Fall and Rise of the Cleveland Indians.* South Bend, Ind.: Diamond Communications, 1995. 303p.

1788. Vass, George. "Cleveland Indians' Lineup Matches Well with the Game's Best." *Baseball Digest,* LIV (September 1995), 24–33.

1789. Verducci, Tom. "Good Home Cookin'" *Sports Illustrated,* LXXXI (July 4, 1994), 28–31.

1790. ____. "Tag Team." *Sports Illustrated,* LXXXV (September 23, 1996), 40–43.

1791. Wiley, George T. *Especially for Cleveland Fans: The 1948 Indians Remembered—A Research Presentation for the Society for American*

Baseball Research. Minneapolis, Minn.: SABR, 1988. Unpaged.

1792. _____. *One Wall and 357 Doubles: The Story of the 1936 Cleveland Indians.* Cleveland, Oh.: Society for American Baseball Research, 1990. Unpaged.

1793. _____. *World's Champion Cleveland Indians, 1920: Selection of Material.* Indiana, Pa.: Priv. pub., 1993. Unpaged.

1794. Wulf, Steve. "It Might Be an Indian Summer." *Time,* CXLVI (July 3, 1995), 48+.

CHICAGO (A.L.)

1795. Devine, J. R. "Baseball's Labor Wars in Historical Context: The 1919 Chicago White Sox as a Case Study in Owner-Player Relations." *Marquette Sports Law Journal,* V (Fall 1994), 1–82.

1796. Farmer, T. "The 1910 White Sox: Hard Times on the South Side." *Baseball Research Journal,* XXIV (1995), 76–78.

1797. Ginneti, Toni. "White Sox Future Bolstered by Young Starters." *Baseball Digest,* LIII (May 1994), 33–35.

1798. Linberg, Richard. *Stealing First in a Two-Team Town: The White Sox from Comiskey to Reinsdorf.* Champaign, Ill.: Sagamore Publications, 1994. 275p.

1799. _____. *The White Sox Encyclopedia.* Philadelphia, Pa.: Temple University Press, 1996. 1,344p.

1800. Stolfa, Ellen. "Baseball 101: Souvenir of Chicago." *Elysian Fields Quarterly,* XII (Summer 1993), 45–48.

1801. Verducci, Tom. "Pop Guns." *Sports Illustrated,* LXXXVI (April 28, 1997), 42–43.

1802. _____. "Quittin' Time." *Sports Illustrated,* LXXXVII (August 11, 1997), 30–35.

1803. Whittingham, Dick. *White Sox: An Illustrated History.* Chicago, Ill.: Quality Sports Publications, 1997. 204p.

DETROIT (A.L.)

1804. Anderson, William M. "They Caught Lightning: The 1968 Detroit Tigers." *Michigan History,* LXXVII (September–October 1993), 17–23.

1805. Callahan, Gerry. "Armed and Dangerous." *Sports Illustrated,* LXXXIV (June 3, 1996), 46–49.

1806. Cantor, George. *The Tigers of '68: Baseball's Last Real Champions.* Dallas, Tx.: Taylor Publishing Co., 1997. 225p.

1807. Crothers, Tim. "Groundwork." *Sports Illustrated,* LXXXII (April 24, 1995), 28–30, 35.

1808. "The Day the Tigers Played Like Kittens." *Good Old Days,* XXX (May 1993), 27+.

1809. Harrigan, Patrick J. *The Detroit Tigers: Club and Community, 1945–1995.* Toronto, Ont.: University of Toronto Press, 1997. 415p.

1810. Okkonen, Marc. "The 1950 Detroit Tigers." *National Pastime,* XV (1995), 154–156.

1811. Verducci, Tom. "It's a Blast." *Sports Illustrated,* LXXVIII (May 31, 1993), 18–24.

KANSAS CITY (A.L.)

1812. Cameron, Steve. *Moments, Memories, and Miracles: A Quarter Century with the Kansas City Royals.* Dallas, Tx.: Taylor, 1993. 230p.

1813. Carothers, Tim. "Royal Improvement." *Sports Illustrated,* LXXXVI (May 26, 1997), 85–86.

1814. Dixon, Phil S. *The Ultimate Kansas City Baseball Quiz Book: Royals, Monarchs, Blues, Athletics, & More.* Shawnee Mission, Ks.: Bon a Tier Publications, 1992.

1815. Eskew, Alan. "A Magical [1985] Season Remembered." In: Kansas City Royals. *The Kansas City Royals 1995 Yearbook.* Kansas City, Mo., 1995. pp. 57–60.

1816. Hodur, Myron Sony. "Ball Four: The IRS Walks for Kansas City

Royals." *Hastings Communications and Entertainment Law Journal,* XIX (Winter 1997), 483–516.

1817. Kaegel, Dick. "Delights of Train Travel Sampled by the Royals in '97." *Baseball Digest,* LVI (December 1997), 78–81.

1818. "The Kansas City Royals: A Salute to the Past 25 Years." In: Kansas City Royals. *The Kansas City Royals 1993 Yearbook.* Kansas City, Mo.: 1993. pp. 51–65.

1819. Murphy, Austin. "Royally Confused." *Sports Illustrated,* LXXVI (April 20, 1992), 32–35.

1820. Newkirk, Stephanie. "Foundation's Ownership of Professional Baseball Team Is Fair Play Under I.R.C. Section 501(c)(3)." *UMKC Law Review,* LXV (Winter 1996), 263–302.

1821. Sheppard, Lee A. "The Kansas City Royals: Populists Defend Their Game." *Tax Notes,* LXI (October 11, 1993), 151–152.

MILWAUKEE (A.L.)

1822. Crothers, Tim. "Something's Brewing." *Sports Illustrated,* LXXXVII (August 11, 1997), 84, 86.

MINNESOTA (A.L.)

1823. DeLand, Dave. "Minnesota Marvels." *Beckett Baseball Card Monthly,* X, no. 93 (March 1993), 100–101.

1824. Robson, Britt. "To Baseball Born." *Minneapolis,* XXI (April 1993), 58+.

1825. Rushin, Steve. "Northern Exposure." *Sports Illustrated,* LXXVI (January 20, 1992), 62–68, 70. On prowess of Minnesota teams.

1826. Wulf, Steve. "Sunk in the Central." *Sports Illustrated,* LXXX (April 4, 1994), 127+.

NEW YORK (A.L.)

1827. Angell, Roger. "Fans Love Yanks." *The New Yorker,* LXXII (November 11, 1996), 5–6.

1828. Bai, Matt. "Yankee Imperialism." *New York,* XXVII (July 25, 1994), 30–35.

1829. Bashe, Phil. *Dog Days: The New York Yankees Fall from Grace & Eventual Redemption.* Indianapolis, Ind.: Random House, 1994.

1830. Callahan, Gerry. "Rebirth in the Bronx." *Sports Illustrated,* LXXXIII (August 14, 1995), 44–48.

1831. Capezzuto, Tom. "Yankees of Old Had Power, But Also Tight Defense." *Baseball Digest,* LII (December 1993), 66–69.

1832. Chadwick, Bruce. *Bronx Bombers: Memories & Memorabilia of the New York Yankees.* New York: Abbeville Press, 1992. 132p.

1833. Curry, Jack. "Pettitte James' Yankee Legends." In: Zander Hollander, ed. *The Complete Book of Baseball '97.* New York: Signet, 1997. pp. 16–23.

1834. Debs, Vic. *They Kept Me Loyal to the Yankees.* Nashville, Tenn.: Rutledge Hill Press, 1993. 160p.

1835. Delavan, John, ed. *New York: 1996 American League Champions.* Northbrook, Ill.: H & S Media, 1996. 80p.

1836. ____. *1996 World Series Champions: New York Yankees.* Northbrook, Ill.: H & S Media, 1996. 80p.

1837. Espada, Pedro, Jr. *Into the 21st Century: Preserving the Yankee Legacy in the Bronx—Report.* Albany, N.Y.: New York (State) Legislature, Senate, 1993. 16p.

1838. "Fifty Years of Old Timers Days." In: Gregg Mazzola, ed. *Yankees 1996 Yearbook.* New York: Yankees Magazine, 1996. pp. 68–69.

1839. Fischer, David. "Destiny Starts with Momentum." In: Gregg Mazzola, ed. *Yankees 1997 Yearbook.* New York: Yankees Magazine, 1997. pp. 8–13.

1840. Frommer, Harvey. *The New York Yankees Encyclopedia: The Complete Record of Yankee Baseball.* New York: Macmillan, 1997.

1841. Gallagher, Mark. *The Yankee*

Encyclopedia. 2nd ed. Champaign, Ill.: Sagamore Press, 1996. 535p.

1842. Gilbert, Thomas W. *Damn Yankees: Casey, Whitey, Yogi and the Mick.* New York: Franklin Watts, 1997.

1843. Harwell, Ernie. "Some Myths About the Mighty '27 Yankees Dispelled." *Baseball Digest,* LII (November 1993), 70–72.

1844. Henrich, Tommy. *Five O'Clock Lightning: Ruth, Gehrig, DiMaggio, Mantle, and the Glory Years of the New York Yankees.* New York: Carol Publishing Group, 1992. 298p.

1845. James, Bill. "New York, New York." *Inside Sports,* XIX (January 1997), 44–49.

1846. "A Legacy of Champions." In: Gregg Mazzola, ed. *Yankees 1994 Yearbook.* New York: Yankees Magazine, 1994. pp. 16–23.

1847. Mercurio, John. *New York Yankee Records: A Year-by-Year Collection of Baseball Stats & Stories.* Canton, Mo.: Sure Seller, 1993. 104p.

1848. "The 1977 Yankees." In: Gregg Mazzola, ed. *Yankees 1992 Yearbook.* New York: Yankees Magazine, 1992. pp. 80–89.

1849. Pepe, Phil. *New York Yankees.* Dallas, Tx.: Taylor, 1995. 240p.

1850. Rizzuto, Phil and Tom Horton. *The October Twelve.* New York: Forge NYC, 1995. 320p.

1851. "Seventy Years of Magic and Memories in the Bronx." In: Gregg Mazzola, ed. *Yankees 1993 Yearbook.* New York: Yankees Magazine, 1993. pp. 72–81.

1852. Smith, C. S. "Winning Isn't Everything." *New York,* XXIX (November 11, 1996), 50–55.

1853. Sullivan, George and John Powers. *The Yankees: An Illustrated History.* Philadelphia, Pa.: Temple University Press, 1997.

1854. Trachtenberg, Leo. *The Wonder Team: The True Story of the Incomparable 1927 New York Yankees.* Bowling Green, Oh.: Bowling Green State University Press, 1995.

1855. Verducci, Tom. "Bright Spot." *Sports Illustrated,* LXXXV (September 2, 1996), 36–38, 46. Retooled in second half of '96 season.

1856. Ward, Geoffrey C. and Ken Burns. "The Capital of Baseball." *U.S. News & World Report,* CXVII (August 29, 1994), 90+.

1857. Wright, R. O. "Which Yankee Teams Were Best?: Not the Babe's." *Baseball Research Journal,* XXIV (1995), 62–65.

OAKLAND (A.L.)

1858. Castle, George. "The 1974 Oakland Athletics." *Sport,* LXXXVI (September 1995), 108–109.

1859. Kroichick, Ron. "The As Last Stand." *Sport,* LXXXIII (October 1992), 72–75. Financial problems.

1860. Kurkjian, Tim. "A's OK." *Sports Illustrated,* LXXVI (April 27, 1992), 14–19.

PHILADELPHIA (A.L.)

1861. Caroulis, John. "When the A's Said Goodbye to Philly." *Baseball Digest,* LIII (October 1994), 59–62.

1862. Nack, William. "Lost in History: From 1929 to '31, the Philadelphia A's Bested Babe Ruth's Yankees, But Few Have Heard of Them." *Sports Illustrated,* LXXXV (August 19, 1996), 74–85.

1863. Orr, Jack. "The Worst Team of All." In: Charles Einstein, ed. *The New Baseball Reader: An All-Star Lineup from the Fireside Book of Baseball.* New York: Penguin, 1992. pp. 284–285. The 1916 club.

ST. LOUIS (A.L.)

1864. Borst, William A. *Still Last in the American League: The St. Louis Browns Revisited.* Birmingham, Ala.: A & M Pub. Co., 1992. 136p.

1865. ____. and Erv Fischer. *A Jockstrap Full of Nails: A Cornucopia of St.*

Louis Browns History and Trivia. St. Louis, Mo.: St. Louis Browns Historical Society, 1992. 133p.

1866. Francis, Jack. "Flashback: When the Browns Bid Farewell to St. Louis." *Baseball Digest,* LII (November 1993), 67–69.

1867. Kashatus, Bill. "A Season in the Sun." *Gateway Heritage,* XII (Summer 1991), 38+. 1944.

1868. Van Lindt, Carson. *One Championship Season: The Story of the 1944 St. Louis Browns.* New York: Marabou Pub., 1994. 180p.

SEATTLE MARINERS (A.L.)

1869. Baker, M. Sharon. "Winning Ways Help Narrow Financial Losses: Popular Club Packs 'Em In, Still Faces Big Cash Demands." *Puget Sound Business Journal,* XVII (April 4, 1997), 2–3.

1870. Caroulis, Jon. "'Other Guys' Vital to Seattle Mariners Besides Club's Superstars." *Baseball Digest,* LVI (October 1997), 68–71.

1871. Jackson, Scoop. "Midnight Marauders." In: Tony Gervino, ed. *Hardball.* New York: Harris Pub. Co., 1997. pp. 76–79.

1872. Thiel, Art. *Magic Season.* Seattle, Wash.: *Seattle Post,* 1995. 100p. Covers 1995 through the ALCS.

1873. Verducci, Tom. "Marinermania." *Sports Illustrated,* LXXXIV (February 5, 1996), 78–82, 84, 87–88, 90–91.

1874. ____. "Midnight Madness." *Sports Illustrated,* LXXXVII (August 11, 1997), 38–39.

SEATTLE PILOTS (A.L.)

1875. Van Lindt, Carson. *The Seattle Pilots Story.* New York: Marabou Pub., 1993. 220p.

TEXAS (A.L.)

1876. Callahan, Gerry. "Home on the Range." *Sports Illustrated,* LXXXV (September 9, 1996), 28–30, 35.

1877. Kurkijan, Tim. "Lone Star Fear." *Sports Illustrated,* LXIII (September 4, 1995), 35–36.

1878. ____. "Special Delivery in Texas." *Sports Illustrated,* LXXXIV (June 24, 1996), 63–64.

1879. Nadel, Eric. *The Texas Rangers: The Authorized History.* Dallas, Tx.: Taylor, 1997. 256p.

1880. "Retired Numbers." In: John Blake, *et al. Texas Rangers 1996 Yearbook.* Arlington, Tx.: Public Relations Dept., Texas Rangers, 1996. pp. 49–67.

1881. Shropshire, Mike. *Seasons in Hell: With Billy Martin, Whitey Herzog, and the Worst Baseball Team in History, the 1973–1975 Texas Rangers.* New York: Donald I. Fine, 1996. 241p.

1882. ____. "Take Me Out to the Boneyard." *Sports Illustrated,* LXXXV (September 23, 1996), 60–68, 71.

1883. Sims, Ken. "20 Years in Texas." In: John Blake, *et al. 1991 Texas Rangers Yearbook.* Arlington, Tex.: Public Relations Dept., Texas Rangers, 1991. pp. 4–9.

TORONTO (A.L.)

1884. Cashman, Frank E. and Russel Gilbert. "Blue Jay Mania." *Canadian Journal of Psychiatry,* XXXVIII (May 1993), 299–300.

1885. Deacon, James. "Play Ball!" *Maclean's,* CVII (April 11, 1994), 46–48.

1886. DiManno, Rosie. *Glory Jays: Canada's World Series Champions.* Champaign, Ill.: Sagamore Pubns., 1993. 300p.

1887. Fulk, David, ed. *A Blue Jays Companion: Thirty-Two Top Writers Expound on the History, Heroes, Heartbreaks & Triumphs of "Canada's Team."* South Pasadena, Calif.: Keystone Communications, 1994. 224p.

1888. Hersch, Hank. "Reeling and Dealing and Lots of Stealing." *Sports*

Illustrated, LXXVII (September 7, 1992), 10–12.

1889. Italia, Bob. *Baseball Champions, 1993: The Toronto Blue Jays.* Minneapolis, Minn.: Abdo & Daughters, 1993. 42p.

1890. ____. *Baseball Champions, 1994: The Toronto Blue Jays.* Minneapolis, Minn.: Abdo & Daughters, 1994. 42p.

1891. Kingwell, M. "The Toronto Blue Jays: Colonialism, Civility, and the Idea of a National Team." *Nine: A Journal of Baseball History and Social Policy Perspective,* II (Spring 1994), 209–232.

1892. Kurkijan, Tim. "The Blue Days." *Sports Illustrated,* LXXXI (July 11, 1994), 54–56+.

1893. ____. "Ready to Leap?" *Sports Illustrated,* LXXXIII (August 14, 1995), 58, 60.

1894. Madden, Bill. "Coming to America?" *Sport,* LXXXV (May 1994), 44–46+. Teams which could prevent the Blue Jays' repeat as A.L. champ.

1895. Milton, Steve. "See You in October." *Beckett Baseball Card Monthly,* X, no. 98 (May 1993), 18–19.

1896. Verducci, Tom. "Truly Foul." *Sports Illustrated,* LXXXVII (July 21, 1997), 90–95.

1897. Wulf, Steve. "The Blue Jay Way." *Sports Illustrated,* LXXVII (November 2, 1992), 28, 31.

WASHINGTON (A.L.)

1898. Alesii, Brenda and Daniel Locche. *Washington-Baltimore Sports Quiz: Colts, Redskins, Senators, Orioles, Capitals.* New York: Carol Publishing Group, 1993.

5. The Minor Leagues

a. General Works

1899. Acton, Jay and Nick Bakalar. *Green Diamonds: The Pleasures and Profits of Investing in Minor League Baseball.* New York: Kensington Pub. Corp., 1993. 214p.

1900. Adelson, Bruce, *et al. The Minor League Baseball Book.* New York: Macmillan, 1995. 255p.

1901. Arthur, A. T. and J. J. Siegried. "Minor League Baseball and Local Economic Development." *Southern Economic Journal,* LXI (January 1995), 899–900.

1902. Ballew, Bill. *Brave Dreams: A Season in the Atlanta Braves Farm System.* Indianapolis, Ind.: Masters Press, 1996. 175p.

1903. Blahnik, Judith and Phillip S. Schulz. *Mud Hens and Mavericks: The New Illustrated Travel Guide to Minor League Baseball.* New York: Viking Studio Books, 1995. 294p.

1904. Bowman, Larry G. "'I Think It Is Pretty Ritzy, Myself': Kansas Minor League Teams and Night Baseball." *Kansas History,* XVIII (Winter 1995–1996), 248–257.

1905. Bowman, R. D. "At Least We Don't Have to Get on the Bus." *Dugout,* III (August 1995), 37–38.

1906. "The Boys of Summer: Minor League Baseball Is of Major Importance in the Small Cities of the South." *Southern Living,* XXVII (August 1992), 60+.

1907. Chadwick, Bruce. *Baseball's Hometown Teams: The Story of the Minor Leagues.* New York: Abbeville Press, 1994. 175p.

1908. Dabscheck, Braham. "Majoring in the Minors: Baseball in the Bush Leagues." *Sporting Traditions,* XIII (November 1996), 145–150.

1909. Davis, Hank. *Small-Town Heroes: Images of Minor League Baseball.* Iowa City: University of Iowa Press, 1997. 357p.

1910. "Down on the Farm: *The Sporting News* Ranks the Minor League Organizations." In: Joe Hoppel, ed. *The Sporting News 1997 Baseball Yearbook.* St. Louis, Mo.: TSN, 1997. pp. 146–147.

1911. Fatsis, Stefan. *Wild & Outside: How a Renegade Minor League Revived the Spirit of Baseball in*

America's Heartland. New York: Walker, 1996. 288p.

1912. Field, R. "Revolutionizing the Minors: Independent Baseball Takes Off." *Dugout,* III (April–May 1995), 15–16.

1913. Fort, Rodney and James Quirk. "Cross-Subsidization, Incentives, and Outcomes in Professional Team Sports Leagues." *Journal of Economic Literature,* XXXIII (September 1995), 1265–1300.

1914. Hemphill, Paul. *The Heart of the Game: The Education of a Minor League Ballplayer.* New York: Simon and Schuster, 1996. 284p.

1915. Hertzel, Laurie. "Baseball for Real." *Minnesota Monthly,* XXVIII (April 1994), 38+.

1916. Johnson, Arthur T. *Minor League Baseball and Local Economic Development.* Urbana: University of Illinois Press, 1993. 273p.

1917. ____. "Professional Baseball at the Minor League Level: Considerations for Cities Large and Small." *State and Local Government Review,* XXII (Spring 1990), 90+.

1918. Johnson, Eric A. "Field of Dreams." *Milwaukee,* XVII (April 1992), 32–33.

1919. Johnson, Lloyd. "The Real National Pastime: The History and Future of the Minor Leagues." *Dugout,* III (August 1995), 7–11.

1920. ____. and Miles Wolff, eds. *The Encyclopedia of Minor League Baseball: The Official Record of Minor League Baseball.* Durham, N.C.: Baseball America, 1993. 416p.

1921. Kelly, Leo. "Oklahoma Baseball." *Chronicles of Oklahoma,* LXX (Spring 1992), 46+. Minor league baseball in the Indian Territory.

1922. Kiefer, Kit. "Play Ball." *Wisconsin Trails,* XXXIII (July–August 1992), 18+.

1923. Knight, Bill. "The Summer Game." *Illinois Issues,* XXII (June 1996), 12+. Minor league play in Illinois.

1924. Kurkijan, Tim. "Feeling Kinda Small." *Sports Illustrated,* LXXXI (July 25, 1994), 77–79.

1925. Lamb, David. "The Major Pleasures of the Minor Leagues." *USA Weekend,* (June 5, 1992), 4–6.

1926. Land, Kenneth C., William R. Davis, and Judith R. Blau. "Organizing the Boys of Summer: The Evolution of U.S. Minor League Baseball, 1883–1990." *American Journal of Sociology,* C (November 1994), 781–813.

1927. Lazzaro, Sam. *More Than a Ballgame: An Inside Look at Minor League Baseball.* Blacksburg, Va.: Pocahontas Press, 1997.

1928. Lott, J. "Hope and a Dream." *Dugout,* III (August 1995), 19–21, 23.

1929. Mahtisian, Charles. "Force Play." *Governing,* VII (April 1994), 18+. Fiscal requirements placed on communities for facility upgrades.

1930. Mandel, Brett H. *Minor Players, Major Dreams.* Lincoln: University of Nebraska Press, 1997. 243p.

1931. *Minor Trips: A Traveler's Guide to Minor League Baseball.* Strongsville, Oh.: Minor Trips, 1991. Unpaged.

1932. Modica, Andrea. *Minor Leagues.* Washington, D.C.: Smithsonian Institution Press, 1993. 64p. A pictorial.

1933. Myers, Gary. "Fewer Are Chosen, Many Are Called." *Inside Sports,* XV (May 1993), 66–69.

1934. Noland, David. "The Old Ball Game." *New York,* XXVI (July 26, 1993), 45–46. Minor league teams in New York State.

1935. Pietrusza, David. *Minor Miracles: The Legend and Curse of Minor League Baseball.* South Bend, Ind.: Diamond Communications, 1995. 232p.

1936. Poff, John. "Please Release Me." *Elysian Fields Quarterly,* XIII (Fall 1994), 3–7. Life in the minor leagues.

1937. "Quakes, Crawdads, and Whiskey Jacks: Minor Leagues' Clever Apparel and Catchy Nicknames Prove Major Hits Nationwide." In: Joe Hoppel, ed.

The Sporting News 1994 Baseball Yearbook. St. Louis, Mo.: TSN, 1994. pp. 44–45.

1938. Rosenthraub, Mark S. and Daniel Soundell. "'Just Say No?': The Economic and Political Realities of a Small City's Investment in Minor League Baseball." *Economic Development Quarterly,* V (May 1991), 152+.

1939. Schwarz, Alan. "No Minor Accomplishment." *Beckett Focus on Future Stars,* V, no. 45 (January 1995), 72–73. Minor league championships.

1940. _____. "Put Me In, Coach: Spring's in the Air, and Talented Farm Systems Have Collectors Ready to Go to the Bench for Prospects Eager to Play." *Beckett Focus on Future Stars,* V, no. 47 (March 1995), 68–73.

1941. Shropshire, Kenneth L. "Minor-League Effort: 50 Years After Jackie Robinson Integrated Baseball." *Emerge,* VIII (April 1997), 60+.

1942. Smith, A. K. "Baseball, for Real." *U.S. News & World Report,* CXXII (April 28, 1997), 73–74.

1943. Snyder, Bob. "The Minor Leagues." In: Gerald Kavanagh, ed. *Street and Smith's Baseball '97.* New York: Street and Smith, 1997. pp. 124–133.

1944. Souders, Paul. "The Summer Game: Baseball in the Minors." *Petersen's Photographic Magazine,* XIX (June 1990), 24+.

1945. Twyman, Gib. "The Royals Fountain of Youth: Talent Sprouts on Royals Farm." In: Kansas City Royals. *The Kansas City Royals 1996 Yearbook.* Kansas City, Mo., 1996. pp. 2–5.

1946. United States. Congress. House. Committee on Small Business. *The Key Issues Confronting Minor League Baseball: Hearings.* 103rd Cong., 2nd sess. Washington, D.C.: GPO, 1994. 92p.

1947. Vrooman, John. "A General Theory of Professional Sports Leagues." *Southern Economic Journal,* LXI (April 1995), 971–991.

1948. Wagner, William. "Minors to Majors: Up the Establishment." *Inside Sports,* XVII (May 1995), 11–12.

1949. Winston, L. "Baseball's Tobacco Road: Touring the Diamonds of the Tar Heel State [North Carolina]." *Dugout,* III (August 1995), 12–16.

1950. Witteman, P. A. "The Only Game in Town." *Time,* CXLIV (August 22, 1994), 76–77.

1951. Zajac, Jennifer. "Get Some Major League Fun at Little League Dollars." *Money,* XXVI (July 1997), 158–160.

b. Specific Leagues,
Arranged Alphabetically

AMERICAN ASSOCIATION

1952. O'Neal, Bill. *American Association: A Baseball History, 1902–1991.* Austin, Tx.: Eakin Publications, 1992. 400p.

1953. Wright, Marshall D. *The American Association: Year-by-Year Statistics for the Baseball Minor League, 1902–1952.* Jefferson, N.C.: McFarland & Co., Inc., 1997. 400p.

CALIFORNIA LEAGUE

1954. Howells, Bob. "Home Team Advantage." *Westways,* LXXXIX (May 1997), 24+.

1955. Mackey, R. S. "The California Winter League: A 'Sure-Fire' Idea That Wasn't." *Baseball Research Journal,* XXIV (1995), 106–107.

1956. Spalding, John E. *Always on Sunday: The California Baseball League, 1886 to 1915.* Manhattan, Ks.: Ag Press, 1992. 172p.

CAPE COD LEAGUE

1957. Blanchard, Jeff. "Summer Treat." *Beckett Focus on Future Stars,* III, no. 28 (August 1993), 14–19.

1958. Kageleiry, John. "Where Tomorrow's Stars Shine Tonight." *Yankee,* LX (July 1996), 58–71+.

CAROLINA ASSOCIATION

1959. Sumner, Jim L. "'The Sole Topic of Conversation': The 1908 Carolina Association and the Dawn of Minor League Baseball in the Carolinas." *Carologue: A Bulletin of South Carolina History,* X (Summer 1994), 8+.

EASTERN SHORE LEAGUE

1960. Sparks, Barry. "Comebacks and Fisticuffs: The Many Lives of the Eastern Shore League, 1922–1949." *Maryland Historical Magazine,* LXXXVII (Summer 1992), 158–170.

HAWAIIAN WINTER LEAGUE

1961. Taketa, Mari. "Back in the Ballgame?" *Hawaii Business,* XXXVIII (October 1992), 56+.

INTERNATIONAL LEAGUE

1962. Field, Robert. "The Tragic Career of Ross Young, International League Innovator." *Dugout,* II (April 1994), 28–29.
1963. Kurkijan, Tim. "We Interrupt the '94 NFL Season to Bring You the '94 Pennant Race." *Sports Illustrated,* LXXXI (September 12, 1994), 48–50+. Between the league's Richmond Braves and Charlotte Knights.
1964. O'Neill, Bill. *The International League: A Baseball History, 1889–1991.* Austin, Tx.: Eakin Press, 1992. 452p.

MEXICAN LEAGUE

1965. Klein, Alan M. "Tender Machos: Masculine Contrasts in the Mexican Baseball League." *Sociology of Sport Journal,* XII, no. 4 (1995), 370–388.

MONTANA LEAGUE

1966. Scott, James A. "'If It Don't End in Bloodshed....': The Montana Baseball League, 1900." *Montana: The Magazine of Western History,* XLVII (Summer 1997), 62+.

NEW YORK-PENNSYLVANIA LEAGUE

1967. Moss, Robert A. "Once Around the Bases: August, 1993." *Elysian Fields Quarterly,* XIII (Winter 1994), 95–102.

NORTH CAROLINA LEAGUE

1968. Sumner, Jim L. "The North Carolina League and the Advent of World War I." *Nine: A Journal of Baseball History and Social Policy Perspective,* IV (Spring 1996), 237–247.

NORTHERN LEAGUE

1969. Shipnuck, Alan. "Northern Exposure." *Sports Illustrated,* LXXXI (August 22, 1994), 68–69.

NORTHWEST LEAGUE

1970. Murphy, Michael. "Play Ball." *Pacific Northwest Quarterly,* XXVIII (May 1994), 64–67.

PACIFIC COAST LEAGUE

1971. Jayroe, Walt. "Boys of Summer." *New Mexico Magazine,* LXXII (May 1994), 22–27.
1972. Mackey, R. Scott. *Barbary Baseball: The Pacific Coast League of the 1920s.* Jefferson, N.C.: McFarland & Co., Inc., 1995. 227p.
1973. McCue, A. "Open Status Delusions: The PCL Attempt to Resist Major League Baseball." *Nine: A Journal of Baseball History and Social Policy Perspective,* V (Spring 1997), 288–304.
1974. Nagata, Yoichi. "The First All-Asian Pitching Duel in Organized Baseball: Japan vs. China in the PCL." *Baseball Research Journal,* XXI (1992), 13–14.

1975. Schulian, John. "Of Stars and Angels." *Sports Illustrated,* LXXVIII (June 21, 1993), 60–64+. PCL history in the 1950s.

1976. Snelling, Dennis. *The Pacific Coast League: A Statistical History, 1903–1957.* Jefferson, N.C.: McFarland & Co., Inc., 1995. 392p.

1977. Zingg, Paul J. and Mark D. Medeiros. *Runs, Hits, and an Era: The Pacific Coast League, 1903–58.* Urbana: Published for the Oakland Museum by the University of Illinois Press, 1994. 170p.

SOUTHERN LEAGUE

1978. Green, Ernest J. *The Diamonds of Dixie: Travels Through the Southern Minor Leagues.* Lanham, Md.: Madison Books, 1995. 247p.

1979. Hemphill, Paul. "The Glory of Their Time." *Atlanta,* XXXIV (April 1995), 32+.

1980. O'Neill, Bill. *The Southern League: Baseball in Dixie, 1885–1994.* Austin, Tx.: Eakin Press, 1994. 361p.

1981. "Southern Bases: Baseball Before the Braves." *Atlanta History,* XXXVII (Summer 1993), 25–40.

TEXAS LEAGUE

1982. Bowman, L. "Night Baseball Comes to the Texas League." *Nine: A Journal of Baseball History and Social Policy Perspective,* V (Spring 1997), 207–227.

1983. Nichols, Max J. "Oklahoma City-Tulsa Baseball." *Chronicles of Oklahoma,* LXXIV (Summer 1996), 174+. Tulsa Oilers and the Oklahoma City Indians battle from 1933 to 1957.

c. Specific Teams,
Arranged Alphabetically

ABERDEEN PHEASANTS

1984. Gertsen, Paul. "The Aberdeen Pheasants." *Elysian Fields Quarterly,*

XIII (Winter 1994), 12–16. 1946–1971 Northern League South Dakota affiliate of the St. Louis Browns/Baltimore Orioles.

ADIRONDACK STARS

1985. Fiesthumel, S. "The Adirondack Stars." *National Pastime,* XIV (1994), 77–79.

AKRON AEROS

1986. "Aeros to Take Off: Tribe's AA Farm Team Creating New Identity to Go with New Ballpark." *Carin's Cleveland Business,* VIII (March 24, 1997), 14–15. Change in name from Canton-Akron Indians.

ALBUQUERQUE DUKES

1987. Briley, Ron. "The Albuquerque Dukes and the Summer of 1981: The Best of Baseball in America." *Nine: A Journal of Baseball History and Social Policy Research,* III (Fall 1994), 66–84.

1988. Chavez, Barbara. "These Dukes Are No Hazard." *Beckett Focus on Future Stars,* II, no. 17 (September 1992), 14–17.

1989. Wall, Dennis. "For the Dukes, Baseball Is Still a Game." *New Mexico Business Journal,* XIX (June 1995), 18–22.

BLUEFIELD ORIOLES

1990. Elliott, Lawrence. "Field of Dreams." *Reader's Digest,* CXLIV (June 1994), 47–51.

BRATTLEBORO ISLANDERS

1991. Kearney, S. "The Brattleboro Islanders: The Twin State League, 1911." *National Pastime,* XV (1995), 5–9.

COLORADO SILVER BULLETS

1992. Ames, K. "A Whole New Ball Game." *Newsweek,* CXXIII (May 9, 1994), 58–59. Colorado Silver Bullets, the first women's minor league team officially recognized by the National Association of Professional Baseball Players.

1993. Farrell, M. H. J. "Say It Ain't So." *People Weekly,* XLI (June 6, 1994), 63–64+.

1994. Miller, Stuart. "A Few More Pitches for Gender Equality." *Inside Sports,* XVI (June 1994), 10–11.

1995. Waterman, G. "The Colorado Silver Bullets: For the Love of the Game." *Nine: A Journal of Baseball History and Social Policy Perspective,* V (Fall 1996), 139–146.

COLUMBUS CLIPPERS

1996. Crawford, Dan. "Columbus Has Big League Potential." *Business First-Columbus,* XIII (May 9, 1997), 1–3.

1997. Lilly, Stephen. "Big Bucks Lure Minor Leaguers." *Business First-Columbus,* X (August 8, 1994), 1–2.

DENVER ZEPHYRS

1998. Klis, Mike. "Mile High Prospects." *Beckett Focus on Future Stars,* II, no. 16 (August 1992), 12–15. Milwaukee Triple-A club.

DURHAM BULLS

1999. Kirkland, Bill. *Eddie Neville and the Durham Bulls.* Jefferson, N.C.: McFarland & Co., Inc., 1993. 230p.

HARRISBURG SENATORS

2000. Zonca, Tony. "All Aboard." *Beckett Focus on Future Stars,* III, no. 28 (August 1993), 20–23. Montreal Double A farm club.

KNOXVILLE SMOKIES

2001. Ballew, Bill. "Smokin' Times in Knoxville." *Beckett Focus on Future Stars,* III, no. 29 (September 1993), 16–21. Toronto Double A farm club.

LAFAYETTE WHITE SOX

2002. Taylor, Doug. "A Community and Its Team: The Evangeline League's Lafayette White Sox, 1934–1942." *Louisiana History,* XXXVI (Spring 1995), 149–170.

LOS ANGELES ANGELS

2003. Schulian, John. "Of Stars and Angels: Once Upon a Time, Tinseltown Was a Heavenly Place to Watch Minor League Baseball." *Sports Illustrated,* LXXVIII (June 21, 1993), 60–68+.

MANILA DODGERS

2004. Kawarsky, I. K. "The Manila Dodgers." *National Pastime,* XIV (1994), 59–60.

NASHUA DODGERS

2005. Roper, S. "The 1949 Nashua Dodgers: The Demise of the New England League." *National Pastime,* XV (1995), 80–84.

NEWARK ORIOLES

2006. Miller, Stuart. "'Play Ball!'" *New Jersey Monthly,* XIX (February 1994), 21+.

ONEONTA YANKEES

2007. Whittemore, Bob. *Baseball Town [Oneonta, New York]: A Place Where Yankees Grow.* Manchester Center, Vt.: M. Jones Co., 1995. 241p.

OTTAWA LYNX

2008. Allen, George. "The Capital Gang." *Maclean's,* CVI (August 9, 1993), 48+.

2009. Gordon, C. "When Smaller Is Better Than Bigger." *Maclean's,* CVI (July 19, 1993), 9+.

PAWTUCKET RED SOX

2010. Giles, J. "Major Pain, Minor Joy." *Newsweek,* CXXIV (August 22, 1994), 53+.

PHOENIX GIANTS

2011. Banks, Leo W. "A Kid Gets His Shot at the Bigs." *Arizona Highways,* LXVIII (March 1992), 35+.

RICHMOND BRAVES

2012. Black, Bob. "Richmond Gets Richer." *Beckett Focus on Future Stars,* III, no. 27 (July 1993), 14–19. Atlanta Triple-A farm club.

2013. Powell, Tom. "Richmond Braves Secure Attendance at a 5,731 Average with Promotionals." *Amusement Business,* CIX (May 26, 1997), 5+.

ROCHESTER RED WINGS

2014. Mandelaro, Jim and Scott Pitoniak. *Silver Seasons: The Story of the Rochester Red Wings.* Syracuse, N.Y.: Syracuse University Press, 1996. 313p.

SAN JOSE BEES

2015. Fimrite, Ron. "There's No Way to San Jose." *Sports Illustrated,* LXXVI (June 15, 1992), 14+.

ST. CATHERINE BLUE JAYS

2016. Nemeth, M. "Diamond in the Rough." *Maclean's,* CVII (September 5, 1994), 48–49.

ST. PAUL SAINTS

2017. Lehman, Stephen. "The Lives of the Saints." *Elysian Fields Quarterly,* XIII (Winter 1994), 90–91. One of six teams in the new (1993) Northern League.

SCOTTSDALE SCORPIONS

2018. Verducci, Tom. "Keeping His Guard Up." *Sports Illustrated,* LXXXI (December 12, 1994), 94–97.

SPOKANE INDIANS

2019. Garrity, John. "Beating the Bushes." *Sports Illustrated,* LXXXI (July 11, 1994), 50–52.

TOLEDO MUD HENS

2020. Wenclas, Karl. "The Last Day of Baseball." *North American Review,* CCLXXIX (November–December 1994), 4–11.

TRENTON GIANTS

2021. Kornberg, Harvey R., ed. *Proceedings of the Trenton City Museum Symposium & Exhibition: "When Trenton Baseball Roared Like Thunder."* Trenton, N.J.: Trenton City Museum, 1995. Celebration of the 1947 team.

WATERLOO DIAMONDS

2022. Panek, Richard. *Waterloo Diamonds.* New York: St. Martin's Press, 1995. 373p. An Iowa minor league team.

6. Stadiums and Equipment

a. Stadiums and Ballparks

1. General Works

2023. "American Food: Hot Dog!" *Restaurants and Institutions,* XCIX (May 29, 1989), 104+.

2024. Ashman, D. "Infield Groomings." *SportsTURF,* XIII (March 1997), 24–26.

2024a. Baim, Dean V. *The Sports Stadium as a Municipal Investment.* Contributions in Economics and Economic History, no. 151. Westport, Conn.: Greenwood Press, 1993.

2025. "Baseball Cops." *Law and Order,* XXXVIII (October 1990), 92+.

2026. Baseball Development, Inc. *Making Baseball and Softball Fields Safe and Playable: A Complete Instructional Guide for Building and Maintaining Ball Diamonds.* Birmingham, Mich., 1995. 62p.

2027. Bess, Philip. "Urban Ballparks and the Future of Cities." *Real Estate Issues,* XXI (December 1996), 27–30.

2028. Blickstein, Steve. *Bouts of Glory and Fields of Dreams: Great Baseball Parks of North America.* Encino, Calif.: Cherbo Pub. Group, 1995. 128p.

2029. Burns, Lori S. and Patti A. Ellison. "First Aid and Emergency Care at a Major League Baseball Stadium." *JEN, Journal of Emergency Nursing,* XVIII (August 1992), 329+.

2030. Casey, Ethan. "The Malling of Major League Baseball: *The Sporting News* and the Media/Corporate Assault on Classic Ballparks." *Elysian Fields Quarterly,* XI (Winter 1992), 6–16.

2031. Caubron, Charles B. "Stadium/Ballpark HVAC Design." *Heating, Piping, and Air Conditioning,* LXVIII (February 1996), 67+.

2032. Colclough, William G., Laurence A. Daellenbach, and Keith R. Sherony. "Estimating the Economic Impact of a Minor League Baseball Stadium." *Managerial and Decision Economics,* XV (September 1994), 497–503.

2033. Crothers, Tim. "The Shakedown Game." *Sports Illustrated,* LXXXII (June 19, 1995), 78–80+. Owners threaten to move unless new stadiums are built or old ones upgraded.

2034. Dawidoff, Nicholas. "Field of Kitsch: Is Nostalgia Wrecking Baseball?" *The New Republic,* CCVII (August 17, 1992), 22–24.

2035. Deckard, Linda. "Baseball Venues Score with Value-Added Packages." *Amusement Business,* CIX (June 16, 1997), 7–10.

2036. "Down the Line: Stretching from Home Plate to the Outfield Wall, Two Simple White Stripes Separate Foul from Fair—and Serve as Sight Lines for a Unique Perspective on the Game." *Sports Illustrated,* LXXXII (May 1, 1995), 74–83.

2037. Edwards, P. "How Much Does That $8 Yankee Ticket Really Cost?: An Analysis of Local Governments' Expenditure of Public Funds to Maintain, Improve, or Acquire an Athletic Stadium for the Use of Professional Sports Teams." *Fordham Urban Law Journal,* XVIII (Summer 1991), 695–723.

2038. Eisner, Milton P. "The Shape of a Baseball Field." *The Mathematics Teacher,* LXXXVI (May 1993), 366+.

2039. Finerty, J. D. "Subverting the Internal Revenue Code in the 'Game' of Sports Stadium Financing." *Marquette Sports Law Journal,* I (Spring 1991), 301–322.

2040. Foster, M. S. "Mile High Greenfields: Denver's Notable Ballparks." *Colorado Heritage,* (Spring 1995), 5–18.

2041. Gershman, Michael. *Diamonds: The Evolution of the Ballpark.* Boston, Mass.: Houghton, Mifflin, 1993. 259p.

2042. Goodale, G. S. "Endangered Diamonds: Preserving Historic Ballparks." *For the Record,* IV (October–November 1993), 5–6.

2043. Goodman, Guy H. and Francis T. McAndrew. "Domes and Astroturf: A Note on the Relationship Between the Physical Environment and the Performance of Major League Baseball Players." *Environment & Behavior,* XXV (January 1993), 121–125.

2044. Hall, Ron. "Safer Pitchers Mounds." *Landscape Management,* XXXIII (June 1994), 27+.

2045. ____. "Rebuilding the Fields." *Landscape Management,* XXXIII (November 1994), 8G+.

2046. Hobbs, Bill and Ray Waddell. "Hot Dog!" *Amusement Business,* CIX (April 28, 1997), 17–21. A look at the old stadium favorite.

2047. "Hot Dogs and Baseball." *Meat Business Magazine,* LVI (May 1995), 16+.

2048. Irani, D. "Public Subsidies to Stadiums: Do the Costs Outweigh the Benefits?" *Public Finance Review,* XXV (March 1997), 238–253.

2049. Keating, R. J. "'We Wuz Robbed!': The Subsidized Stadium Scam." *Policy Review,* no. 82 (March–April 1997), 54–57.

2050. Kinnard, William, Jr., *et al.* "Team Performance, Attendance, and Risk for Major League Stadiums, 1970–1994." *Real Estate Issues,* XXII (April 1997), 8+.

2051. Kurkijan, Tim. "Mounds of Doubt." *Sports Illustrated,* LXXXII (June 19, 1995), 94+. On the possibility of raising the heights of MLB pitching mounds.

2052. Lane, R. "Bread and Circuses." *Forbes,* CLIII (June 6, 1994), 62–64. Taxpayers pay for new stadiums.

2053. Levin, Ted. "Of Birds and Baseball: Anyone Can Make a Double Play at the Ballpark." *Living Bird,* XIII (Spring 1994), 16+. Bird watching at ball games.

2054. Lianes, R. "The Urban Ballpark: Fundamental Qualities of an American Original." *Nine: A Journal of Baseball History and Social Policy Perspective,* III (Fall 1994), 168–179.

2055. Lindstrom, Chuck. "All Lighting Systems Are Not Created Equal." *Scholastic Coach,* LXIV (November 1994), 64+.

2056. Long, James D. "Baseball Field Maintenance: A Novel Twist to Upkeep." *American School and University,* LXI (April 1989), 40+.

2057. Lowry, Philip J. "Ballparks." In: John Thorn and Pete Palmer, eds. *Total Baseball.* 3rd ed. New York: Harper-Perenial, 1993. pp. 114–142.

2058. ____. *Green Cathedrals: The Ultimate Celebration of All 271 Major League and Negro League Ballparks Past and Present.* Reading, Mass.: Addison-Wesley Pub. Co., 1992. 275p.

2059. "Major League Baseball Parks Built Before 1940." *For the Record,* IV (October–November 1993), 6–7.

2060. Maloy, B. P. "Dangerous Base Paths: Baseball and Softball Field Operators Have a Host of Legal Obligations to Participants and Spectators." *Athletic Business,* XIX (January 1995), 59–62.

2061. Miller, Raymond. "Here's a Salute to Four Old Ballparks." *Baseball Digest,* LV (September 1996), 66–76.

2062. Noden, M. "Give Me the Wide-Open Spaces: As Baseball's Fences Move In, Some of the Game's Most Exciting Plays Move Out." *Sports Illustrated,* LXXXVI (June 23, 1997), 110+.

2063. Odenwald, Ryan. "I Went to 24 Ballparks." *Sports Illustrated for Kids,* VIII (April 1996), 44–47.

2064. Ozanian, M. K., *et al.* "Suite Deals: Why New Stadiums Are Shaking Up the Pecking Order of Sports Franchises." *Financial World,* CLXIV (May 9, 1995), 42–43, 46–48, 50, 52–54, 56.

2065. Pastier, J. "Play Ball: Five New Stadiums Devoted to Big League Baseball." *Landscape Architecture,* LXXXV (June 1995), 70–73.

2066. Perry, Floyd, Jr. "Cover All Your Bases." *Athletic Business,* XVIII (January 1994), 54+. Protecting the playing field.

2067. "Preparing Ball Diamonds for Spring." *SportsTURF,* XII (February 1996), 8–9.

2068. Puhalla, J. "Spring Training for Your Baseball Stadium." *SportTURF,* XIII (March 1997), 14–16, 18.

2069. Raitz, Karl B., ed. *The Theater of Sport.* Baltimore, Md.: Johns Hopkins

University Press, 1996. 384p. Includes Camden Yards and Jacobs Field A.L. ballparks.

2070. Richmond, Peter. "Enthusiasms." *GQ: Gentlemen's Quarterly,* LXV (April 1995), 89+.

2071. Ritter, Lawrence S. *Lost Ballparks: A Celebration of Baseball's Legendary Fields.* New York: Viking Press, 1992. 210p.

2072. Rushin, Steve. "Dog Days: Baseball Fans Are Chowing Down Big-Time, on Everything from Wieners to Nachos to Sushi to Rocky Mountain Oysters." *Sports Illustrated,* LXXXV (July 8, 1996), 48–57.

2073. ____. "Into a Golden State: Our Intrepid Scribe's Tour of California Ballparks Gave Him License to Celebrate." *Sports Illustrated,* LXXVII (July 13, 1992), 24–29.

2074. Ryan, Steve. "A Little Give and Take: Ballpark Giveaways...." *Beckett Baseball Card Monthly,* VII, no. 149 (August 1997), *passim.* **<http://www. beckett.com/products/bbpd.html>.**

2075. Santee, Earl F. "Major League Cities." *Real Estate Issues,* XXI (December 1996), 31+.

2076. Schieffer, Tom and Leigh Steinberg. "Pro & Con: Should Public Money Be Used to Finance Pro Sports Stadium Projects?" *Inside Sports,* XVII (December 1995), 14–15.

2077. Schimmel, K. S. "Professional Team Sport and the American City: Urban Politics and Franchise Relocations." In: A. G. Ingham and J. W. Loy, eds. *Sport in Social Development.* Champaign, Ill.: Human Kinetics Pub., 1993. pp. 211–244.

2078. Schlesinger, H. "Fields of Dreams." *Popular Mechanics,* CLXXIII (April 1996), 54–57. Designing ballparks.

2079. Shald, Scott and Paula Gottlob. "Stadium-Building in the Minors." *Concrete International,* XVI (June 1994), 55+.

2080. "Speaking Frankly: We Came, We Saw, We Scarfed." *Sports Illustrated,* LXXXV (July 8, 1996), 56–57, 59.

Rating the 28 big league ballparks, as well as their culinary offerings.

2081. "Sports Venues." *TCI,* XXXI (May 1997), 31–45.

2082. Tackach, James and Joshua B. Stein. *The Fields of Summer: America's Great Ballparks and the Players Who Triumphed in Them.* New York: Crescent Books, 1992. 160p.

2083. Vass, George. "Power Surge in Majors Due to 'Homer Friendly' Parks?" *Baseball Digest,* LVI (September 1997), 26–35.

2084. Vincent, David, ed. *Home Runs in the Old Ballparks: Who Hit the First, the Last, and the Most Round-Trippers in Our Former Major League Parks, 1876–1994.* Cleveland, Oh.: Society for American Baseball Research, 1995. 47p.

2085. Waddell, Ray. "New and Renovated Minor League Facilities Hit Home Run." *Amusement Business,* CVIII (February 26, 1996), 17–19.

2086. Westcott, Rich. *Philadelphia's Old Ballparks.* Philadelphia, Pa.: Temple University Press, 1996. 206p.

2. Specific Stadiums, Arranged Alphabetically

ARLINGTON STADIUM (Texas)

2087. Langendorf, Dan. "Arlington Stadium's Rightful Place." In: John Blake, *et al. Texas Rangers 1993 Yearbook.* Arlington, Tx.: Public Relations Dept., Texas Rangers, 1993. pp. 40–63.

2088. ____. "Building the Ballpark in Arlington." In: John Blake, *et al. 1994 Official Texas Ranger Yearbook.* Arlington, Tx.: Public Relations Dept., Texas Rangers, 1994. pp. 43–48.

BAKER BOWL (Pennsylvania)

2089. Doyle, E. F. "The Baker Bowl." *National Pastime,* XV (1995), 24–31.

CANDLESTICK PARK (California)

2090. Muret, Don. "Volume [Services] Signs New [Concession] Contract with Giants." *Amusement Business,* CIX (June 30, 1997), 1–2.

2091. Rubin, Bob. "The Stick Could Still Blow It for the Giants." *Inside Sports,* XV (April 1993), 12–15.

COMISKEY PARK (Illinois)

2092. Bess, Philip. "Mallpark." *Inland Architect,* XXXV (September 1991), 32+.

2093. Bukowski, Douglas. *Baseball Palace of the World: The Last Year of Comiskey Park.* Chicago: Lyceum Books, 1991. 256p.

2094. ____. "Just a Crack or Two." *Elysian Fields Quarterly,* XIII (Winter 1994), 3–5.

2095. Grosshandler, Stanley. "How a Home Run at Comiskey Park Cost Club $5,000." *Baseball Digest,* LII (April 1993), 87–91.

2096. Krizek, Bob. "Goodbye, Old Friend." *OMEAGA: The Journal of Death and Dying,* XXV (February 1992), 87–93. Old Comiskey.

2097. Lalich, Richard. "Political Hardball." *Chicago,* XLI (September 1992), 69+.

2098. Sullivan, Terry. "Da Dome." *Chicago,* XLI (March 1992), 61–62.

2099. No entry.

COORS FIELD (Colorado)

2100. Bakke, Diane. *Places Around the Bases: A Historic Tour of the Coors Field Neighborhood.* Newport Beach, Calif.: Westcliff Pubn., Inc., 1995.

2101. Guss, Greg. "Pitcher Purgatory." *Sport,* LXXXIX (July 1997), 58–61.

2102. "It's a Blast." In: Joe Hoppel, ed. *The Sporting News 1997 Baseball Yearbook.* St. Louis, Mo.: TSN, 1997. pp. 30–33.

2102. Linn, C. "Coors Field." *Architectural Record,* CLXXXIV (August 1996), 110–113.

2103. Sage, G. H. "Stealing Home: Political, Economic, and Media Power and a Publicly-Funded Baseball Stadium in Denver." *Journal of Sport and Social Issues,* XVII (August 1993), 110–124.

2104. Verducci, Tom. "The Scare of Thin Air." *Sports Illustrated,* LXXX (April 4, 1994), 110+.

CROSLEY FIELD (Ohio)

2105. Rhodes, Gregory L. and John G. Erardi. *Cincinnati's Crosley Field: The Illustrated History of a Classic Ballpark.* Cincinnati, Oh.: Road West Pub. Co., 1995. 216p.

FENWAY PARK (Massachusetts)

2106. Boswell, J. and D. Fisher. *Fenway Park: Legendary Home of the Boston Red Sox.* Boston, Mass.: Little, Brown, 1992. Unpaged.

2107. Huntington, Tom. "There Is No Finer Place in the World to Watch Baseball." *Smithsonian,* XXV (October 1994), 64–66+.

2108. Kageleiry, John. "In Joe Mooney's Perfect World." *Yankee,* LXIX (September 1995), 94–95. Groundskeeping.

FIELD OF DREAMS (Iowa)

2109. Aden, Roger C. "Iowa's Elysian Fields: Spiritual Rejuvenation at the Field of Dreams." Elysian Fields Quarterly, XIII (Summer 1994), 3–9. The field, named after the film, maintained by Al Ameskamp and. Don Lansing near Dyersville.

FORBES FIELD (Pennsylvania)

2110. Bonk, Daniel L. "Ballpark Figures: The Story of Forbes Field." *Pittsburgh History,* LXXVI (Summer 1993), 52–71.

2111. Shanley, John. "Forbes: One Kid's Memory." *Elysian Fields Quarterly,* XIV (Spring 1995), 54–57.

JACOBS FIELD (Ohio)

2112. Bartimole, Roldo. "'If You Build It, We Will Stay.'" *The Progressive,* LVIII (June 1994), 28–31.

2113. "Cleveland Baseball Stadium Scores with Welded Tube Framework."

Welding Journal, LXXII (November 1993), 57+.

2114. "Cleveland's Field of Screams." *U.S. News & World Report,* CXX (April 1, 1996), 50+.

2115. Glassfield, Brian. "And the Beginning." *Elysian Fields Quarterly,* XIII (Fall 1994), 67–69.

2116. Jacobs, Jay. "A Baseball Pilgrimage: Sweet Dreams and a Rude Awakening." *Gourmet,* LV (May 1995), 146–149+.

2117. Muret, Don. "Cleveland's New Ballpark Opens, Shows City Has Promising Future." *Amusement Business,* CVI (April 11, 1994), 1–2.

2118. Verducci, Tom. "Grand Opening." *Sports Illustrated,* LXXX (April 11, 1994), 42–44, 48.

2119. Walsh, Edward J. *Gateway, Blueprint of the Future: Book I, Jacobs Field.* Cleveland, Oh.: Gateway Press, 1994.

KAUFFMAN STADIUM (Missouri)

2120. "Kauffman Stadium Celebrates 25 Years." In: Kansas City Royals. *The Kansas City Royals 1997 Yearbook.* Kansas City, Mo., 1997. pp. 2–5.

LABATT PARK (London, Ontario)

2121. Humber, William. "Labatt Park (nee Tecumseh Park): London, Ontario." *Nine: A Journal of Baseball History and Social Policy Perspective,* II (Spring 1994), 355–361.

LEAGUE PARK (Ohio)

2122. Jedick, Peter and D. L. Swearingen. *League Park.* Cleveland, Oh.: Jedick, 1978. 24p. Rpr. 1992.

McCORMICK FIELD (North Carolina)

2123. Terrell, Bob. *McCormick Field— Home of Reality: The Story of the Oldest Minor League Baseball Park in America and Memories of It.* Asheville, N.C.: Worldcomm Press, 1997. Home of the Asheville Tourists.

McKECHNIE FIELD (Florida)

2124. Popke, M. "The Green, Green Grass of Home." *Athletic Business,* XVIII (January 1994), 51–53. Pirates' spring training facility.

MEMORIAL STADIUM (Maryland)

2125. Miller, James E. "The Dowager of 33rd Street: Memorial Stadium and the Politics of Big-Time Sports in Maryland, 1954–1991." *Maryland Historical Magazine,* LXXXVII (Summer 1992), 187–200.

MILWAUKEE COUNTY STADIUM (Wisconsin)

2126. Dries, Mike. "The Brewers' 'Endless Saga.'" *Business Journal-Milwaukee,* XIII (June 5, 1996), 1–2.

MUNICIPAL STADIUM (Ohio)

2127. Glassman, Brian. "The End." *Elysian Fields Quarterly,* XIII (Fall 1994), 65–66.

2128. Shaw, Bud. "Farewell: Municipal Indians." *Ohio,* XVII (April 1994), 15–16.

ORIOLE PARK AT CAMDEN YARDS (Maryland)

2129. "Bird's Eye View: The Baltimore Orioles' New Playground Combines the Best of the Old and the New." *Sport,* LXXXIII (July 1992), 63–65.

2130. "Camden Yards: A Photo Tour." In: Bob Brown, ed. *The 1996 Official Yearbook of the Baltimore Orioles.* Baltimore, Md.: Public Relations Dept., Baltimore Orioles, 1996. pp. 88–92.

2131. Cohen, Eliot. "Baltimore's Jewell Has Built-in Flaws." *Inside Sports,* XV (August 1993), 16–19.

2132. Kurkijan, Tim. "A Splendid Nest."

Sports Illustrated, LXXVI (April 13, 1992), 34–36, 41.

2133. Kurtz, Mara. "Deja Vu All Over Again." *Metropolis,* XIII (October 1993), 37+.

2134. Richmond, Peter. *Ballpark: Camden Yards and the Building of an American Dream.* New York: Simon and Schuster, 1993.

2135. Thomas, William E. "B&O to the Ball Game: Fans Are Flocking—by Train—to Baltimore's Oriole Park at Camden Yards." *Trains,* LII (September 1992), 28–29.

RICKWOOD FIELD
(Alabama)

2136. Miller, Stuart. "Raising—Not Razing—A Rich Heritage." *Inside Sports,* XVIII (April 1996), 9–10.

2137. Whitt, Timothy. *Bases Loaded With History: Story of Rickwood Field, America's Oldest Baseball Park.* Birmingham, Ala.: R. Boozer Press, 1996. 109p. Former home of the Birmingham Barons and the Negro League Birmingham Black Barons.

SHIBE PARK
(Pennsylvania)

2138. Skilton, R. H. "Memories of Shibe Park (Later Renamed Connie Mack Stadium), Philadelphia, Pennsylvania." *Wisconsin Law Review,* VI (November–December 1992), 1747–1754.

TIGER STADIUM
(Michigan)

2139. Betzhold, Michael and Ethan Casey. "Memories of a Grand Old Ballpark: Tiger Stadium." *Baseball Digest,* LI (July 1992), 34–40.

2140. Rasmussen, Larry. "Here's a List of Ten Historic and Memorable Home Runs at Tiger Stadium." *Baseball Digest,* LVI (July 1997), 72–79.

TURNER FIELD (Georgia)

2141. Weathersby, W. "Turner Field—Centennial-Olympic-Stadium, the Site of Last Summer's Olympic Games, Has Been Scaled Back to a Baseball Park for the Atlanta Braves." *TCI,* XXXI (May 1997), 36–39.

WRIGLEY FIELD
(Illinois)

2142. Castle, George. "Wrigley Field: Baseball's House of Strange Happenings." *Baseball Digest,* LIII (November 1994), 62–68.

2143. Kalmut, A. R. "The Friendly Confines: A Historical Tour of Wrigley Field." *Dugout,* II (December 1994), 17–20.

2144. Royko, Mike. "Dad's Field of Dreams." *Reader's Digest,* CXLVIII (February 1996), 69–70. Reprinted from the July 26, 1995 issue of the *Chicago Tribune.*

YANKEE STADIUM
(New York)

2145. Bernstein, S. L. "Impact of Yankee Stadium Bat Day on Blunt Trauma in Northern New York City." *Annals of Emergency Medicine,* XXIII (March 1994), 555–559.

2146. Greenberg, David. "Yankee, Stay Home." *The New Republic,* CCXIII (October 30, 1995), 14+.

2147. Lowry, R. "Bronx Cheer." *National Review,* XLIX (May 19, 1997), 57–58.

2148. Tucker, W. "Get Out of Town." *The American Spectator,* XXIX (July 1996), 26–28. Opposition to building a new Yankee Stadium on the West Side of New York.

2149. Wolfson, Howard. "Yankee Stadium." *Metropolis,* XIII (April 1994), 33–38.

b. Equipment

1. General Works

2150. Blanding, Sharon L. *What Makes a Boomerang Come Back: How Things in Sports Work.* Stamford, Conn.: Longmeadow Press, 1992. 248p.

2151. Gutman, Bill. *Banana Bats and Ding-Dong Balls: A Century of Unique Baseball Inventions.* New York: Macmillan, 1995. 251p.

2152. Walker, Marica. *Sports Equipment Management.* Boston, Mass.: Jones & Bartlett Publishing, 1992. 146p.

2. Specific Equipment Types

a. The Baseball

2153. Adair, Robert K. "The Physics of Baseball." *Physics Today,* XLVIII (May 1995), 26–31.

2154. Bahill, Terry and William J. Karnavas. "The Perceptual Illusion of Baseball's Rising Fastball and Breaking Curveball." *Journal of Experimental Psychology: Human Perception & Performance,* XIX (February 1993), 3–14.

2155. Beideck, Dan J. "Coefficient of Lift for a Spinning Baseball: Aerodynamics of a Curve Ball." *The Journal of Undergraduate Research in Physics,* XI (May 1993), 57+.

2156. Hyllegard, Randy. "The Role of the Baseball Seam Pattern in Pitch Recognition." *Journal of Sport & Exercise Psychology,* XIII (March 1991), 80–84.

2157. Lopez, F. J. "Is There a Physical Property That Determines the Curse Which Defines the Seam of a Baseball?" *American Journal of Physics,* LXIV (September 1996), 1097+.

2158. Slavsky, David B. "The Astro Physics of Baseball." *Mercury,* XXI (September 1992), 160+.

b. The Baseball Bat

2159. Bahill, Terry and M. M. Freitas. "Two Methods of Recommending Bat Weights." *Annals of Biomedical Engineering,* XXIII (July 1995), 436–444.

2160. _____. and William J. Karnavas. "Determining Ideal Baseball Bat Weights Using Muscle Force-Velocity Relationships." *Biological Cybernetics,* LXX (Summer 1989), 89+.

2161. Black, J. T. "A Slugger's Paradise."

Southern Living, XXXII (January 1997), 24–25. Hillerich & Bradsby Company's Louisville Slugger Museum and Visitors Center in Kentucky.

2162. "The First Baseball Bat." *The Woodworker's Journal,* XVIII (March 1994), 46+.

2163. Fleischman, Marvin, *et al. Waste Minimization Assessment for a Manufacturer of Baseball Bats and Golf Clubs.* EPA/600/S-93/007. Cincinnati, Oh.: Risk Reduction Engineering Laboratory, U.S. Environmental Protection Agency, 1993. 6p.

2164. Forbes, Steve. "Strike Out Aluminum Bats." *Forbes,* CLVIII (July 15, 1996), 24+.

2165. "Getting Good Wood (or Aluminum) on the Ball." *Mechanical Engineering,* CXII (October 1990), 40+.

2166. Herzlich, Adam. "Baseball Bats." *Boston,* LXXXVI (September 1994), 12+.

2167. Hester, Leslie R. and Keith Koenig. "Performance Measurement of Baseball Bats." *Journal of the Mississippi Academy of Sciences,* XXXVIII (August 1993), 7+.

2168. House, G. C. "Baseball and Softball Bats." In: E. Kreighbaum and M. A. Smith, eds. *Sport and Fitness Equipment Design.* Champaign, Ill.: Human Kinetics Pub., 1996. Chpt. 1.

2169. Kurkijan, Tim. "Going Batty: Forget the Juiced Ball—It's the Bats That May Account for All Those Homers." *Sports Illustrated,* LXXXIV (June 24, 1996), 62–63.

2170. "The Louisville Slugger: Up to Bat." *Compressed Air Magazine,* XCVI (April 1991), 6+.

2171. Miller, L. K. "The Rise of the Louisville Slugger in the Mass Market." *Sport Marketing Quarterly,* II (September 1993), 9–16.

2172. Noble, L. and H. Walker. "Baseball Bat Inertial and Vibrational Characteristics and Discomfort Following Ball-Bat Impacts." *Journal of*

Applied Biomechanics, X (May 1994), 132–144.

2173. Schuessler, Raymond. "A Brief History of the Baseball Bat." *The Northern Logger and Timber Processor,* XLII (May 1994), 32+.

c. The Baseball Cap

2174. Buckley, Steve. "Cap Culture." *Boston,* LXXXIV (August 1992), 100+.

2175. Kunke, L. James. "Mad Hatters: The Minor League Cap Business Receives Top Billing These Days." *Beckett Focus on Future Stars,* V, no. 49 (May 1995), 16–20.

2176. Toomy, Toni. "A Baseball Cap to Call Your Own." *Threads Magazine,* LIX (July 1995), 53+. Making a cap.

2177. Trinkaus, John. "Wearing Baseball-Type Caps: An Informal Look." *Psychological Reports,* LXXIV (April 1994), 585+.

d. The Baseball Glove

2178. Bushing, Dave. "Equipment: Collecting Vintage Baseball Gloves." *Beckett Vintage Sports,* I, no. 7 (June 1997), *passim.* **<http://www.beckett.com/products/vtpd.html>.**

2179. Krakofsky, S. "Selecting a Baseball Mitt." *Queen's Quarterly,* CII (September 1995), 791+.

2180. Schwab, Gary. "Aging Baseball Glove Leaves a Touching Legacy." *Baseball Digest,* LIV (April 1995), 73–76.

2181. Stone, Adrian. "Glove Story: A Subjective Self-Portrait." *Petersen's*

Photographic Magazine, XXII (May 1993), 12–13.

e. Baseball Protective Equipment

2182. Booth, Stephen A. "Tools of Ignorance." *Popular Mechanics,* CLXX (April 1993), 36–40. History of catchers' gear.

2183. Gromer, C. "Blue Plate Special." *Popular Mechanics,* CLXXIV (April 1997), 58–59. Catcher's masks.

2184. Kaplan, Ben. "Masked Ball." *Sports Illustrated for Kids,* IX (September 1997), 93–94. Catcher's masks.

f. The Baseball Uniform

2185. Coffey, Wayne. "Uniform Numbers Are a Unique Aspect of Baseball History." *Baseball Digest,* LVI (June 1997), 56–60.

2186. Edwards, Owen. "Uniform Code." *GQ: Gentlemen's Quarterly,* LXII (September 1992), 117, 122.

2187. Hoffman, Frank W. and William G. Bailey. "Classic Baseball Shirt Reproductions." In: their *Sports and Recreation Fads.* Binghampton, N.Y.: Haworth, 1991. pp. 81–82.

2188. King, D. C. "Notes on the Uniform Distribution." *National Pastime,* XV (1995), 38–40.

2189. Stang, Mark M. and Linda Harkness. *Baseball by the Numbers: A Guide to the Uniform Numbers of Major League Teams.* American Sports History Series, no. 4. Lanham, Md.: Scarecrow Press, 1997. 1,124p.

D. Youth League, College, Foreign, and Amateur/Semi-Pro Baseball

1. High School and College Baseball

2190. Abbott, C. L. *"The Relationship Between Sport Commitment, Sport Salience, and Choice Behavior in Division I College Baseball Players."* Unpublished M.A. Thesis, California State University at Fullerton, 1996. 72p.

2191. Baker, Scott. "The Four as in Recruiting College Baseball." *Scholastic Coach & Athletic Director,* LXV (May–June 1996), 90+.

2192. Brown, W. E. "The Yale Nine, 1880: A Turning Point in Collegiate Sport." *Nine: A Journal of Baseball History and Social Policy Perspective,* V (Fall 1996), 94–115.

2193. Burns, Marty. "College World Series." *Sports Illustrated,* LXXXII (June 19, 1995), 86+. Cal State-Fullerton vs. USC.

2194. Ciborowski, Tom. "'Headiness' or 'Intelligence' for Baseball in the Collegiate Athlete." *Perceptual & Motor Skills,* LXXXI (December 1995), 795–801.

2195. Delmonico, Rod. "Tennessee Calls It Incredible!" *Scholastic Coach,* LXIV (November 1994), 22–24.

2196. DeMarco, Tony. "Express Route to Stardom." *Beckett Focus on Future Stars,* III, no. 29 (September 1993), 6–11.

2197. "Destination Omaha: City Boosters and TV Help Propel the College World Series to the 'Big Time.'" In: Joe Hoppel, ed. *The Sporting News 1993 Baseball Yearbook.* St. Louis, Mo.: TSN, 1993. p. 136+.

2198. Farmer, Neal. *Southwest Conference Baseball's Greatest Hits.* Austin, Tx.: Eakin Press, 1996. 343p.

2199. Fleisher, Arthur A. *National Collegiate Athletic Association: A Study in Cartel Behavior.* Chicago, Ill.: University of Chicago Press, 1992.

2200. Fleming, David. "Tiger Mania." *Sports Illustrated,* LXXXVI (June 16, 1997), 60–61. College World Series won by LSU.

2201. Goldstein, Warren. "It Happens Every Spring: Lingua Franca." *The Review of Academic Life,* I (June 1991), 26+.

2202. "Jock Schools USA." *Sports Illustrated,* LXXXVI (April 28, 1997), 52–90.

2203. Kim, A. "The Waves Roll In: Led by an Orel Hershiser Look-Alike, the Pepperdine Waves Crashed on Cal State-Fullerton to Win the College World Series." *Sports Illustrated,* LXXVI (June 15, 1992), 22–23.

2204. Klonsky, Bruce G. "Leaders' Characteristics in Same-Six Sport Groups: A Study of Interscholastic Baseball and Softball Teams." *Perceptual & Motor Skills,* LXXII (June 1991), 943–946.

2205. Kurkijan, Tim. "Agony and Ecstasy: LSU Steals the College World Series from Miami with a 9th-Inning Homer." *Sports Illustrated,* LXXXIV (June 17, 1996), 78+.

2206. Largent, Jim. "Building a Successful Baseball Program at the Small School." *Texas Coach,* XXXVIII (February 1994), 20+.

2207. Littlefield, Bill. "The Old Man in the Bleachers at the Dartmouth Baseball Game was More Than a Casual Fan: He Was a Messenger from the Past, Bearing Gifts." *Yankee,* LVIII (May 1994), 152+.

2208. Miller, P. B. "To Bring the Race Along Rapidly: Sport, Student Culture, and Educational Mission at Historically Black Colleges During the Interwar Years." *History of Education Quarterly,* XXXV (June 1995), 111–133.

2209. Nestel, Daniel. "'Batter Up!': Are Youth Baseball Leagues Overlooking the Safety of Their Players?" *Seton Hall Journal of Sport Law,* IV, no. 1 (1994), 77+.

2210. Nygaard, Tom. "34 Tips for Your [High School] Baseball Program." *Scholastic Coach,* LXII (April 1993), 28+.

2211. Payne, Mike. "The College and the Semipros: Maryland's Washington College and Its Early Role." *National Pastime,* XV (1995), 151–153.

2212. Ross, George. "Building a [High School] Baseball Program for the Long Run." *Scholastic Coach & Athletic Director,* LXVI (December 1996), 27–28.

2213. Russell, D. "Baseball Try Outs at Nacogdoches High School." *Texas Coach,* XLI (March 1997), 50–52.

2214. Schwartz, Alan. "Is This Heaven?: No, It's Omaha." *Beckett Baseball Card Monthly,* X, no. 99 (June 1993), 10–14. College World Series.

2215. Shattuck, Debra A. "Bats, Balls, and Books: Baseball and Higher Education for Women at Three Women's Colleges, 1866–1910." *Journal of Sport History,* XIX (Summer 1992), 91+.

2216. Smith, Gene. "The Girls of Summer." *American Heritage,* XLV (July–August 1994), 110–111. Female baseball team at Vassar College.

2217. Thompson, Richard J. "Giving It That Old College Try." *Elysian Fields Quarterly,* XII (Fall 1993), 40–43. Harvard vs. Boston Red Sox in an exhibition game, April 10, 1916.

2218. United States. Congress. House. Committee on Energy and Commerce. Subcommittee on Commerce, Consumer Protection, and Competitiveness. *Intercollegiate Sports: Hearings.* 102nd Cong., 1st sess. Washington, D.C.: GPO, 1992. 217p.

2219. Walters, John. "Adventures in Baby-Sitting: At Mansfield U, the Baseball Team Raises Money by Taking Care of Kids." *Sports Illustrated,* LXXXII (May 15, 1995), 10, 12.

2220. Whalen, S. C. *"The Relationship Between Precompetitive Affect and Collegiate Baseball Performance."* MA Thesis, University of North Carolina at Chapel Hill, 1995. 94p.

2221. "Well, That's Oberlin." *Sports Illustrated,* LXXX (June 6, 1994), 15–16. Bizarre defense by the Ohio team.

2222. Whiteside, Kelly. "At the College World Series." *Sports Illustrated,* LXXX (June 20, 1994), 117–121. Oklahoma over Georgia Tech.

2223. ____. "Short Hops." *Sports Illustrated,* LXXX (June 20, 1994), 120–122.

2. Youth Leagues, Amateur, and Semi-Pro Baseball

a. General Works

2224. Anderson, William M. "Ludington's Boys of Summer." *Michigan History,* LXXVI (May–June 1992), 14–22.

2225. Berlau, John. "Play (Regulated) Ball!" *Reason,* XXVIII (December 1996), 71–73. Recommendations of the Consumer Products Safety Commission for children's baseball.

2226. Bertman, Skip. *Youth League Baseball: Coaching and Playing.* Indianapolis, Ind.: Masters Press, 1993. 184p. First published as *Spalding Youth League Baseball* and distributed by the *Sporting News* in 1989.

2227. Brindley, Les. "Diamond Mine." *American Legion Magazine,* CXXXIV (May 1993), 30+. American Legion baseball.

2228. Brockway, Michael D. "Play (BEEP) Ball." *Mainstream,* XVIII (June 1994), 44+. Baseball for blind youngsters.

2229. Dash, Judi. "Field of Dreams: Where All the Kids Are Winners." *Family Circle,* CX (March 4, 1997), 19–20. Baseball for disabled children.

2230. Davendorf, Ann. "A Whole New Ballgame." *Jack & Jill,* LIX (June 1997), 10–12. Variations on youth baseball.

2231. Dawson, David D. "Baseball Calls: Arkansas Town Baseball in the Twenties." *Arkansas Historical Quarterly,* LIV (Winter 1995), 409–426.

2232. Doyle, Daniel. *Hardball: A Season in the Projects.* New York: G. P. Putnam's Sons, 1993. 317p. Concerns the First Chicago Near North Kikuyus baseball team.

2233. Epstein, Miles Z. "Buick and American Legion Baseball." *The American Legion,* CXL (January 1996), 43+.

2234. Feldman, Jay. "Baseball Behind Barbed Wire." *Whole Earth Review,* no. 69 (Winter 1990), 36+.

2235. Gent, Peter. *The Last Magic Summer: A Season with My Son.* New York: William Morrow, 1995. 225p.

2236. Gildner, Gary. *The Warsaw Sparks.* Iowa City: University of Iowa Press, 1996. 255p.

2237. Gregorich, Barbara. "John Olson and His Barnstorming Baseball Teams." *Michigan History,* LXXIX (May–June 1995), 38–49.

2238. Harmon, Cecil Munroe. "The Purple Sages Ride to Victory Once More: 12th Consecutive Win for History's Most Amazing Baseball Team." *Purple Sages Review,* I (March 15, 1990), 3+.

2239. Harms, Richard. "Jess Elster and the Grand Rapids Athletics." *Michigan History,* LXXIX (January 1993), 9+. Black semi-pros.

2240. Heilman, Robert. "The Field of Reality." *Elysian Fields Quarterly,* XIII (Summer 1994), 16–20. American Legion world series.

2241. Hill, Grant H. "Youth Sport Participation of Professional Baseball Players." *Sociology of Sport Journal,* X (March 1993), 107+.

2242. Hollander, R. "Father Playing Catch with Sons: A Living Symbol." *Nine: A Journal of Baseball History and Social Policy,* V (Spring 1997), 305–315.

2243. Leimbach, Patricia P. "Baseball Then and Now." *Mother Earth News,* CXXXVII (April–May 1993), 96+. An excerpt from the author's *A Thread of Blue Denim.*

2244. McCarthy, John P., Jr. *Youth Baseball: A Guide for Coaches & Parents.* 2nd ed. Crozet, Va.: Betterway Books, 1996. 166p. Revision of the author's 1989 *A Parent's Guide to Coaching Baseball.*

2245. Pekkanen, John. "Season of Miracles." *Reader's Digest,* CXLII (May 1993), 85–90. Success of a junior team in North Charleston, S.C.

2246. Perry, Thomas K. *Textile League*

Baseball: South Carolina's Mill Teams, 1880–1955. Jefferson, N.C.: McFarland & Co, Inc., 1993. 327p. Semi-pro.

2247. Reynolds, Doug. "Hardball Paternalism, Hardball Politics: Blackstone Valley Baseball, 1925–1955." *Labor's Heritage,* III (April 1991), 24+.

2248. "Rookie League Youth Baseball: Everybody Plays, Everybody Wins." *Perspective,* XIX (March 1993), 35+.

2249. Ryan, Mike and Luke. *It's Where You Played the Game: How Youth Baseball Determines the Personality of the American Male.* New York: Holt, 1996. 152p.

2250. "Stickball: Baseball for Two." *Child Life,* LXXII (April 1993), 36+.

2251. Tahant, Mark. "America's Pastime a History at Laguna: Fans Cheer on Pueblo Baseball Heroes." *New Mexico Magazine,* LXX (August 1992), 128–132. Semi-pro play.

2252. United States. Department of Housing and Urban Development. *Rookie League Baseball: How to Give Youngsters a Head Start.* Washington, D.C.: GPO, 1994. 19p. Includes Little League.

2253. Wheeler, Lonnie. "The Great American Hit." *Family Life,* II (May–June 1994), 99–101.

2254. Wong, G. M. "Called Out: One Strike Was All It Took to Snuff Out a Youth Baseball Team's Eligibility." *Athletic Business,* XIX (December 1995), 10, 14, 16.

2255. Youth Sports Institute. *Youth Baseball, Section I: Skills and Strategies.* Madison, Wisc.: Brown & Benchmark Publishers, 1993.

b. Little League

2256. Baker, Jim. "U.S. Kids Sing the World Series Blues." *TV Guide,* XLI (August 21, 1993), 31+.

2257. Beamer, Buzz. "Happy Birthday, Little League World Series." *Sports Illustrated for Kids,* VIII (August 1996), 53–59.

2258. Bodmer, Judy. "Confessions of a Sports Mom." *Reader's Digest,* CXLVIII (May 1996), 113–114.

2259. Chafetz, Janet Saltzman and Joseph A. Kotarba. "Son Worshipers: The Role of Little League Mothers in Recreating Gender." *Studies in Symbolic Interaction,* no. 18 (1995), 217–245.

2260. Clark, Brooks. "Nightmare Parents." *Sports Illustrated for Kids,* VII (April 1995), Supplement 22–23.

2261. Coyle, Dave. "Diamonds in the Rough: In Chicago, Little League Has Taken Root on Two Gritty Inner-City Baseball Fields." *Sports Illustrated,* LXXVI (June 1, 1992), 6, 8–11.

2262. Curtis, Gary. "The Game's Over." *Texas Monthly,* XXII (April 1994), 5–6+. Father's disappointment when a son outgrows Little League.

2263. Dixon, Ramon "Tru" and David Aromatorio. *How Far Do You Wanna Go?: The True Story of the Man Who Turned Sixteen Inner City Kids Into a Team of Champions.* Far Hills, N.J.: New Horizon Press, 1997. 316p.

2264. "For the Kids: Williamsport, Pa., the 1994 Little League World Series." *Referee,* XX (January 1995), 28+.

2265. "For the Kid's Sake: Lets Make Some Changes That Will Keep Baseball Fun." *Perspective,* XVI (March 1990), 28+.

2266. Fortanasce, Vincent. *Life Lessons from Little League: A Guide for Parents and Coaches.* Garden City, N.Y.: Doubleday, 1995. 303p.

2267. Geist, Bill. *Little League Confidential: One Coach's Completely Unauthorized Tale of Survival.* New York: Macmillan, 1992. 217p.

2268. Gelin, D. "A Victory Dance for Taipei: Dominant Little League Champs." *Sports Illustrated,* LXXXV (September 2, 1996), 16, 18.

2269. Gent, Peter. *The Last Magic Summer: A Season with My Son [Carter]—A Memoir.* New York: William Morrow, 1996. 225p. A father coaches his son at Bangor, Mich.

2270. Grossman, Ellie. "Who's at Bat in Little League Baseball?" *Family Safety and Health,* XLIX (Summer 1990), 12+.

2271. Hoffer, Richard. "Field of Schemes." *Sports Illustrated,* LXXVIII (January 18, 1993), 58–67. Filipino team forced to give up 1992 title.

2272. Hohenstein, Kurt. *The Rules of the Game: Simple Truths Learned From Little League.* Nashville, Tn.: T. Nelson, 1996. 221p.

2273. Kaplan, Ben. "Batter Up." *Sports Illustrated for Kids,* VII (April 1995), Supplement 24–25.

2274. King, L. L. "The Old Man and the Kid." *Washingtonian,* XXIX (May 1994), 45–50+.

2275. Lichtenberg, Gregory. "To Catch a Mother." *New York Times Magazine,* (November 7, 1993), 28+. A son's memories of playing catch with his mother.

2276. Millburg, Steve. "Let the Game Begin." *Southern Living,* XXX (April 1995), 40–41.

2277. Morris, Bob. "An Enduring Game of Catch." *Reader's Digest,* CXLII (March 1993), 83–84. A father plays catch with his 10-year old son.

2278. Noden, Michael. "Child's Play: A Team from the Philippines Manhandled Long Island to Win the Little League World Series." *Sports Illustrated,* LXXVII (September 7, 1992), 14–15.

2279. Rathbun, Mickey. "Hero Worship." *Sports Illustrated for Kids,* VII (April 1995), Supplement 26–28.

2280. Scher, Jon. "Last, But Not Least." *Sports Illustrated,* LXXIX (September 6, 1993), 30+. Long Beach team captures title.

2281. Smith, Chris S. "Diamond Visions." *New York,* XXX (June 1997), 44–46. Staten Island's South Shore Little League.

2282. Therrien, Victoria Leclerc. "Challenger Little League: Children with Disabilities Not Only Play Baseball, But Become Team Players." *The*

Exceptional Parent, XXII (April 1992), 20+.

2283. Whiteside, Kelly. "Coming of Age." *Sports Illustrated,* LXXXI (August 23, 1994), 42–44+. 1989 Trumbull, Conn., championship team.

2284. Zweibel, Alan. "Barbarians at the Plate." *Los Angeles,* XXXIX (September 1994), 122–127.

c. T-ball

2285. Broido, Bing. *The Official T-Ball USA Family Guide to Tee Ball.* Indianapolis, Ind.: Masters Press, 1996. 139p.

2286. Gabriel, Daniel. "My Brother Learned It Early." *Elysian Fields Quarterly,* XIII (Fall 1994), 41–42.

2287. Landers, Melissa A. and Gary Alan Fine. "Learning Life's Lessons in Tee Ball: The Reinforcement of Gender and Status in Kindergarten Sport." *Sociology of Sport Journal,* XIII, no. 1 (1996), 87–93.

2288. McIntosh, Ned. *The Little League Guide to Tee Ball.* Chicago, Ill.: Contemporary Books, 1993. 146p.

2289. "The Name of the Game Is...Tee Ball." *Aussie Sport Action,* VII (Summer 1996), 37–39.

2290. Tola, S. "If the Swing's the Thing, Then the Tee's the Key." *Pennsylvania Journal of Health, Physical Education, Recreation, and Dance,* LXII (Winter 1992), 9, 20.

3. Foreign Baseball

a. General Works

2291. Ballew, Bill. "The International Pastime." *Beckett Focus on Future Stars,* IV, no. 39 (July 1994), 6–10.

2292. Laidlaw, Robert and Adelaide. *Baseball's Bulldogs: The History of the Central Districts [South Africa] Baseball Clubs, 1962–1995.* Evanston Gardens, S.A.: Priv. print., 1996. Unpaged.

2293. Vanverre, Lawrence. "World

Championships of Amateur Baseball." *Journal of Sports Philately,* XXXIII (November–December 1994), 4–9.

b. Olympic and International Championship Baseball

2294. "Beisbol Olimpico: Deports de Exhibition—Olympic Baseball: Exhibition Sport." *World Baseball Magazine,* I (1996), 10–13.

2295. Betz, Tom. "Medalists with Mettle." *Beckett Baseball Card Monthly,* IX, no. 89 (August 1992), 20–24.

2296. Greenspan, B. "My Favorite Olympic Moments: Baseball." *Sports Illustrated,* LXXXIV (May 13, 1996), 5–6, 8, 10, 12, 14, 16.

2297. Griffith-Roberts, C. "The Road to Atlanta." *Southern Living,* XXXI (July 1996), 28+.

2298. Hoffer, Richard. "Day Ten: Where the Cold War Is Still Hot." *Sports Illustrated,* LXXXV (August 5, 1996), 80–81. Atlanta Olympic baseball.

2299. Kaplan, David A. "A Real World Series." *Newsweek,* CXXVIII (July 8, 1996), 70+. The idea of allowing pro players to participate in Olympics.

2300. Lewis, Brad Alan and Gabriella Goldstein. *Olympic Results, Barcelona 1992: A Complete Compilation of Results from the Games of the XXV Olympiad.* New York: Garland Publishing, 1993.

2301. Montville, Leigh. "The One That Got Away." *Sports Illustrated,* LXXXII (March 27, 1995), 42–44. St. John's University team represents the U.S. in the Pan Am Games.

2302. Nesbitt, R. A. "When the Boys Taught Their Coach." *Reader's Digest,* CXLIX (August 1996), 121–123. Special Olympics.

2303. Rondon, T. "The Pan-American Series of 1958: A Latin Series That Happened Only Once." *National Pastime,* XIV (1994), 70–71.

2304. Rushin, Steve. "Best of Both Worlds." *Sports Illustrated,* LXXXV (August 5, 1996), 82–84. Cuba vs. U.S.

2305. Spackler, Carl. "The Golden Boys of Summer." *Topps Magazine,* (Spring 1992), 15–19.

2306. Wulf, Steve. "Head-to-Head: Cuba vs. the United States." *Sports Illustrated,* LXXVII (July 22, 1992), 68–69. 1992 Olympic Games.

2307. ____. "Long Ball." *Sports Illustrated,* LXXVII (August 10, 1992), 87+.

c. Baseball in Asia:
Australia, Taiwan, and Japan

2308. Abe, I., *et al.* "Fascism, Sport, and Society in Japan." *International Journal of the History of Sport,* IX (April 1992), 1–28.

2309. "Baseball and Softball: Improving Steadily—That's the Verdict." *Sports Link (Australia),* (June 1996), 7, 10.

2310. "Baseball in Taiwan: A New League Is Born." *Travel in Taiwan,* XI (October 1996), 30+. The Republic of China becomes the only country other than the U.S. to have two professional baseball leagues.

2311. "The Big Pitch: Brisbane Bandits." *Inside Sport (Australia),* XIV (February 1993), 78–87.

2312. Carothers, R. "The Talent Drain." *Baseball Australia,* V (April 1992), 11–12.

2313. Collins, Ken. "Ballarat Goldiggers: The Realisation of a Master's Dream." *Australian Leisure,* VII (June 1996), 5–6.

2314. Dabscheck, B. "Australian Baseballers Form a Team of Their Own." *Sporting Traditions (Australia),* XII (November 1995), 61–101. Australian Baseball Players Association.

2315. Fruehling-Springwood, Charles. "Space, Time, and Hardware Individualism in Japanese Baseball: Non-Western Dimensions of Personhood." *Play and Culture,* V (August 1992), 280–294.

2316. Fujimori, Tatsuo. "The Effects of

Formal Structure of an Organization on Career and Performance." *Japanese Journal of Psychology,* LXIII (October 1992), 273–276. In English.

2317. Horotitz, Ira. "Betto-San and the White Rat: Evaluating Japanese Major League Baseball Managers Viz-a-Viz Their American Counterparts." *International Review of the Sociology of Sport,* XXX, no. 2 (1995), 165+.

2318. Hudson, D. *The History of the Carlton Baseball Club, 1898–1969.* Melbourne, Australia: Priv. print. for the Club, 1993. 100p.

2319. Liang-fu, Yin. "An Analysis of the Foundation of Yumiuri Giants Baseball Team and the Newspaper Reports on Professional Baseball Through a Comparative Study Between the Yumiuri and Asahi Newspapers." *Hitotsubashi Rouse,* CXVII (February 1979), 39+. In Japanese.

2320. Linnell, S. "The Face of Australia." *Baseball Australia,* V (April 1992), 14–17.

2321. Mitchell, B. "A National Game Goes International: Baseball in Australia." *International Journal of the History of Sport,* IX (August 1992), 288–301.

2322. Mossop, B. "Field of Dreams: Baseball Gains Popularity." *Australian Magazine,* (February 22, 1992), 8–13.

2323. Nagara, Yoichi. *Beisuboru no Shakaishi: Jimi Horio to Nichi-Bei Yakyu (A Social History of Baseball: Jimmy Horio and Baseball in Japan and America).* Osaka, Japan: Toho Shuppan, 1994. 338p. In Japanese.

2324. Nauright, John. "'Try to Reach Home!': 'Real' Baseball, Nostalgia, and Hegemonic Masculine Dreams." *Sporting Traditions (Australia),* XIII (May 1997), 91+.

2325. "The Next Nomo." In: Joe Hoppel, ed. *The Sporting News 1996 Baseball Yearbook.* St. Louis, Mo.: TSN, 1996. pp. 138–139.

2326. Oga, J. "Recent Trends in the Sports Industry in Japan." *Journal of Sport Management,* VII (September 1993), 249–255.

2327. Ohtake, Fumio and Yasushi Ohkusa. "The Relationship Between Supervisor and Workers: The Case of Professional Baseball in Japan." *Japan and the World Economy,* VIII (December 1996), 475–488.

2328. ____. "Testing the Matching Hypothesis: The Case for Professional Baseball in Japan, With Comparisons to the United States." *Journal of the Japanese and International Economic Association,* VIII (June 1994), 204+.

2329. Parker, John. "Yomiuri Giants: The LDP of Baseball—The Team Foreigners Love to Hate." *Journal of the American Chamber of Commerce,* XXX (October 1993), 64+.

2330. Rauch, Jonathan. "Why Is Japanese Baseball So Dull?" *Reason,* XXIV (August 1992), 24+.

2331. Shropshire, Kenneth L. "Baseball Salary Arbitration in Japan." *Entertainment and Sports Lawyer,* IX (Winter 1992), 17–18.

2332. "Swinging Away." *Look Japan,* XXXVIII (September 1992), 22+.

2333. Taylor, Jane, comp. *Australian Baseball League Media Guide.* St. Leonards, NSW: Australian Baseball League, 1996. 220p.

2334. Verducci, Tom. "Away Games." *Sports Illustrated,* LXXXI (October 31, 1994), 30–32+. 1994 Japanese World Series between the Seibu Lions and Yomijuri Giants.

2335. ____. "Giants Come Up Big." *Sports Illustrated,* LXXXI (November 7, 1994), 70–72. More on the '94 series.

2336. Webster, J. "Rosy Pitcher: Australian Baseball Is Set to Become an Even Bigger Summer Sport." *Bulletin,* CXVI (December 17, 1996), 86+. Australian Baseball League.

2337. Wilson, Jeffrey. "A Sport on the Rebound." *Free China Review,* XLIV (December 1994), 56+.

2338. Wulf, Steve. "Plenty More After Nomo: Thanks to Hideo Nomo, Major

League Teams Now Look Upon Japan as the Landing of the Rising Fastball." *Time,* CXLIX (March 24, 1997), 84+.

d. Baseball in Canada

2339. Anderson, Robin. "'On the Edge of the Map' with the 1908 Vancouver Beavers." *The Canadian Historical Review,* LXXVII (December 1996), 538+.

2340. Deacon, James. "A Time to Play." *Maclean's,* CVI (April 5, 1993), 48–50.

2341. Field, Robert. "Before the Lynx Went on the Prowl: 95 Years of Professional Baseball in the Nation's Capital." *Dugout,* I (October 1993), 25–30. Ottawa.

2342. ____. "Rounders on the Rock: Baseball Takes Hold on Newfoundland Before the Great War." *Dugout,* II (October 1994), 21–25.

2343. Howell, Colin D. *Northern Sandlots: A Social History of Maritime Baseball.* North York, Ont., and Buffalo: University of Toronto Press, 1995. 285p. Maritime Provinces of Canada.

2344. ____. "They Played the 'Old-Fashioned' Way: Native Baseball in Atlantic Canada." *Dugout,* III (June–July 1995), 24–26.

2345. Humber, William. *Diamonds of the North: A Concise History of Baseball in Canada.* North York, Ont., and New York: Oxford University Press, 1995. 238p.

2346. ____. and John St. James, eds. *All I Thought About Was Baseball: Writings on a Canadian Pastime.* North York, Ont., and Buffalo: University of Toronto Press, 1996. 352p.

2347. Kendall, B. *Great Moments in Canadian Baseball.* Toronto, Ont.: Lester Publishing, 1995. 64p.

2348. Kirwin, B. "A Colony Within a Colony: The Western Canada Baseball League of 1912." *Nine: A Journal of Baseball History and Social Policy Perspective,* IV (Spring 1996), 282–297.

2349. Prentice, Bruce L. and Merritt Clifton. "Baseball in Canada." In: John Thorn and Pete Palmer, eds. *Total Baseball.* 3rd ed. New York: Harper-Perennial, 1993. pp. 542–546.

2350. Stubbs, Lewis St. G. *Shoestring Glory: Semi-Pro Ball on the Prairies, 1886–1994.* Toronto: Turnstone Press, 1996. 335p.

2351. "Warming Up to Baseball." In: Joe Hoppel, ed. *The Sporting News 1994 Baseball Yearbook.* St. Louis, Mo.: TSN, 1994. pp. 140–153.

e. Baseball in Europe

2352. Benning, D. and D. Bloyce. "Baseball in Britain, 1874–1914." In: B. Svoboda and A. Rychtecky, eds. *Physical Activity for Life, East and West, North and South: Proceedings of the 9th International Society for Comparative Physical Education and Sport Conference, 1995.* Aachen, Germany: Meyer & Meyer Verlag, 1995. pp. 396–400.

2353. Chelminiski, Rudolph. "Take Me Out to the Bourron-Ball Game." *Smithsonian,* XXV (April 1994), 94+. Baseball in France.

2354. Cohen, Ed. "The Latest Fashion in French Diamonds." *Sports Illustrated,* LXXVI (June 15, 1992), 6–8.

2355. Dewey, Don. "Making a Pitch for Baseball: The Sport Is No Longer a Curiosity in Europe." *Europe,* no. 300 (October 1990), 34+.

2356. Di Gesu, E. "Baseball: Un Sport Qui Emerge." *SportEurope (Italy),* VI (Juil 1995), 40–43. "Baseball: An Emerging Sport."

2357. Kapnick, T. "Czech Baseball: Emerging from the Cold." *Baseball Research Journal,* XXIV (1995), 73–75.

2358. Laird, L. "Letter from Moscow." *Europe,* (June 1994), 37–38. Government-subsidized Russian baseball.

2359. Sahker, H. "'Snapshots' of Britball." *Dugout,* III (June–July 1995), 27–30.

2360. Smyth, I. "Baseball Put to the Test: And England Beats the U.S." *Baseball Research Journal,* XXIV (1995), 131–133.

2361. ____. "The Development of Baseball in Northern England, 1935–39." *International Journal of the History of Sport,* X (August 1993), 252–258.

f. Baseball in Latin America

2362. Bjarkman, Peter C. *Baseball with a Latin Beat: A History of the Latin American Game.* Jefferson, N.C.: McFarland & Co., Inc., 1994. 486p.

2363. Cartwright, Gary. "Chasing the Red Eagle." *Texas Monthly,* XXI (August 1993), 92–97. American players boost the Veracruz (Mexico) Red Eagle team.

2364. Echevarria, Roberto G. "The Game in Matanzas: On the Origins of Cuban Baseball." *Yale Review,* LXXXIII (July 1995), 62+.

2365. Heuer, Robert. "Look What They've Done to My Game!" *Americas,* XLVII (May–June 1995), 36–41.

2366. Horenstein, Henry. *Baseball in the Barrios.* New York: Gulliver Books, 1997. Venezuela.

2367. Katel, Peter. "The Best Team Money Can't Buy." *Newsweek,* CXIX (June 8, 1992), 62–63. Cuban.

2368. Klein, Alan M. "American Hegemony, Dominican Resistance, and Baseball." *Dialectical Anthropology,* XIII (Fall 1988), 301+.

2369. ____. "Baseball as Underdevelopment: The Political Economy of Sport in the Dominican Republic." *Sociology of Sport Journal,* VI (June 1989), 95+.

2370. ____. "Borderline Treason: Nationalisms and Baseball on the Texas-Mexican Border." *Journal of Sport and Social Issues,* XX (August 1996), 296–313.

2371. ____. "Culture, Politics, and Baseball in the Dominican Republic." *Latin American Perspectives,* XXII (June 1995), 111–130.

2372. ____. *Sugarball: The American Game, The Dominican Dream.* New Haven, Conn.: Yale University Press, 1991. 179p.

2373. ____. "Trans-Nationalism, Labour Migration, and Latin American Baseball." In: J. Bale and J. Maguire, eds. *The Global Sports Arena: Athletic Talent Migration in an Interdependent World.* London, Eng.: Frank Cass & Co., Ltd., 1994. pp. 183–205.

2374. LaFrance, David G. "Labor, the State, and Professional Baseball in Mexico in the 1980s." *Journal of Sport History,* XXII (Summer 1995), 111–134.

2375. McCarthy, Eugene J. "Diamond Diplomacy." *Elysian Fields Quarterly,* XIV (Summer 1995), 12–15. U.S.-Cuba.

2376. Montville, Leigh. "A Latin Beat." *Sports Illustrated,* LXXXII (January 16, 1995), 42–47. Puerto Rican Winter League.

2377. Oleksak, Michael M. and Mary A. *Beisbol: Latinoamericanos en las Grandes Ligas.* Mexico City: Edamex, 1995. 366p.

2378. Perez, Louis A., Jr. "Between Baseball and Bullfighting: The Quest for Nationality in Cuba, 1868–1898." *Journal of American History,* LXXXI (September 1994), 493+.

2379. Ruck, Rob. "Baseball Diplomacy." *Pittsburgh,* XXV (July 1994), 38+. U.S. aid to youth baseball in Nicaragua.

2380. ____. "Three Kings Days in Consuelo: Crickett, Baseball, and the Cocolos in San Pedro de Macoris." *Studies in Latin American Popular Culture,* XIII (1994), 129+.

2381. Schell, William, Jr. "Lions, Bulls, and Baseball: Colonel R. C. Pate and Modern Sports Promotion in Mexico." *Journal of Sport History,* XX (Winter 1993), 259+.

2382. Van Hyning, Thomas E. *Puerto Rico's Winter League: A History of Major League Baseball's Launching Pad.* Jefferson, N.C.: McFarland & Co., Inc., 1995. 304p.

4. Scouts, Scouting, and Career Opportunities

2383. Arenofsky, Janice. "Baseball: It's More Than Just a Game." *Career World,* XXIII (September 1994), 23–28.

2384. Black, R. J. *"Occupational Employment Patterns by Gender in Major League Baseball."* Unpublished Ph.D. Dissertation, University of Minnesota, 1996. 121p.

2385. Helitzer, Mark. *The Dream Job: Sports Publicity, Promotion, and Public Relations.* Athens, Ohio: University Sports Press, 1992. Unpaged.

2386. Hofacre, S. and S. Branvold. "Baseball Front Office Careers: Expectations and Realities." *Journal of Sport Management,* IX (May 1995), 173–181.

2387. Hookway, Bob. "Former Major League Scout Talks About Talent Hunting." *Baseball Digest,* LV (October 1996), 72–78.

2388. Klis, Mike. "Some Pass, Some Play." *Beckett Baseball Card Monthly,* XI, no. 114 (September 1994), 14–19.

2389. DeMarco, Tony. "Educational Choices." *Beckett Baseball Card Monthly,* X, no. 101 (August 1993), 10–13.

2390. O'Shei, Tim. "Major League Scouts Seek 'Diamonds in the Rough.'" *Baseball Digest,* LII (June 1993), 52–59.

2391. Muff, Red and Mike Cappa. *The Scout: Searching for the Best in Baseball.* Fort Worth, Tx.: Word Press, 1996. 258p.

2392. Price, Lew. "Scouts Will Always Remain Baseball's Indispensable Men." *Baseball Digest,* LI (November 1992), 46–49.

E. Baseball
Rules and Techniques

In the introduction to this chapter in *Baseball: A Comprehensive Bibliography*, we suggested that this part be labeled our chapter on instruction. In addition to an initial review of rules and regulations, information is provided on coaching and managing, signs, and officiating; general works on techniques; and studies of such specific actions as baserunning, catching, fielding, hitting, and pitching.

1. Rules and Regulations

Covered here is the literature surrounding baseball's laws (rules and regulations). Users should note that additional overviews will be found in Chapter B:1:a (General Works and Histories) above and in this chapter's subpart 3 (General Studies of Technique, Strategy, and Baseball Science) below.

2393. Adair, F. "Reengineering Baseball: This Is the Way the Game Should Be Played in the Age of Nintendo." *Across the Board,* XXXI (October 1994), 53–54.

2394. Aschburner, Steve. "After Two Decades, DH Rule Still a Matter of Debate." *Baseball Digest,* LI (December 1992), 48–53.

2395. "Bird Brainer." *Sports Illustrated for Kids,* IX (September 1997), 93–94.

Is a ball that hits a bird in midair and lands in fair territory a single?

2396. Burnett, Kevin. "A Modest Proposal; or, Switchpath Baseball." *Elysian Fields Quarterly,* XIII (Winter 1994), 10–13. A new rule designed to eliminate the DH.

2397. Cohen, Ted. "There Are No Ties at First Base." *Elysian Fields Quarterly,* XI (Winter 1992), 41–49.

2398. "The Common Law Origins of the Infield Fly Rule." *Boston Bar Journal,* XXXI (July–August 1987), 37–41.

2399. Dickson, Paul. *The Joy of Keeping Score: How Scoring the Game Has Influenced and Enhanced the History of Baseball.* New York: Walker, 1996. 117p.

2400. Dudley, Bill. *The Instant Referee: A Simplified Easy-to-Read Guide to the Rules of Professional Baseball, Basketball, Football, and Hockey.*

Vancouver, B.C.: Titan Publishing, 1993. Unpaged.

2401. DuPont, Kevin. "Players Are Usually Governed by the Game's Unwritten Rules." *Baseball Digest,* LV (September 1996), 51–54.

2402. Eisensohn, E. "Faire Evoluer le Reglement." *E.P.S. Education Physique et Sport (France),* XLIV (Janv/Fevr. 1994), 44–47. "How to Improve the Regulations."

2403. Fagen, Herb. "Five Former Major Leaguers Cite Changes in Game." *Baseball Digest,* LV (November 1996), 72–81.

2404. Feinstein, John. "One Game, One Rule: Tradition Be Damned, It's Time for All of Baseball to Adopt the Designated Hitter." *Inside Sports,* XVIII (May 1996), 74–76.

2405. Guidi, Gene. "After 20 Years, the DH Rule Still Has Advocates, Foes." *Baseball Digest,* LII (August 1993), 58–61.

2406. Gutman, Dan. *The Way Baseball Works.* New York: Simon and Schuster, 1996. 215p.

2407. Healey, Dennis and Patrick McRae. *The Illustrated Rules of Baseball.* Nashville, Tn.: Ideals Children Books, 1995. 32p.

2408. Hertzel, Bob. "Modern Changes in Baseball Have Affected Style of Play." *Baseball Digest,* LII (September 1993), 44–47.

2409. Holtzman, Jerome. "American League DH Rule Survives the Test of Time." *Baseball Digest,* LIV (March 1995), 47–48.

2410. ____. "Should Owners and Players Unite on a New Commissioner?" *Baseball Digest,* LIV (November 1995), 27–28.

2411. Kelley, Brent P. *Baseball's Biggest Blunder: The Bonus Rule of 1953–1957.* Lanham, Md.: Scarecrow Press, 1997. 232p.

2412. Kuenster, John. "Trickery, Fair or Foul, Has Always Been Part of Major League Baseball." *Baseball Digest,* LVI (September 1997), 17–21.

2413. Kurlantzick, Lawrence. "A Needed Change in the Rules of Baseball." *Seton Hall Journal of Sport Law,* II, no. 1 (1992), 279–300.

2414. Lehigh, S. "By the Rules: Those Pesky Batters' Box Rules." *Referee,* XXI (April 1996), 46–48, 50–52, 54–55.

2415. ____. "Dead-Ball Lines." *Referee,* XXI (July 1996), 52–59.

2416. Lewis, Allen. "How Sacrifice Fly Rule Affected .400 Hitters in the Majors." *Baseball Digest,* LIV (March 1995), 90–92.

2417. Luksa, Frank. "Commentary: It's Time for Majors to Leave DH on Bench Permanently." *Baseball Digest,* LIV (October 1995), 59–60.

2418. Malley, T. "If I Were Commissioner." *Nine: A Journal of Baseball History and Social Policy Perspectives,* V (Spring 1997), 406–407.

2419. Miller, Marvin and Bowie Kuhn. "Should the Baseball Commissioner's Job Be Restructured?" *Inside Sports,* XV (January 1993), 24–25.

2420. Mowen, Karrie. "Baseball Etiquette Built on Respect for Opponents." *Baseball Digest,* LVI (December 1997), 75–77.

2421. Nemec, David. *The Rules of Baseball: An Anecdotal Look at the Rules of Baseball and How They Came to Be.* New York: Lyons & Buford, 1994. 270p.

2422. Pedersen, Craig. "For the Best or Worst Interests of Baseball: The Commissioner's Powers Lie in Doubt." *Loyola Entertainment Law Journal,* XIII, no. 3 (1993), 587+.

2423. Post, Paul. "Ex-Major Leaguers Express Pros and Cons of the DH Rule." *Baseball Digest,* LV (November 1996), 55–57.

2424. Rainey, David W., Nicholas R. Santilli, and Kevin Fallon. "Development of Athletes' Conceptions of Sport Officials' Authority." *Journal of Sport & Exercise Psychology,* XIV (December 1992), 392–404.

2425. Reinsdorf, Jonathan M. "The Pow-

ers of the Commissioner in Baseball."
Marquette Sports Law Journal, VII
(Fall 1996), 211–255.

2426. Ryan, Jeff. "The Game: If I Were
Commissioner...." *Sport,* LXXXIV
(March 1993), 40+.

2427. Sanoff, Alvin P. "Yawn. What
Inning Is It?" *U.S. News & World
Report,* CXXI (December 30, 1996),
43–44. Proposes changing rules to
speed up the game.

2428. Schieffer, Tom and Marvin Miller.
"Pro & Con: Does Baseball Need a
Commissioner?" *Inside Sports,* XVIII
(August 1996), 20–21.

2429. Shlain, Bruce. *Baseball Inside
Out: The Unspoken Rules of the
Game.* New York: Viking Press, 1992.
175p.

2430. Topkin, Marc. "The DH Rule: Is
It a Hit or a Miss?" *Baseball Digest,*
LV (July 1996), 36–42.

2431. Utz, Stephen G. "The Authority of
the Rules of Baseball: The Commissioner as Judge." *The Journal of the
Philosophy of Sport,* XVI (January
1989), 89+.

2432. Van Dyck, Dave. "Corked Bats,
Scuffed Balls Are as Old as the Game
Itself." *Baseball Digest,* LIV (June
1995), 65–68.

2433. Wulf, Steve. "A Blueprint for
Baseball." *Sports Illustrated,* LXXVI
(April 6, 1992), 32–37.

2434. "Your Cheating Heart: Tactics
Used to Defy Rules Often Are Real
Corkers." In: Joe Hoppel, ed. *The
Sporting News 1995 Baseball Year-
book.* St. Louis, Mo.: TSN, 1995. pp.
28–31.

2. Coaching and Managing, Signs, Officiating

The sources in this part consider the
techniques involved in coaching and managing on various levels, officiating, and
the intricacies of signs and sign-stealing.
For ease of access, three sub-parts are
provided: Coaching and Managing,
Signs, and Officiating.

a. Coaching and Managing

2435. American Coaching Effectiveness
Program. *Coaching Youth Baseball.*
2nd ed. Champaign, Ill.: Human
Kinetics Pub., 1996. 143p. Revision of
the next title.

2436. ____. *Rookie Coaches Baseball
Guide.* Officially Endorsed by the
USA Baseball. Champaign, Ill.:
Human Kinetics Pub., 1993. 73p.

2437. Arconati, A. V. *"The Application
of Markov State Probabilities in
Developing Artificially Intelligent
Managerial Strategies: A Case Study
Based on Major League Baseball."*
Unpublished Ph.D. dissertation, Uni-
versity of Missouri, 1994. 255p.

2438. Barnett, Nancy P., Frank L. Smoll,
and Ronald E. Smith. "Effects of
Enhancing Coach-Athlete Relationships on Youth Sport Attrition." *Sport
Psychologist,* VI (June 1992), 111–127.

2439. Behn, Robert D. "Baseball Man-
agement and Public Management: The
Testable vs. the Important." *Journal of
Policy Analysis and Management,* XI
(Spring 1992), 315+.

2440. Bradley, Jeff. "Baseball's Unend-
ing Battle: Managers Versus Umpires." *Baseball Digest,* LII (September 1993), 32–35.

2441. Cannella, Albert A. and W. Glenn
Rowe. "Leader Capabilities, Succes-
sion, and Competitive Context: A
Study of Professional Baseball
Teams." *Leadership Quarterly,* VI
(Spring 1995), 69–88.

2442. Doumit, Pete. "Coaching First
Base." *Scholastic Coach,* LXIV (December 1994), 14+.

2443. Elderkin, Phil. "Setting Up a Batting Order: It's Like Fine-Tuning a
Car." *Baseball Digest,* LV (September
1996), 31–33.

2444. Fabianic, Daniel. "Managerial
Change and Organizational Effectiveness in Major League Baseball: Find-
ings From the Eighties." *Journal of
Sport Behavior,* XVII (September
1994), 135–147.

2445. Gelinas, Mark and Albert Marier. *Growing Into Baseball*. Gloucester, Ont.: Sport Information Resource Centre, 1989. 79p. Coaching youngsters ages 5–11.

2446. Gorman, Kevin. "If Teams Get Behind, They Should Never, Ever Give Up." *Baseball Digest*, LVI (August 1997), 70–73.

2447. Graham, Stedman. "The Age of Insecurity." *Inside Sports*, XIX (June 1997), 9–10. Rapid turnover of losing skippers.

2448. Hofmann, David A., Rick Jacobs, and Steve J. Gerras. "Mapping Individual Performance Over Time." *Journal of Applied Psychology*, LXXVII (April 1992), 185–195.

2449. Horowitz, Ira. "Betto-San and the White Rat: Evaluating Japanese Major League Baseball Managers Vis-a-Viz Their American Counterparts." *International Review for the Sociology of Sport*, XXX, no. 2 (1995), 165–178.

2450. ____. "Pythagoras, Tommy Lasorda, and Me: On Evaluating Baseball Managers." *Social Science Quarterly*, LXXV (March 1994), 187–194.

2451. Hoynes, Paul. "Big League Bench Coaches: Valuable Aides to Managers." *Baseball Digest*, LVI (July 1997), 56–59.

2452. James, Bill. "What Makes a Great Manager?" *The New York Times Magazine*, (April 13, 1997), 46–51.

2453. Jenkins, Chris. "How the Job of Managing Has Changed in the Majors." *Baseball Digest*, LI (September 1992), 60–66.

2454. Kahn, Lawrence M. "Managerial Quality, Team Success, and Industrial Player Performance in Major League Baseball." *Industrial and Labor Relations Review*, XLVI (April 1993), 531+.

2455. Katz, Evan T. M. "I Manage a Professional Baseball Team." *PM, Public Management*, LXXI (March 1989), 9+.

2456. Kichmer, Bob and Bryan. *Coaching Youth Baseball*. Tulsa, Okla.: Baseball Advantage, 1993. 122p. Spiral-bound.

2457. Kindall, Jerry. *Science of Coaching Baseball*. Champagne, Ill.: Human Kinetics Press, 1992. 200p.

2458. Kuenster, John. "In Plotting to Win, Managers Are Usually Governed by 'the [Rule] Book.'" *Baseball Digest*, LII (June 1993), 17–19.

2459. Kurkjian, Tim. "A Manager's Survival Guide." *Sports Illustrated*, LXXVI (April 6, 1992), 38–41.

2460. Lanning, B. "The Art of Baseball." *Elysian Fields Quarterly*, XI (Winter 1992), 32–40. Principles of winning adapted from Sun Tzu's *The Art of War*.

2461. Lopez, Andy and John Kirkgard. *Coaching Baseball Successfully*. Champagne, Ill.: Human Kinetics Press, 1993. 192p.

2462. ____. *Coaching Baseball Successfully*. Rev. ed. Champaign, Ill.: Human Kinetics Pub., 1996. 204p.

2463. Macht, Norman L. "Whatever Happened to All That Chatter on the Field?" *Baseball Digest*, LI (January 1992), 46–49.

2464. Mazzoni, Wayne. "A Signal Honor: The Pitching Coach as a Conduit for the Catcher." *Scholastic Coach & Athletic Director*, LXVI (April 1997), 17+.

2465. McKnight, Chris and Brad Howland. "Baseball Coaching with Video." *Scholastic Coach*, LXIII (March 1994), 34+.

2466. Pascarelli, Peter. *The Toughest Job in Baseball: What Managers Do, How They Do It, and Why It Gives Them Ulcers*. New York: Simon and Schuster, 1993. 252p.

2467. Risker, D. C. "Baseball and Management Theory: Similar Concerns—Different Fields." *Nine: A Journal of Baseball History and Social Policy Perspective*, V (Fall 1996), 49–60.

2468. Ryan, Bob. "Third Base Coach: He's 'Traffic Cop' of the Game." *Baseball Digest*, LIII (July 1994), 40–43.

2469. Shields, D. L. L., *et al.* "The Relationship Between Leadership Behaviors and Group Cohesion in Team Sports." *Journal of Psychology,* CXXXI (March 1997), 196–210.

2470. Shlain, Bruce. *Baseball Inside Out: Winning the Games Within the Games.* New York: Viking Press, 1992. 185p.

2471. Silvestri, Lynette. "Survey of Volunteer Coaches." *Perceptual & Motor Skills,* LXXII (April 1991), 409–410.

2472. Singell, Larry D., Jr. "Managers, Specific Human Capital, and Firm Productivity in Major League Baseball." *Atlantic Economic Journal,* XXI (September 1993), 47+.

2473. Sport Information Resource Centre. *Getting Started in Baseball: Helpful Tips for First-Time Coaches.* Gloucester, Ont., 1993. 50p.

2474. Topel, Brett. "First Base Coaches: They're Baseball's Unknown Soldiers." *Baseball Digest,* LV (December 1996), 54–57.

2475. Vass, George. "Are Major League Baseball Managers Running Scared?" *Baseball Digest,* LIII (February 1994), 56–61.

2476. _____. "Why Teams Switch Players from One Position to Another." *Baseball Digest,* LI (July 1992), 26–32.

2477. Verducci, Tom. "Minnesota 24, Detroit 11: Vikings-Lions? No, Twins, Tigers. Baseball Is Now So Explosive, Managers Have Thrown Away 'The Book.'" *Sports Illustrated,* LXXXIV (May 13, 1996), 44–46, 53–54, 56.

2478. Villanueva, R. "Baseball Practice Organization." *Texas Coach,* XLI (February 1997), 54–55.

2479. "Winning Team Plays: How You Compare to Four Major League Baseball Managers." *Supervisory Management,* XXXIX (July 1994), 8+.

2480. Witt, Rickey. "Checklist for Baseball Organization." *Texas Coach,* XXXVIII (January 1994), 30+.

b. Signs

2481. Kurkijan, Tim. "Sign Language." *Sports Illustrated,* LXXXVII (July 28, 1997), 58–63.

2482. Lockwood, Wayne. "Sign Language: The Art of Baseball Communication." *Baseball Digest,* LVI (October 1997), 40–43.

2483. Olney, Buster. "Signs to Batters: They're Part Art, Part Con." *Baseball Digest,* LII (December 1993), 57–60.

2484. Priebe, Brian. "Signing On and Off." *Scholastic Coach & Athletic Director,* LXVI (January 1997), 78–80+.

2485. Southworth, Harold S. *The Complete Book of Baseball Signs.* New York: Avon Books, 1993. 357p.

c. Officiating

2486. Anshel, M. H. "Sources of Acute Stress in American and Australian Baseball Referees." *Journal of Applied Sport Psychology,* VII (March 1995), 11–22.

2487. Ford, G. G., *et al.* "Perceptual Factors Affecting the Accuracy of Ball and Strike Judgments from the Traditional American League and National League Umpiring Perspective." *International Journal of Sport Psychology,* XXVII (January–March 1996), 50–58.

2488. Goldsteain, Richard. *You Be the Umpire: The Baseball Controversy Quiz Book.* New York: Dell, 1993. 307p.

2489. Grossi, Tony. "Umpires: They're Guardians of the Game's Integrity." *Baseball Digest,* LII (October 1993), 42–45.

2490. "Handling Plays Made at First Base." *Referee,* XIX (January 1994), 57+.

2491. Holway, John B. "Calling Balls and Strikes Remains an Imperfect Art." *Baseball Digest,* LIV (April 1995), 68–72.

2492. "How to Score Plays While Working the Plate." *Referee,* XVIII (May 1993), 42+.

2493. "Interference or Obstruction?: An Age-Old Question Remains." *Referee,* XX (November 1995), 60–61.

2494. Kuenster, John. "Major League Umpires: Love 'Em or Not, They're Vital to the Game." *Baseball Digest,* LV (July 1996), 17–19.

2495. ____. "Relentless Eye of TV Puts Big League Umpires Under More Stress." *Baseball Digest,* LIII (October 1994), 17–19.

2496. ____. "Sparky Anderson Favors Allowing Umpires to Work Both Leagues." *Baseball Digest,* LV (May 1996), 17–20.

2497. Larsen, Janet D. and David W. Rainey. "Judgment Bias in Baseball Umpires' First Base Calls: A Computer Simulation." *Journal of Sport & Exercise Psychology,* XIII (March 1991), 75–79.

2498. Lehigh, S. "Baseball: Does the Run Score?" *Referee,* XXI (June 1996), 46–48, 50–53.

2499. Major League Baseball Umpire Development Staff and National Association of Professional Baseball Leagues. *N.A.P.B.L. Umpire Manual.* Chicago, Ill.: Triumph Books, 1996. 100p.

2500. *Make the Right Call.* Chicago, Ill.: Triumph Books, 1994. 217p.

2501. Rainey, David W. "Magnitude of Stress Experienced by Baseball and Softball Umpires." *Perception & Motor Skills,* LXXIX (August 1994), 255–258.

2502. ____. "Sources of Stress Among Baseball and Softball Umpires." *Journal of Applied Sport Psychology,* VII (March 1995), 1–10.

2503. ____. "Stress, Burnout, and Intention to Terminate Among Umpires." *Journal of Sport Behavior,* XVIII (December 1995), 312–323.

2504. ____., et al. "Normative Rules Among Umpires: The 'Phantom Tag' at Second Base." *Journal of Sport Behavior,* XVI (September 1993), 147–155.

2505. Robertson, S. A. *"An Evaluation of the Characteristics of Successful Students at the Brinkman-Froemming Umpire School."* Unpublished M.A. thesis, University of North Carolina at Chapel Hill, 1993. 78p.

2506. Wells, S. "Safes, Outs, and Big League Dreams: Those Are Just Three of the Things Shared by More Than 150 Students Who Attended the 1992 Harry Wendelstedt School for Umpires." *Referee,* XVIII (January 1993), 28–33.

3. General Studies of Technique, Strategy, and Baseball Science

Drawing together into one location these general studies of baseball technique, strategy, and science is the purpose of this subpart. While the specific techniques of baserunning, catching, fielding, hitting, and pitching are covered below, here readers will find sources which combine information on those techniques into single works. Additionally, references to baseball strategy and winning are also located here; although, readers should note that certain of the works in subpart 2:a ("Coaching and Managing") above also are relevant. Finally, we have included here those works which deal with baseball science, e.g., why does a baseball curve.

2507. Adair, R. K. "The Physics of Baseball." *Physics Today,* XLVIII (May 1995), 26–31.

2508. Angell, Roger. "Put Me in, Coach." *The New Yorker,* LIX (May 3, 1993), 47–56+. On the decline in desire and skills in the modern game.

2509. Barber, D. and C. Cieminski. "Shoulder and Elbow Training for Baseball." *Strength and Conditioning,* XVII (October 1995), 42–50.

2510. Bush, J. T. "Indoor Baseball Practice Organization." *Texas Coach,* XXXVI (May 1992), 36+.

2511. Cluck, Bob. *How to Hit, How to Pitch: A Complete Self-Coaching*

System for Winning Baseball. Chicago, Ill.: Contemporary Books, 1995. 140p.

2512. ____. *Play Better Baseball: Winning Techniques and Strategies for Coaches & Players.* Chicago, Ill.: Contemporary Books, 1993. 240p.

2513. *Converse All-Star Baseball: How to Play Like a Pro.* New York: John Wiley, 1997.

2514. Cunningham, Bob. "Weight Training Now an Accepted Practice in the Majors." *Baseball Digest,* LV (October 1996), 68–71.

2515. Darden, Gib. "Two Critical Concepts in Baseball Conditioning." *Scholastic Coach,* LXII (January 1993), 82–86.

2516. Delmonico, Rod. "Baseball Conditioning & Strength Program." *Scholastic Coach,* LXII (February 1993), 56–60.

2517. Denis, Pierre. "Les Fondamentaux Techniques." *E.P.S. Education Physique et Sport (France),* XLIV (Janv/Fevr. 1994), 40–42. "The Fundamental Techniques."

2518. Forney, Jeff and Pat Murphy. *Complete Conditioning for Baseball.* Champagne, Ill.: Human Kinetics Press, 1997.

2519. French, K. E., *et al.* "Expert-Novice Differences in Cognitive and Skill Execution Components of Youth Baseball Performance." *Research Quarterly for Exercise and Sport,* LXVI (September 1995), 194–201.

2520. ____. "Knowledge Representation and Problem Solution in Expert and Novice Youth Baseball Players." *Research Quarterly for Exercise and Sport,* LXVII (December 1996), 386–395.

2521. Gambetta, Vern. "Concepts of Baseball Conditioning: The White Sox Experience." *Strength and Conditioning,* XIX (August 1997), 7+.

2522. George, Daniel P. "Big League Basics." *Boy's Life,* LXXXIV (June 1994), 18–21.

2523. George, Thomas R. "Self-confidence and Baseball Performance: A Casual Examination of Self-Efficacy Theory." *Journal of Sport & Exercise Psychology,* XVI (December 1994), 381–399.

2524. Gerstein, Phyllis. "Baseball: Getting in Shape." *Current Health,* XXI (April 1995), 20–23.

2525. Gillespie, Gordon and James Peterson. *Spalding Baseball Drill Book.* Indianapolis, Ind.: Masters Press, 1993. 217p.

2526. Goldstein, Stephen R. and Charlotte A. Young. "'Evolutionary' Stable Strategy of Handedness in Major League Baseball." *Journal of Comparative Psychology,* CX (June 1996), 164–169.

2527. Hoffman, C. M. *"The Difference Between Successful and Unsuccessful Baseball Players on the Trait of Learned Effectiveness."* Unpublished Ph.D. Dissertation, University of Kansas, 1995. 86p.

2528. Keller, Bob. "Winning with the Little Things." *Scholastic Coach & Athletic Director,* LXV (April 1996), 68–69.

2529. Kuenster, John. "Survival and Success in the Majors Depends on a Player's Ability to Adjust." *Baseball Digest,* LI (August 1992), 17–19.

2530. Lockwood, Wayne. "Ability to Switch Positions a Valued Talent in the Majors." *Baseball Digest,* LVI (November 1997), 62–65.

2531. ____. "A 'Career Year' in the Majors Often Defies Explanation." *Baseball Digest,* LVI (September 1997), 58–61.

2532. McEvoy, K. P. and R. V. Newton. "Baseball Throwing Velocity: A Comparison of Medicine Ball Training and Weight Training." *Journal of Strength & Conditioning,* VIII (August 1994), 198–203.

2533. ____. "Effects of Dynamic Weight Training on Baseball Throwing Velocity and Base Running Speed." In: Australian Coaching Council. *1994, the Year of the Coach: Proceedings of the*

National Coaching Conference, Canberra, 1–3 December 1994. Canberra, Aust., 1994. pp. 123–128.

2534. Murphy, Pat and Jeff Forney. *Complete Conditioning for Baseball.* Champaigne, Ill.: Human Kinetics, 1997. 194p.

2535. Olrich, T. "Off-Season Weight Training for Baseball and Softball Players." *Spotlight,* XVIII (Summer 1995), 3–4.

2536. Paull, G. and D. Glencross. "Expert Perception and Decision Making in Baseball." *International Journal of Sport Psychology,* XXVIII (January–March 1997), 35–56.

2537. Ploeger, Robert. *"The Effects of Three Selected Training Programs on Shoulder External Rotation Strength, Flexibility, and Throwing Velocity in Collegiate Baseball Players."* Unpublished M.S. thesis, Brigham Young University, 1993. 113p.

2538. Ravizza, Ken and Tom Hanson. *Heads-Up Baseball: Playing the Game One Pitch at a Time.* Indianapolis, Ind.: Masters Press, 1995. 175p.

2539. Stepich, Don. "The Simplicity of Baseball and the Complexity of Training." *Performance and Instruction,* XXXI (July 1992), 32+.

2540. Taylor, Jim and Kenneth L. Cuave. "The Sophomore Jinx Among Professional Baseball Players: Real or Imagined?" *International Journal of Sport Psychology,* XXV (April–June 1994), 230–239.

2541. Tom, Kenneth. "The Baseball Player: Athlete or Physicist?" *California Engineer,* LXXII (March 1994), 3+.

2542. Urschel, Joe. "Batter vs. Pitcher: A Battle of Wits and Reaction Time." *Baseball Digest,* LV (February 1996), 36–40.

2543. Weatherly, J. and C. Schinck. "Concepts for Baseball Conditioning." *Strength & Conditioning,* XVIII (April 1996), 32–39.

2544. Weinstein, Jerry, with Andy McKay. *SSC Baseball Instructional Manual.* Sacramento, Ca.: Sacramento City College, 1996. Unpaged.

2545. Winkin, John, with Jay Kemble and Michael Coutts. *Maximizing Baseball Practice.* Champagne, Ill.: Human Kinetics, 1995. 130p.

2546. Wolff, Rich. *Playing Better Baseball.* Champagne, Ill.: Human Kinetics, 1997.

4. Specific Techniques

Many separate titles have been prepared on the individual techniques of baseball. These are located in the subparts below: Base Running (which includes base stealing); Catching; Fielding; Hitting; and Pitching. The reader should note the subsection preceding this one ("General Studies of Technique, Strategy, and Baseball Science"). To save space, the historical introductions provided these categories in *Baseball: A Comprehensive Bibliography* are not repeated here.

a. Base Running

2547. Beale, Wade J. "Aggressiveness on the Basepaths." *Scholastic Coach,* LXIV (February 1995), 16–17.

2548. ____. "Stealing Second Base Against a Left-Hander." *Scholastic Coach,* LXIII (March 1994), 73+.

2549. Castle, George. "Baserunning: A Neglected Skill in the Major Leagues?" *Baseball Digest,* LII (February 1993), 42–46.

2550. Fiffer, Steve. *Speed.* Alexandria, Va.: Redefinition, 1992. 191p.

2551. Gabella, Jim. "Absolutes of Base Stealing." *Scholastic Coach,* LXII (February 1993), 12–13.

2552. ____. "Baserunning Fundamentals: Home to Home." *Scholastic Coach,* LXI (May–June 1992), 32–35.

2553. ____. "Preventing the Hit & Run." *Scholastic Coach,* LXIII (March 1994), 74–75.

2554. "The Second Base Steal in Baseball." *Referee,* XXI (July 1996), 30–31.

b. Catching

2555. Adams, Samuel. "Catching in the Majors: Is It a Form of Art or Science?" *Baseball Digest,* LII (November 1993), 48–51.

2556. Davis, Bob. "Working with the Catcher." *Referee,* XX (May 1995), 47–48, 50–51.

2557. Doyle, Al. "Never Underestimate a Good, Defensive Catcher." *Baseball Digest,* LVI (June 1997), 38–41.

2558. Grossi, Tony. "Catching Remains the Game's Most Hazardous Position." *Baseball Digest,* LIV (October 1995), 38–42.

2559. Heck, Bobby. "Blocking the Pitch in the Dirt." *Scholastic Coach,* LXIV (November 1994), 68–69.

2560. Piergustavo, Rich. "Two Little Words for the Catcher: Just Catch." *Scholastic Coach,* LXII (March 1993), 24–25.

2561. Rogers, Phil. "Catching Remains Baseball's Most Demanding Position." *Baseball Digest,* LIV (June 1995), 40–42.

2562. Sakurai, Shinji. "Age-Related Differences in Throwing Techniques Used by the Catcher in Baseball." *Pediatric Exercise Science,* VI (August 1994), 225–235.

2563. Weinstein, Jerry. "In the Hands of the Receiver." *Scholastic Coach & Athletic Director,* LXVII (January–February 1997), 62–67, 24–26.

c. Fielding

2564. Biondi, Greg. "Infield Repetitions with Two Fungoes." *Scholastic Coach,* LXII (November 1992), 74–76.

2565. Collins, Tom R. "Minimizing the Big Inning." *Scholastic Coach,* LXIII (May–June 1994), 20+.

2566. Cramblitt, Steve. "Four Ways to Defense the 1st & 3rd Double Steal." *Scholastic Coach & Athletic Director,* LXVI (May–June 1997), 46–51.

2567. Crasnick, Jerry. "Ex-Stars Discuss the Demands of Playing Shortstop." *Baseball Digest,* LII (September 1993), 36–39.

2568. Cunningham, Bob. "Middle Infielders Discuss Techniques of 'Turning Two.'" *Baseball Digest,* LIV (July 1995), 36–40.

2569. Dannemiller, James L., Timothy G. Babler, and Brian L. Babler. "On Catching Fly Balls." *Science,* CCLXXIII (July 1996), 256–257.

2570. Delmonico, Rod. *Defensive Baseball.* Indianapolis, Ind.: Masters Press, 1996. 145p.

2571. DelPiano, Marc. "A Backhand Complement." *Scholastic Coach,* LXIII (May–June 1994), 69–70. Infielding.

2572. ____. "Fielding the Slow Roller." *Scholastic Coach,* LXII (March 1993), 34+.

2573. Donald, Tom. "Outfielding: The Last Line of Defense." *Scholastic Coach,* LXIII (March 1994), 24–25.

2574. Doyle, Al. "Fourth Outfielder, Valuable 'Insurance' for Contenders." *Baseball Digest,* LVI (October 1997), 60–63.

2575. Ehret, S. "What Is a Force Play?" *Referee,* XXI (August 1996), 68–69, 71.

2576. Eisensohn, E. "Baseball: Enchainement 'Attraper-Relancer.'" *E.P.S. Education Physique et Sport (France),* no. 253 (Mai/Juin 1995), 50–51. "Baseball: Catching and Throwing Again."

2577. Feezell, Travis. "Play the Perimeter in Double-Relay Situations." *Scholastic Coach & Athletic Director,* LXVI (February 1997), 60–63.

2578. Fornaciari, James. "How to Win Friends and Get People Out." *Scholastic Coach & Athletic Director,* LXV (February 1996), 28–29.

2579. Gustafson, M. "Covering All the Bases." *Texas Coach,* XL (April 1996), 60–61.

2580. Jacobs, T. M., *et al.* "On Catching Fly Balls." *Science,* CCLXXIII (July 1996), 257–258.

2581. Kluger, Jeffrey. "Catcher of the

Fly: How Outfielders Catch Fly Balls." *Discovery,* XVI (September 1995), 52+. The research of Michael K. McBeath.

2582. Lane, Mike. "If at First the Left-Hander Wants to Succeed." *Scholastic Coach & Athletic Director,* LXV (December 1995), 24–26+.

2583. Mazzoni, Wayne. "Left-Handed Pickoff Moves." *Scholastic Coach,* LXIV (March 1995), 18–20.

2584. ____. "A Priority System for Defensing the 1st & 3rd Situation." *Scholastic Coach,* LXIV (December 1994), 22–23.

2585. McBeath, Michael K., Dennis M. Shaffer, and Mary K. Kaiser. "How Baseball Outfielders Determine Where to Run to Catch Fly Balls." *Science,* CCLXVIII (April 1995), 569–573.

2586. ____. "On Catching Fly Balls: Reply." *Science,* CCLXXIII (July 1996), 258–260.

2587. Michaels, Claire F. and Raoul R. Oudejans. "The Optics and Actions of Catching Fly Balls: Zeroing Out Optical Acceleration." *Ecological Psychology,* IV, no. 4 (1992), 199–222.

2588. Moore, Terrence. "Major League Defense Shifts to the Computer Age." *Baseball Digest,* LIII (May 1994), 73–74.

2589. Oudejans, Raoul R. D., *et al.* "The Relevance of Action in Perceiving Affordances: Perceptions of Catchableness of Fly Balls." *Journal of Experimental Psychology: Human Perception & Performance,* XXII (August 1996), 879–891.

2590. Pollack, H. N., *et al.* "Play Ball!" *Science,* CCLXVIII (June 23, 1995), 1681–1685. Fly ball trajectories and fielding.

2591. Ridenour, Carl. "Pre-Game Infield Drill." *Scholastic Coach,* LXIV (April 1995), 26+.

2592. Rubin, Bob. "First Base: A Position That Still Demands a 'Good Glove.'" *Baseball Digest,* LII (February 1993), 59–61.

2593. ____. "Success at Second Base Means Getting the DP [Double Play]." *Baseball Digest,* LI (December 1992), 62–67.

2594. ____. "Third Base: It's No Place for the Faint of Heart!" *Baseball Digest,* LII (June 1993), 20–23.

2595. Solomon, Alan. "Outfield Throws: Accuracy Offsets Lack of Arm Strength." *Baseball Digest,* LI (July 1992), 42–45.

2596. Sotir, S. "Special Defensive Plays: Double Steal Defenses." *IBA World Baseball,* (Winter 1993), 18–19.

2597. Stallings, Jack. "Back to the Basics: Catching and Throwing." *Scholastic Coach,* LXIV (February 1995), 36–38.

2598. ____. "Holding the Runners on Base." *Scholastic Coach & Athletic Director,* LXVI (February–March 1997), 14–18, 24–29.

2599. ____. "If at First [Base] You Want to Succeed...." *Scholastic Coach,* LXIII (February 1994), 48–51.

2600. Tessicini, Dennis. "Pre-Game 12-Minute Outfield/Infield Drill." *Scholastic Coach,* LXIII (February 1994), 52–54.

2601. Weinstein, Jerry. "In Outer Space." *Scholastic Coach & Athletic Director,* LXVI (March–April 1997), 70–72, 18–21.

d. Hitting

2602. Baker, Dusty. "Fundamental Hitting." *KidSports,* VI (March–April 1994), 16–21.

2603. ____, Jeff Mercer, and Mary Bittinger. *You Can Teach Hitting.* Carmel, Ind.: Bittinger Books; dist. by Masters Press, 1993. 234p.

2604. Beale, Wade J. "Curing the Common Cold [Bat]." *Scholastic Coach,* LXII (March 1993), 66–68+.

2605. Blount, Roy, Jr. "Plink-Rumba-Barumba-Boom: Without the Pizzazz of Doubles and Triples, Baseball Would Be Nothing But Plink-Boom, and What Fun Would That Be?" *Sports*

Illustrated, LXXIX (August 9, 1993), 64–72, 74.

2606. Boswell, Thomas. "And the First Shall Be Best: The Numbers Prove Ted Williams Wrong—You Should Swing at the First Pitch." *Inside Sports,* XV (August 1993), 58–65.

2607. Bram, A. D. and D. L. Feltz. "Effects of Batting Performance Feedback on Motivational Factors and Batting Performance in Youth Baseball." *Perceptual and Motor Skills,* LXXXI (December 1995), 1367–1378.

2608. Crasnick, Jerry. "Leadoff Hitters: They're Baseball's 'Table Setters.'" *Baseball Digest,* LV (September 1996), 34–39.

2609. ____. "Tape-Measure Homers Spice Up the Game." *Baseball Digest,* LVI (November 1997), 54–59.

2610. Cunningham, Bob. "Definitions Vary When It Comes to the Ideal No. 2 Hitter." *Baseball Digest,* LV (September 1996), 40–43.

2611. Daly, John. *Grip It and Rip It: John Daly's Guide to Hitting the Ball Farther Than You Ever Have Before.* New York: HarperCollins, 1992. 142p.

2612. Davis, Mark H. and Jonathan C. Harvey. "Declines in Major League Batting Performance as a Function of Game Pressure: A Drive Theory Analysis." *Journal of Applied Social Psychology,* XXII (May 1992), 714–735.

2613. Delmonico, Rod. "Getting in Your Batting Licks at Tennessee." *Scholastic Coach & Athletic Director,* LXV (March 1996), 20–21.

2614. ____. *Hit and Run Baseball.* Champagne, Ill.: Human Kinetics Press, 1992. 184p.

2615. ____. *Offensive Baseball Drills.* Champagne, Ill.: Human Kinetics Press, 1996. 167p.

2616. ____. "Put Your Hitters in a Cage." *Scholastic Coach & Athletic Director,* LXV (November 1995), 20–22.

2617. Denis, Pierre. "Baseball: Frapper la Balle." *E.P.S. Education Physique et Sport (France),* XLVI (Janv/Fevr.

1996), 52–53. "Baseball: Hitting the Ball."

2618. DeRenne, C., *et al.* "Effects of Weighted Bat Implement Training on Bat Swing Velocity." *Journal of Strength and Conditioning Research,* IX (November 1995), 247–250.

2619. Dohrmann, George. "What's Happened to the Art of Bunting in the Majors?" *Baseball Digest,* LIII (November 1994), 47–51.

2620. Doumit, Pete. "Look for That Quality at Bat." *Scholastic Coach & Athletic Director,* LXVI (November 1996), 58–63.

2621. Dunlavy, Bruce. "Hitting Power and Good Bat Control: A Rare Combination." *Baseball Digest,* LII (November 1993), 60–61.

2622. Elderkin, Phil. "Batting Coach Reggie Smith Says Young Hitters Need Patience at the Plate." *Baseball Digest,* LIV (May 1995), 45–47.

2623. Gabella, Jim. "Seven Steps to Good Hitting." *Scholastic Coach,* LXIII (May–June 1994), 100–101.

2624. ____. "Why Focus on Hitting Up the Middle?" *Scholastic Coach,* LXIV (April 1995), 25+.

2625. Hall, Rich. "Swinging in the Rain." *Scholastic Coach,* LXII (November 1992), 68+.

2626. Holladay, Kolin. "Disciplined Hitting." *Scholastic Coach & Athletic Director,* LXV (April 1996), 64–65.

2627. Holtzman, Jerome. "Increase in Home Runs Bemoaned by Traditionalists." *Baseball Digest,* LVI (May 1997), 32–33.

2628. ____. "Late-Season Pressure a Formidable Barrier to Hitting .400." *Baseball Digest,* LV (June 1996), 29–30.

2629. Jackson, Trent. "Changing from Slow Swings to Quick Swings." *Scholastic Coach,* LXIII (November 1993), 32+.

2630. Johnson, Michael A. "An 8-Station Hitting Rotation." *Scholastic Coach,* LXIII (April 1994), 30+.

2631. ____. "More Control Needed for Bat Performance." *NCAA News,* XXXIV (June 9, 1997), 4–5.

2632. Johnson, Randy and Wade Boggs. "Pro & Con: Do Hitters Have Too Many Advantages Over Pitchers?" *Inside Sports,* XVII (September 1995), 10–11.

2633. Kasai, T. and T. Matsuo. "Timing Strategy of Baseball Hitting." *Journal of Human Movement Studies,* XXVII (June 1994), 253+.

2634. Kernan, Kevin. "Baseball's Shop Talk Begins Around the Batting Cage." *Baseball Digest,* LII (September 1993), 29–31.

2635. LaBranch, M. J. *"Effect of Batting Stance on Ground Reaction Forces, Bat Velocity, and Response Time."* Unpublished M.S. Thesis, Springfield College, 1994. 91p.

2636. Leonard, W. M. "The Decline of the .400 Hitter: An Explanation and a Test." *Journal of Sport Behavior,* XVIII (September 1995), 226–236. Explores a theory put forward by science writer Stephen Jay Gould.

2637. Lockwood, Wayne. "A Batter's Top Challenge: Winning the Triple Crown." *Baseball Digest,* LVI (December 1997), 60–63.

2638. McPherson, Sue L. "The Influence of Player Experience on Problem Solving During Batting Preparation in Baseball." *Journal of Sport & Exercise Psychology,* XV (September 1993), 304–325.

2639. Mihoces, Gary. "Bunting for Base Hits: A Lost Art in the Majors." *Baseball Digest,* LVI (November 1997), 48–50.

2640. Monteleone, John J. and Mark Gola. *The Louisville Slugger Ultimate Book of Hitting.* New York: Henry Holt, 1997. 237p.

2641. Noble, Marty. "Mystique of the Longball Grips Major League Players and Fans." *Baseball Digest,* LII (February 1993), 67–72.

2642. Pfeil, Bill. "Stylistics for High School Hitters." *Scholastic Coach &* *Athletic Director,* LXV (November 1995), 26–28.

2643. Purl, J. "Learning Hitting Techniques Through Station Drills." *Texas Coach,* XLI (March 1997), 60–61.

2644. Schwendel, P. J. *"Traditional Baseball Weight Training Versus Power Weight Training Effects on Bat Velocity."* Unpublished M.S. Thesis, Washington State University, 1991. 105p.

2645. Tucker, Mark A. "The 3-H Approach to Hitting." *Scholastic Coach & Athletic Director,* LXV (December 1995), 62–63.

2646. Verduccci, Tom. "Boom!" In: David Bauer, ed. *SI Presents Baseball 1997.* New York: Sports Illustrated, 1997. pp. 22–33.

2647. Welch, C. M., *et al.* "Hitting a Baseball: A Biomechanical Description." *Journal of Orthopaedic & Sports Physical Therapy,* XXII (November 1995), 193–201.

2648. Williams, G. "Guidelines for the Stance, Riggering Action, Stride, and Actual Hitting Action." *Scholastic Coach,* LXII (February 1993), 20–21.

2649. Williams, Stan. "Strikes & Strings." *Scholastic Coach,* LXII (April 1993), 74–75.

2650. Wulf, Steve. "Distinguished History." *Sports Illustrated,* LXXVIII (April 5, 1993), 44–50. History of designated hitting.

e. Pitching

2651. Anderson, Kelli. "The K Factor." *Sports Illustrated,* LXXXVII (August 18, 1997), 77–78.

2652. Aschburner, Steve. "Are Five-Man Rotations Good for Today's Starters?" *Baseball Digest,* LI (April 1992), 58–62.

2653. "A Call for Arms." In: Joe Hoppel, ed. *The Sporting News 1997 Baseball Yearbook.* St. Louis, Mo.: TSN, 1997. pp. 34–39.

2654. Castle, George. "Will Knuckleball and Cut Fastball Be the New 'In'

Pitches in the Majors?" *Baseball Digest,* LII (March 1993), 20–24.

2655. Childress, C. "Pitching: Illegal Acts." *Referee,* XX (June 1995), 42–44, 46.

2656. ____. "Pitching: The Set Position." *Referee,* XX (April 1995), 42–43, 46–48, 50, 69.

2657. ____. "Pitching: The Windup Position." *Referee,* XX (May 1995), 42–43, 46–47.

2658. ____. "Pitching: Uniforms and Substitutions." *Referee,* XX (July 1995), 42–44.

2659. Crasnick, Jerry. "'Burnout' Problems, Always a Threat to Middle Relievers." *Baseball Digest,* LV (December 1996), 68–73.

2660. ____. "Life in the Bullpen Can Be Fretful, Funny, or Boring." *Baseball Digest,* LVI (December 1997), 50–57.

2661. Cunningham, Bob. "'Bust 'Em Inside': A Big Key to Pitching Success." *Baseball Digest,* LIII (August 1994), 20–23.

2662. Curran, William. *Strikeout: A Celebration of the Art of Pitching.* New York: Crown, 1995. 244p.

2663. Decenzo, John A. "What's So Foul About a Foul Ball?" *Baseball Digest,* LIII (July 1994), 44–47.

2664. Doyle, Al. "Winning Pitchers Don't All Have to Be Tall." *Baseball Digest,* LVI (September 1997), 48–52.

2665. Fleisig, G. S., *et al.* "Kinetics of Baseball Pitching with Implications About Injury Mechanisms." *American Journal of Sports Medicine,* XXIII (March–April 1995), 233–239.

2666. Forhlich, Cliff. "Pitching No Hitters." *Chance,* VII (March 1994), 24+.

2667. Freed, Roger. "Here Are Some Inside Tips on the Art of Pitching." *Baseball Digest,* LVI (August 1997), 42–44.

2668. Gammons, Peter. "Pitchers Help Themselves by Perfecting Their Defense." *Baseball Digest,* LI (September 1992), 44–48.

2669. Gazel, Neil R. "Should the Major Leagues Legalize the Spitball?" *Baseball Digest,* LI (May 1992), 38–47.

2670. Hardin, William. "A Fundamental Checklist for Young Pitchers." *Scholastic Coach & Athletic Director,* LXVI (November 1996), 54–55.

2671. ____. "If at First the Pitcher Wants to Succeed." *Scholastic Coach & Athletic Director,* LXVI (March 1997), 42+. Pick-offs.

2672. Hasty, Vern. "Lead Front Foot to the Mit." *Scholastic Coach,* LXIII (April 1994), 34–35.

2673. Hendrickson, W. R. *"The Effects of Recovery Time on Throwing Velocity and Accuracy of College Baseball Pitchers."* Unpublished M.S. Thesis, Brigham Young University, 1993. 81p.

2674. House, Tom. *Fit to Pitch.* Champagne, Ill.: Human Kinetics Press, 1996. 203p.

2675. ____. *The Pitching Edge.* Champagne, Ill.: Human Kinetics Press, 1994. 151p.

2676. Jansen, Larry and George A. and Karl van Loo. *The Craft of Pitching.* Indianapolis, Ind.: Masters Press, 1997.

2677. Johnson, Michael A. "The Philosophy of Setting Up the Hitters." *Scholastic Coach,* LXIV (January 1995), 20–21.

2678. Jordan, Pat. *Sports Illustrated Pitching: The Keys to Excellence.* Sports Illustrated Winner's Circle Books. New ed. Lanham, Md.: Sports Illustrated, 1993. 138p.

2679. Kaat, Jim. "The Mechanics of a Breaking Pitch." *Popular Mechanics,* CLXXIV (April 1997), 52–57.

2680. Kirkland, Paul. "Get That First Strike." *Scholastic Coach,* LXII (May–June 1993), 42, 44.

2681. Kuenster, John. "Livelier Ball, a Big Factor in Surge of Monster Home Runs." *Baseball Digest,* LV (November 1996), 17–19.

2682. ____. "Should Major League Umpires Go Back to a Higher Strike Zone?" *Baseball Digest,* LI (September 1992), 17–19.

2683. Kurkijan, Tim. "When Four Is More." *Sports Illustrated,* LXXVIII (April 5, 1993), 42–43. The four-man rotation; simultaneously published in *Sports Illustrated Canada,* I (April 5, 1993), 50–51.

2684. Lehigh, S. "Take Your Base." *Referee,* XXI (May 1996), 46–48.

2685. Lenihan, Jeff. "Will Big Leagues Ever Feature a Switch-Pitcher?" *Baseball Digest,* LI (September 1992), 38–39.

2686. Lockwood, Wayne. "Is the Speed Gun Over-Rated as a Gauge for Pitchers?" *Baseball Digest,* LVI (August 1997), 45–49.

2687. Macht, Norman L. "Big League Catchers Express Their Views on the Strike Zone." *Baseball Digest,* LII (June 1993), 38–41.

2688. Maitland, William J. *Young Ballplayer's Guide to Safe Pitching.* Phoenix, Az.: Maitland Enterprises, 1992. 127p.

2689. Mazzoni, Wayne. "Pitching, for Goodness Sake." *Scholastic Coach & Athletic Director,* LXV (February 1996), 52–53.

2690. ____. "Left-Handed Pickoff Moves." *Scholastic Coach,* LXIV (March 1995), 18–20.

2691. ____. "Teaching Progression for the Changeup." *Scholastic Coach & Athletic Director,* LXV (April 1996), 58–59.

2692. McCann, Sean. "You Can Throw Harder!" *Scholastic Coach,* LXIII (November 1993), 22–25.

2693. ____. "What's the Pitch?" *Scholastic Coach,* LXIV (November 1994), 72–73.

2694. Olney, Buster. "Squeezed: The Incredible Shrinking Strike Zone." In: George Leonard, ed. *Athlon's 1997 Baseball.* Nashville, Tn.: Athlon Pub. Co., 1997. pp. 22–29.

2695. Pappas, A. M., *et al.* "Wrist Kinematics During Pitching: A Preliminary Report." *American Journal of Sports Medicine,* XXIII (May–June 1995), 312–315.

2696. Peticca, Mike. "A Good Curveball: It's Still an Important Key to Winning." *Baseball Digest,* LV (November 1996), 42–46.

2697. Post, Paul. "Is It Time to Say Goodbye to 300-Game Winners in the Majors?" *Baseball Digest,* LVI (May 1997), 44–47.

2698. Priebe, Brian. "The Pitcher's Second Shift." *Scholastic Coach & Athletic Director,* LXV (March 1996), 34+.

2699. Purl, J. "Pitching: Somewhat of a Non-Exact Science." *Texas Coach,* XL (March 1996), 48–49.

2700. Rogers, Phil. "Who's to Blame for the Rise in Ball Counts on Batters?" *Baseball Digest,* LII (January 1993), 50–57.

2701. Romano, John. "Some Relievers Are Caught in the Middle." *Baseball Digest,* LVI (July 1997), 62–63.

2702. Stallings, Jack. "Getting the Most Out of the 20-Second Break Between Pitches." *Scholastic Coach,* LXII (November 1992), 26–29.

2703. ____. "The Pitching Delivery: Don't Rush It." *Scholastic Coach & Athletic Director,* LXV (January 1996), 28–30.

2704. Stewart, Wayne. "Intimidation Helps Pitchers Psyche Out Batters." *Baseball Digest,* LIV (March 1995), 68–72.

2705. ____. "What Sort of Pitch Gets Hit for the Longest Distance?" *Baseball Digest,* LV (October 1996), 56–62.

2706. Sutherland, Jason. *Curves, Sliders, and Sinkers: Pitch Like a Pro with a Wiffle Ball.* New York: Random House, 1996. 32p.

2707. Tuttle, Dennis. "Zoned Out." *Inside Sports,* XIX (June 1997), 28–37. On the shrinking MLB strike zone.

2708. Van Dyck, Dan. "Dilution of Pitching Leads to a Power Feast for Hitters." *Baseball Digest,* LV (August 1996), 52–55.

2709. Vass, George. "Should the High Strike Be Given Back to the Pitchers?"

Baseball Digest, LIII (August 1994), 24–26.

2710. Verducci, Tom. "Major League Pitching: 'It Ain't What It Used to Be.'" *Baseball Digest,* LI (August 1992), 49–54.

2711. ____. "Whiplash." *Sports Illustrated,* LXXX (April 25, 1994), 14–19. Poor pitching at the MLB level.

2712. Wang, Y. T., *et al.* "Three Dimensional Kinematic Analysis of Baseball Pitching in Acceleration Phase." *Perceptual and Motor Skills,* LXXX (February 1995), 43–48.

2713. Warde, Robert. "Fate and the Starting Pitcher." *The Minneapolis Review of Baseball,* X (Fall 1991), 5–7. Rise of the relief pitcher.

2714. Weinstein, Jerry, with Andy McKay. *USA Baseball Pitching & Catching Manual.* Sacramento, Ca.: Sacramento City College, 1996. 32p. Used as the basic manual for the U.S. Olympic baseball team.

2715. Wolpin, Stewart. "The Mystery of the Knuckleball." *Popular Science,* CCL (April 1997), 74+.

2716. Wygonik, Jim. "Don't Overlook the Bullpen." *Scholastic Coach,* LXII (April 1993), 14–16. Pregame activity.

F. Collective Biography

As was the case with *Baseball: A Comprehensive Bibliography,* the coverage of the literature surrounding baseball biography remains a high priority in this supplement. To that end, the citations in this chapter are to general or collective biographies (about two or more individuals) concerning major league participants (players, managers, umpires, executives, coaches, and officials) in the sport or others (e.g., sportscasters) associated with it.

Chapter F is divided into eight parts. First, general biographies, which cover a variety of individuals. Then come sources on first year players or rookies while the third part is devoted to pitchers. Part 4 which follows is devoted to catchers, Part 5 to both hitters and fielders, Part 7 to team owners and executives (of both teams and leagues), and Part 8, to umpires.

Chapter G which follows is devoted strictly to given individuals.

1. General Biographies

2717. Anderson, Robert C. "Baseball Genealogy." *APG Quarterly,* VI (Fall 1991), 59+.

2718. Anderson, William M. "From the Ballfield to the Battlefield ... and Back." *Michigan History,* LXXIX (September–October 1995), 10–18.

2719. Baseball America. *The Minor League Register.* Durham, N.C., 1994–. Annual.

2720. *Baseball Legends: 100 All-Time Greats.* Lincolnwood, Ill.: Publications International, 1997. 320p.

2721. Benson, John. *Baseball Players Guide A-Z.* Wilton, Conn.: Diamond Lib., 1995. 320p.

2722. ____. ____: *1996–1997.* Wilton, Conn.: Diamond Lib., 1996. 300p.

2723. Bevis, Charlie. "Disenfranchised All-Stars of 1945." In: John Blake, ed. *Texas Rangers 1995 Yearbook.* Arlington, Tex.: Public Relations Dept., Texas Rangers, 1995. pp. 50–56.

2724. Blake, Mike. "Major Leaguers of the 1990s Recall Special Moments." *Baseball Digest,* LV (January 1996), 54–60.

2725. ____. "Stars from the 1970s Recall Special Baseball Moments." *Baseball Digest,* LIV (November 1995), 56–63.

2726. ____. "Stars of the '50s Recall Some of Their Special Memories." *Baseball Digest,* LIV (September 1995), 52–57.

2727. ____. "Stars of the 1960s Recall Some Special Baseball Moments." *Baseball Digest,* LIV (October 1995), 50–58.

2728. ____. "Stars of the 1980s Recall Some Special Baseball Moments." *Baseball Digest,* LIV (December 1995), 54–62.

2729. Bodley, Hal. "Managers List Top 'Unsung' Players in Both Leagues." *Baseball Digest,* LVI (October 1997), 64–67.

2730. Bortolin, Greg. "'Play Ball!': A Saga of Stars, Silver Sox, and Nevada-Grown Baseball Players." *Nevada,* L (March 1990), 57+.

2731. Boswell, Thomas. "Gamers: Let Us Now Forget the Strike, and Praise Some Famous Baseball Men." *The Washington Post Magazine,* (August 6, 1995), 8–17.

2732. Broeg, Bob. "Five Ex-Stars Again Eligible for Hall of Fame Election." *Baseball Digest,* LII (December 1993), 83–85.

2733. ____. *Superstars of Baseball: Their Lives, Their Laments.* South Bend, Ind.: Diamond Communications, 1994. 531p. Originally published by The Sporting News in 1970 as *Super Stars of Baseball.*

2734. Bump, L. "The Walk-a-Game Club: An Exclusive Group." *Baseball Research Journal,* XXIV (1995), 108–110.

2735. Callahan, Tom. "The Enduring Pros: Fans Today Seem to Appreciate the Hangers-On." *U.S. News & World Report,* CXII (June 8, 1992), 72+.

2736. Caroulis, Jon. "Some Future Major League Stars Persevered in the Minors." *Baseball Digest,* LV (July 1996), 62–65.

2737. Cazeneuvre, Brian. *Ken Griffey, Jr./Frank Thomas.* Syosset, N.Y.: East End Publishing, 1995. 88p.

2738. Clark, Jerry E. *Anson to Zuber: Iowa Boys in the Major Leagues.* Omaha, Neb.: Making History, 1992. 298p.

2739. ____. *Nebraska Diamonds: A Brief History of Baseball Major Leaguers from the Cornhusker State.* Omaha, Neb.: Making History, 1991. 86p.

2740. Cockcroft, James D. *Latinos in Beisbol.* New York: Franklin Watts, 1996. 207p. Biographies of Hispanic players.

2741. Collier, Gene. "Players Who Spent One, Brief 'Moment' in the Big Leagues." *Baseball Digest,* LII (September 1993), 56–60.

2742. Consumer Guides, Editors of. *Baseball Legends.* New York: Signet Books, 1997.

2743. Crescioni, Jose A. *Los Boricuas en Las Grandes Ligas.* Catano, P.R.: Priv. print, 1996. 457p. Bios of 181 Puerto Rican players.

2744. Crothers, Tim. "The Anti-All Stars." *Sports Illustrated,* LXXXVII (July 14, 1997), 55–56. Biggest flops of early 1997.

2745. Dewey, Donald and Nicholas Acocella. *The Biographical History of Baseball.* New York: Carroll and Graf, 1995. 533p.

2746. Ekin, Larry. *Baseball Fathers and Sons: From Orator Jim to Cal, Barry, and Ken—Every One a Player.* White Hall, Va.: Betterway Publications, 1992. 191p.

2747. Faber, Charles F. *Baseball Pioneers: Ratings of 19th Century Players.* Jefferson, N.C.: McFarland & Co., Inc., 1997. 180p.

2748. ____. *Baseball Ratings: The All-Time Best Players at Each Position.* 2nd ed. Jefferson, N.C.: McFarland & Co., Inc., 1995. 269p.

2749. Feagler, Linda. "Where Are They Now?" *Cleveland,* XXIV (October 1995), 64–67. Former Indians players.

2750. Feinstein, John. "If It's September, This Must Be New York: Today, Even Baseball's Stars Are Journeymen, Picked Up for a Pennant Stretch, Only to Leave When the Job Is Done." *Inside Sports,* XVII (November 1995), 74–75.

2751. ____. "The Lust for the Light: Washed Up or Fed Up, the Great Competitors Hate to Say Goodbye for Good." *Inside Sports,* XVI (June 1994), 48–49.

2752. Figone, Albert J. "Larry McPhail and Dolph Camilli: Heart of the Dodgers." *National Pastime,* XIV (1994), 106–109.

2753. Fraley, Gerry. "The X Factor: Baseball's Generation X—Players 25 Years Old or Younger—Has Emerged in a Big Way." *Inside Sports,* XVIII (September 1996), 24–29.

2754. George, Daniel P. "Diamond Kings." *Boy's Life,* LXXXV (July 1995), 8–9.

2755. Gill, John Freeman. "Heroes Take a Fall." *The New York Times Magazine,* (August 30, 1992), 14–16. Gooden and Strawberry.

2756. Goodwin, S. "Hall-of-Famers on the Early Gridiron: They Tackled Other Sports." *National Pastime,* XIV (1994), 97–98.

2757. Gowdy, Dave. *Baseball Superstars.* New York: Grosset & Dunlap, 1994. 62p.

2758. Green, Lee and Joe Morgenstein. "Beauty and the Beast." *California,* XV (September 1990), 64+. Will Clark and Jose Canseco.

2759. Greshman, Michael. "The 100 Greatest Players." In: John Thorn and Pete Palmer, eds. *Total Baseball.* 3rd ed. New York: HarperPerenial, 1993. pp. 156–193.

2760. Guss, Greg. "Lone Stars." *Sport,* LXXXVII (June 1996), 75–80. Standouts on losing teams.

2761. Hart, Stan. *Scouting Reports: The Original Reviews of Some of Baseball's Greatest Stars.* New York: Macmillan, 1996. 198p.

2762. Hay, D. "Off to the Ball Game: Australians Moving Into America's Major Leagues." *Bulletin (Australia),* CXIV (October 27, 1993), 110–112.

2763. Holtzman, Jerome. "Majors Used 'Replacement' Players During World War II." *Baseball Digest,* LIV (June 1995), 76–78.

2764. Hubbard, Steve. "When the Wall Comes Down: Must Athletes Give Up Their Privacy—and Their Physical Safety—for Stardom?" *Inside Sports,* XVI (June 1996), 70–75.

2765. "Iron Eagles: Veteran Players Who've Stayed Loyal to Their Teams." *Sport,* LXXXV (September 1994), 55–56+.

2766. Itaia, Bob. *Baseball's Best.* Edina, Minn.: Abdo & Daughters, 1993. 32p.

2767. Ivor-Campbell, Frederick. *Baseball's First Stars: Biographies of the Greatest 19th Century Players, Managers, Umpires, Executives, and Writers.* 2 vols. Cleveland, Oh.: SABR, 1989 and 1996.

2768. Jacobs, William Jay. *They Shaped the Game: Ty Cobb, Babe Ruth, Jackie Robinson.* New York: C. Scribner's Sons, 1994. 85p.

2769. James, Bill. *The Bill James Player Ratings Book.* New York: Collier Books, 1994.

2770. ____, Larry King, and Keith Olbermann. "Focused on Cooperstown: Hall of Fame Chances of Thirty Current Players." *Beckett Baseball Card Monthly,* XII, no. 121 (April 1995), 10–21.

2771. Johnson, Lloyd. *Baseball's Dream Teams: The Greatest Major League Players, Decade by Decade.* Updated and rev. New York: Crescent Books, 1994. 208p.

2772. Keegan, Tom. "Here's the Real Lowdown on Some Oriole Stars of the Past." *Baseball Digest,* LIII (October 1994), 56–58.

2773. Kelley, Brent P. *Baseball Stars of the 1950s: Interviews with All-Stars of the Game's Golden Era.* Jefferson, N.C.: McFarland & Co., Inc., 1993. 201p.

2774. ____. *The Early All-Stars: Conversations with Standout Baseball Players of the 1930s and 1940s.* Jefferson, N.C.: McFarland & Co., Inc., 1997. 199p.

2775. ____. *In the Shadow of the Babe: Interviews with Baseball Players Who Played With or Against Babe Ruth.*

Jefferson, N.C.: McFarland & Co., Inc., 1995. 200p.

2776. ____. *Voices from the Negro Leagues: Conversations with 52 Baseball Standouts of the Period 1924–1960.* Jefferson, N.C.: McFarland & Co., Inc., 1997. 304p.

2777. Kiersh, Edward. "Honor Thy Father." *Inside Sports,* XIV (July 1992), 72–77.

2778. Klapisch, Bob. *High and Tight: The Rise and Fall of Dwight Gooden and Darryl Strawberry.* New York: Villard, 1996. 228p.

2779. ____. and Ringolsby, Tracy. "The Best Players." *Inside Sports,* XIV (February 1992), 26–43.

2780. Kreuz, Jim. "How Ted Williams and Bob Feller Fared as High School Players." *Baseball Digest,* LIII (June 1994), 59–64.

2781. Kuenster, Bob. "Baseball's All-Time Greatest: Multi-Position Players." *Baseball Digest,* LIV (February 1995), 32–40.

2782. ____. "Let the Bells Ring for the Majors' Unsung Heroes." *Baseball Digest,* LI (October 1992), 17–19.

2783. ____. "Love of the Game, One Motive That Keeps Veterans Striving in Majors." *Baseball Digest,* LII (July 1993), 17–19.

2784. ____. "Some Memorable At-Bats by Major League Stars." *Baseball Digest,* LIII (June 1994), 74–79.

2785. Kuenster, John. "Characters of the Past Lent Spicy Flavor and Zest to the Game." *Baseball Digest,* LIV (April 1995), 17–20.

2786. ____. "Major League Managers and Coaches Select Players with Best Skills." *Baseball Digest,* LV (January 1996), 15–16.

2787. ____. "Random Recollections of Some Hall of Fame Players and Managers." *Baseball Digest,* LIII (February 1994), 14–18.

2788. Kurkijan, Tim. "Dream On: Sorting Through Big League Wannabes Seems as Futile as Efforts to Solve the Baseball Strike." *Sports Illustrated,* LXXXII (February 13, 1995), 30–35.

2789. ____. "If Close Counted." *Sports Illustrated,* LXIII (August 21, 1995), 71–72. Triple Crown contenders.

2790. ____. "Swing Shift: Anxious Baseball Players Are Trying to Resolve Career Crises Brought On by the Strike." *Sports Illustrated,* LXXII (January 23, 1995), 58–61.

2791. Ladewski, Paul. "So Long…Good Riddance." *Inside Sports,* XV (July 1993), 58–63. On the different retirements of Nolan Ryan and Carlton Fisk.

2792. Ladson, William. "The Ten Worst Free Agents in History." *Sport,* LXXXIII (August 1992), 12+.

2793. Lee, George L. "Baseball Players." In: his *Interesting Athletes: Black American Sports Heroes.* New York: Ballantine Books, 1993. pp. 71–107.

2794. Lenihan, Jeff. "Coming Home." *Sport,* LXXXIV (July 1995), 66–69. Free agent class of 1992–93.

2795. Lidz, Franz. "Flashes in the Pan." *Sports Illustrated,* LXXVI (May 4, 1992), 56–69.

2796. Lupica, Mike. "Fall of the Legends." *Esquire,* CXXII (November 1994), 62+.

2797. MacCarl, Neil. "Managers Rate Major League Players with the Best Skills." *Baseball Digest,* LII (January 1993), 22–27; LIII (January 1994), 22–27.

2798. Madden, Bill and Joe Rutter. "Mr. October Then … Mr. October Now." *Sport,* LXXXVII (November 1997), 58–59. Reggie Jackson and Mark Lemke.

2799. Madden, W. C. *The Women of the All-American Girls Professional Baseball League: A Biographical Dictionary.* Jefferson, N.C.: McFarland & Co., Inc., 1997. 288p.

2800. Marino, John. *MVPs: Baseball's Most Valuable Players.* New York: MetroBooks, 1996. 80p.

2801. McDonald, J. "Signings of the Times: Aussies Climb the Ladder of

Success in the U.S." *Baseball Australia,* V (March 1993), 4–5.

2802. Miller, Stuart. "The Time of Their Lives: An Athlete's Moment in the Spotlight Often Is Over Quickly, But Life Goes On." *Inside Sports,* XVII (August 1995), 76–81.

2803. Moffi, Larry and Jonathan Kronstadt. *Crossing the Line: Black Major Leaguers, 1947–1959.* Jefferson, N.C.: McFarland & Co., Inc., 1994. 251p.

2804. Morey, Janet and Wendy Dunn. *Famous Hispanic Americans.* New York: Cobblehill Books, 1996. 190p. Includes ballplayers.

2805. Morgan, Joe L., with William Ladson. "Joe Morgan's 1993 Baseball Dream Team." *Sport,* LXXXIV (June 1993), 66–69.

2806. Mowen, Karrie. "Where Have All the Baseball Heroes Gone?" *Baseball Digest,* LVI (September 1997), 40–43.

2807. Munro, Neil, ed. *The Stats Canadian Players Encyclopedia.* Skokie, Ill.: Stats, Inc., 1996. Unpaged.

2808. Nagel, Rob and Sharon Rose, eds. *Hispanic American Biography.* Detroit, Mich.: U.X.L., 1995. 238p. Includes ballplayers.

2809. Newlin, Dale. *Baseball's Greatest Careers (Non-Pitcher).* 2nd ed. New York: Dorrance, 1996. 96p.

2810. Nighttingale, Dave, *et al.* "Rating the All-Time Greats." *Inside Sports,* XVI (June 1994), 30–47.

2811. O'Shei, Tim. "How Some Players Recall Their Major League Debuts." *Baseball Digest,* LIII (October 1994), 51–55.

2812. Palmer, Jim. "Hard Acts to Follow." *Inside Sports,* XVI (July 1994), 46–51. Retirements of Nolan Ryan, George Brett, Robin Yount, Carlton Fisk, and Dale Murphy.

2813. Pare, Michael A. *Sports Stars.* Detroit, Mich.: U.X.L., 1994. 622p. Includes ballplayers.

2814. Porter, David L., ed. *African-American Sports Greats: A Biographical Dictionary.* Westport, Conn.: Greenwood Press, 1995. 429p.

2815. ____. *Biographical Dictionary of American Sports, 1989–1992: Supplement for Baseball, Football, Basketball, and Other Sports.* Westport, Conn.: Greenwood Press, 1992. 750p.

2816. ____, ed. *Biographical Dictionary of American Sports, 1992–1995: Supplement for Baseball, Football, Basketball, and Other Team Sports.* Westport, Conn.: Greenwood Press, 1995. 811p.

2817. Riley, James A. *Biographical Encyclopedia of the Negro Leagues, 1885–1949.* Westport, Conn.: Meckler, 1993.

2818. Pueschel, Brad. "He Plays for *Them?*" *Beckett Baseball Card Monthly,* XI, no. 115 (October 1994), 19–22. Some of the players who did not finish their careers with the teams they are most often associated with.

2819. Ringolsby, Tracy. "Baseball's Best: The Top Stars of the Diamond are Rated by the Pro Scouts Themselves." *Inside Sports,* XVII (August 1995), 56–65.

2820. ____. "Beyond Money: Baseball's Millionaires Are Driven by the Dream of Being Champions." *Inside Sports,* XIV (February 1992), 60–63.

2821. Robb, James. "Voices of Summer: Baseball Announcers—The All-Time Greats." *The World & I,* IX (July 1994), 160+.

2822. Rubin, Bob. "Are Big League Mercenaries Lessening the Game's Appeal?" *Baseball Digest,* LII (August 1993), 54–57.

2823. ____. "Fractured Funnies from the Mavens of Malaprop." *Inside Sports,* XV (June 1993), 12–15. Mets announcer Ralph Kiner and Padres announcer Jerry Coleman.

2824. Rubinstein, W. D. "Kosher Heroes: Jewish-American Baseball Stars." *Australian Journal of Jewish Studies,* IX, nos. 1/2 (1995), 124+.

2825. Schwartz, Alan. "Hits & Misses." *Beckett Baseball Card Monthly,* XI, no. 111 (June 1994), 14–18. No. 1 draft picks.

2826. Shearon, Jim. *Canada's Baseball Legends: True Stories, Records, and Photos of Canadian-Born Players in Baseball's Major Leagues Since 1879*. Kanata, Ont.: Malin Head Press, 1994. 248p.

2827. Snelling, Dennis. *A Glimpse of Fame: Brilliant But Fleeting Major League Careers*. Jefferson, N.C.: McFarland & Co., Inc., 1993. 257p.

2828. "The Son Also Rises." *Sport*, LXXXV (July 1994), 63–67. Fathers and sons in MLB.

2829. Souders, Cathy. "Famous Myth Makers: Great Sportswriters." *Media History Digest*, XII (Fall 1992), 15–23.

2830. "South Carolina Names in Baseball History." *Carologue: A Bulletin of South Carolina History*, IX (Fall 1993), 17+.

2831. Spalding, John E. *Pacific Coast League Stars: One Hundred of the Best, 1903–1957*. Manhattan, Ks.: Ag Press, 1994. 123p.

2832. Stewart, Wayne. "Major League Players Noted for Their Distinctive Mannerisms." *Baseball Digest*, LIII (November 1994), 28–33.

2833. ____. "Players Recall Their Most Memorable Baseball Sights." *Baseball Digest*, LV (June 1996), 28–29.

2834. Streisand, Betsy. "Never Too Old for Games: The Hair May Be Graying or Gone, But Fading Jocks Can Still Cavort on Their Fields of Dreams." *U.S. News & World Report*, CXII (June 8, 1992), 68–72.

2835. Sugar, Bert R. *The One Hundred Greatest Athletes of All Time: A Sports Editor's Personal Rankings*. New York: Carol Publishing Group, 1994.

2836. Sullivan, George. *Twenty Seven Baseball Greats*. New York: Atheneum, 1996. 72p.

2837. Sullivan, Paul. "Are These Players '30–Day Wonders' or Genuine Stars?" *Baseball Digest*, LV (August 1996), 38–40.

2838. Summer, Jim. "The South Carolina All-Star Team." *Carologue: A Bulletin of South Carolina History*, X (Fall 1994), 14+.

2839. Swirsky, Seth. *Baseball Letters: A Fan's Correspondence with His Heroes*. New York: Kodansha International, 1996. 179p.

2840. Topei, Brett. "Post-Season Heroes Recall Their Moments of Glory." *Baseball Digest*, LI (July 1992), 20–25.

2841. Truex, Alan. "The Second Year Jinx: A Difficult Pitch to Dodge." *Baseball Digest*, LI (August 1992), 42–46.

2842. *The 20th Century: Great Athletes*. 20 vols. Englewood Cliff, N.J.: The Salem Press, 1992.

2843. Van Blair, Rick. *Dugout to Foxhole: Interviews with Baseball Players Whose Careers Were Affected by World War II*. Jefferson, N.C.: McFarland & Co., Inc., 1994. 226p.

2844. Vass, George. "Bo Jackson and Fernando Valenzuela Head '93 'Comeback List.'" *Baseball Digest*, LII (November 1993), 22–30.

2845. ____. "Club-by-Club Reports on Top Big League Prospects." *Baseball Digest*, LIV (March 1995), 20–34.

2846. ____. "From Ty Cobb to Alex Rodriguez: Baseball's Super Kids." *Baseball Digest*, LVI (February 1997), 28–34.

2847. ____. "Here Are a Dozen Players 'on the Spot' for '97 Season." *Baseball Digest*, LVI (May 1997), 20–25.

2848. ____. "Here Are Nine Prime Candidates for Comeback Honors in '93." *Baseball Digest*, LII (May 1993), 22–27.

2849. ____. "Here Are the Eight Leading 'Comeback' Players of '95." *Baseball Digest*, LIV (November 1995), 37–45.

2850. ____. "Here Are the Majors' Best 25-and-Under Stars." *Baseball Digest*, LII (September 1993), 24–28.

2851. ____. "Here Are the Prime Comeback Candidates for '94 Season." *Baseball Digest*, LIII (May 1994), 26–32.

2852. ____. "Here Are the Seven Great-

est Comeback Players of All Time."
Baseball Digest, LV (February 1996),
46–53.

2853. ____. "Here Are the Seven Leading 'Comeback' Players of the Year."
Baseball Digest, LI (November 1992),
22–27.

2854. ____. "Here's an 'All-Overpaid'
Team of Major Leaguers." *Baseball
Digest,* LIV (June 1995), 20–22.

2855. ____. "MVP Award: It's a Coveted
But Controversial Honor." *Baseball
Digest,* LIII (June 1994), 53–58.

2856. ____. "Players in Their Late 30s
Can Still Shine in the Majors." *Baseball Digest,* LIII (October 1994),
24–31.

2857. ____. "'Problem Players' Have
Always Been on the Big League
Scene." *Baseball Digest,* LV (Sep-
tember 1996), 25–30.

2858. ____. "These Are the All-Time
Best and Worst Free-Agent Signings."
Baseball Digest, LVI (August 1997),
30–37.

2859. ____. "These Are the Majors' Top
'Comeback Players' of 1994." *Baseball Digest,* LIII (November 1994),
20–24.

2960. ____. "These Are the Ten Leading
Comeback Players of '96." *Baseball
Digest,* LV (November 1996), 24–32.

2861. ____. "These Ten Big Leaguers
Are 'Under the Gun' in '94." *Baseball
Digest,* LIII (July 1994), 48–52.

2862. ____. "These Ten Major Leaguers
Are 'On the Spot' in '96." *Baseball
Digest,* LV (June 1996), 54–62.

2863. ____. "Were These '95 Performances in the Majors One-Year
Flukes?" *Baseball Digest,* LV (May
1997), 28–34.

2864. ____. "What Players Are Destined
to Play in the 21st Century?" *Baseball
Digest,* LI (September 1992), 20–24.

2865. Verducci, Tom. "Be Like Ernie
[Banks]." *Sports Illustrated,* LXXXIII
(September 25, 1995), 36–39. Big-
name players from the past who never
made it into postseason play.

2866. ____. "The Best." *Sports Illus-*

trated, LXXXII (May 1, 1995),
64–70+.

2867. ____. "The Best Years of Their
Lives." *Sports Illustrated,* LXXXV
(July 29, 1996), 90–92+. Baltimore
Orioles' players.

2868. ____. "The High Price of Hard
Living." *Sports Illustrated,* LXXXII
(February 27, 1995), 16–24+. Dwight
Gooden and Darryl Strawberry.

2869. ____. "A Sign of the Times."
Sports Illustrated, LXXVIII (May 3,
1993), 14–21. How a lack of true
heroes hurts MBL.

2870. Waterman, Guy. "Big Leaguers
Love Old Parks, Fine Cars, and Ital-
ian Cooking." *Baseball Digest,* LIV
(June 1995), 28–35.

2871. Weinberg, Rick. "Baseball's Best."
Sport, LXXXVI (April 1995), 32+.
Top five MLB players at each position.

2872. Weiss, Peter. "Who Were the Biggest 'Goats' in Major League History?" *Baseball Digest,* LI (February
1992), 46–51.

2873. Westcott, Rich. *Masters of the
Diamond: Interviews with Players
Who Began Their Careers More Than
50 Years Ago.* Jefferson, N.C.: McFarland & Co., Inc., 1994. 187p.

2874. White, Sarah Gardner. *Like Father,
Like Son: Baseball's Major League
Families.* New York: Scholastic, 1993.
152p.

2875. Whiteside, Kelly. "Oh, Brother."
Sports Illustrated, LXXX (March 21,
1994), 32–36. Brother combinations in
baseball.

2876. Wilber, Cynthia J. *For the Love of
the Game: Baseball Memories from
the Men Who Were There.* New York:
William Morrow, 1992. 320p.

2877. Wildavsky, Racel Flick. "They
Dared Cocaine—and Lost." *Reader's
Digest,* CXLI (July 1992), 55–61.
Includes Otis Nixon, Steve Howe,
Alan Wiggins, and LaMarr Hoyt

2878. Williams, Pete. "Ten to Watch."
Beckett Baseball Card Monthly, X, no.
98 (May 1993), 10–13.

2879. Wills, Chuck and Pat. *Beyond*

Home Plate: On the Trail of Yesterday's Baseball Heroes. Ocala, Fla.: Special Publications, 1993. 197p.

2880. ____. *Beyond Home Plate II: Catching Up with Former Major Leaguers.* Ocala, Fla.: Special Publications, 1995. 146p.

2881. Wilson, J. P. "Taiwan Enters the Big Leagues: A Look at Disputes Involving Foreign Professional Baseball Players." *For the Record,* IV (October–November 1993), 3–4.

2882. Winston, Lisa. "Roll Call: Draft Class of '93." *Beckett Baseball Card Monthly,* XI, no. 111 (June 1994), 21–23.

2883. Zia, Helen and Susan B. Gall, eds. *Notable Asian Americans.* Detroit, Mich.: Gale Research, 1995. 468p. Includes team executives like Paul Isaki.

2. Rookies

2884. Black, Stu. "The Best Rookies: Poppin' Good Stuff." *Inside Sports,* XIV (February 1992), 44–51.

2885. ____. and Dave Nighttingale. "Thrown Into the Big Time." *Inside Sports,* XVI (May 1994), 52–61.

2886. Craft, David. *Rookies of the Year: New Kids Who Took the Field.* New York: MetroBooks, 1995. 79p.

2887. Crasnick, Jerry. "Grand Entrance." *Beckett Focus on Future Stars,* IV, no. 34 (February 1994), 78–81.

2888. DeLand, Dave. "On the Rise: Outstanding in Their Fields." *Beckett Baseball Card Monthly,* X, no. 95 (February 1993), 14–16.

2889. Friedman, Myles. "Baseball's Top 100 Prospects: Rating the Top Rookie Prospects." *Spring Training: Grapefruit and Cactus League Yearbook,* V (1992), 4–17; VI (1993), 4–19; VII (1994), 4–19; VII (1995), 4–19; IX (1996), 4–19; X (1997), 4–19.

2890. George, Daniel P. "Baseball's Best Beginners." *Boy's Life,* LXXXIV (May 1994), 16+.

2891. Herman, Bruce. "Heading for Home." *Beckett Focus on Future Stars,* II, no. 14 (June 1992), 6–11.

2892. ____. "Invasion of the Spotlight Snatchers." *Beckett Focus on Future Stars,* III, no. 22 (February 1993), 6–9.

2893. ____. "See You in September." *Beckett Focus on Future Stars,* II, no. 17 (September 1992), 6–9. Minor leaguers called to the majors at season's end.

2894. Langill, Mark. "Draft Dodgers." *Sport,* LXXIV (July 1993), 49–51.

2895. ____. "Opportunity Knocks [for Rookies at Pittsburgh]." *Beckett Focus on Future Stars,* III, no. 23 (March 1993), 65–67.

2896. Margolick, David. "The Boys of Spring." *Vanity Fair,* no. 442 (May 1997), 102+.

2897. Rains, Rob. "Hot Shots." In: Gerald Kavanagh, ed. *Street and Smith's Baseball '97.* New York: Street and Smith, 1997. pp. 48–51.

2898. Schwartz, Alan. "Dynamic Draftees." *Beckett's Future Stars,* VII, no. 74 (June 1997), *passim.* <http://www.beckett.com/products/fspd.html>.

2899. ____. "Fast Trackers." *Beckett Focus on Future Stars,* III, no. 26 (June 1993), 6–11.

2900. ____. "A Peek Into the Future." *Beckett Baseball Card Monthly,* X, no. 96 (March 1993), 10–15.

2901. ____. "Saddle Up." *Beckett Focus on Future Stars,* III, no. 23 (March 1993), 6–11.

2902. ____. "Seasons in the Sun." *Beckett Focus on Future Stars,* IV, no. 36 (April 1994), 6–11.

2903. Van Blair, Rick. "Compared to the 1930s, Rookies Have Easier Going Today." *Baseball Digest,* LIV (March 1995), 64–67.

2904. Vass, George. "*Baseball Digest*'s Rookie All-Star Team for 1992." *Baseball Digest,* LI (December 1992), 22–32.

2905. ____. "*Baseball Digest*'s Rookie All-Star Team for 1994." *Baseball Digest,* LIII (December 1994), 20–30.

2906. ____. "Club-by-Club Reports on Top Rookie Prospects of '96." *Baseball Digest,* LV (March 1996), 18–28.

2907. ____. "Here Are the Top '97 Rookies for Each Major League Club." *Baseball Digest,* LVI (March 1997), 20–33.

2908. ____. "Here They Come!: The Best Big League Rookies of '92." *Baseball Digest,* LI (March 1992), 60–73.

2909. ____. "Here's *Baseball Digest's* 1993 Rookie All-Star Team." *Baseball Digest,* LII (December 1993), 20–30.

2910. ____. "Here's *Baseball Digest's* Rookie All-Star Team for '95." *Baseball Digest,* LIV (December 1995), 20–32.

2911. ____. "Here's *Baseball Digest's* Rookie All-Star Team for '96." *Baseball Digest,* LV (December 1996), 22–35.

2912. ____. "Here's the Lowdown on the Most Promising Rookies of '93." *Baseball Digest,* LI (March 1993), 40–50.

2913. ____. "1997 All-Star Rookie Team, One of the Best in Years." *Baseball Digest,* LVI (December 1997), 22–35.

2914. ____. "Who Will Emerge as the Top Big League Rookies in 1994?" *Baseball Digest,* LIII (March 1994), 20–32.

2915. Verducci, Tom. "The Class of Their Fields." *Sports Illustrated,* LXXXVII (September 1, 1997), 28–33. Rookies.

2916. ____. "Kids' Stuff." *Sports Illustrated,* LXXX (April 4, 1994), 50–58, 60–61.

3. Pitchers

2917. Barra, Allen. "Back Off!" *Inside Sports,* XIV (June 1992), 52–55.

2918. Beaton, Rod. "These Big League Pitchers Thrive on Throwing 'Heat.'" *Baseball Digest,* LVI (October 1997), 48–51.

2919. Blahous, C. "If Not Larson, Who?: Don Did It, But Which Pitcher Was Most Likely to Do It?" *Baseball Research Journal,* XXIV (1995), 17–20. Considers other pitchers who might have thrown a World Series perfect game.

2920. Blengino, T, A.S. Kaufman, and J. C. Kaufman. "Dominant Pitchers." *Baseball Research Journal,* XV (1995), 39–52.

2921. Boren, Stephen D. "These Pitchers Won 200 Games, But Never 20 in a Season." *Baseball Digest,* LII (September 1993), 40–43.

2922. ____. "They Pitched No-Hitters Without Recording a Single Strikeout." *Baseball Digest,* LI (August 1993), 70–72.

2923. Bradley, Mark. "Braves' Starting Rotation: It's Loaded with 'Quality Arms.'" *Baseball Digest,* LII (July 1993), 24–28.

2924. Camps, Mark. "Surprise Packages." *Beckett Focus on Future Stars,* IV, no. 43 (November 1994), 70–75. John Hudek and William VanLandingham.

2925. Capezzuto, Tom. "Lefty Pitchers and Yankee Stadium: A Friendly Fit." *Baseball Digest,* LII (August 1993), 27–29.

2926. Caroulis, Jon. "Four 20-Game Winners Paced Orioles to '71 A.L. Pennant." *Baseball Digest,* LV (October 1996), 64–66.

2927. Castle, George. "Pitchers with Control Are Usually Winners in the Majors." *Baseball Digest,* LIV (January 1995), 40–44.

2928. Chastain, Bill. "Complete Games by Starters Fading Way in Majors." *Baseball Digest,* LIII (January 1994), 28–30.

2929. Crasnick, Jerry. "Young Pitchers Make Their Mark in the Major Leagues." *Baseball Digest,* LVI (November 1997), 38–45.

2930. Cunningham, Bob. "Set-Up Relievers: They're Baseball's Unsung Troopers." *Baseball Digest,* LV (May 1996), 21–27.

2931. DeMarco, Tony. "On the Rise: [A.L.] Battery Power." *Beckett Base-*

ball Card Monthly, X, no. 96 (March 1993), 16–19.

2932. ____. "Why High School Pitchers Are Risky Draft Picks." Baseball Digest, LIV (June 1995), 58–62.

2933. Drysdale, Don. "Don Drysdale's Top Fifteen Starting Pitchers." Sport, LXXXIV (May 1993), 14+.

2934. Eisenbath, Mike. "Hall of Famers Bob Gibson and Fergie Jenkins Still on Opposite Sides as Coaches." Baseball Digest, LIV (August 1995), 54–56.

2935. Farmer, T. "Joss vs. Walsh, October 2, 1908: The Greatest Pitching Duel in Baseball History?" National Pastime, XV (1995), 71–73.

2936. Freese, Mel R. Charmed Circle: Twenty-Game Winning Pitchers in Baseball's 20th Century. Jefferson, N.C.: McFarland & Co., Inc., 1997. 282p.

2937. Fudin, R., et al. "Analysis of Data from Reichler's (1979) The Baseball Encyclopedia: Right-Handed Pitchers Are Taller and Heavier Than Left-Handed Pitchers." Perceptual and Motor Skills, LXXVIII (June 1994), 1043–1048.

2938. George, Daniel P. "A Pair of Aces." Boy's Life, LXXXV (June 1995), 8+. Randy Johnson and Greg Maddox.

2939. Gold, Eddie. "Father-Son Pitching Duos Topped by Dizzy and Steve Trout." Baseball Digest, LII (March 1993), 74–76.

2940. Grosshandler, Stanley. "These 'Losing' Pitchers Also Were Winners in the Majors." Baseball Digest, LII (June 1993), 44–48.

2941. Guilfoile, William. "Hall of Famers Reveal: 'The Toughest I Ever Faced.'" Baseball Digest, LIV (July 1995), 70–74.

2942. Holway, John B. "Middle Relievers Deserve More Credit in Majors." Baseball Digest, LIII (May 1994), 20–23.

2943. Johnson, P. "Bullpen Blues: Where Have All the Great Closers Gone?" Dugout, III (June–July 1995), 7–10.

2944. Kaat, Jim. "Masters of the Mound." Inside Sports, XVII (April 1996), 84–95.

2945. Karp, Josie. "Low Supply of Left-Handed Pitchers Creates Demand." Baseball Digest, LIII (November 1994), 25–27.

2946. Kaufman, Alan S. and James C. The Worst Baseball Pitchers of All Time: Bad Luck, Bad Arms, Bad Teams, and Just Plain Bad. Jefferson, N.C.: McFarland & Co., Inc., 1993. 232p.

2947. Kavanagh, Jack. "Dizzy Dean vs. Carl Hubbel: Duels to Remember." Baseball Research Journal, XXI (1992), 33–35.

2948. Keegan, Tom. "Facing the Heat: Baseball's Pitching Aces Possess More Than Good Stuff—They Have the Strength to Lead." Inside Sports, XVII (September 1995), 72–77.

2949. Kuenster, Bob. "Coaches Pick Majors' Best Starters and Relievers." Baseball Digest, LII (May 1993), 28–31.

2950. ____. "Here Are the Majors' All-Time Best Right-Handed Pitchers." Baseball Digest, LIV (March 1995), 54–56.

2951. ____. "Here Are the Ten Greatest Left-Handed Pitchers Ever." Baseball Digest, LIV (April 1995), 36–41.

2952. ____. "These Are the Ten All-Time Best Major League Relievers." Baseball Digest, LIV (May 1995), 36–38.

2953. Kuenster, John. "Curt Schilling and Mike Mussina: Experts at Keeping Runners Off the Basepaths." Baseball Digest, LII (May 1993), 17–21.

2954. ____. "Infield Defense Helped Seaver and Fingers Gain Hall of Fame." Baseball Digest, LI (November 1992), 19–21.

2955. Kurkijan, Tim. "No Hitters." Sports Illustrated, LXXVIII (April 5, 1993), 54–56+. Batting ability of certain MLB pitchers.

2956. Lawson, Earl. "How Injuries Shortened Careers of Four Reds Pitchers." Baseball Digest, LII (May 1993),

67–70. Jim Maloney, Gary Nolan, Don Gullet, and Wayne Simpson.

2957. ____. "Reds' Relief Corps Has Been Populated by 'Free Spirits.'" *Baseball Digest,* LI (November 1992), 64–67.

2958. Lester, L. "Smokey and the Bandit: One of Baseball's Greatest Pitching Duels." *National Pastime,* XIV (1994), 18–20.

2959. Marino, John. *Pitchers of Perfection: The Cy Young Award Winners.* New York: MetroBooks, 1996. 80p.

2960. Markus, Robert. "Starting Pitchers of Years Gone By Had Fan Appeal." *Baseball Digest,* LIII (July 1994), 61–63.

2961. Miller, Stuart. "How Voters Decide the Cy Young Award." *Baseball Research Journal,* XXIV (1995), 157–159.

2962. Murray, Jim. "When Glory Is Dealt Out, Save Some for Relievers." *Baseball Digest,* LVI (August 1997), 50–53.

2963. Niedzielka, Amy. "Will the Majors Ever Produce Another 30-Game Winner?" *Baseball Digest,* LII (August 1993), 70–75.

2964. Noll, G. "Pinch-Hitting Pitchers: A Survey of a Once-Special Breed of Player." *Baseball Research Journal,* XXIV (1995), 69–72.

2965. Palmer, Jim. "Tough Acts to Follow." *Inside Sports,* XVI (July 1994), 46+.

2966. Pickard, Chuck. "Pitchers Who Posted the Best Proficiency Ratings in '96." *Baseball Digest,* LVI (April 1997), 78–83.

2967. ____. "These Pitchers Posted Best Proficiency Ratings in '95." *Baseball Digest,* LV (April 1996), 95–97.

2968. ____. "These Starters Had the Best Strikeout-to-Walk Proficiency." *Baseball Digest,* LII (May 1993), 50–53.

2969. "A Pitching Metamorphosis." In: Joe Hoppel, ed. *The Sporting News 1996 Baseball Yearbook.* St. Louis, Mo.: TSN, 1996. pp. 32–37. Pitchers of the New York Mets.

2970. Rogers, Phil. "Armed and Ready." *Beckett Focus on Future Stars,* III, no. 32 (December 1993), 16–19.

2971. Rosen, Charley. "How to Tame a Wild Fastball." *Men's Journal,* II (October 1993), 48+. As demonstrated by Randy Johnson and Nolan Ryan.

2972. Rosenblatt, Roger. "Pitchers and Catchers." *Men's Journal,* II (July–August 1993), 23–24.

2973. Ruben, Bob. "How Do They Spell Relief?" *Inside Sports,* XV (September 1993), 68–69.

2974. Rushin, Steve. "Five Aces." *Sports Illustrated,* LXXVIII (April 5, 1993), 34–41. On the staff of the Atlanta Braves.

2975. ____. "Making a Splash." *Sports Illustrated,* LXXX (April 4, 1994), 70–72, 74–76. Chicago (A.L.) pitching staff.

2976. Ryan, Nolan and Herskowitz, Mickey. *Kings of the Hill: An Irreverent Look at the Men on the Mound.* New York: HarperCollins, 1992. 288p.

2977. Schlossberg, Dan. "Circuit Breakers." In: Gerald Kavanagh, ed. *Street and Smith's Baseball '97.* New York: Street and Smith, 1997. pp. 41–43.

2978. Schwartz, Alan. "Pair Beyond Compare." *Beckett Focus on Future Stars,* V, no. 49 (May 1995), 6–10. White Sox hurlers James Baldwin and Scott Ruffcorn.

2979. Shea, Tom. "The Next Closers." *Beckett Focus on Future Stars,* II (January 1992), 6–9.

2980. Shouler, Kenneth. "Maintaining a 20-Win Pace, Mark of Pitching Greatness." *Baseball Digest,* LII (November 1993), 40–41.

2981. Singer, Tom. "Hey, Lefty!" *Sport,* LXXXIII (March 1992), 40–46.

2982. Tenbarge, Larry. "Kings of the Hill." *National Pastime,* XV (1995), 141–143. Cubs' pitching staff, 1904–1910.

2983. Thornley, S. "Lost in the Ninth: Near No-Hitters from a Different Perspective." *Baseball Research Journal,* XXIV (1995), 137–140.

2984. Tiemann, R. L. "Clutch Pitching Does Exist: It's a Historical Reality, Not a Statistical Calculation." *National Pastime,* XIV (1994), 11–13.

2985. Tuttle, Dennis. "The Unhittable Target: Who Will Be Baseball's Next 300 Game Winner?" *Inside Sports,* XVIII (June 1996), 58–63. Does not believe there will be another.

2986. Verducci, Tom. "Alone on the Hill." *Sports Illustrated,* LXXXVI (May 31, 1997), 52–60+. Dominant pitchers.

2987. ____. "Atlanta for Starters." *Sports Illustrated,* LXXXV (October 7, 1996), 34+.

2988. ____. "Just for Starters." *Sports Illustrated,* LXXXIII (October 23, 1995), 42+. Cleveland pitching staff.

2989. ____. "The M & M Boys: Plain and Peanut." *Sports Illustrated,* LXXXI (July 18, 1994), 16–22. Baltimore (A.L.) pitchers Mike Mussian and Ben McDonald.

2990. ____. "No Relief [Pitchers] in Sight." *Sports Illustrated,* LXXXVII (August 18, 1997), 44–51. Burned out hurlers.

2991. ____. "No You See It, Now You Don't." *Sports Illustrated,* LXXXIII (September 11, 1995), 30–33, 35. Tim Wakefield and Hideo Nomo.

2992. ____. "Orient Express." *Sports Illustrated,* LXXX (March 28, 1994), 24–26+. Los Angeles (N.L.) and Seattle (A.L.) pitchers.

2993. ____. "Save Stats for Relievers Are Over-rated, but Not Closers." *Baseball Digest,* LI (December 1992), 60–61.

2994. ____. "Staff Infection." *Sports Illustrated,* LXXXVI (May 19, 1997), 84–85, 88–89. New York Mets pitchers Jason Isringhausen, Bill Pulsipher, and Paul Wilson.

2995. ____. "Strike Back." *Sports Illustrated,* LXXXVI (June 2, 1997), 44–49. Improved pitching in both leagues.

2996. Wayman, J. M. "The Matty-Alex Tie: A Look at Lifetime Victories." *Baseball Research Journal,* XXIV (1995), 25–26.

2997. Young, Ken. *Cy Young Award Winners.* New York: Walker, 1994. 152p.

4. Catchers

2998. Cafardo, Nick. "Catchers Had Trouble Nabbing Base Stealers in 1996 Season." *Baseball Digest,* LV (December 1996), 50–52.

2999. Cunningham, Bob. "Catchers Pride Themselves on Calling a Good Game." *Baseball Digest,* LIV (June 1995), 36–39.

3000. Kuenster, Bob. "All-Time Greatest Players: Catchers." *Baseball Digest,* LIII (June 1994), 36–41.

3001. Kuenster, John. "Many Catchers in Majors Struggling Through Learning Process." *Baseball Digest,* LI (July 1992), 17–19.

3002. Kurkijan, Tim. "Catching Fire." *Sports Illustrated,* LXXXV (July 1, 1996), 68, 70. Dan Wilson and Todd Hundley.

3003. ____. "Hitting Is Catching." *Sports Illustrated,* LXXIX (July 5, 1993), 16–17. Hitting by certain MLB catchers.

3004. Roessing, Walter. "Baseball's Tough and Dirty Job." *Boy's Life,* LXXXII (June 1992), 24+.

3005. Schlossberg, Dan. "Catching On." *Beckett Focus on Future Stars*, IX (March 1992), 8–13.

3006. Singer, Tom. "Passing the Plate." *Sport,* LXXXIV (July 1993), 63–65. Latino catchers replace Afro-Americans.

3007. Storey, K. "A Bad Year for Catchers: Think Good Ones Are Rare Now?" *National Pastime,* XV (1995), 111+.

3008. Van Blair, Rick. "Are Catchers Today as Good Defensively as in the Past?" *Baseball Digest,* LIII (March 1994), 58–61.

3009. Verducci, Tom. "Catch of the Day." *Sports Illustrated,* LXXXVI (March 24, 1997), 38–40+. Backup catchers.

5. Hitters, Fielders, and Runners

3010. Adams, Samuel. "Switch Hitters Hammer Out a Legacy of Double Trouble." *Baseball Digest,* LIII (November 1994), 34–39.

3011. Aschburner, Steve. "Power Surge." In: Gerald Kavanagh, ed. *Street and Smith's Baseball '97.* New York: Street and Smith, 1997. pp. 37–40.

3012. Assicurato, Thomas. *Batting 1000: Baseball's Leading Hitters—A Tribute to Lou Gehrig.* New York: Priv. pub., 1996. 124p.

3013. Axelrod, Phil. "Major League Pinch Hitters Can't Be Afraid to Fail." *Baseball Digest,* LIII (November 1994), 40–43.

3014. Barra, Allen. "An Embarrassment of Richies." *Philadelphia,* LXXXVI (August 1995), 53+. Dick Allen and Richie Ashburn.

3015. Bjarkman, Peter C. *Top Ten Base Stealers.* Springfield, N. J.: Enslow Publishers, 1995. Unpaged.

3016. Bloom, Barry. "Griffey and [Alex] Rodriguez." *Sport,* LXXXVII (October 1997), 70–75.

3017. Boren, Stephen O. "These Big League Leadoff Batters Ruined No-Hitters." *Baseball Digest,* LI (April 1992), 90–96.

3018. Boswell, Thomas. "And the First Shall Be the Best." *Inside Sports,* XV (August 1993), 58+.

3019. Brady, Erik. "For the Alomars, Baseball Is a Family Affair." *Baseball Digest,* LV (September 1996), 22–24.

3020. Callahan, Gerry. "New York … New York." *Sports Illustrated,* LXXXIV (May 6, 1996), 44–48. Mets shortstop Ray Ordonez and Yankees shortstop Derek Jeter.

3021. Coen, Jerry. "Should Triple Crown Award Requirements Be Modified?" *Baseball Digest,* LIII (July 1994), 18–21.

3022. Crasnick, Jerry. "Triple Exposure." *Beckett Focus on Future Stars,* IV, no. 40 (August 1994), 74–81.

Manny Ramirez, Carlos Delgado, and Jeffrey Hammonds.

3023. Cunningham, Bob. "Strong-Armed Outfielders Still Excite Modern Fans." *Baseball Digest,* LIII (December 1994), 46–51.

3024. Daniel, P. K. "Bobby Grich Rates the Second Basemen." *Sport,* LXXXIV (June 1993), 16+.

3025. Deane, Bill. *Top Ten Baseball Home Run Hitters.* Hillsdale, N.J.; Enslow Publications, 1997. 64p.

3026. DeLand, Dave. "On the Rise: The Hot Corners." *Beckett Baseball Card Monthly,* X, no. 94 (January 1993), 18–20. First- and Third- Basemen.

3027. DeMarco, Tony. "On the Rise: Keystone Kids." *Beckett Baseball Card Monthly,* IX, no. 93 (December 1992), 8–11. Second Basemen.

3028. Dieffenbach, Dan and Darryl Howerton. "The Strike Zone." *Sport,* LXXXVII (May 1996), 26–30. Frank Thomas and Ken Griffey, Jr.

3029. Elderkin, Phil. "Will 'Sophomore Hex' Catch Up with Tim Salmon and Mike Piazza?" *Baseball Digest,* LIII (July 1994), 30–33.

3030. Fraley, Gerry. "Having a Blast." *Inside Sports,* XVIII (June 1996), 60–67.

3031. Gagnon, Cappy. "The Six Greatest Throwing Outfielders in History." *Baseball Research Journal,* XXIV (1995), 96–100.

3032. Gilbert, B. "Triple Milestone Hitters: A New Generation." *Baseball Research Journal,* XXIV (1995), 27–29.

3022. Gleisser, Benjamin. "In Defense of Defense." *Beckett Baseball Card Monthly,* IX (February 1992), 16–18. Fielder profiles.

3033. Gostick, Glenn. "Rosters: Left-Handed Catchers, Second Basemen, Third Basemen, and Shortstops (1876–1989)." *Elysian Fields Quarterly,* XIII (Winter 1994), 14–15.

3034. Green, E. J. "Minor League Big Guns: A Comparison of the Top Ten Individual Single-Season Home Run

Records." *Baseball Research Journal,* XXIV (1995), 53–57.

3035. Grosshandler, Stanley. "Batting Champs in the World Series: How Have Season Leaders Done in the Fall Classic?" *Baseball Research Journal,* XXIV (1995), 94–95.

3036. ____. "'92 Tigers Featured Three 30-Plus Home Run Hitters." *Baseball Digest,* LII (January 1993), 64–66. Cecil Fielder, Mickey Tettleton, and Rob Deer.

3037. ____. "These Players Narrowly Missed .300 Career Batting Average." *Baseball Digest,* LI (May 1992), 18–21.

3038. Harris, Arthur. "Baseball's Top Sluggers." *Baseball Illustrated Annual,* XXXII (1997), 58–63.

3039. Harwell, Ernie. "Majors Featured Many Top Leadoff Hitters in '96." *Baseball Digest,* LV (November 1996), 49–50.

3040. Herman, Bruce. "Distant Thunder." *Beckett Focus on Future Stars,* II, no. 15 (July 1992), 10–15. Minor league home run hitters.

3041. Heyman, Jon. "Today's Hitters Are Taking Over the Game." *Baseball Digest,* LVI (August 1997), 20–25.

3042. Hoffer, Richard. "Strokes of Luck." *Sports Illustrated,* LXXVIII (June 28, 1993), 22–24+. Andres Galarraga and John Olerud.

3043. ____. "Try, Try Again." *Sports Illustrated,* LXXX (March 14, 1994), 38–40. Jose Canseco and Darryl Strawberry.

3044. Holway, John B. "Base Stealers: Are They Spinning Their Wheels?" *Baseball Digest,* LI (April 1992), 80–83.

3045. ____. "With a .400 Season [1921] on the Line, Did Hornsby and Cobb Hit or Sit?" *Elysian Fields Quarterly,* XI (Spring 1992), 56–58.

3046. Honig, Donald. *The Greatest Shortstops of All-Time.* Madison, Wisc.: Elysian Fields Press, 1992. 164p.

3047. ____. *The Power Hitters.* New York: Crescent Books, 1993. 241p. First published by the *Sporting News* in 1989.

3048. "Just a Blur: In Today's 'Wait for the Home Run' Style of Offense, the Number of Elite Basestealers is Falling." In: Joe Hoppel, ed. *The Sporting News 1997 Baseball Yearbook.* St. Louis, Mo.: TSN, 1997. pp. 24–29.

3049. Kaegel, Dick. "For the Boones, Baseball Remains a Family Matter." *Baseball Digest,* LVI (September 1997), 54–56.

3050. Kramer, Sydella. *Baseball's Greatest Hitters.* New York: Random House, 1995. 48p.

3051. Kreuz, Jim. "How Mickey Mantle and Stan Musial Fared as High School Athletes." *Baseball Digest,* LIII (December 1994), 58–64.

3052. Kuenster, Bob. "All-Time Greatest Players: Center Fielders." *Baseball Digest,* LIII (December 1994), 36–45.

3053. ____. "All-Time Greatest Players: First Basemen." *Baseball Digest,* LIII (July 1994), 64–69.

3054. ____. "All-Time Greatest Players: Left Fielders." *Baseball Digest,* LIII (November 1994), 52–60.

3055. ____. "All-Time Greatest Players: Right Fielders." *Baseball Digest,* LIV (January 1995), 46–48.

3056. ____. "All-Time Greatest Players: Second Basemen." *Baseball Digest,* LIII (August 1994), 38–42.

3057. ____. "All-Time Greatest Players: Shortstops." *Baseball Digest,* LIII (October 1994), 38–46.

3058. ____. "Baseball's Most Productive Hitters with Men in Scoring Position." *Baseball Digest,* LV (May 1996), 36–40.

3059. ____. "Best Defensive Players Chosen by Ten Hall of Fame Members." *Baseball Digest,* LVI (November 1997), 17–21.

3060. ____. "Frank Thomas and Barry Bonds, Leading Candidates for MVP Honors." *Baseball Digest,* LII (November 1993), 19–21.

3061. ____. "How Batters Fared in '96 with Runners in Scoring Position." *Baseball Digest,* LVI (February 1997), 35–41.

3062. ____. "How Stars Fared in Their First Major League At-Bat." *Baseball Digest,* LI (June 1992), 20–24.

3063. ____. "Leading Run Producers in the Majors for the '96 Season." *Baseball Digest,* LVI (March 1997), 88–89.

3064. Kuenster, John. "Majors' Best 3–4 Hitting Combo?: How About Bonds and Williams." *Baseball Digest,* LV (August 1995), 17–18.

3065. ____. "Ripken and Alomar Form a Special Middle Infield Combo for the Orioles." *Baseball Digest,* LV (June 1996), 17–21.

3066. ____. "Wealth of Talented Young Shortstops to Brighten '97 Major League Season." *Baseball Digest,* LVI (January 1997), 19–23.

3067. ____. "Will There Ever Be Another Triple Crown Winner?: Maybe Not." *Baseball Digest,* LI (June 1992), 17–19.

3068. Kurkjian, Tim. "Good Hands People." *Sports Illustrated,* LXXXIV (April 1, 1996), 52–60, 64, 66.

3069. ____. "The Health Club." *Sports Illustrated,* LXXXV (July 8, 1996), 44–45. How several players, if healthy, could hit 500 homers in their careers.

3070. ____. "New Power Supply." *Sports Illustrated,* LXXIX (July 26, 1995), 18–22. New, young MLB home run hitters.

3071. ____. "Who's on Third?" *Sports Illustrated,* LXXVI (April 6, 1992), 60–75.

3072. Leahy, Leo. *Lumber Men: Nontraditional Statistical Measurements of the Batting Careers of Over 900 Major League Regulars from 1876 to 1992.* Jefferson, N.C.: McFarland & Co., Inc., 1994. 531p.

3073. Lewis, Allen. "How Hall of Famers Performed as Pinch-Hitters?" *Baseball Digest,* LI (June 1992), 76–78.

3074. Lidz, Franz. "Right Off the Bat." *Sports Illustrated,* LXXXII (June 12,

1995), 44–48. Barry Larkin and Ron Gant.

3075. Liebman, Glenn. "Some Major Leaguers Were Disasters on Defense." *Baseball Digest,* LI (November 1992), 40–42.

3076. Lingo, Will. "A Cut Above." *Beckett Focus on Future Stars,* IV, no. 44 (December 1994), 16–20. Brien Taylor and Chipper Jones.

3077. Little, Rod and Doug Stern. "Then … and Now." *U.S. News & World Report,* CXXII (March 24, 1997), 58–59. Careers of Jackie Robinson and Ken Griffey, Jr.

3078. McConnell, Bob and Daniel Vincent, eds. *SABR Presents the Home Run Encyclopedia: The Who, What, and Where of Every Home Run Hit Since 1876.* New York: Macmillan, 1996. 1,310p.

3079. McGregor, Ed. "Why the Triple Crown Remains So Elusive in the Majors." *Baseball Digest,* LII (February 1993), 22–27.

3080. McNeil, William F. *The King of Swat: An Analysis of Baseball's Home Run Hitters from the Major, Minor, Negro, and Japanese Leagues.* Jefferson, N.C.: McFarland & Co., Inc., 1997. 208p.

3081. Minsky, Alan. *Home Run Kings.* New York: MetroBooks, 1995. 80p.

3082. Mizell, Hubert. "Ted Williams Names His Top 20 All-Time Hitters." *Baseball Digest,* LIV (June 1995), 48–53.

3083. Nightingale, Dave. "Club 3000." *Sport,* LXXXV (May 1994), 74+.

3084. ____. "Junior or the Giant?" *Inside Sports,* XVI (September 1994), 70+. Attributes of Ken Griffey, Jr. and Barry Bonds.

3085. Pickard, Chuck. "Biggest Batting Gainers and Losers in Majors." *Baseball Digest,* LI (March 1992), 22–23+; LII (February 1993), 28–30; LIII (February 1994), 44–47; LIV (February 1995), 54–57; LV (February 1996), 32–34; LVI (March 1997), 59–61.

3086. ____. "These Batters Ranked High

in Runs Produced in '95." *Baseball Digest,* LV (April 1996), 68–69.

3087. Poiley, Joel. "Life on the Run." *Beckett Baseball Card Monthly,* XII, no. 121 (April 1995), 120–123.

3088. Rasmussen, Larry F. "Batting Champions Who Gained or Lost Most Points in Successive Seasons." *Baseball Digest,* LIII (May 1994), 56–57.

3089. ____. "These Home Run Hitters Were Tough to Strike Out." *Baseball Digest,* LVI (April 1997), 76–77.

3090. ____. "These Major League Batters Excelled But Finished Second Best." *Baseball Digest,* LVI (July 1997), 64–65.

3091. ____. "These Teammates Combined for 80 Homers in One Season." *Baseball Digest,* LIV (May 1995), 54–58.

3092. Rozin, Skip. "Willie, Mickey, and the Duke." *Topps Magazine,* (Winter 1992), 33–35.

3093. Ryan, Jeff. "A Field of Dreams Deferred." *Inside Sports,* XV (June 1993), 58–61. Yankee centerfielders.

3094. ____. "Hot Times at the Hot Corner." *Inside Sports,* XV (January 1993), 68–71.

3095. Sands, Jack and Peter Gammons. *Coming Apart at the Seams.* New York: Macmillan, 1993. 266p. Dwight Evans and Carlton Fisk.

3096. Shaw, Bud. "Indians' Middle Infielders Combine Bat and Glove Skills." *Baseball Digest,* LV (July 1996), 58–59.

3097. Simon, T. "Goslin vs. Manush: Head to Head for the 1928 American League Batting Title." *National Pastime,* XV (1995), 102–105.

3098. Stewart, Wayne. "Frank Thomas and Albert Belle Rank as Majors' Top Power Duo." *Baseball Digest,* LVI (May 1997), 26–31.

3099. ____. "Mammoth Homers by Active Longball Hitters Recalled." *Baseball Digest,* LII (May 1993), 32–35.

3100. ____. "Power Surge." *Beckett Baseball Card Monthly,* IX, no. 90 (September 1992), 18–23.

3101. ____. "Tape-Measure Artists." *Beckett Baseball Card Monthly,* XI, no. 110 (May 1994), 20–23.

3102. ____. "These Are the Major Leagues' Most Intimidating Hitters." *Baseball Digest,* LIV (June 1995), 44–47.

3103. ____. "These Batters of the Past Intimidated Pitching Foes." *Baseball Digest,* LIV (July 1995), 30–33.

3104. ____. "These Major Leaguers Hit Longest Home Runs in '95." *Baseball Digest,* LV (March 1996), 90–92.

3105. ____. "30/30." *Beckett Baseball Card Monthly,* IX, no. 84 (March 1992), 14–16.

3106. Sullivan, George. *Glovemen: Twenty Seven of Baseball's Greatest.* New York: Atheneum, 1996. 71p.

3107. Surdam, David G. "Five 40-Home Run Hitters Made Impact on '93 Season." *Baseball Digest,* LIII (January 1994), 38–39. Juan Gonzalez, Ken Griffey, Frank Thomas, Barry Bonds, and David Justice.

3108. Torres, John Albert. *Home-Run Hitters: Heroes of the Four-Home-Run Game.* New York: Bradbury Press, 1995. Unpaged.

3109. Tully, Mike. "Center of Attention." *Sport,* LXXXIV (June 1993), 56–59. Centerfielders.

3110. Vass, George. "Baseball's Age-Old Motto: 'Have Glove, Will Travel.'" *Baseball Digest,* LV (January 1996), 44–53.

3111. ____. "Experts Rate Major Leagues' Most Dangerous Hitters." *Baseball Digest,* LI (December 1992), 36–40.

3112. ____. "Why Don't Second Basemen Get More Respect in the Majors?" *Baseball Digest,* LII (August 1993), 30–34.

3113. Verducci, Tom. "Long on Shortstops." *Sports Illustrated,* LXXXVI (February 24, 1997), 50–57. Derek Jeter and Alex Rodriguez.

3114. ____. "Perplexed Players." *Sports*

Illustrated, LXXXII (May 29, 1995), 78–79. Early season batting slumps.

3115. ____. "Shooting Stars." *Sports Illustrated,* LXXX (June 6, 1994), 18–22. Hitters chasing records.

3116. "Wall Crashers." *Sport,* LXXXIV (July 1993), 58–62.

3117. Williams, Ted, with Jim Prince. *Ted William's Hit List: The Ultimate Ranking of Baseball's Greatest Hitters.* Indianapolis, Ind.: Masters Press, 1996. 245p.

6. Managers, Coaches, and Batboys/Girls

3118. "Deans of the Dugout." In: Joe Hoppel, ed. *The Sporting News 1996 Baseball Yearbook.* St. Louis, Mo.: TSN, 1996. 22–27. Senior managers in length of service.

3119. Isaacs, Neil. *Batboys and the World of Baseball.* Studies in Popular Culture. Jackson: University of Mississippi Press, 1995. 232p.

3120. ____. *Innocence and Wonder: Baseball Through the Eyes of Batboys.* Indianapolis, Ind.: Masters Press, 1994. 242p.

3121. James, Bill. *Bill James' Guide to Baseball Managers: From 1870 to Today.* New York: Charles Scribner's Sons, 1997.

3122. Koppett, Leonard. *The Man in the Dugout: Baseball's Top Managers and How They Got That Way.* New York: Crown Publishers, 1993. 404p.

3123. Leavy, Walter. "Baseball's Minority Managers: Taking Charge on the Field." *Ebony,* XLVIII (May 1993), 110–112+.

3124. Smith-Wallace, G. L. *"The Background and Experience of NCAA Division I Head Baseball Coaches."* Unpublished M.A. thesis, Ball State University, 1995. 38p.

3125. Stern, William. "Secrets of the Survivors." *Business Week,* (October 9, 1995), 78+. Includes Sparky Anderson and Tommy Lasorda.

7. Team Owners and Executives/League Officials

3126. Gurnick, Ken. "The State of the Game." *Sport,* LXXXIII (March 1992), 47–51. Baseball commissioners past and present discuss the game.

3127. Hoffacre, Susan and Scott Branvold. "Baseball Front Office Careers: Expectations and Realities." *Journal of Sport Management,* IX (May 1995), 173+.

3128. Ingham, John N. and Lynne B. Feldman. *African-American Business Leaders: A Biographical Dictionary.* Westport, Conn.: Greenwood Press, 1994. 806p. Includes former ballplayers turned executives and officials.

3129. Mayberry, Jodine. *Business Leaders Who Built Financial Empires.* Austin, Tex.: Raintree Steck-Vaughn Publications, 1995. 48p. Includes owners like Ted Turner and Ray Kroc.

3130. Reinsdorf, Jonathan. "The Powers of the Commissioner of Baseball." *Marquette Sports Law Journal,* VII (Fall 1996), 211+.

3131. Shlain, Bruce. "The GM's Burden." In his: *Baseball Inside Out: Winning the Games Within the Games.* New York: Viking Press, 1992. pp. 145–181.

3132. Steinbreder, H. J. "The Owners." *Sports Illustrated,* LXXIX (September 13, 1993), 64–72, 74, 76, 78, 80, 82, 84–86. Ranked by net worth.

3133. Verducci, Tom. "Have You Seen This Man?" *Sports Illustrated,* LXXIX (July 5, 1993), 76–80. Search for a new commissioner.

8. Umpires

3134. Holtzman, Jerome. "Here's a Big League First: Umpires 'Numbers' Retired." *Baseball Digest,* LIV (December 1995), 74–75.

3135. "Major Leagues: The Umpires." *Referee,* XIV (August 1989), 68+.

3136. Skipper, John C. *Umpires: Classic Baseball Stories from the Men*

Who Made the Calls. Jefferson, N.C.: McFarland & Co., Inc., 1997. 168p.

Profiles and moments from Don Denkinger, "Red" Flaherty, Bill Kinnamon, Bill Jackowski, Bill Haller, John Rice, Dutch Renert, John Kibler, Vill Valentine, Terry Cooney, Andy Olsen, Marty Springstead, Hank Morganweck, Art Frantz, Jerry Neudecker, and "Steamboat" Johnson.

3137. Tullio, T. "Major League Umpires: What Makes a Rookie a Rookie?" *Baseball Research Journal,* XXIV (1995), 111–112.

3138. Watt, R. L. "Memories." *Sport,* LXXXIV (July 1993), 70–71. Interviews with Dutch Rennert and Bruce Froemming.

G. Individual Biography

The purpose of this chapter, the largest both here and in the original *Baseball: A Comprehensive Bibliography*, is to draw attention to the sources available on specific players, managers, coaches, umpires, executives, and media personnel. It is arranged alphabetically by the last name of the biographee, beginning with Henry Aaron. Again, the criterion for inclusion is not significance, but whether or not published, non-newspaper data are available and were uncovered prior to the completion of this supplement.

Despite followup on reviews of the main 1986 bibliography, ardent additional research, correspondence with SABR members and team officials, and further generous assistance by personnel at the National Baseball Library, it is again probable that several individuals have been omitted because writings about them were not found. Once more we ask, in the event that users have or find non-newspaper printed items on excluded individuals or items which we have missed on people included, that information should be forwarded to the publisher for use in our next supplement.

In addition to providing bibliographic data on the people noted below, we again make an effort to provide biographical data. In order to save space, however, it has been decided to cut down the amount of information given. Thus we will reference names, functions, and team/league associations of individuals. Users should note that, regardless of the number, team/league affiliations are represented once per individual. We have starred (*) those elected to the National Baseball Hall of Fame.

FUNCTION

Broadcaster   Pitcher   Catcher   First Baseman
Second Baseman   Third Baseman   Shortstop   Outfielder
Manager   Executive   Coach   Umpire
Entertainer   Novelist   Sportswriter

MAJOR LEAGUE

NABBP = National Association of Base Ball Players
N.L. = National League   A.L. = American League
A.A. = American Association   U. = Union Association
P. = Player (Brotherhood) League   F.L. = Federal League
AAGPBL = All-American Girls Professional Baseball League
* = Elected to National Baseball Hall of Fame

HENRY ("HANK") AARON*

Outfielder
Milwaukee (N.L.), Atlanta (N.L.)
Executive
Atlanta

3139. "Braves Pay Tribute to Aaron on 20th Year of Breaking Ruth's Record." *Jet,* LXXXV (May 2, 1994), 52–53.

3140. Capuzzo, Mike. "A Prisoner of Memory." *Sports Illustrated,* LXXVII (December 7, 1992), 80–84, 86, 89–92.

3141. Ethier, B. "Henry Aaron Remembers." *American History,* XXXII (March–April 1997), 38–41+.

3142. Fimrite, Ron. "Henry Aaron." *Sports Illustrated,* LXXXI (September 19, 1994), 88–89.

3143. "Final Look: Hank Aaron." *Beckett Baseball Card Monthly,* XI, no. 114 (September 1994), 105–106.

3144. "Hank Aaron." In: Laurie L. Harris, ed. *Biography Today: Profiles of People of Interest to Young Readers.* Detroit, Mich.: Omnigraphics, 1996. pp. 16–19.

3145. Hanson, T. "The Mental Aspects of Hitting in Baseball: A Case Study of Hank Aaron." *Contemporary Thought on Performance Enhancement,* I (October 1992), 49–70.

3146. Hoffman, Frank W. and William G. Bailey. "Hank Aaron Hits His 715th Home Run." In: their *Sports and Recreation Fads.* Binghampton, N.Y.: Haworth, 1991. pp. 1–4.

3147. Ladson, William. "The *Sport*

Q & A: Hank Aaron." *Sport,* LXXXIV (February 1993), 70–75.

3148. Lowitt, Bruce. "Hank Aaron Says Pursuit of Home Run Record Extracted a Big Toll." *Baseball Digest,* LIII (August 1994), 59–62.

3149. Margolies, Jacob. *Hank Aaron.* New York: Franklin Watts, 1992. 64p.

3150. Plimpton, George. "Final Twist of the Drama." *Sports Illustrated,* LXXX (April 11, 1994), 86–88+. Reprinted from the April 1974 issue.

3151. Rennert, Richard S. *Baseball Legends: Hank Aaron.* New York: Chelsea House, 1993. 127p.

3152. Whiteside, Larry. "Hank Aaron: His Home Run Mark May Never Be Matched." *Baseball Digest,* LV (June 1996), 72–77.

KURT ABBOTT

Shortstop
Oakland (A.L.), Florida (N.L.)

3153. Klis, Mike. "Rookie Report: Kurt Abbott." *Beckett Baseball Card Monthly,* XI, no. 115 (October 1994), 126–127.

JIM ABBOTT

Pitcher
California (A.L.), New York (A.L.), Chicago (A.L.), Anaheim (A.L.)

3154. Bernotas, Bob. *Nothing to Prove: The Jim Abbott Story.* New York: Kodansha International, 1995. 182p.

3155. Gutman, Bill. *Jim Abbott: Star*

Pitcher. Brookfield, Conn.: Millbrook Press, 1992. 48p.

3156. Hertzel, Bob. "Closer Look: Jim Abbott." *Beckett Baseball Card Monthly,* X, no. 99 (June 1993), 6–9.

3157. Iacono, John. "Jim Dandy." *Sports Illustrated for Kids,* VI (September 1994), 40–49.

3158. Kiersh, Edward. "Interview: Jim Abbott." *Inside Sports,* XV (May 1993), 26–33.

3159. Kramer, Jon. *Jim Abbott.* Austin, Tx.: Raintree Steck-Vaughan, 1996. 48p.

3160. Lee, Gregory. *Jim Abbott, Left-Handed Wonder.* Vero Beach, Fla.: Rourke Corp., 1993. 15p.

3161. Macht, Norman L. *Jim Abbott.* New York: Chelsea House, 1994. 64p.

3162. "A Marvel on the Mound." *National Geographic World,* CCX (February 1993), 30–31.

3163. Rambeck, Richard. *Jim Abbott.* Plymouth, Minn.: Child's World, 1994. 31p.

3164. Reiser, Howard. *Jim Abbott: All-American Pitcher.* Chicago, Ill.: Children's Press, 1993. 48p.

3165. Savage, Jeff. *Sports Great Jim Abbott.* Hillside, N.J.: Enslow, 1993. 64p.

3166. Stewart, Mark. *Jim Abbott.* New York: Children's Press, 1996. 48p.

3167. "Superstar Gallery: Jim Abbott." *Beckett Baseball Card Monthly,* X, no. 98 (May 1993), 14–17.

3168. Verducci, Tom. "A Special Delivery." *Sports Illustrated,* LXXIX (September 13, 1993), 62–63. No hitter against Cleveland (A.L.).

DANIEL LUCIUS ADAMS

Shortstop/Executive
New York Base Ball Club

3169. Thorn, John. "The Father of Baseball: You Probably Never Heard of Him." *Elysian Fields Quarterly,* XI (Winter 1992), 85–91. 1850s.

TONY ADAMSON

Outfielder
Australian Baseball League

3170. Palmer, Michael. "The Natural." *Baseball Australia,* V (March 1993), 8–9.

JOSEPH ("JOE") ADCOCK

Outfielder, First Baseman
Cincinnati (N.L.), Milwaukee (A.L.),
Cleveland (A.L.), Los Angeles (A.L.),
California (A.L.)
Manager
Cleveland (A.L.)

3171. Macht, Norman L. "Power Hitter Joe Adcock Recalls the "Glory of His Time."" *Baseball Digest,* LII (October 1993), 60–64.

HARRY ("THE GOLDEN GREEK") AGGANIS

First Baseman
Boston (A.L.)

3172. Tsiotos, Nick and Andy Dabilis. *Harry Agganis, the Golden Greek: An All-American Story.* Brookline, Mass.: Hellenic College Press, 1995. 245p.

GROVER CLEVELAND ("OL PETE") ALEXANDER*

Pitcher
Philadelphia (N.L.), Chicago (N.L.),
St. Louis (N.L.)

3173. Clark, Jerry E. and Marth E. Webb. *Alexander the Great: The Story of Grover Cleveland Alexander.* Omaha, Neb.: Making History, 1993. 59p.

3174. Kavanagh, Jack. *Ol' Pete: The Grover Cleveland Alexander Story.* South Bend, Ind.: Diamond Communications, 1996.

3175. Lewis, Allen. "Grover Alexander's Shutout Record May Never Be

Topped." *Baseball Digest,* LIII (December 1994), 76–79.

DICK/RICHIE ALLEN

Outfielder, Third Baseman,
First Baseman
Philadelphia (N.L.),
Los Angeles (N.L.),
St. Louis (N.L.), Chicago (A.L.),
Oakland (A.L.)

3176. Wright, C. R. "Another View of Dick Allen: The Most Misunderstood Player of His Generation." *Baseball Research Journal,* XXIV (1995), 2–14.

JOHN THOMAS ("JOHNNY") ALLEN

Pitcher
New York (A.L.), Cleveland (A.L.),
St. Louis (N.L.),
Brooklyn (N.L.),
New York Giants (N.L.)

3177. Sumner, Jim L. "Almost Perfect: Johnny Allen's 1937 Season." *National Pastime,* XIV (1994), 51–54.

ROBERTO ALOMAR

Second Baseman
San Diego (N.L.), Toronto (A.L.),
Baltimore (A.L.)

3178. Alomar, Roberto, with S. Brunt. *Second to None: The Roberto Alomar Story.* Toronto, Ont.: Penguin Books Canada, 1993. 224p.
3179. Bloom, Bob. "Roberto Alomar." *Sport,* LXXXVIII (January 1997), 12+. Reflections on the spitting incident.
3180. George, Daniel P. "Tops in Toronto." *Boy's Life,* LXXXIV (April 1994), 8–9.
3181. Kaplan, David A. "When the Spit Hit the Fan." *Newsweek,* CXXVIII (October 14, 1996), 96+.
3182. Kernan, Kevin. "Canada! O Alomar!" In: Zander Hollander, ed. *The*

Complete Handbook of Baseball, 1993. New York: Signet Books, 1993. pp. 14–21.
3183. Kuenster, John. "Versatile Roberto Alomar Earns Top Spot in 1992 Player of the Year Poll." *Baseball Digest,* LII (January 1993), 17–21.
3184. Kurkjian, Tim. "Do Not Disturb." *Sports Illustrated,* LXXXIV (January 29, 1996), 142–144, 146.
3185. ____. "Public Enemy No. 1." *Sports Illustrated,* LXXXV (October 14, 1996), 28–30+.
3186. Milton, Steve. "Closer Look: Roberto Alomar." *Beckett Baseball Card Monthly,* X, no. 97 (April 1993), 6–9.
3187. Newman, Bruce. "Home Suite Home." *Sports Illustrated,* LXXVI (June 8, 1992), 36–39.
3188. Posen, Michael. "Local Hero." *Toronto Life,* XXVII (May 1993), 37+.
3189. Remnick, David. "Hock Tooey." *The New Yorker,* LXXII (October 14, 1996), 7–8. The spitting incident.
3190. Wulf, Steve. "The Spit Hits the Fan." *Time,* CXLVIII (October 14, 1996), 82+. *See also* John Hirschbeck.

SANDY ALOMAR, JR.

Catcher
San Diego (N.L.), Cleveland (A.L.)

3191. Crothers, Tim. "The Other Alomar." *Sports Illustrated,* LXXXVI (April 28, 1997), 92+.
3192. Hoynes, Paul. "Hard Work Pays Off for the Indians' Sandy Alomar, Jr." *Baseball Digest,* LVI (October 1997), 44–47.

FELIPE ROJAS ALOU

Outfielder
San Francisco (N.L.),
Milwaukee (A.L.), Atlanta (N.L.),
Oakland (A.L.), New York (A.L.),
Montreal (N.L.)
Manager
Montreal (N.L.)

3193. Blair, J. "Managing Miracles." *Maclean's,* CVII (August 1, 1994), 43+.

3194. Came, Barry. "Up from the Ashes." *Maclean's,* CV (September 28, 1992), 52–53.

3195. Farber, Michael. "Diamond Heirs." *Sports Illustrated,* LXXXII (June 19, 1995), 88–92, 96, 98, 101–103. Family playing heritage.

3196. Kurkijan, Tim. "Northern Exposure." *Sports Illustrated,* LXXVII (July 27, 1992), 54–55.

WILSON ALVAREZ

Pitcher
Texas (A.L.), Chicago (A.L.), San Francisco (N.L.)

3197. Rushin, Steve. "Making a Splash." *Sports Illustrated,* LXXX (April 4, 1994), 70–72+.

3198. Shook, Richard. "Zeroing in on Stardom." *Beckett Focus on Future Stars,* II, no. 15 (July 1992), 6–9.

BRADY ANDERSON

Outfielder
Boston (A.L.), Baltimore (A.L.)

3199. Bamberger, Michael. "Brady Hits 'Em in Bunches." *Sports Illustrated,* LXXXVI (April 14, 1997), 50–52+.

3200. Boswell, Thomas. "Late Boomer: Brady Anderson." *Washington Post Magazine,* (March 30, 1997), 6–11.

3201. Gelin, Dana. "Hidden Power." In: David Bauer, ed. *SI Presents Baseball 1997.* New York: Sports Illustrated, 1997. pp. 40–45.

3202. Henneman, Jim. "Second Look: Brady Anderson." *Beckett Baseball Card Monthly,* X, no. 98 (May 1993), 97–99.

3203. Holtzman, Jerome. "Orioles' Brady Anderson Ups His Power as a Leadoff Hitter." *Baseball Digest,* LV (August 1996), 60–63.

3204. MacMullan, J. "Brady's Big Binge." *Sports Illustrated,* LXXXIV (May 13, 1996), 84+.

3205. Schmuck, P. "One-on-One [with] Brady Anderson: Interview." *Sport,* LXXXIV (March 1993), 20–21.

3206. Shaughnessy, Dan. "Brady Anderson: Another Good One Red Sox Let Get Away." *Baseball Digest,* LV (November 1996), 47–48.

GEORGE ("SPARKY") ANDERSON

Second Baseman
Philadelphia (N.L.)
Manager
Cincinnati (N.L.), Detroit (A.L.)

3207. Henning, Lynn. "Crazy Like a Fox." *Detroit,* XVII (June 1994), 66–67.

3208. Kuenster, John. "George Anderson Still 'Sparky' When It Comes to Talking Baseball." *Baseball Digest,* LII (December 1993), 17–19.

3209. Lawson, Earl. "Memories of a Younger Sparky Anderson." *Baseball Digest,* LI (August 1992), 58–60.

3210. Rushin, Steve. "The New Perfesser." *Sports Illustrated,* LXXVIII (June 28, 1993), 54–58+.

3211. Ryan, Bob. "Sparky Anderson Looks Back on His Brief Career as a Player." *Baseball Digest,* LIV (November 1995), 90–92.

RYAN ANDERSON

Pitcher
Divine Child High School

3212. Crothers, Tim. "Carbon Copy [of Randy Johnson]." *Sports Illustrated,* LXXXVI (June 2, 1997), 75–76.

ROGER ANGELL

Sportswriter

3213. Freitag, P. J. "Roger Angell's Baseball Myth: Defeat as Affliction and

Gift." *Aethlon: The Journal of Sport Literature,* XII (Fall 1995), 103–111.

PETER ANGELOS

Executive
Baltimore (A.L.)

3214. Goode, E. E. "Trying to Shrink the Strike Zone." *U.S. News & World Report,* CXVIII (February 13, 1995), 69+. Refusal to employ replacement players during the 1994–95 strike.

3215. Kurkijan, Tim. "One Quick Fix." *Sports Illustrated,* LXXX (February 21, 1994), 54–57.

3216. "Peter Angelos." In: Louise Mooney Collins and Geri J. Speace, eds. *Newsmakers, 1995: The People Behind the Headlines.* Detroit, Mich.: Gale Research, 1995. pp. 8–11.

3217. Starr, Mark. "An Owner Who Won't Play [Replacement] Ball with the Other Boys." *Newsweek,* CXXV (March 13, 1995), 64+.

ADRIAN ("CAP") ANSON*

First Baseman
Rockford Forest City (Ind.),
Philadelphia (Ind.), Chicago (N.L.)
Manager
Chicago (N.L.)

3218. Jantz, Steve. "Hall of Famer Cap Anson Was Baseball's Best Player and Most Strident Racist." *Sport,* LXXXIV (May 1993), 70+.

3219. Nawrocki, T. "Captain Anson's Platoon." *National Pastime,* XV (1995), 34–37.

KEVIN APPIER

Pitcher
Kansas City (A.L.)

3220. Eskew, Alan. "Royals' Kevin Appier Joins Elite Group of A.L.

Starters." *Baseball Digest,* LIII (April 1994), 87–90.

3221. Kaegel, Dick. "Kevin Appier Finds Success with a 'Different Pitch.'" *Baseball Digest,* LIV (September 1995), 34–35.

RENE AROCHA

Pitcher
St. Louis (N.L.)

3222. Garlick, David. "Starting Over." *Beckett Focus on Future Stars,* II, no. 20 (December 1992), 73–74.

3223. Wheatley, Tom. "Deeper Look: Rene Arocha." *Beckett Baseball Card Monthly,* XI, no. 106 (January 1994), 120–121.

RICHIE ASHBURN*

Outfielder
Philadelphia (N.L.), Chicago (N.L.),
New York Mets (N.L.)

3224. Caroulis, John. "Richie Ashburn Savors 50 Years of Baseball Memories." *Baseball Digest,* LIII (December 1994), 84–89.

3225. Mathers, J. "The Greatest Fielding Outfielder: Richie Ashburn." *National Pastime,* XV (1995), 43–44.

BILL ASHLEY

Outfielder
Los Angeles (N.L.)

3226. Langill, Mark. "Tall Order." *Beckett Focus on Future Stars,* III, no. 25 (May 1993), 6–9.

SISTER MARY ASSUMPTA

Broadcaster

3227. "Nun Sense." *People Weekly,* XLVII (June 2, 1997), 181+. Baseball analyst for WEWS-TV, Cleveland.

ELDEN ("BIG SIX") AUKER

Pitcher
Detroit (A.L.), Boston (A.L.),
St. Louis (N.L.)

3228. Auker, Elden, as told to George Vass. "'The Game I'll Never Forget.'" *Baseball Digest,* LIII (March 1994), 89–92.
3229. Macht, Norman L. "Sidearmer Elden Auker Remembers How It Was in the 1930s." *Baseball Digest,* LII (February 1993), 62–66.

STEVE AVERY

Pitcher
Atlanta (N.L.), Boston (A.L.)

3230. "Superstar Gallery: Steve Avery." *Beckett Baseball Card Monthly,* X, no. 101 (August 1993), 14–15.

CARLOS BAERGA

First Baseman
Cleveland (A.L.),
New York Mets (N.L.)

3231. Lidz, Franz. "Slick with the Stick." *Sports Illustrated,* LXXX (April 4, 1994), 62–64, 66.
3232. Pluto, Terry. "Carlos Baerga of the Indians: Another Latin Star on the Rise." *Baseball Digest,* LII (January 1993), 47–49.
3233. "Superstar Gallery: Carlos Baerga." *Beckett Baseball Card Monthly,* X, no. 97 (April 1993), 13–15.

JEFF BAGWELL

First Baseman
Boston (A.L.), Houston (N.L.)

3234. Bianchine, Jim. "Astros' Jeff Bagwell: Another Good One the Red Sox Let Get Away." *Baseball Digest,* LIII (May 1994), 36–41.
3235. Graeff, Burt. "Odd Batting Stance Doesn't Inhibit Astros' Jeff Bagwell." *Baseball Digest,* LVI (October 1997), 56–59.
3236. Hagen, Paul. "Focus on Jeff Bagwell." *Beckett Focus on Future Stars,* II, no. 16 (August 1992), 18–21.
3237. Kuenster, Bob. "Jeff Bagwell Earns 1994 Player of the Year Honors." *Baseball Digest,* LIV (January 1995), 22–23.
3238. Molony, Jim. "Closer Look: Jeff Bagwell." *Beckett Baseball Card Monthly,* XI, no. 114 (September 1994), 8–13.
3239. Montville, Leigh. "Trade Deficit." *Sports Illustrated,* LXXIX (July 26, 1993), 44–46+.
3240. Peterson, Gary. "Jeff Bagwell: A Consistent 'Hitting Machine' for the Astros." *Baseball Digest,* LV (October 1996), 44–45.
3241. Weinberg, Rick. "One-on-One [with] Jeff Bagwell: Interview." *Sport,* LXXXVI (May 1995), 18–23.

HAROLD BAINES

Outfielder
Chicago (A.L.), Texas (A.L.),
Oakland (A.L.), Baltimore (A.L.)

3242. Van Dyck, Dave. "Harold Baines: He Lets His Bat Do the Talking." *Baseball Digest,* LV (September 1996), 48–50.

JOHNNIE ("DUSTY") BAKER

Outfielder
Atlanta (N.L.), Los Angeles (N.L.),
San Francisco (N.L.), Oakland (N.L.)
Coach, Manager
San Francisco (N.L.)

3243. "Dusty Baker." In: L. Mpho Mabunda, ed. *Contemporary Black Biography: Profiles from the International Black Community.* Detroit, Mich.: Gale Research, 1995. pp. 14–17.

ERNIE BANKS*

Shortstop, First Baseman
Chicago (N.L.)

3244. "Banks Memorabilia Sold in Public Sports Auction." *Jet,* LXXXIV (August 9, 1993), 56–57.
3245. Bjarkman, Peter C. *Baseball Legends: Ernie Banks.* New York: Chelsea House, 1994. 64p.
3246. Verducci, Tom. "Be Like Ernie." *Sports Illustrated,* LXXXIII (September 25, 1995), 36–39.

WALTER ("RED") BARBER

Broadcaster

3247. Edwards, Bob. *Fridays with Red: A Radio Friendship.* New York: Simon and Schuster, 1993. 240p.
3248. _____. "The Voice on the Radio." *Modern Maturity,* XXXVI (October–November 1993), 94–95.
3249. "Red Barber." In: Louise Mooney, ed. *Newsmakers, 1993: The People Behind the Headlines.* Detroit, Mich.: Gale Research, 1993. pp. 541–542.
3250. Scully, Vin. "Unforgettable Red Barber." *Reader's Digest,* CXLII (April 1993), 91–95.

AL BARLICK*

Umpire
National League

3251. Forman, Ross. "Al Barlick: He Considered Umpiring a Sacred Trust." *Baseball Digest,* LII (February 1993), 80–86.

REX EDWARD BARNEY

Pitcher
Brooklyn (N.L.)
Broadcaster

3252. Barney, Rex, with Norman L. Macht. *Rex Barney's Thank You for*

Fifty Years of Baseball, from Brooklyn to Baltimore. Centreville, Md.: Tidewater Publishers, 1993. 264p.

BILL BARTHOLOMAY

Executive
Atlanta (N.L.)

3253. Webster, Donovan. "Hey, Bill." *Chicago,* XLII (September 1993), 80+.

RICHARD WILLIAM ("DICK" OR "ROWDY RICHARD") BARTELL

Shortstop, Third Baseman
Pittsburgh (N.L.),
Philadelphia (N.L.),
New York Giants (N.L.),
Chicago (N.L.), Detroit (A.L.)
Coach

3254. Van Blair, Rick. "Dick Bartell Looks Back on Baseball as It Was in the 1930s." *Baseball Digest,* LIV (July 1995), 50–56.

RICHARD ("DICK") BASS

Pitcher
Washington (A.L.)

3255. Boynton, B. "Dick Bass: A Case Study of a One-Game Major League Career." *Nine: A Journal of Baseball History and Social Policy Perspective,* III (Fall 1994), 189–203.

JOE BAUMAN

Outfielder
Roswell Rockets

3256. Pietrusza, David. "Roswell's 'Sultan of Swat': Joe Bauman Duels Babe Ruth for Home Run Crown." *New Mexico Magazine,* LXXII (May 1994), 24+.

**FRANK CONRAD
("FRANKIE") BAUMHOLTZ**

Outfielder
Cincinnati (N.L.), Chicago (N.L.),
Philadelphia (N.L.)

3257. Ahrens, Art. "Frankie Baumholtz: He Covered a Lot of Outfield Ground." *Baseball Digest,* LI (September 1992), 76–82.

DON BAYLOR

Outfielder
Baltimore (A.L.), Oakland (A.L.),
California (A.L.),
New York (A.L.), Boston (A.L.),
Minnesota (A.L.)
Manager
Colorado (N.L.)

3258. Kiszla, Mark. "Don Baylor Set to March a Long Rocky Road." *Baseball Digest,* LII (April 1993), 65–67.
3259. Leavy, Walter. "Don Baylor: On Top of the World." *Ebony,* LI (August 1996), 44+.
3260. Pierce, Charles. "Don Baylor Carries a Big Stick." *GQ: Gentlemen's Quarterly,* LXIII (July 1993), 45–46+.
3261. Poses, Jon W. "On Deck." *St. Louis,* XXIV (July 1992), 11–13.
3262. Reinert, Al. "'I'm Not Going to Be Intimidated!'" *USA Weekend,* (April 2, 1993), 4–6.

VINCE BEALL

Outfielder
California State University

3263. Dimmitt, Barbara S. "Heading for Home." *Reader's Digest,* CL (April 1997), 128–133. Player who died of lung cancer.

**PAUL ("THE BEAST")
BEESTON**

Executive
Toronto (A.L.)

3264. Banks, B. "Nature of 'the Beast.'" *CA Magazine,* XXVI (June–July 1993), 20–23.
3265. Peltz, M. "How the Blue Jays Stay Financially Healthy." *Institutional Investor,* XXVII (July 1993), 77–78+.

ROBERT ("BO") BELINSKY

Pitcher
California (A.L.), Philadelphia (N.L.),
Houston (N.L.),
Pittsburgh (N.L.), Cincinnati (N.L.)

3266. Jordan, Pat. "Once He Was an Angel." *Sports Illustrated,* LXXX (March 28, 1994), 74–78+. Reprinted from the March 6, 1973 issue.

**JAMES THOMAS
("COOL PAPA") BELL***

Pitcher, Outfielder
St. Louis Stars, Homestead Grays,
Pittsburgh Crawfords, Kansas City Stars

3267. Kram, Mark. "No Place in the Shade." *Sports Illustrated,* LXXX (June 20, 1994), 65–68. Reprinted from the August 20, 1973, issue.
3268. Pratkanis, A. R. "The Year Cool Papa Bell Lost the Batting Title." *Nine: A Journal of Baseball History and Social Policy Perspective,* II (Spring 1994), 260–276.

JAY BELL

Shortstop
Cleveland (A.L.), Pittsburgh (N.L.),
Kansas City (A.L.)

3269. Kaegel, Dick. "Royals' Jay Bell Rings 'Em Up with Steady Defense." *Baseball Digest,* LVI (July 1997), 52–55.

ALBERT BELLE

Outfielder
Cleveland (A.L.), Chicago (A.L.)

3270. "Albert Belle." In: Louis M. Collins and Frank V. Castronova, eds. *Newsmakers, 1996: The People Behind Today's Headlines.* Detroit, Mich.: Gale Research, 1997. pp. 31–34.

3271. Bamberger, Michael. "He Thrives on Anger." *Sports Illustrated,* LXXXIV (May 6, 1996), 72–76, 79–82, 87.

3272. Callahan, Gerry. "Double Play." *Sports Illustrated,* LXXXV (December 2, 1996), 32–33.

3273. Crothers, Tim. "50/50." *Sports Illustrated,* LXXXIII (October 9, 1995), 54–55.

3274. Hoynes, Paul. "Closer Look: Albert Belle." *Beckett Baseball Card Monthly,* X, no. 102 (September 1993), 6–13.

3275. ____. "Tribe's Albert Belle Reveals Inside Story on 'Batgate.'" *Baseball Digest,* LIV (August 1995), 42–45.

3276. Johnson, Paul M. "Hangtime [with] Albert Belle." *Sport,* LXXXVIII (November 1996), 22–26.

3277. Kiersh, Edward. "Albert Belle: Interview." *Inside Sports,* XV (June 1993), 22–27.

3278. Kuenster, Bob. "Albert Belle, *Baseball Digest's* 1995 Player of the Year." *Baseball Digest,* LV (January 1996), 20–32.

3279. ____. "Albert Belle's Words and Actions Dishonored Major League Baseball." *Baseball Digest,* LV (October 1996), 17–20.

3280. Kurkijan, Tim. "Overboard Belle." *Sports Illustrated,* LXXXIV (June 10, 1996), 88–89.

3281. Leavy, Walter. "Albert Belle: A New Beginning for Baseball's $55 Million Man." *Ebony,* LII (May 1997), 28+.

3282. Livingston, Bill. "Albert Belle: An Indian Who Swings a Mean War Club." *Baseball Digest,* LII (November 1993), 33–34.

3283. Mikaly, Mary. "The Real Albert Belle." *Cleveland,* XXI (March 1992), 54+.

3284. Tuttle, Dennis. *Albert Belle.* New York: Chelsea House, 1997. 64p.

3285. Weinberg, Rick. "Inside Interview: Albert Belle." *Inside Sports,* XVIII (April 1996), 20–27.

3286. ____. "Malcontent." *Sport,* LXXXIX (May 1997), 18–22.

3287. Whiteside, Larry. "Did Albert Belle's Conduct Cost Him the 1995 American League MVP Award?" *Baseball Digest,* LV (April 1996), 58–61.

RAFAEL BELLIARD

Shortstop
Pittsburgh (N.L.), Atlanta (N.L.)

3288. Crothers, Tim. "The Drought Continues." *Sports Illustrated,* LXXXVI (May 12, 1997), 95+.

JOHNNY BENCH*

Catcher
Cincinnati (N.L.)
Broadcaster

3289. Sorci, Rick. "Baseball Profile: Hall of Fame Catcher Johnny Bench." *Baseball Digest,* LII (October 1993), 65–67.

ANDY BENES

Pitcher
San Diego (N.L.), Seattle (A.L.),
St. Louis (N.L.)

3290. Geschke, Jim. "Second Look: Andy Benes." *Beckett Baseball Card Monthly,* X, no. 105 (December 1993), 105–107.

3291. Pickard, Chuck. "Padres' Andy Benes Posted Best SO Over Walks Rating in '94." *Baseball Digest,* LIV (April 1995), 32–34.

3292. Whiteside, Kelly. "The Survival Game." *Sports Illustrated,* LXXX (February 14, 1994), 136–138+.

JASON BERE

Pitcher
Chicago (A.L.)

3293. Rushin, Steve. "Making a Splash." *Sports Illustrated,* LXXX (April 4, 1994), 70–72+.

JUAN BERENGUER

Pitcher
New York Mets (N.L.),
Kansas City (A.L.), Detroit (A.L.),
San Francisco (N.L.), Minnesota (A.L.),
Atlanta (N.L.),
Toronto (A.L.)

3294. Buerenguer, Juan, as told to George Vass. "'The Game I'll Never Forget.'" *Baseball Digest,* LI (August 1992), 47–48.

MOE BERG

Catcher
Brooklyn (N.L.), Chicago (A.L.),
Cleveland (A.L.),
Washington (A.L.), Boston (A.L.)
Scholar, Intelligence Agent

3295. Andryszewski, Tricia. *The Amazing Life of Moe Berg: Catcher, Scholar, Spy.* Brookfield, Conn.: Millbrook Press, 1996. 127p.
3296. Dawidoff, Nicholas. "The Fabled Moe." *The American Scholar,* LXIII (Summer 1994), 433–439.
3297. Grey, Vivian. *Moe Berg: The Spy Behind Home Plate.* Philadelphia, Pa.: Jewish Publications Society, 1996. Unpaged.

WALTER ANTON ("WALLY") BERGER

Outfielder
Boston (N.L.),
New York Giants (N.L.),
Cincinnati (N.L.),
Philadelphia (N.L.)

3298. Berger, Walter A., with George M. Snyder. *Freshly Remembered.* Redondo Beach, Calif.: Schnedier-McGuirk, 1993. 233p.
3299. Rosenberg, Norman L. "Bosey Berger." *National Pastime,* XV (1995), 144–145.

RAY BERRES

Catcher
Brooklyn (N.L.), Pittsburgh (N.L.),
Boston (N.L.), New York Giants (N.L.)
Coach

3300. Macht, Norman L. "Ray Berres: Old-Time Pitching Coach Reveals Some Helpful Tips." *Baseball Digest,* LVI (February 1997), 72–76.

SKIP BERTMAN

Coach
Louisiana State University

3301. Nolan, Timothy. "Tiger, Tiger Burning Bright: Interview." *Scholastic Coach & Athletic Director,* LXVI (November 1996), 64–71.

DANTE BICHETTE

Outfielder
California (A.L.), Milwaukee (A.L.),
Colorado (N.L.)

3302. Capezzuto, Tom. "Dante Bichette: His Hitting Helps Energize the Rockies." *Baseball Digest,* LIV (October 1995), 35–37.
3303. "Dante's Inferno: When You're Hot, You're Hot." In: Joe Hoppel, ed. *The Sporting News 1996 Baseball Yearbook.* St. Louis, Mo.: TSN, 1996. pp. 28–31.
3304. Guss, Greg. "Bichette Happens." *Sport,* LXXXVII (June 1996), 81–84.
3305. Holtzman, Jerome. "Dante Bichette: He Learned About Hitting from the Greats." *Baseball Digest,* LIII (August 1994), 44–45.

3306. Kiszla, Mark. "Dante Bichette Goes by the Book to Gain an Edge on Pitchers." *Baseball Digest,* LV (November 1996), 66–67.

3307. Kurkijan, Tim. "Mere Child's Play." *Sports Illustrated,* LXXXIII (July 3, 1995), 50–53.

CRAIG BIGGIO

Catcher, Second Baseman
Houston (N.L.)

3308. Bamberger, Michael. "Second Effort." *Sports Illustrated,* LXXXIV (April 1, 1996), 102–106.

3309. Fraley, Gerry. "Craig Biggio: From Catcher to All-Star Second Baseman." *Baseball Digest,* LIV (November 1995), 72–75.

3310. Graeff, Burt. "Versatility Pays Dividends for Astros' Craig Biggio." *Baseball Digest,* LVI (December 1997), 72–73.

PAUL BLAIR

Outfielder
Baltimore (A.L.), New York (A.L.),
Cincinnati (A.L.)

3311. Menfus, Ron. "Center Fielder Paul Blair: He Was a Gifted Ball Hawk." *Baseball Digest,* LI (June 1992), 48–50.

JEFF BLAUSER

Shortstop
Atlanta (N.L.)

3312. Odum, Charles. "Shortstop Jeff Blauser of the Braves: A Winner, But Who Notices?" *Baseball Digest,* LIII (July 1994), 26–27.

TERRY BLOCKER

Outfielder
New York Mets (N.L.),
Atlanta (N.L.)

3313. Plummer, William. "Playing for Keeps." *People Weekly,* XLIII (April 17, 1995), 123–124.

RON BLOMBERG

First Baseman, Outfielder
New York (A.L.), Chicago (A.L.)

3314. Blomberg, Ron, as told to George Vass. "'The Game I'll Never Forget.'" *Baseball Digest,* LIII (February 1994), 48–51.

3315. Wulf, Steve. "Distinguished History." *Sports Illustrated,* LXXVIII (April 5, 1993), 44–50. First DH.

ROY BLOUNT, JR.

Sportswriter

3316. Moseley, Merritt W. "Roy Blount, Jr." In: Robert Bain and Joseph M. Flora, eds. *Contemporary Poets, Dramatists, Essayists, and Novelists of the South: A Bio-Bibliographical Sourcebook.* Westport, Conn.: Greenwood Press, 1994. pp. 75–83.

VIDA BLUE

Pitcher
Oakland (A.L.),
San Francisco (N.L.),
Kansas City (A.L.)

3317. Forman, Ross. "Final Look: Vida Blue." *Beckett Baseball Card Monthly,* X, no. 95 (February 1993), 118–119.

3318. Romano, John. "Vida Blue Recalls His MVP and Cy Young Award Year." *Baseball Digest,* LV (August 1996), 56–59.

BERT BLYLEVEN

Pitcher
Minnesota (A.L.), Texas (A.L.),
Cleveland (A.L.),
Pittsburgh (N.L.),
California (A.L.)

3319. Blyleven, Bert, as told to George Vass. "'The Game I'll Never Forget.'" *Baseball Digest,* LI (December 1992), 54–56.

DOUG BOCHTLER

Pitcher
San Diego (N.L.)

3320. Crothers, Tim. "The Magic Padre." *Sports Illustrated,* LXXXVI (May 19, 1997), 86–87.

WADE BOGGS

Third Baseman
Boston (A.L.), New York (A.L.)

3321. Haudricourt, Tom. "Wade Boggs Taking Aim at 3,000 Career Hits and More." *Baseball Digest,* LVI (August 1997), 62–63.

3322. Pedulla, Tom. "Pre-Game Regimen Helps Wade Boggs Maintain Edge." *Baseball Digest,* LV (October 1996), 42–43.

3323. Verducci, Tom. "A Quiet .300." *Sports Illustrated,* LXXXIV (January 15, 1996), 70–72, 75.

BARRY BONDS

Outfielder
Pittsburgh (N.L.), San Francisco (N.L.)

3324. Barney, Chuck. "Closer Look: Barry Bonds." *Beckett Baseball Card Monthly,* X, no. 101 (August 1993), 6–9.

3325. "Barry Bonds Not Charged in Dispute with Wife Over Birth Control Pills." *Jet,* LXXXIV (October 11, 1993), 51–53.

3326. "Barry Bonds' Big Bat and a $7 Million Salary Make Him the Best in Baseball." *Jet,* LXXXIV (August 9, 1993), 52–55.

3327. Bloom, Barry M. "Hangtime [with] Barry Bonds." *Sport,* LXXXVII (October 1996), 16–20.

3328. Boswell, Thomas. "Unbreakable Bonds." *Inside Sports,* XV (March 1993), 74–81.

3329. Crothers, Tim. "Yes, Indeed, I'm Walkin'." *Sports Illustrated,* LXXXVI (May 5, 1997), 69–70.

3330. Dodd, J. "Family of Giants." *People Weekly,* XL (October 4, 1993), 101–102.

3331. George, Daniel P. "Running Home." *Boy's Life,* LXXXIV (May 1994), 8+.

3332. Goodman, Michael E. *Barry Bonds.* Minneapolis, Minn.: Lerner, 1997.

3333. Harvey, Miles. *Barry Bonds: Baseball's Complete Player.* Chicago, Ill.: Children's Press, 1994. 48p.

3334. Hertzel, Bob. "The Two Barry Bonds." In: Zander Hollander, ed. *The Complete Book of Baseball, 1993.* New York: Signet Books, 1993. pp. 6–13.

3335. Hoffer, Richard. "The Importance of Being Barry." *Sports Illustrated,* LXXVIII (May 24, 1993), 12–21.

3336. Kaplan, David A. "The Rising Stock of Bonds." *Newsweek,* CXXI (May 31, 1993), 64+.

3337. Kuenster, John. "Barry Bonds: Best All-Around Player in the Majors Today?" *Baseball Digest,* LII (August 1993), 17–19.

3338. ____. "Barry Bonds Gets the Call as *Baseball Digest*'s 1993 Player of the Year." *Baseball Digest,* LIII (January 1994), 17–21.

3339. Leavy, Walter. "Barry Bonds: Baseball's $60 Million Man." *Ebony,* XLVIII (September 1993), 118–120+.

3340. Lupica, Mike. "Barry Bonds for President." *Esquire,* CCXXVI (August 1996), 46+.

3341. Perrotto, John. "A Second Look: Barry Bonds." *Beckett Baseball Card Monthly,* IX, no. 89 (August 1992), 105–107.

3342. Rambeck, Richard. *Barry Bonds.* Plymouth, Minn.: Child's World, 1996. 31p.

3343. Richmond, Peter. "Why Isn't Barry

Bonds Willie Mays?" *GQ: Gentle-men's Quarterly,* LXIV (April 1994), 174+.

3344. Savage, Jeff. *Barry Bonds, Mr. Excitement.* Minneapolis, Minn.: Lerner Publications, 1997. 64p.

3345. Schoenfeld, Bruce. "Unfinished Business." *Sport,* LXXXV (April 1994), 80–82+.

3346. Sullivan, Michael J. *Sports Great Barry Bonds.* Hillside, N.J.: Enslow, 1995. 64p.

3347. Weinberg, Rick. "Interview: Barry Bonds." *Inside Sports,* XVIII (October 1996), 22–29.

3348. Weinstock, Jeff. "The *Sport* Q & A: Barry Bonds." *Sport,* LXXIV (April 1993), 60–65.

3349. Wuhl, Robert. "Celebrity Interview: Arli$$ & Bonds." *Sport,* LXXXVII (October 1997), 42–57.

BOBBY BONDS

Outfielder
San Francisco (N.L.), New York (A.L.), California (A.L.), Texas (A.L.), Cleveland (A.L.), St. Louis (N.L.)
Chicago (N.L.)
Coach

3350. Dodd, J. "Family of Giants." *People Weekly,* XL (October 4, 1993), 101–102.

BOBBY BONILLA

Outfielder
Chicago (A.L.), Pittsburgh (N.L.), New York Mets (N.L.), Baltimore (A.L.), Florida (N.L.)

3351. Knapp, Ron. *Sports Great Bobby Bonilla.* Hillside, N.J.: Enslow, 1993. 64p.

3352. Noble, Marty. "Bad Boy Bo?" *Florida Sports Fan,* IV (April–May 1997), 40–44.

3353. Rappoport, Ken. *Bobby Bonilla.* New York: Walker, 1993. 115p.

BRET BOONE

Second Baseman
Seattle (A.L.), Cincinnati (N.L.)

3354. Finnigan, Bob. "Boon(e) Times Ahead." *Beckett Focus on Future Stars,* III, no. 24 (April 1993), 12–15.

3355. Posnanski, Joe. "Second Baseman Bret Boone: 'Heart' of Division Champion Reds." *Baseball Digest,* LV (January 1996), 37–39.

RAY BOONE

Third Baseman, Shortstop
Cleveland (A.L.), Detroit (A.L.)
Chicago (A.L.),
Kansas City (A.L.),
Milwaukee (N.L.), Boston (A.L.)

3356. Fagen, Herb. "Ray Boone: Three-Generation Baseball Family Patriarch." *Baseball Digest,* LIV (March 1995), 73–77.

JOSH BOOTY

Catcher
Florida (N.L.)

3357. "The Marlins' Big Catch." In: Joe Hoppel, ed. *The Sporting News 1995 Baseball Yearbook.* St. Louis, Mo.: TSN, 1995. pp. 144–145.

3358. Walters, John. "Josh Booty." *Sports Illustrated,* LXXX (June 13, 1994), 46–47.

ILA BORDERS

Pitcher
Southern California College

3359. Brown, A. "Girl Throws Curve Into Men's Baseball." *Career World,* XXIII (January 1995), 21+.

3360. Smith, Shelly. "Ila Borders." *Sports Illustrated,* LXXX (March 7, 1994), 66–67. First woman to pitch on a men's college team.

CHRIS BOSIO

Pitcher
Milwaukee (A.L.),
Seattle (A.L.)

3361. Kurkijan, Tim. "Chris Bosio." *Sports Illustrated,* LXXVIII (May 3, 1993), 64+. No hitter against Boston.

LOUIS ("LOU") BOUDREAU*

Shortstop
Cleveland (A.L.),
Boston (A.L.)
Manager
Cleveland (A.L.),
Boston (A.L.),
Kansas City (A.L.),
Chicago (N.L.)
Broadcaster

3362. Boudreau, Lou, with Russell Schneider. *Lou Boudreau: Covering All the Bases.* Champagne, Ill.: Sagamore Publishing, 1993. 203p.

JIM BOUTON

Pitcher
New York (A.L.), Seattle (A.L.),
Houston (N.L.), Atlanta (N.L.)
Sportswriter

3363. Barra, Allen. "The Mr. Inside *and* Mr. Outside of the Diamond." *Inside Sports,* XVI (August 1994), 16, 20.
3364. Cohen, Jeffrey. "The Player." *Entrepreneur,* XXII (June 1994), 142+.

MIKE BORDICK

Shortstop
Oakland (A.L.), Baltimore (A.L.)

3365. Fimrite, Ron. "A View from the Treetops." *Sports Illustrated,* LXXVI (June 8, 1992), 71+.
3366. Olney, Buster. "How Undrafted Mike Bordick Earned His Niche in the Majors." *Baseball Digest,* LVI (June 1997), 48–53.

ROBERT RANDALL ("BOBBY") BRAGAN

Shortstop, Catcher
Philadelphia (N.L.), Brooklyn (N.L.)
Manager
Pittsburgh (N.L.), Cleveland (A.L.),
Milwaukee (N.L.), Atlanta (N.L.)

3367. Bragan, Bobby, with Jeff Guinn. *You Can't Hit the Ball with the Bat on Your Shoulder: The Baseball Life and Times of Bobby Bragan.* Fort Worth, Tx. : The Summit Group, 1992. 362p.

HARRY ("THE CAT") BRECHEEN

Pitcher
St. Louis (N.L.), St. Louis (A.L.)

3368. Mayer, Bob. "Flashback: Harry Brecheen Recalls '46 World Series Wins Over the Red Sox." *Baseball Digest,* LV (October 1996), 37–41.

GEORGE BRETT

Third Baseman, First Baseman
Kansas City (A.L.)

3369. Althaus, Bill. "George Brett, the Loyal Royal." *Boy's Life,* LXXXIII (August 1993), 6–7.
3370. Askew, Alan. "George Brett Closed Out His Career with a Flourish." *Baseball Digest,* LIII (January 1994), 56–60.
3371. Brett, George, as told to George Vass. "'The Game I'll Never Forget.'" *Baseball Digest,* LIV (January 1995), 63–69.
3372. Cameron, Steve. *George Brett— Last of a Breed: With Chapter 7, "In My Own Words," by George Brett.* Dallas, Tx.: Taylor, 1993. 190p.
3373. Click, Paul. "George Brett Looks Back on His Long Climb to 3,000 Hits." *Baseball Digest,* LII (March 1993), 26–29.
3374. Crasnick, Jerry. "Deeper Look:

George Brett." *Beckett Baseball Card Monthly,* XII, no. 119 (February 1995), 108–115.

3375. Eskew, Alan. "Closer Look: George Brett." *Beckett Baseball Card Monthly,* X, no. 98 (May 1993), 6–9.

3376. "Final Look: George Brett." *Beckett Baseball Card Monthly,* XI, no. 107 (February 1994), 105–106.

3377. Kaegel, Dick. "As His Career Winds Down, George Brett Adjusts to Age." *Baseball Digest,* LII (July 1993), 40–43.

3378. *Kansas City Star,* Editors of. *Number 5: George Brett and the Kansas City Royals.* Kansas City, Mo.: Andrews and McMeel, 1993. 88p.

3379. "Superstar Gallery: George Brett." *Beckett Baseball Card Monthly,* IX, no. 90 (September 1992), 13–14.

3380. Wulf, Steve. "That's All, Folks." *Sports Illustrated,* LXXIX (October 11, 1993), 112+.

JACK BRICKHOUSE

Broadcaster

3381. Petterchak, Janice A. *Jack Brickhouse: A Voice for All Seasons.* Chicago, Ill.: Contemporary Books, 1996. 226p.

JOE BRINKMAN

Umpire
American League

3382. Forman, Ross. "Veteran Ump Joe Brinkman Cites Changes in the Game." *Baseball Digest,* LII (January 1993), 59–62.

LOU BROCK*

Outfielder
Chicago (N.L.), St. Louis (N.L.)

3383. Eisenbath, Mike. "Lou Brock Looks Back on His 19-Year Hall of Fame Career." *Baseball Digest,* LIII (December 1994), 66–70.

BOBBY BROWN

Third Baseman
New York (A.L.)
Executive
President, American League

3384. Boston, T. "Hitting Hard to All Fields: The Life of Bobby Brown." *Baseball Research Journal,* XXIV (1995), 58–61.

GATES BROWN

Catcher
Detroit (A.L.)

3385. Schneider, Russell. "Baseball Gave Gates Brown New Outlook and a New Life." *Baseball Digest,* LIII (March 1994), 73–76.

KEVIN BROWN

Pitcher
Texas (A.L.), Baltimore (A.L.), Florida (N.L.)

3386. Ballew, Bill. "Kevin Brown of the Rangers: In Pursuit of Major League Stardom." *Baseball Digest,* LII (June 1993), 32–34.

3387. Iverson, Kurt. "Second Look: Kevin Brown." *Beckett Baseball Card Monthly,* X, no. 101 (August 1993), 105–107.

BILL ("BILLY BUCKS") BUCKNER

Outfielder, First Baseman
Los Angeles (N.L.), Chicago (N.L.), Boston (A.L.), California (A.L.), Kansas City (A.L.)
Coach

3388. "Catching Up with Bill Buckner." In: Joe Hoppel, ed. *The Sporting News 1996 Baseball Yearbook.* St. Louis, Mo.: TSN, 1996. pp. 160–161.

3389. Mulgannon, T. "The $93,500

Question: The Ball Gets Buckner Again." *Sport,* LXXXIV (January 1993), 12+. Baseball that went through his legs during 1986 World Series sold at Leland's auction.

JAY BUHNER

Outfielder
New York (A.L.), Seattle (A.L.)

3390. Callahan, Gerry. "A Real Cutup." *Sports Illustrated,* LXXXIV (March 18, 1996), 88–92, 94, 96–97, 99.
3391. Ryan, Bob. "Mariners' Jay Buhner: He's the Majors' Most Efficient Hitter." *Baseball Digest,* LVI (January 1997), 50–52.

JIM BUNNING*

Pitcher
Detroit (A.L.), Philadelphia (N.L.), Pittsburgh (N.L.), Los Angeles (N.L.)
Politician

3392. Falls, Joe. "Hall of Famer Jim Bunning Kept a 'Book' on Batters." *Baseball Digest,* LV (December 1996), 86–89.
3393. Hofmann, H. S. "The Forgotten Pitcher: Remembering Jim Bunning." *National Pastime,* XV (1995), 106–110.
3394. Warren, Dan. "Final Look: Jim Bunning." *Beckett Baseball Card Monthly,* X, no. 96 (March 1993), 118–119.

GLENN BURKE

Outfielder
Los Angeles (N.L.), Oakland (A.L.)

3395. Burke, Glenn, with Erik Sherman. *Out at Home: The Glenn Burke Story.* Napa, Calif.: Excel Publishing, 1995. 128p.
3396. Plummer, William. "The Outfielder Who Came Out." *People Weekly,* XLII (November 21, 1994), 151–152.

TIM BURKE

Pitcher
Montreal (N.L.),
New York Mets (N.L.),
New York (A.L.)

3397. Burke, Tim and Christine, with Gregg Lewis. *Major League Dad.* Dallas, Tx.: Word Books, 1994. 261p. Excerpted in *Ladies Home Journal,* CXI (July 1994), 100+.

ELLIS BURKS

Outfielder
Boston (A.L.), Chicago (A.L.), Colorado (N.L.)

3398. Armstrong, Jim. "Rockies' Ellis Burks Revives His Major League Career." *Baseball Digest,* LV (November 1996), 50–52.
3399. Gelin, D. "Ellis Burks." In: David Bauer, ed. *SI Presents Baseball 1997.* New York: *Sports Illustrated,* 1997. pp. 100–103.

KEN BURNS

Documentary Film Producer

3400. Adelman, K. L. "Perfect Game: An Interview with Ken Burns." *Washingtonian,* XXIX (September 1994), 25–26+.
3401. Browne, Murray. "Keeping Track of Ken Burns." *Elysian Fields Quarterly,* XIV (Spring 1995), 76–77.
3402. Burns, Ken. "Diamonds Are Forever: An Interview." *People Weekly,* XLII (September 19, 1994), 205+.
3403. Clark, Tim. "New England Scene: Ken Burns Wants to Hurt You." *Yankee,* XXXVIII (October 1994), 88+. Making his documentary "Baseball."
3404. Connelly, Christopher. "At the Top of His Game." *Premiere,* VIII (September 1994), 76–78+.
3405. Edgerton, G. R. "Ken Burns: A Conversation with Public Television's Resident Historian." *Journal of*

American Culture, XVIII (September 1995), 1–12.

3406. ____. "Ken Burns' American Dream: Histories-for-TV from Walpole, New Hampshire: An Interview." *Television Quarterly,* XXVII (Spring 1994), 56–64.

3407. Jackson, D. D. "Ken Burns Puts His Special Spin on the Old Ball Game." *Smithsonian,* XXV (July 1994), 38–42+.

3408. "Ken Burns" In: Louise Mooney Collins and Geri J. Speace, eds. *Newsmakers, 1995: The People Behind Today's Headlines.* Detroit, Mich.: Gale Research, 1995. pp. 60–63.

3409. McConnell, F. D. "No Fall Classic." *Commonweal,* CXXI (November 18, 1994), 31–32.

3410. McDowell, Robert. "When Baseball Made Out: Ken Burns' Television Documentary *Baseball." Hudson Review,* XLVIII (September 1995), 411–424.

3411. Pastier, John. "Ken Burns' *Baseball*: Big Runs, Key Hits, and Quite a Few Errors." *Elysian Fields Quarterly,* XIV (Summer 1995), 78–82.

3412. Shouler, Kenneth. "Burns Back at Bat." *Emmy,* XVI (July–August 1994), 6+.

3413. "The Sounds of Summer." *The New Yorker,* LXX (February 21, 1994), 37–38. Making of the documentary.

3414. Stein, Herb. "Baseball's *Civil War." TV Guide,* XLII (September 10, 1994), 30–33.

3415. Sullivan, Robert. "Visions of Glory." *Life,* XVII (September 1994), 40–44+.

3416. Thomson, David. "Ken Burns' 'Baseball.'" *Film Comment,* XXX (September–October 1994), 20–21+.

3417. Ward, Geoffrey C. "Learning to Like Baseball." *American Heritage,* XLV (October 1994), 86–90+.

3418. Weigel, George. "Politically-Correct Baseball." *Commentary,* XCVIII (November 1994), 46–51.

3419. "'You Can't Tell the Players Without a Scorecard.'" *Television Quarterly,* XXVII, no. 1 (1994), 65–66.

MIKE BUSCH

Third Baseman
Los Angeles (N.L.)

3420. "Busch League Behavior." *Sports Illustrated,* LXXXIII (September 11, 1995), 14–16.

GEORGE W. BUSH

Executive
Texas (A.L.)
Politician

3421. "George W. Bush." In: Mooney Collins and Frank V. Castronova, eds. *Newsmakers, 1996: The People Behind Today's Headlines.* Detroit, Mich.: Gale Research, 1997. pp. 63–66.

3422. Gwynne, S. C. "The Sons Also Rise." *Time,* CXLIV (September 26, 1994), 39-40.

3423. Hollandsworth, S. "Born to Run." *Texas Monthly,* XXII (May 1994), 112–117+.

BRETT BUTLER

Outfielder
Atlanta (N.L.), Cleveland (A.L.),
San Francisco (N.L.),
Los Angeles (N.L.)

3424. Click, Paul. "Dodgers' Brett Butler: An MVP On and Off the Field." *Baseball Digest,* LII (September 1993), 48–51.

3425. Kirkijan, Tim. "Dodger Blue." *Sports Illustrated,* LXXXIV (May 20, 1996), 66+.

3426. Verducci, Tom. "Back in Style." *Sports Illustrated,* LXXXV (September 16, 1996), 52–53.

TOMMY BYRNE

Pitcher
New York (A.L.), St. Louis (A.L.),
Chicago (A.L.), Washington (A.L.)

3427. Van Blair, Rick. "Flashback: Tommy Byrne—He Was One of the Best Ever." *Baseball Digest,* LIII (May 1994), 63–70.

KEN CAMINITE

Third Baseman
Houston (N.L.), San Diego (N.L.)

3428.Crasnick, Jerry. "Padres' Ken Caminite Strives for Continued Excellence." *Baseball Digest,* LV (July 1997), 47–48.
3429. Johnson, Ted. "Sgt. Rock." In: Tony Gervino, ed. *Hardball.* New York: Harris Pub. Co., 1997. pp. 60–65.
3430. Verducci, Tom. "Scary Man." *Sports Illustrated,* LXXXV (September 9, 1996), 48–50, 55.

ROY CAMPANELLA*

Catcher
Baltimore Elites, Brooklyn (N.L.)
Executive
Los Angeles (N.L.)

3431. Broeg, Bob. "Roy Campanella Never Lost His Enthusiasm for the Game." *Baseball Digest,* LII (October 1993), 68–71.
3432. Campanella, Roy. "From *It's Good to Be Alive.*" In: Charles Einstein, ed. *The New Baseball Reader: An All-Star Lineup from the Fireside Book of Baseball.* New York: Penguin Books, 1992. pp. 69–83.
3433. Macht, Norman L. *Roy Campanella, Baseball Star.* New York: Chelsea House, 1996. 64p.

JOSE CANSECO

Outfielder
Oakland (A.L.), Texas (A.L.),
Boston (A.L.)

3434. Bloom, Bob. "Monster Basher." *Sport,* LXXXVI (June 1995), 87–91.

3435. Callahan, Gerry. "Playing Wall Ball." *Sports Illustrated,* LXXXII (May 8, 1995), 25+.
3436. Celeste, Eric. "The Player." *D Magazine,* XX (April 1993), 38+.
3437. "A Closer Look: Jose Canseco." *Beckett Baseball Card Monthly,* XII, no. 121 (April 1995), 6–7.
3438. Edes, Gordon. "Interview: Jose Canseco." *Inside Sports,* XVII (June 1995), 26–35.
3439. Hoffer, Richard. "Try, Try Again." *Sports Illustrated,* LXXX (March 14, 1994), 38–40.
3440. Levine, Felicia. "Miami's 'Bad Boy' Slugger." *South Florida,* XLV (May 1992), 36–37.
3441. Ling, Bettina. *Jose Canseco.* Austin, Tx.: Raintree Steck-Vaughn, 1995. 48p.
3442. Montville, Leigh. "Texas-Sized Trade: The Oakland A's Sent Superstar Jose Canseco to the Rangers in a Deal That Was Both Bold and Bewildering." *Sports Illustrated,* LXXVII (September 14, 1992), 36–38.
3443. Rogers, Phil. "Deeper Look: Jose Canseco." *Beckett Baseball Card Monthly,* XI, no. 116 (November 1994), 114–116.
3444. ____. "Second Look: Jose Canseco." *Beckett Baseball Card Monthly,* X, no. 100 (July 1993), 105–106.
3445. Rothaus, James R. *Jose Canseco.* Mankato, Minn.: Child's World, 1991. Unpaged.
3446. Sonnenschein, Allan. "No Way, Jose." *Penthouse,* XXIII (May 1992), 96+.

OZZIE CANSECO

Outfielder
Oakland (A.L.), St. Louis (N.L.)

3447. Wheatley, Tom. "Hi, Brother." *Beckett Focus on Future Stars,* III, no. 21 (January 1993), 17–19.

HARRY CARAY

Broadcaster

3448. Watt, R. L. "Caray Me Away: 50 Years of Harry Caray." *Sport,* LXXXV (July 1994), 51+.

ROD CAREW*

Second Baseman, First Baseman
Minnesota (A.L.), California (A.L.)
Coach

3449. Fraley, Gerry. "Young Angel Hitters Thrive Under Guidance of Rod Carew." *Baseball Digest,* LIV (November 1995), 30–33.
3450. Marshall, R. "1969: Carew Steals Home—Seven Thefts Tied What Was Then Thought to Be the Record." *Baseball Research Journal,* XXIV (1995), 66–68.
3451. Rosen, Max. "The Game of His Life." *People Weekly,* XLIV (December 4, 1995), 133–135. Search for bone marrow donors for his daughter Michelle.
3452. Verducci, Tom. "Carew's Crew." *Sports Illustrated,* LXXXIII (July 17, 1995), 28–30, 32, 36.

STEVE CARLTON*

Pitcher
St. Louis (N.L.), Philadelphia (N.L.),
San Francisco (N.L.),
Chicago (A.L.), Cleveland (A.L.),
Minnesota (A.L.)

3453. Barrett, W. M. "Saluting the Sphinx of the Slab." *USA Today,* CXXIII (July 1994), 93+.
3454. Caroulis, Jon. "Steve Carlton Defied Odds for Lowly '72 Phillies." *Baseball Digest,* LVI (February 1997), 82–87.
3455. Curreri, Joe. "The Silence Was Golden." *Beckett Baseball Card Monthly,* XII, no. 122 (May 1995), 106–109.
3456. "Final Look: Steve Carlton." *Beck-ett Baseball Card Monthly,* XI, no. 109 (April 1994), 105–106.
3457. Jordan, Pat. "Thin Mountain Air." *Philadelphia,* LXXXV (April 1994), 88+.
3458. Kuenster, Bob. "Steve Carlton's Slider, His Ticket to the Hall of Fame." *Baseball Digest,* LIII (April 1994), 57–59.
3459. Silary, Ted. "Steve Carlton's Long Winning Streak in '72 Still Amazing." *Baseball Digest,* LI (November 1992), 56–60.
3460. Wulf, Steve. "Steve Carlton." *Sports Illustrated,* LXXX (January 24, 1994), 48–49.

CHUCK CARR

Outfielder
New York Mets (N.L.), St. Louis (N.L.),
Florida (N.L.), Milwaukee (A.L.)

3461. LeBatard, Dan. "Marlins' Chuck Carr Plays Center Field with a Flair." *Baseball Digest,* LII (December 1993), 44–45.
3462. Perrotto, John. "Rookie Report: Chuck Carr." *Beckett Baseball Card Monthly,* X, no. 102 (September 1993), 114–116.

GARY CARTER

Catcher
Montreal (N.L.), New York Mets (N.L.),
Los Angeles (N.L.)
Broadcaster

3463. Branon, Dave and Lee Pellegrino. "Gary Carter." In: their *Safe at Home.* Chicago, Ill.: Moody Press, 1992. pp. 73–84.
3464. Carter, Gary, with Ken Abraham. *The Gamer.* Dallas, Tx.: Word Books, 1993. 272p.
3465. Kuenster, John. "Gary Carter Finished a Noteworthy Career on His Own Terms." *Baseball Digest,* LII (March 1993), 15–19.
3466. Peck, Burton L., 4th. "Final Look:

Gary Carter." *Beckett Baseball Card Monthly,* X, no. 94 (January 1993), 118–119.

3467. Rubin, Bob. "Strangers in a Strange Land." *Inside Sports,* XVI (June 1994), 16–18.

JOE CARTER

Outfielder, First Baseman
Chicago (N.L.), Cleveland (A.L.),
San Diego (N.L.), Toronto (A.L.)

3468. Henneman, Jim. "Joe Carter of the Jays: He Swings a Productive Bat." *Baseball Digest,* LII (September 1993), 22–23.

3469. Milton, Steve. "Closer Look: Joe Carter." *Beckett Baseball Card Monthly,* X, no. 96 (March 1993), 6–9.

3470. ____. "A Deeper Look: Joe Carter." *Beckett Baseball Card Monthly,* XI, no. 109 (April 1994), 108–109.

3471. Weinberg, Rich. "Super Joe." *Sport,* LXXXIII (June 1992), 22–23, 26, 28–29.

ALEXANDER CARTWRIGHT*

Executive
Knickerbocker Base Ball Club

3472. Theroux, Joseph. "The Father of Baseball." *Honolulu,* XXVI (May 1992), 30–31+.

VINNY CASTILLA

Third Baseman
Atlanta (N.L.), Colorado (N.L.)

3473. Crasnick, Jerry. "Vinny Castilla: A Rising Young Star for the Rockies." *Baseball Digest,* LIV (November 1995), 34–36.

ORLANDO CEPEDA

First Baseman
San Francisco (N.L.), St. Louis (N.L.),
Atlanta (N.L.),

Oakland (A.L.), Boston (A.L.),
Kansas City (A.L.)
Coach

3474. Fagen, Herb. "Orlando Cepeda Still Hopes for Hall of Fame Admission." *Baseball Digest,* LIV (September 1995), 68–76.

HENRY CHADWICK*

Sportswriter

3475. Tygiel, Jules. "Henry Chadwick and the Invention of Baseball Statistics." *Nine: A Journal of Baseball History and Social Policy Perspective,* IV (Spring 1996), 198–216.

SPURGEON FERDINAND ("SPUD") CHANDLER

Pitcher
New York (A.L.)

3476. Rafal, Sam. "Yankee's Spud Chandler: He Had a Brief, but Shining Career." *Sports Illustrated,* LII (August 1993), 46–50.

HAROLD HARRIS ("HAL" or "PRINCE HAL") CHASE

First Baseman
New York (A.L.), Chicago (A.L.),
Buffalo (F.L.), Cincinnati (N.L.),
New York Giants (N.L.)
Manager
New York (A.L.)

3477. LaCasse, G. "Hal Chase in Victoria." *National Pastime,* XV (1995), 88–90.

RUSSELL ORMAND ("RUSS") CHRISTOPHER

Pitcher
Philadelphia (A.L.), Cleveland (A.L.)

3478. Tekulsky, J. D. "Russ Christopher—Courageous Athlete: A Key to the Indians' 1948 Pennant." *National Pastime,* XV (1995), 112–113.

JACK ("THE RIPPER") CLARK

Outfielder
San Francisco (N.L.), St. Louis (N.L.),
New York (A.L.),
San Diego (N.L.), Boston (A.L.)

3479. Kurkijan, Tim. "Crash in the Fast Lane." *Sports Illustrated,* LXXVII (August 17, 1992), 97–98.
3480. Ladson, William. "Riches to Rags." *Sport,* LXXXV (January 1994), 34–37+.
3481. Lieber, Jill. "Jack Clark." *Sports Illustrated,* LXXXI (August 1, 1994), 46–47.
3482. Montville, Leigh. "The 18-Car Barrage." *Sports Illustrated,* LXXVII (August 24, 1992), 8+. Bankruptcy.
3483. Pierce, Charles P. "The Designated Hitter." *Boston,* LXXXIV (April 1992), 58+.

TONY CLARK

First Baseman
Detroit (A.L.)

3484. Crothers, Tim. "Tony the Tiger." *Sports Illustrated,* LXXXVI (May 12, 1997), 94+.
3485. Jenkins, Chris. "Tony Clark of the Tigers: Emergence of a New Longball Hitter." *Baseball Digest,* LVI (August 1997), 54–57.

WILL CLARK

First Baseman
San Francisco (N.L.), Texas (A.L.)

3486. DeMarco, Tom. "Will to Win." *Sport,* LXXXV (May 1994), 38–41.
3487. Keown, Tim. "A Second Look: Will Clark." *Beckett Baseball Card Monthly,* IX, no. 90 (September 1992), 105–107.
3488. Knapp, Ron. *Sports Great Will Clark.* Hillside, N.J.: Enslow, 1993. 64p.
3489. Payne, Mike. "Deeper Look: Will Clark." *Beckett Baseball Card Monthly,* XI, no. 115 (October 1994), 116–118.

ROYCE CLAYTON

Shortstop
San Francisco (N.L.), St. Louis (N.L.)

3490. Whiteside, Kelly. "Royce Clayton." In: David Bauer, ed. *SI Presents Baseball 1997.* New York: Sports Illustrated, 1997. pp. 86–89.

ROGER ("THE ROCKET") CLEMENS

Pitcher
Boston (A.L.), Toronto (A.L.)

3491. Buckley, Steve. "Rocket Science." *Sport,* LXXXIV (May 1993), 56–59.
3492. Cafardo, Nick. "Deeper Look: Roger Clemens." *Beckett Baseball Card Monthly,* X, no. 93 (March 1993), 112–117.
3493. Callahan, Gerry. "Commanding Presence." *Sports Illustrated,* LXXXVI (March 31, 1997), 120–124+.
3494. Chastain, Bill. "Roger Clemens, a Welcome Addition to Blue Jays' Starting Staff." *Baseball Digest,* LVI (June 1997), 61–63.
3495. Clemens, Roger. "How to Pitch." *KidSports,* IV, no. 3 (1992), 28–31.
3496. Schmuck, Peter. "Roger Clemens: He's Back in Command with the Blue Jays." *Baseball Digest,* LVI (September 1997), 22–25.
3497. Weinberg, Rick. "Special Delivery." *Sport,* LXXXIX (May 1997), 34–38.

AMANDA CLEMENT

Umpire

3498. Gregorich, Barbara. "Amanda Clement: The First Woman Baseball

Ump." *Referee,* XVIII (March 1993), 25+.

ROBERTO CLEMENTE*

Outfielder
Pittsburgh (N.L.)

3499. Allen, Maury. "Final Look: Roberto Clemente." *Beckett Baseball Card Monthly,* X, no. 102 (September 1993), 126+.

3500. Engel, Trudie. *We'll Never Forget You, Roberto Clemente.* New York: Scholastic, 1997.

3501. Feldman, Jay. "Roberto Clemente Went to Bat for All Latino Ballplayers." *Smithsonian,* XXIV (September 1993), 128–136+.

3502. Loftus, Joanne. "The Heart of the Game: Baseball Hall of Famer Roberto Clemente." *Cobblestone,* X (April 1989), 36+.

3503. Macht, Norman L. *Baseball Legends: Roberto Clemente.* New York: Chelsea House, 1994. 64p.

3504. Miro Fernando, Roman. *Roberto Clemente, the Untold Story: En el Cielo lo Que se Juega es Beisbol.* Bayamon, P.R.: L. B. B. A., 1992. 198p. Biographical novel in English and Spanish.

3505. O'Brien, Jim. *Remember Roberto: Roberto Clemente Recalled by Teammates, Family, Friends, and Fans.* Pittsburgh, Pa.: James A. O'Brien, 1994. 448p.

3506. O'Connor, Jim. *The Story of Roberto Clemente, All-Star Hero.* N.p.: George Stevens, 1995. 108p.

3507. Peterson, Robert W. "The Pride of Puerto Rico." *Boy's Life,* LXXXI (November 1991), 10–11.

3508. Rudeen, Kenneth. *Roberto Clemente.* New York: HarperTrophy, 1996. 53p.

3509. Ruck, Rob. "Remembering Roberto Clemente." *Pittsburgh,* XXIII (December 1992), 36–42.

3510. Smizik, Bob. "Roberto Clemente Would Have Been Proud of Memorial

Statue." *Baseball Digest,* LIII (November 1994), 79–82.

3511. West, Alan. *Roberto Clemente: Baseball Legend.* Brookfield, Conn.: Millbrook Press, 1993. 32p.

3512. Wulf, Steve. "Arriba Roberto." *Sports Illustrated,* LXXVII (December 29, 1992), 114–118, 120, 122, 125–128.

3513. ____. "Roberto Clemente." *Sports Illustrated,* LXXXI (September 19, 1994), 110–112.

3514. Zeske, Mark. "Mementoes of Roberto." *Beckett Vintage Sports,* no. 10 (September 1997), *passim.* **<http://www.beckett.com/products/vtpd.html>.**

TONY LEE CLONINGER

Pitcher
Milwaukee (N.L.), Atlanta (N.L.), Cincinnati (N.L.), St. Louis (N.L.)

3515. Adelson, Bruce. "Tony Cloninger Relieves the Day He Hit Two Grand Slams." *Baseball Digest,* LII (May 1993), 54–58.

TY ("THE GEORGIA PEACH") COBB*

Outfielder
Detroit (A.L.), Philadelphia (A.L.)
Manager
Detroit (A.L.)

3516. Alvarez, Mark. "Say It Ain't So, Ty." *National Pastime,* XIV (1994), 21–28.

3517. Bak, Richard. *Ty Cobb, His Tumultuous Life and Times.* Dallas, Tx.: Taylor, 1994. 194p.

3518. Barra, Allen. "A Rotten Peach." *Inside Sports,* XVII (January 1995), 72–77. Ron Shelton's motion picture *Cobb* deconstructs a hero and a film genre.

3519. Burns, Ken. "'A Grain of Sand That Reveals the Universe': An Interview." *U.S. News & World Report,* CXVII (August 29, 1994), 56–58.

3520. Cobb, Ty. "The Other Side of Ty Cobb." *Nevada Magazine,* LIV (September–October 1994), 88–91.

3521. ____. *Selection of Letters Between Ty Cobb and Taylor Spink, 1941–1958* <http://www.thesportingnews.com/archives/ty> is an Internet site from the Archives of *The Sporting News* which reproduces a series of actual letters between "The Georgia Peach" and the baseball newspaper's chief.

3522. Kramer, Sydella. *Ty Cobb, Bad Boy of Baseball.* New York: Random House, 1995. 48p.

3523. Macht, Norman L. *Baseball Legends: Ty Cobb.* New York: Chelsea House, 1993. 64p.

3524. ____. "Cobb Never Supported Cochrane: The Facts, Not the Myth." *National Pastime,* XV (1995), 21–23.

3525. Montville, Leigh. "The Last Remains of a Legend." *Sports Illustrated Classic,* LXXVII (Fall 1992), 60–67.

3526. Stump, Al. "Bobby and Ty—One Legend to Another: Bobby Jones Introduced Ty Cobb to Golf, But for the Georgia Peace, It Was the Pits." *Golf Magazine,* XXXII (April 1990), 68+.

3527. ____. *Cobb: A Biography.* Chapel Hill, N.C.: Algonquin Books of Chapel Hill, 1994. 436p. Simultaneously published in Canada by the Markham, Ont., firm of Thomas Allen & Son, Ltd.

3528. Trimble, P. "Cobb." *Journal of Sport History,* XXIII (Spring 1996), 78–80. Review of the Warner Brothers 1995 feature film, starring Tommy Lee Jones.

3529. Ward, Geoffrey C. and Ken Burns. "A Tiger Named Ty." *U.S. News & World Report,* CXVII (August 29, 1994), 64–65.

GORDON COBBLEDICK

Sportswriter

3530. Odenkirk, James E. *Plain Dealing: A Biography of Gordon Cobbledick.*

N.p.: Spider-naps Publications, 1990. 195p.

ROCCO DOMENICO ("ROCKY") COLAVITO

Outfielder, Pitcher
Cleveland (A.L.), Detroit (A.L.),
Kansas City (A.L.),
Chicago (A.L.), Los Angeles (N.L.),
New York (A.L.)

3531. Stewart, Wayne. "Rocky Colavito Recalls [1959] Game in Which He Hit Four Homers." *Baseball Digest,* LII (February 1993), 48–52.

GARNOLD LEANDER ("LEFTY") COLE

Pitcher
Albany Senators
Coach

3532. Patrick, Philip. "Lefty Cole." *Elysian Fields Quarterly,* XIII (Winter 1993), 42–45.

LEONARD S. COLEMAN, JR.

Executive
President, National League

3533. "Baseball Owners Name Leonard S. Coleman, Jr., President of the National League with a Strong Show of Support." *Jet,* LXXXV (March 21, 1994), 52–53.

3534. "Len Coleman, the National League's New President, Takes Charge." *Ebony,* XLIX (June 1994), 116–118.

VINCE COLEMAN

Outfielder
St. Louis (N.L.), New York Mets (N.L.), Kansas City (A.L.), Seattle (A.L.)

3535. Kurkjian, Tim. "A Bad Sign." *Sports Illustrated,* LXXVII (September 14, 1992), 66–67.

3535a. Marx, Linda. "Night Games."
Penthouse, XXIV (September 1992),
78+.

3536. "A Moral Vacuum." *Sports Illustrated,* LXXIX (August 9, 1993), 9–10.
Charged after L.A. firecracker incident.

MARLA COLLINS

Ballgirl
Chicago (N.L.)

3537. Muskat, Carrie. "Enjoy the Sunshine, and Then Move On." *Inside
Sports,* XVII (June 1995), 18–20. Ballgirl, 1982–1986, fired after posing for
Playboy.

DAVID CONE

Pitcher
Kansas City (A.L.),
New York Mets (N.L.),
New York (A.L.)

3538. Bradley, John Ed. "The Head-
liner." *Sports Illustrated,* LXXVIII
(April 5, 1993), 92–102, 104. Published
simultaneously in *Sports Illustrated
Canada,* I (April 5, 1993), 82–98.

3539. "The Itinerant Ace." In: Joe Hoppel, ed. *The Sporting News 1996 Baseball Yearbook.* St. Louis, Mo.: TSN,
1996. pp. 16–21.

3540. Klapisch, Bob. "The *Sport* Q & A:
David Cone." *Sport,* LXXXIV (July
1993), 52–57.

3541. Ringolsby, Tracy. "Inside Interview: David Cone." *Inside Sports,*
XIX (March 1997), 24–32.

3542. Smith, C. S. "The Cone Zone."
New York, XXIX (October 7, 1996),
20–21.

3543. Verducci, Tom. "A Moving Experience." *Sports Illustrated,* LXXXIV
(January 8, 1996), 57+.

WIL CORDERO

Second Baseman
Montreal (N.L.), Boston (A.L.)

3544. Giuliotti, Ed. "Where There's Wil,
They're Amazed." *Beckett Focus on
Future Stars,* II, no. 13 (May 1992),
10–13.

MARTY CORDOVA

Outfielder
Minnesota (A.L.)

3545. Forman, Ross. "Marty Cordova,
A.L.'s Leading Rookie of '95, Looks
Ahead." *Baseball Digest,* LV (May
1996), 52–54.

BOB COSTAS

Broadcaster

3546. Goodman, M. S. "Bob Costas."
People Weekly, XXXIX (February 1,
1993), 71–74.

JOE COWLEY

Pitcher
Atlanta (N.L.), New York (A.L.),
Chicago (N.L.), Philadelphia (N.L.)

3547. Lidz, Franz. "Flash in the Pan."
Sports Illustrated, LXXVI (May 4,
1992), 56–61, 63–64, 67–68.

BOBBY COX

Third Baseman
New York (A.L.)
Manager
Toronto (N.L.), Atlanta (N.L.)

3548. Freeman, Scott. "What About
Bobby?" *Atlanta,* XXXV (October
1995), 44+.

3549. Wolff, Alexander. "Out of Control." *Sports Illustrated,* LXXXII
(May 15, 1995), 34–36+.

JAMES CREIGHTON

Pitcher
Brooklyn Excelsiors

3550. Thorn, John. "Jim Thorn: To a Ballplayer Dying Young." *Elysian Fields Quarterly,* XI (Spring 1992), 59–63.

3551. Ward, Geoffrey C. and Ken Burns. "Jim Creighton [1841–1862]." *U.S. News & World Report,* CXVII (August 29, 1994), 62+.

JOHN W. ("JIMMIE") CRUTCHFIELD

Outfielder
Pittsburgh Crawfords, Newark Eagles,
Toledo Crawfords,
Chicago American Giants,
Cleveland Buckeyes

3552. Cohen, Sheldon and Jim Keenan. "Jimmy Crutchfield's Baseball World." *Elysian Fields Quarterly,* XIII (Winter 1994), 26–35. First published in the Spring 1993 issue of *Loyola Magazine.*

JOSE CRUZ, JR.

Outfielder
Seattle (A.L.), Toronto (A.L.)

3553. Bradley, Lance. "Cruz Control." *Beckett Future Stars & Sports Collectibles,* VII, no. 75 (July 1997), *passim.* **<http://www.beckett.com/products/fspd.html>.**

3554. Crothers, Tim. "Cruz Control." *Sports Illustrated,* LXXXVI (June 30, 1997), 72, 74.

JIM CZAJKOWSKI

Pitcher
Colorado (N.L.)

3555. Berler, Ron. "Just Give Me One Chance." *Inside Sports,* XV (May 1993), 56+.

JOHN D'ACQUISTO

Pitcher
San Francisco (N.L.), St. Louis (N.L.),
San Diego (N.L.), Montreal (N.L.), California (A.L.), Oakland (A.L.)

3556. Miller, Stuart. "An Irresistible Pitch: How Did a Former Big-League Hurler with Little Financial Training Talk His Way Into the Middle of a $200 Million Fraud Case?" *Inside Sports,* XVIII (October 1996), 72–74.

ARTHUR J. DALEY

Sportswriter

3557. Harper, J. "Daley's Diamond: The Baseball Writing of Arthur J. Daley." *Nine: A Journal of Baseball History and Social Policy Perspective,* IV (Fall 1995), 34–50.

JOHNNY DAMON

Outfielder
Kansas City (A.L.)

3558. Johnson, Paul M. "Speed Damon." *Sport,* LXXXVIII (July 1996), 24–25.

HARRY ("HORSE") DANNING

Catcher
New York Giants (N.L.)

3559. Van Blair, Rick. "Flashback: Harry Danning—Catching Star of Another Era." *Baseball Digest,* LIII (October 1994), 63–67.

DARREN DAULTON

Catcher
Philadelphia (N.L.), Florida (N.L.)

3560. Buchholz, Brad. "Safe at Home." *Inside Sports,* XV (April 1993), 52–56.

3561. Hagen, Paul. "The Blue-Collar Catcher." *Sport,* LXXXIV (May 1993), 51–53.

3562. _____. "A Deeper Look: Darren Daulton." *Beckett Baseball Card*

Monthly, IX, no. 91 (October 1992), 110–111.

3563. Kurkijan, Tim. "A Catcher Catches Fire." *Sports Illustrated,* LXXVI (June 22, 1992), 65+.

3564. Montville, Leigh. "Leading Man." *Sports Illustrated,* LXXIX (October 11, 1993), 46–48.

CHARLES THEODORE ("CHILI") DAVIS

Outfielder
San Francisco (N.L.), California (A.L.), Minnesota (A.L.)

3565. Kaegel, Dick. "Chili Davis Keeps Climbing on the Switch-Hitter Charts." *Baseball Digest,* LVI (June 1997), 64–65.

ERIC DAVIS

Outfielder
Cincinnati (N.L.), Los Angeles (N.L.), Detroit (A.L.), Baltimore (A.L.)

3566. Crothers, Tim. "Mr. Comeback." *Sports Illustrated,* LXXXVII (July 7, 1997), 85–86.

3567. Davis, Eric, as told to George Vass. "'The Game I'll Never Forget.'" *Baseball Digest,* LIII (April 1994), 81–83.

3567a. Tresniowski, Alex. "No Surrender." *People Weekly,* XLVIII (November 3, 1997), 97098.

GERRY DAVIS

Umpire
N.L.

3568. Davis, Gerry. "Interview." *Referee,* XX (May 1995), 72+.

GLENN DAVIS

First Baseman
Houston (N.L.), Baltimore (A.L.)

3569. Macht, Norman. "A Deeper Look: Glenn Davis." *Beckett Baseball Card*

Monthly, IX, no. 90 (September 1992), 110–111.

SHERRY DAVIS

Broadcaster

3570. Gmeich, G. "Sherry Davis, Announcer, San Francisco Giants." *Nine: A Journal of Baseball History and Social Policy Perspective,* IV (Spring 1996), 353–361.

ANDRE DAWSON

Outfielder
Montreal (N.L.), Chicago (N.L.)

3571. Cafardo, Nick. "Will '94 Season Be the Last Hurrah for Andre Dawson?" *Baseball Digest,* LIII (June 1994), 50–52.

3572. Dawson, Andre, with Tom Bird. *Andre Dawson.* Grand Rapids, Mich.: Zondervan, 1994. 117p. Excerpted from the next entry.

3573. ____. *Hawk: An Inspiring True Story of Success at the Game of Life and Baseball.* Grand Rapids, Mich.: Zondervan, 1994. 207p.

JAY ("DIZZY") DEAN*

Pitcher
St. Louis (N.L.), Chicago (N.L.), St. Louis (A.L.)
Broadcaster

3574. Bickett, William. "Dizzy Dean." *Mississippi,* XI (July–August 1993), 71+.

3575. Gunn, Pete. "The Song of the Cicadas: An Interpretive Biographical Sketch." *Elysian Fields Quarterly,* XI (Spring 1992), 22–23.

RAOUL ("ROD") DEDEAUX

Coach
University of Southern California

3576. Lawlor, Chris. "Rapping with Rod Deadeaux: Interview." *Scholastic Coach,* LXIII (November 1993), A20–A22+.

FRANK DEFORD

Sportswriter

3577. Goodrich, C. "PW Interviews Frank Deford." *Publishers Weekly,* CCXL (December 6, 1993), 52–53.

ED ("BIG ED") DELAHANTY*

Outfielder, First Baseman
Philadelphia (N.L.),
Cleveland (P.), Washington (A.L.)

3578. Sowell, Mike. *July 2, 1903: The Mysterious Death of Hall-of-Famer Big Ed Delahanty.* New York: Macmillan, 1992. 326p.

CARLOS DELGADO

Catcher
Toronto (A.L.)

3579. Milton, Steve. "Focus on Carlos Delgado." *Beckett Focus on Future Stars,* IV, no. 33 (January 1994), 14–17.
3580. ____. "Rookie Report: Carlos Delgado." *Beckett Baseball Card Monthly,* XI, no. 112 (July 1994), 126–127.

RUSSELL ("BUCKY") DENT

Shortstop
Chicago (A.L.), New York (A.L.),
Texas (A.L.), Kansas City (A.L.)
Manager
New York (A.L.)

3581. Dent, Bucky, as told to George Vass. "'The Game I'll Never Forget.'" *Baseball Digest,* LI (September 1992), 83–86.

DELINO DESHIELDS

Second Baseman
Montreal (N.L.), Los Angeles (N.L.),
St. Louis (N.L.)

3582. Hummel, Rick. "Delino Deshields: He's a Good Fit with the Cardinals." *Baseball Digest,* LVI (June 1997), 72–73.
3583. Kurkijan, Tim. "A Dazzling Deal." *Sports Illustrated,* LXXX (April 4, 1994), 86–88.

ROBERT ("ROB") DIBBLE

Pitcher
Cincinnati (N.L.), Chicago (A.L.),
Milwaukee (A.L.)

3584. Sorci, Rick. "Baseball Profile: Relief Pitcher Rob Dibble." *Baseball Digest,* LII (April 1993), 77–78.
3585. Steinberg, Alan. "Interview: Rob Dibble." *Inside Sports,* XV (January 1993), 26–32.

WILLIAM MALCOLM ("BILL") DICKEY*

Catcher
New York (A.L.)
Manager
New York (A.L.)
Coach

3586. Broeg, Bob. "Bill Dickey: He Was One of the All-Time Great Receivers." *Baseball Digest,* LIII (March 1994), 62–65.

JASON DICKSON

Pitcher
California (A.L.), Anaheim (A.L.)

3587. Crothers, Tim. "Heavenly Angel." *Sports Illustrated,* LXXXVI (May 5, 1997), 70, 73.

LARRY DIERKER

Pitcher
Houston (N.L.), St. Louis (N.L.)
Manager
Houston (N.L.)
Broadcaster

3588. Rushin, Steve. "The Retro Astro." *Sports Illustrated,* LXXXVII (October 6, 1997), 38–40.

JOE DIMAGGIO*

Outfielder
New York (A.L.)

3589. *Beckett Great Sports Heroes: Joe DiMaggio.* Dallas, Tx.: Beckett Publications, 1997. 100p.

3590. Bredeson, Carmen. "Joe DiMaggio." In: his *Presidential Medal of Freedom Winners.* Hillsdale, N.J.: Enslow Publications, 1996. pp. 49–55.

3591. Chapin, Dwight. "As a Minor Leaguer, Joe DiMaggio Hit in 61 Straight Games." *Baseball Digest,* LII (November 1993), 62–66.

3592. "DiMaggio: The Enduring Image." *Sports Illustrated,* LXXIX (July 19, 1993), 66–74.

3593. Durso, Joseph. *DiMaggio: The Last American Knight.* Boston, Mass.: Little, Brown, 1995. 272p.

3594. Engel, Trudie. *Joe DiMaggio: Baseball Star.* New York: Scholastic, 1994. 68p.

3595. Hoffman, Frank W. and William G. Bailey. "Joe DiMaggio's Consecutive Game Hitting Streak." In: their *Sports and Recreation Fads.* Binghampton, N.Y.: Haworth, 1991. pp. 99–101.

3596. Holland, Vinny. "The DiMaggio Man." *Topps Magazine,* (Spring 1993), 18–19.

3597. Lupica, Mike. "The Eternal Yankee." *Esquire,* CXXXI (May 1994), 51–52.

3598. "Marilyn Monroe and Joe DiMaggio: An Unlikely Marriage Took the Ballplayer Into a Major League Romance." *People Weekly,* XLV (February 12, 1996), 77+.

3599. Ostler, Scott. "Chasing the Trail of 'Joltin' Joe' DiMaggio." *Baseball Digest,* LV (June 1996), 63–67.

3600. Sanford, William R. and Carl R. Green. *Joe DiMaggio.* New York: Crestwood House, 1993. 48p.

3601. Stout, Glenn. *Joe DiMaggio: An Illustrated Life.* Edited by Dick Johnson. New York: Walker, 1995. 272p.

3602. Ward, Geoffrey C. and Ken Burns. "Joe DiMaggio." *U.S. News & World Report,* CXVII (August 29, 1994), 89+.

MIKE DI MURO

Umpire
Japan League

3603. Gibney, Frank, Jr. "Yankee, You're Out." *Time,* CXLIX (June 23, 1997), 46+. Called back from Japan due to fears over his safety.

3604. Whiting, Robert. "The Umpire Strikes Out." *U.S. News & World Report,* CXXII (June 23, 1997), 11+.

LARRY DOBY

Outfielder
Cleveland (A.L.), Chicago (A.L.), Detroit (A.L.)
Manager
Chicago (A.L.)
Coach

3605. Berkow, Ira. "Larry Doby: An Overlooked Black Pioneer in the American League." *Baseball Digest,* LVI (July 1997), 66–71.

3606. Caroulis, Jon. "Larry Doby: He Played in the Shadow of Jackie Robinson." *Baseball Digest,* LIV (July 1995), 47–49.

3607. Stewart, Wayne. "Flashback: Larry Doby—He Pioneered with Jackie Robinson." *Baseball Digest,* LIII (August 1994), 57–58.

TIM DONAHUE

Catcher
Boston (A.A.), Chicago (N.L.), Washington (A.L.)

3608. Donahue, Bill. "Remembering Tim Donahue." *Elysian Fields Quarterly,* XIV (Summer 1995), 83–87.

HARRY ("FRITZ") DORISH
Pitcher
Boston (A.L.), St. Louis (A.L.),
Chicago (A.L.), Baltimore (A.L.)

3609. Woody, Clay. "Flashback: Harry Dorish—The Pitcher Who Stole Home." *Baseball Digest,* LIII (November 1994), 75–78.

ABNER DOUBLEDAY
General, Executive

3610. Dunham, Montrew. *Abner Doubleday, Young Baseball Pioneer.* New York: Alladin Books, 1995. 192p.

ANTHONY DOUGLAS
Sports Artist

3611. Threatt, Jana. "Drawing Closer to His Goal." *Beckett Focus on Future Stars,* III, no. 25 (May 1993), 23–24.

DAVE DRAVECKY
Pitcher
San Diego (N.L.), San Francisco (N.L.)

3612. Dravecky, Dave and Jan, with Ken Gire. *When You Can't Come Back.* San Francisco, Ca.: HarperSan Francisco, 1992. 199p. Excerpted in *Reader's Digest,* CXLI (October 1992), 89–92, under the title "My Finest Hour."
3613. Gire, Judy. *A Boy and His Baseball: The Dave Dravecky Story.* Grand Rapids, Mich.: Zondervan, 1992. 32p.
3614. Schachter, C. L., P. B. Canham, and M. F. Mottola. "Biomechanical Factors Affecting Dave Dravecky's Return to Competitive Pitching: A Case Study." *Journal of Orthopedic and Sports Physical Therapy,* XVI (July 1992), 2–5.

DARREN DREIFORT
Pitcher
Los Angeles (N.L.)

3615. Johnson, Jeff. "Focus on Darren Dreifort." *Beckett's Focus on Future Stars,* IV, no. 40 (August 1994), 70–73.
3616. ____. "Rookie Report: Darren Dreifort." *Beckett Baseball Card Monthly,* XI, no. 114 (September 1994), 126–127.

J. D. DREW
Outfielder
Florida State University

3617. Fleming, David. "Draft Dodger." *Sports Illustrated,* LXXXVII (July 21, 1997), 86–87.

WALT DROPO
First Baseman
Boston (A.L.), Detroit (A.L.),
Chicago (A.L.), Cincinnati (N.L.)

3618. Montville, Leigh. "What Ever Happened to Walt Dropo?" *Sports Illustrated,* LXXIX (July 19, 1993), 82–83.

DON DRYSDALE*
Pitcher
Brooklyn (N.L.), Los Angeles (N.L.)
Broadcaster

3619. Broeg, Bob. "National League Batters Didn't Crowd the Plate on Drysdale." *Baseball Digest,* LII (November 1993), 52–55.
3620. "Big D." *Sports Illustrated,* LXXIX (July 12, 1993), 13–14.
3621. "Don Drysdale." In: Louise Mooney Collins, ed. *Newsmakers, 1994: The People Behind the Headlines.* Detroit, Mich.: Gale Research, 1994. pp. 588–589.
3622. No entry.

SHAWON DUNSTON
Shortstop
Chicago (N.L.), San Francisco (N.L.),
Pittsburgh (N.L.)

3623. Farber, Michael. "Look Who's Back." *Sports Illustrated,* LXXX (May 9, 1994), 66–68.

DANIEL ("DAN") DUQUETTE

Executive
Boston (A.L.)

3624. Wulf, Steve. "Diamond Vision." *Sports Illustrated,* LXXX (April 4, 1994), 80–83.

LEO ("THE LIP") DUROCHER*

Shortstop
New York (A.L.), Cincinnati (N.L.),
St. Louis (N.L.), Brooklyn (N.L.)
Manager
Brooklyn (N.L.),
New York Giants (N.L.),
Chicago (N.L.), Houston (N.L.)

3625. Eskenazi, Gerald. *The Lip: A Biography of Leo Durocher.* New York: William Morrow, 1993. 336p.

LEN ("NAILS") DYKSTRA

Outfielder
New York Mets (N.L.),
Philadelphia (N.L.)

3626. "Awesome Dude." In: Joe Hoppel, ed. *The Sporting News 1994 Baseball Yearbook.* St. Louis, Mo.: TSN, 1994. pp. 4–11.
3627. Buschel, Bruce. "Lips Gets Smacked." *Philadelphia,* LXXXIV (January 1993), 25–29.
3628. Crasnick, Jerry. "Lenny Dykstra: The Phillies' Spirited Leadoff Hitter." *Baseball Digest,* LII (December 1993), 38–39.
3629. Fraley, Gerry. "Lenny Dykstra of the Phils: This 'Dude' Comes to Play." *Baseball Digest,* LIV (September 1995), 36–39.
3630. Hagen, Paul. "Deeper Look: Lenny Dykstra." *Beckett Baseball Card Monthly,* XI, no. 107 (February 1994), 108–110.

3631. Klapisch, Bob. "Body by Dykstra." *Men's Journal,* III (June–July 1994), 119–120.
3632. Kuenster, John. "Larry Dykstra Moves to the Top Among Majors' Leadoff Hitters." *Baseball Digest,* LIII (May 1994), 17–19.
3633. Pugliese, Nick. "Phils' Lenny Dykstra: He's on a Mission in '92." *Baseball Digest,* LI (June 1992), 46–47.
3634. Stark, Jayson. "One-on-One [with] Lenny Dykstra: Interview." *Sport,* LXXXV (July 1994), 28+.
3635. Thomsen, Ian. "Oo-la-la, Lenny." *Sports Illustrated,* LXXIX (December 6, 1993), 44–47.

DENNIS ECKERSLEY

Pitcher
Cleveland (A.L.), Boston (A.L.),
Chicago (N.L.), Oakland (A.L.),
St. Louis (N.L.)

3636. Hanson, Dave. "Outstanding in His Field." *Runner's World,* XXVIII (May 1993), 38–40.
3637. Holtzman, Jerome. "Competitive Fires Still Burn in Dennis Eckersley." *Baseball Digest,* LII (June 1993), 42–43.
3638. _____. "Dennis Eckersley: Baseball's Top One-Inning Reliever." *Baseball Digest,* LIII (June 1994), 42–43.
3639. Kroichick, Ron. "The Eck: From Fear to A's Saving Grace." In: Zander Hollander, ed. *The Complete Book of Baseball, 1993.* New York: Signet Books, 1993. pp. 30–39.
3640. Maloney, Tom. "The Secret of Dennis Eckersley's Success: Pinpoint Control." *Baseball Digest,* LI (November 1992), 32–34.
3641. Pfager, Mickey. "Eck!" *Sports Illustrated for Kids,* V (June 1993), 32–41.
3641a. Plummer, William, Lisa Twyman Bessone, and Sue Avery Brown. "A Saving Grace." *People Weekly,* XXXVIII (October 12, 1992), 137–138.

3642. Ratio, Ray. "Dennis Eckersley Helped Define the A's Championship Era." *Baseball Digest,* LV (July 1996), 60–62.

3643. Schlossberg, Dan. "From Bum to Hero." *Topps Magazine,* (Fall 1992), 22–27.

3644. Stier, Kit. "A Deeper Look: Dennis Eckersley." *Beckett Baseball Card Monthly,* IX, no. 93 (December 1992), 112–113.

3645. Wulf, Steve. "The Paintmaster." *Sports Illustrated,* LXXVII (August 24, 1992), 62–66, 68–70, 72, 76.

JIM EISENREICH

Outfielder
Minnesota (A.L.), Kansas City (A.L.), Philadelphia (N.L.), Florida (N.L.)

3646. Capezzuto, Tom. "Jim Eisenreich: He Learned to Persevere Against the Odds." *Baseball Digest,* LV (June 1996), 40–43.

3647. Gutman, Bill. *Jim Eisenreich.* Austin, Tx.: Raintree Stech-Vaughan, 1996. 48p..

3648. Valenzano, Joseph M., 3rd. "Batting 1000 Against Tourette Syndrome." *Exceptional Parent,* XXVII (February 1997), 40–42.

CAL ELDRED

Pitcher
Milwaukee (A.L.)

3649. Haudricourt, Tom. "'Corn-Fed' Cal." *Beckett Focus on Future Stars,* III, no. 22 (February 1993), 10–13.

ELWOOD ("WOODY") ENGLISH

Second Baseman
New York Giants (N.L.), Detroit (A.L.), Boston (N.L.), Brooklyn (N.L.)
Manager
Grand Rapids Chicks (AAGPBL)

3650. Helmer, Diana. "Woody English's Final League." *Elysian Fields Quarterly,* XXII (Summer 1993), 26–27.

SCOTT ERICKSON

Pitcher
Minnesota (A.L.), Baltimore (A.L.)

3651. Kurkijan, Tim. "Scott Erickson." *Sports Illustrated,* LXXX (May 9, 1994), 74+. Pitches no-hitter.

SHAWN ESTES

Pitcher
San Francisco (N.L.)

3652. Crothers, Tim. "Giant Leap." *Sports Illustrated,* LXXXVII (July 14, 1997), 57–58.

ELROY ("ROY") FACE

Pitcher
Pittsburgh (N.L.), Detroit (A.L.), Montreal (N.L.)

3653. Orlansky, F. E. "The Baron of the Bullpen: Elroy Face's Magnificent 1959 Season." *National Pastime,* XV (1995), 74–79.

FERRIS ROY ("BURRHEAD") FAIN

First Baseman
Philadelphia (A.L.), Chicago (A.L.), Detroit (A.L.), Cleveland (A.L.)

3654. Fagen, Herb. "Ferris Fain: An Old-Time Star Recalls How It Was in the 1950s." *Baseball Digest,* LIV (August 1995), 29–33.

JEFF FASSERO

Pitcher
Montreal (N.L.), Seattle (A.L.)

3655. Capezzuto, Tom. "Years of Labor in the Minors Pay Off for Jeff

Fassero." *Baseball Digest,* LVI (August 1997), 66–69.

DONALD FEHR

Executive
Major League
Baseball Players Association

3656. Swift, E. M. "The Perfect Square." *Sports Illustrated,* LXXVIII (March 8, 1993), 32–35.

BOB FELLER*

Pitcher
Cleveland (A.L.)

3657. Feller, Bob, as told to Carl Lundquist. "Then and Now: Why I Still Love Baseball." *Baseball Digest,* LIV (March 1995), 78–84.
3658. Rushefsky, N. "'Rapid Robert' Feller." *Journal of Sports Philately,* XXXV (May–June 1997), 13–14.
3659. Stewart, Wayne. "Pioneer of Penmanship." *Beckett Vintage Sports,* I, no. 6 (May 1997), *passim.* **<http:// www.beckett.com/products/vtpd.ht ml>**. His appearances at baseball card shows.
3660. Van Blair, Rick. "Bob Feller: He Was One Phenom Who Didn't Fizzle." *Baseball Digest,* LIII (February 1994), 77–81.

ALEX FERNANDEZ

Pitcher
Chicago (A.L.)

3661. Rushin, Steve. "Making a Splash." *Sports Illustrated,* LXXX (April 4, 1994), 70–72+.
3662. Sorci, Rick. "Baseball Profile: Pitcher Alex Fernandez." *Baseball Digest,* LIII (December 1994), 35+.

DAVID MEADOW ("DAVE" or "BOO") FERRISS

Pitcher
Boston (A.L.)

3663. Macht, Norman L. "Boo Ferriss: How an Overhand Curve Ruined a 20-Game Winner." *Baseball Digest,* LII (July 1993), 66–74.

MARK ("THE BIRD") FIDRYCH

Pitcher
Detroit (A.L.)

3664. Hoffman, Frank W. and William G. Bailey. "Mark 'Bird' Fidrych." In: their *Sports and Recreation Fads.* Binghampton, N.Y.: Haworth, 1991. pp. 125–127.
3665. Shook, Richard. "Final Look: Mark Fidrych." *Beckett Baseball Card Monthly,* X, no. 98 (May 1993), 118–119.

CECIL FIELDER

First Baseman
Toronto (A.L.), Detroit (A.L.),
New York (A.L.)

3666. "The Big Bopper." *Sports Illustrated for Kids,* VIII (August 1996), 30–33.
3667. Creager, Reid. "'Yes, I Can!'" In: Gary Levy, ed. *The Sporting News 1992 Baseball Yearbook.* St. Louis, Mo.: TSN, 1992. pp. 26–29.
3668. Dye, Dave. "Cecil Fielder's Thunderous Bat Silences His Critics." *Baseball Digest,* LI (August 1992), 24–27.
3669. Plummer, William. "Livin' Large." *People Weekly,* XL (July 19, 1993), 56–57.
3670. Rasmussen, Larry F. "Cecil Fielder Adds His Name to Exclusive RBI Club." *Baseball Digest,* LII (January 1993), 44–46.

3671. Stewart, Mark. *Cecil Fielder.* New York: Children's Press, 1996. 48p.

RON FIMRITE

Sportswriter

3672. Fimrite, Ron. "In the Name of the Father." *Sports Illustrated,* LXXX (February 7, 1994), 142–143.

ROLLIE FINGERS*

Pitcher
Oakland (A.L.), San Diego (N.L.), Milwaukee (A.L.)

3673. Barney, Chuck. "A Deeper Look: Rollie Fingers." *Beckett Baseball Card Monthly,* IX, no. 87 (June 1992), 116–118.

CHARLES O. FINLEY

Executive
Kansas City (A.L.), Oakland (A.L.)

3674. "Friend, T. O. Is for Oddball." *The New York Times Magazine,* (December 29, 1996), 20–21.

STEVE FINLEY

Outfielder
Baltimore (A.L.), Houston (N.L.), San Diego (N.L.)

3675. Johnson, Paul M. "Encore." *Sport,* LXXXIX (July 1997), 67–69.
3676. Sorci, Rick. "Baseball Profile: Outfielder Steve Finley of the Astros." *Baseball Digest,* LI (October 1992), 56–57.

BILL FISCHER

Pitcher
Detroit (A.L.), Washington (A.L.), Kansas City (A.L.), Minnesota (A.L.)
Coach

3677. Harris, Elliott. "Bill Fischer: The Pitcher Who Hated to Surrender Walks." *Baseball Digest,* LVI (December 1997), 82–84.

CARLTON FISK

Catcher
Boston (A.L.), Chicago (A.L.)

3678. "Final Look: Carlton Fisk." *Beckett Baseball Card Monthly,* XI, no. 108 (March 1994), 105–106.
3679. Fisk, Carlton. "How to Catch." *KidSports,* IV, no. 2 (1992), 26–29.
3680. Jordan, Pat. "Conversations with a Dinosaur." *Men's Journal,* II (May–June 1993), 116+.
3681. Ladewski, Paul. "Interview: Carlton Fisk." *Inside Sports,* XIV (August 1992), 24+.; XV (July 1993), 59+.
3682. Montville, Leigh. "Bitter Ending." *Sports Illustrated,* LXXVIII (May 31, 1993), 36–38+.
3683. "Superstar Gallery: Carlton Fisk." *Beckett Baseball Card Monthly,* IX, no. 89 (August 1992), 13–15.

DAVE FLEMING

Pitcher
Seattle (A.L.), Kansas City (A.L.)

3684. Finnigan, Bob. "Killing Them Softly." *Beckett Focus on Future Stars,* II, no. 17 (September 1992), 65–67.
3685. ____. "Rookie Report: Dave Fleming." *Beckett Baseball Card Monthly,* IX, no. 90 (September 1992), 108–109.
3686. "Superstar Gallery: Dave Fleming." *Beckett Baseball Card Monthly,* X, no. 93 (March 1993), 20–21.

ELMER FLICK*

Outfielder
Philadelphia (N.L.),
Philadelphia (A.L.), Cleveland (A.L.)

3687. Longert, S. "Elmer Flick: The Demon of the Stick." *National Pastime,* XV (1995), 32–33.

CLIFF FLOYD

Outfielder
Montreal (N.L.)

3688. Giulotti, Ed. "Focus on Cliff Floyd." *Beckett Focus on Future Stars,* IV, no. 37 (May 1994), 12–14.
3689. Lastinger, Mark. "Maximum Exposure." *Beckett Focus on Future Stars,* II, no. 19 (November 1992), 6–9.
3690. Linker, Andrew. "Rookie Report: Cliff Floyd." *Beckett Baseball Card Monthly,* XI, no. 110 (May 1994), 126–127.

CURT FLOOD

Outfielder
Cincinnati (N.L.), St. Louis (N.L.), Washington (A.L.)

3691. McCallum, J. "Curt Flood." *Sports Illustrated,* LXXXVI (January 27, 1997), 19–20.
3692. Mulgannon, Terry. "The Return of Curt Flood." *Sport,* LXXXIII (July 1992), 8+.

JACOB NELSON ("NELLIE") FOX*

Second Baseman
Philadelphia (A.L.), Chicago (A.L.), Houston (N.L.)
Coach

3693. Kuenster, John. "Nellie Fox, a Worthy New Member of the Baseball Hall of Fame." *Baseball Digest,* LVI (June 1997), 17–21.

JIMMIE FOXX*

First Baseman
Philadelphia (A.L.), Boston (A.L.), Chicago (N.L.), Philadelphia (N.L.)

3694. Harrison, Daniel W. *Jimmie Foxx: The Life and Times of a Baseball Hall of Famer.* Jefferson, N.C.: McFarland & Co., Inc., 1996. 246p.

3695. Kelly, Brent. "What If Jimmie Foxx Had Played for the Yankees?" *Baseball Digest,* LIV (April 1995), 58–59.
3696. No entry.
3697. Macht, Norman L. *Baseball Legends: Jimmie Foxx.* New York: Chelsea House, 1991. 64p.

JOHN FRANCO

Pitcher
Cincinnati (N.L.),
New York Mets (N.L.)

3698. Stewart, Mark. *John Franco.* New York: Children's Press, 1996. 48p.

RON FRASER

Coach
University of Miami (Fla.)
U.S. Olympic Baseball Team

3699. Wulf, Steve. "A Last Hurrah." *Sports Illustrated,* LXXVII (July 22, 1992), 150–152.

FRANK FRANCIS ("FRANKIE" or "THE FORDHAM FLASH") FRISCH*

Second Baseman, Third Baseman
New York Giants (N.L.),
St. Louis (N.L.)
Manager
St. Louis (N.L.), Pittsburgh (N.L.), Chicago (N.L.)

3700. Broeg, Bob. "Flashback: Frankie Frisch—He Played the Game with Gusto!" *Baseball Digest,* LII (June 1993), 65–70.

TRAVIS FRYMAN

Third Baseman
Detroit (A.L.)

3701. Sorci, Rick. "Player Profile: Third Baseman Travis Fryman of the

Tigers." *Baseball Digest,* LIII (October 1994), 47–48.

EDDIE GAEDEL

Pinch Hitter
St. Louis (A.L.)

3702. Wheatley, Tom. "This Was the Craziest At-Bat in Major League History." *Baseball Digest,* LIV (February 1995), 66–69.

3703. ____. "Wonder of Eddie Gaedel's Feat Gets Larger with the Years." *Baseball Digest,* LIV (December 1995), 76–80.

GARY GAETTI

Third Baseman
Minnesota (A.L.), California (A.L.),
Kansas City (A.L.), St. Louis (N.L.)

3704. Reusse, Patrick. "Gary Gaetti: The 'G-Man' Played Like a Kid for Cardinals in '96." *Baseball Digest,* LVI (March 1997), 72–73.

GREG GAGNE

Shortstop
Minnesota (A.L.), Kansas City (A.L.),
Los Angeles (N.L.)

3705. Capie, Jim. "Greg Gagne of the Twins: An Unheralded Shortstop." *Baseball Digest,* LI (July 1992), 70–72.

3706. Caroulis, Jon. "Greg Gagne: There's More to His Game Than Fielding." *Baseball Digest,* LV (August 1996), 64–68.

ANDRES GALARRAGA

First Baseman
Montreal (N.L.), St. Louis (N.L.),
Colorado (N.L.)

3707. Farber, Michael. "Cat Quick." *Sports Illustrated,* LXXXVI (June 2, 1997), 68–70, 72.

3708. Hoffer, Richard. "Strokes of Luck." *Sports Illustrated,* LXXVIII (June 28, 1993), 22–24+.

3709. Sorci, Rick. "Baseball Profile: Andres Galarraga." *Baseball Digest,* LIV (July 1995), 68–69.

PETER GAMMONS

Sportswriter

3710. "Mr. Know-It-All." In: Joe Hoppel, ed. *The Sporting News 1994 Baseball Yearbook.* St. Louis, Mo.: TSN, 1994. pp. 135–137.

RON GANT

Outfielder
Atlanta (N.L.), Cincinnati (N.L.),
St. Louis (N.L.)

3711. Bisher, Furman. "How Ron Gant Developed as a Key Producer for the Braves." *Baseball Digest,* LI (September 1992), 49–51.

3712. Creager, Reid. "'Yes, I Can!'" In: Gary Levy, ed. *The Sporting News 1992 Baseball Yearbook.* St. Louis, Mo.: TSN, 1992. pp. 26–29.

3713. Johnson, Paul M. "Hangtime [with] Ron Gant." *Sport,* LXXXVIII (July 1996), 16–20.

3714. Van Dyck, Dave. "Hard Work Paid Off for '95 'Comeback' Star Ron Gant." *Baseball Digest,* LIV (December 1995), 42–44.

3715. Verducci, Tom. "Mister Clutch." *Sports Illustrated,* LXXIX (September 27, 1993), 28–29.

NOMAR GARCIAPARRA

Shortstop
Boston (A.L.)

3716. Crothers, Tim. "Nomar, No Less." *Sports Illustrated,* LXXXVI (May 19, 1997), 92+.

3717. Daley, Ken. "Reaching the Show." *Beckett Future Stars and Sports Col-*

lectibles, no. 73 (May 1997), *passim.* <http://www.beckett.com/products/fspd.html>.

3718. Edes, Gordon. "Nomar Garciaparra Lived Up to His Advance Billing in '97." *Baseball Digest,* LVI (December 1997), 40–43.

3719. Garciaparra, Norman. "Questions and Answers." *Beckett Future Stars and Sports Collectibles,* no. 77 (September 1997), *passim.* <http://www.beckett.com/products/fspd.html>.

PHIL GARNER

Third Baseman
Oakland (A.L.), Pittsburgh (N.L.),
Houston (N.L.), Los Angeles (N.L.),
San Francisco (N.L.)
Manager
Milwaukee (A.L.)

3720. Baldassaro, Larry. "'I've Always Loved Playing This Game': Conversations with Phil Garner." *Elysian Fields Quarterly,* XIII (Winter 1994), 46–49.

3721. Korn, Peter. "'We'll Do It My Way!'" *Inside Sports,* XIV (July 1992), 62–67.

3722. Lamer, Perry M. "Tough Guys Don't Dance." *Milwaukee,* XVII (April 1992), 24–28.

AUGIE GARRIDO

Coach
Cal-State Fullerton

3723. Nolan, Timothy. "High and Inside with a Titan Named Augie." *Scholastic Coach & Athletic Director,* LXV (November 1995), 70–75.

STEVE GARVEY

First Baseman
Los Angeles (N.L.), San Diego (N.L.)

3724. Goodman, M. S. "A Swinger No More." *People Weekly,* XL (December 6, 1993), 99–102.

3725. Taylor, Keith. "A Final Look: Steve Garvey." *Beckett Baseball Card Monthly,* IX, no. 87 (June 1992), 126–127.

CITO GASTON

Outfielder
Atlanta (N.L.),
San Diego (N.L.),Pittsburgh
Manager
Toronto (A.L.)

3726. Frayne, Trent. "The Quiet Texan in the Jay's Dugout." *Maclean's,* CV (October 12, 1992), 79+.

3727. Leavy, Walter. "Cito Gaston on Top of the Baseball World." *Ebony,* XLIX (May 1994), 144+.

ELMER GEDEON

Outfielder
Washington (A.L.)

3728. Tekulsky, J. D. "Elmer Gedeon: A Major League War Hero." *National Pastime,* XIV (1994), 68–69. Died at St. Pol, France, on April 20, 1944.

LOU GEHRIG*

First Baseman
New York (A.L.)

3729. Adler, Gary A. *Lou Gehrig: The Luckiest Man.* San Diego, Calif.: Gulliver Books, 1997. Unpaged.

3730. Bak, Richard. *Lou Gehrig, American Classic.* Dallas, Tx.: Taylor, 1995. 192p.

3731. Bloom, Bob. "Straight from the Iron Horse's Mouth." *Sport,* LXXXVI (September 1995), 87–88+.

3732. Dolgan, Bob. "Iron Man Lou Gehrig Played in the Shadow of Babe Ruth." *Baseball Digest,* LIV (November 1995), 76–78.

3733. "Final Look: Lou Gehrig." *Beckett Baseball Card Monthly,* XI, no. 110 (May 1994), 105–106.

3734. Macht, Norman L. *Baseball Legends: Lou Gehrig.* New York: Chelsea House, 1993. 64p.

3735. Rambeck, Richard. *Lou Gehrig.* Plymouth, Minn.: Child's World, 1994. 31p.

3736. Topel, Brett. "Yankee Teammates Recall the Greatness of Lou Gehrig." *Baseball Digest,* LIV (July 1995), 28–29.

CHARLES LEONARD ("CHARLIE" or "MECHANICAL MAN") GEHRINGER*

Second Baseman
Detroit (A.L.)
Executive
Detroit (A.L.)

3737. Green, Jerry. "Charlie Gehringer: He Was a First-Class Second Baseman." *Baseball Digest,* LI (November 1992), 75–82.

BOB GIBSON*

Pitcher
St. Louis (N.L.)

3738. Gibson, Bob, with Lonnie Wheeler. *Stranger to the Game: The Autobiography of Bob Gibson.* New York: Viking, 1994. 280p.

3739. Rushin, Steve. "The Season of High Heat." *Sports Illustrated,* LXXIX (July 19, 1993), 30–37.

JOSH GIBSON*

Catcher
Pittsburgh Homestead Grays,
Pittsburgh Crawfords

3740. Holway, John B. *Baseball Legends: Josh Gibson.* New York: Chelsea House, 1995. 64p.

3741. ____. "Josh Gibson: The Heartbreak Kid." *Pennsylvania Heritage,* XX (Fall 1994), 18–25.

3742. Ribowsky, Marty. *The Power and the Darkness: The Life of Josh Gibson in the Shadows of the Game.* New York: Simon and Schuster, 1996. 319p. A brief excerpt appears in *Interview,* XXVI (April 1996), 64.

KIRK GIBSON

Outfielder
Detroit (A.L.), Los Angeles (N.L.),
Kansas City (A.L.), Pittsburgh (N.L.)

3743. Shook, Richard. "A Final Look: Kirk Gibson." *Beckett Baseball Card Monthly,* IX, no. 91 (October 1992), 126–127.

BENJI GIL

Shortstop
Texas (A.L.)

3744. Iverson, Kurt. "No Sweat." *Beckett Focus on Future Stars,* III, no. 27 (July 1993), 65–67.

DENNIS GILBERT

Agent

3745. Mulgannon, Tom. "The Player." *Sport,* LXXXV (January 1994), 66–69.

PAT GILLICK

Executive
Toronto (A.L.), Baltimore (A.L.)

3746. Feinstein, John. "The Comeback Kid." *Inside Sports,* XVIII (August 1996), 62–63.

3747. Frayne, Trent. "The Man Who Built the Blue Jays." *Maclean's,* CVII (March 7, 1994), 57+.

3748. Kurkijan, Tim. "He's Not Standing Pat." *Sports Illustrated,* LXXXIV (January 8, 1996), 50–52, 57.

TOM GLAVINE

Pitcher
Atlanta (N.L.)

3749. Cawthon, Read. "Braves' Tom Glavine Makes It Look Easy." *Baseball Digest,* LI (November 1992), 28–31.

3750. Glavine, Tom, with Nick Cafardo. *None But the Braves: A Pitcher, a Team, a Champion.* New York: Harper-Collins, 1996. 226p.

3751. Montville, Leigh. "A Gripping Tale." *Sports Illustrated,* LXXVII (July 13, 1992), 42–45.

3752. Rosenberg, I. J. "Braves' Gritty Tom Glavine Wins Without Much Fanfare." *Baseball Digest,* LV (February 1996), 28–31.

3753. Zinczenko, David. "Perfect Pitch." *Men's Health,* IX (September 1994), 84–85.

PRESTON GOMEZ

Shortstop
Washington (A.L.)
Manager
San Diego (N.L.), Houston (N.L.),
Chicago (N.L.)
Coach

3754. Holtzman, Jerome. "Preston Gomez: Twice He 'Lifted' a No-Hit Pitcher." *Baseball Digest,* LIII (December 1994), 74–75.

JUAN GONZALES

Outfielder
Texas (A.L.)

3755. Egan, Terry. "Juan Gonzales: The Rangers' Unheralded Power Hitter." *Baseball Digest,* LV (November 1996), 53–54.

3756. Gonzalez, Simon. "Juan Gonzalez Sets Sights on 500 Career Home Runs." *Baseball Digest,* LIII (August 1994), 50–52.

3757. Guttman, Bill. *Juan Gonzales, Outstanding Outfielder.* Brookfield, Conn.: Millbrook Press, 1995. 48p.

3758. Harvey, Miles. *Juan Gonzales: Home Run Hero.* New York: Children's Press, 1995. 48p.

3759. Iverson, Kurt. "A Closer Look: Juan Gonzales." *Beckett Baseball Card Monthly,* IX, no. 93 (December 1992), 6–7.

3760. Johnson, Chuck. "Juan Gonzalez: The Soaring Star of the Texas Rangers." *Baseball Digest,* LII (December 1993), 53–56.

3761. Johnson, Paul M. "Going Deep." *Sport,* LXXXIX (July 1997), 62–65.

3762. Rogers, Phil. "Lone Ranger." *Sport,* LXXXIV (May 1993), 61–63.

3763. "Superstar Gallery: Juan Gonzales." *Beckett Baseball Card Monthly,* X, no. 95 (February 1993), 17–18.

3764. Tuttle, Dennis R. *Juan Gonzales.* New York: Chelsea House, 1995. 64p.

3765. ____. "No Man Is an Island." *Inside Sports,* XVII (March 1995), 58–65.

3766. Verducci, Tom. "Puerto Rico's New Patron Saint." *Sports Illustrated,* LXXVIII (April 5, 1993), 60–64, 67.

3767. Veseley, Ron. "Smash Hit." *Sports Illustrated for Kids,* VI (April 1994), 36–43.

RENE GONZALEZ

First Baseman
Montreal (N.L.), Baltimore (A.L.),
Toronto (A.L.),
California (A.L.), Cleveland (A.L.),
Texas (A.L.)

3768. Kurkijan, Tim. "Texas Tornado." *Sports Illustrated,* LXXXV (August 12, 1996), 118+.

DWIGHT GOODEN

Pitcher
New York Mets (N.L.),
San Diego (N.L.), New York (A.L.)

3769. "Gooden Evil." *Sports Illustrated,* LXXXII (April 24, 1995), 13–14.

3770. Horowitz, C. "Undamned Yankee." *New York,* XXIX (August 12, 1996), 22–29.

3771. Kurkijan, Tim. "What's Up, Doc?"

Sports Illustrated, LXXXIV (April 22, 1996), 74+.

3772. Verducci, Tom. "From Phenom to Phantom." *Sports Illustrated,* LXXVIII (March 22, 1993), 34–37.

3773. _____. "The Hero Trap: Dwight Gooden's Suspension Is Further Evidence of the Folly of Worshipping Sports Stars." *Sports Illustrated,* LXXXI (July 11, 1994), 88+.

3774. _____. "A New High." *Sports Illustrated,* LXXXIV (May 27, 1996), 32–34, 39.

RICH ("GOOSE") GOSSAGE

Pitcher
Chicago (A.L.), Pittsburgh (N.L.),
New York (A.L.),
San Diego (N.L.), San Francisco (N.L.),
Texas (A.L.),
Oakland (A.L.), Seattle (A.L.),
Toronto (A.L.),
Los Angeles (N.L.)

3775. Verducci, Tom. "Making Hay." *Sports Illustrated,* LXXXI (September 12, 1994), 68–70+.

HARRY MORGAN ("HANK") GOWDY

Catcher
New York Giants (N.L.), Boston (N.L.)

3776. Farmer, T. "Hank Gowdy and the Call to Arms: Major League Baseball and World War I." *Nine: A Journal of Baseball History and Social Policy Perspective,* V (Spring 1997), 285–287.

MARK GRACE

First Baseman
Chicago (N.L.)

3777. Bickley, Dan. "First Baseman Mark Grace: A Star in the Shadows." *Baseball Digest,* LI (November 1992), 43–45.

3778. Castle, George. "Cubs' Mark Grace Talks About First Base Defense." *Baseball Digest,* LII (April 1993), 68–72.

3779. Kiley, Mike. "First Baseman Mark Grace: The Cubs' 'Mr. Consistency.'" *Baseball Digest,* LVI (June 1997), 42–45.

3780. Sorci, Rick. "Baseball Profile: First Baseman Mark Grace of the Cubs." *Baseball Digest,* LI (August 1992), 55–56.

3781. Wojciechowski, Gene. "Cub's Mark Grace: Chicago's 'Other' First Baseman." *Baseball Digest,* LV (June 1996), 32–34.

MIKE GRACE

Pitcher
Philadelphia (N.L.)

3782. Kurkijan, Tim. "Amazing Grace." *Sports Illustrated,* LXXXIV (May 27, 1996), 64+.

JEFF GRANGER

Pitcher
Kansas City (A.L.)

3783. Schwarz, Alan. "False Start." *Beckett Focus on Future Stars,* IV, no. 38 (June 1994), 12–13.

3784. Whiteside, K. "Sports People." *Sports Illustrated,* LXXVIII (May 10, 1993), 48–49.

PETE GRAY

Outfielder
St. Louis (A.L.)

3785. Kashatus, William. *One-Armed Wonder: Pete Gray, Wartime Baseball, and the American Dream.* Jefferson, N.C.: McFarland & Co., Inc., 1995. 161p. Excerpted in *American History Illustrated,* XXX (June 1995), 42–43.

3786. Steadman, John. "How Outfielder Pete Gray Met Challenge of Big

League Baseball." *Baseball Digest,* LV (July 1996), 74–77.

DICK GREEN

Shortstop
Kansas City (A.L.), Oakland (A.L.)

3787. McMurray, John. "Dick Green: An Unheralded Key to Champion A's of the Early 1970s." *Baseball Digest,* LVI (June 1997), 74–77.

SHAWN GREEN

Outfielder
Toronto (A.L.)

3788. Milton, Steve. "Rookie Report: Shawn Green." *Beckett Baseball Card Monthly,* XII, no. 121 (April 1995), 126–127.

TYLER GREEN

Pitcher
Philadelphia (N.L.)

3789. Zonca, Tony. "Knuckling Under." *Beckett Focus on Future Stars,* II, no. 15 (July 1992), 57–59.

HANK GREENBERG*

First Baseman, Outfielder
Detroit (A.L.), Pittsburgh (N.L.)
Executive
Cleveland (A.L.), Chicago (A.L.)

3790. Eisler, Kim Isaac. "'Such a Hitter!'" *The Washingtonian,* XXXII (September 1997), 76+.
3791. Gietschier, Steve. "Against the Odds." *Beckett Baseball Card Monthly,* XII, no. 118 (January 1995), 100–104.

WILLIE GREENE

Third Baseman
California (A.L.)

3792. Garlick, David. "Ready to Rebound." *Beckett Focus on Future Stars,* III, no. 29 (September 1993), 73–75.

TOM GRIEVE

Outfielder
Washington (A.L.), Texas (A.L.),
New York Mets (N.L.), St. Louis (N.L.)
Executive
Texas (A.L.)

3793. Schwartz, Alan. "Ben There. Done That." *Beckett Focus on Future Stars,* V, no. 51 (July 1995), 26–29. With son Ben, about whom most of the article is concerned, formed first father and son first round draft team.

KEN ("THE KID") GRIFFEY, JR.

Outfielder
Seattle (A.L.)

3794. *Beckett Tribute: Ken Griffey, Jr.* Dallas, Tx.: Beckett Publications, 1997. 64p.
3795. Beck, Robert. "Let Junior Do It." *Sports Illustrated for Kids,* VIII (April 1996), 34–41.
3796. Christopher, Matt. *At the Plate with Ken Griffey, Jr.* Boston, Mass.: Little, Brown, 1997. Unpaged.
3797. Daley, Ken. "Ken Griffey, Jr., Pays a Price for His Baseball Fame." *Baseball Digest,* LV (August 1996), 47–49.
3798. ____. "The Kid Who Could Be King." *Beckett Baseball Card Monthly,* VII, no. 149 (August 1997), *passim.* **<http://www.beckett.com/ products/bbpd.html>**.
3799. Dieffenbach, D. "One-on-One [with] Ken Griffey, Jr.: Interview." *Sport,* LXXXV (March 1994), 20+.
3800. Finnigan, Bob. "A Closer Look: Ken Griffey, Jr." *Beckett Baseball Card Monthly,* X, no. 95 (February 1993), 6–9.
3801. ____. "Focus on Ken Griffey, Jr."

Beckett Focus on Future Stars, II, no. 13 (May 1992), 14–16.

3802. ____. "The Job of Being 'Junior.'" *Beckett Baseball Card Monthly,* XII, no. 124 (July 1995), 6–12.

3803. Goddard, Joe. "Ken Griffey, Jr., Gradually Coming of Age as a Big League Star." *Baseball Digest,* LII (November 1993), 29–30.

3804. Graeff, Burt. "Ken Griffey, Jr.: Mariners' 'Leading Man' in the Big Show." *Baseball Digest,* LVI (August 1997), 26–29.

3805. Griffey, Ken, Jr. *Junior: Griffey on Griffey.* Edited by Mark Vancil. New York: HarperCollins, 1997.

3806. Gutman, Bill. *Ken Griffey, Jr. and Ken Griffey, Sr.: Father and Son Teammates.* Brookfield, Conn.: Millbrook Press, 1993. 48p.

3807. Joseph, Paul. *Ken Griffey, Jr.* Edina, Minn.: Abdo and Daughters, 1997. 30p.

3808. "Ken Griffey, Jr. " In: Louise Mooney Collins, ed. *Newsmakers, 1994: The People Behind Today's Headlines.* Detroit, Mich.: Gale Research, 1994. pp. 217–220.

3809. "The Kid." In: Joe Hoppel, ed. *The Sporting News 1993 Baseball Yearbook.* St. Louis, Mo.: TSN, 1993. pp. 10–13.

3810. Kramer, Barbara. *Ken Griffey, Jr.: All-Around All-Star.* Minneapolis, Minn.: Lerner Publications, 1996. 64p.

3811. Laskaris, Sam. "A Bright Future in Store for Mariners' Ken Griffey, Jr." *Baseball Digest,* LI (September 1992), 31–33.

3812. Lupica, Mike. "Roger and Him." *Esquire,* CXXII (September 1994), 96+.

3813. MacNow, Glen. *Ken Griffey, Jr., Star Outfielder.* Hillside, N.J.: Enslow Publications, 1997. 64p.

3814. Nicholson, Lois P. *Today's Stars: Ken Griffey, Jr.* Philadelphia, Pa.: Chelsea House, 1997. 64p.

3815. Press, Skip. *Ken Griffey, Jr. and Ken Griffey, Sr.* Parsippany, N.J.: Crestwood House, 1996. 48p.

3816. Reiser, Howard. *Ken Griffey, Jr.: The Kid.* Chicago, Ill.: Children's Press, 1994. 48p.

3817. Richmond, Peter. "The Supernatural." *GQ: Gentlemen's Quarterly,* LXVI (April 1996), 198–205.

3818. Rolfe, John. *Ken Griffey, Jr.* New York: Bantam Books, 1995. 110p.

3819. Rothaus, James R. *Ken Griffey, Jr.* Mankato, Minn.: Child's World, 1991. 31p.

3820. Sandground, Grant. "Junior Achievement." *Beckett Baseball Card Monthly,* XII, no. 124 (July 1995), 13–17.

3821. Shipnuck, Alan. "Junior Comes of Age." *Sports Illustrated,* LXXXI (August 8, 1994), 24–30.

3822. Smith, Vern E. and Mark Starr. "Junior's League." *Newsweek,* CXXX (September 29, 1997), 60–61.

3823. Stewart, Wayne. "'Mr. Griffey! Mr. Griffey!'" *Beckett Baseball Card Monthly,* X, no. 97 (April 1993), 10–12.

3824. "Superstar Gallery: Ken Griffey, Jr." *Beckett Baseball Card Monthly,* X, no. 105 (December 1993), 17–19.

3825. Verducci, Tom. "Hitting His Prime." *Sports Illustrated,* LXXXVI (May 12, 1997), 86–88, 90.

MARQUIS GRISSOM

Outfielder
Montreal (N.L.), Atlanta (N.L.),
Cleveland (A.L.)

3826. Montville, Leigh. "We Are Fa Base Stealer, Grew Up with 14 Siblings. Now He's a Big Part of Another Happy Clan, the Fast-Improving Expos." *Sports Illustrated,* LXXVII (September 28, 1992), 38–41.

3827. Sorci, Rick. "Baseball Profile: Outfielder Marquis Grissom." *Baseball Digest,* LII (December 1993), 51–52.

ROBERT ("LEFTY") GROVE*

Pitcher
Philadelphia (A.L.), Boston (A.L.)

3828. Meyers, Francis J. "Wild Dreams and Harsh Realities: Lefty Grove and the Life of Organized Baseball in Allegheny County, 1900–1924." *Maryland Historical Magazine,* LXXXVII (Summer 1992), 147–157.

BILL GULLICKSON

Pitcher
Montreal (N.L.), Chicago (N.L.),
New York (A.L.),
Yomiuri Giants (Japan League),
Houston (N.L.),
Detroit (A.L.)

3829. Dye, Dave. "Stint in Japan Revitalized Bill Gullickson's Career." *Baseball Digest,* LI (October 1992), 60–61.

OZZIE GUILLEN

Shortstop
Chicago (A.L.)

3830. Sullivan, Paul. "Ozzie Guillen Still Retains His Defensive Edge at Short." *Baseball Digest,* LV (July 1996), 44–46.

CLIFF GUSTAFSON

Coach
University of Texas at Austin

3831. Kurkijan, Tim. "Cliff Gustafson." *Sports Illustrated,* LXXX (May 2, 1994), 65+. College ball's winningest coach.

JUAN GUZMAN

Pitcher
Toronto (A.L.)

3832. DeMarco, Tony. "Flying High." *Beckett Focus on Future Stars,* II, no. 19 (November 1992), 10–13.
3833. Kurkijan, Tim. "The Accidental Blue Jay." *Sports Illustrated,* LXXVI (May 25, 1992), 72+.

3834. Kennedy, T. "Juan Guzman." In: David Bauer, ed. *SI Presents Baseball 1997.* New York: Sports Illustrated, 1997. pp. 114–117.

TONY GWYNN

Outfielder
San Diego (N.L.)

3835. Bloom, Barry. "One-on-One [with] Tony Gwynn: Interview." *Sport,* LXXXV (September 1994), 26–27.
3836. Doyle, Al. "Tony Gwynn Continues to Build Strong Hall of Fame Credentials." *Baseball Digest,* LVI (August 1997), 58–61.
3837. Geschke, Jim. "Closer Look: Tony Gwynn." *Beckett Baseball Card Monthly,* XI, no. 122 (May 1995), 6–9.
3838. Gwynn, Tony, as told to George Vass. "'The Game I'll Never Forget.'" *Baseball Digest,* LII (August 1993), 43–45.
3839. Hoffer, Richard. "Fear of Failure." *Sports Illustrated,* LXXXIII (September 18, 1995), 66–70, 73–74.
3840. Hood, Robert E. "Tony Gwynn: Practice Makes Perfect." *Boy's Life,* LXXXII (September 1992), 26–28.
3841. Krasovic, Tom. "Ted Williams' Batting Tips Absorbed by Tony Gwynn." *Baseball Digest,* LIV (August 1995), 38–40.
3842. Kuenster, John. "With Five Batting Titles, Tony Gwynn Moves Up Among Elite Hitters." *Baseball Digest,* LIV (February 1995), 17–19.
3843. Leavy, Walter. "Is Tony Gwynn the Greatest Hitter in Baseball History?" *Ebony,* LII (August 1997), 132+.
3844. Lieber, Jill. "Tony Gwynn: He's Always Honing His Baseball Skills." *Baseball Digest,* LV (August 1996), 42–46.
3845. Lupica, Mike. "The Unnatural." *Esquire,* CXXIV (August 1995), 40+.
3846. Ryan, Jeff. "Partners at the Plate." *Inside Sports,* XVI (June 1994), 10–11. Tony and wife Alicia.
3847. Silverman, Jay. "Mr. Contact."

California, XVI (September 1991), 66+.

3848. Verducci, Tom. "Bat Man." *Sports Illustrated,* LXXXVII (July 28, 1997), 40–47.

3849. Williams, Pete. "Deeper Look: Tony Gwynn." *Beckett Baseball Card Monthly,* XI, no. 108 (March 1994), 112–113.

HOWIE HAAK

Scout

3850. Bird, Tom. "Howie Haak: Veteran Scout Looks Back on Long Career." *Baseball Digest,* LIII (February 1994), 62–66.

HARVEY ("THE KITTEN") HADDIX

Pitcher
St. Louis (N.L.), Philadelphia (N.L.), Cincinnati (N.L.), Pittsburgh (N.L.), Baltimore (A.L.)

3851. Modeno, Bill. "Legacy of 'The Kitten.'" *Pittsburgh,* XXV (April 1994), 30+.

DICK HALL

Pitcher
Pittsburgh (N.L.), Kansas City (A.L.), Baltimore (A.L.), Philadelphia (N.L.)

3852. Patterson, Ted. "Whatever Became of … Former Oriole Reliever Dick Hall?" *Baseball Digest,* LII (December 1993), 90–92.

BARRY HALPER

Baseball Memorabilia Collector

3853. Lidz, Franz. "The Sultan of Swap." *Sports Illustrated,* LXXXII (May 22, 1995), 66–70, 72, 74–77.

BOB ("HAMMER") HAMELIN

First Baseman
Kansas City (A.L.)

3854. Rand, Jonathan. "Bob Hamelin: He Provides New Longball Power for the Royals." *Baseball Digest,* LIII (November 1994), 69–70.

JOEY HAMILTON

Pitcher
San Diego (N.L.)

3855. Geschke, Jim. "Rookie Report: Joey Hamilton." *Beckett Baseball Card Monthly,* XII, no. 118 (January 1995), 126–127.

JEFFREY HAMMONDS

Outfielder
Baltimore (A.L.)

3856. Topkin, Marc. "Oriole on the Fly." *Beckett's Focus on Future Stars,* III, no. 26 (June 1993), 65–67.

3857. Williams, Pete. "Closer Look: Jeffrey Hammonds." *Beckett Baseball Card Monthly,* XI, no. 111 (June 1994), 10–13.

BILL HANDS

Pitcher
San Francisco (N.L.), Chicago (N.L.), Minnesota (A.L.), Texas (A.L.)

3858. Hands, Bill, as told to Tom Capezzuto. "'The Game I'll Never Forget.'" *Baseball Digest,* LIV (July 1995), 57–59.

ERIK HANSON

Pitcher
Seattle (A.L.), Cincinnati (N.L.), Boston (A.L.), Toronto (A.L.)

3859. McGee, Todd. "Erik Hanson Turns a New Page as Starter for the Reds." *Baseball Digest,* LIII (May 1994), 52–53.

MELVIN LEROY ("MEL" or "CHIEF" or "WIMPY") HARDER

Pitcher
Cleveland (A.L.)
Coach

3860. Harder, Mel, as told to John L. Fox. "The Day I Pitched the Opening Game in Cleveland Municipal Stadium." *Baseball Digest,* LII (September 1993), 80–82.

PETE HARNISH

Pitcher
Baltimore (A.L.), Houston (N.L.),
New York Mets (N.L.),
Milwaukee (A.L.)

3861. Anderson, Kellie. "Courageous Comeback." *Sports Illustrated,* LXXXVII (August 18, 1997), 78–79.

DERRELL ("BUD") HARRELSON

Shortstop
New York Mets (N.L.),
Philadelphia (N.L.),
Texas (A.L.)
Manager
New York Mets (N.L.)
Executive
Peninsula Pilots

3862. Comte, Liz. "He Likes the Game So Much, He Bought a Team." *Inside Sports,* XV (January 1993), 8, 10.

JOHN HART

Executive
Cleveland (A.L.)

3863. Farber, Michael. "The Big Picture." *Sports Illustrated,* LXXXVI (April 7, 1997), 82–84+.

BRYAN HARVEY

Pitcher
California (A.L.), Florida (A.L.)

3864. Rubin, Bob. "Marlins' Bryan Harvey Baffles Hitters with His Forkball." *Baseball Digest,* LII (October 1993), 30–32.

DOUG HARVEY

Umpire
National League

3865. Holtzman, Jerome. "Doug Harvey: An Old Umpiring Soldier Fades Away." *Baseball Digest,* LI (October 1992), 65–67.
3866. Olney, Buster. "Umpire Doug Harvey Reviews Highlights of 31-Year Career." *Baseball Digest,* LII (April 1993), 74–76.

ERNIE HARWELL

Broadcaster

3867. Branon, Dave and Lee Pellegrino. "Ernie Harwell." In: their *Safe at Home.* Chicago, Ill.: Moody Press, 1992. pp. 277–290.
3868. Charlotte, Susan, *et al.*, eds. "Ernie Harwell." In: their *Creative Conversations with 28 Who Excel.* Troy, Mich.: Momentum Books, 1993. pp. 145–157.
3869. Harwell, Ernie. *The Babe Signed My Shoe: Baseball As It Was and Will Always Be—Tales of the Grand Old Game.* Edited by Geoff Upward. South Bend, Ind.: Diamond Communications, 1994. 226p.

HARRY HEILMANN*

Outfielder, First Baseman
Detroit (A.L.), Cincinnati (N.L.)
Broadcaster

3870. Selko, J. "Harry Who?" *National Pastime,* XV (1995), 45–50.

RICK HELLING

Pitcher
Texas (A.L.), Florida (N.L.)

3871. Rogers, Phil. "Cardinal Rule." *Beckett Focus on Future Stars,* IV, no. 36 (April 1994), 16–17. Written while

Helling a hurler in the Cardinal's farm system.

RICKY HENDERSON

Outfielder
Oakland (A.L.), New York (A.L.),
San Diego (N.L.),
Toronto (A.L.), Houston (N.L.),
Anaheim (A.L.)

3872. "Blue Jays Acquire Rickey Henderson for Stretch Drive." *Jet,* LXXXIV (August 23, 1993), 46+.
3873. Bruning, F. "Rickey the Insufferable: Snagging Henderson Will Make Toronto More Hated Than Ever." *Maclean's,* CVI (April 16, 1993), 45+.
3874. Henderson, Ricky, as told to George Vass. "'The Game I'll Never Forget.'" *Baseball Digest,* LI (October 1992), 49–51.
3875. ____. with John Shea. *Off Base: Confessions of a Thief.* New York: HarperCollins, 1992. 210p.
3876. Kroichick, Ron. "Stealing Time." *Sport,* LXXXIV (May 1993), 46–50.
3877. Leavy, Walter. "The Game's Most Exciting Player." *Ebony,* XLVII (June 1992), 108–110.

PAT HENTGEN

Pitcher
Toronto (A.L.)

3878. Doyle, Al. "How Blue Jays' Pat Hentgen Rebounded to Win Cy Young Award." *Baseball Digest,* LVI (March 1997), 66–71.

WILLIE ("BILLY") HERMAN*

Second Baseman, Third Baseman
Chicago (N.L.), Brooklyn (N.L.),
Boston (N.L.), Pittsburgh (N.L.)
Manager
Pittsburgh (N.L.), California (A.L.)

3879. Holtzman, Jerome. "Farewell to Billy Herman: A Classic Second Base-man." *Baseball Digest,* LI (December 1992), 81–86.

KEITH HERNANDEZ

First Baseman
St. Louis (N.L.), New York Mets (N.L.),
Cleveland (A.L.)

3880. Hernandez, Keith, with Mike Bryan. *Pure Baseball.* New York: HarperCollins, 1994. 259p.
3881. Smith, C. S. "The Afterlife." *New York,* XXVII (April 4, 1994), 56–57.
3882. Stein, Harry. "The Extra Innings of Keith Hernandez." *Men's Health,* VIII (June 1993), 68–71.

LIVAN HERNANDEZ

Pitcher
Florida (N.L.)

3883. Price, S. L. "Delivering a Strong Pitch." *Sports Illustrated,* LXXXIV (March 25, 1996), 72–74, 79.

OREL HERSHISER

Pitcher
Los Angeles (N.L.), Cleveland (A.L.)

3884. Branon, Dave and Lee Pellegrino. "Orel Hershiser." In: their *Safe at Home.* Chicago, Ill.: Moody Press, 1992. pp. 298–299.
3885. Callahan, Gerry. "Mind Over Muscle." *Sports Illustrated,* LXXXIII (October 16, 1995), 28+.
3886. Hershiser, Orel, as told to George Vass. "'The Game I'll Never Forget.'" *Baseball Digest,* LIV (February 1995), 41–42.
3887. Holtzman, Jerome. "Orel Hershiser Expounds on His Pitching Theories." *Baseball Digest,* LIV (September 1995), 49–50.
3888. Hoynes, Paul. "Orel Hershiser Beats Foes with His Patented Sinker." *Baseball Digest,* LV (December 1996), 48–49.

DORREL ("WHITEY") HERZOG

Outfielder, First Baseman
Washington (A.L.), Kansas City (A.L.),
Baltimore (A.L.), Detroit (A.L.)
Manager
Texas (A.L.), California (A.L.),
Kansas City (A.L.), St. Louis (A.L.)
Executive
St. Louis (N.L.), California (A.L.)

3889. Cairns, Bob. "Here Are Whitey
Herzog's Views on Bullpen Strategy."
Baseball Digest, LI (July 1992),
46–50.
3890. Cunningham, Dave. "No More
Mickey Mouse: Angels Anoint 'Rat'
as Big Cheese in Bid to End Medioc-
rity." In: Gary Levy, ed. *The Sporting
News 1992 Baseball Yearbook.* St.
Louis, Mo.: TSN, 1992. pp. 22–24.

JOE HEYDLER

Umpire
National League
Executive
President, National League

3891. Harwell, Ernie. "Idea for DH Rule
Originated with (Gasp!) N.L. President." *Baseball Digest,* LII (December 1993), 74–75.

PHIL HIATT

Third Baseman
Kansas City (A.L.), Detroit (A.L.)

3892. Eskew, Alan. "Unexpected Divi-
dend." *Beckett Focus on Future Stars,*
III, no. 28 (August 1993), 65–66.

JOHN HIRSCHBECK

Umpire
American League

3893. Rosen, Marjorie. "In a League of
Their Own." *Good Housekeeping,*
CCXXV (September 1997), 86–89,

152. Hirschbeck, his wife Denise, and
his ill child. *See also* Roberto Alomar.

**DONALD ALBERT ("DON" or
"TIGER") HOAK**

Third Baseman
Brooklyn (N.L.), Chicago (N.L.),
Cincinnati (N.L.), Pittsburgh (N.L.),
Philadelphia (N.L.)

3894. Santamarina, E. J. "The Hoak
Hoax." *National Pastime,* XIV (1994),
29–30.

CLELL L. ("BUTCH") HOBSON

Third Baseman
Boston (A.L.), California (A.L.),
New York (A.L.)
Manager
Boston (A.L.)

3895. Pierce, Charles P. "Hobson's
Choice." *Boston,* LXXXIV (April
1993), 40+.

GIL HODGES*

First Baseman
Brooklyn (N.L.), Los Angeles (N.L.),
New York Mets (N.L.)
Manager
Washington (A.L.),
New York Mets (N.L.)

3896. Harris, Randy. "Gil Hodges Still
Remembered by His Indiana Home
Town." *Baseball Digest,* LIV (Febru-
ary 1995), 70–74.

RICH HOFMAN

Coach
Westminster Christian High School

3897. Nolan, Timothy. "Person-to-Per-
son: Once in a Baseball Coach's Lifetime." *Scholastic Coach & Athletic
Director,* XLVI (February 1997),
46–53.

TREVOR HOFFMAN

Pitcher
Florida (N.L.), San Diego (N.L.)

3898. Kurkijan, Tim. "A Blessed Padre." *Sports Illustrated,* LXXXIV (June 10, 1996), 89–90.

DAVE HOLLINS

Third Baseman
Philadelphia (N.L.), Boston (A.L.), Minnesota (A.L.), Seattle (A.L.), Anaheim (A.L.)

3899. Hagen, Paul. "Second Look: Dave Hollins." *Beckett Baseball Card Monthly,* X, no. 103 (September 1993), 105–107.

3900. O'Shei, Tim. "Phils' Dave Hollins: He Should Be Called 'Mr. Intensity.'" *Baseball Digest,* LIII (May 1994), 42–44.

HARRY HOOPER*

Outfielder
Boston (A.L.), Chicago (A.L.)

3901. Zingg, Paul J. *Harry Hooper: An American Baseball Life.* Sport and Society Series. Urbana, Ill.: University of Illinois Press, 1993. 281p.

ROGERS ("THE RAJAH") HORNSBY*

Second Baseman, Shortstop, Third Baseman
St. Louis (N.L.), Boston (N.L.), New York Giants (N.L.), Chicago (N.L.), St. Louis (A.L.)
Manager
St. Louis (N.L.), Boston (N.L.), Chicago (N.L.), St. Louis (A.L.), Cincinnati (N.L.)

3902. Alexander, Charles C. *Rogers Hornsby: A Biography.* New York: Henry Holt, 1995. 366p.

3903. Ward, Geoffrey C. and Ken Burns. "Rogers Hornsby." *U.S. News & World Report,* CXVII (August 29, 1994), 77+.

KATIE HORSTMAN

Pitcher
Fort Wayne Daisies

3904. "A League of Her Own: Interview." *Scholastic Coach,* LXII (November 1992), 84–87.

TONY HORTON

First Baseman
Boston (A.L.), Cleveland (A.L.)

3905. Madden, Bill. "Tragic Saga of Tony Horton Still Clouded in Mystery." *Baseball Digest,* LVI (November 1997), 72–75.

CHARLIE HOUGH

Pitcher
Los Angeles (N.L.), Texas (A.L.), Chicago (A.L.), Florida (N.L.)

3906. Kurkijan, Tim. "Florida's Aflutter." *Sports Illustrated,* LXXVIII (April 12, 1993), 32–34+. First pitcher to win a game for the expansion team.

FRANK HOWARD

Outfielder, First Baseman
Los Angeles (N.L.), Washington (A.L.), Detroit (A.L.)
Manager
San Diego (N.L.), New York Mets (N.L.)

3907. Nathans, Aaron. "A Final Look: Frank Howard." *Beckett Baseball Card Monthly,* IX, no. 93 (December 1992), 126–127.

ARTHUR ("ART") HOWE, JR.

Third Baseman, Second Baseman, First Baseman

Pittsburgh (N.L.), Houston (N.L.),
St. Louis (N.L.)
Manager
Houston (N.L.), Oakland (A.L.)

3908. Sorci, Rick. "Baseball Profile: Manager Art Howe of the Astros." *Baseball Digest,* LII (July 1993), 57–58.

STEVE HOWE

Pitcher
Los Angeles (N.L.), Minnesota (A.L.), Texas (A.L.), San Diego (N.L.), New York (A.L.)

3909. Kirshenbaum, Jerry. "Mercy Me." *Sports Illustrated,* LXXVII (November 23, 1992), 13+.

WAITE HOYT*

Pitcher
New York Giants (N.L.), Boston (A.L.), New York (A.L.), Pittsburgh (N.L.), Brooklyn (N.Y.)
Broadcaster

3910. Knight, T. "Remembering Waite Hoyt, Signed by McGraw at 15." *National Pastime,* XV (1995), 100–101.

ROBERT CAL HUBBARD*

Umpire
American League

3911. Reed, William F. "Early Master." *Sports Illustrated,* LXXXI (September 5, 1994), 64–65.

CARL OWEN ("KING CARL" or "MEAL TICKET") HUBBELL*

Pitcher
New York Giants (N.L.)

3912. Curran, W. "Dodgers End Hubbell's Record [Sixteen Game Winning] Streak [of 1936]." *National Pastime,* XIV (1994), 61–65.

JOHN HUDEK

Pitcher
Houston (N.L.)

3913. Molony, Jim. "Rookie Report: John Hudek." *Beckett Baseball Card Monthly,* XI, no. 116 (November 1994), 126–127.

REX HUDLER

Second Baseman
New York (A.L.), Baltimore (A.L.), Montreal (N.L.),
St. Louis (N.L.), California (A.L.)

3914. Kindred, Dave. "'For Me, Baseball Is a Joy.'" In: Joe Hoppel, ed. *The Sporting News 1996 Baseball Yearbook.* St. Louis, Mo.: TSN, 1996. pp. 8–9.

WAYNE HUIZENGA

Executive
Florida (N.L.)

3915. Anderson, D. M. and M. Warshaw. "The No. 1 Entrepreneur in America." *Success,* XLII (March 1995), 32–43.
3916. DeGeorge, Gail. *The Making of a Blockbuster: How Wayne Huizenga Built a Sports and Entertainment Empire from Trash, Grit, and Videotape.* New York: John Wiley, 1996. 354p.
3917. Jordan, Pat. "Wayne Huizenga." *The New York Times Magazine,* (December 5, 1993), 54–57.
3918. Nocera, Joseph. "Wayne's World." *GQ: Gentlemen's Quarterly,* LXII (June 1992), 60, 63–64.

TODD HUNDLEY

Catcher
New York Mets (N.L.)

3919. Center, Bill. "Opposing Pitchers Fear Todd Hundley Without the

Mask." *Baseball Digest,* LVI (August 1997), 74–79.

3920. Harper, John. "The Future Is Now." *Beckett Focus on Future Stars,* II, no. 13 (May 1992), 6–8.

3921. Hill, Thomas. "Mets Receiver Todd Hundley Finally Hits His Stride." *Baseball Digest,* LV (September 1996), 20–21.

3922. "Roy Campanella's Widow Gives Mets Catcher Her Blessing." *Jet,* XC (September 16, 1996), 49–50.

MARK HUTTON

Pitcher
New York (A.L.), Florida (N.L.)

3923. McDonald, J. "Biting the Big Apple: Mark Hutton Off to Work in a Pinstripe Suit." *Baseball Australia,* V (November 1992), 4–5.

3924. Sexton, M. "The Big Pitcher: Mark Hutton." *Inside Sports (Australia),* XXVIII (April 1994), 84–90, 93.

ROBERT ("HAM") HYATT

Outfielder, First Baseman
Pittsburgh (N.L.), St. Louis (N.L.), New York (A.L.)

3925. Hannon, J. T. "Ham Hyatt and the Development of Pinch-Hitting: An Early—But Long-Term—Record-Holder." *Baseball Research Journal,* XXIV (1995), 146–149.

MIKE ILLITCH

Executive
Detroit (A.L.)

3926. Oneal, Michael. "Pizza Pizza and Tigers, Too." *Business Week,* (September 14, 1992), 108–109.

HIDEKI IRABU

Pitcher
Chiba Lotte Marines (Japan);
New York (A.L.)

3927. Neuman, A. Lin. "Shooting Star: Hideki Irabu Only Lasted 18 Days in the U.S. Major Leagues." *Far Eastern Economic Review,* CLX (August 21, 1997), 52–54.

3928. Verducci, Tom. "Magnetic!" *Sports Illustrated,* LXXXVII (July 21, 1997), 34–37.

3929. Wulf, Steve. "Plenty More After Nomo." *Time,* CXLIX (March 24, 1997), 84+.

MONFORD ("MONTE") IRVIN*

Outfielder, First Baseman
Newark Eagles,
New York Giants (N.L.),
Chicago (N.L.)
Executive
Commissioner's Office

3930. Irvin, Monte, with James A. Riley. *Monte Irvin: Nice Guys Finish First.* New York: Carroll and Graf, 1996. 252p.

JAMIE IRVING

Pitcher
Harvard

3931. Montville, Leigh. "Jamie Irving." *Sports Illustrated,* LXXVIII (May 17, 1993), 63+. Ambidextrous college hurler.

JASON ISRINGHAUSEN

Pitcher
New York Mets (N.L.)

3932. Guss, Greg. "Izzy, the Next Seaver?" *Sport,* LXXXVII (June 1996), 20–21.

BO JACKSON

Outfielder
Kansas City (A.L.), Chicago (A.L.), California (A.L.)

3933. "Bo Jackson Beats Odds, Returns to Chicago White Sox After Hip Surgery." *Jet,* LXXXIII (April 19, 1993), 48–49+.

3934. "Bo Jackson Quits Baseball; Says 'Family Looks Better Than $10 Million Contract.'" *Jet,* LXXXVII (April 24, 1995), 46–47.

3935. Howe, R. "Above the Fray." *People Weekly,* XLV (January 15, 1996), 59–60.

3936. DeMarco, Tony. "Deeper Look: Bo Jackson." *Beckett Baseball Card Monthly,* X, no. 99 (June 1993), 126–129.

3937. Etkin, Jack, Joe Hoppel, and Steve Zesch, eds. *Bo Stories.* St. Louis, Mo.: The Sporting News, 1990. 176p.

3938. Hoffer, Richard. "What Bo Knows Now." *Sports Illustrated,* LXXXIII (October 30, 1995), 52–56+.

3939. Holland, Dave. "Bo Jackson's Comeback Complete with Dramatic Home Run to Help White Sox Clinch Division Title." *Jet,* LXXXIV (October 18, 1993), 52–55.

3940. Kramer, Jon. *Bo Jackson.* Austin, Tx.: Raintree Stech-Vaughan, 1996. 48.

3941. Kurkijan, Tim. "Can Bo Go?" *Sports Illustrated,* LXXVIII (March 1, 1993), 12–18.

3942. Verducci, Tom. "Hip, Hip Hooray." *Sports Illustrated,* LXXVIII (April 19, 1993), 22–24+. Homers in first game back with artificial hip.

3943. Weaver, M. "Bo Knows Family, Pain, and Glory." *Ebony,* XLVIII (August 1993), 72–74+.

3944. Wulf, Steve. "It Hurts Just to Watch Him." *Sports Illustrated,* LXXVI (March 16, 1992), 80+.

3945. ____. "'Say It Ain't So, Bo!'" *Sports Illustrated,* LXXIV (April 1, 1991), 34–37.

JOE ("SHOELESS JOE") JACKSON

Outfielder
Philadelphia (A.L.), Cleveland (A.L.),
Chicago (A.L.)

3946. Camp, Emily. "Final Look: Joe Jackson." *Beckett Baseball Card Monthly,* XII, no. 118 (January 1995), 105–106.

3947. Dalleo, Peter T. and Vincent Watchorn, 3rd. "Slugger or Slacker?: Shoeless Joe Jackson and Baseball in Wilmington, 1918." *Delaware History,* XXVI (Fall-Winter 1994–1995), 95–123.

3948. Frommer, Harvey. *Shoeless Joe and Ragtime Baseball.* Dallas, Tx.: Taylor, 1992. 255p.

3949. Gropman, Donald. *Say It Ain't So, Joe: The True Story of Shoeless Joe Jackson.* Rev. ed. New York: Citadel Press, 1992. 256p.

3950. Kavanagh, Jack. *Early Legends: Shoeless Joe Jackson.* New York: Chelsea House, 1995. 64p.

3951. Ward, Geoffrey C. and Ken Burns. "Shoeless Joe Jackson." *U.S. News & World Report,* CXVII (August 29, 1994), 71+.

REGGIE JACKSON*

Outfielder
Kansas City (A.L.), Oakland (A.L.),
Baltimore (A.L.),
New York (A.L.), California (A.L.)
Executive
New York

3952. Angeli, Michael. "The Gall of Fame." *Sports Illustrated,* LXXIX (August 2, 1993), 58–64, 66, 69.

3953. Angell, Roger. "Swingtime." *The New Yorker,* LXIX (August 2, 1993), 40–41.

3954. Bussard, Camron E. "Reggie Jackson." *Cycle World,* XXIX (January 1990), 44+.

3955. Hirsch, A. "Mr. October?: Not." *Baseball Research Journal,* XXIV (1995), 142–143.

3956. Holtzman, Jerome. "Reggie Jackson Produced Best When in the Spotlight." *Baseball Digest,* LII (April 1993), 79–82.

3957. Lupica, Mike. "'I, Reggie, Take

Thee, George...." *Esquire,* CXIX (June 1993), 69–71.

3958. Macht, Norman L. *Modern Day Legends: Reggie Jackson.* New York: Chelsea House, 1994. 64p.

3959. "Mr. October Goes to Cooperstown." In: Gregg Mazzola, ed. *Yankees 1993 Yearbook.* New York: *Yankees Magazine,* 1993. pp. 82–86.

3960. Wulf, Steve. "In the Hall, He'll Need a Wall." *Sports Illustrated,* LXXVIII (January 18, 1993), 68+.

JOHN JAHA

First Baseman
Milwaukee (A.L.)

3961. Bianchine, Jim. "John Jaha: A Throwback to Brewer Sluggers of the Past." *Baseball Digest,* LVI (February 1997), 62–67.

3962. Haudricourt, Tom. "He Speaks Softly, and Carries a Big Stick." *Beckett Focus on Future Stars,* III, no. 27 (July 1993), 8–9.

GREG JEFFERIES

First Baseman, Outfielder
New York Mets (N.L.),
Kansas City (A.L.),
St. Louis (N.L.), Philadelphia (N.L.)

3963. Garrity, John. "Sweet Swinger." *Sports Illustrated,* LXXXI (July 18, 1994), 50–53.

3964. Murray, Jim. "Gregg Jefferies: As a Hitter, He's a Clone of Pete Rose." *Baseball Digest,* LII (December 1993), 40–43.

3965. Sorci, Rick. "Baseball Profile: Greg Jefferies." *Baseball Digest,* LIII (November 1994), 61+.

FERGUSON JENKINS*

Pitcher
Philadelphia (N.L.), Chicago (N.L.),
Texas (A.L.), Boston (A.L.)

3966. Threatt, Jana. "Deeper Look: Ferguson Jenkins." *Beckett Baseball Card Monthly,* X, no. 95 (February 1993), 110–111.

DEREK JETER

Shortstop
New York (A.L.)

3967. Curry, J. "My Shortstop Is Better Than Yours." *The New York Times Magazine,* (August 11, 1996), 38–39.

3968. Kaplan, Jim. "Local Hero." *Sports Illustrated,* LXXXVI (April 7, 1997), 24–31.

3969. King, George. "Derek Jeter: His Pursuit of Excellence Continues." *Baseball Digest,* LVI (November 1997), 46–47.

3970. Schwarz, Alan. "Short-Stops." *Beckett Focus on Future Stars,* V, no. 46 (February 1995), 68–71.

3971. Webb, V. "Derek Jeter: Interview." *Interview,* XXVII (June 1997), 88–89.

3972. Winston, Lisa. "Rookie Report: Derek Jeter." *Beckett Baseball Card Monthly,* XII, no. 119 (February 1995), 126–127.

BYRON BANCROFT ("BAN") JOHNSON*

Sportswriter, Executive
President, Western League
President, American League

3973. "American Originals: Byron Bancroft Johnson." *Ohio,* XVIII (August 1995), 13–14.

CHARLES JOHNSON

Catcher
Florida (N.L.)

3974. Giuliotti, Ed. "A Fine Catch." *Beckett Focus on Future Stars,* II, no. 14 (June 1992), 12–13.

3975. Johnson, Paul M. "A Fine Catch." *Sport,* LXXXVIII (July 1996), 82–83.

3976. Niedzielka, Amy. "Rookie Report: Charles Johnson." *Beckett Baseball Card Monthly,* XII, no. 123 (June 1995), 126–127.
3977. Verducci, Tom. "Somebody's Perfect." *Sports Illustrated,* LXXXVII (September 22, 1997), 52–55.

DAVEY JOHNSON

Second Baseman
Baltimore (A.L.), Atlanta (N.L.)
Philadelphia (N.L.), Chicago (N.L.)
Coach
Florida State University
Manager
New York (A.L.), Kansas City (A.L.),
New York Mets (N.L.), Cincinnati (N.L.),
Baltimore (A.L.)

3978. Madden, Bill. "Manager for Hire." *Sport,* LXXXIV (June 1993), 63–65.
3979. Reed, William F. "Seeing Red in Cincinnati." *Sports Illustrated,* LXXVIII (June 7, 1993), 63–65.
3980. Verducci, Tom. "Who's the Boss?" *Sports Illustrated,* LXXXIII (September 18, 1995), 46–48+.

HOWARD ("HOJO") JOHNSON

Third Baseman, Shortstop
Detroit (A.L.), New York Mets (N.L.),
Colorado (N.L.), Chicago (N.L.)

3981. Branon, Dave and Lee Pellegrino. "Howard Johnson." In: their *Safe at Home.* Chicago, Ill.: Moody Press, 1992. pp. 139–149.
3982. Johnson, Howard, as told to George Vass. "'The Game I'll Never Forget.'" *Baseball Digest,* LII (September 1993), 73–75.
3983. Klapisch, Bob. "Silent Superstar." *Topps Magazine,* (Summer 1992), 26–29.

LANCE JOHNSON

Outfielder

St. Louis (N.L.), Chicago (A.L.),
New York Mets (N.L.)

3984. Beaton, Rod. "Mets' Lance Johnson: He's a True 'Triple Threat' Talent." *Baseball Digest,* LV (August 1996), 50–51.
3985. Hill, Thomas. "For Lance Johnson, It's Been a Long, Hard Climb to Success." *Baseball Digest,* LVI (January 1997), 40–42.
3986. Kuenster, John. "How About a Little More Recognition for Players Like Lance Johnson." *Baseball Digest,* LIII (July 1994), 15–17.

RANDY JOHNSON

Pitcher
Seattle (A.L.)

3987. DeMarco, Tony. "Closer Look: Randy Johnson." *Beckett Baseball Card Monthly,* XI, no. 110 (May 1994), 10–13.
3988. "The Next Nolan?" In: Joe Hoppel, ed. *The Sporting News 1994 Baseball Yearbook.* St. Louis, Mo.: TSN, 1994. pp. 26–31.
3989. Pickard, Chuck. "Randy Johnson Posted Best Strikeouts Over Walks Rating in '93." *Baseball Digest,* LIII (April 1994), 64–67.
3990. "Randy Johnson." In: Louise M. Collins and Frank V. Castronova, eds. *Newsmakers, 1996: The People Behind Today's Headlines.* Detroit, Mich.: Gale Research, 1997. pp. 259–262.
3991. Shaughnessy, Dan. "Randy Johnson: The Most Feared Man in Baseball." *Baseball Digest,* LVI (October 1997), 52–53.
3992. Stewart, Mark. *Randy Johnson.* Chicago, Ill.: Childrens Press, 1997. 32p.
3993. Street, Jim. "Randy Johnson Ages Well as the A.L.'s Most Dominant Pitcher." *Baseball Digest,* LV (June 1996), 46–49.
3994. Verducci, Tom. "An Armful."

Sports Illustrated, LXXXVII (July 7, 1997), 52–57.

3995. ____. "The Intimidator." *Sports Illustrated,* LXXXII (June 26, 1995), 58–62.

3996. Tuthill, Bill. "Randy Johnson Sets Sights on Even Better Season in '94." *Baseball Digest,* LIII (February 1994), 26–29.

3997. Weinberg, Rick. "The King of K." *Sport,* LXXXV (June 1994), 42–44+.

WALTER ("BIG TRAIN") JOHNSON*

Pitcher
Washington (A.L.)
Manager
Washington (A.L.), Cleveland (A.L.)

3998. Fortunato, F. "Walter Johnson's Debut." *Nine: A Journal of Baseball History and Social Policy Perspective,* IV (Fall 1995), 84–93.

3999. Kavanagh, Jack. *Early Legends: Walter Johnson.* New York: Chelsea House, 1992. 64p.

4000. ____. *Walter Johnson: A Life.* South Bend, Ind.: Diamond Communications, 1995. 300p.

4001. Thomas, Henry W. "Big Train." *Washingtonian,* XXX (April 1995), 41–46.

WILLIAM ("JUDY") JOHNSON*

Third Baseman
Bacharach's Philadelphia All-Stars,
Hilldales,
Pittsburgh Homestead Grays,
Darby Daisies, Pittsburgh Crawfords

4002. Rendle, Ellen. *Judy Johnson: Delaware's Invisible Hero.* Wilmington, Del.: Cedar Tree Press, 1994. 82p.

ANDREW JONES

Outfielder
Atlanta (N.L.)

4003. Gordon, Dan. "Hot Shot: Andrew Jones." *Sport,* LXXXIX (May 1997), 72+.

4004. Kurkijan, Tim. "Brave Moves." *Sports Illustrated,* LXXXV (August 26, 1996), 120+.

CHARLIE JONES

Broadcaster

4005. Rubin, Bob. "Still Waiting in Line for Stardom." *Inside Sports,* XVI (May 1994), 18, 20–21. Colorado Rockies announcer.

LARRY ("CHIPPER") JONES

Third Baseman
Atlanta (N.L.)

4006. Ballew, Bill. "Chipper Jones Emerges as a Clutch Hitter for the Braves." *Baseball Digest,* LVI (November 1997), 22–25.

4007. Bamberger, Michael. "Riding High." *Sports Illustrated,* LXXXV (September 16, 1996), 60–63, 66.

4008. Beaton, Rod. "Braves' Chipper Jones: He Was Born to Play Baseball." *Baseball Digest,* LVI (March 1997), 54–56.

4009. "Bravo for Chipper." In: Joe Hoppel, ed. *The Sporting News 1996 Baseball Yearbook.* St. Louis, Mo.: TSN, 1996. pp. 38–41.

4010. Flanagan, Jeffrey. "Chipper Jones Makes the Braves Feel Chipper About the Future." *Baseball Digest,* LIV (September 1995), 45–48.

4011. Hayes, Matt. "Chipping Away at Stardom." *Beckett Focus on Future Stars,* II, no. 20 (December 1992), 10–13.

4012. Holtzman, Jerome. "Braves Have a 'Blue Chip' Player in Chipper Jones." *Baseball Digest,* LV (March 1996), 54–55.

4013. Hudson, Don. "The Fall Guy." *Sport,* LXXXVII (April 1996), 62, 64.

4014. Kurkijan, Tim. "Pressure-Treated."

Sports Illustrated, LXXXIII (October 16, 1995), 26–27.

4015. "Mr. Hustle." *Sports Illustrated for Kids,* IX (June 1997), 36+.

4016. "Prime Time Talent: Chipper Jones." *Beckett Focus on Future Stars,* V, no. 52 (August 1995), 40–41.

4017. Schwartz, Alan. "The People's Choice." *Inside Sports,* XIX (July 1997), 62+.

BRIAN JORDAN

Outfielder
St. Louis (N.L.)

4018. Crothers, Tim. "One and Only." *Sports Illustrated,* LXXXIV (January 22, 1996), 52–55.

4019. Gordon, Dan. "Hot Shot: Brian Jordan." *Sport,* LXXXIX (May 1997), 83+.

4020. Wheatley, Tom. "Prime Time Talent." *Beckett Focus on Future Stars,* II, no. 14 (June 1992), 16–17.

MICHAEL JORDAN

Outfielder
Birmingham Barons

4021. Bickley, Dan. "See Ya, Mike." *Beckett Baseball Card Monthly,* XII, no. 123 (June 1995), 116–117.

4022. Bukowski, Douglas. "The Myth Plays Double-A." *Elysian Fields Quarterly,* XIII (Winter 1994), 6–7, 22.

4023. "A Closer Look: Michael Jordan." *Beckett Baseball Card Monthly,* XI, no. 109 (April 1994), 10–13.

4024. Crepeau, Richard C. "An Evening with Michael in the Minors." *Elysian Fields Quarterly,* XIII (Winter 1994), 2–6.

4025. Grant, Rubin. "A Minor Sensation." *Beckett Focus on Future Stars,* IV, no. 39 (July 1994), 16–19.

4026. Greene, Bob. "The Road Home." *People Weekly,* XLIV (October 9, 1995), 89–90+.

4037. "Jordan Earns $850 Per Month in Minors, But $31 Million in Endorsements." *Jet,* LXXXV (April 25, 1994), 46+.

4028. Kurkijan, Tim. "Reading the Signs." *Sports Illustrated,* LXXX (February 28, 1994), 64–65.

4029. Mathur, L. K., I. Mathur, and N. Rangan. "The Wealth Effects Associated with a Celebrity Endorser: The Michael Jordan Phenomenon." *Journal of Advertising Research,* XXXVII (May–June 1997), 67–73.

4030. "Michael in the Minors." *Ebony,* XLIX (July 1994), 108–110+.

4031. "Minor Memories of Michael." *Beckett Focus on Future Stars,* V, no. 49 (May 1995), 14–15.

4032. Patton, Jim. *Rookie: When Michael Jordan Came to the Minor Leagues.* Reading, Mass.: Addison-Wesley, 1995. 220p.

4033. Rushin, Steve. "A Lot of Hot Air?" *Sports Illustrated,* LXXX (January 17, 1994), 32–35.

4034. Waddell, Ray. "Jordan Gives AA Teams Lesson in Crowd Management." *Amusement Business,* CVI (May 9, 1994), 1–2.

4035. Wall, J. M. "Not Afraid to Fail." *Christian Century,* CXI (February 23, 1994), 187–188.

4036. Wulf, Steve. "Err Jordan." *Sports Illustrated,* LXXX (March 14, 1994), 20–23.

FELIX JOSE

Outfielder
Oakland (A.L.), St. Louis (N.L), Kansas City (A.L.)

4037. Wheatley, Tom. "A Second Look: Felix Jose." *Beckett Baseball Card Monthly,* IX, no. 91 (October 1992), 105–106.

JEFF JUDEN

Pitcher
Montreal (N.L.), Cleveland (A.L.)

4038. Crothers, Tim. "Rockin' and Firin'." *Sports Illustrated,* LXXXVII (July 14, 1997), 57–58.

DAVID JUSTICE

Outfielder
Atlanta (N.L.), Cleveland (A.L.)

4039. Ballew, Bill. "David Justice: One Brave Who Swings a 'Sweet' Club." *Baseball Digest,* LIII (February 1994), 30–32.
4040. Bradley, John Ed. "Justice Prevails." *Sports Illustrated,* LXXX (June 6, 1994), 66–70+.
4041. Carothers, Tim. "Man in the Middle." *Sports Illustrated,* LXXXVI (June 2, 1997), 76, 78.
4042. Coppola, Vincent. "Beauty and the Brave." *Redbook,* CLXXXIII (July 1994), 46+. Justice helps Halle Berry to trust again.
4043. "David Justice's Homer Powers Atlanta to World Series Win Over Cleveland." *Jet,* LXXXIX (November 13, 1995), 54–55.
4044. Grossi, Tony. "Indians' David Justice: He's a Man on a Mission." *Baseball Digest,* LVI (September 1997), 72–75.
4045. Howerton, Darryl. "Hangtime [with] David Justice." *Sport,* LXXXVII (June 1996), 22–26.
4046. Kurkjian, Tim. "Justice Prevails." *Sports Illustrated,* LXXXIII (November 6, 1995), 32+.
4047. "Love Strikes Out." *People Weekly,* XLV (March 11, 1996), 46–47. Personal life.
4048. Rosenberg, I. J. "Closer Look: David Justice." *Beckett Baseball Card Monthly,* XI, no. 106 (January 1994), 6–9.
4049. ____. "One-on-One [with] David Justice: Interview." *Sport,* LXXXV (June 1994), 26+.
4050. Schneider, K. S. "Hurts So Bad." *People Weekly,* XLV (May 13, 1996), 102–106+. Personal life.

BILLY JURGES

Shortstop
Chicago (N.L.),
New York Giants (N.L.),
Chicago (N.L.), Boston (A.L.)

4051. Grosshandler, Stanley. "Billy Jurges Recalls How It Was in Majors in 1930s." *Baseball Digest,* LI (October 1992), 68–72.

ROGER KAHN

Sportswriter

4052. Kahn, Roger. *Memories of Summer: When Baseball Was an Art and Writing About It a Game.* New York: Hyperion, 1997. 290p.
4053. Little, C. "PW Interviews Roger Kahn." *Publisher's Weekly,* CCXL (October 4, 1993), 49–50.
4054. Peale, Cliff. "When Boys Become Men: Roger Kahn and *The Boys of Summer* 20 Years Later." *Elysian Fields Quarterly,* XI (Winter 1992), 97–102.

AL KALINE*

Outfielder
Detroit (A.L.)
Broadcaster

4055. "Final Look: Al Kaline." *Beckett Baseball Card Monthly,* XI, no. 116 (November 1994), 105–106.

ERIC KARROS

First Baseman
Los Angeles (N.L.)

4056. Dilbeck, Steve. "The Longshot." *Sport,* LXXXIV (April 1993), 66–68.
4057. Langill, Mark. "Focus on Eric Karros." *Beckett Focus on Future Stars,* III, no. 23 (March 1993), 12–14.
4058. ____. "Prime Time Talent." *Beckett Focus on Future Stars,* II, no. 7 (July 1992), 20–21.

4059. Rocca, Lawrence. "Eric Karros of the Dodgers Follows One Simple Creed: Win." *Baseball Digest,* LIV (December 1995), 52–53.

STEVE KARSAY

Pitcher
Oakland (A.L.)

4060. Rausch, Gary. "City Slicker." *Beckett Focus on Future Stars,* IV, no. 37 (May 1994), 18–19.

4061. Winston, Lisa. "Rookie Report: Steve Karsay." *Beckett Baseball Card Monthly,* XI, no. 113 (August 1994), 126–127.

EWING MARION KAUFFMAN

Executive
Kansas City

4062. Morgan, Anne Hodges. *Prescription for Success: The Life and Values of Ewing Marion Kauffman.* Kansas City, Mo.: Andrews & McMeel, 1995. 415p. The Royals founder died in 1993.

LES KEITER

Broadcaster

4063. Keiter, Les, with Dennis Christianson. *50 Years Behind the Microphone: The Les Keiter Story.* Honolulu: University of Hawaii Press, 1991.

GEORGE CLYDE KELL*

Third Baseman
Philadelphia (A.L.), Detroit (A.L.),
Boston (A.L.),
Chicago (A.L.), Baltimore (A.L.)
Broadcaster

4064. Schneider, Russell. "George Kell: From Rejected Prospect to Hall of Famer." *Baseball Digest,* LIII (August 1994), 63–66.

MICHAEL JOSEPH ("KING") KELLY*

Outfielder, Catcher, Third Baseman,
Second Baseman, First Baseman,
Pitcher
Cincinnati (N.L.), Chicago (N.L.),
Boston (N.L.), Boston (P.),
Cincinnati-Milwaukee (A.A.),
Boston (A.A.),
Boston (N.L.), New York (N.L.)
Manager
Boston (P.), Cincinnati-Milwaukee (A.A.)

4065. Appel, Marty. *Slide, Kelly, Slide: The Wild Life and Times of Mike "King" Kelly, Baseball's First Superstar.* Lanham, Md.: Scarecrow Press, 1996. 211p.

4066. Tully, Mike. "The King of Diamonds." *New Jersey Monthly,* XIX (November 1994), 108+.

ROBERTO KELLY

Outfielder
New York (A.L.), Cincinnati (N.L.),
Atlanta (N.L.),
Montreal (N.L.), Los Angeles (N.L.),
Minnesota (A.L.)

4067. Capezzuto, Tom. "Roberto Kelly on the Road to Stardom with the Yankees." *Baseball Digest,* LI (September 1992), 34–37.

TOM KELLY

Manager
Minnesota (A.L.)

4068. Rushin, Steve. "Stress Management." *Sports Illustrated,* LXXVII (August 3, 1992), 70–74.

DON KESSINGER

Shortstop
Chicago (N.L.), St. Louis (N.L.),
Chicago (A.L.)
Manager
Chicago (A.L.)

4069. Macht, Norman L. "Don Kessinger Looks Back on His Big League Career." *Baseball Digest,* LVI (November 1997), 78–81.

JIMMY KEY

Pitcher
Toronto (A.L.), New York (A.L.), Baltimore (A.L.)

4070. Capezzuto, Tom. "Left-Hander Jimmy Key: Why Yankee Stadium Gives Him an Edge." *Baseball Digest,* LIII (October 1994), 20–23.

MICHAEL BROOKS KIESCHNICK

Outfielder
Chicago (N.L.)

4071. Bohls, Kirk. "Two-Way Terror." *Beckett's Focus on Future Stars,* III, no. 26 (June 1993), 16–17.
4072. Schwarz, Alan. "Bold Move." *Beckett Focus on Future Stars,* IV, no. 42 (October 1994), 76–79.

DARRYL KILE

Pitcher
Houston (N.L.)

4073. Eisenbath. Mike. "How Darryl Kile Matured Into a Winner for Astros." *Baseball Digest,* LVI (November 1997), 52–53.

HARMON KILLEBREW*

First Baseman, Third Baseman, Outfielder
Washington (A.L.), Minnesota (A.L.), Kansas City (A.L.)

4074. "Final Look: Harmon Killebrew." *Beckett Baseball Card Monthly,* XI, no. 115 (October 1994), 105–106.

STEPHEN KING

Author

4075. King, Stephen. "Diamonds Are Forever." *Life,* XVII (May 1994), 26+. Memories of Little League baseball.

W. P. KINSELLA

Sportswriter

4076. Levin, B. "Tales from Left Field." *Maclean's,* CVI (July 12, 1993), 60–61.

SACHIO KINUGASA

Catcher
Hiroshima Carp (Japan)
Broadcaster

4077. Ikei, Masara. "The Man Ripken's Still Chasing." *Inside Sports,* XVII (December 1995), 12–13. Had a 2,215 consecutive game playing streak at the time of his 1987 retirement.

CHUCK KLEIN*

Outfielder
Philadelphia (N.L.), Chicago (N.L.), Pittsburgh (N.L.)

4078. Nelson, D. "Nobody Did It Better: Chuck Klein's Fabulous Five-Year Run." *National Pastime,* XV (1995), 118–119.

RYAN KLESKO

Outfielder
Atlanta (N.L.)

4079. Black, Bob. "Focus on Ryan Klesko." *Beckett Focus on Future Stars,* III, no. 22 (February 1993), 14–17.
4080. ____. "Rookie Report: Ryan Klesko." *Beckett Baseball Card Monthly,* XI, no. 108 (March 1994), 126–127.

4081. Callahan, Gerry. "Sultan of SWAT." *Sports Illustrated,* LXXXIV (April 8, 1996), 66–68, 73–74.

4082. Rosenberg, I. J. "Closer Look: Ryan Klesko." *Beckett Baseball Card Monthly,* XI, no. 115 (October 1994), 8–11.

4083. Winston, Lisa. "Prime Time Talent." *Beckett Focus on Future Stars,* IV, no. 42 (October 1994), 18–20.

RAY KNIGHT

Third Baseman
Cincinnati (N.L.), Houston (N.L.),
New York Mets (N.L.)
Baltimore (A.L.), Detroit (A.L.)
Manager
Cincinnati (N.L.)

4084. Knight, Ray, as told to George Vass. "'The Game I'll Never Forget.'" *Baseball Digest,* LV (March 1996), 71–73.

CHUCK KNOBLAUCH

Second Baseman
Minnesota (A.L.)

4085. Baufeke, Ann. "Chuck Knoblauch." *Minneapolis,* XXII (April 1994), 45+.

4086. Holler, John. "Biography of Mr. Chuck." In: Tony Gervino, ed. *Hardball.* New York: Harris Pub. Co., 1997. pp. 66–69.

4087. Kurkijan, Tim. "Prime Chuck." *Sports Illustrated,* LXXXV (August 5, 1996), 127–129.

4088. Lowe, John. "Chuck Knoblauch: He Strives for Constant Improvement." *Baseball Digest,* LV (November 1996), 58–61.

4089. Miller, Cary S. "Closer Look: Chuck Knoblauch." *Beckett Baseball Card Monthly,* X, no. 94 (January 1993), 6–7.

4090. Souhan, Jim. "Why Chuck Knoblauch Ranks Among Top Second Basemen." *Baseball Digest,* LV (July 1996), 50–53.

MARK ANTHONY KOENIG

Shortstop, Second Baseman,
Third Baseman
New York (A.L.), Detroit (A.L.),
Chicago (N.L.), Cincinnati (N.L.)

4091. Bisher, Furman. "Mark Koenig: He Played in the Shadows of Famed 'Murders' Row.'" *Baseball Digest,* LII (September 1993), 83–86.

SANDY KOUFAX*

Pitcher
Brooklyn (N.L.), Los Angeles (N.L.)

4092. Grabowski, John F. *Baseball Legends: Sandy Koufax.* New York: Chelsea House, 1992. 64p.

4093. Olsen, Jack. "The Very Best Act in Town." *Sports Illustrated,* LXXX (April 25, 1994), 38–40+. Reprinted from the July 29, 1963 issue.

4094. Rothe, Emil. "Boxscore to Remember: When Sandy Koufax Notched Perfect Game vs. Cubs." *Baseball Digest,* LV (March 1996), 67–68.

4095. Sanford, William R. and Carl R. Green. *Sandy Koufax.* New York: Crestwood House, 1993. 48p.

ED KRANEPOOL

First Baseman, Outfielder
New York Mets (N.L.)

4096. Kranepool, Ed, as told to George Vass. "'The Game I'll Never Forget.'" *Baseball Digest,* LII (April 1993), 83–86.

RAY KROC

Executive
San Diego (N.L.)

4097. Love, John F. *McDonald's: Behind the Arches.* Rev. ed. New York: Bantam Books, 1995. 486p.

JOHN KRUK

First Baseman
San Diego (N.L.), Philadelphia (N.L.), Chicago (A.L.)

4098. "Cardboard Kruk." In: Joe Hoppel, ed. *The Sporting News 1993 Baseball Yearbook.* St. Louis, Mo.: TSN, 1993. pp. 14–17.

4099. Hagen, Paul. "A Closer Look: John Kruk." *Beckett Baseball Card Monthly,* IX, no. 90 (September 1992), 6–7.

4100. ____. "A Deeper Look: John Kruk." *Beckett Baseball Card Monthly,* XI, no. 113 (August 1994), 118–120.

4101. Kruk, John, with Paul Hagen. *"I Ain't an Athlete Lady!": My Well-Rounded Life and Times.* New York: Simon and Schuster, 1994. 255p.

4102. Kuenster, John. "Major League Baseball Needs More Characters Like Phils' John Kruk." *Baseball Digest,* LII (October 1993), 15–17.

4103. Lidz, Franz. "What's a Kruk?" *Sports Illustrated,* LXXVI (May 25, 1992), 30–32, 37.

4104. Platt, Larry. "Sixteen Reasons Why We Love John Kruk." *Philadelphia,* LXXXIII (May 1992), 75+.

4105. Sorci, Rick. "Baseball Profile: First Baseman John Kruk." *Baseball Digest,* LII (May 1993), 49–50.

4106. "Superstar Gallery: John Kruk." *Beckett Baseball Card Monthly,* X, no. 102 (September 1993), 14–17.

GEORGE ("WHITEY") KUROWSKI

Third Baseman
St. Louis (N.L.)

4107. Mayer, Bob. "Whitey Kurowski Excelled Despite a Shortened Arm." *Baseball Digest,* LIV (June 1995), 69–72.

JIM LANDIS

Outfielder
Chicago (A.L.), Kansas City (A.L.),
Cleveland (A.L.), Detroit (A.L.), Boston (A.L.)

4108. Fagen, Herb. "Jim Landis: He Played Center Field in Classic Style." *Baseball Digest,* LIII (July 1994), 76–80.

KENESAW MOUNTAIN LANDIS*

Executive
Commissioner of Baseball

4109. Fimrite, Ron. "His Own Biggest Fan." *Sports Illustrated,* LXXIX (July 19, 1993), 76–80.

4110. Pretruza, David. *Judge & Jury: The Life and Times of Judge Kenesaw Mountain Landis.* Southbend, Ind.: Diamond Communications, 1997.

RAY LANKFORD

Outfielder
St. Louis (N.L.)

4111. Hummel, Rick. "Ray Lankford: A Vital Key to the Cardinals' Hopes in '96." *Baseball Digest,* LV (June 1996), 44–47.

DON LARSEN

Pitcher
St. Louis (A.L.), Baltimore (A.L.),
New York (A.L.),
Kansas City (A.L.), Chicago (A.L.),
San Francisco (N.L.),
Houston (N.L.), Chicago (N.L.)

4112. Alvarez, Mark. *The Perfect Game.* Dallas, Tx.: Taylor Pub., 1993.

4113. Larsen, Don, with Mark Slow. *The Perfect Yankee: The Incredible Story of the Greatest Miracle in Baseball History.* Champaign, Ill.: Sagamore Pub. Co., 1996. 250p.

TONY LA RUSSA

Second Baseman, Shortstop
Kansas City (A.L.), Oakland (A.L.),

Atlanta (N.L.), Chicago (N.L.)
Manager
Chicago (A.L.), Oakland (A.L.),
St. Louis (N.L.)

4114. Bailey-Kelly, Barbara. "An 'A' for Effort." *California,* XVI (May 1991), 50+.

4115. Fraley, Gerry. "Inside Interview: Tony La Russa." *Inside Sports,* XVIII (August 1996), 22–29.

4116. Rogers, Phil. "Deeper Look: Tony La Russa." *Beckett Baseball Card Monthly,* X, no. 102 (September 1993), 122–125.

4117. Verducci, Tom. "Brave New World." *Sports Illustrated,* LXXXV (July 15, 1996), 66–68, 73.

BARRY LARKIN

Shortstop
Cincinnati (N.L.)

4118. Fraley, Gerry. "Barry Larkin of the Reds: Is He the Majors' New No. 1 Shortstop?" *Baseball Digest,* LIV (October 1995), 29–31.

4119. Madden, Bill. "Safe at Home." *Sport,* LXXXVIII (July 1996), 76–78.

GENE LARKIN

Outfielder
Minnesota (A.L.)

4120. McMurray, John. "Former Twin Gene Larkin: He Was a Big Hit in '91 World Series." *Baseball Digest,* LVI (May 1997), 65–69.

TOMMY LASORDA*

Pitcher
Brooklyn (N.L.), Kansas City (A.L.)
Manager
Los Angeles (N.L.)

4121. Elderkin, Phil. "Tom Lasorda Still Running the Show for the Dodgers." *Baseball Digest,* LV (February 1996), 64–69.

4122. Langill, Mark. "Deeper Look: Tommy Lasorda." *Beckett Baseball Card Monthly,* X, no. 98 (May 1993), 110–117.

4123. Lupica, Mike. "The Skinny on Tommy Lasorda." *Esquire,* CXVII (May 1992), 57–58.

4124. O'Brien, Pat. "Lean Times in Dodger Blue." *Inside Sports,* XV (August 1993), 8–9.

4125. Singer, Tom. "The *Sport* Q&A: Tom Lasorda." *Sport,* LXXXV (June 1994), 60–65.

4126. "True Blue: Lasorda Hangs 'Em Up." *Sports Illustrated,* LXXXV (August 5, 1996), 18, 20.

VERNON LAW

Pitcher
Pittsburgh (N.L.)

4127. Van Blair, Rick. "Vernon Law: Forgotten Hero of the 1960 World Series." *Baseball Digest,* LIV (October 1995), 26–28.

BRETT LAXTON

Pitcher
Louisiana State University

4128. Kim, A. "Brett Laxton." *Sports Illustrated,* LXXVIII (June 21, 1993), 52+. Victor Over Wichita State in 1993 College World Series.

BILL ("SPACEMAN") LEE

Pitcher
Boston (A.L.), Montreal (N.L.)

4129. Collins, J. "Still Spaceman After All These Years." *Yankee,* LVII (August 1993), 76–83+.

4130. Gross, J. "Bill Lee Finds Serenity in the Good Life." In: William Humber and John St. James, eds. *All I Thought About Was Baseball: Writings on a Canadian Pastime.* North York, Ont.: University of Toronto Press, 1996. pp. 137–139.

4131. Lingo, Will. "Bill Lee." *Beckett Focus on Future Stars,* V, no. 47 (March 1995), 74–75.

4132. Lott, J. "Still Pitching from a Different Mound: The Spaceman Bill Lee at 47." *Dugout,* III (April–May 1995), 11–14.

CHARLIE LIEBRANDT

Pitcher
Cincinnati (N.L.), Kansas City (A.L.), Atlanta (A.L.)

4133. Moll, Randall. "Charlie Liebrant Remembers *That* Home Run." *Baseball Digest,* LI (June 1992), 56–57.

DAVE LEIPER

Pitcher
Oakland (A.L.), San Diego (N.L.), Montreal (N.L.)

4134. Kurkijan, Tim. "Dave Leiper." *Sports Illustrated,* LXXX (June 27, 1994), 69+.

WALTER FENNER ("BUCK") LEONARD*

First Baseman
Baltimore Stars,
Pittsburgh Homestead Grays,
Torreon (Mex.), Durango (Mex.)

4135. Leonard, W. F. "Buck," with James A. Riley. *Buck Leonard, the Black Lou Gehrig.* New York: Carroll and Graf, 1995. 273p.

ALEXANDER H. P. LEUF

Physician

4136. Teigen, P. M. "Sore Arms and Selective Memories: Alexander H. P. Leuf and the Beginning of Baseball Medicine." *Journal of the History of Medicine and Allied Sciences,* L (July 1995), 391–408.

RUBE LEVY

Executive

4137. Franks, Joel S. "Rube Levy: A San Francisco Shoe Cutter and the Origins of Professional Baseball in California." *California History,* LXX (Summer 1991), 714+. Also published in *Western States Jewish History,* XXV (October 1992/January 1993), 35–51, 141–150.

JOHN KELLY ("BUDDY") LEWIS

Third Baseman
Washington (A.L.)

4138. Van Blair, Rick. "Buddy Lewis: Opposing Pitchers Couldn't Stop Him, but a War Did." *Baseball Digest,* LIII (July 1994), 56–60.

JIM LEYLAND

Manager
Pittsburgh (N.L.), Florida (N.L.)

4139. Gmelch, G. "Jim Leyland, Manager, Pittsburgh Pirates." *Nine: A Journal of Baseball History and Social Policy Perspective,* V (Fall 1996), 176–184.

4140. Lupica, Mike. "Season in the Sun." *Esquire,* CXXVII (June 1997), 36+.

4141. Pierce, Charles S. "The Last Pittsburgh Innocent." *GQ: Gentlemen's Quarterly,* LXVI (May 1996), 61–62+.

4142. Rushin, Steve. "Glad to Be in the Game." *Sports Illustrated,* LXXVIII (January 25, 1993), 42–46.

4143. Starr, Mark. "Touching All the Bases." *Newsweek,* CXXIX (March 10, 1997), 77+.

JIM LEYRITZ

Catcher
New York (A.L.), Anaheim (A.L.)

4144. Montville, Leigh. "Stepping to the Fore." *Sports Illustrated,* LXXXVI (May 5, 1997), 38–40.

PAT LISTACH

Second Baseman, Shortstop
Milwaukee (A.L.), New York (A.L.)

4145. Perrotto, John. "Second Look: Pat Listach." *Beckett Baseball Card Monthly,* X, no. 94 (January 1993), 97–98.

KENNY LOFTON

Outfielder
Houston (N.L.), Cleveland (A.L.),
Atlanta (N.L.)

4146. Castle, George. "One-on-One [with] Kenny Lofton: Interview." *Sport,* LXXXVI (August 1995), 12+.
4147. "Catch Me If You Can." *Sports Illustrated for Kids,* VIII (June 1996), 36–43.
4148. Chastain, Bill. "Indians' Kenny Lofton Has Earned the Respect of His Foes." *Baseball Digest,* LIII (December 1994), 52–54.
4149. Di Simone, Bonnie. "Indians' Kenny Lofton: He Was Born to Lead Off." *Baseball Digest,* LVI (May 1997), 34–37.
4150. Graham, Tim. "Closer Look: Kenny Lofton." *Beckett Baseball Card Monthly,* XI, no. 108 (March 1994), 8–12.
4151. Hackler, Tracy. "Life in the Fast Lane." *Beckett's Baseball Card Monthly,* no. 148 (July 1997), *passim.* **<http:// www.beckett.com/products/bbpd. html>.**
4152. Howerton, Darryl. "Wheels of Fortune." *Sport,* LXXXVIII (August 1997), 80–83.
4153. "The New Man of Steal." In: Joe Hoppel, ed. *The Sporting News 1995 Baseball Yearbook.* St. Louis, Mo.: TSN, 1995. pp. 46–49.
4154. Perrotto, John. "Rookie Report: Kenny Lofton." *Beckett Baseball Card Monthly,* X, no. 95 (February 1993), 112–113.
4155. Pluto, Terry. "Kenny Lofton: His Talents Brighten the Indians' Future." *Baseball Digest,* LIV (April 1995), 24–25.
4156. Silver, Michael. "Close to the Heart." *Sports Illustrated,* LXXXII (May 1, 1995), 96–98, 100–101.
4157. Williams, Pete. "Closer Look: Kenny Lofton." *Beckett Baseball Card Monthly,* XII, no. 123 (June 1995), 6–9.

JACK WAYNE ("LUCKY") LOHRKE

Third Baseman, Second Baseman
New York Giants (N.L.),
Philadelphia (N.L.)

4158. Fimrite, Ron. "O Lucky Man: A Twist of Fate Saved Jack Lohrke from the Worst Tragedy in Minor League History." *Sports Illustrated,* LXXXI (November 14, 1994), 194, 196, 198–199.

MICHAEL ("MICKEY") LOLICH

Pitcher
Detroit (A.L.), New York Mets (N.L.),
San Diego (N.L.)

4159. Forman, Ross. "Mickey Lolich: He Was a Dependable Starter." *Baseball Digest,* LIII (February 1994), 52–55.

JIM ("GENTLEMAN JIM") LONBORG

Pitcher
Boston (A.L.), Milwaukee (A.L.),
Philadephia (N.L.)

4160. Lonborg, Rosemary. *The Quiet Hero: A Baseball Story.* Brookline, Mass.: Branden Books, 1993. Unpaged.

GEORGE LONG

Manager
Muscatine Red Sox

4161. "Manager of the Ages." *Sports Illustrated,* LXXXV (July 1, 1996), 13–14.

ALFONSO RAYMOND ("AL") LOPEZ*

Catcher
Brooklyn (N.L.), Boston (N.L.), Pittsburgh (N.L.), Cleveland (A.L.)
Manager
Cleveland (A.L.), Chicago (A.L.)

4162. Singletary, Wes. "The Early Baseball Career of Al Lopez." *Tampa Bay History,* XVI (Spring-Summer 1994), 5–21.
4163. ____. *"Señor: The Life of Al Lopez."* Unpublished Ph.D. Dissertation, Florida State University, 1996. 326p.

JAVIER ("JAVY") LOPEZ

Catcher
Atlanta (N.L.)

4164. Hagen, Paul. "Into the Void." *Beckett Focus on Future Stars,* IV, no. 37 (May 1994), 6–9.
4165. Rosenberg, I. J. "Prize Catch." *Beckett Focus on Future Stars,* III, no. 25 (May 1993), 14–15.

RON LUCIANO

Umpire
American League

4166. Cerio, G. "Behind the Mask." *People Weekly,* XLIII (February 6, 1995), 99–100.
4167. Gohde, M. "Luciano's Last Call." *Referee,* XX (April 1995), 70–71.

ROBERT ("BOB") LURIE

Executive
San Francisco (N.L.)

4168. Fimrite, Ron. "Oh Give Me a Home!" *Sports Illustrated,* LXXVI (June 1, 1992), 50–52, 57. Efforts to move the Giants.

RYAN ("BABY BULL") LUZINSKI

Catcher
Holy Cross

4169. Delany, Maureen. "Bull's Eye." *Beckett Focus on Future Stars,* III, no. 29 (September 1993), 22–23. Son of MLB catcher and K.C. coach Greg Luzinski.

STEVE LYONS

Outfielder, Third Baseman
Boston (A.L.), Chicago (A.L.), Atlanta (N.L.), Montreal (N.L.)

4170. Lyons, Steve. *Steve Lyons: Psychoanalysis.* Champagne, Ill.: Sagamore Publishing, 1995. 224p.

TED LYONS*

Pitcher
Chicago (A.L.)
Manager
Chicago (A.L.)

4171. Spatz, L. "Ted Lyons' Complete Season of 1942: Closer? Who Needs a Closer?" *National Pastime,* XV (1995), 129–130.

SHANE MACK

Outfielder
San Diego (N.L.), Minnesota (A.L.), Japan League, Boston (A.L.)

4173. Aschburner, Steve. "Twins' Shane Mack Learned from the Experts."

Baseball Digest, LI (November 1992), 35–38.

LELAND STANFORD ("LARRY") MacPHAIL*

Executive

4174. Dewey, Donald. "Major League Maverick: Baseball's Larry Mac-Phail." *Timeline,* IX (August–September 1992), 30–39.

BILL MADLOCK

Third Baseman
Texas (A.L.), Chicago (N.L.),
San Francisco (N.L.),
Pittsburgh (N.L.), Los Angeles (N.L.),
Detroit (A.L.)

4175. Ladson, William. "Riches to Rags." *Sport,* LXXXV (January 1994), 34–37+.

GREG MADDUX

Pitcher
Atlanta (N.L.)

4176. Castle, George. "One-on-One [with] Greg Maddux: Interview." *Sport,* LXXXIV (May 1993), 19–20.

4177. Chastain, Bill. "Greg Maddux Wins Acclaim as Best Pitcher in the Majors." *Baseball Digest,* LIII (March 1994), 52–54.

4178. Christopher, Matt. *On the Mound with Greg Maddux.* Boston, Mass.: Little, Brown, 1997. Unpaged.

4179. Cox, Ted. *Greg Maddux: Pitching Ace.* Chicago, Ill.: Children's Press, 1996. 48p.

4180. Dieffenbach, D. "Sport Lifestyle: Off the Mound with Greg Maddux." *Sport,* LXXXVI (January 1995), 34–35.

4181. Fraley, Gerry. "Greg Maddux: He's a Master in the Art of Pitching." *Baseball Digest,* LIV (August 1995), 46–49.

4182. "Greg Maddux." In: Louis M. Collins and Frank V. Castronova, eds. *Newsmakers, 1996: The People Behind Today's Headlines.* Detroit, Mich.: Gale Research, 1997. pp. 298–301.

4183. Hill, Thomas and John Harper. "Greg Maddux: Analysis of the '90s Winningest Pitcher." *Baseball Digest,* LVI (February 1997), 68–71.

4184. Kaat, Jim. "The Pitcher's Pitcher." *Inside Sports,* XVIII (March 1996), 32–43.

4185. Kirkpatrick, Curry. "Mastery of the Mound." *Newsweek,* CXXVI (October 9, 1995), 71+.

4186. Kuenster, Bob. "Greg Maddux, *Baseball Digest's* 1995 Pitcher of the Year." *Baseball Digest,* LV (January 1996), 20–32.

4187. Macht, Norman L. *Today's Stars: Greg Maddux.* New York: Chelsea House, 1997. 64p.

4188. Maddux, Greg. "The Throw." *Outside,* XXII (July 1997), 80–81.

4189. Mazzoni, Wayne. "What Makes Greg Maddux So Good and Can We Teach It?" *Scholastic Coach & Athletic Director,* LXV (December 1995), 58–60.

4190. Rambeck, Richard. *Greg Maddux.* Plymouth, Minn.: Child's World, 1996. 31p.

4191. Rozner, Barry. "Second Look: Greg Maddux." *Beckett Baseball Card Monthly,* X, no. 95 (February 1993), 97–99.

4192. Sheehan, Jack. "Greg Maddux." *Golf Magazine,* XXXVIII (February 1996), 38–39.

4193. Thornley, Stew. *Sports Great Greg Maddux.* Hillside, N.J.: Enslow, 1997. 64p.

4194. Torres, John A. *Greg Maddux, Ace.* Minneapolis, Minn.: Lerner, 1997.

4195. Verducci, Tom. "Drive for Show, Pitch for Dough." *Sports Illustrated,* LXXXII (May 1, 1995), 110–119.

4196. ____. "Once in a Lifetime." *Sports Illustrated,* LXXXIII (August 14, 1995), 22–28, 30.

SALVATORE ANTHONY ("SAL" or "THE BARBER") MAGLIE

Pitcher
New York Giants (N.L.),
Cleveland (A.L.),
Brooklyn (N.L.), New York (A.L.),
St. Louis (N.L.)

4197. Madden, Bill. "Sal (The Barber) Maglie Gives Hitters Closest of Shaves." *Baseball Digest,* LII (May 1993), 40–42.

JOHN MALANGONE

Catcher
New York (A.L.)

4198. Smith, Gary. "Damned Yankee." *Sports Illustrated,* LXXXVII (October 13, 1997), 114–132.

MARTY MALLORY

Second Baseman
Durham Bulls

4199. Hemphill, Paul. *The Heart of the Game: The Education of a Minor League Ballplayer.* New York: Simon and Schuster, 1996. 284p.

SAM MALONE

Fictional pitcher
Boston (A.L.)

4200. Rushin, Steve. "Everybody Knows His Name." *Sports Illustrated,* LXXVIII (May 24, 1993), 62–70. Bar owner of the TV bar *Cheers.*

FRANK JAMES MALZONE

Third Baseman
Boston (A.L.), California (A.L.)
Scout

4201. Kuenster, John. "Veteran Scout Says Style of Play Has Changed in Majors." *Baseball Digest,* LIII (April 1994), 17–19.

FRANK MANCUSO

Catcher
St. Louis (A.L.), Washington (A.L.)

4202. Pickard, Chuck. "Flashback: Frank Mancuso Recalls the Old St. Louis Browns." *Baseball Digest,* LIV (March 1995), 85–89.

EFFA MANLEY

Executive
Newark Eagles

4203. Overmyer, James. *Effa Manley and the Newark Eagles.* American Sports History Series, no. 1. Secaucus, N.J.: The Scarecrow Press, 1993. 297p.

MICKEY MANTLE*

Outfielder
New York (A.L.)

4204. Allen, Maury. *Memories of the Mick.* Dallas, Tx.: Taylor, 1997.
4205. Beckett Publications, Staff of. *Mickey Mantle.* New York: House of Collectibles, 1995. 127p.
4206. *Beckett Great Sports Heroes: Mickey Mantle.* Dallas, Tx.: Beckett Publications, 1997. 100p.
4207. Cinque, Chris. "Mickey Mantle Still Grappling with Old Knee Injuries." *Physician and Sports Medicine,* XVII (June 1989), 170+.
4208. Creamer, Robert W. *Sports Illustrated Presents: Mickey Mantle Remembered.* New York: Warner Books, 1995. 95p.
4209. Dabney, John J. "Mickey Mantle: An American Legend." *Seton Hall Journal of Sport Law,* VII (Winter 1997), 1–4.
4210. Debs, Victor. "Mickey Mantle: The Star Shines Brightest at Twilight." In: his *They Kept Me Loyal to the Yankees.*

Nashville, Tn.: Tennessee Rutledge Hill Press, 1993. pp. 3–22.

4211. Falkner, David. *The Last Hero: The Life of Mickey Mantle.* New York: Simon and Schuster, 1995. 255p.

4212. Fox, William Price. "Mickey Mantle." *Golf,* XXXIII (April 1991), 106+.

4213. Herskowitz, Mickey. *Mickey Mantle: An Appreciation.* New York: William Morrow, 1995. 100p.

4214. Hines, Rick, Mark K. Larson, and Dave Platta. *Mickey Mantle Memorabilia.* Iola, Wis.: Krause Publications, 1993. 208p.

4215. Hoffer, Richard. "Mickey Mantle: The Legacy of the Last Great Player on the Last Great Team." *Sports Illustrated,* LXXXIII (August 21, 995), 18–28, 30.

4216. Hoffman, Frank W. and William G. Bailey. "Mickey Mantle's Race with Ruth." In: their *Sports and Recreation Fads.* Binghampton, N.Y.: Haworth, 1991. pp. 215–216.

4217. Kuenster, John. "Mickey Mantle: As a Player, He Was the 'Whole Package.'" *Baseball Digest,* LIV (September 1995), 17–19.

4218. *Letters to Mikey, by the Friends and Fans of Mickey Mantle.* New York: HarperCollins, 1995. 138p.

4219. Mantle, Mickey, with Jill Lieber. "My Time in a Bottle." *Sports Illustrated,* LXXX (April 18, 1994), 66–72+. Excerpted in *Reader's Digest,* CXLV (December 1994), 88–92.

4220. _____., with Lewis Early. *Mickey Mantle, the American Dream Comes to Life: The Companion Volume to the Public Television Videograph Program Special.* Edited, Compiled, and Sequenced by Douglas Mackey. Champagne, Ill.: Sagamore Publishing, 1994. 143p.

4221. _____., with Mickey Herskowitz. *All My Octobers: My Memories of Twelve World Series When the Yankees Ruled Baseball.* New York: HarperCollins, 1994. 224p.

4222. _____. "Yankee Doodle Dandy." *Sports Illustrated,* LXXIX (October

11, 1993), 50, 52–54, 56, 58, 63–64, 66, 68–70, 72..

4223. Mantle Family (Merlyn, Mickey Jr., David, and Dan), with Mickey Herskowitz. *A Hero All His Life: A Memoir.* New York: HarperCollins, 1996. 260p.

4224. "Mickey Mantle." In: Laurie L. Harris, ed. *Biography Today, 1996: Profiles of People of Interest to Young Readers.* Detroit, Mich.: Omnigraphics, 1996. pp. 226–234.

4225. "Mickey Mantle." In: Louis M. Collins and Frank V. Castronova, eds. *Newsmakers, 1996: The People Behind Today's Headlines.* Detroit, Mich.: Gale Research, 1997. pp. 535–537.

4225a. Nuttall, David S. *Mickey Mantle's Greatest Hits: Dramatic Highlights of a Legendary Career.* Bedford Hills, N.Y.: S.P.I. Books, 1997.

4226. O'Brien, Pat. "Another Season with the Mick." *Inside Sports,* XVI (September 1994), 18–19.

4227. "Remembering Mickey Mantle." In: Gregg Mazzola, ed. *Yankees 1996 Yearbook.* New York: Yankees Magazine, 1996. pp. 18–29.

4228. Schoor, Gene. *The Illustrated History of Mickey Mantle.* New York: Carroll and Graf, 1996. 213p.

4229. Shah, Dana K. "The Legend of Number 7." *Newsweek,* CXXV (June 19, 1995), 70+.

4230. Shaughnessy, Dan. "Young Mickey Mantle: He Was the Ultimate in Speed and Power." *Baseball Digest,* LIV (February 1995), 26–31.

4231. Sherrington, Kevin. "Closer Look: Mickey Mantle." *Beckett Baseball Card Monthly,* XI, no. 116 (November 1994), 6–9.

4232. Siegel, Morris. "Here's the Inside Story on Mickey Mantle's Epic Homer in '53." *Baseball Digest,* LII (August 1993), 52–53.

4233. Smith, Marshall and John Rohde. *Memoirs of Mickey Mantle, by Very Best Friends.* Bronxville, N.J.: AdventureQuest, 1996. 210p.

4234. Susman, Paul. "Physical Ailments Took a Toll on Mickey Mantle's Career." *Baseball Digest,* LV (June 1996), 50–53.

4235. Taylor, John. "Live and Let Die." *Esquire,* CXXIV (December 1995), 120–122.

4236. Van Dyck, Dave. "Farewell to Mickey Mantle, One of Baseball's Greatest." *Baseball Digest,* LIV (November 1995), 22–25.

ROGER MARIS

Outfielder
Cleveland (A.L.), Kansas City (A.L.), New York (A.L.), St. Louis (N.L.)

4237. Gergen, Joe. "Who Won't Break Roger Maris' Record?" In: Zander Hollander, ed. *The Complete Book of Baseball '97.* New York: Signet, 1997. pp. 6–15.

4238. Holway, John B. "Will '96 See Roger Maris' Home Run Record Shattered?" *Baseball Digest,* LV (April 1996), 70–72.

4239. Kahn, Roger. "Pursuit of No. 60: The Ordeal of Roger Maris." *Sports Illustrated,* LXXXI (September 26, 1994), 54–56+. Reprinted from the 1961 issue.

4240. Kuenster, John. "Only a Matter of Rime Before Roger Maris' Home Run Record Falls." *Baseball Digest,* LVI (August 1997), 17–19.

4241. Parks, T. "You Are There, October 1, 1961: Roger Maris' 61st Home Run." *Referee,* XXI (May 1996), 52–53.

4242. Strasberg, Andy. "Roger Maris' Greatest Fan." *KidSports,* III, no. 2 (1991), 26–29.

RICHARD ("RUBE") MARQUAND*

Pitcher
New York Giants (N.L.), Brooklyn (N.L.), Cincinnati (N.L.), Boston (N.L.)

4243. Hynd, Noel. *Marquand and Seeley: This Is Their Captivating Story.*

Hyannis, Mass.: Parnassus Imprints, 1996. 259p. The pitcher and actress Blossom Seeley.

WILLARD MARSHALL

Outfielder
New York Giants (N.L.), Boston (N.L.), Cincinnati (N.L.), Chicago (A.L.)

4244. Mayer, Bob. "Willard Marshall Recalls His Banner Year with the Giants in 1947." *Baseball Digest,* LV (February 1996), 76–79.

MACRO MARTELLI

Batboy
Cal-State Fullerton

4245. Whiteside, Kelly. "Marco the Magnificent." *Sports Illustrated,* LXXX (June 20, 1994), 118–119. Predictions by the 7 year old.

BILLY MARTIN

Second Baseman
New York (A.L.), Kansas City (A.L.), Detroit (A.L.), Cleveland (A.L.), Cincinnati (N.L.), Milwaukee (N.L.), Minnesota (A.L.)
Manager
Minnesota (A.L.), Detroit (A.L.), Texas (A.L.), New York (A.L.), Oakland (A.L.)

4246. Golenbock, Peter. *Wild, High, and Tight: The Life and Death of Billy Martin.* New York: St. Martin's Press, 1994. 545p.

4247. Kucko, John. "A Final Look: Billy Martin." *Beckett Baseball Card Monthly,* IX, no. 88 (July 1992), 126–127.

DENNIS MARTINEZ

Pitcher
Baltimore (A.L.), Montreal (N.L.), Cleveland (A.L.)

4248. Snyder, Brad. "How Indians' Dennis Martinez Transformed His Career." *Baseball Digest,* LIV (October 1995), 32–34.

EDGAR MARTINEZ

Third Baseman
Seattle (A.L.)

4249. Bianchine, Jim. "Mariners' Edgar Martinez: An Unsung Batting Champion." *Baseball Digest,* LIV (December 1995), 38–41.
4250. Tuthill, Bill. "Edgar Martinez Makes His Mark with the Mariners." *Baseball Digest,* LI (December 1992), 43–45.

PEDRO MARTINEZ

Pitcher
San Diego (N.L.), Houston (N.L.),
New York Mets (N.L.), Cincinnati (N.L.)

4251. Etkin, Jack. "Pedro Martinez: A Little Guy Makes It Bigtime." *Baseball Digest,* LVI (November 1997), 34–37.
4252. Kurkijan, Tim. "A Dazzling Deal." *Sports Illustrated,* LXXX (April 4, 1994), 86–88.

RAMON MARTINEZ

Pitcher
Los Angeles (N.L.)

4253. Verducci, Tom. "Martinez Mania." *Sports Illustrated,* LXXXIII (July 24, 1995), 26–28, 30. No hitter.

CONSTANTINO ("TINO") MARTINEZ

First Baseman
Seattle (A.L.), New York (A.L.)

4254. Capezzuto, Tom. "Tino Martinez: The Yankees' New Offensive Leader." *Baseball Digest,* LVI (October 1997), 22–25.

4255. Chastain, Bill. "Tino Martinez Finds Success by Adjusting at the Plate." *Baseball Digest,* LIV (November 1995), 46–49.
4256. ____. "Tito Martinez: He's Ready for Another Pennant Run." *Baseball Digest,* LVI (May 1997), 40–43.
4257. Topkin, Marc. "Will Tino Martinez Win the Hearts of Yankee Fans?" *Baseball Digest,* LV (June 1996), 30–31.
4258. Verducci, Tom. "Teeing Off." *Sports Illustrated,* LXXXVI (June 9, 1997), 56–58, 63.

CHRISTY MATHEWSON*

Pitcher
New York Giants (N.L.),
Cincinnati (N.L.)
Manager
Cincinnati (N.L.)

4259. Macht, Norman. "Class of His Era." *Beckett Baseball Card Monthly,* IX, no. 90 (September 1992), 73–74.
4260. ____. "Final Look: Christy Mathewson." *Beckett Baseball Card Monthly,* X, no. 101 (August 1993), 126–127.
4261. Mayer, Ronald A. *Christy Mathewson: A Game-by-Game Profile of a Legendary Pitcher.* Jefferson, N.C.: McFarland & Co., Inc., 1993. 367p.
4262. Robinson, Ray. *Matty, an American Hero: Christy Mathewson of the New York Giants.* New York: Oxford University Press, 1993. 236p.
4263. Ward, Geoffrey C. and Ken Burns. "Christy Mathewson." *U.S. News & World Report,* CXVII (August 29, 1994), 65+.

DON MATTINGLY

First Baseman
New York (A.L.)

4264. "Don Mattingly." In: Gregg Mazzola, ed. *Yankees 1996 Yearbook.* New York: *Yankees Magazine,* 1996. pp. 14–17.

4265. Johnson, Chuck. "Farewell to Don Mattingly: A Loyal Yankee to the End." *Baseball Digest,* LVI (May 1997), 38–39.

4266. Kay, Michael. "Don Mattingly: An Appreciation." In: Gregg Mazzola, ed. *Yankees 1997 Yearbook.* New York: Yankees Magazine, 1997. pp. 20–29.

4267. Kuenster, John. "Yankees' Don Mattingly Still One of the Top Fielding First Basemen." *Baseball Digest,* LIV (May 1995), 17-21.

4268. Lupica, Mike. "The Last Great Yankee." *Esquire,* CXXIV (July 1995), 29–31.

4269. Mattingly, Don, as told to George Vass. "'The Game I'll Never Forget.'" *Baseball Digest,* LI (November 1992), 61–62.

4270. Rushin, Steve. "First Rate." *Sports Illustrated,* LXXIX (August 30, 1993), 14–17.

4271. Shook, Richard. "A Second Look: Don Mattingly." *Beckett Baseball Card Monthly,* IX, no. 88 (July 1992), 105–109.

JONATHAN TRUMPBOUR ("JON") MATLACK

Pitcher
New York Mets (N.L.), Texas (A.L.)

4272. Post, Paul. "Jon Matlack Recalls His Days with the Mets." *Baseball Digest,* LVI (August 1997), 80–85.

GENE MAUCH

Shortstop
Brooklyn (N.L.), Pittsburgh (N.L.),
Chicago (N.L.),
Boston (N.L.), St. Louis (N.L.),
Boston (A.L.)
Manager
Philadelphia (N.L.), Montreal (N.L.),
Minnesota (A.L.), California (A.L.)

4273. Kaegel, Dick. "Gene Mauch Returns to the Game He Loves as Royals Coach." *Baseball Digest,* LIV (July 1995), 42–46.

ROBERT MAYER

Sportswriter

4274. Mayer, Robert. *Baseball in Men's Lives: The True Confessions of a Skinny-Marink.* New York: Delta, dist. by Dell Publishing, 1994. 275p.

WILLIE MAYS*

Outfielder
New York Giants (N.L.),
San Francisco (N.L.),
New York Mets (N.L.)

4275. Auster, Paul. "Willie Mays: A Writer Remembers His Brush with a Baseball Great." *Scholastic Scope,* XLIII (October 21, 1994), 3+.

4276. Einstein, Charles. *Willie's Time: A Memoir.* New York: Penguin Books, 1992.

4277. "Final Look: Willie Mays." *Beckett Baseball Card Monthly,* XI, no. 112 (July 1994), 105–106.

4278. Gammons, Peter. "Hall of Famer Willie Mays Helped Shape Today's Game." *Baseball Digest,* LIV (April 1995), 52–56.

4279. Merz, T. E. "Willie Mays Meet John Nash." *Journal of Economic Education,* XXVII (Winter 1996), 45–48.

4280. Rediger, Pat. "Willie Mays." In: his *Great African Americans in Sports.* New York: Crabtree Pub., 1996. pp. 40–45.

4281. Spatz, Lyle. "Boxscores to Remember: When Willie Mays Homered in His Debut with the Mets." *Baseball Digest,* LV (July 1996), 78–82.

4282. Vass, George. "Will There Ever Be Another Center Fielder Like Willie Mays?" *Baseball Digest,* LII (June 1993), 24–28.

4283. Ward, Geoffrey C. and Ken Burns. "Willie Mays." *U.S. News & World Report,* CXVII (August 29, 1994), 96+.

DAVE McCARTHY

Outfielder
Minnesota (A.L.), San Francisco (N.L.)

4284. Lenihan, Jeff. "Intent Twin." *Beckett Focus on Future Stars,* III, no. 29 (September 1993), 12–14.
4285. White, Russ. "Dave McCarthy." *Beckett Focus on Future Stars,* II, no. 17 (September 1992), 18–21.

JOE McCARTHY*

Manager
Chicago (N.L.), New York (A.L.), Boston (A.L.)

4286. Boynton, B. "Managers and Close Games: 'Push-Button' Joe McCarthy and the D-Score." *Baseball Research Journal,* XXIV (1995), 81–87.

THOMAS ("TOMMY") McCARTHY*

Outfielder
Boston (U.), Boston (N.L.), Philadelphia (N.L.), St. Louis (A.A.), Brooklyn (N.L.)
Manager
St. Louis (A.A.)

4287. Gold, E. "Tommy McCarthy: How Heavenly Was This 'Heavenly Twin?'" *Baseball Research Journal,* XXIV (1995), 88+.

TIM McCARVER

Catcher
St. Louis (N.L.), Philadelphia (N.L.), Montreal (N.L.), Boston (A.L.)
Broadcaster

4288. Nevius, C. W. "Tim McCarver Knows All, Tells All." *TV Guide,* XLIV (October 5, 1996), 26–28.

BENJAMIN ("BENNY") McCOY

Second Baseman
Detroit (A.L.), Philadelphia (A.L.)

4289. Feldman, Jay. "Benny McCoy: Free Agency, 1940s Style." *National Pastime,* XIV (1994), 39–41.

RAY McDAVID

Outfielder
San Diego (N.L.)

4290. Rausch, Gary. "Man on a Mission." *Beckett Focus on Future Stars,* III, no. 22 (February 1993), 18–19.

BEN ("BIG BEN") McDONALD

Pitcher
Baltimore (A.L.), Milwaukee (A.L.)

4291. Hinneman, Jim. "Times Have Changed for Orioles' 'Big Ben' McDonald." *Baseball Digest,* LI (June 1992), 34–36.
4292. Williams, Pete. "Closer Look: Ben McDonald." *Beckett Baseball Card Monthly,* XI, no. 112 (July 1994), 6–9.

JACK ("BLACK JACK") McDOWELL

Pitcher
Chicago (A.L.), New York (A.L.), Cleveland (A.L.)

4293. "Black Jack." In: Joe Hoppel, ed. *The Sporting News 1994 Baseball Yearbook.* St. Louis, Mo.: TSN, 1994. pp. 20–25.
4294. Brashler, Bill. "Unplugged." *Men's Journal,* III (June–July 1994), 60+.
4295. Daily, Bob. "The Ballad of Black Jack." *Chicago,* XLIII (April 1994), 67+.
4296. Hoffer, Richard. "The Bandleader." *Sports Illustrated,* LXXIX (August 2, 1993), 30–32, 35.
4297. Holtzman, Jerome. "Jack McDowell of White Sox: He Knows the Formula for Winning." *Baseball Digest,* LII (August 1993), 24–26.
4298. Keegan, Tom. "Jack McDowell: 'I'm Always Going to Be a Baseball Player First and Foremost, But You

Have to Draw a Line..." *Sport,*
LXXXIII (August 1992), 16, 18–19.
4299. Ladewski, Paul. "Interview: Jack
McDowell." *Inside Sports,* XVI
(March 1994), 24–32.
4300. McDowell, Jack. "My First
Glove." *Sports Illustrated for Kids,* IX
(July 1997), 58+.
4301. ____. "Strength Training Benefits
White Sox Pitcher McDowell: Inter-
view." *National Strength and Condi-
tioning Association Journal,* XV
(July–August 1993), 50–54.
4302. Williams, Pete. "Deeper Look:
Jack McDowell." *Beckett Baseball
Card Monthly,* X, no. 105 (December
1993), 122–125.

ROGER McDOWELL

Pitcher
New York Mets (N.L.),
Philadelphia (N.L.),
Los Angeles (N.L.),
Texas (N.L.), Baltimore (N.L.),
Chicago (A.L.)

4303. McDowell, Roger, as told to
George Vass. "'The Game I'll Never
Forget.'" *Baseball Digest,* LIII (November 1994), 71–74.
4304. McSpadden, Wyatt. "You're Outrageous." *Sports Illustrated for Kids,*
VII (November 1995), 38–47.

JOHN JOSEPH ("LITTLE NAPOLEON") McGRAW*

Third Baseman, Shortstop
Baltimore (A.A.), Baltimore (N.L.),
St. Louis (N.L.),
Baltimore (A.L.), New York Giants (N.L.)
Manager
Baltimore (N.L.), Baltimore (A.L.),
New York Giants (N.L.)

4305. Ward, Geoffrey C. and Ken Burns.
"John McGraw." *U.S. News & World
Report,* CXVII (August 19, 1994),
63+.

FRED McGRIFF

First Baseman
Toronto (A.L.), San Diego (N.L.),
Atlanta (N.L.)

4306. Ballew, Bill. "Fred McGriff: The
Braves' Dependable Run Producer."
Baseball Digest, LV (September
1996), 44–47.
4307. Keidan, Bob. "ComPadres." *Sport,*
LXXXIV (March 1993), 58–61.
4308. Kuenster, John. "Unsung Fred
McGriff Earns His Keep with the
Atlanta Braves." *Baseball Digest,* LIV
(June 1995), 17–19.
4309. "The Quiet Man." In: Joe Hoppel,
ed. *The Sporting News 1994 Baseball
Yearbook.* St. Louis, Mo.: TSN, 1994.
pp. 138–139.
4310. Rosenberg, I. J. "Deeper Look:
Fred McGriff." *Beckett Baseball Card
Monthly,* XII, no. 121 (April 1995),
22–23.
4311. Sorci, Rick. "Braves' Fred McGriff:
He Thrives as a Steady Run Producer."
Baseball Digest, LIII (October 1994),
34–37.
4312. "Superstar Gallery: Fred McGriff."
Beckett Baseball Card Monthly, XI,
no. 113 (August 1994), 14–15.
4313. Williams, Pete. "Second Look:
Fred McGriff." *Beckett Baseball Card
Monthly,* X, no. 97 (April 1993),
97–98.

MARK McGWIRE

First Baseman
Oakland (A.L.), St. Louis (N.L.)

4314. Crasnick, Jerry. "Mark McGwire:
The Oakland A's Mighty 'Home Run
Machine.'" *Baseball Digest,* LV
(November 1996), 20–23.
4315. Dickey, Glenn. "The Table Is Set."
Inside Sports, XV (July 1993), 68–71.
4316. Graeff, Burt. "Power Hitter Mark
McGwire Slams 'Em Far and Often."
Baseball Digest, LVI (September 1997),
36–39.

4317. Hickey, John. "Going…Going… Gone!" *Beckett Baseball Card Monthly,* no. 151 (October 1997), *passim.* **<http: //www.beckett.com/products/bbpd.h tml>.**

4318. Howe, Art. "He's in a League by Himself." In: Tony Gervino, ed. *Hardball.* New York: Harris Pub. Co., 1997. pp. 56–59.

4319. Ladson, William. "Bay Area Bambino." *Sport,* LXXXIX (April 1997), 48–53.

4320. Murphy, Austin. "In Sight." *Sports Illustrated,* LXXXV (August 26, 1996), 32–34. The Maris record.

4321. Rogers, Phil. "Mark McGwire of the A's: The Bash Is Back!" *Baseball Digest,* LI (August 1992), 20–23.

4322. Stier, Kit. "Closer Look: Mark McGwire." *Beckett Baseball Card Monthly,* IX, no. 89 (August 1992), 6–7.

4323. Wulf, Steve. "Most Happy Fella." *Sports Illustrated,* LXXVI (June 1, 1992), 42–45.

JOE McILVAINE

Executive
New York Mets (N.L.)

4324. Verducci, Tom. "Front-Office Flap." *Sports Illustrated,* LXXXVII (July 28, 1997), 66–67.

WILLIAM BOYD ("BILL" or "DEACON") McKECHNIE*

Third Baseman, Second Baseman
Pittsburgh (N.L.), Boston (N.L.),
New York Giants (N.L.),
Indianapolis (F.L.),
Newark (F.L.), Cincinnati (N.L.)
Manager
Newark (F.L.), Pittsburgh (N.L.),
St. Louis (N.L.), Boston (N.L.),
Cincinnati (N.L.)

4325. Boston, Talmage. "The Deacon of Cincinnati: Hall of Fame Manager Bill McKechnie Leads the Reds to the

[1939] National League Pennant." *Elysian Fields Quarterly,* XIII (Fall 1994), 17–29.

DENNY McLAIN

Pitcher
Detroit (A.L.), Washington (A.L.),
Oakland (A.L.), Atlanta (N.L.)

4326. Ladson, William. "Can We Talk?" *Sport,* LXXXIV (October 1993), 63–65.

4327. Rushin, Steve. "The Season of High Heat." *Sports Illustrated,* LXXIX (July 19, 1993), 30–37.

DRAYTON McLANE, JR.

Executive
Houston (N.L.)

4328. Sheehy, Sandy. "Major League McLane." *Houston Metro,* XIX (March 1993), 32+.

GREG McMICHAEL

Pitcher
Atlanta (N.L.)

4329. Kurkijan, Tim. "Greg McMichael." *Sports Illustrated,* LXXIX (September 20, 1993), 42–43.

TIM McNAMARA

Pitcher
Boston (N.L.), New York Giants (N.L.)

4330. Kreuz, J. "Tim McNamara: Fordham, the Braves, the Giants…and SABR." *Baseball Research Journal,* XXIV (1995), 160–161.

JOHN A. ("BID") McPHEE

Second Baseman
Cincinnati (A.A.), Cincinnati (N.L.)
Manager
Cincinnati (N.L.)

4331. Moses, R. C. "Bid McPhee: The King of 19th Century Second Basemen." *National Pastime,* XIV (1994), 48–50.

HAL McRAE

Outfielder
Cincinnati (N.L.), Kansas City (A.L.)
Manager
Kansas City (A.L.)

4332. Kurkijan, Tim. "Father's Days." *Sports Illustrated,* LXXVIII (June 21, 1993), 32–35.

JOHN McSHERRY

Umpire

4333. Kaplon, A. "My Idol, My Mentor, My Friend John McSherry." *Referee,* XXI (June 1996), 44–45.
4334. "Tragedy Behind the Plate." *Sports Illustrated,* LXXXIV (April 8, 1996), 23+. Dies of heart attack.

ORLANDO MERCED

Outfielder
Pittsburgh (N.L.)

4335. Stewart, Mark. *Orlando Merced.* New York: Children's Press, 1996. 48p.

KENT MERCKER

Pitcher
Atlanta (N.L.), Baltimore (A.L.), Cleveland (A.L.)

4336. Kurkijan, Tim. "Surprise, Surprise, Surprise." *Sports Illustrated,* LXXX (April 18, 1994), 35–38, 41–42, 44.

FREDERICK CHARLES ("FRED" or "BONEHEAD") MERKLE

First Baseman
New York Giants (N.L.),
Brooklyn (N.L.),
Chicago (N.L.), New York (A.L.)

4337. Bowman, R. D. "In Defense of Bonehead Merkle." *Dugout,* II (December 1994), 40+.

JOSE MESA

Pitcher
Baltimore (A.L.), Cleveland (A.L.)

4338. Hoynes, Paul. "Will Indians' Jose Mesa Repeat His Relief Heroics in '96?" *Baseball Digest,* LV (June 1996), 22–25.

MATT MIESKE

Outfielder
Milwaukee (A.L.)

4339. Haudricourt, Tom. "Welcoming Matt." *Beckett Focus on Future Stars,* III, no. 27 (July 1993), 6–9.

MARVIN MILLER

Executive
Major League
Baseball Players' Association

4340. Verducci, Tom. "Marvin Miller." *Sports Illustrated,* LXXXI (September 19, 1994), 64–65.

SATURING ORESTES ARRIETA ARMAS ("MINNIE") MINOSO

4341. Minoso, S. O. A. A. ("Minnie"), with Herb Fagan. *Just Call Me Minnie: My Six Decades in Baseball.* Champaign, Ill.: Sagamore Publications, 1994. Unpaged.

JACKIE MITCHELL

Pitcher

4342. Gregorich, Barbara. "Jackie Mitchell and the Northern Lights: Was She

Ready for a Shot at the Major Leagues?—After All, She Had Struck Out Babe Ruth and Lou Gehrig." *Timeline,* XII (May 1995), 50+. The feat was accomplished in an exhibition game at Chattanooga, Tennessee, on April 3, 1931.

4343. Yoakam, Cy. "She Struck Out Babe Ruth." *Sports Heritage,* I (March–April 1987), 23–27.

KEVIN MITCHELL

Outfielder, Third Baseman
New York Mets (N.L.),
San Diego (N.L.), San Francisco (N.L.),
Seattle (A.L.), Cincinnati (N.L.),
Fukuoka Daiel Hawks (Japan League);
Boston (A.L.); Cleveland (A.L.)

4344. Dickey, Glenn. *Sports Great Kevin Mitchell.* Hillside, N.J.: Enslow, 1993. 64p.

4345. Korn, Peter. "Silent Thunder." *Inside Sports,* XIV (August 1992), 70–77.

4346. Rushin, Steve. "Diary of a Lame Lefthander." *Sports Illustrated,* LXXIX (August 23, 1993), 70+.

4347. Verducci, Tom. "Living Large." *Sports Illustrated,* LXXXVI (June 16, 1997), 78–81, 85–86.

JOHN ("JOHNNY/THE BIG CAT") MIZE*

First Baseman
St. Louis (N.L.), New York Giants (N.L.),
New York (A.L.)

4348. "'The Big Cat'—Johnny Mize: Reminiscences of a Baseball Hall of Famer." *Foxfire,* XXIII (Summer 1989), 115+.

4349. Roush, Chris. "Final Look: Johnny Mize." *Beckett Baseball Card Monthly,* X, no. 97 (April 1993), 118–119.

PAUL MOLITOR

Third Baseman, Second Baseman
Milwaukee (A.L.), Toronto (A.L.),
Minnesota (A.L.)

4350. Antonen, Mel. "With the Twins, Paul Molitor Relives His Boyhood Dreams." *Baseball Digest,* LV (June 1996), 36–38.

4351. Aschburner, Steve. "Strictly Business." *Inside Sports,* XVI (June 1994), 56–61.

4352. Branon, Dave and Lee Pellegrino. "Paul Molitor." In: their *Safe at Home.* Chicago, Ill.: Moody Press, 1992. pp. 304–305.

4353. Broomer, Stuart. *Paul Molitor: Good Timing.* Toronto, Ont.: ECW Press, 1994. 217p.

4354. Buckley, Steve. "One-on-One [with] Paul Molitor: Interview." *Sport,* LXXXV (April 1994), 22+.

4355. Feinstein, John. "Tick...Tick... Tick." *Inside Sports,* XVII (August 1995), 52–55.

4356. Haudricourt, Tom. "Closer Look: Paul Molitor." *Beckett Baseball Card Monthly,* XI, no. 107 (February 1994), 8–10.

4357. Hoffer, Richard. "Career Move." *Sports Illustrated,* LXXVIII (March 29, 1993), 44–46, 49.

4358. Holtzman, Jerome. "Blue Jays' Paul Molitor Proves You're Never Too Old to Learn." *Baseball Digest,* LIII (July 1994), 28–29.

4359. Kurkjian, Tim. "No Asterisk Necessary." *Sports Illustrated,* LXXXV (September 9, 1996), 76–77.

4360. Reusse, Patrick. "How the Twins' Paul Molitor Makes the Game Look Easy." *Baseball Digest,* LV (December 1996), 40–41.

4361. Verducci, Tom. "The Complete Player." *Sports Illustrated,* LXXIX (November 1, 1993), 28+.

THOMAS MONAGHAN

Executive
Detroit (A.L.)

4362. Landrum, Gene N. "Tom Monaghan." In: his *Profiles in Genius: Thirteen Creative Men Who Changed the World.* Buffalo, N.Y.: Prometheus Books, 1993. pp. 96–105.

RAUL MONDESI

Outfielder
Los Angeles (N.L.)

4363. Chavez, Barbara. "Ready to Explode." *Beckett Focus on Future Stars,* II, no. 14 (June 1992), 57–59.

4364. DeMarco, Tony. "Promise Fulfilled." *Beckett Focus on Future Stars,* IV, no. 44 (December 1994), 68–69.

4365. Geschke, Jim. "Closer Look: Raul Mondesi." *Beckett Baseball Card Monthly,* XI, no. 117 (December 1994), 6–9.

4366. Howard, Johnette. "The Next Clemente?" *Sports Illustrated,* LXXXII (May 29, 1995), 38–40, 42.

4367. Johnson, Terry. "Having a Ball." *Beckett Focus on Future Stars,* IV, no. 41 (September 1994), 6–9.

4368. Kuenster, John. "Raul Mondesi, Another Budding Star Brightens Dodgers' Future." *Baseball Digest,* LIV (March 1995), 17–19.

4369. Singer, Tom. "Armed and Dangerous." *Sport,* LXXXV (October 1994), 71–73.

JEFF MONTGOMERY

Pitcher
Cincinnati (N.L.), Kansas City (A.L.)

4370. Flanagan, Jeffrey. "Jeff Montgomery, Spurned by the Reds, Blooms in K.C." *Baseball Digest,* LI (November 1993), 44–45.

DONNIE MOORE

Pitcher
Chicago (N.L.), St. Louis (N.L.), Milwaukee (A.L.), Atlanta (N.L.), California (A.L.)

4371. Poff, John. "Donnie Moore: A Racial Memoir." *Elysian Fields Quarterly,* XIV (Spring 1995), 11–22.

TERRY BLUFORD MOORE

Outfielder
St. Louis (N.L.)

Manager
Philadelphia (N.L.)

4372. Van Blair, Rick. "Terry Moore: An Overlooked Star from Another Era." *Baseball Digest,* LIII (August 1994), 69–74.

JOE L. MORGAN*

Second Baseman
Houston (N.L.), Cincinnati (N.L.), San Francisco (N.L.), Philadelphia (N.L.), Oakland (A.L.)
Broadcaster

4373. Armstrong, Jim. "Joe Morgan: Been There, Done That." *Sport,* LXXXVII (November 1997), 60–63.

4374. Morgan, Joe L., with David Falkener. *Joe Morgan: A Life in Baseball.* New York: W. W. Norton, 1993. 303p.

MIKE MORGAN

Pitcher
Oakland (A.L.), New York (A.L.), Toronto (A.L.), Seattle (A.L.), Baltimore (A.L.), Los Angeles (N.L.), Chicago (N.L.), St. Louis (N.L.)

4375. Sorci, Rick. "Baseball Profile: Pitcher Mike Morgan." *Baseball Digest,* LII (November 1993), 35–36.

JACK MORRIS

Pitcher
Detroit (A.L.), Minnesota (A.L.), Toronto (A.L.), Cleveland (A.L.)

4376. Falls, Joe. "Jack Morris Reflects on His Long and Varied Career." *Baseball Digest,* LIII (June 1994), 44–46.

4377. McCoy, Hal. "Jack Morris Bids the Game Farewell with His Pride Intact." *Baseball Digest,* LIV (August 1995), 50–53.

4378. Milton, Steve. "Second Look: Jack Morris." *Beckett Baseball Card*

Monthly, X, no. 99 (June 1993), 109–111.

4379. Morris, Jack, as told to George Vass. "'The Game I'll Never Forget.'" *Baseball Digest,* LIII (December 1994), 71–73.

VAN LINGLE MUNGO

Pitcher
Brooklyn (N.L.),
New York Giants (N.L.)

4380. Van Blair, Rick. "In the 1930s, Van Lingle Mungo Was a Scourge for N.L. Hitters." *Baseball Digest,* LV (May 1996), 68–69.

RED MURFF

Scout

4381. Murff, Red, with Mike Capps. *The Scout.* Dallas, Tx.: Word Publishing Co., 1996. 334p.

DALE MURPHY

Outfielder
Atlanta (N.L.), Philadelphia (N.L.),
Colorado (N.L.)

4382. Hagen, Paul. "Final Look: Dale Murphy." *Beckett Baseball Card Monthly,* X, no. 105 (December 1993), 126–127.

4383. Sheeley, Glenn. "Farewell to Dale Murphy: A Class Performer to the End." *Baseball Digest,* LII (September 1993), 52–55.

EDDIE MURRAY

First Baseman
Baltimore (A.L.), Los Angeles (N.L.),
New York Mets (N.L.),
Cleveland (A.L.),
California (A.L.), Anaheim (A.L.)

4384. Kuenster, John. "Eddie Murray Quietly Polishes His Hall-of-Fame

Credentials." *Baseball Digest,* LIV (August 1995), 17–19.

4385. Lowitt, Bruce. "Eddie Murray Rang the Bell with His 500th Career Homer." *Baseball Digest,* LV (December 1996), 42–44.

4386. Verducci, Tom. "At Arm's Length." *Sports Illustrated,* LXXXII (May 22, 1995), 56–58, 60. Pursuit of 3,000 hits.

JIM MURRAY

Sportwriter

4387. Murray, Jim. *Jim Murray: An Autobiography.* New York: Macmillan, 1993. 268p.

STAN ("THE MAN") MUSIAL*

Outfielder, Pitcher
St. Louis (N.L.)

4388. Giglio, James N. "Prelude to Greatness: Stanley Musial and the Springfield Cardinals of 1941." *Missouri Historical Review,* XC (July 1996), 429–452.

4389. Grabowski, John F. *Baseball Legends: Stan Musial.* New York: Chelsea House, 1993. 64p.

4390. Kelley, Brent. "How Stan Musial Pitched in His Lone Major League Start." *Baseball Digest,* LIII (May 1994), 75–76.

4391. Lansche, Jerry. *Stan "The Man" Musial: Born to Be a Ballplayer.* Dallas, Tx.: Taylor, 1994. 212p.

MIKE ("MOOSE") MUSSINA

Pitcher
Baltimore (A.L.)

4392. Markus, Don. "No Stopping Him Now." *Beckett Focus on Future Stars,* II, no. 16 (August 1992), 8–9.

4393. Sorci, Rick. "Baseball Profile: Mike Mussina." *Baseball Digest,* LVI (October 1997), 54–55.

4394. "Superstar Gallery: Mike Mussina."

Beckett Baseball Card Monthly, X, no. 99 (June 1993), 15–19.

4395. Whiteside, Larry. "Orioles' Mike Mussina Learning How to Master Art of Pitching." *Baseball Digest,* LI (November 1992), 50–54.

CHARLES NAGY

Pitcher
Cleveland (A.L.)

4396. Grossi, Tony. "Charles Nagy: A Vital Link in Indians' Starting Corps." *Baseball Digest,* LV (November 1996), 38–41.
4397. Shaw, Bud. "Charles Nagy of Indians Lives Up to Billing as No. 1 Starter." *Baseball Digest,* LI (December 1992), 46–47.

DENNY NEAGLE

Pitcher
Minnesota (A.L.), Pittsburgh (N.L.), Atlanta (N.L.)

4398. Farber, Michael. "Matinee Idol." *Sports Illustrated,* LXVII (September 15, 1997), 81–87.
4399. Neal, Lavelle E. "Denny Neagle Hit Stride in First 20-Win Season." *Baseball Digest,* LVI (December 1997), 58–59.

RICHARD A. NESBITT

Coach
Special Olympics

4400. Nesbitt, Richard A. "When the Boys Taught Their Coach." *Reader's Digest,* CXLIX (August 1996), 121–123.

EDDIE NEVILLE

Pitcher
Toledo Mudhens, Durham Bulls

4401. Kirkland, Bill. *Eddie Neville of the Durham Bulls.* Jefferson, N.C.: McFarland & Co., Inc., 1993. 230p.

PHIL NEVIN

Third Baseman
Houston (N.L.), Detroit (A.L.)

4402. Giuliotti, Ed. "Focus on Phil Nevin." *Beckett Focus on Future Stars,* II, no. 20 (December 1992), 18–21.
4403. Rausch, Gary. "Prime Time Talent." *Beckett Focus on Future Stars,* IV, no. 35 (March 1994), 18–19.

MARC NEWFIELD

Outfielder
Seattle (A.L.), San Diego (N.L.), Milwaukee (A.L.)

4404. Hayes, Matt. "Focus on Marc Newfield." *Beckett Focus on Future Stars,* IV, no. 36 (April 1994), 18–20.
4405. ____. "Great Expectations." *Beckett Focus on Future Stars,* II, no. 16 (August 1992), 65–67.
4406. ____. "Rookie Report: Marc Newfield." *Beckett Baseball Card Monthly,* XI, no. 109 (April 1994), 126–127.

HAROLD ("HAL" OR "PRINCE HAL") NEWHOUSER*

Pitcher
Detroit (A.L.), Cleveland (A.L.)

4407. Schneider, Russell. "Hal Newhouser Looks Back on His Hall-of-Fame Career." *Baseball Digest,* LIV (May 1995), 48–52.

LOUIS ("BOBO") NEWSOM

Pitcher
Brooklyn (N.L.), Chicago (N.L.), St. Louis (A.L.), Washington (A.L.), Boston (A.L.), Detroit (A.L.), Philadelphia (A.L.)

4408. Lardner, John. "The One and Only Bobo." In: Charles Einstein, ed. *The New Baseball Reader: An All-Star*

Lineup from the Fireside Book of Baseball. New York: Penguin Books, 1992. pp. 195–209.

WILLIAM B. ("SWISH") NICHOLSON

Outfielder
Philadelphia (A.L.), Chicago (N.L.)

4409. Mayer, B. "Swish Nicholson." *National Pastime,* XV (1995), 129–130.

DAVID NIED

Pitcher
Atlanta (N.L.), Colorado (N.L.)

4410. Klis, Mike. "Expanding Opportunities: David Nied/Rockies." *Beckett Focus on Future Stars,* III, no. 24 (April 1993), 6–9.

4411. ____. "Focus on David Nied." *Beckett Focus on Future Stars,* III, no. 27 (July 1993), 10–13.

4412. ____. "Rookie Report: David Nied." *Beckett Baseball Card Monthly,* X, no. 93 (March 1993), 110–111.

PHIL ("KNUCKSIE") NIEKRO*

Pitcher
Milwaukee (N.L.), Atlanta (N.L.), New York (A.L.), Cleveland (A.L.), Toronto
Coach

4413. Kuenster, Bob. "Knuckleball Master Phil Niekro: A Deserving, New Hall of Fame Member." *Baseball Digest,* LVI (April 1997), 84–85.

4414. Pluto, Terry. "How About a Hall of Fame Spot for Pitcher Phil Niekro?" *Baseball Digest,* LV (January 1996), 33–36.

DAVE NILSSON

Outfielder, First Baseman
Milwaukee (A.L.)

4415. Scher, Jon. "Thunder from Down Under: Brisbane's Own Dave Nilsson Has Cracked the U.S. Major Leagues." *Sports Illustrated Australia,* I (October 1992), 68–71, 75, 77.

4416. Skipwich, Alan. "Dave Nilsson." In: David Bauer, ed. *SI Presents Baseball 1997.* New York: *Sports Illustrated,* 1997. pp. 128–131.

4417. Weber, R. "The Natural: What's a Nice Left-Handed Catcher from Brisbane Like Dave Nilsson Doing in a Place Like Milwaukee?" *Inside Sport (Australia),* I (October 1992), 82–84, 87–88.

OTIS NIXON

Outfielder
New York (A.L.), Cleveland (A.L.), Montreal (N.L.), Atlanta (N.L.), Boston (A.L.), Texas (A.L.), Toronto (A.L.), Los Angeles (N.L.)

4418. "Braves Baseball Star, Once Hooked on Drugs, Funds Anti-Drug Movie." *Jet,* LXXXII (September 21, 1992), 52–55.

4419. Haywood, R. L. "Juanita Leonard Tells Why She Secretly Married Atlanta Braves Star Otis Nixon." *Jet,* LXXXIII (February 22, 1993), 54–57.

TROT NIXON

Outfielder
Boston (A.L.)

4420. Cafardo, Nick. "Hot to Trot." *Beckett Focus on Future Stars,* IV, no. 36 (April 1994), 12–13.

HIDEO NOMO

Pitcher
Los Angeles (N.L.)

4421. "A Buffalo No Mo." *Sports Illustrated,* LXXXII (February 6, 1995), 16, 18.

4422. Dougherty, S. "Tornado Watch."

People Weekly, XLIV (July 17, 1995), 103–104.

4423. Fagen, Bob. *Nomo: The Inside Story of Baseball's Hottest Sensation.* New York: Penguin Books, 1996. 199p.

4424. "Hideo Nomo." In: Louis M. Collins and Frank V. Castronova, eds. *Newsmakers, 1996: The People Behind Today's Headlines.* Detroit, Mich.: Gale Research, 1997. pp. 344–346.

4425. Kuenster, John. "Dodgers' Hideo Nomo, One of the Bright Spots of '95 Season." *Baseball Digest,* LIV (October 1995), 15–17.

4426. Langill, Mark. "No-Mo, No Mo." *Beckett Focus on Future Stars,* V, no. 52 (August 1995), 24–25.

4427. "Lost in Translation." *Harper's,* CCXCII (March 1996), 21–23. Misquotes in an earlier interview.

4428. Lupica, Mike. "Nomo, Mr. Nice Guy." *Esquire,* CXXIV (September 1995), 72+.

4429. Masaru, Ikei. "Nomo's Heroics and U.S.–Japan Relations." *Japan Echo,* XXII (Winter 1995), *passim.* **<http://ifrm.glocom.ac.jp/japanecho>.**

4430. Newmann, A. Linn. "Wonder Boy." *Far Eastern Economic Review,* CLVIII (August 31, 1996), 46–49.

4431. "No More Nomo?" *Sports Illustrated,* LXXXIII (August 21, 1995), 12–14.

4432. Rodman, Edmond J. *Nomo: The Tornado Who Took America by Storm.* Chicago, Ill.: Contemporary Books, 1996. 111p.

4433. "The Tornado." *Sports Illustrated for Kids,* VIII (August 1996), 42–47.

4434. Verducci, Tom. "He's Over Here." *Sports Illustrated,* LXXXII (May 15, 1995), 44–46.

JIM NORTHRUP

Outfielder
Detroit (A.L.), Montreal (N.L.), Baltimore (A.L.)

4435. Woody, Clay. "Jim Northrup: They Called Him 'the Grand Slam Kid.'"

Baseball Digest, LIV (April 1995), 60–67.

JOE NUXHALL

Pitcher
Cincinnati (N.L.), Kansas City (A.L.)

4436. Lawson, Earl. "Joe Nuxhall Recalls Final Time He Faced Stan Musial." *Baseball Digest,* LV (July 1996), 66–69.

JOHNNY OATES

Catcher
Baltimore (A.L.), Atlanta (N.L.), Philadelphia (N.L.),
Los Angeles (N.L.), New York (A.L.)
Manager
Baltimore (A.L.), Texas (A.L.)

4437. Bayliss, Skip. "Managing Himself." *Sport,* LXXXVIII (September 1997), 38–42.

4438. Kurkjian, Tim. "Dugout Doldrums." *Sports Illustrated,* LXXX (June 20, 1994), 50–52+.

ALEX OCHOA

Outfielder
New York Mets (N.L.)

4439. Smith, C. S. "The Cuban Missile." *New York,* XXIX (August 19, 1996), 38–39.

WILLIAM OLIVER ("BILLY" or "DIGER") O'DELL

Pitcher
Baltimore (A.L.), San Francisco (N.L.), Milwaukee (N.L.),
Atlanta (N.L.), Pittsburgh (N.L.)

4440. Patterson, Ted. "Flashback: Whatever Became of ... Billy O'Dell?" *Baseball Digest,* LIII (March 1994), 77–80.

SADAHARU OH

Outfielder
Japan League

4441. "Bambino San." *Psychology Today,* XXV (May–June 1992), 47, 90.
4442. Herbold, John O., 2nd and Tony Muser. "The Hitter Who Went Oh for 868." *Scholastic Coach,* LXIII (April 1994), 22+.

JOHN OLERUD

First Baseman
Toronto (A.L.), New York Mets (N.L.)

4443. Click, Paul. "John Olerud: The Jays' Magnificent 'Hitting Machine.'" *Baseball Digest,* LII (October 1993), 37–41.
4444. Crothers, Tim. "On the Right Track." *Sports Illustrated,* LXXXVI (June 9, 1997), 90, 92.
4445. Deacon, James. "The Swing's the Thing." *Maclean's,* CVI (July 12, 1993), 58–59.
4446. Milton, Steve. "Deeper Look: John Olerud." *Beckett Baseball Card Monthly,* X, no. 101 (August 1993), 120–121.
4447. Taylor, Phil. "A Swing So Sweet." *Sports Illustrated,* LXXVIII (May 10, 1993), 44–46. Published simultaneously in *Sports Illustrated Canada,* I (May 10, 1993), 28–30.

AL OLIVER

Outfielder
Pittsburgh (N.L.), Texas (A.L.),
Montreal (N.L.),
San Francisco (N.L.),
Philadelphia (N.L.),
Los Angeles (N.L.), Toronto (A.L.)

4448. Topel, Brett. "Al Oliver Deserves More Recognition for His Career." *Baseball Digest,* LI (December 1992), 66–68.

C. E. ("PAT") OLSEN

Pitcher
New York (A.L.)

4449. Harrison, Robert L. "The Iron Fan of Baseball: An Interview." *The Minneapolis Review of Baseball,* X (Fall 1991), 22–24.

JOHN ("BUCK") O'NEILL

First Baseman
Memphis Red Sox, KC Monarchs

4450. Goodman, R. S. "A League of His Own." *People Weekly,* XLII (September 26, 1994), 105–106.
4451. O'Neill, John ("Buck"), with Steve Wulf and David Conrads. *I Was Right on Time.* New York: Simon & Schuster, 1996. 254p.
4452. Wulf, Steve. "The Guiding Light." *Sports Illustrated,* LXXXI (September 19, 1994), 148–150+.

PAUL O'NEILL

Outfielder
Cincinnati (N.L.), New York (A.L.)

4453. Hertzel, Bob. "Closer Look: Paul O'Neill." *Beckett Baseball Card Monthly,* XI, no. 113 (August 1994), 6–9.
4454. Lidz, Franz. "Paul O'Neill." *Sports Illustrated,* LXXIX (July 26, 1993), 86–87.

DONOVAN OSBORNE

Pitcher
St. Louis (N.L.)

4455. Solomon, Sally. "Kicking Into Gear." *Beckett Focus on Future Stars,* II, no. 16 (August 1992), 16–17.

MARTY O'TOOLE

Pitcher
Pittsburgh (N.L.)

4456. Rogers, Jim. "The $22,500 Beauty." *Elysian Fields Quarterly,* XI (Winter 1992), 29–31.

RAY OYLER

Shortstop
Detroit (A.L.), Seattle (A.L.),
California (A.L.)

4457. "Rodriguez's Forefather: Seattle's First Shortstop Sensation." *Sports Illustrated,* LXXXV (September 30, 1996), 14, 16.

ANDREW ("ANDY" or "PRUSCHKA" or "HANDY ANDY") PAFKO

Outfielder
Brooklyn (N.L.), Milwaukee (N.L.)

4458. Chapman, Lou. "Andy Pafko Still Remembers Shot Heard 'Round the World.'" *Baseball Digest,* LI (November 1992), 68–74.

LEROY ("SATCHEL") PAIGE*

Pitcher
Chattanooga Black Lookouts,
Birmingham Black Barons,
Cleveland Cubs, Pittsburgh Crawfords,
KC Monarchs,
New York Black Yankees,
Philadelphia Stars,
Cleveland (A.L.), St. Louis (A.L.),
Kansas City (A.L.)

4459. Macht, Norman L. *Baseball Legends: Satchel Paige.* New York: Chelsea House, 1991. 64p.
4460. McKissack, Pat. *Satchel Paige: The Best Arm in Baseball.* Hillside, N.J.: Enslow, 1992. 64p.
4461. Ribowsky, Marty. *Don't Look Back: Satchel Paige and the Shadows of Baseball.* New York: Simon and Schuster, 1994. 351p.
4462. Van Blair, Rick. "Was Satchel Paige as Great as They Said He Was?"

Baseball Digest, LV (June 1996), 68–71.
4463. Ward, Geoffrey C. and Ken Burns. "Satchel Paige." *U.S. News & World Report,* CXVII (August 29, 1994), 84–85.

STEVE PALERMO

Umpire
American League

4464. Knopf, David. "Inch by Inch: Three-and-a-Half Years After Being Partially Paralyzed by a Mugger's Bullet, Steve Palermo Still Fights for What He Hopes Will Be a Full Recovery." *Referee,* XX (February 1995), 28–35.
4465. Newman, Bruce. "Pain and Progress." *Sports Illustrated,* LXXVII (July 6, 1992), 28–33.
4466. Palermo, Steve. "The Umpire Won't Call Himself Out." *People Weekly,* XXXVII (April 27, 1992), 105–108.

JIM PALMER*

Pitcher
Baltimore (A.L.)
Broadcaster

4467. Palmer, Jim. "The Inside Pitch." *Inside Sports,* XVI (May 1994), 48–51.
4468. _____., with Jim Dale. *Together We Were Eleven Foot Nine: The Twenty Year Friendship of Hall of Fame Pitcher Jim Palmer and Orioles Manager Earl Weaver.* Kansas City, Mo.: Andrews and McMeel, 1996. 169p.
4469. _____., with Tracy Ringolsby. "Making the Final Stride." *Inside Sports,* XVI (April 1994), 28+.

RAFAEL PALMEIRO

First Baseman
Chicago (N.L.), Texas (A.L.),
Baltimore (A.L.)

4470. Eisenberg, John. "Rafael Palmeiro Wants to Do More to Spark Orioles." *Baseball Digest,* LVI (July 1997), 60–61.

4471. Howard, Johnette. "A Star in the Shadows." *Sports Illustrated,* LXXXVII (September 8, 1997), 42–47.

4472. Rogers, Phil. "Interview: Rafael Palmeiro." *Inside Sports,* XVI (May 1994), 24–31.

4473. Sorci, Rick. "Baseball Profile: First Baseman Rafael Palmeiro." *Baseball Digest,* LIV (December 1995), 47–48.

CHAN HO PARK

Pitcher
Los Angeles (N.L.)

4474. Johnston, Jeff. "Deeper Look: Chan Ho Park." *Beckett Baseball Card Monthly,* XI, no. 112 (July 1994), 20–21.

DAVE ("THE COBRA") PARKER

Outfielder
Pittsburgh (N.L.), Cincinnati (N.L.),
Oakland (A.L.), Milwaukee (A.L.)

4475. Perotto, John. "Final Look: Dave Parker." *Beckett Baseball Card Monthly,* X, no. 99 (June 1993), 130–131.

MELVIN LLOYD ("MEL" or "DUSTY") PARNELL

Pitcher
Boston (A.L.)

4476. Macht, Norman L. "How Red Sox Lefty Mel Parnell Mastered the 'Green Monster.'" *Baseball Digest,* LII (August 1993), 64–69.

4477. Newville, Todd. "Mel Parnell Wasn't Awed by Fenway's 'Green Monster.'" *Baseball Digest,* LVI (March 1997), 77–79.

JAMES ("RUBE") PARNHAM

Pitcher
Philadelphia (A.L.)

4478. Ross, M. "Rube Parnham: He May Have Been the Game's Best Pitcher in 1923." *Baseball Research Journal,* XXIV (1995), 92–93.

LARRY PARRISH

Third Baseman
Montreal (N.L.), Texas (A.L.),
Boston (A.L.)
Minor League Manager

4479. O'Reilly, P. "Back to the Bushes." *Dugout,* I (October 1993), 5–7.

CAMILO ALBERTO PASCUAL

Pitcher
Washington (A.L.), Minnesota (A.L.),
Cincinnati (N.L.), Los Angeles (N.L.),
Cleveland (A.L.)
Coach

4480. Rubin, Bob. "Camilo Pascual: He Was a Master of the Curveball." *Baseball Digest,* LII (July 1993), 44–47.

CLAUDE WILLIAM PASSEAU

Pitcher
Pittsburgh (N.L.), Philadelphia (N.L.),
Chicago (N.L.)

4481. Fagen, Herb. "Claude Passeau: He Usually Finished What He Started." *Baseball Digest,* LIV (December 1995), 84–90.

4482. Macht, Norman L. "Claude Passeau: He Pitched a World Series One-Hitter." *Baseball Digest,* LII (November 1993), 75–85.

MAX PATKIN

Entertainer

4483. Patkin, Max, with Stan Hochman. *The Clown Prince of Baseball.* Waco, Tx.: WRS Pub., 1994. 167p.

TERRY PENDLETON

Second Baseman
St. Louis (N.L.), Atlanta (N.L.),
Florida (N.L.), Cincinnati (N.L.)

4484. "The Real Thing." In: Joe Hoppel,
ed. *The Sporting News 1993 Baseball
Yearbook.* St. Louis, Mo.: TSN, 1993.
pp. 46–48.
4485. Rosenberg, I. J. "A Second Look:
Terry Pendleton." *Beckett Baseball
Card Monthly,* IX, no. 93 (December
1992), 105–107.
4486. Schlossberg, Dan. "From Bum to
Hero." *Topps Magazine,* (Fall 1992),
22–27.

TROY PERCIVAL

Pitcher
California (A.L.), Anaheim (A.L.)

4487. Johnson, Paul M. "Heavenly
Heat." *Sport,* LXXXVII (May 1996),
92+.

EDUARDO PEREZ

Third Baseman
California (A.L.), Cincinnati (N.L.)

4488. Nightengale, Bob. "Prime Time
Talent." *Beckett Focus on Future
Stars,* IV, no. 38 (June 1994), 18–19.

TONY PEREZ

First Baseman
Cincinnati (N.L.), Montreal (N.L.),
Boston (A.L.), Philadelphia (N.L.)
Coach
Manager
Cincinnati (N.L.)

4489. Reed, William F. "Seeing Red
in Cincinnati." *Sports Illustrated,*
LXXVIII (June 7, 1993), 28–30.
4490. Sorci, Rick. "Baseball Profile:
Coach Tony Perez of the Reds." *Baseball Digest,* LI (December 1992),
57–59.

ANDY PETTITTE

Pitcher
New York (A.L.)

4491. Capezzuto, Tom. "Yankee's Andy
Pettitte Learns the Fine Art of Pitching." *Baseball Digest,* LV (November
1996), 34–37.
4492. Glickson, Grant. "By Any Means
Necessary." In: Tony Gervino, ed.
Hardball. New York: Harris Pub. Co.,
1997. pp. 28–33.
4493. Sorci, Rick. "Baseball Profile:
Yankee Pitcher Andy Pettitte." *Baseball Digest,* LVI (August 1997),
64–65.

KEITH ANTHONY ("TONY") PHILLIPS

Outfielder
Oakland (A.L.), Detroit (A.L.),
California (A.L.), Chicago (A.L.)

4494. Guss, Greg. "All the Rage." *Sport,*
LXXXVII (October 1996), 71–73.
4495. Howard, Johnette. "Dynamite."
Sports Illustrated, LXXXVI (June 30,
1997), 64–66, 71.
4496. Kurkjian, Tim. "A Short Fuse."
Sports Illustrated, LXXXIV (June 10,
1996), 86, 88.
4497. Ryan, Bob. "Tony Phillips Masters
the Art of Gaining a Winning Edge."
Baseball Digest, LIV (December
1995), 70–73.

MIKE PIAZZA

Catcher
Los Angeles (N.L.)

4498. *Beckett Tribute: Mike Piazza.* Dallas, Tx.: Beckett Publications, 1997.
64p.
4499. Cunningham, Bob. "Deeper Look:
Mike Piazza." *Beckett Baseball Card
Monthly,* XI, no. 110 (May 1994),
120–121.
4500. Fry, George B., 3rd. "Catching the

Beat." *Sports Illustrated for Kids,* VII (June 1995), 32–38.

4501. Hoffer, Richard. "Catch a Rising Star." *Sports Illustrated,* LXXXIV (May 13, 1996), 74–77.

4502. Langill, Mark. "No Backing Off." *Beckett Focus on Future Stars,* III, no. 21 (January 1993), 6–9.

4503. ____. "Rookie Report: Mike Piazza." *Beckett Baseball Card Monthly,* X, no. 97 (April 1993), 20–21.

4504. Nightengale, Bob. "Work Ethic Thrusts Dodgers' Mike Piazza Among Elite Catchers." *Baseball Digest,* LV (July 1997), 32–35.

4505. Olney, Bustr. "Dodgers' Mike Piazza Ignores Rookie of Year Hype." *Baseball Digest,* LII (October 1993), 33–36.

4506. Owen, Tom. *Mike Piazza.* New York: Rosen Pub. Group's PowerKid's Press, 1997. 24p.

4507. Romano, John. "Dodger Catcher Mike Piazza Hits at a High Level." *Baseball Digest,* LV (January 1996), 40–43.

4508. Schwarz, Alan. "Closer Look: Mike Piazza." *Beckett Baseball Card Monthly,* X, no. 105 (December 1993), 8–16.

4509. ____. "Interview: Mike Piazza." *Inside Sports,* XIX (May 1997), 22–27.

4510. Singer, Tom. "One-on-One [with] Mike Piazza." *Sport,* LXXXV (May 1994), 26+.

4511. No entry.

4512. Whiteside, Kelly. "A Piazza with Everything." *Sports Illustrated,* LXXIX (July 5, 1993), 12–17.

JACK PIERCE

First Baseman
Atlanta (N.L.), Detroit (A.L.)

4513. Cartwright, Gary. "Chasing the Red Eagle." *Texas Monthly,* XXI (August 1993), 92–97.

JIMMY PIERSALL

Outfielder
Boston (A.L.), Cleveland (A.L.),
Washington (A.L.), California (A.L.)

4514. Piersall, Jimmy. and Al Hirschberg. "From *Fear Strikes Out.*" In: Charles Einstein, ed. *The New Baseball Reader: An All-Star Lineup from The Fireside Book of Baseball.* New York: Penguin Books, 1992. pp. 296–301.

EMIL PIETRANGELI

Umpire
All-American Girls
Professional Baseball League

4515. "When Ballplayers Wore Skirts." *Referee,* XVIII (April 1993), 36+.

LOU ("SWEET LOU") PINELLA

Outfielder
Baltimore (A.L.), Cleveland (A.L.),
Kansas City (A.L.), New York (A.L.)
Manager
New York (A.L.), Cincinnati (N.L.),
Seattle (A.L.)

4516. Buckley, Steve. "One on One [with] Lou Pinella: Interview." *Sport,* LXXXIV (June 1993), 20–21.

GEORGE PLIMPTON

Sportswriter

4517. Plimpton, George. "From *Out of My League.*" In: Charles Einstein, ed. *The New Baseball Reader: An All-Star Lineup from the Fireside Book of Baseball.* New York: Penguin Books, 1992. pp. 301–305.

JOHNNY PODRES

Pitcher
Brooklyn (N.L.), Los Angeles (N.L.),

Detroit (A.L.), San Diego (N.L.)
Coach

4518. Kurkijan, Tim. "Johnny Podres." *Sports Illustrated,* LXXIX (October 25, 1993), 26–27. As pitching coach.
4519. Lucas, Edward. "Johnny Podres' High Mark: World Series Win in '55." *Baseball Digest,* LI (August 1992), 68–71.

CLETUS ELWOOD ("BOOTS") POFFENBERGER

Pitcher
Detroit (A.L.), Brooklyn (N.L.)

4520. Steadman, John. "'Boots' Poffenberger: Last of Great Baseball Characters." *Baseball Digest,* LI (December 1992), 89–95.

PAM POSTEMA

Umpire
Triple A-Alliance

4521. Berlage, G. I. "Women Umpires as Mirrors of Gender Roles." *National Pastime,* XIV (1994), 34–38.
4522. Comte, Liz. "She Calls It as She Sees It." *Inside Sports,* XV (April 1993), 18–19.
4523. McEvoy, Sharlene A. "When the Umpire Strikes Out: Gender Discrimination in Professional Baseball." *Women Lawyer's Journal,* LXXIX (September 1993), 17+.
4524. Reed, Susan and Lyndon Stambler. "The Umpire Strikes Back." *People Weekly,* XXXVII (May 25, 1992), 87–88.

ALBERT ("AL" or "UNCLE AL") PRATT

Pitcher
Cleveland Forest Cities (NABBP)
Manager
Pittsburgh (A.A./N.L.)
Umpire

American Association,
National League
Executive
Union Association, Pittsburgh (N.L.)

4525. Pietrusza, David. "Al Pratt: Present at the Creations." *Elysian Fields Quarterly,* XIV (Spring 1995), 43–47. Pratt pitched in the 1870s and managed Pittsburgh (A.A.) in 1882–1883 and N.L. in 1890.

JOHN A. PREGENZER

Pitcher
San Francisco (N.L.)

4526. Laiolo, Tony. "A Great Cup of Coffee: The John Pregenzer Story." *Elysian Fields Quarterly,* XIII (Winter 1994), 38–50.

CURTIS PRIDE

Outfielder
Montreal (N.L.), Detroit (A.L.)

4527. Bowker, Michael. "The Loudest Cheer." *Reader's Digest,* CXLIV (May 1994), 79–83. Pride's success despite his deafness.
4528. Giuliotti, Ed. "Pride of the Expos." *Beckett Focus on Future Stars,* IV, no. 35 (March 1994), 14–16.
4529. Jordan, Pat. "Pride of the Expos." *Men's Journal,* III (April 1994), 64+.
4530. Whiteside, Kelly. "Curtis Pride." *Sports Illustrated,* LXXIX (July 12, 1993), 57+.

KIRBY PUCKETT

Outfielder
Minnesota (A.L.)

4531. Aaseng, Nathan. *Sports Great Kirby Puckett.* Hillside, N.J.: Enslow, 1993. 64p.
4532. Aschburner, Steve. "For Kirby Puckett, Success a Product of Hard

Work." *Baseball Digest,* LI (October 1992), 20–23.

4533. Bauleke, Ann. *Kirby Puckett: Fan Favorite.* Minneapolis, Minn.: Lerner Publications, 1993. 64p.

4534. Caple, Jim. "Deeper Look: Kirby Puckett." *Beckett Baseball Card Monthly,* X, no. 97 (April 1993), 112–113.

4535. Crasnick, Jerry. "Farewell to Kirby Puckett, One of the Game's Class Acts." *Baseball Digest,* LV (November 1996), 62–65.

4536. DeLand, Dave. "Deeper Look: Kirby Puckett." *Beckett Baseball Card Monthly,* XI, no. 114 (September 1994), 22–24.

4537. Italia, Bob. *Kirby Puckett.* Edina, Minn.: Abdo & Daughters, 1993. 32p.

4538. Kennedy, K. "Baseball's Loss." *Sports Illustrated,* LXXXIV (June 3, 1996), 13–14.

4539. Lenihan, Jeff. "A Closer Look: Kirby Puckett." *Beckett Baseball Card Monthly,* IX, no. 87 (June 1992), 6–7.

4540. Lupica, Mike. "The Short, Happy Life of Kirby Puckett." *Esquire,* CXVII (April 1992), 61–62.

4541. Puckett, Kirby. *I Love the Game: My Life and Baseball.* New York: HarperCollins, 1993. 238p.

4542. ____. "Kirby Talks Baseball." *Minnesota Monthly,* XXVII (March 1994), 46+.

4543. ____. "When I Was Your Age." *KidSports,* IV, no. 4 (1992), 28–29.

4544. ____. and Andrew Gutelle. *Kirby Puckett's Baseball Games.* New York: Workman Publishers, 1996. 100p. Instructional and biographical.

4545. ____., as told to George Vass. "'The Game I'll Never Forget.'" *Baseball Digest,* LII (November 1993), 37–39.

4546. Rambeck, Richard. *Kirby Puckett.* Mankato, Minn.: Child's World, 1993. 31p.

4547. Robson, Britt. "Watch Him While You Can." *Minneapolis,* XXI (June 1993), 49+.

4548. Rushin, Steve. "A Bright Outlook." *Sports Illustrated,* LXXXVI (May 19, 1997), 74–76, 79–80.

4549. ____. "Does the Puck Stop Here?" *Sports Illustrated,* LXXVI (June 22, 1992), 22–24, 29–30.

4550. Young, A. D. "Doc." "Coping." *People Weekly,* XLVII (March 3, 1997), 67+. Glaucoma drives Puckett from the game.

BILL PULSIPHER

Pitcher
New York Mets (N.L.)

4551. Lingo, Will. "Hard Nut to Crack." *Beckett Focus on Future Stars,* V, no. 47 (March 1995), 74–75.

4552. Schwartz, Alan. "Rookie Report: Bill Pulsipher." *Beckett Baseball Card Monthly,* XII, no. 124 (July 1995), 126–127.

LUIS QUINONES

Third Baseman,
Second Baseman, Shortstop
Oakland (A.L.), San Francisco (N.L.),
Chicago (N.L.), Cincinnati (N.L.)

4553. Quinones, Luis, as told to George Vass. "'The Game I'll Never Forget.'" *Baseball Digest,* LI (July 1992), 63–64.

TED ("DOUBLE DUTY") RADCLIFFE

Pitcher, Catcher, Manager
Detroit Stars, St. Louis Stars,
Pittsburgh Homestead Grays,
Pittsburgh Crawfords,
Chicago American Giants,
Brooklyn Eagles, Claybrook Tigers,
Memphis Red Sox,
Cleveland Red Sox,
Birmingham Black Barons

4553. McNary, Kyle P. *Ted "Double Duty" Radcliffe: 36 Years of Pitching & Catching in Baseball's Negro*

Leagues. Minneapolis, Minn.: McNary Pub., 1994. 277p.

BRAD RADKE

Pitcher
Minnesota (A.L.)

4554. Eisenbath, Mike. "Why Twins' Brad Radke Blossomed Into a No. 1 Starter." *Baseball Digest,* LVI (November 1997), 60–61.

KEN RAFFENSBERGER

Pitcher
St. Louis (N.L.), Chicago (N.L.),
Philadelphia (N.L.), Cincinnati (N.L.)

4555. Sparks, Barry. "Ken Raffensberger: The Pitcher Who Baffled Stan Musial." *Baseball Digest,* LIV (May 1995), 59–60.

MANUEL ("MANNY") RAMIREZ

Outfielder
Cleveland (A.L.)

4556. Gleisser, Benjamin. "Rookie Report: Manny Ramirez." *Beckett Baseball Card Monthly,* XI, no. 107 (February 1994), 126–127.
4557. Ocker, Sheldon. "Manny Happy Returns." *Beckett Focus on Future Stars,* III, no. 25 (May 1993), 16–17.

JOSEPH ("GOLDIE") RAPP

Third Baseman
New York Giants (N.L.),
Philadelphia (N.L.)

4558. Selko, Jamie. "The Strange Case of Rapp's Missing Raps: Something was Not Right About Goldie Rapp's Rookie Hitting Streaks." *Baseball Research Journal,* XXIV (1995), 134–136.

JEFF REARDON

Pitcher
New York Mets (N.L.),
Montreal (N.L.),
Minnesota (A.L.), Boston (A.L.),
Atlanta (N.L.), Cincinnati (N.L.),
New York (A.L.)

4559. Reardon, Jeff, as told to George Vass. "'The Game I'll Never Forget.'" *Baseball Digest,* LIII (October 1994), 69–73.
4560. Rushin, Steve. "The Pen Ultimate." *Sports Illustrated,* LXXVI (June 8, 1992), 54–57.

HAROLD ("PEE WEE") REESE*

Shortstop
Brooklyn (N.L.),
Los Angeles (N.L.)

4561. Gershman, Michael. "A Final Look: Pee Wee Reese." *Beckett Baseball Card Monthly,* IX, no. 90 (September 1992), 126–127.

JIMMIE REESE

Second Baseman
New York (A.L.),
St. Louis (N.L.)

4562. Smith, J. D. "Jimmie Reese: In His Own Words." *Baseball Research Journal,* XXIV (1995), 89–91.

JERRY REINSDORF

Executive
Chicago (A.L.)

4563. Greising, David. "The Toughest #&?!% in Sports: In Just Over a Decade, Jerry Reinsdorf Has Become a Major Power in Two Major Leagues." *Business Week,* (June 15, 1992), 100–101, 104.

HAROLD PATRICK ("PETE") REISER

Outfielder
Brooklyn (N.L.), Boston (N.L.),
Pittsburgh (N.L.), Cleveland (A.L.)
Coach

4564. Moss, Robert A. "'Hit It to Me!':
Pete Reiser and *The Natural.*" *Elysian
Fields Quarterly,* XII (Fall 1993),
92–98.

LAURENCE ("DUTCH") RENNERT

Umpire
National League

4565. Watt, R. L. "Memories: An Interview." *Sport,* LXXXIV (July 1993),
70–71.

ALLIE REYNOLDS

Pitcher
Cleveland (A.L.), New York (A.L.)

4566. Nichols, Max J. "Allie Pierce
Reynolds." *Chronicles of Oklahoma,*
LXXIII (Spring 1995), 4+.

GRANTLAND RICE

Sportwriter

4567. Fountain, Charles. *Sportswriter:
The Life and Times of Grantland Rice.*
New York: Oxford University Press,
1993. 327p.

EDGAR ("SAM") RICE*

Outfielder
Washington (A.L.), Cleveland (A.L.)

4568. Wulf, Steve. "The Secrets of
Sam." *Sports Illustrated,* LXXIX (July
19, 1993), 58–64.

J. R. RICHARD

Pitcher
Houston (N.L.)

4569. "Former Houston Star Says Bad
Investments Left Him Homeless." *Jet,*
LXXXVII (February 13, 1995), 47–48.

BOBBY RICHARDSON

Second Baseman
New York (A.L.)
Head Coach
University of South Carolina

4570. Olson, Stan. "Bobby Richardson
Looks Back on the Yankee Dynasty
Years." *Baseball Digest,* LIV (Sep-
tember 1995), 64–67.

J. LEE RICHMOND

Pitcher
Boston (N.L.), Worcester (N.L.),
Providence (N.L.), Cincinnati (A.A.)

4571. Husman, John R. "The First Perfect Game." *Ohio,* XV (May 1992),
39+. In 1879.

BRANCH ("THE MAHATMA") RICKEY*

Catcher
St. Louis (A.L.), New York (A.L.)
Coach
University of Michigan
Manager
St. Louis (A.L.), St. Louis (N.L.)
Executive
St. Louis (A.L.), St. Louis (N.L.),
Brooklyn (N.L.), Pittsburgh (N.L.)
President, Continental League

4572. Stevens, J. D. "As the Branch is
Bent: Rickey as College Coach at the
University of Michigan." *Nine: A
Journal of Baseball History and
Social Policy Perspective,* II (Spring
1994), 277–286.

DAVE RIGHETTI

Pitcher
New York (A.L.), San Francisco (N.L.),
Oakland (A.L.), Toronto (A.L.)

4573. Righetti, Dave, as told to George Vass. "'The Game I'll Never Forget.'" *Baseball Digest,* LII (June 1993), 49–51.

JOSE RIJO

Pitcher
New York (A.L.), Oakland (A.L.),
Cincinnati (N.L.)

4574. Rijo, Jose, as told to George Vass. "'The Game I'll Never Forget.'" *Baseball Digest,* LIII (August 1994), 53–55.

CAL RIPKEN, JR.

Shortstop
Baltimore (A.L.)

4575. *Beckett Tribute: Cal Ripken, Jr.* Dallas, Tx.: Beckett Publishers, 1995. 80p.

4576. Bloom, Barry M. "Paradise Lost." *Sport,* LXXXIX (June 1997), 68–72.

4577. ____. "Pride of the Orioles." *Sport,* LXXXVI (September 1995), 84+.

4578. Broome, Tol. "Jock Talk: Cal Ripken, Jr." *Beckett Baseball Card Monthly,* VII, no. 149 (August 1997), *passim.* <**http://www.beckett.com/ products/bbpd.html**>.

4580. "Cal Ripken, Jr." In: Laurie L. Harris, ed. *Biography Today, 1996: Profiles of People of Interest to Young Readers.* Detroit, Mich.: Omnigraphics, 1996. pp. 126–137.

4581. Campbell, Jim. *Today's Stars: Cal Ripken, Jr.* Philadelphia, Pa.: Chelsea House, 1997. 64p.

4582. Cramer, Richard Ben. "A Native Son's Thoughts." *Sports Illustrated,* LXXXIII (September 11, 1995), 56–64, 66, 68.

4583. Crothers, Tim. "Is It Time to Sit Down?" *Sports Illustrated,* LXXXVII (August 4, 1997), 83–84.

4584. Dodd, Mike. "One-on-One with Baseball 'Ironman' Cal Ripken." *Baseball Digest,* LIV (December 1995), 45–46.

4585. Edelson, M. "Pride of the Orioles." *Washingtonian,* XXX (September 1995), 64–67+.

4586. Ey, Craig S. "Cal-ebration: Everyone's Cashing In on the Streak." *Baltimore Business Journal,* XIII (August 11, 1995), 1–2.

4587. Gottlieb, Nat. "How Cal Ripken Proved His Critics Wrong." *Baseball Digest,* LI (July 1992), 51–53.

4588. "He Keeps Going and Going." *Sports Illustrated for Kids,* VII (August 1995), 32–42.

4589. Hoffer, Richard. "Sportsman of the Year." *Sports Illustrated,* LXXXIII (December 18, 1995), 70–76, 78, 83–84, 86–88, 90.

4590. Hood, Robert E. "Cal Ripken: The Perfect Shortstop." *Boy's Life,* LXXXII (August 1992), 22–24.

4591. Joseph, Paul. *Cal Ripken, Jr.* Edina, Minn.: Abdo and Daughters, 1997. 30p.

4592. Kiersh, Edward. "Interview: Cal Ripken, Jr." *Inside Sports,* XIV (June 1992), 22+.

4593. Kirkpatrick, Curry. "Cal Ripken, Jr." *TV Guide,* XLIII (July 8, 1995), 10–14.

4594. ____. "The Pride of the Orioles." *Newsweek,* CCVI (September 11, 1995), 79+.

4595. Kurkjian, Tim. "Man of Iron." *Sports Illustrated,* LXXXIII (August 7, 1995), 22–32, 34, 37.

4596. ____. "Shortchanging Cal: Why Moving Ripken to Third Would Be an Error by the Orioles." *Sports Illustrated,* LXXXIV (June 3, 1996), 74, 76.

4597. Lord, L. J. "For the Fans, Day in and Day Out." *U.S. News & World Report,* CXIX (September 18, 1995), 16–17.

4598. Lupica, Mike. "The Cherry O's." *Esquire,* CXXV (May 1996), 48–49.

4599. ____. "Let's Play 2000." *Esquire,* CXXIII (April 1995), 48+.

4600. Macnow, Glen. *Sports Great Cal Ripken, Jr.* Hillside, N.J.: Enslow, 1993. 64p.

4601. Mansfield, Stephanie. "My Husband the Hero." *Ladies Home Journal,* CXIII (August 1996), 98+. Views of Kelly Ripken.

4602. Nicholson, Lois. *Cal Ripken, Jr.: Quiet Hero.* 2nd ed. Centreville, Md.: Tidewater Publishers, 1995. 116p. A 100-page first edition was published in 1993.

4603. Palmer, Sally. "People's Choice." *Beckett Future Stars & Sports Collectibles,* VII, no. 75 (July 1997), *passim.* **<http://www.beckett.com/ products/fspd.html>.**

4604. Plummer, William. "Man at Work." *People Weekly,* XLIV (September 18, 1995), 68–70.

4605. Rainie, H. "Chasing Lou Gehrig." *U.S. News & World Report,* CXVII (December 26, 1994), 87–88.

4606. Rambeck, Richard. *Cal Ripken, Jr.* Mankato, Minn.: Child's World, 1993. 31p.

4607. Richmond, Paul. "Local Hero." *Gentlemen's Quarterly,* LXIII (May 1993), 166–171+.

4608. Ripken, Cal, Jr. "Learn to Play Cal's Way." *Sports Illustrated for Kids,* IV (June 1992), 28–33.

4609. ____. "Position Perfect." *KidSports,* III, no. 2 (1991), 22–25.

4610. ____. *Ripken: Cal on Cal.* Edited by Mark Vincent. Arlington, Tx.: Summit Publishing Group, 1995. 112p. Largely pictorial.

4611. ____. "Standing Tall at Short Stop." *KidSports,* III, no. 1 (1991), 14–21.

4612. ____., as told to George Vass. "'The Game I'll Never Forget.'" *Baseball Digest,* LII (January 1993), 69–72.

4613. ____., with Mike Bryan. *The Only Way I Know.* New York: Viking Press, 1997. 326p.

4614. Roberts, S. V. "'Remember, Baseball Is a Great Game.'" *U.S. News & World Report,* CXIX (August 14, 1995), 6–7.

4615. Rosenfeld, Harvey. *Iron Man: The Cal Ripken, Jr. Story.* New York: St. Martin's Press, 1995. 276p.

4616. Savage, Jeff. *Cal Ripken, Jr.: Star Shortstop.* Hillside, N.J.: Enslow, 1994. 64p.

4617. Schmuck, Peter. "Cal Ripken, Jr.: On Course to Make Baseball History." *Baseball Digest,* LIII (February 1994), 34–37.

4618. ____. "A Matter of Record." *Sport,* LXXXIII (May 1992), 22–27.

4619. ____. "Shortstop of Steel." In: Gary Levy, ed. *The Sporting News 1992 Baseball Yearbook.* St. Louis, Mo.: TSN, 1992. pp. 12–14.

4620. Strazzabosco, Jeanne. *Learning About the Work Ethic from the Life of Cal Ripken, Jr.* New York: Rosen Pub. Group's PowerKids Press, 1996. 24p.

4621. "A True Baseball Hero: Why Cal Ripken, Jr., Stands by His Union." *American Teacher,* LXXIX (April 1995), 3+.

4622. "2131: A Baseball Odyssey." In: Joe Hoppel, ed. *The Sporting News 1995 Baseball Yearbook.* St. Louis, Mo.: TSN, 1995. pp. 14–21.

4623. Verducci, Tom. "The Pleasures of His Company: 'The Worst Thing Anyone Ever Said About Cal Ripken Is That He Never Misses a Game.'" *Sports Illustrated,* LXXXIII (September 18, 1995), 98+.

4624. ____. "The Solitary Man." *Sports Illustrated,* LXXVIII (June 28, 1993), 40–42+.

4625. Wulf, Steve. "Iron Bird." *Time,* CXLVI (September 11, 1995), 68–73.

MARIANO RIVERA

Pitcher
New York (A.L.)

4626. Bamberger, Michael. "Strikeouts by the Boatload." *Sports Illustrated,* LXXXVI (March 24, 1997), 50–53.

4627. Giannone, John. "Mariano Rivera Faces New Challenges as Yankee Closer." *Baseball Digest,* LVI (June 1997), 70–71.

RUBEN RIVERA

Outfielder
New York (A.L.)

4628. Schwarz, Alan. "Rookie Report: Ruben Rivera." *Beckett Baseball Card Monthly,* XII, no. 122 (May 1995), 126–127.

EPPA ("EPPA JEPHTHA") RIXEY*

Pitcher
Philadelphia (N.L.),
Cincinnati (N.L.)

4629. Driver, David. "Eppa Rixey: A Son of the Old Dominion." *National Pastime,* XV (1995), 85–87.

PHIL ("SCOOTER") RIZZUTO*

Shortstop
New York (A.L.)
Broadcaster

4630. Baldassaro, Larry. "Schmmozing with the Scooter: A Conversation with Phil Rizzuto." *Elysian Fields Quarterly,* XIII (Fall 1994), 70–81.
4631. Corliss, Rich. "Willie, Mickey... and Scooter?" *Time,* CXLIV (August 1, 1994), 56–57.
4632. Hirshberg, Dan. *Phil Rizzuto: A Yankee Tradition.* Champagne, Ill.: Sagamore Publishing, 1993. 197p.
4633. "Justice Is Served: Phil Rizzuto Enters the Hall." In: Gregg Mazzola, ed. *Yankees 1994 Yearbook.* New York: Yankees Magazine, 1994. pp. 80–84.
4634. Rizzuto, Phil. *O Holy Cow!: The Selected Verse of Phil Rizzuto.* Edited by Tom Peyer and Hart Seely. Hopewell, N.J.: Ecco Press, 1993. 107p.
4635. Sahadi, Lou. "Baseball's Shame." *Penthouse,* XXIV (May 1993), 84–85. On the delay in his Hall of Fame election.

LEON JOSEPH ("BIP") ROBERTS

Second Baseman
San Diego (N.L.), Cincinnati (N.L.),
Kansas City (A.L.), Cleveland (A.L.)

4636. Banks, Don. "'Mr. Utilityman' Bip Roberts Settles In at Second Base." *Baseball Digest,* LII (July 1993), 36–37.
4637. Crasnick, Jerry. "One-on-One [with] Bip Roberts: Interview." *Sport,* LXXXIV (July 1993), 20–21.

BROOKS ROBINSON*

Third Baseman
Baltimore (A.L.)

4638. O'Shei, Tim. "Tips on Third Base Defense Shared by Brooks Robinson." *Baseball Digest,* LIV (June 1995), 54–57.
4639. Robinson, Brooks, with Jon Scher. "World Series [1970]: The Human Vacuum Cleaner." *Sports Illustrated,* LXXXIII (October 23, 1995), 51–52, 55–56, 58, 62, 64–66, 69.

FRANK ROBINSON*

Outfielder
Cincinnati (N.L.), Baltimore (A.L.),
Los Angeles (N.L.),
California (A.L.), Cleveland (A.L.)
Manager
Cleveland (A.L.), San Francisco (N.L.),
Baltimore (A.L.)

4640. Macht, Norman L. *Baseball Legends: Frank Robinson.* New York: Chelsea House, 1991. 64p.
4641. Post, Paul. "Frank Robinson Revives Some Choice Baseball Memories." *Baseball Digest,* LV (May 1996), 44–47.

JACKIE ROBINSON*

Second Baseman, Third Baseman
K.C. Monarchs, Brooklyn (N.L.)

4642. Adler, Gary A. *A Picture Book of Jackie Robinson.* New York: Holiday House, 1994. Unpaged.

4643. Angell, Roger. "Box Score." *The New Yorker,* LXXIII (April 14, 1997), 5–6.

4644. Bergman, Irwin B. *Baseball Legends: Jackie Robinson.* New York: Chelsea House, 1994. 79p.

4645. Boston, Talmage. "Jackie Robinson and the Papini Doctrine." *Elysian Fields Quarterly,* XI (Spring 1992), 41–44, 58.

4646. Brandt, Keith. *Jackie Robinson: A Life of Courage.* Mahwah, N.J.: Troll Associates, 1992. 48p.

4647. Carpozi, George, Jr. *Jackie Robinson, a Tribute.* New York: Princeton Pub. Co., 1997. 66p. Magazine format.

4648. Chace, S. "The True Color of Heroism." *Good Housekeeping,* CCXXIII (October 1996), 18–19.

4649. Coombs, Karen M. *Jackie Robinson: Baseball's Civil Rights Legend.* Hillside, N. J.: Enslow Publications, 1997. 128p.

4650. "Conference Celebrates Legacy of Jackie Robinson." *Jet,* XCI (April 21, 1997), 51–52. "Jackie Robinson: Race, Sports, and the American Dream" held at Long Island University.

4651. Davis, Hal. "The Court Martial of Jackie Robinson: 50 Years Later, a Defense Lawyer Remembers His Client, the Future Baseball Legend." *National Law Journal,* XVII (September 19, 1994), A12+.

4652. Dawidoff, Nicholas. "Recalling Jackie Robinson: Carl Erskine Visits an Exhibition Celebrating His Teammate." *Sports Illustrated,* LXV (September 28, 1987), 70+.

4653. Deford, Frank. "Crossing the [Color] Bar." *Newsweek,* CXXIX (April 14, 1997), 52–55.

4654. Diamond, Arthur. *Jackie Robinson.* San Diego, Ca.: Lucent Books, 1992. 112p.

4655. Ecenbarger, William. "Year of Fire, Year of Grace." *Reader's Digest,* CXLVII (August 1995), 61–65. Rookie season.

4656. Eddings, Jerelyn. "A Grandfather's Greatest Gift: Jackie Robinson Fought to Play, His Grandson [Jesse Simms] Doesn't Have To." *U.S. News & World Report,* CXXII (March 24, 1997), 52–54+.

4657. Falkner, David. *Great Time Coming: The Life of Jackie Robinson, from Baseball to Birmingham.* New York: Simon & Schuster, 1995. 382p.

4658. Griffin, Richard. "Jackie Robinson's 'Real' Anniversary." *World Press Review,* XLVIII (August 1996), 38–39. Breaking color barrier in 1946 while playing for Montreal Royals.

4659. Harris, Mark. "Where've You Gone, Jackie Robinson?" *The Nation,* CCLX (May 15, 1995), 674–676.

4660. Hayes, Henry L. *Hey Jackie, We Love You.* Nashville, Tn.: Winston-Drek Pub. Co., 1997.

4661. Henry, Patrick. "Jackie Robinson: Athlete and American *Par Excellence.*" *The Virginia Quarterly Review,* LXXIII (Spring 1997), 189–203.

4662. Herzog, Brad. "A Home Run for the Ages." *Sports Illustrated,* LXXXIV (April 1, 1996), 1+.

4663. Hoffman, Frank W. and William G. Bailey. "Jackie Robinson and Baseball's Color Line." In: their *Sports and Recreation Fads.* Binghampton, N.Y.: Haworth, 1991. pp. 307–309.

4664. Howerton, Darryl. "Spike [Lee] on Sports: America's Most Famous Fan Talks Reggie Miller, Scottie Pippen, Charles Barkley, Patrick Ewing, and Jackie Robinson." *Sport,* LXXXVI (February 1995), 76+.

4665. Hyman, S. E. "The Other Jackie Robinson." *The New Leader,* LXXX (April 21, 1997), 8–16.

4666. "Jackie Robinson, President Eisenhower, and the Little Rock Crisis." *Social Education,* LXI (April 1997), 218+.

4667. "Jackie Robinson's Grandson Carries on His Sports Legacy." *Jet,* XCI (December 23, 1996), 53–54.

4668. Jerome, R. "Man on Fire." *People Weekly,* XLVII (April 28, 1997), 71–74.

4669. Kashatus, B. "Baseball's Noble Experiment." *American History,* XXXII (March–April 1997), 32–37+.

4670. Kindred, Dave. "Remembering Jackie Robinson." In: Joe Hoppel, ed. *The Sporting News 1997 Baseball Yearbook.* St. Louis, Mo.: TSN, 1997. pp. 10–11.

4671. Kuenster, John. "Jackie Robinson Left an Enduring Legacy as a Courageous Pioneer." *Baseball Digest,* LVI (March 1997), 17–19.

4672. Leavy, Walter. "Baseball's Biggest Superstars Salute a 'Legend.'" *Ebony,* LII (July 1997), 52–55.

4673. Lupica, Mike. "Now Batting for Brooklyn...." *Esquire,* CXXVII (April 1997), 94–98.

4674. Macht, Norman. "Final Look: Jackie Robinson." *Beckett Baseball Card Monthly,* X, no. 100 (July 1993), 126–127.

4675. "Major League Baseball Dedicates Season to 50th Anniversary of Jackie Robinson's Breaking Color Barrier." *Jet,* XCI (March 17, 1997), 48–49.

4676. "The Man Who Changed America." *Sports Illustrated for Kids,* IX (February 1997), 24–35.

4677. Massaquoi, Hans. "The Breakthrough Stars." *Ebony,* XLVII (August 1992), 44+.

4678. McCollum, S. "Jackie Robinson: Leading the Way." *Scholastic Update,* CXXIX (April 11, 1997), 18–19.

4679. Nack, William. "The Breakthrough." *Sports Illustrated,* LXXXVI (May 5, 1997), 56–67.

4680. "Nation Celebrates Anniversary of Jackie Robinson's Breaking the Color Barrier." *Jet,* XCI (May 5, 1997), 46–48.

4681. National Baseball Hall of Fame Library, Staff of. *Jackie Robinson: A Selective Bibliography.* Cooperstown, N.Y.: National Baseball Hall of Fame Library, 1997. 11p. Based, without acknowledgment, on the Robinson sections in the 1985 original edition and 1992 supplement of *Baseball: A Comprehensive Bibliography*; also available from the library's World Wide Web site <**http://www.enews.com/bas_hal_fame/library/bibs/jrobbib.html**>.

4682. "Player of the Half Century." *Sport,* LXXXVII (September 1996), 18+.

4683. Ralph, John J. "Breaking Barriers: Remembering April 15, 1947." In: Kansas City Royals. *The Kansas City Royals 1997 Yearbook.* Kansas City, Mo., 1997. pp. 56–57.

4684. Rampersad, Arnold and Jackie. *Jackie Robinson: A Biography.* New York: Alfred A. Knopf, 1997. 448p.

4685. Rediger, Pat. "Jackie Robinson." In: his *Great African Americans in Sports.* New York: Crabtree Pub., 1996. pp. 58–60.

4686. Reiser, Howard. *Jackie Robinson: Baseball Pioneer.* New York: Franklin Watts, 1992. 64p.

4687. Resnick, Joe. "Jackie Robinson: He Paved the Way for Some of Baseball's Greatest." *Dodgers Scoreboard Magazine,* (May 1987), 12–13.

4688. Robinson, Rachel, and Lee Daniels. *Jackie Robinson: An Intimate Portrait.* New York: Harry N. Abrams, 1996. 240p. Excerpted in *Essence,* XXVII (November 1996), 52+.

4689. Robinson, Sharon. *Stealing Home: An Intimate Family Portrait by the Daughter of Jackie Robinson.* New York: HarperCollins, 1996. 213p.

4690. Rudeen, Kenneth. *Jackie Robinson.* New York: HarperTrophy, 1996. 53p.

4691. Sabin, Francene. *Jackie Robinson.* Mahwah, N.J.: Troll Associates, 1985. 187p.

4692. Sailer, Steve. "How Jackie Robinson Desegregated America." *National Review,* XLVIII (April 8, 1996), 38+.

4693. Sanford, William R. and Carl R. Green. *Jackie Robinson.* New York: Crestwood House, 1993. 48p.

4694. Santella, Andrew. *Jackie Robinson Breaks the Color Line.* New York: Children's Press, 1996. 30p.

4695. Shumard, Bill. "In Memorium to Jackie Robinson." In: Bill Shumard, ed. *Los Angeles Dodgers 1987 Yearbook.* Los Angeles, Calif.: George Rice & Sons, 1987. pp. 17–19.

4696. *The Sporting News. Archives. Soul of the Game: Jackie Robinson 50th Anniversary* <**http://www.thesport ingnews.com/features/jackie**> is an Internet site offering documents, photos, press coverage of the 1946–1947 events.

4697. Thorn, John and Jules Tygiel. "Jackie Robinson's Signing: The Real Untold Story." In: their *Total Baseball.* 3rd ed. New York: HarperPerenial, 1993. pp. 148–153.

4698. Tygiel, Jules. *Baseball's Great Experiment: Jackie Robinson and His Legacy.* New York: Oxford University Press, 1997.

4699. ____., ed. *The Jackie Robinson Reader.* New York: E. P. Dutton, 1997. 278p.

4700. Voigt, David Q. "They Shaped the Game: Jackie Robinson." *Baseball History,* I (Spring 1986), 5–22.

4701. Ward, Geoffrey C. and Ken Burns. "Jackie! Jackie! Jackie!" *U.S. News & World Report,* CXVII (April 29, 1994), 85–86+.

4702. Weidhorn, Manfred. *Jackie Robinson.* New York: Atheneum, 1993. 207p.

4703. Wilkins, Roy W. "Jack & Rachel Robinson." *The Nation,* CCLXIV (April 21, 1997), 4–5.

4704. Williams, Alex. "Jackie Under Her Skin: 50 Years After Jackie Robinson Broke Baseball's Color Line, His Widow, Rachel Robinson, Revisits the Man Behind the Legend." *New York,* XXIX (September 23, 1996), 46–47.

4705. Young, Andrew S. "Doc." "Jackie Robinson Remembered." *Ebony,* LII (February 1, 1997), 103+.

ALEX RODRIGUEZ

Short Stop
Seattle (A.L.)

4706. Antonen, Mel. "Mariners' Alex Rodriguez Has the Makings of Major Stardom." *Baseball Digest,* LV (October 1996), 48–51.

4707. Callahan, Gerry. "The Fairest of Them All." *Sports Illustrated,* LXXXV (July 8, 1996), 38–42.

4708. Emmons, Mark. "Setting Sail." *Beckett Focus on Future Stars,* IV, no. 38 (June 1994), 14–16.

4709. "Great Expectations, Greater Results." In: Joe Hoppel, ed. *The Sporting News 1997 Baseball Yearbook.* St. Louis, Mo.: TSN, 1997. pp. 18–23.

4710. Hayes, Matt. "Focus on Alex Rodriguez." *Beckett Focus on Future Stars,* IV, no. 43 (November 1994), 76–79.

4711. Kuenster, Bob. "Alex Rodriguez, *Baseball Digest's* 1996 Player of the Year." *Baseball Digest,* LVI (January 1997), 24–39.

4712. Kuenster, John. "Alex Rodriguez Joined an Elite Group of Shortstops with His '96 Production." *Baseball Digest,* LV (December 1996), 17–19.

4713. Ladson, William. "Thinking Big." *Sport,* LXXXIX (June 1997), 65–67.

4714. Lockwood, Wayne. "Mariners' Alex Rodriguez: Standing Tall at Short." *Baseball Digest,* LVI (July 1997), 38–41.

4715. Nolan, Timothy. "Once in a Baseball Coach's Lifetime: An Interview." *Scholastic Coach & Athletic Director,* LXVI (February 1997), 46–54. Thoughts of Coach Rich Hofman regarding his best player.

4716. Whiteside, Kelly. "Alex Rodriguez." *Sports Illustrated,* LXXVIII (March 22, 1993), 74–75.

HENRY RODRIGUEZ

Outfielder
Los Angeles (N.L.), Montreal (N.L.)

4717. Crasnick, Jerry. "Henry Rodriguez Enjoyed a Break-Through Year in '96." *Baseball Digest,* LVI (March 1997), 62–65.

4718. Johnson, Paul M. "Oh Henry." *Sport,* LXXXVIII (October 1996), 22–23.

IVAN RODRIGUEZ

Catcher
Texas (A.L.)

4719. Caldwell, Dave. "Ivan Rodriguez: His Pickoff Talents Keep Baserunners Honest." *Baseball Digest,* LVI (January 1997), 58–59.
4720. Crothers, Tim. "Catch as Catch Can." *Sports Illustrated,* LXXXVI (May 19, 1997), 92, 96.
4721. DeMarco, Tony. "Ivan the Terrific." *Beckett Focus on Future Stars,* II, no. 15 (July 1992), 16–19.
4722. Howard, Johnette. "Pudge Factor." *Sports Illustrated,* LXXXVII (August 11, 1997), 40–44.
4723. Mayoral, Luis R. "Ivan Rodriguez of the Rangers Comes of Age as a Major League Star." *Baseball Digest,* LIII (December 1994), 55–57.
4724. Tarrant, David. "Rangers' Ivan Rodriguez: The Majors' No. 1 All-Around Catcher." *Baseball Digest,* LVI (July 1997), 20–23.

TOM RODRIGUEZ

Baseball Artist

4725. Buckley, J., Jr. "An Artist's Field Day." *Sports Illustrated,* LXXIX (September 6, 1993), 8, 12.

BILLY ROGELL

Shortstop
Boston (A.L.), Detroit (A.L.),
Chicago (N.L.)

4726. Grosshandler, Stanley. "Billy Rogell Looks Back on Glory Days with the Tigers." *Baseball Digest,* LII (December 1993), 70–72.

KENNY ROGERS

Pitcher
Texas (A.L.), New York (A.L.)

4727. Kurkjian, Tim. "As Good as It Gets." *Sports Illustrated,* LXXXI (August 8, 1994), 32–33. Perfect game.

SCOTT ROLEN

Third Baseman
Philadelphia (N.L.)

4728. Etkin, Jack. "Third Baseman Scott Rolen, a Budding Star for the Phillies." *Baseball Digest,* LVI (December 1997), 46–49.

EDWIN AMERICUS ("EDDIE") ROMMEL

Pitcher
Philadelphia (A.L.)
Coach
Umpire
American League

4729. Rothe, Emil. "This Was the Most Bizarre Relief Job in the Majors." *Baseball Digest,* LI (June 1992), 72–75.

PETE ROSE

Outfielder, First Baseman
Cincinnati (N.L.), Philadelphia (N.L.),
Montreal (N.L.)
Manager
Cincinnati (N.L.)

4730. Bloom, Barry. "Pete Rose: Banished But Still a Baseball Man at Heart." *Baseball Digest,* LII (May 1993), 36–39.
4731. Dolson, Frank. "How Pete Rose Helped Nudge Mike Schmidt to Greatness." *Baseball Digest,* LIV (May 1995), 61–62.
4732. Fimrite, Ron. "Pete Rose." *Sports Illustrated,* LXXXI (September 19, 1994), 15–16.

4733. Gilbert, Thomas W. *Pete Rose.* New York: Chelsea House, 1995. 64p.

4734. Hoffman, Frank W. and William G. Bailey. "The Pete Rose Gambling Scandal." In: their *Sports and Recreation Fads.* Binghampton, N.Y.: Haworth, 1991. pp. 311–314.

4735. Kahn, Roger. "A Rose by Another Name." *Playboy,* XXXVIII (December 1991), 174+.

4736. Klein, Michael. "Rose is Black, Black Sox Are Blue: A Comparison of 'Rose v. Giamatti' and the 1921 Black Sox Trial." *Comm/Ent.,* XIII (Spring 1991), 551+.

4737. Lupica, Mike. "Gooooood Morning, Cooperstown: Pete Rose May Be a Hit on the Radio, But He's Still Gambling with Reinstatement." *Esquire,* CXVIII (September 1992), 135, 138.

4738. Reilly, Rick. "A Rose Is a Rose." *Sports Illustrated,* LXXIX (August 16, 1993), 30–36.

PETE ROSE, JR.

Third Baseman
Cincinnati (N.L.)

4739. Bradley, John Ed. "Honor Thy Father." *Sports Illustrated,* LXXXVII (August 11, 1997), 70–80, 82–83.

CHARLES L. ("PANTS") ROWLAND

Outfielder
Philadelphia (A.L.)

4740. Murphy, J. P. "The Busher from Dubuque." *Baseball Research Journal,* XXIV (1995), 17–22.

KIRK RUETER

Pitcher
Montreal (N.L.), San Francisco (N.L.)

4741. Peck, Burton L., 4th. "Rookie Report: Kirk Rueter." *Beckett Base-*

ball Card Monthly, XI, no. 106 (January 1994), 126–127.

GEORGE HERMAN ("BABE") RUTH*

Pitcher, Outfielder
Boston (A.L.), New York (A.L.), Boston (N.L.)

4742. Ardolino, F. "Born is the Savior of Baseball: Babe Ruth as Christ-Figure in *The Babe Ruth Story." Aethlon: The Journal of Sport Literature,* XII (Spring 1995), 87–93.

4743. "Babe Ruth's 100th Anniversary." In: Gregg Mazzola, ed. *Yankees 1995 Yearbook.* New York: Yankees Magazine, 1995. pp. 16–29.

4744. Boswell, Thomas. "Everyman and Superman." *Inside Sports,* XVII (May 1995), 60–64.

4745. Brown, Chip. "The Babe and the Mid-Ocean Club." *Men's Journal,* I (May–June 1992), 92+.

4746. Castle, George. "The Babe Myth: The Call That Was Never Made." *Sport,* LXXXIII (October 1992), 16, 19.

4747. Creamer, Robert W. "Ruth?: He Is Still in the Spotlight, Still Going Strong." *Smithsonian,* XXV (February 1995), 68–70+. Abridged in *Reader's Digest,* CXLVI (June 1995), 71–75, under the title "Forever 'The Babe'" and published in *Reader's Digest,* Editors of, *Reader's Digest Winner's Circle* (Hicksville, N.Y.: Reader's Digest Association, 1996), pp. 18–23.

4748. Deedy, John. "The Day I Collected Babe Ruth's Autograph." *Baseball Digest,* LVI (February 1997), 56–60.

4749. De Marco, Mario. "The King of Baseball: Baseball Collector's Treasure—The Babe." *Antiques and Collecting Hobbies,* XCVI (December 1991), 56+.

4750. Drooz, Alan. "The Legend That Ruth Built." *Beckett Baseball Card Monthly,* XII, no. 119 (February 1995), 6–7.

4751. ____. "Sultan of $uccess." *Beckett Baseball Card Monthly,* XII, no. 119 (February 1995), 8–10. Curtis Management Group, owners to the rights to the player's name.

4752. Dunne, Michael. "Postwar Cultural Construction in *The Babe Ruth Story.*" *Studies in Popular Culture,* XIX, no. 1 (1996), 1+.

4753. Gold, Eddie. "Babe Ruth Still the Champ in Home Run Frequency." *Baseball Digest,* LIII (March 1994), 82–83.

4754. Hoffman, Frank W. and William G. Bailey. "Babe Ruth Calls His Shot." In: their *Sports and Recreations Fads.* Binghampton, N.Y.: Haworth, 1991. pp. 315–318. Compare with George Castle's article.

4755. Holtzman, Jerome. "Babe Ruth's Last Stand Still a Vivid Memory." *Baseball Digest,* LI (August 1992), 63–65.

4756. Hore, T. "'God, We Liked That Big Son of a Bitch': Babe Ruth, Still a Legend at 100." *Dugout,* III (April–May 1995), 21–24.

4757. Jackendoff, Ray. "Babe Ruth Homered His Way Into the Hearts of America." *Syntax and Semantics,* XXVI (1992), 155+.

4758. Jarvis, Robert M. "Babe Ruth as Legal Hero." *Florida State University Law Review,* XXII (Spring 1995), 885–897.

4759. Keene, Kerry, Raymond Sinbaldi, and David Hickey. *The Babe in Red Stockings: An In-Depth Chronicle of Babe Ruth with the Boston Red Sox, 1914–1919.* Champagne, Ill.: Sagamore Publications, 1997. 307p.

4760. Liebowitz, Herbert. "The Babe Ruth Syndrome." *Parnassus: Poetry in Review,* XVII, no. 2 (1992), 9+.

4761. Lorenz, Stacy L. "Bowing Down to Babe Ruth: Major League Baseball and Canadian Popular Culture, 1920–1929." *Canadian Journal of the History of Sport,* XXVI (May 1995), 22–39.

4762. Mercurio, John A. *Babe Ruth's Incredible Records and the 44 Players Who Broke Them.* New York: S. P. I. Books, 1993. 217p.

4763. Nicholson, Lois. *Babe Ruth: Sultan of Swat.* Westport, Conn.: Greenwood Press, 1994. 119p.

4764. Rambeck, Richard. *Babe Ruth.* Mankato, Minn.: Child's World, 1993. 31p.

4765. Sanford, William R. and Carl R. Green. *Babe Ruth.* New York: Crestwood House, 1992. 48p.

4766. Scahill, Edward H. "Did Babe Ruth Have a Comparative Advantage as a Pitcher?" *Journal of Economic Education,* XXI (Fall 1990), 402+.

4767. Steadman, John. "Dolph Camilli: Old-Time National League Star Recalls the Babe." *Baseball Digest,* LVI (June 1997), 78–81.

4768. ____. "Lab Tests Proved That Babe Ruth Was Indeed Superior." *Baseball Digest,* LI (October 1992), 57–59.

4769. Trimble, P. "Babe Ruth and American Baseball: The Media Construction of a 1920s Sport Personality." *Colby Quarterly,* XXXII (March 1996), 45–57.

4770. Turley, Bob. "A Babe in the Woods: A Boy Who Caddied for Babe Ruth Remembers." *Yankee,* LVII (June 1993), 92+.

4771. Van Loon, N. "Babe Ruth Comes to Pickle River." In: William Humber and John St. James, eds. *All I Thought About Was Baseball: Writings on a Canadian Pastime.* North York, Ont.: University of Toronto Press, 1996. pp. 292–303.

4772. Walsh, John E. "Babe Ruth and the Legend of the Called Shot." *Wisconsin Magazine of History,* LXXVII (Summer 1994), 243+.

4773. Ward, Geoffrey C. and Ken Burns. "The Sultan of Swat." *U.S. News & World Report,* CXVII (August 29, 1994), 75–78+.

NOLAN RYAN

Pitcher
New York Mets (N.L.), California (A.L.), Houston (N.L.), Texas (A.L.)

4774. *Beckett Tribute to Nolan Ryan.* Dallas, Tx.: Beckett Publications, 1993. 80p.

4775. "Final Look: Nolan Ryan." *Beckett Baseball Card Monthly,* XI, no. 106 (January 1994), 105–106.

4776. Greenberg, Keith E. *Nolan Ryan, Ageless Superstar.* Vero Beach, Fla.: Rourke Enterprises, 1993. 48p.

4777. Herskowitz, Mickey. "Baseball Without Nolan Ryan." In: John Blake, *et al. Texas Rangers Official 1994 Yearbook.* Arlington, Tex.: Public Relations Dept., Texas Rangers, 1994. pp. 50–54.

4778. ____. "Farewell to Nolan Ryan: He Was a Baseball Treasure." *Baseball Digest,* LIII (February 1994), 38–43.

4779. Iverson, Kurt. "A Deeper Look: Nolan Ryan." *Beckett Baseball Card Monthly,* IX, no. 88 (July 1992), 110–114.

4780. ____. "May Day Alert: Ryan Unhittable." In: John Blake, *et al. Texas Rangers Official 1996 Yearbook.* Arlington, Tex.: Public Relations Dept., Texas Rangers, 1996. pp. 41–47. Seventh no-hitter on May 1, 1991.

4781. Kreuz, Jim. "High School Coach Recalls Nolan Ryan as a Young Pitcher." *Baseball Digest,* LV (March 1996), 60–64.

4782. Kuenster, Bob. "Baseball's Dramatic Moments: Nolan Ryan Establishes a New Strikeout Record." *Baseball Digest,* LIV (August 1995), 41–42.

4783. Kurkijan, Tim. "Nolan Ryan." *Sports Illustrated,* LXXIX (October 4, 1993), 46–47. Career ends with elbow injury.

4784. Lace, William W. *Sports Great Nolan Ryan.* Hillsdale, N.J.: Enslow, 1993. 64p.

4785. McLemore, Ivy. "Nolan Ryan's Long Career Built on Strong Work Ethic." *Baseball Digest,* LII (August 1993), 38–39.

4786. Mulgannon, Tom. "The Nolan Ryan Scrapbook." *Sport,* LXXXIV (October 1993), 66–69.

4787. Nicholson, Lois P. *Nolan Ryan.* Philadelphia, Pa.: Chelsea House, 1995. 64p.

4788. "Nolan Ryan." *KidSports,* IV, no. 2 (1992), 12–17.

4789. Patoski, J. N. "A Farewell to Arm." *Texas Monthly,* XXI (May 1993), 114–115+.

4790. Rappoport, Ken. *Nolan Ryan: The Ryan Express.* New York: Dillon Press, 1992. 64p.

4791. Reiser, Howard. *Nolan Ryan: Strikeout King.* Chicago, Ill.: Children's Press, 1993. 48p.

4792. Roberts, Jack. *Nolan Ryan.* New York: Scholastic, 1992. 50p.

4793. Rolfe, John. *Nolan Ryan.* Boston, Mass.: Little, Brown, 1992. 124p.

4794. Ryan, Nolan, with Jerry Jenkins. *Miracle Man: The Autobiography of Nolan Ryan.* Dallas, Tx.: Word Books, 1992. 272p. A largest text edition was published by the Boston firm of G. K. Hall in 1993.

4795. Trujillo, Nick. *The Meaning of Nolan Ryan.* College Station, Tx.: Texas A & M University Press, 1994. 163p.

BRET SABERHAGEN

Pitcher
Kansas City (A.L.),
New York Mets (N.L.),
Colorado (N.L.), Boston (A.L.)

4796. McBride, M. "The SABeRhagen Syndrome: Pitching Streaks of a Special Kind." *Baseball Research Journal,* XXIV (1995), 34–38.

4797. Noble, Marty. "A Deeper Look: Bret Saberhagen." *Beckett Baseball Card Monthly,* XII, no. 123 (June 1995), 22–23.

4798. Rudeen, L. "Home Run." *Motor Boating & Sailing,* CLXXVIII (October 1996), 52–55+.

JOHN FRANKLIN ("JOHNNY") SAIN

Pitcher
New York (A.L.), Kansas City (A.L.)
Coach

4799. Fagen, Herb. "Johnny Sain Did It His Way … As a Pitcher and Coach." *Baseball Digest,* LII (December 1993), 76–80.

TIM SALMON

Outfielder
California (A.L.), Anaheim (A.L.)

4800. Rausch, Gary. "Focus on Tim Salmon." *Beckett Focus on Future Stars,* III, no. 26 (June 1993), 12–14.
4801. ____. "Headed Upstream." *Beckett Focus on Future Stars,* II, no. 17 (September 1992), 10–13.

RYNE SANDBERG

Second Baseman
Philadelphia (N.L.), Chicago (N.L.)

4802. Castle, George. "Passing Up the Buck." *Sport,* LXXXIII (December 1992), 12+.
4803. "Final Look: Ryne Sandberg." *Beckett Baseball Card Monthly,* XI, no. 113 (August 1994), 105–106.
4804. Muskat, Carrie. "Second to None." *Topps Magazine,* (Summer 1992), 24–29.
4805. Ringolsby, Tracy. "Ryne Sandberg Has Achieved It All … Except for the [World Series] Ring." *Baseball Digest,* LII (March 1993), 30–31.
4806. Sandberg, Ryne, as told to George Vass. "'The Game I'll Never Forget.'" *Baseball Digest,* LII (June 1993), 77–78.
4807. ____. with Barry Rozner. *Second to Home: Ryne Sandberg Opens Up.* Chicago, Ill.: Bonus Books, 1995. 313p.
4808. "Superstar Gallery: Ryne Sand-

berg." *Beckett Baseball Card Monthly,* IX, no. 88 (July 1992), 10–14.
4809. Van Dyke, Dave. "Farewell to Ryne Sandberg: A Class Act to the End." *Baseball Digest,* LIII (November 1994), 44–46.
4810. Verducci, Tom. "Second Time Around." *Sports Illustrated,* LXXXIV (March 11, 1996), 34–41.

DEION ("PRIME TIME") SANDERS

Outfielder
New York (A.L.), Atlanta (N.L.),
Cincinnati (N.L.), San Francisco (N.L.)

4811. Callahan, Gerry. "Running Start." *Sports Illustrated,* LXXXVI (May 19, 1997), 58–62.
4812. Chadwick, Bruce. *Deion Sanders.* Philadelphia, Pa.: Chelsea House, 1996. 64p.
4813. "Deion Sanders." In: Laurie L. Harris, ed. *Biography Today, 1996: Profiles of People of Interest to Young Readers.* Detroit, Mich.: Omnigraphics, 1996. pp. 145–154.
4814. Harvey, Miles. *Deion Sanders: Prime Time.* Chicago, Ill.: Children's Press, 1996. 48p.
4815. King, Peter. "Time for a Game Plan." *Sports Illustrated,* LXXVII (August 24, 1992), 20–23.
4816. Klein, Aaron. *Deion Sanders.* New York: Walker, 1995. 149p.
4817. Ladson, William. "The *Sport* Q&A: Deion Sanders." *Sport,* LXXXVI (February 1995), 32–36.
4818. Lupica, Mike. "The Neon Nineties." *Esquire,* CXVII (June 1992), 59–60.
4819. "No Passing Zone." *Sports Illustrated for Kids,* IX (October 1997), 38–47.
4820. "Prime Time." *Sports Illustrated for Kids,* VI (August 1994), 34–41.
4821. Rosenberg, I. J. "A Closer Look: Deion Sanders." *Beckett Baseball Card Monthly,* IX, no. 88 (July 1992), 6–9.

4822. Rushin, Steve. "Catch-21." *Sports Illustrated,* LXXXIII (July 31, 1995), 54–59.

4823. Savage, Jeff. *Deion Sanders: Star Athlete.* Springfield, N.J.: Enslow, 1996. 104p.

4824. Thornley, Stew. *Deion Sanders.* Minneapolis, Minn.: Lerner, 1997.

4825. "Two-Sport Phenom Sanders Ponders Quitting Baseball." *Jet,* LXXXVIII (October 2, 1995), 46–47.

REGGIE SANDERS

Outfielder
Cincinnati (N.L.)

4826. Crasnick, Jerry. "Prime Time Talent." *Beckett Focus on Future Stars,* II, no. 13 (May 1992), 18–19.

4827. Kurkijan, Tim. "Red-Faced." *Sports Illustrated,* LXXXIII (October 23, 1995), 41–42.

RON SANTO

Third Baseman
Chicago (N.L.), Chicago (A.L.)
Broadcaster

4828. Dray, Bill. "Ron Santo: A Hall of Fame Plaque in His Future?" *Baseball Digest,* LI (July 1992), 66–69.

4829–4838 No entries.

4839. Santo, Ron, with Randy Minhoff. *Ron Santo—For Love of Ivy: The Autobiography of Ron Santo.* Chicago, Ill.: Bonus Books, 1993. 224p.

ALEXANDER ("AL" or "THE CLOWN PRINCE OF BASE-BALL") SCHACHT

Pitcher
Washington (A.L.)
Coach

4840. Schacht, Mike. *Mudville Diaries: A Book of Baseball Memories.* New York: Avon Books, 1996. 208p.

DICK SCHAAP

Sportswriter/Broadcaster

4841. Schaap, Dick. "Magazine Memories." *Sport,* LXXXVII (September 1996), 77–78+.

CURT SCHILLING

Pitcher
Philadelphia (N.L.)

4842. Henderson, John. "In '97, Curt Schilling Joined Ranks of Top Whiff Artists." *Baseball Digest,* LVI (December 1997), 64–65.

MIKE SCHMIDT*

Third Baseman
Philadelphia (N.L.)

4843. "Final Look: Mike Schmidt." *Beckett Baseball Card Monthly,* XI, no. 111 (June 1994), 105–106.

4844. Holtzman, Jerome. "Mike Schmidt Joins Elite Hall of Fame Vote Leaders." *Baseball Digest,* LIV (April 1995), 21–23.

4845. Platt, Larry. "Unloved Mike Schmidt." *Philadelphia,* LXXXVI (September 1995), 53+.

4846. Schmidt, Mike, with Rob Ellis. *The Mike Schmidt Study: Building a Hitting Foundation.* Atlanta, Ga.: McGriff & Bell, 1994. 78p. Emphasis on technique.

4847. Westcott, Rick. *Mike Schmidt.* New York: Chelsea House, 1995. 64p.

4848. Whitford, David. "The Unhappiness of Mike Schmidt." *GQ: Gentlemen's Quarterly,* LXII (July 1992), 62, 66+.

JOHN ALBERT ("JOHNNY" or "BEAR TRACKS") SCHMITZ

Pitcher
Chicago (N.L.), Brooklyn (N.L.),
New York (A.L.), Cincinnati (N.L.),

Washington (A.L.), Boston (A.L.), Baltimore (A.L.)

4849. Macht, Norman L. "Johnny Schmitz: Old Brooklyn Dodgers Were 'Patsies' for Him." *Baseball Digest,* LV (September 1996), 77–81.

ALBERT ("RED") SCHOENDIENST

Second Baseman
St. Louis (N.L.), New York Giants (N.L.), Milwaukee (N.L.)
Manager-Executive
St. Louis (N.L.)

4850. Kuenster, John. "Red Schoendienst Lives Up to His Surname as a Baseball 'Lifer.'" *Baseball Digest,* LV (March 1996), 15–17.

MARGE SCHOTT

Executive
Cincinnati

4851. Bass, Mike. *Marge Schott: Unleashed.* Champagne, Ill.: Sagamore Pub. Co., 1993. 309p.
4852. "Departing Schott." *Sports Illustrated,* LXXXIV (June 24, 1996), 20, 22.
4853. Kurkijan, Tim. "Dog Days." *Sports Illustrated,* LXXVII (October 19, 1992), 28–30.
4854. O'Brien, Richard. "Block That Schott." *Sports Illustrated,* LXXVII (December 7, 1992), 15–16.
4855. Plummer, William and Civia Tamarkin. "Big Red Embarrassment." *People Weekly,* XXXVIII (December 14, 1992), 79, 82.
4856. Reilly, Rick. "Heaven Help Marge Schott." *Sports Illustrated,* LXXXIV (May 20, 1996), 72–78, 80, 83–84, 87.
4857. "Schott Out of the Park." *Time,* CXLI (February 15, 1993), 18–19. Racial comments.

4858. Verducci, Tom. "Who's the Boss?" *Sports Illustrated,* LXXXIII (September 18, 1995), 46–48, 50.
4859. "Will Alleged 'Nigger' Slur by White Owner of Cincinnati Reds Hurt Baseball?" *Jet,* LXXXIII (December 21, 1992), 52–55.

JOHN SCHUERHOLZ

Executive
Atlanta (N.L.)

4860. Cattau, Daniel. "Boss of the Braves: Atlanta's John Schuerholz Talks Baseball." *The Lutheran,* VII (August 1994), 8+.

HAL ("PRINCE HAL") SCHUMACHER

Pitcher
New York Giants (N.L.)

4861. Van Blair, Rick. "When [in 1935] the Majors Almost Suffered Second Fatality." *Baseball Digest,* LII (November 1993), 73–74. Heat prostration on July 25.

CLAY SCHWARTZ

Catcher
University of Wisconsin at Milwaukee

4862. "Battered, But on Base." *Sports Illustrated,* LXVI (May 12, 1997), 23+. Holds NCAA record for being the most-hit batter.

MIKE SCIOSCIA

Catcher
Los Angeles (N.L.)

4863. Scioscia, Mike, as told to George Vass. "'The Game I'll Never Forget.'" *Baseball Digest,* LIII (January 1994), 61–62.

HERB SCORE

Pitcher
Cleveland (A.L.), Chicago (A.L.)
Broadcaster

4864. Dolgan, Bob. "How Line Drive Damaged the Career of Herb Score." *Baseball Digest,* LVI (September 1997), 80–83.

VIN SCULLY

Broadcaster

4865. Hodges, Jim. "Vin Scully Nears Half Century." In: Zander Hollander, ed. *The Complete Book of Baseball '97.* New York: Signet, 1997. pp. 24–31.

TOM SEAVER*

Pitcher
New York Mets (N.L.), Cincinnati (N.L.), Chicago (A.L.), Boston (A.L.)
Sportswriter/Broadcaster

4866. Cohen, Linda J. "Seaver's Bad Pitch." *Inside Sports,* XV (July 1993), 8, 12. Broadcasting difficulties.
4867. Mauro, James. "Mound Olympus: A Heroic Conversation with Tom Seaver." *Psychology Today,* XXV (July–August 1992), 22–23.
4868. Mueller, Rob. "Final Look: Tom Seaver." *Beckett Baseball Card Monthly,* IX, no. 89 (August 1992), 126–127.

KEVIN SEITZER

First Baseman
Kansas City (A.L.), Milwaukee (A.L.), Oakland (A.L.), Cleveland (A.L.)

4869. Seitzer, Kevin. "Fear Strikes Back: An All-Star Player Describes the Horror of Being Hit in the Head by a Big League Fastball." *Sports Illustrated,* LXXXIII (July 24, 1995), 118+.

ALLAN H. ("BUD") SELIG

Executive
Milwaukee (A.L.),
President, American League
Interim Commissioner,
Major League Baseball

4870. "Bud Selig." In: Louise Mooney Collins and Gert J. Speace, eds. *Newsmakers, 1995: The People Behind the Headlines.* Detroit, Mich.: Gale Research, 1995. pp. 466–469.
4871. "The Buddy System." *Sports Illustrated,* LXXXIV (May 6, 1996), 22+.
4872. "Interview with Allan H. "Bud" Selig, President of the MLB Executive Council." *World Baseball Magazine,* III (1996), 8–11.
4873. Whiteside, Kelly. "This, Bud, Is for You." *Sports Illustrated,* LXXXII (May 8, 1995), 24+.

JAMES LUTHER ("LUKE") SEWELL

Catcher
Cleveland (A.L.), Washington (A.L.), Chicago (A.L.), St. Louis (A.L.)
Manager
St. Louis (A.L.), Cincinnati (N.L.)

4874. Lundquist, Carl. "The Manager Who Used Nine Pitchers in One Game." *Baseball Digest,* LI (June 1992), 58–61.

GARY SHEFFIELD

Shortstop
Milwaukee (A.L.), San Diego (N.L.), Florida (A.L.)

4875. Kurkjian, Tim. "A Blessing for the Padres." *Sports Illustrated,* LXXVI (April 27, 1992), 13–14.
4876. Martin, Bruce. "A Closer Look: Gary Sheffield." *Beckett Baseball Card Monthly,* IX, no. 91 (October 1992), 6–7.
4877. Reilly, Rick. "Can't Take Nothin'

Off Nobody." *Sports Illustrated,*
LXXVII (September 14, 1992), 54–56,
59–61.
4878. Schlossberg, Dan. "From Bum to
Hero." *Topps Magazine,* (Fall 1992),
22–27.
4879. "Too Good to Be True." In: Joe
Hoppel, ed. *The Sporting News 1993
Baseball Yearbook.* St. Louis, Mo.:
TSN, 1993. pp. 2–9.
4880. Topkin, Marc. "Gary Sheffield Sets
His Sights on a Banner Year." *Baseball
Digest,* LVI (June 1997), 66–67.
4881. Verducci, Tom. "Part of the
Crowd." *Sports Illustrated,* LXXXIV
(May 27, 1996), 68–70, 72.

BOB SHEPPARD

Public address announcer
New York (A.L.)

4882. "Yan-kee Ac-Cent." *The New
Yorker,* LXIX (October 4, 1993), 69–70.

LARRY SHERRY

Pitcher
Los Angeles (N.L.), Detroit (A.L.),
Houston (N.L.), California (N.L.)
Coach

4883. Schlossberg, Dan. "How a Rookie
Pitcher Rallied Dodgers to Title in
'59." *Baseball Digest,* LII (November
1993), 42–43.

CRAIG SHIPLEY

Infielder
Australian Baseball League

4884. McDonald, J. "A Craig of All
Trades." *Baseball Australia,* V (March
1993), 6–7.

BURTON EDWIN
("BURT/BARNEY") SHOTTON

Outfielder
St. Louis (A.L.), Washington (A.L.),

St. Louis (N.L.)
Manager
Philadelphia (N.L.), Cincinnati (N.L.),
Brooklyn (N.L.)

4885. Gough, David. *Burt Shotton,
Dodgers Manager: A Baseball Biog-
raphy.* Jefferson, N.C.: McFarland &
Co., Inc., 1994. 141p.
4886. ____. "A Tribute to Burt Shotton:
One of Baseball's Unique Heroes."
National Pastime, XIV (1994), 99–101.

ERIC SHOW

Pitcher
San Diego (N.L.), Oakland (N.L.)

4887. Jordan, Pat. "The Last Inning." *Los
Angeles,* XL (June 1993), 88–96+.
4888. "A Troubled Soul." *Sports Illustrated,* LXXX (March 28, 1994), 9–10.

WILLIAM ("BUCK")
SHOWALTER

Manager
New York (A.L.), Arizona (N.L.)

4889. Pierce, Charles. "Southern Yankee:
Buck Showalter." *New York Times
Magazine,* (July 10, 1994), 24–27.
4890. Verducci, Tom. "Bucking Up the
Yanks." *Sports Illustrated,* LXXX
(May 16, 1994), 48–50+.
4891. ____. "One Luck Buck." *Sports
Illustrated,* LXXXV (July 1, 1996),
50–54.

RUBEN SIERRA

Outfielder
Texas (A.L.), Oakland (A.L.),
New York (A.L.)

4892. DeMarco, Tony. "A Second Look:
Ruben Sierra." *Beckett Baseball Card
Monthly,* IX, no. 87 (June 1992),
105–106.
4893. Jamail, Milton. "Who Is Ruben

Sierra?" *Hispanic,* (April 1990),
26–29.

GEORGE SISLER*

First Baseman
St. Louis (A.L.), Washington (A.L.),
Boston (N.L.)
Manager
St. Louis (A.L.)

4894. Losada, Luis A. "George Sisler,
Manolin's Age, and Hemingway's Use
of Baseball." *The Hemingway Review,*
XIV (Fall 1994), 79+.

ENOS ("COUNTRY") SLAUGHTER*

Outfielder
St. Louis (N.L.), New York (A.L.),
Kansas City (A.L.)

4895. Eisenbath, Mike. "Enos Slaughter:
He Set the Standard for Hustle." *Baseball Digest,* LI (September 1992),
56–59.

LEE SMITH

Pitcher
Chicago (N.L.), Boston (A.L.),
St. Louis (N.L.),
New York (A.L.), California (A.L.),
Cincinnati (N.L.)

4896. Hummel, Rick. "Lee Smith: The
Pitcher with an Identity Crisis." *Baseball Digest,* LI (June 1992), 38–41.
4897. Kurkijan, Tim. "Case Closed?:
California's Closer Quandary." *Sports
Illustrated,* LXXXIV (May 6, 1996),
71+.
4898. Ringolsby, Tracy. "No Hits, No
Hype." *Inside Sports,* XIV (September 1992), 74–77.

OSBORNE ("OZZIE" or "THE WIZARD") SMITH

Shortstop
San Diego (N.L.), St. Louis (N.L.)

4899. Eisenbath, Mike. "Cardinal Teammates Bid a Fond Farewell to Ozzie
Smith." *Baseball Digest,* LV (October
1996), 52–55.
4900. Smith, Ozzie, as told to George
Vass. "'The Game I'll Never Forget.'"
Baseball Digest, LI (June 1992),
69–71.
4901. Topkin, Marc. "Deeper Look:
Ozzie Smith." *Beckett Baseball Card
Monthly,* XII, no. 124 (July 1995),
114–115.

JOHN SMOLTZ

Pitcher
Atlanta (N.L.)

4902. Johnson, Paul M. "Smoke Signals." *Sport,* LXXXVII (November
1996), 74–78.
4903. Kaat, Jim. "Armed for Success."
Inside Sports, XIX (March 1997),
40–51.
4904. Kuenster, Bob. "John Smoltz,
Baseball Digest's 1996 Pitcher of the
Year." *Baseball Digest,* LVI (January
1997), 24–39.
4905. Plummer, William. "Faith Healer."
People Weekly, XLVI (July 15, 1996),
173–174.
4906. Verducci, Tom. "Eye-Opener."
Sports Illustrated, LXXXIV (June 10,
1996), 46–48, 50, 55.
4907. Whiteside, Larry. "Braves' John
Smoltz Making a Pitch for Cy Young
Award." *Baseball Digest,* LV (October
1996), 22–25.

EDWIN ("DUKE") SNIDER*

Outfielder
Brooklyn (N.L.), Los Angeles (N.L.),
New York Mets (N.L.)

4908. Bjarkman, Peter C. *Baseball Legends: Duke Snider.* New York: Chelsea
House, 1994. 64p.

J. T. SNOW

First Baseman
New York (A.L.), California (A.L.),
San Francisco (N.L.)

4909. Langill, Mark. "Rookie Report:
J. T. Snow." *Beckett Baseball Card
Monthly,* X, no. 101 (August 1993),
20–21.
4910. McCarthy, Charlie. "Prime Time
Talent." *Beckett Focus on Future
Stars,* III, no. 24 (April 1993), 16–
17.
4911. Nightengale, Bob. "Heaven Sent."
Beckett Focus on Future Stars, III, no.
28 (August 1993), 6–9.
4912. Stewart, Mark. *J. T. Snow.* New
York: Children's Press, 1996. 48p.

JIMMIE LEE SOLOMON

Executive
MLB Director of
Minor League Operations

4913. Lombardo, John. "Jimmie Lee
Solomon: He's Majoring in Minor
League Baseball and Plans to
Move Up." *Washington Business
Journal,* XIII (October 14, 1994),
22–23.

SAMMY SOSA

Outfielder
Texas (A.L.), Chicago (A.L.),
Chicago (N.L.)

4914. Castle, George. "Cubs' Sammy
Sosa: Ready to Fulfill His Potential?"
Baseball Digest, LIII (April 1994),
74–76.
4915. Holtzman, Jerome. "Cubs' Sammy
Sosa Destined to Join Game's Hitting
Elite." *Baseball Digest,* LV (October
1996), 46–47.
4916. Van Schouwen, Daryl. "Sammy
Sosa Produces But Still Has His Critics." *Baseball Digest,* LIV (December
1995), 49–51.

WARREN SPAHN*

Pitcher
Boston (N.L.), Milwaukee (N.L.),
New York Mets (N.L.),
San Francisco (N.L.)

4917. Bjarkman, Peter C. *Baseball Legends: Warren Spahn.* New York: Chelsea House, 1995. 64p.

ED SPRAGUE, JR.

Third Baseman
Toronto (A.L.)

4918. Milton, Steve. "Cleared for Take-
off." *Beckett Focus on Future Stars,*
III, no. 24 (April 1993), 18–19.
4919. Montville, Leigh. "Home Alone,
Two." *Sports Illustrated,* LXXVIII
(January 11, 1993), 58–60, 64–66. Ed
and his Olympic gold medal-winning
wife Kristen Babb-Sprague.

GEORGE TWEEDY ("THE MIRACLE MAN") STALLINGS

Catcher, Outfielder, First Baseman
Brooklyn (N.L.), Philadelphia (N.L.)
Manager
Philadelphia (N.L.), Detroit (A.L.),
New York (A.L.), Boston (N.L.)

4920. Meany, Tom. "The Miracle Man."
In: Charles Einstein, ed. *The New
Baseball Reader: An All-Star Lineup
from The Fireside Book of Baseball.*
New York: Penguin Books, 1992. pp.
250–263.

JACK STALLINGS

Coach
Georgia Southern

4921. Lawlor, Chris. "Georgia Southern
Hospitality: Interview." *Scholastic
Coach,* LXIV (November 1994), A20–
A24.

MIKE STANLEY

Catcher
Texas (A.L.), New York (A.L.),
Boston (A.L.)

4922. Capezzuto, Tom. "Mike Stanley Made the Most of His Opportunity in '93." *Baseball Digest,* LIII (January 1994), 52–55.

MIKE STANTON

Pitcher
Atlanta (N.L.), Boston (A.L.),
Texas (A.L.)

4923. Chastain, Bill. "Braves' Bullpen Ace Mike Stanton Thrives in Closing Role." *Baseball Digest,* LII (August 1993), 40–42.

WILLIE ("POPS") STARGELL*

Outfielder
Pittsburgh (N.L.)

4924. Shannon, Mike. *Willie Stargell.* New York: Chelsea House, 1992. 64p.

DANIEL ("RUSTY") STAUB

Outfielder
Houston (N.L.), Montreal (N.L.),
New York Mets (N.L.),
Detroit (A.L.), Texas (A.L.)

4925. Lape, Bob. "Rusty Staub, Restauranteur." *Ovation,* X (July 1989), 42+.

TERRY STEINBACH

Catcher
Oakland (A.L.), Minnesota (A.L.)

4926. Swift, E. M. "Cold Sweet Home." *Sports Illustrated,* LXXXVI (January 27, 1997), 56–58+.

GEORGE ("THE BOSS") STEINBRENNER

Executive
New York (A.L.)

4927. Coffey, Frank. *The Wit and Wisdom of George Steinbrenner.* New York: Signet Books, 1993. 210p.
4928. Downey, Mike. "Cleveland, By George!" *Inside Sports,* XIV (July 1992), 68–71.
4929. Lieber, Jill. "Will 'the Boss' Behave Himself?" *Sports Illustrated,* LXXVIII (March 1, 1993), 18–21.
4930. Madden, Bill. "The Big Payback." *Sport,* LXXXIV (March 1993), 52–57.
4931. Pooley, Eric. "Let Him Walk." *New York,* XXVIII (February 13, 1995), 82–87.
4932. Toropov, Brandon. *101 Reasons to Hate George Steinbrenner.* New York: Citadel Press, 1997.
4933. "The Trouble with George." *The New Yorker,* LXIX (August 2, 1993), 4–5.

GUS STEINER

Umpire
N.C.A.A., Olympics

4934. Steiner, Gus. "Interview." *Referee,* XVII (May 1992), 28+.

CHARLES ("CASEY") STENGEL*

Outfielder
Brooklyn (N.L.), Pittsburgh (N.L.),
Philadelphia (N.L.)
Manager
Brooklyn (N.L.), Boston (N.L.),
New York (A.L.), New York Mets (N.L.)

4935. Bak, Richard. *Casey Stengel: A Splendid Baseball Life.* Dallas, Tx.: Taylor, 1997. 198p.
4936. Frayne, Trent. "The Loveable Old Perfesser." *Maclean's,* CV (May 11, 1992), 50 l.

4937. Kaplan, Jim and Ira Berkow. *The Gospel According to Casey: Casey Stengel's Inimitable, Instructional, Historical Baseball Book.* New York: St. Martin's Press, 1992. 172p.

RENNIE STENNETT

Second Baseman
Pittsburgh (N.L.), San Francisco (N.L.)

4938. Powell, Larry. "Rennie Stennet Recalls His 7-for-7 Game." *Baseball Digest,* LI (December 1992), 69–71.

DAVE STEWART

Pitcher
Los Angeles (N.L.), Texas (A.L.),
Philadelphia (N.L.), Oakland (A.L.),
Toronto (A.L.)

4939. Johnson, P. "From the Dodgers to the Dome: Is Dave Stewart's Long Journey Over?" *Dugout,* II (October 1994), 8–10.
4940. Stewart, Dave, as told to George Vass. "'The Game I'll Never Forget.'" *Baseball Digest,* LII (December 1993), 49–50.
4941. Wulf, Steve. "Dave Stewart." *Sports Illustrated,* LXXIX (December 27, 1993), 80+.

DAVE STIEB

Pitcher
Toronto (A.L.), Chicago (A.L.)

4942. Stieb, Dave, as told to George Vass. "'The Game I'll Never Forget.'" *Baseball Digest,* LII (March 1993), 77–78.

TONI STONE

Second Baseman
Indianapolis Clowns,
Kansas City Monarchs

4943. Gregorich, Barbara. "1954: Toni Stone." *American Visions,* VIII (June–July 1993), 27+. Negro leagues female player.

HANNAH STORM

Broadcaster

4944. Young, C. "Storm Watch." *TV Guide,* XLI (June 26, 1993), 24–27.

GEORGE W. STOVEY

Pitcher
Cuban Giants, Newark Giants, Trenton

4945. Hunsinger, L., Jr. "George W. Stovey: A Pitcher in the Shadows." *National Pastime,* XIV (1994), 80–82. Famous 19th century black hurler.

DARRYL STRAWBERRY

Outfielder
New York Mets (N.L.),
Los Angeles (N.L.),
San Francisco (N.L.), New York (A.L.)

4946. Fimrite, Ron. "The Long Shot." *Sports Illustrated,* LXXXI (July 18, 1994), 34+.
4947. Hoffer, Richard. "Try, Try Again." *Sports Illustrated,* LXXX (March 14, 1994), 38–40.
4948. Roberts, Jack. *Darryl Strawberry.* New York: Scholastic, 1992. 50p.
4950. Starr, Mark. "One More Time at Bat." *Newsweek,* CXXVI (July 3, 1995), 60–61.
4951. Strawberry, Darryl, as told to George Vass. "'The Game I'll Never Forget.'" *Baseball Digest,* LII (May 1993), 62–62.

WILLIAM ASHLEY ("BILLY" or "PARSON" or "THE BASEBALL EVANGELIST") SUNDAY

Outfielder
Chicago (N.L.), Pittsburgh (N.L.),
Philadelphia (N.L.)

4952. Bruns, Roger A. *Preacher: Billy Sunday and Big-Time American Evangelism.* New York: W. W. Norton, 1992. 351p.
4953. Warnock, J. "'Playing Centerfield in the Lord's Ball Club': Billy Sunday's 1914 Denver Campaign." *Nine: A Journal of Baseball History and Social Policy Perspective,* IV (Fall 1995), 62–83.

WILLIAM JAMES ("B.J.") SURHOFF

Outfielder, Catcher
Milwaukee (A.L.), Baltimore (A.L.)

4954. Doyle, Al. "B. J. Surhoff Gave the Brewers Their Money's Worth in '95." *Baseball Digest,* LV (February 1995), 41–45.

DON SUTTON

Pitcher
Los Angeles (N.L.), Houston (N.L.),
Milwaukee (A.L.), Oakland (A.L.),
California (A.L.)

4955. Sorci, Rick. "Baseball Profile: Former Pitcher Don Sutton." *Baseball Digest,* LIV (January 1995), 45–46.

BILL SWIFT

Pitcher
Seattle (A.L.), San Francisco (N.L.),
Colorado (N.L.)

4956. Buckley, Steve. "A Deeper Look: Bill Swift." *Beckett Baseball Card Monthly,* IX, no. 89 (August 1992), 122–123.

GREG SWINDELL

Pitcher
Cleveland (A.L.), Cincinnati (N.L.),
Houston (N.L.), Minnesota (A.L.)

4957. Glassman, Brian. "Guaranteed." *Elysian Fields Quarterly,* XI (Spring 1992), 70–72.

FRANK TANANA

Pitcher
California (A.L.),
Boston (A.L.),
Texas (A.L.)

4958. Tanana, Frank, as told to George Vass. "'The Game I'll Never Forget.'" *Baseball Digest,* LII (July 1993), 55–56.

DANNY TARTABULL

Outfielder
Seattle (A.L.),
Kansas City (A.L.),
New York (A.L.), Oakland (A.L.),
Chicago (A.L.)

4959. Gergen, Joe. "Danny Tartabull: He Goes Beyond His Father's Footsteps." *Baseball Digest,* LI (June 1992), 42–45.

FREDERICK TAYLOR

Executive
Management Consultant

4960. Risker, D. C. "Frederick Taylor's Use of the Baseball Team Metaphor: A Historical Perspective on Scientific Management and Baseball." *Nine: A Journal of Baseball History and Social Policy Perspective,* IV (Fall 1995), 1–10.

RON TAYLOR

Pitcher
Cleveland (A.L.),
St. Louis (N.L.),
Houston (N.L.),
New York Mets (N.L.),
San Diego (N.L.)

4961. Forman, Ross. "Down Memory Lane: Whatever Became of Ron Taylor?" *Baseball Digest,* LIV (September 1995), 77–78.

KENTON CHARLES ("KENT") TEKULVE

Pitcher
Pittsburgh (N.L.), Philadelphia (N.L.), Cincinnati (N.L.)

4962. Forman, Ross. "Durability was the Key to Success for Reliever Kent Tekulve." *Baseball Digest,* LII (September 1993), 76–78.

WILLIAM HAROLD ("BILL" or "MEMPHIS BILL") TERRY*

First Baseman
New York Giants (N.L.)
Manager
New York Giants (N.L.)

4963. Salisbury, L. "Bill Terry: Baseball Memory and Mere Excellence." *Nine: A Journal of Baseball History and Social Policy Perspective,* III (Fall 1994), 122–125.
4964. Williams, Peter. *When the Giants Were Giants: Bill Terry and the Golden Age of New York Baseball.* Chapel Hill, N.C.: Algonquin Books, 1994. 331p.

FRANK ("THE BIG HURT") THOMAS

First Baseman
Chicago (A.L.)

4965. Aschburner, Steve. "Frank Thomas of White Sox Puts Big Hurt on Enemy Pitching." *Baseball Digest,* LII (December 1993), 34–37.
4966. *Beckett Tribute: Frank Thomas.* Dallas, Tx.: Beckett Publications, 1997. 64p.
4967. Buckley, Dan. "White Sox Slugger Frank Thomas Remains Unspoiled by Success." *Baseball Digest,* LIII (June 1994), 27–29.
4968. Cox, Ted. *Frank Thomas: The Big Hurt.* Chicago, Ill.: Children's Press, 1994. 48p.

4969. Dunn, Stephen. "Tower of Power." *Sports Illustrated for Kids,* VIII (May 1996), 56–61.
4970. George, Daniel P. "Big Man on Base." *Boy's Life,* LXXXIV (July 1994), 16+.
4971. Graham, Tim. "Talkin' with Frank Thomas." *Beckett Baseball Card Monthly,* XII, no. 124 (July 1995), 22–23.
4972. Gutman, Bill. *Frank Thomas, Power Hitter.* Brookfield, Conn.: Millbrook Press, 1996. 48p.
4973. Hotzman, Jerome. "Frank Thomas of the White Sox Debunks Sophomore Jinx Theory." *Baseball Digest,* LII (January 1993), 29–31.
4974. Keegan, Tom. "The Big Hurt." *Sport,* LXXXV (May 1994), 54–57.
4975. Muskat, Carrie. *Frank Thomas.* Philadelphia, Pa.: Chelsea House, 1997. 64p.
4976. ____. "Frankly Speaking." *Topps Magazine,* (Spring 1992), 34–36.
4977. Payne, Mike. "The Big Hot." *Beckett Baseball Card Monthly,* XI, no. 116 (November 1994), 10–15.
4978. Reilly, Rick. "The Big Heart." *Sports Illustrated,* LXXXI (April 8, 1994), 16–22.
4979. Robbins, Liz. "Frank Thomas of the White Sox Piling Up Hall of Fame Statistics." *Baseball Digest,* LVI (September 1997), 44–47.
4980. Ruda, Mark. "Closer Look: Frank Thomas." *Beckett Baseball Card Monthly,* X, no. 100 (July 1993), 6–9.
4981. Schnert, Chris W. *Frank Thomas.* Edina, Minn.: Abdo & Daughters, 1996. 31p.
4982. Spiros, Dean. *Frank Thomas: Star First Baseman.* Springfield, N.J.: Enslow, 1996. 104p.
4983. Stewart, Mark. *Frank Thomas.* New York: Children's Press, 1996. 48p.
4984. "Superstar Gallery: Frank Thomas." *Beckett Baseball Card Monthly,* X, no. 94 (January 1993), 21–22.
4985. Thornley, Stew. *Frank Thomas.* Minneapolis, Minn.: Lerner Publications, 1997.

4986. Wulf, Steve. "The Big Hurt." *Sports Illustrated,* LXXIX (September 13, 1993), 40–43.

JUSTIN THOMPSON

Pitcher
Detroit (A.L.)

4987. Crothers, Tim. "Griffey's Nemesis." *Sports Illustrated,* LXXXVI (June 23, 1997), 72, 74.

ROBBIE THOMPSON

Second Baseman
San Francisco

4988. Stone, Larry. "In '93, Robby Thompson Came of Age as a Clutch Hitter." *Baseball Digest,* LII (December 1993), 46–48.

RYAN THOMPSON

Outfielder
New York Mets (N.L.), Cleveland (A.L.)

4989. Schwarz, Alan. "Rookie Report: Ryan Thompson." *Beckett Baseball Card Monthly,* X, no. 98 (May 1993), 100–102.

JIM THOME

Third Baseman/First Baseman
Cleveland (A.L.)

4990. Johnson, P. M. "The Throwback." *Sport,* LXXXVI (November 1995), 94+.
4991. Rosewater, Amy. "Indians' Jim Thome Thrives on Overcoming Challenges." *Baseball Digest,* LVI (January 1997), 44–48.

EUSTACE TILLEY

Baseball Cartoonist

4992. Altherr, T. L. "Eustace Tilley

Draws the Game: The Image of Baseball in *The New Yorker,* 1925 to the Present." *Nine: A Journal of Baseball History and Social Policy Perspective,* III (Fall 1994), 14–35.

JOSEPH PAUL ("JOE") TORRE

Catcher, First Baseman, Third Baseman
Milwaukee (N.L.), Atlanta (N.L.),
St. Louis (N.L.),
New York Mets (N.L.)
Manager
New York Mets (N.L.), Atlanta (N.L.),
St. Louis (N.L.), New York (A.L.)
Broadcaster

4993. Jerome, R. "Torre, Torre, Torre." *People Weekly,* XLVI (November 11, 1996), 52–55.
4994. Jordan, Pat. "The Patience of Joe." *The New York Times Magazine,* (September 15, 1996), 34–37.
4995. Kurkjian, Tim. "Who's on First, Joe?" *Sports Illustrated,* LXXII (March 6, 1995), 44–46+.
4996. Torre, Joe, with Tom Verducci. *Chasing the Dream: My Lifelong Journey to the World Series.* New York: Bantam Books, 1997. 272p.
4997. Verducci, Tom. "Regular Joe." *Sports Illustrated,* LXXXV (October 28, 1996), 40–44.
4998. Wulf, Steve. "The Torre of Love." *Time,* CXLVIII (October 28, 1996), 115+.

CECIL TRAVIS

Shortstop, Third Baseman
Washington (A.L.)
Scout

4999. Holway, John B. "Does Cecil Travis Belong in the Hall of Fame?" *Baseball Digest,* LII (May 1993), 63–66.

GUS TRIANDOS

Catcher

New York (A.L.), Baltimore (A.L.), Detroit (A.L.), Philadelphia (N.L.), Houston (N.L.)

5000. Fagen, Herb. "Gus Triandos Looks Back on His Catching Career." *Baseball Digest,* LVI (June 1997), 82–88.

TIM TSCHIDA

Umpire

5001. Galt, Margot F. "Vitae: St. Paul's Own Tim Tschida." *Minnesota Monthly,* XXIV (April 1990), 40+.

TED TURNER

Executive
Atlanta (N.L.)

5002. Bibb, Porter. *It Ain't as Easy as It Looks: Ted Turner's Amazing Story.* New York: Crown Publishers, 1993. 468p.
5003. ____. "Ted Turner's Wild Ride to the Top." *Success,* XL (November 1993), 35–39.
5004. Fischer, David M. *Ted Turner.* Vero Beach, Fla.: Rourke, 1993. 109p.
5005. Goldberg, Robert and Gerald Jay. *Citizen Turner: The Wild Rise of an American Tycoon.* San Diego, Calif.: Harcourt, Brace & Co., 1995. 525p.
5006. Landrum, Gene N. "Ted Turner." In: his *Profiles of Genius: Thirteen Creative Men Who Changed the World.* Buffalo, N.Y.: Prometheus Books, 1993. pp. 213–229.

BOBBY VALENTINE

Shortstop, Outfielder
Los Angeles (N.L.), California (A.L.), San Diego (N.L.),
New York Mets (N.L.), Seattle (A.L.)
Manager
Texas (A.L.),
Chiba Lotte Marines (Japan)
New York Mets (N.L.)

5007. Esham, Robin. "The Bobby Valentine Story." *The Journal of the American Chamber of Commerce,* XXXIII (March 1996), 34+.
5008. Starr, Mark. "Losing in a New Language." *Newsweek,* CXXV (May 22, 1995), 46+.
5009. Verducci, Tom. "Valentine Days." *Sports Illustrated,* LXXXVII (August 4, 1997), 30–33.

FERNANDO VALENZUELA

Pitcher
Los Angeles (N.L.), California (A.L.), Baltimore (A.L.),
Philadelphia (N.L.), San Diego (N.L.), St. Louis (N.L.)

5010. Pedulla, Tom. "Perseverance Paid Dividends for Fernando Valenzuela." *Baseball Digest,* LV (December 1996), 74–76.
5011. Valenzuela, Fernando, as told to George Vass. "'The Game I'll Never Forget.'" *Baseball Digest,* LIII (July 1994), 81–82.
5012. Wulf, Steve. "It's That Screwball Again." *Sports Illustrated,* LXXVIII (March 22, 1993), 37+.

TODD VAN POPPEL

Pitcher
Oakland (A.L.), Detroit (A.L.)

5013. Stier, Kit. "Focus on Todd van Poppel." *Beckett Focus on Future Stars,* II, no. 14 (June 1992), 18–21.

ANDY ("SLICK") VAN SLYKE

Outfielder
St. Louis (N.L.), Pittsburgh (N.L.), Baltimore (A.L.), Philadelphia (N.L.)

5014. Branon, Dave and Lee Pellegrino. "Andy Van Slyke." In: their *Safe at Home.* Chicago, Ill.: Moody Press, 1992. pp. 308–310.
5015. Fletcher, Christopher. "Angel of

the Outfield." *Pittsburgh,* XXV (July 1994), 17+.

5016. Meyer, Paul. "Interview: Andy Van Slyke." *Inside Sports,* XVI (June 1994), 22–29.

5017. Perrotto, John. "Deeper Look: Andy Van Slyke." *Beckett Baseball Card Monthly,* X, no. 94 (January 1993), 108–109.

5018. Rushin, Steve. "Playing for Laughs." *Sports Illustrated,* LXXVII (September 21, 1992), 56–62, 64.

WILLIAM VANLANDINGHAM

Pitcher
San Francisco (N.L.)

5019. Camps, Mark. "Rookie Report: William VanLandingham." *Beckett Baseball Card Monthly,* XI, no. 117 (December 1994), 126–127.

MO ("BIG MO") VAUGHN

First Baseman
Boston (A.L.)

5020. Arnold, Eric. *A Day in the Life of Baseball Player Mo Vaughn.* New York: Scholastic, 1996. Unpaged.

5021. Cafardo, Nick. "Closer Look: Mo Vaughn." *Beckett Baseball Card Monthly,* XII, no. 118 (January 1995), 6–9.

5022. Callahan, Gerry. "Sox Appeal." *Sports Illustrated,* LXXXIII (October 2, 1995), 42–44, 47–49.

5023. Christopher, Matt. *At the Plate With—Mo Vaughn.* Boston, Mass.: Little, Brown, 1997. Unpaged.

5024. Dieffenbach, Dan. "Hitting It with Mo Vaughn." *Sport,* LXXVII (May 1996), 86–87.

5025. ____. "Mo Vaughn's Prize." *Sport,* LXXXVIII (July 1996), 79–81.

5026. "Mo's Town." In: Joe Hoppel, ed. *The Sporting News 1995 Baseball Yearbook.* St. Louis, Mo.: TSN, 1995. pp. 32–35.

5027. Santella, Andrew. *Mo Vaughn,*

"Big Mo." Danbury, Conn.: Children's Press, 1996. 48p.

5028. Vaughn, Mo, with Greg Brown. *Follow Your Dreams.* Dallas, Tx.: Taylor, 1996. 300p.

MICHAEL VEECK

Executive
St. Paul Saints

5029. Richmond, Peter. "Veeck II: Meet Mr. Minors." *GQ: Gentlemen's Quarterly,* LXV (April 1995), 211+.

ROBIN VENTURA

Third Baseman
Chicago (A.L.)

5030. Holtzman, Jerome. "Robin Ventura Seeks a Repeat of His Productive '96 Season." *Baseball Digest,* LVI (April 1997), 74–75.

JAMES BARTON ("MICKEY") VERNON

First Baseman
Washington (A.L.), Cleveland (A.L.), Milwaukee (N.L.), Pittsburgh (N.L.)
Manager
Washington (A.L.)
Coach

5031. Hirshberg, Dan. "Flashback— Mickey Vernon: Twice He Led the A.L. in Hitting." *Baseball Digest,* LIV (January 1995), 56–62.

FRANCIS T. ("FAY") VINCENT, JR.

Executive
Commissioner of Baseball

5032. Angell, Roger. "The Rules of the Game." *The New Yorker,* LXVIII (October 5, 1992), 178+.

5033. Brunning, Fred. "Baseball and Politics: Lessons in Hardball." *Maclean's,* CV (September 28, 1992), 13+.

5034. Corliss, Richard. "Fay Vincent Gets Beaned." *Time,* CXL (September 14, 1992), 61+.

5035. Demak, Richard. "Baseball Strikes Out." *Sports Illustrated,* LXXVII (September 14, 1992), 13+.

5036. Hammer, Joshua, David A. Kaplan, and Todd Barrett. "Paradise Lost: Why Baseball's Economic Troubles May Force Fay Vincent Out of the Box." *Newsweek,* CXX (September 14, 1992), 72–74.

5037. Kaplan, David A. "Take Him Out to a Ball Game: Does the Beleaguered Commissioner Need Relief?" *Newsweek,* CXX (July 20, 1992), 56+.

5038. "A League of Their Own: Baseball's Bosses Are Back in Charge After Fay Vincent Resigns." *Time,* CXL (September 21, 1992), 20–21.

5039. Neff, Craig and Jill Lieber. "Behind the Scenes with George [Steinbrenner] and Fay." *Sports Illustrated,* LXXIII (August 13, 1990), 13–14.

5040. Vincent, Francis T. ("Fay"), Jr. "An Agenda for the Most Original Game Ever Invented: Baseball in the 1990s." *Vital Speeches of the Day,* LVIII (June 15, 1992), 541+.

OMAR VISQUEL

Shortstop
Seattle (A.L.), Cleveland (A.L.)

5041. Kurkijan, Tim. "Playmaker." *Sports Illustrated,* LXXXIV (April 1, 1996), 68–72.

5042. Robbins, Liz. "Omar Visquel: His Smooth Glove Work Heartens the Indians." *Baseball Digest,* LIV (November 1995), 64–70.

CHRIS VON DER AHE

Executive
St. Louis (A.A.), St. Louis (N.L.)

5043. Rygelski, Jim. "Baseball's 'Boss President': Chris von der Ahe and the 19th Century St. Louis Browns." *Gateway Heritage,* XIII (Summer 1992), 42–53.

HIAWATHA TERRELL WADE

Pitcher
Atlanta

5044. Schwartz, Alan. "A Brave Named Hiawatha." *Beckett Focus on Future Stars,* IV, no. 34 (February 1994), 82–83.

BILLY WAGNER

Pitcher
Houston (N.L.)

5045. Kurkijan, Tim. "Billy Hits the Big Time." *Sports Illustrated,* LXXXV (August 19, 1995), 72–73.

JOHN ("HONUS/THE FLYING DUTCHMAN") WAGNER*

Shortstop
Louisville (N.L.), Pittsburgh (N.L.)
Manager
Pittsburgh (N.L.)

5046. De Valeria, Dennis and Jeanne Burke. *Honus Wagner: A Biography.* New York: Holt, 1996. 334p.

5047. Hageman, William. *Honus: The Life and Times of a Baseball Hero.* Champaign, Ill.: Sagamore Pub., 1996. 218p.

5048. Hittner, Arthur D. *Honus Wagner: The Life of Baseball's "Flying Dutchman."* Jefferson, N.C.: McFarland & Co., Inc., 1996. 306p.

5049. Kavanagh, John. *Baseball Legends: Honus Wagner.* New York: Chelsea House, 1994. 64p.

EDWARD ("EDDIE") WAITKUS

First Baseman
Chicago (N.L.), Philadelphia (N.L.), Baltimore (A.L.)

5050. "From *A Report to Felony Court: File No.—, the Behavior Clinic.*" In: Charles Einstein, ed. *The New Baseball Reader: An All-Star Lineup from The Fireside Book of Baseball.* New York: Penguin Books, 1992. pp. 124–132.

TIM WAKEFIELD

Pitcher
Pittsburgh (N.L.), Boston (A.L.)

5051. Hartsock, John. "Pirates' Tim Wakefield Frustrated Foes with His Knuckleball." *Baseball Digest,* LII (June 1993), 53–56.

SUSYN WALDMAN

Broadcaster

5052. Viles, Peter. "First for Mets, WFAN: A Woman in the Booth—Waldman Does Color, Not Play-by-Play; Fans May Already Know Her Singing Voice." *Broadcasting & Cable,* (June 1993), 61+.

BOB WALK

Pitcher
Philadelphia (N.L.), Atlanta (N.L.), Pittsburgh (N.L.)

5053. Walk, Bob, as told to George Vass. "'The Game I'll Never Forget.'" *Baseball Digest,* LIV (March 1995), 50–53.

LARRY WALKER

Outfielder
Montreal (N.L.), Colorado (N.L.)

5054. Callahan, Gerry. "See It, Hit It." *Sports Illustrated,* LXXXVII (July 14, 1997), 40–49.
5055. Came, Barry. "The Homegrown Hero." *Maclean's,* CV (August 24, 1992), 56+.
5056. Cassoff, Derek. "Larry Walker of Expos Makes an Impact as Canadian Big Leaguer." *Baseball Digest,* LI (October 1992), 52–55.
5057. Joyce, Gary. "Yerrr Out!" *Saturday Night,* CIX (October 1994), 71–72+.
5058. Montville, Leigh. "The Accidental Ballplayer." *Sports Illustrated,* LXXVIII (April 5, 1993), 78–80+. Published simultaneously in *Sports Illustrated Canada,* I (April 5, 1993), 70–72, 75, under the title "Southern Exposure."
5059. Morrissey, Rick. "Rockies' Larry Walker: A Natural in Disguise." *Baseball Digest,* LVI (October 1997), 32–38.
5060. O'Shei, Tim. "Larry Walker of Expos Chases Big-Time Stardom." *Baseball Digest,* LIII (August 1994), 31–36.
5061. Perrotto, John. "Second Look: Larry Walker." *Beckett Baseball Card Monthly,* X, no. 94 (January 1993), 97–98.
5062. Rubin, Bob. "Larry Walker of Expos Climbing the Stairs to Stardom." *Baseball Digest,* LII (July 1993), 29–31.
5063. Verducci, Tom. "MVP?" *Sports Illustrated,* LXXXVII (October 6, 1997), 43–48.

MOSES FLEETWOOD WALKER

Catcher
Toledo (A.A.)

5064. Giancaterino, Randy. "1884: Moses Fleetwood Walker." *American Visions,* VIII (June–July 1993), 25–26.
5065. Nutt, A. "An All-But-Forgotten First: Long Before Jackie Robinson's Dodger Debut, Moses Walker Played Ball for Toledo." *Sports Illustrated,* LXXVI (June 15, 1992), 26+.
5066. Wheeler, Lonnie. "Hounded Out of Baseball." *Ohio,* XVI (May 1993), 22+.
5067. Zang, D. W. *Fleet Walker's Divided*

Heart: The Life of Baseball's First Black Major Leaguer. Lincoln: University of Nebraska Press, 1995. 200p.

WILLIAM ADOLPH ("BILL") WAMBGSGANSS

Second Baseman, Shortstop
Cleveland (A.L.), Boston (A.L.),
Philadelphia (A.L.)

5068. Holway, John B. "First and Only World Series Triple Play Recalled." *Baseball Digest,* LII (February 1993), 73–76. In 1920.

PAUL ("BIG POISON") WANER*

Outfielder
Pittsburgh (N.L.), Brooklyn (N.L.),
Boston (N.L.), New York (A.L.)

5069. Lalire, Gregory. "Perspective: Asked by a Fan Why He Was in the Yankee Outfield, Paul Waner Replied: 'Because Joe D Is in the Army!'" *World War II,* VIII (September 1993), 64+.

DUANE WARD

Pitcher
Atlanta (N.L.), Toronto (A.L.)

5070. Kurkijan, Tim. "Hanging On to One Man's Arm." *Sports Illustrated,* LXXX (April 4, 1994), 114+.
5071. Shelton, Gary. "Jays' Duane Ward Steps into 'Prime Time' as Reliever." *Baseball Digest,* LII (July 1993), 38–39.

HERBERT ("HERB") WASHINGTON

Pinch runner
Oakland (A.L.)

5072. Lidz, Franz. "Whatever Happened to…Herb Washington?" *Sports Illus-*

trated, LXXIX (July 19, 1993), 86+. Employed exclusively to run bases during a two year career.

ALLEN WATSON

Pitcher
St. Louis (N.L.), San Francisco (N.L.)

5073. Wheatley, Tom. "Rookie Report: Allen Watson." *Beckett Baseball Card Monthly,* X, no. 105 (December 1993), 112–113.

BOB WATSON

Executive
Houston

5074. Wulf, Steve. "Bob Watson." *Sports Illustrated,* LXXIX (October 18, 1993), 74+. G.M.

EARL WEAVER*

Manager
Baltimore (A.L.)
Broadcaster

5075. Barrett, Wayne M. "The Earl of Baltimore." *USA Today,* CXXV (July 1996), 65+.
5076. Palmer, Jim, and Jim Dale. *Together We Were Eleven Foot Nine: The Twenty-Year Friendship of Hall of Fame Pitcher Jim Palmer and Orioles Manager Earl Weaver.* Kansas City, Mo.: Andrews and McMeel, 1996. 169p.
5077. Shafer, Kevin. *Earl Weaver: Hall of Fame Manager.* Berkeley, Ca.: Osborne McGraw-Hill, 1992. 490p.

EARL WEBB

Outfielder
New York Giants (N.L.),
Chicago (N.L.),
Boston (A.L.), Detroit (A.L.)

5078. Barumba-Boom." *Sports Illustrated,* LXXIX (August 9, 1993), 64–72+.

5079. Holway, John B. "Earl Webb: His One-Season Doubles Mark Still Stands." *Baseball Digest,* LIII (December 1994), 80–83.

ALTA WEISS

Pioneer Female Player

5080. Gregorich, Barbara. "'You Can't Play in Skirts': Alta Weiss, Baseball Player." *Timeline,* XI (July 1994), 38+.

TIM WELKE

Umpire
A.L.

5081. Welke, Tim. "Interview." *Referee,* XIX (July 1994), 72+.

DAVID ("BOOMER") WELLS

Pitcher
Toronto (A.L.), Detroit (A.L.),
Cincinnati (N.L.), Baltimore (A.L.),
New York (A.L.)

5082. Farber, Michael. "A Doggone Red." *Sports Illustrated,* LXXXIII (October 16, 1995), 33+.
5083. Lidz, Franz. "The Unvarnished Ruth." *Sports Illustrated,* LXXXVII (September 8, 1997), 70–79.

HARRY WENDELSTEDT

Umpire
N.L.

5084. Wendelstedt, Harry. "Interview." *Referee,* XVIII (August 1993), 72+.

JOHN WETTELAND

Pitcher
Los Angeles (N.L.), Montreal (N.L.),
New York (A.L.)

5085. Farber, Michael. "Going to Extremes." *Sports Illustrated,* LXXXI (July 4, 1994), 44–48+.

LOU WHITAKER

Second Baseman
Detroit (A.L.)

5086. Shook, Richard. "Second Look: Lou Whitaker." *Beckett Baseball Card Monthly,* X, no. 93 (March 1993), 97–98.

BILL WHITE

First Baseman
New York Giants (N.L.),
San Francisco (N.L.),
St. Louis (N.L.), Philadelphia (N.L.)
Executive
President, National League

5087. Randolph, Laura B. "Bill White, National League President." *Ebony,* XLVII (August 1992), 52–54.

SOL WHITE

Historian

5088. Malloy, Jerry. "The Strange Career of Sol White, Black Baseball's First Historian." *Nine: A Journal of Baseball History and Social Policy Perspective,* IV (Spring 1996), 217–236.

BURGESS URQUHART ("WHITEY") WHITEHEAD

Second Baseman, Third Baseman
St. Louis (N.L.),
New York Giants (N.L.),
Pittsburgh (N.L.)

5089. Grosshandler, Stanley. "Burgess Whitehead: Last of the Old 'Gas House Gang.'" *Baseball Digest,* LI (June 1992), 66–68.

MARK WHITEN

Outfielder
Toronto (A.L.), Cleveland (A.L.),
St. Louis (N.L.), Boston (A.L.),
New York (A.L.)

5090. "Cardinals' Whiten Jolts 4 Homers, 12 RBI in Game." *Jet,* LXXXIV (September 27, 1993), 46+.

5091. Fimrite, Ron. "Mark Whiten." *Sports Illustrated,* LXXIX (September 20, 1993), 45+.

GEORGE F. WILL

Baseball historian

5092. Wright, William W. "Safe at Home for What?: George F. Will and the Republic of Baseball." *Diversity,* I (Spring 1993), 57+.

BERNIE WILLIAMS

Outfielder
New York (A.L.)

5093. Bodley, Hal. "Yankees' Bernie Williams: He Makes Sweet 'Music' at the Plate." *Baseball Digest,* LVI (January 1997), 53–57.

5094. Ryan, Jeff. "All Tied Up with a Neat Bow." *Inside Sports,* XV (June 1993), 59+.

5095. ____. "In Tune with Greatness." *Sport,* LXXXIX (July 1997), 71–74.

5096. Tringali, Rob, Jr. "Yankee Doodle Dandy." *Sports Illustrated for Kids,* IX (April 1997), 24–27.

BILLY WILLIAMS*

Outfielder
Chicago (N.L.), Oakland (A.L.)

5097. Kuenster, John. "Hall of Famer Billy Williams Talks About the Fine Art of Hitting." *Baseball Digest,* LVI (July 1997), 17–19.

GLENN WILLIAMS

Pitcher
Australian Baseball League

5098. Crawley, P. "Fast Ball: Glenn Williams." *Sports Weekly (Australia),* (February 27, 1996), 28–29.

JOE WILLIAMS

Sportswriter

5099. Williams, Pete. "When Chipmunks Become Wolves: The Scapegoating of Sportswriter Joe Williams by His Peers." *Nine: A Journal of Baseball History and Social Policy Perspective,* IV (Fall 1995), 51–61.

MATT WILLIAMS

Third Baseman
San Francisco (N.L.), Cleveland (A.L.)

5100. Fimrite, Ron. "The Strong, Silent Type." *Sports Illustrated,* LXXXI (July 25, 1994), 30–32+.

5101. Kaplan, Ben. "Get Into Baseball." *Sports Illustrated for Kids,* VII (April 1995), 22–27.

5102. Kuenster, John. "Matt Williams Building Credentials as Majors' Premier Third Baseman." *Baseball Digest,* LIII (August 1994), 17–19.

5103. Pluto, Terry. "Matt Williams Turns a New Page as A.L. Power Hitter." *Baseball Digest,* LVI (June 1997), 34–37.

5104. Whiteside, Kelly. "Big Matt Attack." *Sports Illustrated,* LXXXII (June 5, 1995), 32–35.

MITCH ("THE WILD THING") WILLIAMS

Pitcher
Texas (A.L.), Chicago (N.L.), Philadelphia (N.L.), Houston (N.L.), California (A.L.), Kansas City (A.L.)

5105. Kurkijan, Tim. "Relief at Last." *Sports Illustrated,* LXXX (June 13, 1994), 42–45.

5106. ____. "A Walk on the Wild Side." *Sports Illustrated,* LXXIX (November 1, 1993), 22–23.

5107. Plummer, William. "Out of Control." *People Weekly,* XLI (May 9, 1994), 158–159.

5108. "The Unforgiven." In: Joe Hoppel, ed. *The Sporting News 1994 Baseball Yearbook.* St. Louis, Mo.: TSN, 1994. pp. 12–19.

5109. Verducci, Tom. "Mitch Williams Traded to Houston." *Sports Illustrated,* LXXIX (December 13, 1993), 62–63.

TED WILLIAMS*

Outfielder
Boston (A.L.)
Manager
Washington (A.L.), Texas (A.L.)
Coach

5110. Hannan, J. "Ted Williams, Premier Batting Coach: Big Improvements for the '68 Senators." *Baseball Research Journal,* XXIV (1995), 101–102.

5111. Hawkins, Burt. "Ted Williams, First Rangers Manager." In: John Blake, *et al. Texas Rangers Official 1994 Yearbook.* Arlington, Tex.: Public Relations Dept., Texas Rangers, 1994. pp. 56–60.

5112. Hoffer, Richard. "Williams Does It!: Bosox Slugger Ends Season with .406 Mark." *Sports Illustrated,* LXXIX (July 19, 1993), 25–26, 28.

5113. Holtzman, Jerome. "Ted Williams: He's Still Connecting with Strong Views." *Baseball Digest,* LVI (June 1997), 54–55.

5114. Linn, Ed. *Hitter: The Life and Turmoils of Ted Williams.* New York: Harcourt, Brace, Jovanovich, 1993. 437p.

5115. Maracin, Paul R. "Ted Williams Struggled in His First Year as a Pro." *Baseball Digest,* LIV (November 1995), 71–72.

5116. Price, S. L. "Rounding Third." *Sports Illustrated,* LXXXV (November 25, 1996), 92–96+.

5116a. Prime, Jim and Bill Nowlin. *Ted Williams: A Tribute.* South Bend, Ind.: Masters Press, 1997.

5117. Ryan, Steve. "Still Splendid." *Beckett Baseball Card Monthly,* X, no. 101 (August 1993), 108–110.

5118. Shaughnessey, Dan. "Opposing Pitcher [Jack Fisher] Recalls Ted Williams' Final Homer." *Baseball Digest,* LII (March 1993), 82–83.

5119. Underwood, John. "Going Fishing with the Kid." *Sports Illustrated,* LXXXI (July 4, 1994), 56–60+. Reprinted from a 1967 issue.

5120. Verducci, Tom. "Triple Threats: Two-Time Triple Crown Winner Ted Williams Nearly Won It Five Times in Six Years." *Sports Illustrated,* LXXXV (July 1, 1996), 25–30, 32, 37.

5121. Williams, Ted, with Don Sider. "A Slugger Goes Back to School." *People Weekly,* XLIII (July–August 1995), 36–43+.

5122. Wolff, Rick. *Baseball Legend Ted Williams.* New York: Chelsea House, 1992. 64p.

MAURY WILLS

Shortstop
Los Angeles (N.L.), Pittsburgh (N.L.), Montreal (N.L.)
Manager
Seattle (A.L.)

5123. Wills, Maury, with Mike Celizic. *On the Run: The Never-Dull and Often-Shocking Life of Maury Wills.* New York: Carroll and Graf, 1991. 334p.

DAN WILSON

Catcher
Cincinnati (N.L.), Seattle (A.L.)

5124. Anderson, Lars. "Dan Wilson." In: David Bauer, ed. *SI Presents Baseball 1997.* New York: Sports Illustrated, 1997. pp. 142–145.

5125. Driver, David. "How Hard Work Paid Off for Mariners' Receiver Dan Wilson." *Baseball Digest,* LV (December 1996), 83–85.

LEWIS ("HACK") WILSON*

Outfielder
New York Giants (N.L.),

Chicago (N.L.),
Brooklyn (N.L.), Philadelphia (N.L.)

5126. Holway, John B. "Hack Wilson Belted Homers and Hecklers with Equal Gusto." *Baseball Digest,* LV (June 1996), 78–84.

NIGEL WILSON

Outfielder
Florida (N.L.), Cincinnati (N.L.), Cleveland (A.L.)

5127. Giuliotti, Ed. "Expanding Opportunities: Nigel Wilson/Marlins." *Beckett Focus on Future Stars,* III, no. 24 (April 1993), 9–11.

PAUL WILSON

Pitcher
New York Mets (N.L.)

5128. Schwarz, Alan. "Fanning the Flames." *Beckett Focus on Future Stars,* IV, no. 41 (September 1994), 16–17.

WILLIE JAMES WILSON

Outfielder
Kansas City (A.L.), Oakland (A.L.), Chicago (N.L.)

5129. Solomon, Alan. "Willie Wilson: Helping Win Games Keeps Him Going." *Baseball Digest,* LII (June 1993), 36–37.

DAVE WINFIELD

Outfielder
San Diego (N.L.), New York (A.L.), California (A.L.),
Toronto (A.L.), Minnesota (A.L.), Cleveland (A.L.)

5130. Banks, Don. "Dave Winfield: Still in Title Chase with the Blue Jays." *Baseball Digest,* LI (June 1992), 32–33.

5132. Caple, Jim. "Deeper Look: Dave Winfield." *Beckett Baseball Card Monthly,* XI, no. 117 (December 1994), 106–109.

5133. Click, Paul. "Dave Winfield Zeroes in on Exclusive 3,000 Hit Club." *Baseball Digest,* LII (July 1993), 32–35.

5134. "He's a Hall of Famer, George." *Sports Illustrated,* LXXXIV (February 19, 1996), 14–15.

5135. Kiersh, Dave. "Interview: Dave Winfield." *Inside Sports,* XV (February 1993), 24–28.

5136. Kurkijan, Tim. "Mr. Longevity." *Sports Illustrated,* LXXIX (September 27, 1993), 55+.

5137. ____. "This Old Man, He Plays Good." *Sports Illustrated,* LXXVII (November 2, 1992), 27+.

5138. Reilly, Rick. "'I Feel a Whole Lot Better Now.'" *Sports Illustrated,* LXXVI (June 29, 1992), 56–60, 62–64, 66, 68.

5139. Saint Paul Pioneer Press and the Minnesota Twins, comps. *Dave Winfield, 3,000 and Counting.* Kansas City, Mo.: Andrews and McMeel, 1993. 88p.

5140. "Slugger Dave Winfield Continues to Shine On and Off the Field." *Jet,* LXXXIV (September 27, 1993), 48+.

5141. Souhan, Jim. "Hitting: A Constant Learning Process for Dave Winfield." *Baseball Digest,* LIII (January 1994), 32–35.

5142. "Superstar Gallery: Dave Winfield." *Beckett Baseball Card Monthly,* IX, no. 91 (October 1992), 12–13.

5143. Winfield, Dave. *Ask Dave: Dave Winfield Answers Kids' Questions About Baseball and Life.* Kansas City, Mo.: Andrews and McMeel, 1994. 102p.

5144. "Winfield Hits 3,000 Mark; Becomes 19th Man to Do It." *Jet,* LXXXIV (October 4, 1993), 46+.

MARK WOHLERS

Pitcher
Atlanta (N.L.)

5145. Verducci, Tom. "Turning Up the Heat." *Sports Illustrated,* LXXXIII (October 9, 1995), 56, 61.

WILBUR FORRESTER WOOD

Pitcher
Boston (A.L.), Pittsburgh (N.L.), Chicago (A.L.)

5146. Forman, Ross. "Knuckleballer Wilbur Wood Recalls How It Was in the '70s." *Baseball Digest,* LII (July 1993), 62–65.

FLORENCE IRENE WOODS

New England Semi-Pro Player

5147. Lannin, Joanne. "Smokey Was a Natural." *Yankee,* LVII (April 1993), 96–99. New England semi-pro league player Florence Irene Woods, who later became a nun.

PHILIP KNIGHT WRIGLEY

Executive
Chicago (N.L.)

5148. Holtzman, Jerome. "When Cubs Owner Phil Wrigley Revolutionized the Managerial System." *Baseball Digest,* LV (May 1996), 60–64.

HAROLD DELANO ("BUTCH") WYNEGAR

Catcher
Minnesota (A.L.), New York (A.L.), California (A.L.)

5149. Sparks, Barry. "Butch Wynegar Enjoyed a Meteoric Rise to the Majors." *Baseball Digest,* LV (July 1996), 70–72.

CARL YASTRZEMSKI*

Outfielder
Boston (A.L.)

5150. "Catching Up with Yaz." In: Joe Hoppel, ed. *The Sporting News 1997 Baseball Yearbook.* St. Louis, Mo.: TSN, 1997. pp. 160–161.
5151. Long, Skip. *Baseball Legends: Carl Yastrzemski.* New York: Chelsea House, 1993. 64p.
5152. Shaughnessy, Dan. "Triple Crown Season in '67 Marked High Point for Yaz." *Baseball Digest,* LI (August 1992), 66–69.

ANTHONY YOUNG

Pitcher
New York Mets (N.L.), Chicago (N.L.), Houston (N.L.)

5153. Whiteside, Kelly. "Sigh Young." *Sports Illustrated,* LXXIX (July 5, 1993), 26–28. On the recording of his 24th straight loss.

DENTON TRUE ("CY") YOUNG*

Pitcher
Cleveland (N.L.), St. Louis (N.L.), Boston (A.L.),
Cleveland (A.L.), Boston (N.L.)
Manager
Boston (A.L.)

5154. Macht, Norman L. *Baseball Legends: Cy Young.* New York: Chelsea House, 1992. 64p.

ERIC YOUNG

Second Baseman
Los Angeles (N.L.), Colorado (N.L.)

5155. Kurkjian, Tim. "Young and Gifted: Oh, to Be Young in Colorado." *Sports Illustrated,* LXXXV (July 1, 1996), 60+.
5156. Lowery, S. "Numbers in Strength: How Colorado Rockies Second Baseman Eric Young Rediscovered Weight Training, Revved Up His Stats, and Revived His Career." *Men's Fitness,* XIII (May 1997), 88–91.

KEVIN YOUNG

First Baseman
Pittsburgh (N.L.), Kansas City (A.L.)

5157. Perrotto, John. "Rookie Report: Kevin Young." *Beckett Baseball Card Monthly,* X, no. 99 (June 1993), 20–21.

ROBIN YOUNT

Shortstop
Milwaukee (A.L.)

5158. Adelson, Bruce. "Robin Yount: He Has a Hall of Fame Approach to Baseball." *Baseball Digest,* LI (September 1992), 26–30.
5159. Baldassaro, Larry. "The Robin Yount Countdown Diary, September 7–9, 1992." *Elysian Fields Quarterly,* XII (Spring 1993), 78–81.
5160. Haudricourt, Tom. "Deeper Look: Robin Yount." *Beckett Baseball Card Monthly,* XI, no. 111 (June 1994), 126–127.
5161. Kurkijan, Tim. "Make Room in Cooperstown." *Sports Illustrated,* LXXVII (September 21, 1992), 48–49.
5162. "Superstar Gallery: Robin Young." *Beckett Baseball Card Monthly,* IX, no. 90 (September 1992), 14–15.
5163. Van Dyck, Dave. "Robin Yount: A Future Hall of Famer Bows Out Quietly." *Baseball Digest,* LIII (May 1994), 24–25.

5164. Wulf, Steve. "Robin Yount." *Sports Illustrated,* LXXX (February 21, 1994), 74+. Retirement.

GUS EDWARD ("OZARK IKE") ZERNIAL

Outfielder
Chicago (A.L.), Philadelphia (A.L.), Kansas City (A.L.), Detroit (A.L.)

5165. Fagen, Herb. "Gus Zernial: A Forgotten Power Hitter of the 1950s." *Baseball Digest,* LIII (January 1994), 46–50.

DON ZIMMER

Third Baseman, Second Baseman
Brooklyn (N.L.), Los Angeles (N.L.), Chicago (N.L.), New York Mets (N.L.), Cincinnati (N.L.), Washington (A.L.)
Manager
San Diego (N.L.), Boston (A.L.), Texas (A.L.), Chicago (N.L.)
Coach

5166. Holtzman, Jerome. "Don Zimmer: A 'Baseball Lifer' Says Goodbye to the Game He Loves." *Baseball Digest,* LIV (October 1995), 63–64.
5167. Whiteside, Larry. "There's Plenty of Vim Still Left in Don Zimmer." *Baseball Digest,* LIII (July 1994), 36–38.

Author Index

Subject Index